A CANADIAN MILLIONAIRE

To Jamie

A CANADIAN MILLIONAIRE

THE LIFE AND BUSINESS TIMES OF
SIR JOSEPH FLAVELLE, BART.
1858—1939

MICHAEL BLISS

MACMILLAN OF CANADA
TORONTO

Canadian Cataloguing in Publication Data

Bliss, Michael, 1941 –
A Canadian millionaire

Includes index.
ISBN 0-7705-1657-2

1. Flavelle, Joseph Wesley, Sir, bart., 1858–1939. 2. Businessmen–Canada–Biography.
3. Capitalists and financiers–Canada–Biography. I. Title.

HC112.5.F53B55   338'.092'4   C78-001103-1

Printed in Canada
for The Macmillan Company of Canada Limited
70 Bond Street
Toronto, Ontario

CONTENTS

PREFACE

I wrote this book because Joseph Wesley Flavelle was a fascinating man. I also knew that the history of his life would help illuminate the history of his country—particularly the history of modern Canadian business. I hope that the book will interest others in Canadian business history, which is still a neglected field.

Modest grants from the Canada Council and the Varsity Fund of the University of Toronto supported my research. Two of Sir Joseph's grandchildren, June McEachren Barrett and the late Flavelle Barrett, enthusiastically welcomed a project over which they would have no control, did everything they could to meet my incessant requests for information, and gave me unrestricted access to their collection of family papers. No biographer could ask for more valuable and gracious cooperation.

The late Stuart Flavelle of Lindsay, Ontario, gave me access to his collection of family records and talked to me for hours about his uncle. Other grandchildren—Frank McEachren, William Barrett, Barbara Barrett, and Betty Love — willingly shared their rich memories. Grace Flavelle Ballem shared documents, memories, and enthusiasm, and has inherited her great-uncle's love of letter-writing.

All of the companies with which Flavelle was associated met my requests for access to their records. I am grateful to National Trust, Simpson's, and the Canadian Imperial Bank of Commerce, for permission to quote from Minutes and other company documents, and for the time their officers spent helping an inquisitive historian. It was at Canada Packers, though, that the historian became most inquisitive — wanting to see how hogs were disassembled, needing a short course in bacon-curing, insisting on the hottest day of summer that a warehouse be searched for records —and Alan Mackenzie and Michael Neprilly responded with understanding, patience, and resource. Mr. A. J. E. Child, formerly with Canada Packers and now president of Burns Foods, helped my project from the beginning by giving me access to his splendid MA thesis on the packing industry, lending me his notes, and answering all of my queries. The Board of Trustees of Toronto General Hospital and the Governing Council of the University of Toronto gave me permission to use their records. The Borden Diaries are used by permission of Henry Borden and R. C. Brown.

Glenn Wright and David Bell each spent a summer doing excellent research on Flavelle. Ian Wilson and his staff at the Queen's University Archives and Glenn Lucas and his staff at the United Church Archives went far beyond the norm of helpfulness to facilitate my research and make the work pleasant. The staff of the University of Toronto Archives was also unfailingly helpful. In the early years of my research the staff of the Rare Books division of the University of Toronto Library continued to wage their relentless war against the scholar and his pen.

I talked with a large number of people who had known Flavelle and his circle. Muriel Gladman, Horace Speakman, Sir John Wheeler-Bennett, and W. E. Bosnell gave me invaluable interviews before their deaths. Others to whom I am indebted for information include Hope Ellsworth Bond, Floyd Chalmers, R. M. Parkinson, O. N. Edwards, George Kirkpatrick, Paul H. Mills, Gordon Miles, Dr. and Mrs. John A. Ralph, Mrs. Miriam Squires, Mrs. Harry Barron, Mrs. L. H. Hamilton, J. G. Hungerford, Alan Ross, James M. Tory, and Jack Kerr.

My colleagues, R. C. Brown, Bob Bothwell, Viv Nelles, and Paul Rutherford, read and commented on sections of the manuscript. Jim Spence has heard more than he ever wanted to know about Flavelle. Ralph Barford checked the entire manuscript for technical errors about business. Doug Richardson and Bill Dendy explained Holwood's architecture to a business historian. Diane Mew is a super editor. Thanks to you all. Everything wrong with this book, except design and typographical errors committed by Macmillan, is my fault.

Stephen Leacock wrote at the end of one of his prefaces: "Acknowledging all these debts, I feel also that I owe a good deal of this book to my own industry and effort." I share this feeling, and also owe a good deal of the book to my wife, Elizabeth.

MICHAEL BLISS
Toronto, January 1978

THE ROBBER BARONET

A wealthy businessman could easily buy a title in 1917. Lloyd George would ennoble anyone who donated enough cash to the Unionist Central Office. In the birthday Honours List, announced on June 3, George V created at his Prime Minister's request three new viscounts, five barons, twenty-five baronets, and fifty knights. Surveying the ranks of newly titled gentlemen, *The Times* declared it a public outrage to have honoured "these serried rows of political climbers" in wartime, when so many thousands of their countrymen were making the supreme sacrifice. It allowed only two deserving exceptions in the "dreary waste of baronets," two men who had earned their titles. One was J. G. Nairne, an Englishman. The other was J. W. Flavelle of Toronto, the Canadian who was serving as Chairman of the Imperial Munitions Board.

He was the only Canadian on the list whose title was hereditary. So long as the Flavelles continued to bear male heirs, the head of the family could have "Sir" in front of his name and "Bart." after it. Several newspaper editors and even some of Flavelle's friends were not sure that hereditary titles were appropriate honours for the citizens of a North American democracy. They all agreed that if hereditary titles were warranted Flavelle deserved his.

In that summer of 1917 the Imperial Munitions Board ran the Canadian munitions industry and Flavelle ran the Imperial Munitions Board. Six hundred factories and some 250,000 workers under his direction were turning out 100,000 shells a day for the armies in France. Tons of high explosive were being shipped from the Board's own "National Factories" in Ontario and Quebec; shipyards from Halifax to Vancouver were welding the hulls of steel ships for the IMB; and the mass production of aeroplanes was about to begin in the IMB's Toronto factory. Every month the Board was spending $50 million. It was the largest enterprise that had ever existed in Canada.

The charges of profiteering on munitions contracts that had brought the IMB into existence late in 1915 had disappeared in the face of Flavelle's stalwart guarding of the public purse. The business genius he had demonstrated in turning his meat-packing company, the William Davies Company, into the largest pork-packer in the British Empire had worked just as well at the IMB. The mammoth organization ran remarkably efficiently under the team of brilliant executives he had assembled from across the country. The men of the IMB were devoted to their Chairman and to the war effort.

Those who had followed Flavelle's career before the war were not surprised at his success, for the soft-spoken fifty-nine-year-old Torontonian had combined an outstanding record in private business with years of public service in educational, hospital, and church work. He was a pillar of the Methodist Church, prominent in its national affairs, but not too busy to have given years of Sundays and Saturday evenings teaching Sunday School. He was a capitalist with a conscience, a millionaire who knew the meaning of stewardship. A man of exceptional integrity and ability, he had been well chosen to serve his country in wartime in a way no other Canadian businessman had ever served.

Of course he worked without pay. And when other businessmen, the munitions manufacturers under contract to the IMB, had put their pay before the need to serve and insisted on higher profit margins, he had lost his temper and said something no other capitalist in Canada had ever said: "Profits! Send profits to the hell where they belong."

His title symbolized more than a reward for war service well done. It was a fitting touch to a classic North American fairy tale, the story of the poor boy who made good. Flavelle's immigrant father had become an alcoholic. His mother had held the family together in poverty, the children leaving school early to earn their own way in life. Joe, the youngest, had left school at thirteen, gone into business on his own at eighteen. Following his mother's and his church's teachings, he practised a code of hard work, honesty, sobriety, and daily prayer. Twenty years later he was a millionaire. He had moved about as far and as fast as anyone could in one lifetime. Now the title certified it. Joe Flavelle, the son of a poor, intemperate shopkeeper in Peterborough, Upper Canada, had become a member of the aristocracy of the world's greatest Empire.

Six weeks a baronet, and then the headlines on July 13:

MILLIONS MADE BY FLAVELLES OUT OF BACON EXPORT

SENSATION IN PARLIAMENT WHEN COST OF LIVING COMMISSION REPORTS

THIS FIRM MADE OVER 5 CENTS A POUND PROFIT, CLEANING UP FIVE
MILLION DOLLARS IN A YEAR ON THIS ALONE.

The most terrible thing a businessman could do in wartime — profiteering. Making millions while men died. Praying in public, preying in private. Hypocrisy, parasitism; some used the word treason. There were bitter jokes about baconets and baconeers, hogging the profits and wallowing at the trough. They had sometimes nicknamed him "Holy Joe," or "Joseph the Provider"; now he was "Old Black Joe." To hell with profits? To Flavelle with profits! In German he was a *Kriegsgewinnern*.

A Royal Commission cleared the William Davies Company of all charges of unethical business practice. The fact remained that it had earned a profit of eighty per cent on its invested capital in the year ending March 31, 1916, and almost as much again the next year. That was all the evidence of profiteering most people needed; a lot of them believed the other charges, whatever the Royal Commission said. The government slapped tight controls on packers' profits. Several newspapers and politicians called for Flavelle's resignation from the Imperial Munitions Board. He considered resigning, but did not, and the Canadian government could not fire him.

He did not consider resigning his title. Popular opinion and Parliament decided that no more Canadians should receive titles. A few more did in 1935, but Flavelle was the last Canadian domiciled in Canada to receive a hereditary title. His reputation as an unconscionable profiteer had done as much as anything to bring such honours into disrepute.

He went on about his work at the IMB, trying as best he could to ignore the hatred of him. "My activity will largely pass with my duties here," he wrote in November 1918. "I can have no effective voice in any activity following the war — the great body of the press — of the public — of my own church, know me as a convicted profiteer — selfish, greedy and pressing burdens on the poor. Of course it hurts. . . ."[1]

As some people's memories of the war faded, as his friends rallied to his support, he regained some of his prominence as a public-spirited businessman — until he was attacked again in the depths of the Depression as one of the worst exploiters of poor Canadians. When he died in 1939 the papers said nothing about 1917. People remembered though. Outside the circle of those who knew him personally most memories of Flavelle revolved around profiteering and spoiled meat. "Be sure to write about the bad meat he sold in the war," white-collar workers at Canada Packers told me when I was searching for records of the William Davies Company. "I want to be known as a business man who with others established a great business and sustained it upon integrity, truthfulness and honest service," Flavelle had written in 1917.[2] In his own industry later generations remembered him as one of those old-time buccaneers who had made a lot of money selling bad meat.

Joseph Wesley Flavelle symbolized as well as any modern Canadian the pure spirit of capitalism. In meat-packing and in his other business activities — as president of National Trust, chairman of the Bank of Commerce, principal owner of Simpson's — Flavelle was at or near the centre of Canadian business during the formative years of our modern economy—though his roots were back in the days of Sir John A. Macdonald and the National Policy. No businessman in the country was more active in non-business service, trying to apply his abilities to further useful public goals. The web of his private philanthropies was incredible. With only a Grade Nine education, he was among the most articulate spokesmen for private enterprise and social conservatism. Flavelle's wartime work with the IMB was not equalled by a businessman in public life until the emergence of C. D. Howe as the czar of Canadian industry in the Second World War. But in a few weeks in that summer of 1917 a man who was thought to represent the best in Canadian business came to stand for the worst. A man who wanted and was thought to be a credit to his generation of businessmen did as much as anyone to bring that generation and its values into disrepute.

A CANADIAN MILLIONAIRE

CHAPTER ONE

THE FLAVVLES OF PETERBOROUGH

The future baronet was born on February 15, 1858, the fifth and youngest child of John and Dorothea Flavelle of Peterborough, Upper Canada. They had emigrated from Ireland in 1847, the worst year of the great famine. Flavelle was pronounced with the accent on the first syllable, *flav'-vle*.

It had lost its original French pronunciation in the generations that the Huguenot Flavelles had lived in Ireland; they had emigrated some time after the 1685 revocation of the Edict of Nantes, settling in Ulster as tenant farmers. John Flavelle was born on a farm near Dungannon, County Tyrone, in 1823, one of six children. As a teenager he was apprenticed to learn the grocery trade in the market town of Cootehill in neighbouring County Cavan, completed his training, and was considered to be a willing, steady worker.

In July 1847 John Flavelle married Dorothea Dundas, a girl his age, who was keeping house for her brother in Cootehill. The Dundases had emigrated to Ireland from Scotland in the seventeenth century and had moderately prospered as flax farmers and linen manufacturers. Dorothea's mother, Katherine Brunker Dundas, was well-educated, a school teacher whose family had deep roots in the Anglo-Irish Ascendency. Its fortune had been dissipated by the nineteeth century, but the Dundases were able to afford a decent education for Dorothea, and perhaps a small dowry. John and "Dolly" were married in Dungannon by a cousin who was a bishop of the Church of England in Ireland.

They were married in a month when three million Irish, almost forty per cent of the island's population, were receiving food rations. Tens of thousands were fleeing a starving, plague-ridden country for sanctuary in the New World. The young couple were not themselves desperately poor or

hungry, but like many others of the comparatively well-to-do classes that
year, they realized there was no future for them in Ireland. They decided not
to risk their capital "in the present condition of affairs," but rather to set out
for Canada "to seek their fortune in the land of promise." They left almost
immediately after the wedding.[1]

I

Having some money of their own, the Flavelles probably enjoyed a relatively comfortable crossing to the port of New York, avoiding the fever-
ridden coffin ships that landed so many dying and destitute Irish on British
North American soil that year. They travelled with Dorothea's younger
brother and his bride, but continued on to Canada when their companions
decided to settle in upstate New York. Peterborough was a town of about
two thousand people, the centre of a lumbering and farming county settled
almost entirely by Irish emigrants. It was a bustling, semi-frontier community, in which an ambitious, hard-working man could get ahead. Already at
least one Cootehill boy, William Cluxton, an orphan who came out to
Canada in his teens, was known to be prospering wonderfully in his own
dry-goods business. The Flavelles may have briefly tried farming just outside the community; if so, the experience cost them most of their remaining
capital and they soon moved into town where John could practise his trade.
In 1848 Dorothea's mother, Katherine, and her four remaining children
joined them in Peterborough.

Steady and industrious as he may have been in Ireland, John Flavelle
turned out to be an unreliable breadwinner in Canada. Starting as book-
keeper for a local grocer, possibly running his own store for a time, he
drifted from job to job, sometimes working in the shanties north of town,
other times returning to clerk in stores or hire himself out as a common
labourer—never finding his fortune. The problem was that, although he was
warm-hearted and God-fearing, John Flavelle developed over the years an
uncontrollable thirst for strong drink. "It was not that my father meant to
conduct himself the way he did," Joe recalled in one of his few references to
his father, "but the appetite for liquor became a desire which would lead him
to drink week after week until he would have to go to bed ill for two or three
weeks. He would then get up and go to work, and do what work he could
get, only to have the same thing break out in the course of a few weeks and
repeat the story again."[2]

A kindly and gentle man in his sober periods, John Flavelle was able to maintain a façade of respectability. He was not without grit in his character —Joe never forgot the time his father walked twenty-three miles into town with a toothache and then held the lantern while the dentist made the extraction. But he was too often incapacitated to hold down a regular job or bring in a steady income. And there was a darker side of his character that survives only in oral tradition: Joe also told stories of the children scattering as their father hurled bottles through windows in drunken rage. He lost touch with his family in Ireland ("I have not had a word from any of you for Six Years so I thought I would try one on you and see . . . if poor Mother is still living").[3] The John Flavelle whose portrait survives from the early 1880s is sad-eyed and spiritless, a man overcome by life. For the rest of their lives his children seldom mentioned their father. Instead they remembered Dorothea as one of the best mothers who ever lived.

Immediately on arriving in the Peterborough area Dorothea began to supplement John's income by offering music and singing lessons. In 1849 her mother founded a private school in the Flavelle house "for the instruction of children in the various branches of an English education and plain and fancy needlework."[4] Both Dorothea and her mother taught in the local grammar school in the early 1850s, but shortly resumed their private classes. In 1854 Dorothea and her sister Lydia took charge of the school.

"We quickly learned that our teacher's displeasure was the one thing in the universe most to be dreaded," a former student wrote of Dorothea, "and only to be avoided by strict attention to our lessons and total abstinence from the unpardonable sin of whispering."[5] The school seems to have prospered in the 1850s, drawing many students from the established families in the Peterborough region, including the children of lumber king Mossom Boyd. In 1862 Dorothea closed it to take charge of the primary department in Central Public School. She taught for another thirteen years, as many as a hundred students at a time, at a salary of $300 to $400 annually,* before retiring in 1875.

---

* Prices and wages remained roughly constant in Canada from the 1870s through the early 1900s. $1.00 a day was a common wage for an unskilled labourer in Central Canada and the Maritimes, $2.00 to $3.50 for a tradesman. Businessmen and professionals — but not lady schoolteachers—enjoyed a much wider differential from blue-collar workers than they do today —$2,000 annually, or about six to seven times a labourer's income, was good but not extraordinary.

By the last quarter of the twentieth century salaries and wages had increased by 2000 to 3000 per cent for workers, 1000 to 2000 per cent for professionals. Prices had risen about 500 per

3

Dorothea's teaching did not lift the Flavelles above a condition of genteel poverty. They lived in rented frame bungalows; Dorothea made her own tallow candles for lighting because kerosene was too expensive. She dressed plainly, Quaker-like a friend recalled, "from principle and through necessity."[6] Her male children left school at an early age to help supplement the family's income. Mary Katherine (Minnie) was the eldest child, born in 1848. She was followed by John Dundas (1850), William McElroy (1853), Margaret (1855), and Joe in 1858. The Flavelles were fortunate for their time in that all their offspring survived the first couple of years of life, although Maggie was crippled by scarlet fever when she was two years old.

Joe's earliest memories were of sitting on his mother's knee for hours while she taught during the day and watching her pour melted tallow into tin moulds for her candles in the evening. He also soon became conscious of his mother's religious devotion, expressed in the family prayers she led morning and night. These prayers were rich with the language of the Anglican Prayer Book because Dorothea had been a faithful member of the Church of England in Ireland. But when she attended St. John's Anglican Church in Peterborough she was shocked by the whiskey-drinking, cock-fighting parson supplied as a missionary from England. Turning to the Methodist Church, which John had favoured in Ireland, Dorothea found a cultivated minister and comfort and satisfaction in her worship. Her children were baptized as Methodists. She learned to pray in the impromptu Methodist manner, volunteering her feelings and fears. "Mother addressed God not in any irreverent, familiar manner, but as though He were right beside her and she was just telling Him. She had a great deal to tell him in her anxiety and care, but as she prayed one felt she was in the presence of a Being in whom she believed."[7]

Like his brothers and sisters, whom Dorothea moulded into a remarkably close-knit family, Joe was raised to be prayerful at home, at church, and in business. Listening to his mother talk with God, "it grew with me as a little fellow that I, too, could pray as Mother did, and ask as she did for guidance and counsel."[8] At an early age he was a member of the George Street Methodist Church Sabbath School, where his mother's training was reinforced by the striking oratory and personal magnetism of the superinten-

cent. One way to make the various figures quoted in this text begin to approach modern values (though still erring on the low side) is mentally to multiply them all by ten. It is less misleading, though, to forget about modern comparisons and to learn the meaning of older scales of prices and incomes on their own terms.

dent, Robinson Rutherford. "Bunty" Joe, small for his years as a boy, helped out in the Sunday School library and distributed the Bibles to the classes. During regular worship he was small enough to romp around behind the high backs of the pews without being noticed, until he slipped and his head rattled like a drumstick against the wood.

His family made a special point every year of attending the church's revival or "protracted" meetings, the annual evangelistic services designed to win converts to God and Methodism. At the protracted meeting when Joe was twelve years old he decided he wanted to join the church, "and it seemed to me the natural way to do so was the way other people did, and so I went to the penitent bench and was admitted into membership in the church."[9] It is hard to imagine what sins he confessed in his conversion experience. Perhaps he was contrite about the time he had been one of the group in the grammar-school play shed who tossed a stone through the back window of the Presbyterian Church and were caught by the mayor. He had been an exuberant enough boy that Dorothea is said to have disciplined him on occasion by dipping him head first in the rainbarrel.[10]

In discipline as in everything else Dorothea Flavelle was by common testimony an extraordinary woman and mother. A Methodist minister's daughter who was deeply influenced by her teaching recalled that there were many men and women in town "over whom she wielded a powerful influence for good, who came to her for counsel in matters worldly as well as spiritual."[11] In her few surviving letters, written in her old age, she shifts easily from the spiritual—thanking the Heavenly Father for his mercies and loving-kindness—to the worldly: "How high pork is this year. Some one will feel it by the end I am afraid."[12] In 1902 she gave her son a piece of business advice that changed the future of the Canadian meat-packing industry.

Giving Joe advice was a habit she began with him as a child, sitting him on her knee and telling him of events that interested her. One of these sessions marked the beginning of his lifelong interest in Western Canada. A missionary from Rupert's Land had spoken at the annual missionary service at George Street. Flavelle remembered his mother as saying, "The missionary told us last night that in the eight hundred miles between Fort Garry and the foothills of the Rocky Mountains, there are rolling plains, occupied by huge herds of buffalo, and by Indians and half-breeds; that some day these plains would produce wheat, cattle and dairy products in quantities that would be an important factor in the world's food supply. Now, my boy, as you grow up, I want you to remember what this wise man said." Several years later, in 1869, she reminded him of the missionary's talk and told him of the sharp criticism being made of the Macdonald government's purchase of these lands from the Hudson's Bay Company. Eleven-year-old Joe was indignant at cheapskates who dared oppose the country's growth.[13]

II

Before he reached his teens Joe was starting to help supplement the family income. The first of the family to go into business had been an uncle, Dorothea's younger brother, Joseph Rutherford Dundas, who was trained in trade by William Cluxton, the now wealthy orphan who probably had known the Dundases in Cootehill. In 1860 Cluxton sent J. R. Dundas to Lindsay to manage a grocery and dry-goods branch of his Peterborough store, not so much for the money Dundas might earn him, but to give him a start on a business career. Rated by the Dun credit reporter as "sober, steady, shrewd & attentive," Dundas was given a partnership in the Lindsay business and bought it when Cluxton retired in 1870. He brought his nephews, Johnnie and Will Flavelle, to Lindsay to work with him, forming Dundas & Flavelle Brothers in 1877. Minnie Flavelle, who had been teaching school but was unusually talented in mathematics, also moved to Lindsay as book-keeper for the firm.

In the meantime Joe had had his first paid-for piece of work when he was ten years old, spending two weeks in the Christmas holidays delivering telegram messages. He had been hired by the local telegraph and express agent for the Grand Trunk, George Albertus Cox, another eager young Methodist, who some thought might get ahead in life if he didn't over-extend himself. Joe was paid ten dollars for his work and promptly spent it at the Nicholls & Hall Drygoods store on a black paramatta dress for his mother. He also spent some time when he was eleven helping another uncle in Lindsay in his boot and shoe shop, catching rats at five cents a head.

After qualifying for entrance into high school, Joe decided to go to work instead. Early in 1871 he got a job selling fancy goods and fingering wool in John Erskine's general dry-goods store at eight dollars a month. Erskine was a kind but strait-laced Scotsman. Joe worked the normal hours of a clerk in the 1870s, eight in the morning until seven-thirty in the evening on week-days and till ten or midnight on Saturdays, relieved by the occasional game of ball in the alley when he could hook out with Sam Wright and the other boys.

Incidents of that first job stood out in his memory. Toward the end of a particularly busy Saturday, "I was as curious as a monkey to see how much our sales had been, and after supper, I went to the till, opened it, took out the money, and commenced to count it. My Scotch employer, shocked at so unheard of a thing, did not say anything to me until I was almost done, then he came and remarked—'What are you doing boy?' 'Trying to find out how much the sales are,' I replied. 'Don't you know you have no business to do that?' I can still remember the sense of injury I felt. I knew what I was doing arose out of my interest in the store, and my employer told me I had no business to do it." [14]

He was still so small that his chin barely cleared the counter, and another time he was keenly wounded when a woman customer announced that she wouldn't be waited on by a snip of a boy. But for all his problems Bunty Flavelle did well and knew it. "I hear a great many talking about Joe, saying what a smart boy he is," Johnnie Flavelle wrote Will in 1871. "Jim Benson says that he is the best little salesman he ever saw. Don't tell Joe for, dear knows, he thinks enough of himself already. That is a failing that belongs to all the young portion of our family." [15]

William Flavelle had been apprenticed to James Best, a general-store keeper and a member of George Street Methodist Church. When Will left at the end of 1871 to work in the Lindsay business, Dorothea persuaded Best to take Joe on as a replacement. He was formally apprenticed to Best for three years at wages of fifty dollars the first year, seventy-five the second, and one hundred the third, with Best to provide breakfast and dinner. Joe got along well with Best, another upstanding churchman, and became Mrs. Best's favourite when he discovered it was the ticks spread from the sheepskins at James Stevenson's neighbouring store that caused her baby to cry so much. They sold everything from needles to anchors in Best's store, but most of their trade involved bartering with farmers, taking in butter, eggs, fruit, vegetables, and Mud Lake fish as payment. One of Joe's first jobs was to sort the lumps of butter farmers brought in into similar colours, pack it into fifty-pound tubs, and salt it for storage. It was the beginning of a fifty-year career handling agricultural produce.

Despite its Horatio Alger-like overtones (Flavelle's was the kind of real life that made Horatio Alger plausible), there is no reason to disbelieve the story Joe often told about his mother's advice when he brought home his first earnings from Best's store. "'Now, Joe, a portion of that is to be put aside for the Church, and a portion set aside for your Party. When you grow up to be a man, and to be a good man as I hope you will be, I want you to have learned that among the things you ought to do is to support your Party with money, because if good men do not support it, bad men will, and the government will do things they should not do because bad men pay them and good men don't.' And so a portion of my first wages was set aside for the Church and a portion for the Party."[16]

Following his mother's Irish Toryism Joe was already a committed Conservative. More important, he was trying to hold fast to his new commitment to the church. The senior clerk at Best's store used to make fun of the little convert, trying to make him do or say things that would discredit a Christian. As a "little altar of refuge" he would creep into a packing case against the stone wall in the cellar and there pray to be kept from anger and temptation. The packing case in the cellar was his sanctuary for the three years he worked for Best.[17]

III

The Flavelles were a conservative family, conscious of class and status in Peterborough and anxious to advance themselves. As a little boy Joe had been taught to touch his hat to members of the established Peterborough families—the Burnhams, the Rogerses, the Haultains, and others—on the street. Even in Peterborough in the 1870s there was a slight stigma attached to going into trade. Will and Johnnie Flavelle hoped that at least one of their family would complete an education and advance into the professions. When Joe finished his apprenticeship Will offered to pay their mother the equivalent of Joe's wages so he could start back to high school and eventually go on to be a lawyer or a doctor "instead of going into business like the rest of us."

Joe returned to high school in 1874, older than the other boys and ready to throw his weight around. By his own account he was a "conceited headstrong boy—angry, insistent, impulsive."[18] The teacher knocked him down the first day. The boys got even by dowsing the stove with red pepper and forcing the school to close. A new principal left Joe's class on their honour while he was out of the room, and they were permanently chastened when a pen missed the beam it was thrown at and put out an eye. Beyond this there are no records of Flavelle's schooling, only his lifelong sensitivity about his lack of higher education.

He probably found school too confining after his apprenticeship, and he did not like being dependent on his brother's charity. When Will repeated the offer for another year Joe found himself saying, "Will, I don't want to do it. I want to go into business and earn for myself. I am not going to let you do it."[19] Now seventeen, he took a job in a flour and feed store where his father had sometimes worked. When the owner died suddenly in 1876, Joe, eighteen years old, bought the business. His uncle and his brothers, all prospering in Lindsay, supplied him with the necessary cash and guaranteed his credit at the bank. Will came to Peterborough for the first year and a half to help him get his bearings. With the exception of Cluxton's patronage of J. R. Dundas, the members of the large family had helped each other up the ladder until Joe, the youngest, was in business on his own. To square the circle Joe gave work to his father when John Flavelle was sober.

His mother had held the family together economically and spiritually. Most of Joe's character was inherited from or moulded by the Dundases. A graphologist might find it significant, though, that the flourish with which Joe began his (left-handed) signature in the 1880s was an exact copy of his father's.

He was now J. W. Flavelle, Dealer in Flour, Feed, Pork, and Provisions. He had developed physically in his teens, reaching his adult height of six feet, enjoying strength and good health which would stay with him into his seventies. In his mid-twenties he cultivated first a mustache and sideburns, then a neatly-trimmed beard, perhaps to mask his ugly, jutting chin, perhaps because his hairline was receding. Later it would be said he grew a beard because he hadn't time to shave. If he was unusually young to be in business on his own, he already had his three years' apprenticeship in general store-keeping and he could always rely on his uncle and brothers in Lindsay for advice and financial support. At least as important, he brought to his vocation the personal characteristics summed up in the framed motto two maiden ladies of the church gave him to hang on his office wall: "Not Slothful in Business, Fervent in Spirit, Serving the Lord."[20]

IV

Since his conversion almost all his free time had been spent in the work and worship of George Street Methodist Church. His friendships, his cultural interests, and probably no small part of his early business connections all developed in the church. His Sabbath, for example, began with a seven a.m. prayer meeting, followed by class meeting at half past nine, regular service at half past ten, Sunday School at two-thirty (he became a teacher in his teens) with a teachers' prayer meeting immediately afterwards, volunteer tract distribution from four-thirty to five, evening service at half past six, and a final prayer meeting to close the day. There would be a midweek prayer meeting to attend, at least one evening spent preparing his Sunday School lessons, and perhaps a Saturday-night teachers' meeting to give thought to the morrow. There were also personal devotions—morning and evening prayers, daily Bible study.

Twelve-year-old Joe Flavelle had been redeemed of his sins, "justified" by the faith he professed when he came to the penitents' bench, and was accepted into the fellowship. But for a Methodist boy who took his faith seriously this was only the beginning of a lifelong striving for personal holiness, what Wesley had called "sanctification" or "Christian perfection."

The genius of John Wesley and the Methodists was their emphasis on man's freedom in his relationship to God. All men, Wesley had taught, could be saved, if only they had the faith to open themselves to God's grace. God had not chosen only his elect few, as the dour Calvinists taught, damning the majority of mankind to eternal suffering. The good news of the Gospel was free grace for all—salvation for anyone and everyone willing to believe.

But God required much from those to whom He gave so much. After conversion, what the Methodists called "the higher life" was a perpetual striving for personal holiness or perfection. It was to be a life of perfect service, of perfect accountability to God. It involved renunciation of the world and worldliness, of self-indulgence and luxuries. Above all there was to be a methodical denial of self and selfishness, a relentless overcoming of temptation—in practice a new puritanism. Living in the "freedom" promised by Wesley in fact required the iron self-discipline of the man determined to transcend human frailty.

Stressing the conversion of the individual and his personal struggle afterwards for self-perfection, Methodism could seem to be a faith for the lone man, atomized and isolated as he made his way through life. But Wesley has also been recognized as an organizational genius for his understanding of fellowship, of the benefits flowing from disciples' banding together to help one another. The fundamental unit of his Methodist societies, the "peculiar institution" of Methodism, was the *class* of disciples, about a dozen in number, meeting together weekly. Class membership was still a condition of church membership in Methodism in the 1870s, and when Joe Flavelle left Sunday School upon joining the church he was immediately enrolled in a young men's class.

At the weekly class meeting the leader, a kind of sub-pastor of the church, would, in the words of the *Discipline,* "inquire how their souls prosper." Each member gave a statement rendering account of his spiritual condition. The leader would then "advise, reprove, comfort, or exhort, as occasion may require." There were also Bible readings and prayers, led by the members in turn, with special prayers for members facing temptation, sick, or for any reason absent from class. Some critics compared the Methodist class to the Catholic confessional. In the late twentieth century it might seem not unlike the secular encounter group. Methodists themselves were proud of its function as a training ground for lay leaders in the church, men who had learned to pray and speak out in public, to profess their faith and work powerfully together towards personal perfection.

Through his teens Flavelle was a faithful attender at class; in his early twenties he became one of the youngest class leaders at George Street. In 1882 he also became superintendent of the Sunday School. Much of the rest of his life reflected his experiences as a young man struggling for Christian perfection and leading other young men along the same path. His Methodist training made him introspective, deeply concerned with the problem of his own motivation, intent on self-mastery, perfect self-control. He learned to account for the state of his spiritual life weekly in class, and as a businessman he stressed formal accounting—the regular rendering of the state of the firm—as the key to success. He would never be backward in advising, reproving, comforting, or exhorting others on the state of their accounts, monetary or moral. Methodists deferred present gratification, looking ahead to future reward; in business Flavelle planned and built for the future, never milking the profits of the moment. Working in large organizations, yet suspicious of organization, he built teams of executives under his direction who operated in ways strikingly like a Methodist class. In business, private life, and politics, he was most true to Wesley in believing that the individual will, aided by spiritual power, could achieve almost anything.

His earliest surviving letter was written about 1880 to "Sister" Clara Ellsworth, who was wrestling with a deep personal problem. Offering her "my earnest prayers during the course of your Trial," Joe tried to convince her of the rightness of the course she was being pressed to take:

Which spirit prompts you to do the act, which not? I know what your answer must be. Well, Clara, if God says do so, can He advise anything which would be mocking to Himself? Are you not safe then in acting? . . .

Just let me notice a remark or two you made use of. "Mockery almost blasphemy for me to attempt to pray in public." Is this true logic—does it come from God or the devil Clara? I think the latter. Do you feel that in your private devotions you are mocking or blaspheming God? I am sure you can say no. Then this being so—tell me —is the God you address in public any different from the one you address in private? *Surely not* Clara. This is nothing but a Temptation I am convinced—all the more powerful because of its peculiar form. . . .

I have spoken plainly, not in the spirit of being better than you, only I have gone through the same difficulty myself. I pray God He may see fit to give you some little comfort from something I have said—before I attempted to reply I went and asked direction from Him. . . .[21]

As part of his renunciation of worldly habits young Flavelle touched no liquor or tobacco, did not attend the theatre, dance, or play cards. He dressed conservatively, favouring greys and blacks — though most often he wore plain workingman's clothes. His givings to the church and other worthy causes approached and went beyond literal tithing. Although he was considered one of the finest Christian young men of George Street, he never seems to have thought of the ministry as a vocation, indeed making it a principle never to speak from a pulpit.

Wesley considered business a legitimate Christian calling, believed deeply in the institution of private property, and had foreseen that the Methodist people would grow wealthy through their hard work and frugality. "Godliness," the Peterborough congregation was told in the 1880s, "was profitable financially because it gave character and reputation to the man that practised it, and these begot confidence, which led to preferment and increased financial gain. When a man was faithful to religious principles, other things being equal, God gave worldly prosperity. . . . The ungodly might flourish, but their prosperity was only temporary."[22]

In Flavelle's youth, worldly prosperity was already being bestowed upon the George Street Methodists and Canadian Methodists in general. Across the country wealthy and devout Methodist laymen, like James Morrow of Halifax, Robert Wilkes and John Macdonald of Toronto, gave the largest subscriptions and laid the cornerstones for Gothic stone temples to replace the wooden meeting-house as the symbol of Methodism. The George Street congregation spent $60,000 on their new church, finished in 1875, which was patterned after Toronto's famous Metropolitan Church. The largest contributor was George Cox. In addition to his telegraph agency and his service as mayor of Peterborough for three terms, Cox had found his *métier* as a Christian businessman. From 1861 he had been preaching the gospel of life insurance in the service of the Canada Life, earnestly and profitably convincing Peterboroughnians to take thought for the morrow and provide for their dear ones. No other business in the nineteenth century seemed to accomplish as much social good as these life-insurance companies promoting thrift and love of family.

Although some Methodists worried about the possible corrupting effects of their new affluence, the denomination was prospering precisely because its wealthy laymen took the idea of Christian stewardship seriously. John Macdonald, the merchant prince of the wholesale trade in Toronto in the 1870s and 1880s, regularly gave away twenty per cent of his income. In the *Canadian Methodist Magazine* he described the endless stream of visitors to the office of a successful Christian businessman — collectors for every charity in the city, tramps in every stage of dilapidation, reformed alcoholics and not-so-reformed alcoholics, people wanting to borrow five dollars and three thousand dollars, "artists, sculptors, men interested in gold mines in Nova Scotia, and silver mines in Mexico, cattle ranches in Colorado and the North-West." Many—most—of these would be frauds, but where there was not time to investigate, "it is better that you should be deceived and this in nine cases rather than that the tenth really deserving should go away unassisted."[23] As he read this Flavelle could hardly have known that all these and more would eventually pass though his own office and that he too would be deceived in a healthy portion of the cases.

v

First there was the problem of making his own way in the world, of turning a profit in his provision business at 139 Simcoe Street, just off the market square. To determine whether he was making money Flavelle kept a careful memo of his transactions in his pocket. Like most country merchants in the nineteenth century he knew nothing of bookkeeping and was probably too independent to listen to advice from his brothers. But just as he kept watch over his spiritual condition in his weekly class meeting, so in business every week he attempted a summing up, reckoning his costs against sales and finding out how nearly he had come to making expenses. "When it did not look well I used to work harder the next week to catch up."[24] As the business developed he began to estimate each week's prospects in advance, comparing the results at week's end with the forecast. To simplify his accounting and to provide him with ready cash for his buying, Flavelle allowed only one month's credit instead of the usual three months, six months, or longer. The insistence on prompt payment and careful accounting distinguished him from the majority of country storekeepers in the 1870s and 1880s, who were notorious for taking heavy losses on credit accounts and who often had no idea of their financial position from one season to the next.

He decided to add a retail trade in town to his general trade with local farmers in grain, feed, seeds, and bulk provisions. He intended to purchase farm products on the Peterborough market in the fall, particularly quarters and sides of meat, and resell to consumers from his store during the rest of the year. He hoped to pay the rent and other costs of the store out of this line of business so his earnings on his main transactions would be clear profit. It is unlikely that he was able to keep separate accounts of this trade, but he considered the idea to be the origin of his later, more sophisticated use of collateral enterprises to balance the costs of his principal business.

In ten years as a provision merchant in Peterborough, Flavelle dealt in a wide variety of agricultural products. To the farmers of the county he sold hay, feed grains, salt, flour, and every kind of seed. He sold salt pork and beef by the side to lumbermen for their camps, cut and packed it by the pound for consumers in the town—specializing in sugar-cured hams at 10¢ to 12¢ per pound. He sold pigs' heads for $2.00 per hundred, spareribs at ten pounds for 25¢, hen feed at $1.00 per hundredweight, Manitoba Hard baker's flour at $2.50 per hundredweight. He bought everything farmers had to sell and often advertised when he was in the market for more potatoes, hogs, or butter. Despite his retail trade he tried to deal in bulk as much as possible and was soon bringing in seed by the carload and offering salt by the ton. As early as 1879 he was prepared to supply feed "in any quantities" and was advertising to purchase five hundred hogs and a thousand tubs of butter. His advertisements stressed quality rather than price, another characteristic of his later business methods. The quality was high, the prices "as low as a living profit will allow."[25]

Although he was in business for himself he operated in close cooperation with Dundas & Flavelle Bros. in Lindsay. Through the 1860s William Cluxton had been a large buyer of farm produce—grain, butter, and cheese—for export through Montreal to the United States and Britain. In Lindsay

J. R. Dundas had acted as Cluxton's agent in this trade, many of the products coming into the store as barter. Eventually Dundas & Flavelle Bros. became produce merchants in their own right. In the early 1880s they were exporting butter, cheese, and eggs to Manitoba and American cities; they also began exporting to Scotland when Johnnie Flavelle decided it should be possible to offset his dry-goods orders there with sales of Canadian farm products.

In Peterborough Joe bought grain, eggs, and cheese for his brothers, and perhaps Cluxton, to export, while taking some of their surpluses of feed and seed for sale in his area. In the 1880s the three brothers formed a separate partnership to deal in butter, dividing up the countryside east and west of Peterborough. Joe took the eastern territory, driving with his team every fall through Keene, Indian River, Norwood, Hastings, and other villages to buy store-packed butter from local merchants. In the Peterborough market he was a large buyer of hundred-pound kegs of farmer-packed butter. Each cask he always tested for quality first by plunging in an auger and bringing out a core to its full depth (the first lesson a buyer learned was to get below the surface of anything a farmer had to offer). The best of the butter would be resold to local customers; some was shipped to one of the commission merchants on Front Street in Toronto; the remainder, usually the lowest quality, was exported to England through Dundas & Flavelles.

His businesses did well. By 1883 twenty-five-year-old Joe Flavelle owned his own home and lot valued at $1,400 and rented store property valued at $3,000. In 1877 and 1878 he had given $26 yearly for the regular work of George Street Church; in 1879 he raised it to $52, making him one of the larger contributors. The George Street congregation were still heavily in debt for their new building; in 1881 Flavelle subscribed $500 towards liquidating its debt. His income in 1883 was $2,000, and in 1885, a year in which he enlarged his premises, he made $2,500. In 1882 the *Examiner* had referred to him as one of the town's "youngest, most enterprising and successful businessmen."[26]

Joe once appeared at the local curling rink in his grimy workclothes, a story goes, to take up an urgent business point with his brother Johnnie. Johnnie urged him to stay and join the game. Joe pointedly said he had no time for curling. Johnnie Flavelle did moderately well in business and became a champion curler. Joe eventually learned to curl and became a millionaire.

VI

By 1880 the Dundases and the Flavelles had prospered to the point of being able to afford trips back to the British Isles. J. R. Dundas, his wife, Will, and one of Joe's sisters took Dorothea back to Ireland in the summer of that year. The next summer it was Joe's turn, travelling with Johnnie and seventeen-year-old Ed Cox, George Cox's eldest son. On the eve of their departure Joe's Bible class presented him with Butt's *Commentaries on the Romans*, the *Homiletic Cyclopedia of Illustrations*, Thompson's *The Land and the Book*, and Whedon's five volumes of *Commentaries on the New Testament*.

The young men spent three months abroad. In England they were typical tourists at Stratford, Warwick, Oxford, Chester, and other historic towns, with Joe being specially impressed by the estates of the Duke of Westminster, the richest nobleman in England. Whether or not he had taken his Bible commentaries along with him, Joe was anxious to improve himself on the trip. "I am learning here," he wrote Clara Ellsworth from London, "and am going to go back I hope a better man, capable of more work and more usefulness." In Ireland they visited distant relatives and saw their parents' old home, hearing an especially fine sermon, "Salvation is Transformation," in Carlisle Methodist Church. "You will look somewhat anxiously for the influence of my trip upon my character, whether I will be a stronger or weaker man in Christ Jesus," Joe wrote from Ireland. "Well, Uncle, my life upon my return will have to give the practical result. Any statement of untried resolutions would give no evidence of permanent improvement. Yet I earnestly pray my Father that the lessons I have learned of my weakness, my lack of knowledge, my want of the Humility of the Master, may be of lasting influence upon me."[27]

In other summers Joe had spent his holidays at Bible camp or just canoeing or camping on the Otonabee River and the Kawartha Lakes. He became an expert canoeist, though never learned to swim, and began a life-time assault on the maskinonge and bass of the Kawarthas.

More and more often Clara Ellsworth was his companion on these outings. She and her mother had come to live in Peterborough in 1867 after the death of her father, a Methodist minister of Loyalist descent. She was the same age as Joe, who apparently fell in love with her when they were teenagers in Sunday School together. Their courtship proceeded through walks home after class and teachers' meetings, after-church dinners at the Ellsworths', church socials on the grounds of the Cox house, and long afternoons canoeing and fishing. They were married from the Ellsworth house in Ashburnham in September 1882. The night before the wedding Joe had taken Clara to see their little house, helping her in through the window so as not to violate the threshold.

Three months later John Flavelle died at age fifty-nine. The newspaper obituary referred to a painful chronic disease; others remember hearing it said that he had started home from a tavern, spent the night sleeping in a snowdrift, and died of pneumonia. Dorothea soon moved to Lindsay to be with her other four children, taking with her the black-walnut davenport presented by the George Street Ladies Aid Society as a token of their esteem for her "zealous and devout" service to the church. Joe was now the last of the Flavelles and Dundases left in Peterborough. In later years it was mistakenly believed that he too had moved to Lindsay.

The J. W. Flavelles settled down to a life of business and church work. Their first child, Mina, was born in 1884. Joe was often out of town on buying trips. He had just hitched the team to leave for Campbellford on one of these, when Mina took a convulsion and he had to rush for the doctor. "I can still see Dr. Halliday," he remembered in 1938, "with a clean handkerchief spread across her mouth, breathe down, stretch her little arms out, and by and by she commenced to breathe, and her life was saved." Religious men and women who lived so close to sudden death or crippling misfortune a century ago were constantly giving thanks for the blessings of health and life. "How good and kind our Heavenly Father has been to us," Joe wrote Clara in 1885 from Toronto. "Now almost three years married and not a heavy shadow across our path in that time. Sometimes I wonder why I am so mercifully dealt with. I find so much weakness in my character that I know the all-seeing Eye also notes. Yet my Father pities and spares me. No gift of all gifts though my love is like yourself."[28]

As Sunday School superintendent he was now the leading layman of George Street. His sister wrote that he showed "remarkable ability in all departments" of his Sunday School work, and in 1884 the *Christian Guardian* reported, "probably no school in the Province is more orderly conducted. Love, reverence, order, study and cheerful obedience are marked features." He was also taking an increasingly active role in volunteer and church-related activities in the community — a member of the fire brigade (run on strict temperance principles), grand-jury foreman at the general sessions, a member of the executive of the Peterborough branch of the Upper Canada Bible Society, one of twenty prominent men at a meeting called by George

Cox to find ways of raising money for the YMCA, chairman of the board of trustees of Nicholls General Hospital. He had apparently been supporting his political party since his mother's advice in 1871 and was an active Conservative in Peterborough local politics in the early 1880s.[29]

Most of his older close acquaintances were politically active. William Cluxton had been Liberal-Conservative MP for Peterborough West from 1872 to 1874. Flavelle's uncle, J. R. Dundas, sat for Victoria as a Conservative from 1882 to 1887. James Stevenson, another Irish Methodist whose first wife had been a Dundas, eventually served fifty-five years on the Board of Education, ten terms as mayor of Peterborough, and nine years as a Conservative MP. In the 1887 federal election Stevenson beat George Cox by sixteen votes, spoiling Cox's second attempt to sit as a legislator. In the 1872 provincial election Cox had won by forty-five votes but was unseated when his agent admitted to bribery.

Cox was the only member of the group who was not a Conservative. But he shared fully these rising businessmen's concern for rapid economic development. It was Cox who took over the presidency of the faltering Midland Railway in 1878 (Cluxton had earlier been president; J. R. Dundas remained one of the directors) and engineered such improvement in service that by 1883 it was possible to travel from Peterborough to Toronto and back on the same day. Flavelle was among the crowd of citizens, accompanied by a brass band, who met the first incoming train heralding the end of what had been an overnight trip. This was real progress; it meant time and money to a busy merchant in the bustling community of 7,800, its outskirts dotted with factories, its streets lit by electricity, its pioneer years as a mud-gutted lumber town fading into memory.

Remembering his mother's stories of missionaries from Rupert's Land, shipping butter and eggs himself to the Canadian frontier in Manitoba, Flavelle was always enthusiastic about the prospect of opening up the resources of the great West. He was excited by the possibilities of agricultural development if the CPR could be pushed through to completion, considered moving to Winnipeg himself for a time in the early 1880s, and may have invested (and lost) some of his savings in western land.[30]

He believed in the development of Canadian industries, and was one of the many businessmen who supported Macdonald's National Policy tariff of 1879 as the kind of violation of orthodox economic theory that a practical, progressive country had to dare to undertake. As a practical, progressive young businessman he was contemptuous of the timid, woolly-minded

Liberals—Sir Richard Cartwright, the economic free-trader, Edward Blake, the constitutional lawyer who fancied himself an expert on railroads, Wilfrid Laurier, the French-Canadian dilettante — who had no faith in the country's capacity for developing its wonderful natural resources.[31] Flavelle's down-to-earth view of Canadian commercial problems blended with the Toryism he inherited from his mother to make him a very partisan Macdonald Conservative. One of the special thrills of his youth was meeting the great man himself on one of John A's campaign swings through the region.

VII

In 1886 Flavelle ran for public office for the only time in his life. He was defeated by R. W. Erret in the Ward 2 School Board Trustee election, 130 votes to 105. The turnout was the largest the ward had ever seen because J. W. Flavelle was now a controversial figure in Peterborough, one of the leaders in a fight that split the community in half in the mid-1880s.

Drink had been the curse of the Flavelle family. Liquor was cheap, strong, and available everywhere. John Flavelle had been the kind of drinker who could not drink moderately or socially. He had to abstain completely, for one nickel-shot of rye led to another and to another. . . . His drinking habits were not untypical of late-nineteenth-century Irishmen or Canadians, whose drinking led to drunkenness with a regularity not nearly so common half a century later. Whatever the causes of drinking, addiction to alcohol was widespread, and, as with the Flavelles, disastrous for drinkers and their families. In the English-speaking world Methodists were among the leaders in the drive to cure society of the drink habit, first by urging individuals to abstain from alcohol, then, when this had only limited success, taking the next logical step of trying to make it impossible for the drinker to procure the liquid fire. By religious persuasion and personal experience the Flavelles were ardent supporters of the Canadian temperance movement. Their father's experience had shown them, of course, that prohibition was the only way to achieve temperance.

In 1878 Parliament had passed the Canada Temperance, or Scott, Act, providing for local prohibition of the sale of liquor and beer on a majority vote in a city or county referendum. Various constitutional and technical problems delayed Scott Act referenda in Ontario until the middle of the 1880s. The Scott Act fight in Peterborough County[32] began in February 1885 with the visit of the Reverend B. B. Keefer of the Dominion Alliance for the Total Suppression of the Liquor Traffic. After preaching on the drink question at local Protestant churches, Keefer organized a meeting at Bradburn's Opera House on the sixteenth at which eight hundred citizens, led by their ministers, appointed a committee to make arrangements for a convention to plan their Scott Act strategy. George Cox was chairman of the committee, J. W. Flavelle its secretary.

The temperance convention and "Grand Mass Meeting" was held in the Opera House on March 4 with F. S. Spence of the Dominion Alliance as featured speaker. A Scott Act Association was formed—Cox the president, Flavelle treasurer. In a room adjoining the Opera House the ladies met to form a local branch of the Woman's Christian Temperance Union (Clara Flavelle soon became its secretary-treasurer). On May 13 Cox submitted the petition necessary for a Scott Act vote, signed by 1,852 citizens, to the county sheriff. After several months' delay the petition was forwarded to Ottawa and polling day was set for September 24, 1885.

Through September the Scott Act Association held rallies at Bradburn's Opera House every three or four days, each rally beginning with a hymn and a prayer. They hired special organizers for the campaign and brought in outside speakers. John Nicholls of Lowell, Massachusetts, told their first rally that the liquor traffic rested on "debased manhood, wronged womanhood and defrauded childhood," and promised that prohibition would reduce crime and benefit business. Susanneh E. Pech, one of the continent's foremost lady speakers on behalf of temperance, told them on September 4 that moral suasion had proven ineffective; they did not expect to make people sober by legislation, she argued, "but they intended to prevent sober people being made drunk by Act of Parliament." F. S. Spence emphasized that prohibition did not violate individual freedom: "Freedom for the right meant suppression of the wrong. The temperance people believed in liberty, but they wanted liberty to do only that which was right." He also indicted alcohol for inflaming the body, hardening the brain, overstimulating the heart, paralysing the nervous system, and leading to obesity.

The anti-Scott forces were organized under the auspices of the National Liberal Temperance Union, a front group for the distillers, the brewers, and the hotelkeepers, but were on the defensive, unable or afraid to use the Opera House and worried about disruptions from Scott Act supporters. Their star speaker was "Professor" C. Gordon Richardson of the NLTU whose specialty was to satirize the prohibitionists by describing in "thrilling and heartrending terms" the fatal effects of overindulgence in salt, to argue that more people died of overeating than overdrinking, and to warn that prohibition gave the socialists a precedent for other arbitrary interferences with rights and property. He delighted in infuriating Christian prohibitionists by citing a report of the superintendent of the Toronto Lunatic Asylum that half the inmates were there because of the effects of "religious excitement" (he was too delicate to add that another third were supposed to be there from the effects of masturbation). More effective opposition to prohibition came from Roman Catholic Archbishop Lynch of Toronto writing to the *Examiner* to oppose the attempt to make people temperate by legislation, urging stricter punishment for drunkenness, and suggesting that fair wages for the labouring man would enable him to have a comfortable breakfast in the morning "and there will be little craving for strong drink and less intemperance."

The campaign reached a climax of sorts at an open meeting on the eve of the plebiscite. The Peterborough drill hall was too jammed for anyone to sit down. All the anti-temperance speakers were heckled throughout their talks. When J. Gordon Mowat dragged on into the time period allotted to a pro-Scott speaker, George Cox and Police Magistrate Dumble (another George Street Methodist), the latter brandishing his cane, insisted on their man's right to speak. Mowat tried to continue but was silenced by a crescendo of hisses, groans, cat calls, and Indian war-whoops—these last from veterans of the North-West campaign against Louis Riel. Mowat resumed his speech by addressing the crowd as "friends and pharisees" and was immediately drowned out again. The audience sang "God Save the Queen," "Rule Britannia," and "We Won't Go Home Till Morning." For an hour the drill hall was "a perfect Babel" and nothing changed when Mowat started again: "Although no one could hear a word he said, he still talked on, gesticulating fiercely, and emphasizing his unheard periods by clinching his fist and thumping the rail vigorously." Finally, after Professor Richardson had tried to arrest one of the disturbers and had to be rescued from the mob by a constable, the chairman adjourned the meeting. The crowd gave three cheers for the Queen and went home.

Polling day was more orderly, perhaps because Cox and Flavelle's association was offering rewards of twenty-five dollars for the conviction of anyone selling liquor and fifty dollars for the conviction of anyone caught tampering with the voting procedures. There was a slight majority against the Act in the town of Peterborough, but a large majority for it in the townships. The final vote was 1,998 for and 1,487 against. Cox, Flavelle, and the Protestants of Peterborough had dried the county up, or, rather, were scheduled to when the Act came into force on May 1, 1886.

That winter Cox, the subject of considerable hate mail for his role in the Scott Act campaign, decided not to run for mayor again. James Stevenson, who had opposed the Scott Act (he did not drink himself, but did not believe in forcing others not to drink), was elected by acclamation. Flavelle was beaten in his campaign for Board of Education, almost certainly in retaliation for his role in the Scott Act struggle.

But he was also spending considerable time in Toronto on business. Sometime in the fall of 1885 or winter of 1886 he went there to examine three thousand fifty-pound packages of two-year-old store-packed butter that had accumulated in the cellars of the commission merchants on Front and West Market streets. For some reason they had not been able to sell it; most of it had gone disgustingly rancid, some had turned to grease. Flavelle bought the seventy-five tons of bad butter on behalf of himself and his brothers at three to five cents per pound (good butter sold for fifteen to twenty cents), sorted and graded it into grease, moderately firm, and firm butter, and re-coopered it himself in Toronto. After a day's work his clothes stank so of rancid butter that the disgust of passengers on the horse-car drove him to sit out on the back rail in shame. The regraded and repacked butter was all shipped to England and sold at a profit.

The same Toronto merchants were taking large losses on eggs in 1886. They had failed to clear their limed eggs from their cellars, carried them over for another year, and suffered a total loss when the young man from Peterborough who had bought their butter declared the eggs unfit for use and would have nothing to do with them. Flavelle came home from Toronto appalled at how badly the produce business was handled. He thought he could do better than that, had proven he could make money where the Toronto people couldn't, and began to ponder the pros and cons of setting up in business himself on Front Street.[33]

In the meantime there was the question of law enforcement in Peterborough. All through the Scott Act campaign, cynics had suggested prohibition could never be enforced in the county, partly because it would be impossible to stop people from drinking, partly because it was known that Sir John A.'s government had little taste for the political consequences of driving the liquor sellers out of business. The Scott Act Association had promised that if the Act were voted in they would see that it was enforced whatever the federal government did or failed to do.

On May 5, 1886, four days after prohibition officially came to Peter-borough, the Scott Act Association met in Bradburn's Opera House to discuss ways of enforcing the Act. The meeting opened with "Rescue the Perishing," was advised by the ubiquitous Spence that the only way to deal with the liquor traffic was to knock it on the head, and decided to raise a fund to prosecute violators of the Act. $4,125 was pledged that night — $1,500 by James Kendry, a local woollen manufacturer, $500 by Cox, and $100 sums by Flavelle and eleven others. The association was not impressed by local grocers' announcements of new stocks of ginger ale, mineral water, and choice teas, or the statement by Henry Calcutt, the leading local brewer, that he had begun to produce ginger ale.

On May 15 one Henry Rossiter, acting on information given him by the association, laid charges against nine hotelkeepers and Henry Calcutt. They were all convicted and fined $50 and costs, with half the fine going to Ros-siter, the informer—who immediately became notorious in town as Rossiter the Informer. Cox and Flavelle, the enforcers, denied in court that their association's fund was used for paying witnesses for the prosecution, reiterated their determination to see that justice was done whatever the public authorities did, and accepted responsibility for Rossiter's actions as their agent.

E. Mannell, a shoemaker like Rossiter, who lived three doors down from him, was awakened in the dead of night on June 3 by a fusillade of stones smashing his windows. A little later more stones were accompanied by three revolver shots and an explosion. "Boys, I guess you have made a mistake! I'm not Rossiter the Informer," Mannell shouted to the mob outside, who soon dispersed. The next morning evidence of a dynamite explosion was found outside his house along with an empty five-gallon beer keg.

Rossiter the Informer struck back with more charges against his enemies. An auctioneer who had publicly called him "a mean sneak of a whisky informer" was convicted of using grossly abusive language. Cavanagh, one of the convicted hotelkeepers, got into a fight with Rossiter over the rights and wrongs of boys shouting "Rats, rats, rats" at him on the street and was convicted of assault despite his defence that Rossiter had tried to pull a revolver on him. Scott Act prosecutions continued.

Finding Rossiter unshakable, some of the wets turned their attention to the men he was fighting for, the group brewer Calcutt considered "a lot of cranks." There were rumours, undoubtedly true, that the hotelkeepers had decided to stop doing business with J. W. Flavelle, known to be the most zealous worker on the committee prosecuting them. Then on Thursday,

October 21, Flavelle found his store's plate-glass window shattered and a five-pound rock lying inside his shop. Windows had also been broken at the YMCA rooms—Flavelle was the Association's president. Everyone knew the reason for the vandalism. Flavelle only commented that his landlords, Cox and Mayor Stevenson, were fully insured. The *Review* warned of the danger of anarchy in Peterborough. Sunday morning at George Street Rev. Tovell denounced the attack on Flavelle's store as cowardly and contemptible. That night passers-by frightened off men apparently trying to set fire to the sheds next to George Street Methodist.

Flavelle had worked behind the scenes through the agitation, raising and distributing the association's money, joining delegations to Ottawa to demand better enforcement, and arranging the prosecutions with Rossiter. On December 30, the day after an Ontario election, he broke his silence in an open letter resigning from the committee. An unequal share of the burden had fallen on him because no one was willing to take his place, he claimed, and the wet sympathies of Mayor Stevenson and J. R. Stratton, editor of the *Examiner*, had undercut much of the work. Now his fellow members of the committee had just allied themselves with the entire liquor interest by supporting Stratton in his successful candidacy for the provincial riding as a Liberal. "I cannot thus endorse such action. I cannot continue to do the larger part of the work of a committee whose members support a gentleman who has been so active in hindering us in our work."[34]

This was the end of Flavelle's temperance work in Peterborough. Within two months he acted on his plan to try his way in business in Toronto.

It was said then and for the rest of his life that Flavelle left Peterborough because of the hotelkeepers' boycott of his business. He never admitted that, always explaining the move in terms of his experience with the rancid butter. At the George Street farewell assembly in his honour he denied that his business had suffered through his opposition to the liquor traffic, and claimed his resolution to go to Toronto "had been made before ever the Scott Act was mooted here. No young man need be afraid to oppose the liquor traffic, for he would not suffer."[35] This was partly true at best. Flavelle may have been restless in Peterborough, may have been thinking of wider horizons before the Scott Act struggle began, but he had not then had his experience with the butter and eggs on Front Street, and as late as January 1887 was still accepting new offices in George Street Church. He was short of money and very anxious about his affairs in the winter and spring of 1887, reasonable evidence that his Peterborough business was being affected by the boycott.

So his decision to come to Toronto was probably influenced by the unhappy outcome of the temperance fight. On the other hand he considered his early months in business in Toronto to be an "experiment" from which he could fall back on his Peterborough base if necessary, and there is no reason to doubt his account of how he developed an interest in the Front Street trade. His ambition might well have led him to Toronto without the influence of the discouraging temperance struggle. Or, had he stayed in Peterborough, he would soon have been urged to move into larger ventures by his former patron, friend, and fellow prohibitionist, George Cox, who in 1888 also moved to Toronto because it was the natural centre of his growing insurance and financial empire.*

VIII

Flavelle began doing business in Toronto on the eve of his twenty-ninth birthday. He was no raw youngster in trade, having sixteen years' experience in business, ten of them as a merchant in his own right. He had mastered the intricacies and uncertainties of buying directly from farmers and reselling at a profit at retail, wholesale, and for export. He was not wealthy—it would be risky starting a second business in Toronto—but he did have important support. His uncle and brothers in Lindsay were well established in their business and would not hesitate to lend their credit and advice. George Cox had probably now surpassed Cluxton as the wealthiest man in Peterborough. When Joe needed a letter of reference to help secure the property he wanted on Front Street, Cox introduced him to Robert Jaffray, owner of the *Globe*, who supplied the necessary testimonial.

But had he been asked who was most responsible for his success in life so far, Flavelle would have immediately credited his mother. Dorothea Flavelle had imprinted her tenacity, her will, her religious beliefs, her very Methodist combination of humility and pride, so successfully on Joe and all her children that their father's failure had few discernible effects on their character, save perhaps to reinforce an identification with their mother that they never rebelled against. Dorothea's influence on Joe was reinforced in every way by the Methodist society of Peterborough so that it became impossible to separate what he owed to his mother from what he owed to his church associations.

* Neither Cox nor Flavelle was present in Peterborough for the second Scott Act referendum in 1889 when the wets defeated the dries 1,926 to 1,564.

Joe Flavelle came to Toronto already successful in business, well connected, happily married, but ambitious to make his way further in life. He had already tasted prominence in community affairs, had spoken out for his beliefs, and had known in a small way some of the consequences of incurring public disfavour. When he was worried about business, about his family, about being criticized as a crank and a Christer, he had learned to find powerful consolation and reinforcement in prayer. Now in Toronto, on the brink of an uncertain future, he wrote to Clara that, "One of my earliest acts was to go to our Father and consecrate myself, my new business, my whole affairs to Him."[36]

CHAPTER TWO

HOGTOWN

Flavelle's assets could not have totalled ten thousand dollars when he set out in business in Toronto in 1887.

It did not seem a good time for new business ventures in Canada. The economy was not obviously prospering in the late 1880s and early 1890s. The last spike had been driven, but settlers did not rush onto the Western prairies the missionaries had described so enthusiastically to the Peterborough Methodists in the 1860s. The climate was too harsh, the sod too tough for the early homesteaders to grow wheat they could sell at a profit halfway round the world. For every person who came to try his luck in Canada, someone else left for the United States. American tariffs cut off what seemed to be the natural market for the country's surplus products. American cities absorbed its surplus people.

In the 1891 election the Liberal party turned to the desperate expedient of advocating unlimited free trade with the United States. John A. Macdonald clung to power only on the strength of his personal prestige, manufacturers' and the CPR's money, and the patriotism of those who regarded the Liberals as annexationists. In the bleak winters following the international financial collapse of 1893, intellectuals debated what should be done about the tramps roaming the countryside, the black flag of anarchism appeared in marches of the unemployed in Toronto, and the post-Macdonald Conservatives disintegrated in a muck of scandal, incompetence, and endless wrangling about French Catholics in Manitoba. Even in 1900, after four years of slow recovery in business, only some forty-two thousand foreigners thought Canada worth coming to, less than a third of the total twenty years earlier.

In these not very easy times Flavelle multiplied his wealth one hundredfold. In 1900 he was a millionaire, managing the largest enterprise of its kind in the British Empire, making plans to build one of the grandest houses in Toronto, pronouncing his name according to the original French, *Fla-velle'*. He had succeeded in business beyond his wildest dreams. He was partly lucky, but had also proven himself a superb business manager and strategist. His efforts had been richly blessed.

I

For the first several months of 1887 he worked in Toronto during the week and rested with his family in Peterborough on the Sabbath. He had rented a shop and warehouse space at 74 Front Street East in the long row of four-storey brick commission and wholesale houses stretching from Church Street to the St. Lawrence Market. Flavelle was one of many middlemen supplying farm products to Ontario's largest urban population (167,000) and shipping surpluses abroad for export. As in Peterborough he dealt at wholesale and retail in flour, grain, cheese, butter, eggs, and meat. But he was a commission merchant now: most of his work was selling the eggs, butter, and poultry that country dealers had taken in barter, keeping a percentage of the sales as his commission. One effect of this was to minimize his need for capital.

He had to keep his costs down because most of his money was still tied up in the Peterborough business, which was not doing well. He was never quite certain when he would be free to go home on weekends, but stopped sending Clara telegrams so he could save an extra twenty-five cents. The second-hand stove for his shop cost him $6.50, his desk $5.50. He worked alone in the early weeks, installing the stove himself, putting his butter up in boxes, living in cheap hotel rooms where he prepared his Sunday School lessons at night while shouts and laughter drifted up from the barroom.[1]

On Monday, February 10, he arrived in Toronto "very blue" with loneliness at the separation from Clara, but was cheered by his first sale — ten one-hundred-pound packages of butter to Christie Brown & Co., the biscuit-makers, at a net profit of twenty-five dollars. By the middle of March he had hired his first Toronto employee. "I am fairly committed to my new venture," he wrote Clara. "My visits at intervals here did not seem to commit me. Now I recognize it is sink or swim."[2]

There was some danger of sinking. The city was oversupplied with butter that winter, and Joe lost "a lot of money" clearing his stocks before the new season's supply came in. Clara had to be pressed into service in Peterborough, helping with the books in his absence. He also had to rely on his banker. Duncan Coulson, Cashier of the Bank of Toronto, was at first doubtful of Flavelle's ability to carry on business in two separate cities. "You do not know how ready I was for Mr. Coulson's question day before yesterday," Joe wrote Clara. " 'But whom have you left behind you Mr. Flavelle with a power of attorney to act for you?' I looked him in the eye and told him, 'My wife.' . . . There were no more questions in that line."³

The separated Methodist couple found comfort in mutual devotion. Each night Clara in Peterborough and Joe in Toronto read an agreed-upon text from Scripture. "Be strong and of good courage," Clara quoted in one of her letters. "The Lord thy God He it is that doth go with thee." Telling her of the inspiration their daily texts provided, Joe explained the course of his business life: "I 'devise' in my own way and according to my own best judgment, and then to save me from error and mistake the Father orders my steps."⁴

Despite the losses on butter, Flavelle found other lines of business opening up satisfactorily. At the end of June he leased a house on Homewood Avenue, just west of Sherbourne Street and north of Carlton. It was old and undistinguished, but "we are surrounded by lovely homes and good people." Immediately after signing the lease he paid the quarterly rent for four seats in Sherbourne Street Methodist Church. He had to take second pew from the back—"still we shall like them—when we are together darling position does not count for much."

So now he could fairly call himself a citizen of Toronto. "I bow my head darling, bow yours with mine and pray The Father that we may leave it better and purer than when we came, because we have walked in righteousness and Truth."⁵

Hardly had Clara and Mina joined him in Toronto when he left for the hinterland to drum up new business. Through the summer and fall he scoured the western- and northern-Ontario countryside, travelling as far as Sault Ste. Marie in search of merchants who wanted to dispose of butter, eggs, "and anything else which would sell." On one of these trips he arrived in London at three in the morning. Thinking it silly to pay for a whole night's lodging, he lay down on a bench in the station to sleep till morning. Half a century later, young businessmen on Bay Street talked about how the white-bearded millionaire in the limousine had once slept on benches to save money.⁶

The young teetotaller from Peterborough placed too much faith in the good effects of water on his constitution, at least the water available to Torontonians. In the fall of 1887 he contracted the typhoid fever endemic in the city because of its polluted water supply. His doctor correctly diagnosed the illness and told him to go to bed. "I am sorry but I must go downtown," Flavelle replied, and went on about his business. A week later he was just passing Jarvis Street Baptist Church on his way home when he collapsed. The next thing he knew Clara was bathing his head at home and the doctor was repeating his orders.

While Joe sweated in bed that winter his business fell apart. He had notes coming due at the Bank of Toronto that he could not meet. Clara was pregnant again. Without telling her husband she wrote Duncan Coulson explaining about the illness and warning that the debts could not be paid until Joe returned to work. "Tell your husband to have his typhoid fever with as much comfort as he can," Coulson wrote back, "I will look after his notes." As the sermons on the profitability of godliness had predicted, good things like that happened to young businessmen who were seen to be earnest and honest.[7]

The first visitor Flavelle was allowed during his illness was Donald Gunn, his neighbour at 78 Front Street, who specialized in pork-packing. Gunn's partner wanted to quit. Gunn had been watching Flavelle work and thought they could get on together. In February 1888 the firm of D. Gunn, Flavelle & Company was formed as an equal partnership with a capital of $15,000. Flavelle must have disposed of his Peterborough business by then to raise the $7,500 capital he needed. But Gunn was worried enough about his new partner's resources to insist that J. R. Dundas, William Flavelle, and John Flavelle sign the partnership agreement, guaranteeing Gunn against any impairment of the firm's capital during the partnership.[8] If only because of his illness and the troubles with the boycott in Peterborough, Flavelle had not done well in his year on his own in Toronto. But he had succeeded well enough, had demonstrated enough character and ability, for an older, more established merchant to want to take him on as an equal partner.

Josie Flavelle was born in January 1888. She died in August. Joe and Clara were comforted by their belief that God had taken her and they would see her again. The lines they had printed on the black mourning card in her memory were from Coleridge's *Epitaph on an Infant*:

> This lovely bud, so young so fair,
> Called hence by early doom,

Just came to show how sweet a flower,
In Paradise would bloom:
Ere sin could harm or sorrow fade,
Death came with friendly care,
The opening bud to Heaven conveyed
And bade it blossom there.

A third daughter, Clara, was born in 1890. She was frail and wracked with asthma. In the climax of the worst bout, at the end of the longest night of their lives, the parents laid their baby dead in her cradle—"only later to find our mistake and again take up the struggle, and to bring the wee form home, barely alive, on a pillow."[9] Clara lived, and she and Mina were joined by Ellsworth in 1892. Joe was delighted to have a son and heir and soon moved the family into a more spacious house at 565 Jarvis Street.* But he had little time for his children and family while he was busy making his way as a merchant.

II

In their quarters at 78 and 80 Front Street East, Gunn, Flavelle & Company combined Joe's produce business with Gunn's trade in pork. Flavelle almost immediately gave the firm a healthy sideline by participating in the first attempt to stabilize the marketing of eggs in Canada. He had been in the habit of obtaining his egg supply directly from rural storekeepers at prices determined by the state of the Toronto market. This tended to cut out the wholesale dealers in the small Ontario cities who acted as middlemen between storekeepers and the big Toronto merchants. In self-defence a group of wholesalers in Chatham, Seaforth, St. Mary's, and Walkerton formed the Egg Dealers' Association of Ontario and asked Gunn, Flavelle to be their exclusive Toronto agent. The firm was promised all the eggs they wanted each week, to be sold at a price and commission fixed in consultation with the association.

There was a brief flurry of comment on this minor attempt to control the egg market in the spring of 1888, a time when price-fixing was coming under parliamentary scrutiny for the first time. One financial journal com-

---

* Before it was torn down in the 1960s, 565 Jarvis was owned for many years by the CCF.

mented that even eggs were passing under the "yolk" of monopoly. In fact the association was much less successful in exercising monopoly power than were government-sponsored egg combines ninety years later. Like most of the early combines it fell apart within a year or so, but not before Gunn, Flavelle had made useful profits.[10]

Another new venture for the firm was brought about by Flavelle's initiative in importing American creamery butter into Toronto. Unlike farmer-made butter, which was manufactured under primitive quality controls and preserved by heavy salting, the new product was made in special butter factories or creameries, kept under refrigeration, and sold to the public while still fresh and sweet. It commanded a substantial premium on the market. In the late spring of each year Flavelle purchased as much creamery butter as he could afford in Chicago at 12½¢ to 15½¢ per pound. He held it there through the summer and fall in cold storage and in winter shipped it to Toronto for resale at 20¢ to 25¢ a pound. After costs of storage and shipping had been met, Gunn, Flavelle & Company found it highly profitable to supply Torontonians with their first fresh butter in winter.

His partnership with Gunn introduced Flavelle to a set of double-entry books, the fundamental tool of modern accounting. With the aid of a decent set of accounts and a skilled bookkeeper he was able to refine his old rough system of a weekly summing up into an exact rendering of the state of the firm's affairs. He further improved Gunn's accounting by breaking sales into their respective parts so he could determine the profitability of each product the firm handled. He was and always would be inflexible in insisting on a thorough keeping of the accounts each day, going so far as to fire one of the young members of the Gunn family for failing to balance the journal before closing the office.[11]

The partnership did very well. Profits in 1888 were $3,000; by 1891 they had swollen to $39,000. By the end of 1891 Flavelle's investment of $7,500 had returned to him something between $35,000 and $45,000, making him a solidly prosperous businessman in the Toronto of the 1890s.[12]

Although there were problems in the Canadian economy as a whole, Flavelle had come to Toronto at the right time. With the Ontario hinterland now tied to it by the railway network radiating from the city, Toronto came of age in the 1880s as the province's commercial, financial, and manufacturing metropolis. Its population almost doubled in that decade and the soaring demand for foodstuffs by city folk was one of the brightest prospects for Ontario agriculture.

So, too, were growing foreign markets for dairy products and meat. Although extra sons often had to move off to new land in the United States or the Canadian West, many Ontario farmers were making a highly successful transition from the old grain crops of mid-century into dairying and livestock. Ontario's cheese, butter, egg, cattle, and hog production grew spectacularly after Confederation. Earlier in Peterborough and now in Toronto, Flavelle was one of the middlemen organizing and directing this flow of foodstuffs to consumers in Canada and abroad. It was a bad time to be an immigrant to the Canadian West, a carpenter in a Maritime port, a subsistence farmer or a farmer's third or fourth son in Central Canada. It was a good time to be in the produce and provision trade in Toronto.

Provided, that is, you knew what you were doing. If Gunn and Flavelle were in the right city at the right time, they also exploited their opportunities more successfully than others. Flavelle often used an incident of these years as an illustration of how business ability rather than good luck made the difference between success and failure. Parke, Blackwell & Company were competitors of Gunn, Flavelle, doing exactly the same kind of trade. According to Flavelle, one day Charlie Blackwell came to him and said, "Look here, J.W., I think you will admit I am as clever as you are, but there is something different in our two houses. What is it? I do not know. It is perfectly plain to me that you are doing well here. We are just struggling along, making ends meet." The fixed costs of their business that year had been $19,500. Gunn, Flavelle's had been higher. Yet the latter firm had made $17,000 profit and Parke, Blackwell had made none. "He had the same opportunity, the same markets, the same location, but we had the advantage of our practice of planned operation, of encouraging men to work together, of keeping our eyes open for openings that would break through."[13]

Flavelle's account of the partnership does not refer to the pork-packing which was the mainstay of the business and seems to have been largely handled by Gunn. Gunn, Flavelle were pork-packers as the term was used in the late nineteenth century, not as it is understood today. They did not slaughter hogs. Farmers killed their own pigs in the late fall or winter, cleaned and trimmed the carcasses, and sold them to local storekeepers from whom they passed to agents like Gunn, Flavelle in Toronto. At some point the meat would be cured in salt as a preservative. Gunn, Flavelle shipped much of their product as barrelled salt pork to lumber and mining camps in northern Ontario and Quebec, east to the Maritimes, and as far west as Winnipeg. The better cuts of ham and bacon, lightly cured and then smoked, were sold for the Toronto retail trade. From his earliest days in Peterborough Flavelle had dealt in hog carcasses and was reasonably knowledgeable about standard methods of curing and packing. But there is no evidence that he had taken any special interest in pork, his strong points being buying, selling, and accounting. In 1890 Gunn, Flavelle & Company were among more than five hundred Canadian merchants who called themselves meat-packers.[14]

Occasionally they would resell carcasses or some of their best cuts to Canada's first and largest modern packing house, owned by the William Davies Company. William Davies had emigrated to Toronto from England in 1854, already an experienced meat-curer at age twenty-one. He was impressed by the quality of hogs he could purchase around Toronto—pigs fed often on peas, whose high protein content produced a specially firm and lean side of meat. Trying to find a market for what he knew was a good product, Davies followed a neighbour's example in 1860 by shipping a case of bacon (the British term for the whole side of a hog) to his brother in England. It was so well received that the next year Davies established at Front and Frederick streets what is said to have been the first building in Canada wholly devoted to the curing and smoking of meats.

Davies found the English demand for his bacon almost unlimited. His main problem was to find enough of the right kind of hogs to meet the demand. During the 1860s he began to buy live hogs and slaughter them at his plant rather than buying the dressed carcasses. This way, as American packers were also discovering, some of the offal could be sold—usually as lard—instead of being buried in a farmer's yard. More important, standardized methods of killing, dressing, and curing, produced a much better and more consistent product. Just as cheese and butter manufacture was passing from farm to factory and creamery in these years, so the modern meat-packers were taking over the killing of the animal from the farmer.

In 1874 Davies erected a much larger packing plant on the block between Front Street and Lake Ontario, bounded by the Don River on the west and Beachell Street (now Overend Avenue) on the east. Using primitive refrigeration facilities he could now slaughter and cure at any time of the year. In 1875 he processed about 30,000 hogs, two-thirds of which were exported to England. A dozen years later, in 1887, he slaughtered 63,500 hogs, and in 1888 more than 80,000, a volume greater than all other packers in Ontario combined. As well as selling at wholesale on British and Canadian markets, William Davies and Company had also opened a retail store at Queen and

Yonge streets in Toronto to sell lard and other perishable edible parts of their hogs; later, a second store was opened on Spadina south of College. A devout, teetotalling Baptist with his eye on the main chance, Davies apparently ploughed his profits back into the business through the 1870s, but by the 1880s was achieving more than the "competence" he had hoped for in hogs. Net profits averaged $25,000 to $35,000 per year in the middle of that decade. In his fifties and growing increasingly deaf, Davies, like most nineteenth-century entrepreneurs, expected his sons to take over his business.[15]

Coming home from work one day in early 1892 Flavelle was surprised to find William Davies on his doorstep. He knew the tall, white-bearded packer by sight, but had never spoken to him. "I have called to see you," Davies bellowed. "My boys are sick unto death, and James says you are decent. Will you come into the William Davies Company?" Flavelle tried to answer, but Davies cut him off. "There is no use speaking to me, I am deaf." He thrust a pad and pencil into the young man's hands. Flavelle had just renewed his partnership with Gunn for a further three years; he wrote this to Davies, adding that it would be impossible for him to consider the proposal. Davies would have none of Flavelle's objections. His two oldest sons were dying of tuberculosis and he was desperate to find someone capable of managing his business. He insisted Flavelle consider the possibility of leaving Gunn and joining his company as general manager.[16]

To his surprise Flavelle found he was being asked to take over a less profitable business than his current one. Davies had net profits of only $28,000 for the year ended March 31, 1892. Gunn, Flavelle's had been $39,000. But Davies' figures seemed an abnormally thin margin on a sales volume of over $800,000. The packing house had earned more on considerably lower sales in other years, so the foundation probably existed for much better earnings. Gunn, Flavelle had done well, but were operating in a bitterly competitive trading world where an upstart firm could easily be knocked down again. Flavelle may also have realized that Davies' integrated approach to meatpacking was the wave of the industry's future and that old-fashioned porkpackers like himself and Gunn would soon have to add slaughtering facilities or be shoved aside. Finally, a devout Methodist, who believed religion should be relevant in business, found it decidedly attractive to join a firm whose operations reflected the founder's reputation for rugged Christian integrity. In the old days Davies' business disputes with fellow Baptists had been arbitrated by a council of elders of the church. An active churchman and philanthropist, Davies was one of the few Canadian businessmen of the 1880s who shared his profits with his employees.

Flavelle withdrew from his partnership by selling part of his interest to one of the Gunn family and having J. R. Dundas take over the remainder. Dundas, who had started the family on the road to economic success, now sold out his Lindsay interests to Johnnie and Willie; by buying into Gunn, Flavelle he made it possible for Joe to take the major business step of his life in joining Davies. This arrangement was worked out smoothly enough. The more difficult question was Flavelle's future with Davies. He would not come into the company as a mere salaried manager.

With his sons literally on their deathbeds, handicapped in the bargaining by the disappointing state of his company's profits and his desire to withdraw capital from it for his sons' estates, William Davies agreed to give Flavelle a substantial interest in the business. The William Davies Company, Limited, was formed to take over all the assets of Davies' old partnership with his boys. The Davies family turned over their business, valued at $150,000, to the new company in return for all 2,500 shares of its stock. Each share had a par value of $100, making the capitalization of the new company $250,000. The difference between the $250,000 the stock was officially "worth" and the $150,000 in tangible assets was set down in the books as the value of "good will," meaning that the prospect of profts from the operation was greater than $150,000 would normally earn. Net profits of, say, $30,000 a year would be a 12 per cent return on $250,000; therefore the company's stock was officially deemed to be worth that figure.

The Davies family then sold 1,101, or 44 per cent, of the shares to Flavelle for a total price of $95,000 ($86 a share). He paid $40,000 in cash—borrowed from the Bank of Commerce, using the stock as collateral—and gave Davies his note for $55,000. J. R. Dundas guaranteed $25,000 of the note and Davies held an insurance policy on Flavelle's life for the balance. Davies was president of the new company, Flavelle its managing director at a salary of $4,000 a year.[17]

Flavelle moved down Front Street to the packing house on the Don in the summer of 1892. He was pleased with the new situation. During a visit to Chicago with Davies he wrote Clara of "the rest which is secured to me by my new business connection. The nervous strain of apprehension for the future, shall I succeed or shall I not! is gone. Mingling here among busy men, I feel that I can hold up my head among them and have courage, not as a struggling fearful man, but as one who has at an early age been helped into a business connection of stability and assurance. Through all these changes and years God has been with us darling. . . ." That morning he was going to the opening of a new Reformed Episcopal Church, "on spec" he wrote, on the general principle that a church opening meant a good preacher.[18]

III

The pig was and is man's best friend in the animal world. He converts cereal to meat more efficiently than any other farm animal, storing in his body 35 per cent of the energy contained in his food, compared with only 11 per cent for sheep and cattle. He gains a pound in weight for every 3 to 5 pounds he consumes; cattle need 10 pounds or more to add a pound of flesh. The hog's carcass yields 65 to 80 per cent dressed meat, his competitors only 45 to 60 per cent. Pork contains the finest-quality protein and provides the greatest energy value of all meats. It takes more kindly to preservation — salting, pickling, smoking — than the meat of any other animal.

Sows give birth to large litters only four months after conception. In another six months the piggies are on their way to market. They are naturally clean animals, made slovenly only by their keepers, and are usually docile and even-tempered. They realize their fate only in the last few feet of the ramp leading to slaughter. No more amiable grunting, oinking, or squealing then. The pig's last sound is a deep-throated shriek of terror, as unsettling as any human scream. Cattle tend to go quietly, more befitting dumb animals.

By the time Flavelle joined the Davies Company, advanced North American packing-house operations had become fairly standardized. Purchased from farmers at a few cents per pound live weight, hogs were shipped to the Don in railway cars, rested and cooled overnight in the pens, and then driven up long ramps to the upper storey of the packing house. In a small pen at the top, each screaming pig was shackled by his left hind leg and hoisted upside down on a moving track. A quick stab in the jugular with a short, sharp knife and the animal was dead meat, its blood flowing cranberry-red on the killing-room floor. After the carcasses had been cleaned in scalding water, passed through a scraping machine, and then singed in a furnace, their hides were perfectly bare. Travelling along the packer's dis-assembly line, the corpses were then disembowelled, decapitated, and split. The sides were next hung for up to forty-eight hours in a

37

cooling or chilling room while their animal heat dissipated. Resuming its journey, the meat was trimmed in the cutting room. Most Davies hogs were manufactured into Wiltshire sides for the British market. The term refers to the method of cutting the sides—a Wiltshire side had only the neck, back, and blade bones removed. In the curing cellars the sides were swabbed with salt, stacked, and stored for several weeks while the salt penetrated the meat to prevent bacterial action and spoilage.

Fully cured forty-five- to sixty-five-pound sides were packed in boxes, nine to twelve to a box, and shipped without refrigeration to England. They were consigned to the company's British agent, J. Wheeler Bennett, who sold them to wholesalers at London's Smithfield market, remitting his proceeds after taking a commission. The wholesaler would smoke the sides and then resell them to retailers, who would cut and sell the bacon for British breakfast tables. All the edible parts of the hog—tail, snout, feet— were sold for consumption in Canada, often through the company's retail stores. The fat was turned into lard. All the inedible offal was ground into fertilizer. In a way, nineteenth—century meat manufacturers could have packed the hog's squeal. Dried and blown-up hog bladders made powerful noisemakers. But the packers found it more profitable to use the bladders as containers for lard.[19]

Finding the most profitable way to sell the meat was, of course, the key to a packer's success. The existence of ample markets for a Canadian packer's product could not be taken for granted. Or, if the markets existed, there was no guarantee that the packer as middleman could secure the raw product cheaply enough to meet the demand and still make a profit.

There was a rapidly expanding market in Great Britain at the end of the nineteenth century. Urban, industrial England demanded far more meat than its inefficient, declining agricultural sector could supply. But Canadians had trouble finding a product they could produce for export to England as cheaply as their potential competitors. Despite repeated attempts by Davies and later by Flavelle, Canada was never able to compete with the United States and Argentina in the export trade in chilled and frozen beef. Sheep and lamb became the specialty of the Australians and New Zealanders. Only pork remained.

But Canadian pork-packers could not produce the fat salt pork commonly eaten in North America and Europe as cheaply as could American packers — in fact they had to have substantial tariff protection to keep Americans out of their own Canadian market. The farmers in the great

Mississippi Valley corn belt supplied Chicago with mountains of cheap hogs grown wonderfully fat and round from following cattle and eating the corn in their excrement. The farmers of Ontario, still Canada's agricultural heartland, had neither the corn nor the cattle to raise hogs this way.

They did raise some hogs, though, feeding them on peas, bran, barley, and other grains, and on the skim-milk refuse from cheese factories and dairies. William Davies had noticed the superior quality of meat in hogs enjoying this high-protein diet and had developed his business in the British market for bacon and hams, leaving the much larger trade in common salt pork to the Americans and others. A Davies "Pea-Fed" Wiltshire side was premium meat, producing hams and breakfast bacon of about the same degree of leanness favoured today. At first this was luxury food; but rising standards of living in the Western world, as well as a reduction in the calorie needs of populations doing less physical work, influenced consumer taste in the late nineteenth century to move rapidly to favour this lean, tasty product instead of the greasy fat pork eaten by industrial and frontier workers alike. "Forty years ago," Davies wrote in 1889, "I sold bacon with the fat four to six inches thick, from which all the lean had been cut away and sold fresh. Today these same consumers, laboring men, would not take it as a gift; they insist on having lean, mild cured meat." [20]

Once the market had been perceived, the next problem for Davies and Flavelle was to get a regular supply of hogs good enough to convert into Wiltshire sides. Not any old porker would do. Ontario farmers had to get over their North American preconception that the ideal hog was a two- or three-hundred-pound symmetrical ball of lard. As early as 1864 Davies had written letters to farm journals pleading for supplies of longer, leaner hogs no heavier than one hundred and eighty pounds. When the supply did not develop he began buying in Chicago, where so many pigs came to market that the minority of light, lean hogs could fill his needs. By the mid-1880s more than eighty per cent of his supply consisted of American hogs slaughtered and cured in bond and exported under his "Royal Standard" brand. [21]

Just before Flavelle joined the company Davies launched a vigorous letter-writing campaign in the *Farmer's Advocate* on behalf of more and leaner Canadian hogs. He wanted Canadian farmers to switch from the prevailing North American breeds — Berkshire, Poland–China, Suffolk, Essex — which ran to too much fat, into the Improved Yorkshire and Tamworth hogs being raised by the Irish and Danes to produce Wiltshire sides for the English market. A gentleman farmer himself, Davies introduced the first herd of Improved Yorkshires into Canada for breeding purposes. William Fearman of Hamilton, another packer who occasionally exported, brought in the first Tamworths. The breeders of Berkshires fought back with claims that their pigs were more robust, better feeders, and more docile than these new "race-horse" hogs. "One breed may rise, another fall/ The Berkshire hog survives them all."[22] The packers began to pay premium prices for leaner hogs. Provincial and federal agricultural experts joined their campaign to improve the breed and methods of feeding. The new breeds gradually crowded their competitors out of Ontario piggeries, thus effecting the Anglicization of the Canadian hog. His parentage, length, leanness, and lightness now sharply distinguished him from his corpulent American neighbour. There were some Canadians who took a certain national pride in not raising hogs fed on cattle turds. It was an altogether cleaner business north of the border.[23]

The Americans themselves provided a vital stimulus to Canadian bacon exports to Britain after 1890 when the McKinley tariff effectively cut Canadian grains out of the American market. The price of barley, wheat, and other Canadian cereals plummeted. But if they could not return their costs of production as grains, they could yield a healthy return when converted into pork. Or, if a farmer switched entirely out of grain, as Ontarians had already been doing through the 1870s and 1880s, and went into dairy farming, pigs were useful to have around to consume the skim-milk refuse of the dairying operation. Either way, the cost of raising hogs was very low in the several years after 1890. The prices the packers offered remained fairly constant at about five cents a pound live weight. There was a hog population explosion in rural Ontario in the 1890s. This, combined with the acceptance of the new breeds, meant the packers no longer had to worry about the constancy or quality of their supply of pigs. Shortly after Flavelle joined Davies, the company stopped importing American hogs, filling all its requirements in Canada.

The incentive the McKinley tariff gave farmers to switch into hogs and the gradual conversion from a lard to a bacon-type hog were responsible for the William Davies Company's extraordinary profits in Flavelle's first year as manager. In the year ending March 31, 1893, the company's sales in Canada remained exactly constant at $300,000. Export sales of Wiltshires almost doubled, however, from $500,000 to $998,000. More than 95,000 hogs were packed that year; profits ballooned from $28,000 to $202,225; the shareholders received a 65 per cent dividend on their $250,000 capitalization (more than 100 per cent on their $150,000 in tangible assets).[24] Flavelle's dividend income in his first year as a packing-house manager was $71,500.

Net profits in that startling first year were 15.8 per cent of sales, an inconceivable figure to modern food merchants, who are satisfied with anything above 1 per cent on sales. The main reason for such a high return, one the company never equalled, stemmed from the fact that it was buying and selling in unrelated markets. Canadian supplies did not significantly affect British demand. The increased flow of hogs in Canada gave Flavelle all the raw product he could absorb at a steady low cost; but British demand was so great, and other foreign suppliers were so unable to fill it, that sharp increases in Canadian exports did not bring down the price received in Britain. With constant costs per pound in Canada and rising prices per pound in Britain, profit margins soared. The William Davies Company, pork-packers, found themselves wallowing in money.

Businessmen seen to be making money quickly face competitors. Davies and Flavelle did their best not to be seen making money. As Flavelle noted, the company had always done its business "in a quiet unassuming manner, little was known of it." The hogs flowed quietly into the Don. Sales and profit figures were not public knowledge. Wheeler Bennett in England said nothing about the prices he was getting for the Canadian product, which did not yet have an identity in market reports. Through 1892 the Davies Company had almost no Canadian competitors in the British market. (Only three other Canadian packers killed their own hogs — James L. Grant & Company of Ingersoll, Fearman of Hamilton, and George Matthews of Peterborough. Matthews did not export and Fearman did so only occasionally. Grant and Davies probably agreed informally on the prices they would ask for "Canadian" in England, or divided the market to avoid competition.) As the dominant company in a trade whose profitability was not instantly evident, the Davies Company briefly reaped windfall profits from would-be competitors' ignorance. The success of its first year of operation under Flavelle was more a matter of good luck than good business ability.

The luck did not last. The increased quantity of Canadian bacon shipments was noticed, as was the volume of hogs moving into the Toronto factory. There were intelligence leaks: according to Wheeler Bennett, Grant of Ingersoll "blew" about his profits in Canada; according to Grant, Wheeler Bennett's boasting about the size of his Canadian account put others on to a good thing. Fearman and Matthews soon turned to exporting in earnest.

New packing houses opened in London and Montreal, at least one of them financed by English provision agents. By 1894 Canadian singed sides were pouring into Smithfield. Davies' "Pea-Fed" (actually more likely to have been raised on a bran meal by now, for peas produced too much firmness) jostled on the market with Grant's "Beaver," Matthews' "Farmer's Fed," Laing of Montreal's "Earl King," and other unbranded Canadian sides.[25]

Davies' sales dropped by one-quarter in the year ending March 31, 1894; profits fell to $95,000 and the dividend to 34 per cent. On much higher sales the next year, profits barely moved to $97,000, the margin on sales having fallen to 5.9 per cent.[26] By any standards it was still a fine business to be in—Flavelle's dividend income was $37,400 and $44,000 in those two years. But the competition was making inroads and the future was very uncertain. More than ordinary business judgment would be required to maintain a predominance the new company had earlier enjoyed almost by default.

IV

As managing director Flavelle had already shown he could improve on the operation he took over from William Davies. The 1891 profits had been disappointing partly because the company had suffered from taint in its product, boxes arriving spoiled in England because for some reason the cure had not "taken." It was an oddly intermittent phenomenon and broke out again a week or two after Flavelle came into the company. In some weeks as much as sixteen per cent of a shipment had to be written off as spoiled, more than enough to wipe out profits.

Both William Davies and William Davies Junior (the latter about to die of tuberculosis) told Flavelle the taint could not be overcome, "but was due to some peculiar condition of the Canadian hog which made him hard to cure." The American sides never tainted, they claimed; whereas Canadian ones often did. But why should taint be any respecter of nationality?

Flavelle found that the Davies family had simply accepted stories that were "the accumulation of a gossipy spirit among the Workmen," and had not bothered to investigate the problem themselves. The owners had left day-to-day factory operations to their foremen. By contrast, as he described it in a memo written a year or so later, Flavelle personally "went into the investigation of the trouble with an earnest spirit."[27]

For the better part of two years he wrestled earnestly with the taint. At first the problem was thought to be in the chilling rooms. When experiments with new procedures failed, Flavelle toured Chicago packing houses to get the best American advice. It was usually contradictory, and the one idea he gleaned—to improve ventilation in the chilling rooms—produced no results. There was another theory that hogs needed considerable rest in the yards before going to slaughter—"it gives them time to say their prayers & to think of their latter end"[28] — so Flavelle personally supervised the resting, watering, and driving to slaughter, with no improvement. He also found that racing the hogs to exhaustion before killing brought no deterioration. He tried singeing the carcasses with less fire, singeing with hard coal instead of soft, singeing without scalding, further chilling after trimming, and other changes. Nothing worked. In desperation he recommended overhauling the whole factory, "hoping that in doing so we would throttle the monster." Thirty thousand dollars' worth of improvements later, the taint returned.

Flavelle finally became curious about conditions in the curing cellars. Davies had assured him the cellar procedures were so superior that the trouble could not possibly be in the curing. When Flavelle personally traced a quantity of sides through the cellars he found complete irregularity in turning them for their second salting. "From this date I took nothing from anyone as truth until I proved it. I stayed in the cellar hours daily." About the same time, advice from Wheeler Bennett led him to a trouble spot on the shoulders, the incision where the blade bone had been removed. This should have been thoroughly salted to prevent the two sides of the fresh meat from sticking together and spoiling. Flavelle found his workmen holding the salt-pushing sticks improperly, inserting them too sharply so they dug down into the shoulder instead of following the incision to the end. The lack of salt at the end of the incision caused the tainted shoulders. He had new curved pushers made to distribute the salt properly; these, combined with a rigid schedule for turning the sides, completely eliminated the taint.

Locating the cause of the taint had cost countless hours of Flavelle's time and about ten thousand dollars in unnecessary renovations. But, as he noted to himself, it was a most useful experience:

My investigations however were invaluable training to me as a packing house manager and curer of bacon. Indeed the exhaustive attention given to every detail gives me confidence and assurance in my judgment which fit me for fully discharging all my duties, and makes me valuable to myself in the rich experience gained—I have not learned in the school of hope so or think so but in the plain school of every day hard and close intelligent work.[29]

V

Fresh from his victory over taint, Flavelle went to England in 1894 to study the bacon situation there for himself. It was his first meeting with John Wheeler Bennett, the exclusive British agent for Davies bacon since 1880. Two years older than Flavelle, the son of a prosperous English civil servant, Bennett had decided to strike out on his own and in the 1870s had invested his inheritance in a bacon-curing business in Ireland. A few years later he established himself as a produce agent in London, selling pork and dairy products on consignment. When Davies gave Bennett, Piery and Company his account, he found them "the most efficient, prompt & energetic men I have ever had to do with." He was particularly pleased with Bennett's practical knowledge of the trade and the hints he passed back to Canada about improving the product. Wheeler(-)Bennett (over the years his middle name became attached and finally hyphenated to his surname) continued to please Davies and was well established as the company's man in England when Flavelle came into the business.[30]

On this and later trips Flavelle spent most of his time in Wheeler Bennett's company. "I was very much impressed with the magnificent energy of Mr. Bennett," he reported to Davies. "He is tireless in his devotion to his business. He is at it shortly after 8, . . . is pressed hard all day only getting home between 7 and 8. . . . I can see that it will be difficult to find anyone else with such a measure of astonishing energy and general good judgment. Everyone bore testimony to his ability and more than one firm said we ought to consider ourselves fortunate in having the best agent in London." Flavelle's own energy and earnest desire to improve the business appealed to Wheeler Bennett, and their partnership soon warmed into friendship.

Despite Wheeler Bennett's brilliance as a salesman, Flavelle found the English situation distressing. The London Produce Exchange was a viciously competitive arena, in which every buyer struggled for advantage against every seller, every seller against every other seller, and every buyer against every buyer—"a hot-bed of envy and hatred," Wheeler Bennett called it. The key skill of a London agent, Flavelle wrote, "is to find out how much his competitor or buyer is lying to him." The situation in Canadian bacon was particularly disturbing, with the four or five agents engaged in tooth-and-claw competition, each hating the others, and all of them forcing their shippers to undergo "cruel punishment" in low returns for their product. Buyers were doing handsomely out of "Canadian," getting it at cut prices and slipping it on the market as Irish or Danish bacon when their prices rose too high. By contrast, the agents for Irish and Danish met in relative friendship and fixed an official price for their product each week. The competition of Canadian agents, Flavelle was convinced, kept the selling price significantly below what the product could command on its merits.[31]

Canadian bacon stayed on the British market only because Canadian packers could get their hogs as much as one-third cheaper than the Danes; if that difference ever disappeared, so would the Canadian trade. Raising the price paid for hogs in Canada, Flavelle told Wheeler Bennett, was "the question which of all others is of pressing importance in the development of the business. . . . if competition in Canada is to be attended by a steady increasing quantity of hogs, . . . it will be necessary for Canadian Bacon to sell at a price in England which will encourage a healthy sentiment in our farmers." Suppose the Canadian exporters and their agents started to cooperate. Flavelle suggested the packers might form an association, "with no idea of controlling or affecting the prices of hogs, but rather to deal with questions which affect the breeding of hogs and the proper time to market them, and to secure a somewhat uniform idea as to grading and inspection in our yards, also to stimulate a feeling of interest in London which will be reflected in our various agents, who might in turn ultimately be able to weekly meet together, and establish an official price for Canadian."[32]

Wheeler Bennett would have none of this. Contemptuous of his competitors—the "mushroom men," "rank duffers," "too low a cut altogether to be trusted"—he was by temperament a supreme individualist. Business was war, his competitors the enemy. "Personally I do not want any combine," he wrote Flavelle, objecting to a later proposal; "I glory in liberty, independence and a free hand. . . . Until we are fairly beaten at the last ditch on these lines, I should be sorry to see you or myself engaged in any combine with the tail ends of this business." From the beginning he lectured Flavelle on the merits of competition ("I can see indeed as you fairly remarked," Flavelle admitted, "that competition drives us into greater excellence and compels the use of better methods in every department"), promising him there would be no problem with sales or prices when Davies could ship across a consistently excellent product.[33]

Wheeler Bennett took the Canadian packer to Smithfield market at 4:30 a.m. to inspect boxes of bacon as they were being unpacked, arranged tours for him of the leading Irish houses, and introduced him to expert Danish and Irish curers. Flavelle had to admit there were problems with the quality of his product. "The failure of Canadian Bacon to take a higher price is to be laid largely at our own door," he confessed to Davies. "We have not been curers as the Irish and Danish understand the term. Regularity of cure and possible selection is nailed to the masthead of every Irish and Danish house. . . . A first class house will not permit any slip-shod management, which overlooks tireless attention to the highest quality of work. . . . Your knowledge of the cure of sides in our house during the long years that have passed will tell you of a failure to appreciate these conditions. . . . it is our own fault if we do not produce an article which will rank the best on the list and the best which can be made."

Whether or not there could be any useful cooperation among the Canadian packers, Flavelle announced to Davies in 1894 a policy of "aggression" for their own company: "I believe we should command and keep the leading place in the trade, that in place of the opposition leading us to timidity and reduced operations, it should make the necessity for a larger output from our factory, and so reduce the cost per lb. of manufacture. I believe our equipment in every respect should not only be good but the best obtainable. . . . In brief, I believe our Company has the possibility of being first in the trade in every department, and that we should be on the alert for all and every means to keep ourselves abreast of the times, and to be just a little ahead of everyone else in conservative aggressiveness."[34]

He set out to improve the quality and consistency of his cure, recording his experiments, formulae, and the intelligence he gathered about other packers' methods in a special journal. He began travelling to England two or three times a year to gather information, trips few Canadian curers ever made. Wheeler Bennett cooperated with detailed reports on the quality of the product he was receiving:

. . . I now revert again to Box 1563 which does you credit except for the pumping which is too fierce. I cut several gammons all to pieces, in different ways and this revealed a perforation of the gammon in many places. Holes the size of your needle and the meat forced apart from the sinews. This in hot weather means so many stinkers when the air gets in and puffs and swells the gammon. I have seen nothing but what is perfectly sweet. We had some of it, Box 1563, for breakfast and barring a little effluvium (musty flavor) arising when the lid of the dish was lifted it was satisfactory. Broiled and boiled this flavor is not noticed, but the frying pan brings it out. It must be the borax? Box 1610 was inspected by me today again after a lapse of 12 days. It opened as ripe as a cherry all running with red pickle. . . . No 2137 came out of the loft today. It was badly selected 65 lbs. a side many sides long & lanky with thick rinds. 3 sides ought to have been a lower grade, not Ontario. Meat cut good color very very mild insipid to taste masticated raw. This box also showed great force in pumping but was sweet in all direction. I am cooking some tomorrow. Boxes 2139, 2240, 2220, 2262, & 2299 I have today inspected. All opened fresh and bright and no appreciable difference could be discovered. . . . At present I like the cure of 1563 better than anything I have yet seen cut, but I shall keep an open mind till I get through with all my trials.[35]

Reliance on pickle and pumping were the most important innovations Flavelle made in his curing methods. Learning from the Danes and the Irish via Wheeler Bennett, he had begun to cure his sides in a liquid brine or pickle solution rather than with the old dry salt. It gave a more consistent cure while much more effectively holding the moisture in the meat. Pumping — shooting the pickle directly into the meat through hollow needles instead of waiting for it to seep in — shortened the curing time while guaranteeing that the brine would treat what were formerly the most likely parts of the meat to go bad. Many of the formulae for pickle solutions and the diagrams indicating where pumping needles should be inserted were procured for Flavelle by a friend of Wheeler Bennett's who worked in a leading Irish plant. It was a mild form of industrial espionage; Wheeler Bennett cut the friend's name out of the letters before he passed them on.

The taint problem had alerted Flavelle to the need for rigid discipline in the cellars. The other change he made in his cellar procedure was to institute uniformity in the total length of cure. Previously the bacon had been left in cure until market conditions seemed to warrant shipping it to England. By enlarging his refrigerated storage space Flavelle was able to have all sides cured for the same length of time, storing those not for immediate shipment. The curing process could now be aimed solely at quality, instead of having to serve shipping schedules and market estimates.[36]

There were probably other innovations, such as importing skilled workers from Denmark and Ireland. In a general way Flavelle had made a determined effort to produce the best bacon he possibly could, an effort not matched by his less earnest, less thorough competitors. The combination of improved curing methods and rigid regularity of cellar procedure had good results. An experienced Danish curer at Canada Packers who examined Flavelle's quality journal for me concluded that his methods were surprisingly close to much later Danish practice (and that the problems with discipline in the cellars were very close to modern packers' problems), and would have produced an excellent product for the time — although the meat was saltier and less flavourful than today's bacon.

As he stated in a private intercompany memo, Flavelle wanted to raise the price of Canadian bacon in Britain so packers could maintain the hog supply by paying higher prices. The Davies company set a weekly price it would pay for hogs based partly on cabled information about the English market, partly on reports of Irish and Danish killings, and partly on the hog supply and competitors' behaviour at home. Through most of the 1890s, though, Flavelle had the great advantage of having no competitors bidding for the hogs arriving at the cattle market in Toronto, the province's most important stockyard. The firms in Hamilton, Ingersoll, London, and other towns might occasionally deflect a few carloads of hogs by offering higher prices, but they could not permanently alter the flow of hogs from the hinterland into Toronto. A competitor buying on the same market, of course, could force the price of all hogs up, even if he bought only odd carloads. Flavelle valued the savings of this semi-monopoly position at a hundred thousand dollars yearly.

On the other hand he had to maintain the advantage by buying all the hogs offered on the Toronto market, whatever the situation in England, at a price that would keep sellers reasonably happy. Where a lesser businessman would have exploited the situation by taking quick monopoly profits, causing farmer complaints and attracting competitors like bees to honey, Flavelle determined to keep his prices high enough to forestall competition as long as possible, even though it sometimes meant doing business at a loss for weeks on end. In 1897 he wrote Wheeler Bennett triumphantly, "I suppose there is no market in the world handling the same quantity of stock, where values are ordinarily largely governed by competition, that only one buyer is found to take care of the stock, and that only having one buyer, the business has been done so well, and on such broad fair lines, that in a period extending over five years not a line has appeared in the public press, not an adverse criticism has been offered among drovers that there was no competition for their hogs on the Toronto Cattle Market."[37] It was not until 1899 that Charlie Blackwell, his old neighbour on Front Street, finally opened another packing house in Toronto and Flavelle had to face a competitor for his region's hog supply — a competitor he had already bested in business.

The 1895–6 statement seemed to indicate the business had stabilized.

Sales fell a bit from the year before, but on a better margin profits rose to $120,000. Flavelle's share of the 45-per-cent dividend was $49,500. Success had made him a rich man. 1895 had been a depression year in Canada and he was congratulated at the shareholders' meeting for "the gratifying results of the year's operation at a time when the general experience was anything but gratifying." But the future was still uncertain. In the summer of 1896 the price of hogs was very low, down to 4¾ cents a pound from 5½ cents in 1893, and many farmers "wavered in their faith" about future profits in pigs. Then the price of wheat advanced sharply in the fall of 1896 and Flavelle found "evidence that everywhere they were returning to their first love." Worried too about the future of the tariff under the new Laurier government, Flavelle decided the limits of expansion in Canadian pork-packing had been reached. For the next year or two the company would barely hold its own. The only bright spot in the situation was Wheeler Bennett's reports that summer that Davies' bacon was now consistently first class, the equal of the finest Danish.[38]

VI

In early 1897 Flavelle admitted to Wheeler Bennett that he had fallen into the near-fatal trap of becoming obsessed with a pessimistic preconception. The hog supply had not fallen—each month more pigs came to the Don than ever before. Costs were still falling: in 1896 the Davies Company bought its hogs at 4¼ cents a pound; the average dropped to 4¹⁄₁₀ cents in 1897 and stayed under 5 cents through 1900. (It seems that Ontario farmers could not compete in grain markets with the wheat starting to flow out of the prairies in the late 1890s. They still found it profitable to convert their grain to pork. In 1897 the *Farmer's Advocate* estimated that a good farmer could raise hogs at a cost of only 2½ to 3 cents a pound. There were handsome profits at even the low prices Davies was paying.)[39]

Moreover, as Flavelle told Davies, even though he had recognized Wheeler Bennett's splendid energy, he had failed to realize what their agent could achieve once he was satisfied with the Davies product and began to sell it single-mindedly. At the height of his power in these years, nicknamed "The Bismarck of the Bacon Trade," Wheeler Bennett bullied, cajoled, seduced his customers into switching from Irish brands like Denny's famous "I.D.K." into Davies' "Pea-Fed." He convinced the conservative Wholesale Produce

Merchants' Association that the quality was now consistently high enough for Davies' brand to have an official listing along with Irish and Danish on the markets, the first Canadian brand to achieve such recognition. This one step, Flavelle wrote, "advanced Canadian bacon into a position of dignity which perhaps could not have been secured by years of effort along any other lines." To Wheeler Bennett, whom he had sometimes criticized for lack of faith in the product, he conceded, "No one in the history of the bacon trade ever put his heart and soul at the back of his conviction more than you have since I was with you in the Summer . . . the difference is really revolutionary."[40]

The new sales had a wonderful impact on quality. Once Wheeler Bennett had found steady customers, Flavelle could be sure each shipment would be sold the week it arrived in Britain instead of being held over indefinitely and peddled a case or two at a time. The meat no longer had to be so strongly preserved. The cure could become milder and shorter, making the bacon less salty, more tender, and still more attractive to the consumer. In the early 1890s Davies' sides had usually sold at a premium of a sixpence per hundredweight over the Canadian competition, say 50 shillings sixpence, as opposed to 50 shillings for Grant's or Fearman's sides. Now the premium edged up to at least a shilling and as much as two and six on prices in the 60-shilling range.[41] At the same time the gap between Canadian and Danish prices closed significantly, though it never disappeared completely.

Flavelle realized his misjudgment quickly enough to be able to expand capacity and production to keep up with demand. In the year ending March 31, 1896, the company had slaughtered 186,000 hogs. In 1897, 254,000 pigs were driven up the ramps to the killing-rooms. A total of 446,000 hogs were packed in 1899 and 439,000 in 1900. Export sales amounted to $1,242,529 in 1896, $3,652,208 in 1900. Margins ranged between 7.9 and 14 per cent, generating profits in 1897, 1898, 1899, and 1900 of $316,461, $292,704, $312,675, and $433,455 respectively. Until 1900 these were returns on a capitalization of still only $250,000. All expansion was financed out of reserves until $150,000 was reinvested by the shareholders in 1899. They received dividends of 110 per cent on their capital in 1897, 100 per cent in 1898, 120 per cent in 1899, and 82 per cent (on the expanded capital) in 1900. Flavelle took home in dividends $121,000, $110,000, $132,000, and $144,500 in these four years. Of course neither the company nor the shareholders had to pay any taxes.[42]

Flavelle had invested $95,000 in the William Davies Company in 1892. His dividends in eight years totalled $710,050. His only reinvestment was $66,400 in 1899. If Flavelle had wanted to sell his 1,764 shares in the company in 1900 and could have found a buyer who believed the performance could be maintained, he would have received at least $400 a share, or $705,600. If the company was thought able to do only half as well in the future, Flavelle's holdings were still worth more than $350,000. By any reckoning of the value of his dividends and shareholdings he was worth more than a million dollars.

VII

There had been good luck involved in the company's spectacular performance during the years from 1897 to 1900. Neither the Danes nor the Irish had been able to supply enough hogs to slow the geometric growth of Canadian exports to Britain. Canadian farmers had multiplied their hog families as fast as the packers could execute them and there had never been serious shortages of supply. It was a splendid opportunity to make money in the interaction between the two markets. Here, as in his whole business career from the 1870s, Flavelle had been operating on the crest of the revolution in Ontario agriculture, the transition from wheat as a staple into mixed farming emphasizing dairy and livestock production. This revolution coincided exactly with improvements in transportation which made it possible for middlemen like Flavelle to provide consumers thousands of miles away with reasonably fresh butter, eggs, and bacon all year round.

That it was Joe Flavelle rather than some other businessman who seized this opportunity so thoroughly and profitably is what separated him from his competitors, both those who had been in business from the beginning and those Englishmen who rushed to Canada to bring home more bacon. Unlike William Davies, who opposed almost all of his innovations, Flavelle had not rested content with traditional methods or traditional profits. His "conservative aggression" in the face of competition, his determination to improve every aspect of his operations, separated his company from the competition and preserved its premier place in the exploding Canadian bacon trade.

In 1892 the William Davies Company controlled 50 per cent of the Canadian bacon trade with England; its two competitors split the other 50 per cent. Canadian bacon exports were worth $591,000 that year. In 1900 they were worth $12,472,000, and thirteen packing houses jostled for the best cut. Davies still did at least one-third of all the business, probably more, and its twelve competitors divided the rest.[43] The William Davies Company was the largest pork-packing company in the British Empire.[44] People were starting to call Toronto "Hogtown." Flavelle was immensely proud of his company's and his own achievement in the 1890s. It confirmed everything his mother and his ministers had taught him about hard work, attention to business, and success.

CHAPTER THREE

ALL IN THE FAMILY

Flavelle never thought of himself as just a pork-packer. He was a general businessman, what the nineteenth century called "a man of affairs." As opportunities developed he was ready to invest and become active in diverse lines of business.

In 1896 he was elected to the Board of Directors of the Canadian Bank of Commerce. In 1897 he became vice-president of the new Imperial Life Assurance Company. In 1898 the National Trust Company opened for business, J. W. Flavelle president. The same year he became vice-president and one-third owner of the Robert Simpson Company. In 1899 he joined the boards of the Canada Life Assurance Company and the Central Canada Savings and Loan Company. In September of that year he was one of the founding directors of both the Canada Cycle and Motor Company and the Carter–Crume Company. The packing-house manager was now involved in banking, life insurance, trusteeship, a department store, bond dealing, bicycles, and supplying merchants' duplicating and triplicating sales books. In most of these enterprises he was closely involved with the Peterborough man who had given him his first job thirty years earlier, George Albertus Cox.

While Flavelle had been earning his fortune in Toronto, Cox had been anything but idle. The telegrapher, life-insurance salesman, and ofttimes mayor had seized his main chance in the reorganization of the Midland Railway between 1878 and 1883. Under Cox's presidency, scattered lines of track running in various directions in the Port Hope, Peterborough, Lindsay, and Orillia regions were completed and consolidated, and the system's tangled finances were reorganized. Cox eventually leased the Midland to the Grand Trunk, making spectacular profits for the bondholders and shareholders, including himself. He then used his railway earnings to embark on a career in financial intermediation — managing other people's money — that by 1900 had made him Toronto's own "wizard of finance," Canada's most prominent capitalist next to Sir William Van Horne. In the early 1900s the Cox "family" of companies dominated the Toronto business scene and was challenging the much older Montreal institutions for leadership in Canadian economic development.

Flavelle was intimately involved in the group's affairs, one of the inner circle of relatives, Peterboroughnians, and other promising young men whose careers Cox advanced. The connections and experiences of the six or seven years around the turn of the century largely defined his role in Toronto business life for the next two generations.

I

Although his tracks are everywhere in Canadian business history, no one has discovered George Cox the man. His personal papers have not been found; his surviving letters are terse and businesslike; associates passed on few recollections of him. He looked suitably patriarchal, a tall, lean man whose long, thin face became longer still as it faded into his beard. His mouth turned up at the corners, set in a slight, zippered half-smile as he went about his business. He had no hobbies, recreations, or amusements, and read only newspapers and books about business. His other interests in life were the Methodist Church, the Liberal party, and the business careers of his sons. His active Liberalism resulted in Laurier's gift of his Senatorship in 1896; in eighteen years in the Senate he made three speeches. For many years he was bursar of Victoria College, president of the Methodist Ladies College at Whitby, and a vice-president of the Ontario Prohibition Alliance. These outside activities were nothing for a man who at one time was president, vice-president, or a director of forty-six distinct companies.

Extraordinarily self-collected, Cox could nap at will, never lost patience or temper, never showed signs of worry or strain. At the height of his power his associates marvelled at his grasp of detail and his memory for figures. At the same time he was thought to be a soft touch for anyone who needed money, especially if that person had a link to the old days in Peterborough. After his death it was said that Cox personally maintained eighty needy acquaintances. His friends in Sherbourne Street Church claimed he was basically a simple man, whose wealth and formality melted as he knelt with them in prayer. Outsiders saw only the silk hat, the long stern face, the forty-six companies, and Senator Cox's fine hand grasping most of the strings that tied Canadian capitalists together.[1]

In 1884 Cox used some of his railway profits to set up the Central Canada Loan and Savings Company in Peterborough. For years he had been dealing on his own account in real estate in the region (his associates also said he had a phenomenal eye for real-estate values). Now the Central Canada took in local deposits and sold sterling debentures in Britain, investing the proceeds in mortgages. J. R. Dundas, Flavelle's uncle, was vice-president of the Central Canada, and old William Cluxton, Dundas's former patron, was a director. One of the first employees was eighteen-year-old E. R. (Eddie) Wood, who moved over from Cox's telegraph office. He was another Peterborough Irish Protestant, who had quit school at fourteen to work as a clerk in a fur store before casting his lot with Cox. The Cox group invested $300,000 of its own money in the Central Canada and soon came to be managing several millions of borrowed money, paying the investors a steady 6 per cent dividend on the par value of their shares.[2]

In 1886 Cox was invited to join the board of the Canadian Bank of Commerce. Since its founding in 1867 by Senator William McMaster, the Baptist wholesale merchant, the Commerce had become Canada's second-largest bank, Ontario's answer to what seemed to be the undue caution of the Bank of Montreal in lending money west of the Ottawa River. But the Commerce was still dwarfed by the older bank, was entirely Ontario-centred, and had been going through the most difficult years in its history since 1882. Assets had shrunk by almost 20 per cent by 1886 and the reserve had been depleted to meet bad debts.

Cox came on the board as part of a general reorganization after McMaster's retirement. Henry Darling, president of the Toronto Board of Trade, became the Commerce's president. Thirty-eight-year-old Byron Edmund Walker was brought back from the New York agency as general manager. He had already served eighteen years with the bank since joining it as a clerk in 1868, and had mastered every position he had filled. With Cox playing an active role in the bank's affairs, Walker began to reorganize and retrench. In 1890 Cox succeeded Darling as president. He was one of the half-dozen largest shareholders in the bank, though still with less than 2 per cent of the shares, a holding worth about $100,000. As president he was in charge of the administration of some $25 million in assets. According to the

bank's historian, he had risen so rapidly because of his reputation as "a financier of the highest acumen and enterprise."[3]

He had also moved to Toronto in 1888, to the fashionable Sherbourne
Street district the Flavelles lived in, and to the same Methodist church. It was
a logical move towards the centre of his business interests—the Commerce
was in Toronto and his Eastern Ontario Branch of the Canada Life had taken
over the company's Toronto business in 1887. Like Flavelle, Cox may also
have found Peterborough less hospitable since the Scott Act campaigns of
1885–6. Neither of them later rewarded Peterborough with the parks, playgrounds, or public buildings often bestowed on old hometowns by native
boys who made good.

Cox was the Canada Life's most successful agent and had become a major
shareholder by buying shares as often as he could afford them. When he
moved to Toronto he quarrelled with the directors for rejecting his plan to
move the Central Canada along with him into the west wing of the Canada
Life's Toronto office. "Then and there I decided to go upon the Board." He
bought up shares as fast as he could, often through agents who did not
disclose their principal. By 1891 some of the directors had become resentful
at the thought of one of their employees buying up the company, and
vaguely nervous about the danger of undue influence if control of a life-
insurance company fell into one person's hands. Cox's holdings were
already so large that he forced his way onto the board in 1892, allowing his
opponents the Pyrrhic victory of setting up a trusteeship to handle most of
his shares while he was a director, a kind of guarantee of Mr. Cox's good
behaviour.

In 1897 he had the trusteeship ended by simply threatening to resign from
the board, regain control of his shares, and elect a new board. The last of the
old guard soon left the board. The triumph of the Cox regime was symbolized in 1899 by the removal of the head office from Hamilton to Toronto.
In 1900 Senator Cox became president and general manager of the Canada
Life, fulfilling an aspiration he said he had had for the thirty-eight years since
he became its agent. He owned or controlled close to 50 per cent of the
company's stock, perhaps more. As head of the company he was in charge of
the investment of about $20 million, about 2½ per cent of which was his
own money.[4]

In 1900 as president of the Central Canada, Bank of Commerce, and
Canada Life, George Cox controlled assets totalling $70,442,935.75. He was
one of the most powerful businessmen in Canada because so many people

had trusted his institutions with their money, and because as yet there were few restrictions on what the institutions could do with their money. His personal fortune at the time might not have exceeded Flavelle's.

The Senator intended to create a family dynasty. Each time he moved on to something bigger, a Cox relative was brought along to handle the old job. E. W. (Ed) Cox, his eldest son, had been his partner in the Eastern Ontario Branch of the Canada Life. When the father became president and general manager Ed moved up as assistant general manager; H. C. (Bert) Cox, the youngest son, took over the Eastern Ontario Branch. F. G. (Fred) Cox, the middle son, had been manager of the Central Canada—or, rather, nominal manager, for Dundas had told Flavelle in 1892 that George A. was doing all the work. Two of the lesser family enterprises, the Toronto Savings and Loan Company and the Provident Investment Company, were managed by a son-in-law, Alfred Ernest Ames. Ames was a Methodist minister's son from Lambeth, Ontario, who had married into the family in 1887. Not content to follow exactly in his father-in-law's footsteps, Ames in 1889 had also founded his own stock-brokerage business in Toronto. He was only twenty-three at the time, but the Toronto Stock Exchange was young too— only 176,000 shares changed hands that year. The bulk of Ames's business must have been trading for his father-in-law, who guaranteed his credit at the Bank.[5]

II

Flavelle does not appear to have had any business connection with Cox during the early 1890s. He made his own way in Toronto, relying only on his family for guarantees at the start of his new enterprises. In 1889 Gunn, Flavelle & Company did switch their banking to the Commerce, which also supported Flavelle's purchase of William Davies stock. At all times in his life, though, Flavelle would have resented the suggestion that he was any other man's creation.

Of course nothing had interfered with his friendship with the Coxes. After they moved to Toronto Flavelle shared with the Coxes and Ames in the services, the prayer and class and board meetings of Sherbourne Street Church. By 1896 Flavelle had shown he could stand on his own as a successful businessman, and Cox may have known he was ready to branch out. Perhaps, too, it was no coincidence that Dundas, long associated with Cox, died in 1896. The uncle having passed away, Cox might have thought it useful to keep the family connection alive by introducing the nephew to the various businesses. In any case Flavelle would be an asset to a Board of Directors, for he was becoming known in Toronto as a successful and upright businessman. He had impressed such an important figure as Zebulon Lash, solicitor for both Cox and the Bank of Commerce, when he first needed legal advice. "You told me it was not a bare legal opinion you wanted," Lash reminded Flavelle years later, "but it was my personal opinion of what it would be right for you to do as between man & man without regard to legal rights—I explained the legal position & gave you my views of the man & man side & you acted on them & voluntarily assumed a liability which you were not legally under. Ever since then our intercourse has been close & delightful."[6] So when Cox asked Flavelle to join the board of the Commerce in 1896 it was as one successful businessman to another, not as patron to protégé.

As it almost always would be in Flavelle's business career, the timing was perfect. In 1896 the Canadian economy's dreary cycle of sharp depressions followed by only moderate recovery gave way to year after year in which business was better than the last. International terms of trade were changing in Canada's favour as urban, industrial England and the United States became hungrier for raw materials. Earlier there had been such products as Canadian cheese and the premium bacon of the Davies Company; soon these would be dwarfed by the great new grain staple from the prairies and the timber and minerals of the Canadian Shield. Within a few years the trickle of settlers into Canada's "Last, Best West" would grow to a stream, then a flood. So would the foreign capital, mostly British, attracted to a new investment frontier. Toronto's bankers and financial men did not know it at the time, but they were poised on the brink of what is often called the Laurier boom (although it is not clear that the Laurier government had anything to do with the good times other than to take credit for them). The Flavelles, the Coxes, the Ameses, and the Walkers had done well in not very good times in the 1880s and early 1890s. Now they were ready to do spectacularly well in boom times.

In ten years, from 1896 to 1906, the Bank of Commerce more than tripled its assets to well over $100 million. Branches were pitched, sometimes literally, wherever there was money to be gathered in or loaned out — in the Yukon, along the CPR's main line on the prairies, in the lumber and mining towns of New Ontario. The Bank of British Columbia was bought out on the Pacific Coast, the Halifax Banking Company on the Atlantic. Between the Great Lakes and the Rockies the Commerce had only its Winnipeg branch in 1898; in 1911 it had 113 branches in the three prairie provinces. The Commerce had transformed itself from a provincial Ontario bank to a national financial institution, a symbol of Toronto's rise to challenge Montreal for national business leadership.

The Imperial Life was not founded to take advantage of the good times a-coming. It was created, Cox admitted later, because of "purely a personal matter" within his family. His second son, Fred, who had been nominal manager of the Central Canada, decided he would do better in life insurance. With his other two sons already holding high positions in the Canada Life, Cox realized it would be carrying nepotism too far to bring Fred in too. So he decided to give Fred his own life-insurance company to manage.[7]

There seemed nothing improper in combining a favour to the Coxes with a good business proposition. Flavelle was the active figure in organizing the company and became first vice-president when it opened for business in October 1897. Sir Oliver Mowat, who had just retired from the perpetual premiership of Ontario to become Minister of Justice in the Laurier cabinet, was the Imperial Life's figurehead president. To right the political balance, Sir Mackenzie Bowell, ex-Prime Minister, Conservative leader in the Senate, and a prominent Methodist, joined the board, along with Ames, E. R. Wood, and Senator Cox. The Cox family owned well over half the stock either directly or through the Central Canada or nominal shareholders — a device which probably concealed the family nature of the firm from the general public. Flavelle did own his eight hundred shares outright, having supplied $45,000 of the $562,500 invested in the company.[8]

Fred Cox did no better in life insurance than he had in the Central Canada. Thomas Bradshaw, the secretary and actuary, was the real manager of the company. Flavelle also took an active part in day-to-day operations for the first year or two. In 1898 Senator Cox briefly owned a controlling interest in two other life-insurance companies, Manufacturers' and the Temperance and General Life, and hoped to merge them with the Imperial. When Bradshaw recommended against the merger, he sold the other companies and the Imperial made its own way in life, though not without growing pains.

It was not able to pay dividends at first. Expenses were so high that Flavelle, Ames, and Cox had to subsidize the company with special contributions each year through 1903, to a total of $91,000 in six years. There were two ways of looking at these subsidies, which were given without legal obligation on the company's part. To Bradshaw, reflecting the views of the donors, they were "an exceedingly generous act, a thing that has never been done in Canada before, and we feel proud of it. . . . it was all done for the benefit of the policyholders — $91,000 paid for their benefit and for no one else's benefit." The Royal Commission on Life Insurance, whose inquiry in 1906 revealed all these details, was more impressed by the failure of the company to list the subsidies in its returns to the government, thus misleading policyholders about the company's ratio of expenses to income.[9] Flavelle left the board in 1900 because of the pressure of his other responsibilities. Ames took over the vice-presidency and became president in 1901 when Sir Oliver Mowat died. After the first few uneven years the business developed nicely.

National Trust was not founded to make work for Cox relatives. Canadian law did not permit life-insurance companies or banks to exercise such trusteeship functions as executing estates or acting as agent in securities transactions. There was no reason why Cox and his associates, already managing tens of millions, should not also perform these functions. In 1898 the National Trust Company was incorporated, with Flavelle as president and A. E. Ames as vice-president. Eddie Wood, who had taken over management of the Central Canada when Fred Cox moved to Imperial Life, was National Trust's first manager in his spare time. The typing was done by young Harry Gundy, stenographer of the Central Canada (and another Methodist minister's son), in *his* spare time. These easy arrangements were possible because National Trust rented space in the rear of the Central Canada office at 26 King Street East. The Imperial Life and the Toronto Stock Exchange were upstairs.

The trust company operated on the same broad principle as the other financial intermediaries run by the Cox group. The shareholders — Cox, his associates, the Central Canada, and the Canada Life — subscribed the original capital of $1 million in fully paid $100 shares. But they paid a premium of 25 per cent on their shares (i.e. $125 per share), so the company started with a reserve of $250,000. Business would be attracted by the security the company offered — $1.25 million protecting its customers' money — and by the reputation of the members of the board. The company's own capital and the money it attracted through the sale of its Guaranteed Trust Certificates (rate of interest guaranteed by the resources of the company) was invested in mortgages, securities, real estate, and call loans. As with the bank, life insurance, and investment companies, profits came from the difference between the interest earned on investments and that paid to customers. There were also fees for other financial services: acting as transfer agent for stock issues, as trustee for bondholders, and as executor of estates. The company particularly hoped to develop the estate business, for as the country's wealth increased it seemed likely that corporate executors would be able to offer better service than private executors. Zebulon Lash, who was by now Toronto's most prominent solicitor, was a member of the board; he could be counted on to advise clients to use the trust company for their estate management. On each transaction the profit or fee would be a small percentage of the sum involved, but as the volume of business mounted, the earnings could return substantial dividends on the original capital (which, except for the reserve, would also be earning normal rates of interest).

In the first three months of its existence National Trust operated in every capacity in its charter, doing business generated by the other Cox companies and by Zebulon Lash. Clara Flavelle gave the company its first estate trusteeship, an estate worth $2,075. In 1899 National Trust moved into its own building at 20 King Street East, dividing the ground floor with A. E. Ames & Company. The Stock Exchange followed, renting the second floor (Ames & Company once had a hole cut in the ceiling so their floor man on the Exchange could drop his memos directly into an office basket; it was plugged up as being an unfair special privilege). Wood was relieved of his management duties in 1901 when William Thomas White was hired as general manager. It is said that Cox hired him as a favour to his uncle, R. J. Fleming, a former mayor of Toronto whose unfortunate real-estate speculations had put him deeply in debt to Cox. A Methodist farmer's son, White had graduated in classics from the University of Toronto in 1895, taken two gold medals in law at Osgoode Hall, and become an expert in real estate by working for Toronto's municipal assessment department. He was no ordinary businessman. Tall, handsome, an excellent conversationalist and writer (he had briefly been a reporter for the *Evening Telegram*), White combined a biblical knowledge equal to Flavelle's with a rich, crude vocabulary quite beyond the president's. He brought two other university graduates onto the staff, W. A. Breckenridge, who had worked with him at City Hall, and Home Smith, a classmate at Osgoode. Another early employee was Will Rundle, who joined the company in 1901 as secretary, the same year he married one of Flavelle's nieces.

At the end of its first full year of operations National Trust was able to pay a six-per-cent dividend to its shareholders. By 1904 it had offices in Montreal,

Winnipeg, and Edmonton—the last two to handle investments in Western mortgages—and was administering total assets of $7,814,000. Of all the Cox companies, National Trust would have the steadiest, least turbulent growth.[10]

III

Flavelle was involved in one new venture which was not promoted by Senator Cox. Harris Henry Fudger was yet another Irish Methodist (though said to be descended from the European merchant house of Fugger), who had been born in Toronto in 1852 and had grown up in Paris, Ontario. He was a brilliant high-school student, who went into business against his teachers' belief that someone so bright should prepare for a profession and his parents' notion that he should be a minister. At seventeen he took a position with Robert Wilkes, a wholesale jeweller and fancy-goods merchant, who was one of Toronto's leading Methodist lay preachers. Thriving under Wilkes's strict discipline, he worked his way up to senior accountant and, with a partner, took over the business when Wilkes was drowned in 1880 at Sturgeon Point in the Kawarthas. By the mid-1890s Fudger had his own wholesale fancy-goods house. Like Flavelle, he had his father on his staff; from time to time son would lecture parent for sleeping on the job. The Fudgers, senior and junior, were founding members of Sherbourne Street Church. H. H. Fudger led the Infant Class in the Sunday School at the time Flavelle joined the congregation. They were soon associated in all aspects of the life of the church.[11]

One evening in early 1898 Fudger called on Flavelle to ask him to take a half-interest in purchasing the Robert Simpson Company, which ran the big store and mail-order house at Queen and Yonge streets. Simpson had died suddenly in 1897, and his estate was offering the business at a good price. Flavelle was not financially able to take a half-interest, but offered to put up one-third of the money. He suggested another of their Sabbath School teachers, A. E. Ames, as a likely person to take the remaining one-sixth interest. Ames agreed, and the Sherbourne Street syndicate bought the capital stock of the Robert Simpson Company for $135,000. Assuming the presidency of the company, Fudger turned the management of his former business over to one of his senior buyers and his twenty-three-year-old chief accountant, C. L. Burton.[12]

The Methodists had bought themselves what was coming to be called a "department store" business. It was the junior of Toronto's two department stores, almost literally in the shadow of Timothy Eaton's mammoth establishment on the other side of Queen Street. Eaton, another Ulster Methodist, had made one innovation after another in cost-cutting and expansion in the 1870s and 1880s. Relying on fellow Methodist John Macdonald for credit, he converted his dry-goods business to a cash-only basis, lured customers by heavy advertising, fixed prices, and a guarantee of satisfaction, and undercut competitors by direct buying from manufacturers. Taking advantage of the maturing of Ontario's railway and postal system in the 1880s, he began his mail- and express-order catalogue business. From dry goods he expanded into every other line of retailing that would make money, multiplying his departments until his store offered everything from ladies' pumps to patent medicines, ploughs, and farmyard pumps. Everything worked. In a splendid entrepreneurial achievement Eaton revolutionized nineteenth-century Canadian retailing, just as Marshall Field, John Wanamaker, William Whitely, and others were seizing the same opportunities in the United States and Great Britain.[13] On the other hand Eaton drove a lot of small merchants out of business, especially in the hard years of the early 1890s, and for many years he and his family were considered much too ruthless to be counted among the "prominent" business or social leaders of Toronto.

Robert Simpson, a canny and hard-working Scot despite his occasional problems with drink, had the good sense to give up his attempt to do a high-class, high-price dry-goods business and instead copied Eaton's methods in every way.[14] There was easily enough business in Ontario for two major department stores. The first reaction of anyone dissatisfied with Eaton's would be to try Simpson's; and as the first and biggest store Eaton's had to bear the brunt of the retailers' criticisms. The duopoly in department stores probably gave a stability to the businesses that no single store could have maintained. Who would try to compete with both Eaton's and Simpson's?

It was the lesser department store, but Simpson's handsome six-storey steel-frame building on the south corner of Queen and Yonge still contained four acres of shopping space, all purchases speeded by its advanced pneumatic-tube cash system. Simpson's catalogues were distributed free across Canada twice a year, giving "every shopper, though a resident of some remote corner of the Dominion . . . the same advantages that belong to those who are citizens of Toronto."[15] It was a measure of either the conservatism of other Toronto merchants, or their shortage of ready capital in the mid-1890s (gruelling times for wholesalers), or both, that the Simpson estate had spent almost a year looking for a purchaser.

Fudger, Flavelle, and Ames paid $135,000 for the company, which owned the fixtures (such as the pneumatic tubes) and the Simpson name, but not the building. Simpson's then leased the building from the Simpson estate, and paid a further $324,000 to buy the inventory. Much of its working capital was advanced by the Bank of Commerce. In the first nine months of operation the returns covered rent and interest charges and left net profits of $48,000, enough to pay a 6-per-cent dividend to the shareholders and add $40,000 to the reserve. From the beginning Fudger and his partners followed an expensive expansionary policy. In 1899 the three shareholders invested another $171,000. In 1900, $75,000 in profits was distributed as a 25-per-cent dividend, but each partner immediately (within the hour) reinvested his $25,000 to buy 250 new shares (by now Ames had increased his holdings to one-third, making it an equal partnership). Eighteen months later another 21.6-per-cent dividend had been paid, but each partner increased his investment by 33⅓ per cent.[16]

By 1902 Flavelle had invested approximately $117,000 more than he had received in dividends from Simpson's and owned 1,667 shares with a par value of $167,000. The business had been profitable,* but expansion had gobbled up all the profits. The minutes record one addition after another to the property and buildings. In 1903, with the first period of expansion completed, the directors were able to promise themselves a steady 6-per-cent cash dividend, with any surplus to be retained and capitalized in stock dividends.[17] The business was apparently running smoothly. The mail and express systems were so perfect that not one in ten thousand parcels was going astray; the big Toronto stores could offer their catalogue buyers prices 25 to 50 per cent lower than the local single-line merchant or general storekeeper.[18] Fudger, always the active partner, never had to innovate. He had to administer the expansion of a complex going concern—no mean job—and keep an eye on Eaton's.

---

* There are no sales figures for any years before the 1920s. A rough estimate, based on turning the $324,000 inventory of 1898 over every six months to earn $48,000 in nine months, suggests a profit of about 7 per cent on sales; if it were turned over every three months the profit would be 4.6 to 5 per cent. The latter rate of turnover is more likely.

IV

The companies Flavelle was involved in naturally did business with each other. Simpson's and the Davies Company did their banking at the Commerce. Imperial Life wrote the $50,000 policy Simpson's took out to insure Fudger's life in 1898. A. E. Ames & Company had acted as agents for the first issues of Imperial Life and National Trust stock. National Trust bought its real estate as well as a block of Central Canada stock from the Provident Investment Company.*[19] And so on. In 1899 Flavelle came fully into the web of interlocking Cox directorates when he joined the boards of the Central Canada and the Canada Life.

Investments took up more and more of the directors' time in the 1890s as a glut on the Ontario mortgage market forced them to cast about for other securities to absorb their cash. The Central Canada had moved increasingly into provincial and municipal bonds. In passing, Cox and Wood discovered a profitable sideline in buying large blocks of bonds and reselling them to individual investors. The Central Canada did most of the bond dealing in the Cox "family"; Ames & Company handled the stocks.[20]

The continuing demand for new investments in the late 1890s was met by a wave of new issues of industrial securities, suspect until then because of the volatility of their fortunes. But the new utilities of the 1890s and 1900s — light and power companies, electric street railways — usually operated on long-term monopoly franchises. Their earnings looked particularly secure, their bonds and perhaps even their stock a safe investment. In 1892 the Bank of Commerce made its first major excursion into the utility-bond business when, in association with Cox acting on his own account, it purchased more than $1 million of the bonds of the Toronto Railway Company, which had the franchise to electrify the city's old horse-drawn street-railway system. Having earlier backed the tender of a rival group for the franchise, the bank had clearly been alert to the business possibilities of the revolutionary new utility.[21] The bond purchase also brought the Cox group back into contact with William Mackenzie, president of the street-railway company, who had recently returned to Toronto after several years' contracting for the CPR in

---

* This $482,000 investment in 1898 effectively reduced by over 40 per cent the cash needed to buy the original National Trust shares. The transaction was explained and justified by a very long entry in the Minutes, which pointed out the necessity of investing in the Central Canada to cement a lasting relationship with a senior financial institution, the soundness of the securities being purchased (at lower than market price), and the fact that the real estate had been independently appraised.

the West (he had done earlier contracting work for Cox on the Midland). Mackenzie, too, was a man of possibilities.

Ordinary industrial companies with sound earning ability could also be attractive investments. They seemed to become more attractive in 1899 when it became legal in Canada to issue preferred stock. If a company divided its stock into preferred and common shares, buyers of the preferred would have first call on its profits up to a specified percentage of the par value of their shares. To many investors preferred stock seemed to offer more security than being part of the ordinary shareholder herd in the old days, although that was not necessarily true. To company promoters there was the intriguing way common stock became a speculative "kicker" in floating even the most solidly-based companies. A company with real assets of, say, $1 million might declare its capital as $2 million. The first million would be in preferred shares, the solid securities backed by the real assets on which dividends were likely to be paid. The second paper million would be in common shares on which it had no obligation to pay anything. Their face value was $1 million; in the beginning their real value might well be zero. Representing wishful thinking, the common stock could be scattered about to promoters, underwriters, and lenders as sweeteners to the deal. If the company prospered and was ever able to pay a dividend on its common stock, the deal would have been very sweet. If not, nothing had been lost.*

Often the money managers themselves — the Coxes, the Woods, the Ameses — were the first to perceive the opportunities for profitable investment of the funds they controlled, and they created new issues simply by organizing new companies. Alternatively, any industrialist planning to go public would want to ally himself with the money managers to ensure a friendly reception of the securities on the market. There was no better way to do that than to invite a Cox, a Wood, or an Ames to join his board and take an interest in the company. Cox, especially, collected directorates by the dozen.

---

* Of course another name for this practice was "stock-watering." In the example given, only half the stock is backed by real assets; the other half is "water," backed by nothing. Appropriately, the term derives from farmers' habit of quenching the thirst of their livestock just before marketing to increase their weight. Stock-watering came in for much condemnation by those who mistakenly assumed it meant that promoters were, in this case, selling one million worth of assets for two million. The real abuse of these fictitious capitalizations came when companies tried to justify a return of, say, thirty per cent on their real assets, as a reasonable fifteen per cent on their "capital." Since the 1920s the almost universal use of no-par stock has made watering a thing of the past.

Flavelle was involved in two of the first flotations in the year that preferred stock became legal. He was a member of the board and later a vice-
president of the Carter—Crume Company, launched in September 1899
with a capitalization of $2 million ($750,000 of 7 per cent first preference
stock, $1,250,000 common). This company bought the businesses of the
Carter—Crume companies of Toronto and Niagara Falls, New York, private firms formed in the early 1880s and managed by S. J. Moore.

Moore was a former printer, who had come to Canada as a youth and was
prominent in Toronto Baptist circles. Holding important patents on business forms involving the use of carbon paper, Moore's companies supplied
nearly 90 per cent of the Merchants' Duplicating and Triplicating Sales
Books in use in North America, as well as selling other ledgers and registers.
The new company was an alliance of Moore with the Cox group of financial
men. The contact may have developed through Simpson's, which, like other
department stores, found the advanced forms pioneered by Moore essential
for its complex record-keeping. Moore and Flavelle were joined on the
board by Ames, Walter Massey (president of Massey—Harris, a director of
the Commerce, another prominent Methodist), and Robert Kilgour (vice-
president of the Commerce, a director of National Trust, a Presbyterian).
Ames & Company underwrote the public issue of the preference stock; National Trust was the transfer agent; Carter—Crume banked at the Commerce. The $550,000 of preference stock offered to the public at par was
oversubscribed.[22]

In the same month National Trust offered the public at par $2 million of
the 7 per cent preference stock of the Canada Cycle and Motor Company
Limited, Walter Massey president, George A. Cox vice-president, Flavelle a
director, banking done with the Commerce. CCM was formed to acquire
five bicycle firms, including the bicycle division of Massey—Harris. Its
capitalization was $6 million, divided equally between preference and
common stock. $500,000 of the preference stock had been subscribed by the
directors and another $500,000 was being held back by the company. The
issue looked attractive because the constituent companies had had combined
profits averaging $267,000 in each of the previous three years, easily enough
to cover the dividend obligation of $175,000 on the preference stock. One of
the more intriguing prospects of the new company was its intention to go
into the manufacture of automobiles.[23] Despite scattered comment in the
financial press that the capitalization seemed high, the issue was largely
oversubscribed. Among the four hundred or so shareholders were a number

of Methodist laymen and ministers attracted by the prominence in their church of most of the directors.

There was a host of other new issues. Down east a Boston financier, H. M. Whitney, had taken hold of various Nova Scotia coal properties and launched a steel-making complex at Sydney. Both Montreal and Toronto financiers were brought onto the boards of Dominion Coal and Dominion Iron and Steel, and Canadian investors put up the millions they raised through securities offerings. Returning to the West in partnership with Donald Mann, another former CPR contractor, Mackenzie of the Toronto Railway Company had bought a decrepit branch railway in Manitoba. With the backing of the Commerce (whose board approved a $500,000 line of credit for Mackenzie and Mann in the same month in 1896 that Flavelle joined it), and later of the Central Canada, Mackenzie & Mann were building, buying, and leasing track at a record pace. By 1902 there was talk of their Canadian Northern Railway going transcontinental, the only unresolved question being their relations with the old Grand Trunk, which was also planning to launch a transcontinental. Whatever happened, the Bank of Commerce would be in on the building of a rival to the CPR (whose bonds it had timidly refused to buy in the 1880s), for Senator Cox would be one of the founding directors of the Grand Trunk Pacific. Flavelle, who had dreamed of being involved in railways since he was a little boy, was also slated to be on the Grand Trunk Pacific's board.

The money flowed on. Van Horne and those who had worked with him building the CPR — Mackenzie, Mann, James Ross, Herbert Holt — knew their railroading. Frederic Nicholls, the German-born president of Canadian General Electric, and the mysterious American engineer, F. S. Pearson, who got to know the Canadians through H. M. Whitney, were alive to the new world of electricity. Cox, E. R. Wood, and other prominent brokers like Henry Mill Pellatt, had the financial connections. Promoting or reorganizing street-railway and power companies became a specialty of Canadian enterprise, not only in Canada but on three continents, beginning with Van Horne's railway work in Cuba after the Spanish–American war. In a ten-year period spanning the turn of the century, some or all of this group— always Mackenzie — were involved in electricity and street railways in Toronto, Winnipeg, Montreal, Saint John, Minneapolis/St. Paul, Detroit, Birmingham (England), Barcelona, Havana, Trinidad, Jamaica, Mexico City, Monterrey, Rio de Janeiro, and São Paulo. The São Paulo Tramway, Light and Power Company, a Cox "family" promotion of 1900, was their most enduring success; it survives today as Brascan. Closest to home, Mackenzie, Nicholls, and Pellatt launched the Electrical Development Company in 1903 to bring Niagara's power to Toronto through the electric-light company and street railway they already owned. At their furthest reaches the Canadian utility magnates considered the prospects for tramway development in Shanghai.[24]

All the Cox companies were involved with these new enterprises — underwriting the securities, investing in the securities, trading the securities, loaning money on the security of the securities. The Central Canada Loan and Savings' bond business became so extensive that in 1901 a subsidiary company, Dominion Securities, was chartered to carry on the group's bond trading. Its address was 4 Victoria Street, the back door of the Central Canada. The officers included E. R. Wood president, Frank W. Baillie managing director, G. H. Wood (no relation to E. R. Wood) secretary, and J. H. Gundy accountant. Despite Gundy's and G. H. Wood's withdrawal in 1905 to form Wood, Gundy & Company (Wood was replaced by E. R. Peacock, a Queen's graduate who had been teaching at Upper Canada College), Dominion Securities was by then the largest bond dealer in the Dominion. One of its best customers had always been the Canada Life, and much of the agency and trusteeship work involved in these issues had gone to National Trust. The Imperial Life became another good customer as its assets grew. Examples of dealing among the Cox companies could be multiplied almost endlessly.

Aside from brief service on the boards of the Crow's Nest Pass Coal Company (another Cox company) and an electric railway company in the Niagara peninsula (affiliated with the Electrical Development Company's projects), Flavelle participated in these new ventures only as an investor. In 1902 he reckoned his total capital as about $1,300,000, more than $850,000 of which was in the William Davies Company and Simpson's. The remaining four or five hundred thousand was invested as opportunities developed. "I do not speculate in stocks," he claimed—and then drew the finest line—"I however from time to time take very substantial holdings of securities not yet fully proven—in the purchase of which I exercise my judgment based upon an intelligent study of the situation. In these holdings I sometimes use only my own capital, and again in addition I lean upon my bankers."[25]

In 1901 he owned São Paulo 5-per-cent debentures with a par value of $50,000 and common stock with a par value of $56,600. As one of the original underwriters of São Paulo (along with Mackenzie, Cox, Nicholls, B. F.

Pearson, the Central Canada, and the Commerce)[26] he had purchased the debentures at about 90 with the common stock thrown in as a bonus. By March 1901, securities that cost him about $45,000 less than a year before were worth $87,500. He held on to them, though, using the stock and bonds as collateral for a $50,000 loan from the Imperial Life.[27] The next year he was in on the ground floor in Dominion Coal and Dominion Iron and Steel. Despite his insider's knowledge of the situation, or rather because of it, he did not anticipate the wave of public speculation in the two properties that began in the spring of 1902.

Even the Prime Minister was trying to make a killing in steel and coal.[28] When Dominion Coal common started shooting up 10 points a day Flavelle sold 1,000 shares at between 80 and 90 and his other thousand at 115 to 120, having probably bought at less than 60. But Coal continued to climb. "It has been a case where I have known too much," he wrote Wheeler-Bennett in April when Coal was at 130, "and where the cautious business man has failed to appreciate what would happen in the situation when a thronging public, illogical and impetuous, took a notion to buy particular securities." Some of the other insiders, including Senator Cox, had "wakened up to the situation" and bought back in heavily after the stock had passed 80. Flavelle was willing to give Wheeler-Bennett, who was dabbling in Canadian stocks, inside information on the state of the steel and coal properties ("I take my financial honor in hand in giving you this"), but was not sure whether to advise him to go into Steel. Although times were good, "as sure as the sun will rise tomorrow this will be followed by commercial depression." He held on to his own Steel stock into the fall of 1902, only to be caught temporarily short of cash in the market decline of September and October.[29] He apparently recovered easily.

V

Because Flavelle was still a nominal shareholder in the Imperial Life in 1901, it was illegal for the Imperial Life to have loaned him the $50,000 on his São Paulo securities. The Dominion Insurance Commissioner did not know about the loan because it was officially paid back on December 31, 1901, so it did not appear in the company's year-end return. It was then renewed on January 2, 1902.

In April 1902 the Imperial Life invested $22,000 in Dominion Iron and

Steel bonds, an unauthorized investment under the company's charter. At year's end the bonds were sold to A. E. Ames & Company so they did not appear on the annual return. On January 2, 1903, the bonds were bought back from Ames & Company along with more steel-company bonds. They were finally sold that fall, a portion to Dominion Securities. In March 1903 the Imperial Life made an unauthorized purchase of Dominion Coal stock.

The Canada Life made no illegal or unauthorized investments, but it did extensive bond trading with Dominion Securities, loaned money to DS, and used its policyholders' money to help support the market value of Dominion Coal stock, in which most of its investors had private holdings, at a time when it could have made a profit by selling. A $389,500 loan to A. E. Ames & Company in 1902 was paid off on December 31 and renewed on January 2; it did not appear on the company's annual return.

These details were revealed when the life-insurance industry was investigated by the McTavish Royal Commission of 1906. Referring to Senator Cox and the Canada Life, the commissioners concluded that his absolute control of the company had "to a marked extent influenced the investments of the company, which have been made to serve not only the interests of the Canada Life Assurance Company, but also his own interests and the interests of other institutions in which he was largely concerned. . . . In many of these transactions the conflict of Mr. Cox's interest with his duty is so apparent that the care of the insurance funds could not always have been the sole consideration."[30]

The insurance commissioners did not believe it was possible for one man or group of men to have so many corporate personalities and to buy and sell from themselves so often without someone's interests being adversely affected, most likely the people who had entrusted money to the companies. They were, in effect, accusing Cox and his associates of abusing their public trust, of mismanaging the public's money. There is no doubt from the revelations before the insurance commission and from other evidence that the pool of other people's money the Cox group had come to administer was managed to help projects in which they were personally interested. Some of the associates, including Flavelle, Frank Baillie (who made a killing in Dominion Coal),[31] and E. R. Wood (who somehow became a millionaire in these years), made healthy sums from their personal investments in these projects. On occasion, as with Imperial Life, the in-family investments were illegal.

Some of the Cox-promoted enterprises were also bad business. There were signs of trouble in Canada Cycle and Motor almost as soon as the issue of preference stock was subscribed. Instead of rising above par, as the directors had expected, the shares showed a definite weakness on the market. Through 1900, Cox, Flavelle, Ames, Massey, and three of the companies they directed, one of which was National Trust, supported the market, buying up more than $400,000 of the stock at between 92 and 100. True, the first year's profits of $195,000 would support only a dividend of 5¾ per cent on the preference stock, but prospects for 1901 looked good enough to issue the full 7 per cent in January and July payments.

When the final returns for the year ending in September were calculated, the directors discovered that Walter Massey's budgeting system may have been fine for binders and reapers, but did not work properly for bicycles. It underestimated costs of manufacture and sale by $6 and overestimated returns by $3 for each "wheel" the company sold, a mis-estimate of $216,000 on 24,000 bicycles. CCM had also bought up the National Cycle Company that year to avoid getting into a price war, and found after the transaction had closed that it had taken a $280,000 loss.* Nothing came of the automobile business. At the peak of the season CCM's St. Catharines plant burned down. The bicycle market, saturated after the craze of the late nineties, was very weak. Net profits for 1901 were $2,035. From these profits the shareholders had already been paid $175,000 in dividends!

By December rumours of the disastrous results had pushed CCM preferred down to $40 on the Toronto Stock Exchange; in the week after the annual meeting it fell to $15. Writs issued from angry shareholders charging the directors with negligence and breach of duty. Rumours circulated on King Street of huge promoters' profits and a directors' conspiracy in the last year to support the shares on the market until they could be unloaded on an unsuspecting public. How much of their holdings had the directors sold before announcing the bad news? Walter Massey had died of typhoid in the fall of 1901 and would answer to God. The other directors, the pillars of Sherbourne Street Methodist Church, would answer to the shareholders.

A special shareholders' meeting on March 29, 1902, considered the situation. The only director who "faced the music like a man," the *Monetary Times* reported, was Flavelle (he was also the only director not subject to a suit brought against the original promoters). For two and a half hours Flavelle

---

* Alternatively the directors may have thought at the time that it was worth $280,000 in a "goodwill" payment to eliminate National Cycle's competition.

answered angry questions from the more than one hundred shareholders present, interspersed with heckling and shouts of "Why isn't Cox here?" "To his credit be it said he never once lost his temper, being quite unruffled throughout the entire proceedings. Indeed, but for his savoir faire the meeting might have had a far different ending," the *Mail and Empire* reported. He outlined all the details of the promotion—the $1,397,500 the original companies had cost, the $250,000 in underwriting costs, and the $72,500 in incidentals. The directors had not unloaded their stock, but rather had increased their holdings to try and protect the other shareholders, and now with their friends and associates they held over $1,300,000 of the original $2,500,000. The *Monetary Times* editors had been allowed to see the company's books to confirm these statements. Flavelle admitted all the errors in management and agreed that too much had been paid for the original properties. After assuring the shareholders that the banks would carry the company's overdraft on the directors' personal guarantees and promising a regime of cost-cutting and reorganization, he succeeded in getting a vote of confidence in CCM's directors.[32]

This did not eliminate the dissatisfaction, especially at the quarter-million dollars spent underwriting a company trumpeted as such an attractive investment. $50,000 had gone to Cox, Massey, and the other three promoters (Flavelle was not among them) who had originally bought the constituent companies. The underwriters made $200,000. Had the CCM directors struck the best possible bargain for underwriting the stock when it appeared that they had been bargaining with themselves under a different set of silk hats?* Was it really credible that Walter Massey should use "jump" estimates and rule-of-thumb methods to justify paying unearned dividends? Where was the surplus that CCM had started in business with after paying all its expenses? "I have said my last word," Flavelle told the press. Those questions—raised afterwards by reporters—should have been asked at the open meeting.[33]

For the next two years Flavelle chaired the annual meetings and led the negotiations to have the litigation dropped and the company reorganized.

---

* As indeed they had. National Trust, the Bank of Commerce, and the Central Canada, had underwritten the CCM stock at 90 cents on the dollar, taking a 10-per-cent profit on the sale to the public. It is not clear whether CCM could have obtained better terms from any other potential underwriters. National Trust was worried enough about its underwriting commitment to arrange secondary underwriting by the Commerce and Central Canada for two-thirds of its share at 95, reducing its profit on the flotation to about $46,000.

Although they were under no legal obligation, the directors put $1 million of their preference shares into trust to be distributed to the least-well-off shareholders. When the better-off shareholders blocked this, the directors agreed to have $900,000 of their holdings cancelled, reducing the preference shares to $1,600,000. These were then written down to $1 million (the common stock, which had gone to the promoters as a bonus and had never been worth anything, was also cancelled). To rebuild the company Flavelle persuaded young T. A. Russell to come in as general manager in 1902. Russell had graduated from the University of Toronto in political science in 1899, lectured there for a year, and just finished an impressive job reorganizing the Canadian Manufacturers' Association. Russell cut back on the bicycle operations, expanded into automobiles with a Ford agency, and gradually revived the company. In 1905 CCM offered its first Canadian automobile, the Russell. Flavelle left the company shortly after the reorganization.[34]

VI

The directors of CCM surrendered only $900,000 of their stock because one of them, who was to put up $100,000 in stock, had failed. By 1902 A. E. Ames had decided to move out of the family nest of companies. Supported by Moore of Carter–Crume, Bradshaw of Imperial Life, and Baillie of Dominion Securities, he founded his own bank, the Metropolitan. He resigned from the board of National Trust and he and Bradshaw bought enough shares in Imperial Life from a reluctant Cox and the Central Canada to make the Ames/Bradshaw and Cox holdings exactly equal, with provision for arbitration if the two interests deadlocked over policy. There was no open quarrel among the financiers — Flavelle seems to have stood somewhere in the middle of the two groups, Fred Cox kept his sinecure with the Imperial Life — but the Senator reprehended his son-in-law and withdrew whatever interest he and his companies had in A. E. Ames & Company, along with his guarantee of Ames's credit at the Commerce. Ames was particularly intent on developing an American brokerage business, a course Byron Walker and Senator Cox considered to be fraught with hazard because of the instability of the American credit system.[35]

For a time the young man was on top of the business world. As retiring president of the Toronto Board of Trade he gave a "severely ethical" presidential address in January 1903, warning businessmen to guard against "the tendency to take on more than can be carried through stress of weather," to be wary of "the contagion of a feverish period during which one's neighbours are picking their mushroom riches."

Using common stock as security, Ames & Company had borrowed $21 million from American banks to finance customers' purchases. The firm had huge holdings of Twin Cities Rapid Transit. In a bear market in the spring of 1903 Twin Cities went straight down. The American banks called their loans to Ames. His customers could not meet calls on their margins. The prodigal son-in-law rushed back to the family.

Fearing a major financial collapse, a consortium of Canadian banks, including the Commerce, advanced several millions to the firm. The Ames/ Bradshaw interest in Imperial Life was bought back by Senator Cox (with a windfall premium to Bradshaw to induce him to let the resale go through). On June 1 when the other directors of the Imperial refused to loan Ames, their president, more money, Cox phoned to take over the obligation himself. The needful was advanced to Ames, although the Imperial itself was running an overdraft. But it was not enough. On June 2, A. E. Ames & Company had to close its doors. Ames, who had given a number of talks to YMCA and church groups on how to succeed in business, had failed.[36]

Thanks to the banks, and because the other Cox companies had disassociated themselves from Ames, there were few falling dominoes. He brought down only two St. Thomas, Ontario, loan companies with him. But he had brought himself down to personal humiliation. He immediately resigned as president of the Imperial Life and the Metropolitan Bank, gave up his other directorships and his membership on Sherbourne Street Church's Board of Trustees, and set about liquidating his assets to pay his creditors. "Poor Ames," Flavelle wrote from Europe. "His strength was his weakness—a less able man would not have been in such a position—he came close to winning—but missed."[37] In a fit of righteousness members of Parliament briefly debated a resolution to outlaw speculation in stocks.

Ames was unable to meet the second payment due his creditors in January 1904. "Poor fellow—he has had his full share of punishment. His failure to meet his promised payment has robbed him of that intangible sort of support, which comes to a man who while down, establishes his resources and ability to pay his debts," Flavelle wrote his wife.[38] A few days later Ames resigned his last directorate, in Simpson's; his father-in-law replaced him on the board, having bought his shares. Flavelle later told a grandson that he, Flavelle, helped Ames get back on his feet. Wherever the money came from,

Ames was eventually able to pay his creditors in full and A. E. Ames & Company soon reopened for business.[39]

VII

Even for Ames the setbacks were only temporary. Markets recovered, companies could be reorganized, losses could be made good out of wealthy directors' pockets. Flavelle and his circle thought the mistakes and dubious ventures of these years paled by comparison with the achievements of their companies in helping to develop Canada's resources. Certainly they had been aggressive. Under Cox's management the Canada Life had expanded throughout the British Empire. In its support of Mackenzie and Mann's Canadian Northern Railway the Commerce was backing the most aggressive railway venture in Canadian history, and in the territory it served one of the most popular.[40] Simpson's was becoming a national retailer. The William Davies Company killed more hogs than anyone in the Empire. Of course the financial institutions had intervened in 1902 to support the market in Dominion Coal. Why not protect their investment, Senator Cox argued? It was one of the most valuable properties on the continent, "one of very great interest to this country, second only in importance to the Transcontinental Railways of our country, and because a number of people get speculating in the stock and kick it about in the market it should not be regarded as an unsafe investment for a life insurance company."[41]

Nor had any of the policyholders of the Canada Life, the depositors in the Bank of Commerce, or the investors in the Central Canada suffered from the policies pursued by the men who had managed their money. If the essence of fiduciary responsibility was safeguarding capital and having it return a reasonable rate of interest, no one could charge Cox and his companies with poor stewardship. That was a lot more than could be said of hundreds of other businessmen, who through incompetence or dishonesty had their names scattered through the "Failures" columns of the business press. Ames had failed, but the money had all been paid back. CCM had been a dreadful series of errors; in restitution the directors had voluntarily given away most, perhaps all, of their holdings.*[42]

---

* Flavelle's role in grappling with the CCM problem may have enhanced his reputation. When he was under public attack during the war, a Toronto businessman offered his support, remarking that "Businessmen have never forgotten how you treated the shareholders of the Canada Cycle & Motor Co."

What about the conflicts of interest, the trading back and forth between companies, the buying and selling from one's self in different corporate dress? Questioned about his stewardship in 1906, Cox's defence was that the transactions had been to the advantage of all parties involved. No one could show unwise purchases or sales or unreasonably high commissions. It was natural for the Canada Life to buy most of its bonds from Dominion Securities because it was by far the largest bond dealer in Canada. In any case the average commission paid to DS was $1\frac{5}{8}$ per cent on all these transactions, a smaller percentage than the province of Ontario was paying to sell its bonds to the Bank of Montreal.[43]

Even if Cox had wanted to manipulate transactions between his companies to his personal advantage, he argued that his fellow directors and officers would not have consented. They were men of the highest standing in the community, trained to be prudent, skilled investors, each loyal to the company he was serving at the time. As he told the Senate in 1907, the Canada Life's board was "chosen from the leading businessmen of this country, whose ability, integrity and independence are beyond question." How could they be considered "mere tools in my hands to vote at my dictation?" Finally, Cox's methods of doing business were not unusual in the early 1900s. It was unusual for people to ask mean questions about conflict of interest. "There has never been any suggestion, nor could there be, that it was illegal for two corporations having the same president and in which some of the same shareholders were interested in both companies, to deal with each other, and it has never until recently, so far as I am aware, been suggested that it was improper to do so."[44]

Cox understood instinctively why these questions had not previously been common. In an uncertain business world, where money managers had almost no technical advice or reliable intelligence about situations they were being asked to support, personal knowledge was vital. A businessman deals with men on whom he can rely. Better to invest in companies formed by your own group of reliable men than to get involved with businessmen of unknown capacity (such as that American promoter, F. H. Clergue, whose fiasco in steel and a dozen other enterprises at Sault Ste. Marie in the early years of the century lost millions in American and Canadian investors' money, but not one cent of the Cox group's funds).[45] Better to loan money to your own directors and shareholders, who you knew were good risks, than to outsiders and companies you knew little about. Better to invest money entrusted to your care in ventures you were confident enough of to risk your own money in, rather than put it into projects you would not back yourself.

There were insiders and outsiders. If an outsider's credentials looked good it was prudent to bring him inside by putting him on one of your boards, or going on to one of his boards, so that you would have advance warning if something was going wrong, or if something promising was turning up. Being an insider on a deal was a natural occurrence in a business world full of information blockages, suspicion, and distrust. Reputable businessmen like the Methodist financiers in the Cox group warned the public that most ordinary speculators were outsiders who lost their shirts ("Don't be a fool," Flavelle once told a servant considering an investment. "If the stock were as good as that you wouldn't be getting a chance at it. We'd have bought it long ago.").[46] Conversely, their own position on the inside being deserved, they did not hesitate to take advantage of it—to a point.

Above all, it was a business world of individuals. The institutional structures they worked in and through were instruments to facilitate their work. The idea of setting up barriers and safeguards based on the novel idea of keeping the instruments — the corporations — at arm's length from each other, limited the craftsman in the use of tools. When bothersome regulations got in the way of confident, arrogant men, when, say, the Insurance Commissioner got "pernickety" about the Imperial Life's investments or its perfectly well secured loan to J. W. Flavelle, there were harmless ways of disregarding them.*[47] Harmless because no money was being lost. If something did go wrong, if an Ames got in trouble or directors authorized an improper loan that didn't work, the personal fortunes of those involved could be drawn on to make good the mistake. Another legal nicety sometimes disregarded by these businessmen was the idea of limited liability.

These rationalizations were very important to Flavelle and his friends, who considered themselves men of the highest moral integrity. They still begged some questions. So much depended on an individual's probity in a

---

* Flavelle explained the loan this way: "I was not a director when the loan was made — no obligations existed either way between the Imperial and myself. The loan was made on its own merits of high order, the security absolute and the option to the Imperial a good one. . . . I do not remember anything about the payment at the end of December and the renewal early in the year. I presume Mr. Bradshaw asked me to do so, and that I did it. The whole transaction was such a one as would take place in any Company, with any one of its many clients and could challenge no comment from the most fastidious as far as the borrower was concerned."

system where neither institutions nor the law effectively protected investors. Was it too much? Could even the most high-minded businessman always sort out the grey areas where the trustee's obligation and his personal
self-interest sometimes conflicted? Could Senator Cox always be trusted to
further the Canada Life's interest if it ever conflicted with that of his other
companies, or with his ambitions for his sons? William Mackenzie had been
known to cross the ethical borderline in some of his business deals (substantial sums of money had found their way into aldermanic pockets just before
his syndicate got the Toronto street-railway franchise). How wise was it of
the directors of the Cox companies to become intimately involved with his
enterprises? Most important, how long would the public, legitimately suspicious of men's aims in a world that revolved around making money, continue to believe that financiers were motivated by high ethical standards
simply because they said they were? The system rested on tenuous, intangible foundations of public trust in the men who ran it.

VIII

Flavelle's strongest feeling about his wider business ventures was pride in the
way most of the Cox companies were contributing to Canada's marvellous
development. Well aware of the need for caution and prudence in individual
transactions ("in the background I always carry as an understood part of the
program a quality of sane prudence which delivers the man of optimism
from the perils of a mere promoter's spirit and from becoming an expan-
sionist who loses all sense of proportion"), he was nevertheless contemptuous of businessmen and politicians who failed to see and respond to
Canada's incredible potential, best described in the phraseology of the old
Methodist camp meetings: "These drops are but the promise of the shower
that is to come."

Foreseeing showers of blessing for Canadian enterprises, he scorned the
"timidity, caution, and anxiety" of some businessmen "where vigor, and
courage, and hope might have been looked for." The banks, especially the
Bank of Montreal, had been "failing to measure up to the requirements of
the country" by timid forecasting, which had allowed a shortage of currency to develop in 1901 and 1902. "The General Manager of the Bank of
Montreal is understood to have said in an indifferent way that there was
ample circulation for the country; that this boom would expend its force and

79

it would be found that a good deal of the scare over want of circulation was of an imaginary character.—This from the Bank of Montreal which pledged its very existence in the Canadian Pacific movement."

The CPR, which had so challenged his imagination in the 1880s, now seemed to have declined in "aggressive force and size." Its construction programme and freight-handling capacity lagged far behind exploding Western needs. It had lost "that quality of vigor which caused it to step out beyond all others, and which made those identified with it leaders in the country; there was creative genius at work in the direction of its affairs. I do not observe this spirit now." Through the Commerce Flavelle was identified with the CPR's apparent successors as great railway builders, Mackenzie and Mann. His advice to them in the early 1900s was to build even faster—"widen your borders, command wider interests, and push your work through with more vigorous energy"—to relieve the West from "the paralysis of the Canadian Pacific Railway Company."[48]

(In his criticism of Montreal enterprise Flavelle might have added that Montreal's department stores, Henry Morgan & Company, and Ogilvy's, had let leadership in national retailing pass to Eaton's and his own Simpson's. Neither of the Montreal stores established an extensive catalogue-mail-order business. The Quebec hinterland around Montreal was relatively poor; Toronto's hinterland was rich with customers—the visitors to the CNE to whom Timothy Eaton handed out his first catalogues, the farm families who took the railways' Friday excursions into Toronto to shop at the big stores. And Toronto's hinterland supplied not only the business, but the businessmen — Flavelle, Cox, Wood, Ames, Moore, Walker, Mackenzie, Mann — who spearheaded Toronto's rise to rival Montreal for Canadian business leadership. Montreal's problem was not so much the alleged conservatism of the Bank of Montreal or the decline of the CPR. It was not having a Peterborough seventy miles away.)

In words more prescient than he intended, Flavelle in 1903 summarized his view of Canada's economic future: "All sorts of errors of judgment, mistaken expenditures, extravagant policies, will be present; and yet the great productive power of her yet unbroken prairie lands, her uncut forests, her undeveloped mines, her exhaustless fisheries, will produce such an amount of wealth year by year that will quite override all these unfavorable circumstances."[49] Still, he was not without reservations after his several years in high finance, particularly the dreadful error of CCM. He had begun to have doubts about this kind of frantic business life, about its utility in developing enduring enterprises, and perhaps about the ethical standards of some of his associates. In August 1903 he wrote S. J. Moore of the Carter–Crume Company a long letter, suggesting that the company either reduce its capitalization or defer dividends. In passing, he described how he now understood the relations between the men who financed companies and those who had to manage them:

> In these recent years of amalgamations, public flotations, and capital enlargement, I have found myself associated with men and conditions, who, with no improper motive, viewed a business primarily from the standpoint of its capacity to earn dividends on a maximum amount of securities. Through lack of training they have not been too capable in commercial discernment and judgment, and have perhaps directed the activities of the enterprises with which they were connected, with their eye chiefly on the stock market, in which they were expert, rather than on the business, with which they were not so familiar....
>
> I remember years ago being very much affected in reading "Adam Bede." You may know the story. At one place you are introduced to Adam in his workshop, where in company with others he is busy with his tools. The signal is given for the noon hour —or for six o'clock, I forget which. Every workman in the shop drops his tools. The man who had raised his hammer to strike a blow sets the hammer down without striking the blow. Adam Bede, who loved his work for the work's sake, is forced to exclaim, "What, have you no pride in your work?" I say reading this left a powerful impression on me, and the spirit that moved Adam Bede has from time to time affected me in relation to various enterprises with which I have been identified, and has helped me, during the last twelve months particularly, to differentiate the ideas I have had concerning business enterprises and the ideas held by some of my associates.
>
> Too many men with financial instincts become associated with business and treat it —as is too common with the workman in his occupation—simply as a hewer of wood and drawer of water. Their chief interest is outside the business. The business is simply a necessary servant to accomplish for them a desired end; in the workman's case to give him bread and butter and something more if he can get it; in the financial man's case to produce dividends which will enable him to make some money out of the stock situation.
>
> I think in our operations in the Carter–Crume Company as a Board of business men, we should simply consider the business situation.... I take it we are essentially trustees, who are commissioned to operate the business in the wisest and most efficient manner possible, safeguarding both the present and the future. We must

have regard to the present need and necessity of the shareholders whom we represent. We must also, however, have regard to the larger interests which require sufficient capital for the easy operation of the business and for its ultimate development.... The business must be directed for the good of the whole and safeguarded for the good of the whole.[50]

He left the Carter—Crume board that fall, also resigning from the board of the Niagara and St. Catharines Railway Company. "The experience of the past year in business and financial matters has told me how mistaken I have been in dividing myself among so many activities, and how foolish my vanity has been in leading me to occupy positions which I filled with but little real quality or excellence," he wrote Senator Cox in November, suggesting that he also leave the Central Canada, Canada Life, and National Trust.[51]

He wanted to concentrate on the enterprises he did lend strength to, and with Clara in poor health he wanted to spend more time with his family. Earlier he had turned down Cox's request that he join the board of the Grand Trunk Pacific because he was now a newspaper proprietor and wanted his paper to be free to pass disinterested judgments on railway policy.[52] Cox persuaded him to stay with National Trust and the Canada Life for the time being; he dropped the Central Canada and got out of CCM as soon as Russell had it reorganized. He tied up most of his capital in his newspaper and more William Davies shares, and was not an active investor after 1903.

In the flush of success and self-confidence he had overextended himself, apparently hoping to follow in Cox's footsteps and become an all-round wizard of finance. Now he had retrenched. Though still involved with Simpson's, National Trust, and the Commerce, his only active management duty was to the William Davies Company. He would run it well, but would not become a slave to half a dozen other companies. There were more important things to life than board meetings and dividend cheques.

CHAPTER FOUR

METHODIST MILLIONAIRE

The family were afraid his health could not stand the pace of his work. Business trips were almost the only breaks in his routine of long days at the packing house, business luncheons, late afternoon board meetings, conferences into the night, and busy Sabbaths at Sherbourne Street Church. In the summers there might be a week or two for family holidaying and fishing at Sturgeon Point north of Lindsay, where the Flavelles and Dundases had a cottage colony. He found time to learn to curl, though not regularly, and in the mid-1890s would squeeze in an occasional game of tennis with his brother-in-law, Will Milner, a lecturer in classics at University College, who had married Margaret Flavelle. In the late 1890s the whole family joined the cycling craze, but Joe's enthusiasm for bicycles seems to have cooled about the time of the CCM affair.

He did much of his relaxing *en route*. Overcoming a tendency to motion sickness on trains, he learned to sleep soundly on the Pullman after a day's business in New York or Chicago or Montreal, and was ready to go straight from the station to the Don for another day's work. Each passage on the Atlantic gave him five or six days' rest. As long as the ship rolled sideways on the swells he was not bothered with seasickness. When the *Lucania* or the *Oceanic* pitched like a rocking-horse in heavy weather, though, he had to take to his berth with lime water, milk, snow apples, and Dr. Howard's Giddy Medicine.[1]

Clara occasionally joined him on the business trips to England. After the bacon trade was dealt with they would spend a fortnight touring rural and historic England. These were some of their happiest times together — "we are sitting right now on the bank of a little stream called the Derwent. And the water is flowing over a lot of stones that make it look like a dam, and make such a nice sound. I am sitting on the rug on the grass and Papa is lying with his head on my knee, nearly asleep. I am writing on top of his head...."[2] Except for his seasickness and occasional eye strain, Flavelle had an iron constitution. Until well into his seventies he seldom missed a day's work.

His first reaction to his new wealth was a certain bewilderment. "I cannot explain my feelings darling," he wrote Clara in 1897. "I find it so strange to get respectful and kindly recognition from good people who are in strong positions. I find it strange to feel no remorseful feeling when I spend a few extra dollars. After all these years of struggle to find myself easy seems strange."[3]

His conscience could relax its grip on his pocketbook, but it seemed necessary to strive even harder to make himself worthy of his new position:

I am deeply sensible that with our increasing means is coming a greater sense of our need of greater faithfulness in all our duties so we may fill our broader place with honor to our Great Father who has bestowed such honor upon us, and if you want to be a better wife so do I want to be a truer and better husband to prove myself worthy of you, and worthy of the dignity and blessed possibilities of the relation.

I was thinking a while ago when I was performing a little act with some tinge of the vulgar in it, and when I found myself saying "No one sees me," how much more careful I should be to be the very best to myself, that if no one else is present I am, and ... I ought to be careful to be always as select in my acts, my thoughts before myself as before others.[4]

Of course it is hard to know what a conscientious Methodist meant by "a little act with some tinge of the vulgar in it." It was probably on the order of spitting on the sidewalk.

Flavelle had been superbly trained by his mother and his church to scramble up the ladder of business success. Now he owned the ladder, enjoying power and freedom most people could barely imagine. But in some ways he was poorly equipped for the "broader place" he was trying to fill. He had little more than an elementary-school education, and was well read only in the Bible, newspapers, and romantic adventure stories. His cultural horizons were narrow, limited to a love of religious music. Most of his social connections had been with like-minded Methodists, narrow, self-righteous, and zealous. Scenes like the departure party on the *Lucania* in 1894 still shocked him: "I can see two Methodists side by side sipping—shall I say it—champagne!"[5]

I

He always held fast to the centre of stability in his life, Clara and the children. "Oh, my darling, shall we not turn to God and offer our prayer of thanksgiving that our increased means, our greater Comforts, our wider outlook have not ever ran as fast as our sympathetic love for one another, and that to both of us the most lovely place on earth is our home with our children?" He felt guilty about being away from home so often, and in his letters to Clara tried to explain how much it meant just to know she was there waiting for him. The first thing he did in his stateroom was unpack her picture, the last act before disembarking was to pack it away again. In 1904 he put down a love story he was reading to dash off a last note to Clara before the *Oceanic* sailed: "You are always before me, all the graces, beauties, loving kindness in the story, I interpret as belonging to my wife. So here when others say goodby, I do the same, when a brave tearful woman stood waving her hand quietly, unobtrusively on the dock, I see my wife, and bid her goodby, and wave my hand sweetheart. Even as I write my eyes moisten."[6]

He learned his love language from Victorian romances and had no other way of expressing his feelings. He also cried easily; in private life—though seldom in business—his emotions were always close to the surface. His love letters are affected and saccharine, but occasionally approach a kind of eloquence: "I can picture you here before me, beside me, and as I wipe away an unbidden tear, my heart sings its psalm of praise and thanksgiving for your love to me which never wavers, and mine for you dear, which ever grows more green, ever more sweetens my life, represses my vanity, and calls me to a more excellent manhood."[7]

Clara was restrained and motherly. Joe was her "dear boy" or "dear heart," whom she always supported, awaited, and quietly urged to cut back on his outside activities. She was a model late-Victorian wife, mother, and Christian woman—gentle, unassuming, gracious, and kind. From her generous allowance she kept the household accounts and spent her free time and money on good works. Inclined to stoutness, and with a round, sharp-featured face, she looked more like a hard society woman than the quiet, retiring wife she was. Nor was she as robust as she appears in pictures. Kidney failure in 1903 almost killed her and she was often bed-ridden in later years. Her illnesses were real, but some of the family thought she was also influenced by the lingering Victorian notion of the gentle lady as a semi-invalid.

Clara's retiring domesticity was offset by a streak of quiet toughness which set some limits to Joe's dominance of her life. Mildly criticizing her in a letter for exposing herself to the cold, he would suddenly remember, "I get back to my old complaint of lecturing," and break off. Not many of Clara's letters survive. Her plainest statement about their life together is a note replying to congratulations on their forty-eighth anniversary: "We are certainly only very ordinary people, but life has always meant a great deal to us, and whether it was to a star we hitched or not, I do not know, only that we happened to hitch together."[8]

Joe's favourite times at home were sitting before the fire with Clara and the children. He prayed often for guidance as a father, that he might lead his children to understand true values. He could appear to be a stern, aloof father, closing a letter to twelve-year-old Mina with "Commit your way unto Him who will never fail you, and be obedient unto His command daily," and signing it, "Your affectionate Father, J. W. Flavelle." But then he would scribble a note to little Ellsworth,

Do you know when we were coming here we came through a Town called "Banbury," and what do you think, this is the place where you "Ride a cock horse to Banbury cross to see an old lady ride a white horse." We did not see the old lady nor the white horse, nor did any one ask us to ride a Cock horse. I think you had better ask Aunt Lizzie to give you a ride right now....

and sign it "Papa."[9]

Mina, Clara, and Ellsworth were expected to obey their parents' and God's commandments, as young Joe and Clara had. Above all, their father did not want them to be self-seeking. "Learn my darlings, learn by every day doing it, to live so as to help others. Make it the pride, the hope of your life that you will cause everyone who meets you to know you mean to keep out selfishness, pride, vanity, and too much love of yourself." But neither were they to be dour and unhappy—"and too my darlings, learn to get sunshine and gladness out of everything. God our Father loves to have his little girls play with dolls, swing, shout, run in the sunshine, and thus bring gladness unto all."[10]

As the family became richer it seemed more important to teach the children that their privileges meant an added obligation to do good. In 1896, when the children were staying with an aunt on the Isle of Wight, Joe's letters from London dwelt on the children around him, who could not play by the sea in sunshine. To six-year-old Clara he wrote:

I saw such a lot of little girls last night who looked so thin and poor that it made me very sorry. They were playing up and down upon the Streets in the East end of this great city, dirty, hungry, neglected, and yet trying to be happy and to have a good time. I fancy not one of them ever had a doll, not one of them ever had a ride on a train, or a bus. Poor wee things, many of them have fathers and mothers who get drunk, and who beat them and neglect them. Is it not sad? and do you not think it ought to teach us to think of others rather than ourselves, and each time a naughty spirit comes around to claim us, to tell him to go right away, as we have so many things to be thankful for we cannot afford to think of things which now and again go wrong?[11]

Joe was passing on his mother's training. In her seventies now, passing her days knitting, reading, and counting her blessings, Dorothea Flavelle wrote loving notes to her grandchildren urging them to be obedient and generous and to "follow your mother and father's example, as they have followed their Christian parents." She marvelled at the children's opportunities for travel and education, but suggested they take as their motto the little text, "Of whom much is given much will be required."[12] As experience and discipline passed from grandparent to parent to child, no one mentioned John Flavelle.

II

The old ways and old values could not be maintained exactly as they had been in the George Street days in Peterborough. Joe's horizons had broadened almost beyond recognition. He still went directly from board to prayer meetings with many of his closest friends — Fudger, Ames, Cox. Family and church were always the centre of his social life. But now he knew businessmen whose beliefs and habits were strange to him, and yet whose character commanded his respect. Many smoked and drank and played cards and lived well without making any visible progress down the road to degradation. Flavelle deeply admired an associate like Byron Walker of the Bank of Commerce—self-educated, devoted to high culture, in love with the idea of public service, and an agnostic. Flavelle had sold his first butter to Robert Christie, who had become an evolutionist openly scornful of established churches after a Presbyterian minister had failed to come to baptize his dying child. Yet Flavelle's lard contract with Christie, based only on a hand-shake, was one of his longest, most satisfying business arrangements.[13] As he became more involved in church and educational affairs Flavelle met preachers who were questioning almost all the details of Christian doctrine, professors who had abandoned all the principles. To a young man brought up in the narrow Methodist society of Peterborough, life in Ontario's capital was positively cosmopolitan.

His Methodist circle of emigrants from small-town Ontario was changing with him. Flavelle had joined Sherbourne Street Church, at the corner of Sherbourne and Carlton streets, a few weeks after the dedication of the congregation's new building in 1887. It was a good Methodist meeting-hall, a squarish Romanesque pile of grey Credit Valley stone trimmed with Credit Valley brownstone. The corner tower was not too high and looked a bit like a castle's keep. The congregation worshipped in a plain, square auditorium, little more than a lecture hall, whose only impressive feature was the clear view every pewholder had of the pulpit. Over the years the church building stayed unattractive, always a contrast to the visual opulence of Metropolitan Methodist and half a dozen Anglican churches in Toronto. The congregation did change. As Flavelle wrote in 1909, they were "a community of Methodists who in one generation passed from being mostly poor people to those who are comfortably off, and in some cases very well-to-do."[14]

Well-to-do indeed. The Sunday School was run by the millionaire Flavelle. The guiding spirit of the Mission Society was the Senator and millionaire George Cox. A. E. Kemp, who had made his million in kitchenware, was the most active member of the Music Committee. H. H. Fudger, well on his way to millions, had taken over stewardship of Sherbourne Street's funds from his father and led the Infants Class in the Sunday School. Thought to be a man of great wealth until the day his firm suspended, A. E. Ames had served as secretary of the Board of Trustees as well as teaching Sunday School. It must have been a curious experience for an ordinary member to pay his $4.50 quarterly pew rent to one of the threesome who perennially made up the Seat Committee, Brothers Ames, Kemp, and Fudger. Torontonians nicknamed Sherbourne Street "The Millionaires' Church."[15]

By the end of the 1890s Sherbourne Street was Canada's richest Methodist congregation, raising more then $17,000 in 1900 and over $35,000 in 1910. Its ministers were paid the highest salary—$2,700 through the 1890s, rising to more than $3,000 by 1910. Men like James Henderson, James Allen, R. P. Bowles, Solomon Cleaver, and George Jackson were among the finest preachers and scholars in the Methodist Connection. If the church's decor was kept simple and unadorned, as befitting plain Methodist people, the preaching was outstanding. The music, especially the anthems and solos at the Sunday-evening services, was always excellent. In the late 1880s the Sherbourne Street congregation had begun paying its soloists. In the 1890s the Sunday School had its own fourteen-piece orchestra.

Not that the congregation could afford velvet-padded kneeling benches, for the millionaires gave much less than a tenth of their income to support the regular work. In 1900 Flavelle was the largest contributor, giving $314 through the collection envelopes (his children, who were being taught to give systematically, added another $46). The other wealthy families gave $100 to $300 each, their contributions totalling less than 20 per cent of the envelope receipts. If the rich were too generous, the ordinary members of the congregation would rely on them to do all the giving. This would be unhealthy for everyone; so the Sherbourne Street millionaires gave a smaller percentage of their income each week than many of their clerks contributed.[16]

The well-to-do's *largesse* was more evident in subscriptions to special funds, which were usually poorly supported by the rank-and-file. In 1900 Flavelle, Fudger, Cox, and Ames contributed $1,850 of the $4,129 Sherbourne Street gave for missions (Flavelle's $800 was the largest donation), $280 of the $538 raised for the Educational Fund, and $375 of the $698 in support of the Fred Victor Mission. These were still not much more than token donations. The wealthy saved their resources for special causes like building campaigns, help to ministers and churches overcome by debt, and other projects for which it was inexpedient to make public appeals. In 1901 it was typical of their approach for Cox and Flavelle to offer to match dollar for dollar the sum raised by the congregation of Toronto's Centennial Methodist Church towards the reduction of their debt. The next year Chester Massey led the effort to save Montreal's St. James Church, contributing $50,000 to help pay its debt. Flavelle, Ames, Cox, Timothy Eaton, and E. R. Wood gave $5,000 each. A few years earlier there had been the great campaign to raise $1 million across Canada for the Methodist Twentieth-Century Thanksgiving Fund. Sherbourne Street contributed a full 10 per cent of the million, $90,000 of that coming from Cox ($50,000), Flavelle ($25,000 in shares of National Trust stock at 130, two points below its market value), and Ames ($15,000). These large gifts were supplemented by hundreds of smaller ones for every conceivable church purpose.[17]

Like Fudger and his other friends, Flavelle gave more of his time to his church than most ordinary laymen. There were the morning and evening services each Sunday, of course, plus Wednesday-evening prayer meeting. For several years Flavelle was a class leader, his Class x meeting every Sunday morning before the service. He soon became a Sunday School teacher as well, and in 1891 was asked to become the School's superintendent. His fifty teachers offered Christian education every Sunday afternoon to some six hundred infants, children, and adult Bible students. Flavelle led the opening hymns and prayers, checked on absentee teachers, tried to stop parents from using the infants' class for free baby-sitting. Visitors reported that Sherbourne Street's was one of the best-organized Sunday Schools in the denomination. The Saturday-night teacher's-preparation meeting attracted many teachers from neighbouring congregations lacking an equally earnest superintendent.[18]

The weekly rhythm of church work and worship did not change much over the years, but the tone and content of Sherbourne Street's Methodism did. Revivalism and respectability did not mix well, for example, and a comfortable, well-established congregation found it had little enthusiasm for fire-and-brimstone "protracted meetings" to gather sinners into the fold. Some of the younger members chafed at the puritanism of the "old-fashioned" Methodism, which seemed to consider harmless dissipations, such as card-playing and dancing, to be mortal sins. The better-educated churchmen were alive to the new currents of theology, stirred by modern biblical scholars, the Higher Critics, who were interpreting parts of Scripture as myth or allegory—divinely-inspired myth to be sure, but not factually true. Some of the more radical ministers within the denomination were also beginning to interpret Christian service as going beyond tract-distribution and temperance campaigns. Perhaps it meant working for social change rather than just the reform of the individual. Perhaps the idea of perfection in Methodist thought could be extended from the individual's quest for a perfectly moral life to encompass society's progress towards equality and justice. In the 1890s the prosperous Methodists at Sherbourne Street heard sermons approving of Christian socialism and raising troublesome questions about rich men, camels, and the eyes of needles.[19]

The questions did not particularly trouble Flavelle. Nor did these changes in denominational thought and practice. His personal faith centred on the individual's experience of God. When he talked about religious life he most often referred to "daily communion with God through prayer," "constant and close conference with Him who is the source of all life," "the young man who in simple sincerity daily goes into his room and shutting the door commits his way to God." Worship, prayer, devotion—mysterious, perhaps mystical, encounters between the human and the Divine—were for him the bases of Christianity.[20]

Theology seemed to Flavelle to raise largely "quibbles and speculative questions" as it groped to describe the relation between man and God. When he quoted Scripture before church and business groups, as he often did, he never commented on whether the stories were literally true, merely using them as illustrations. When forced to take sides on religious questions, he found it incomprehensible that reason and faith could be contradictory, and always came down on the side of learning and scholarship. "It is never true, never, never true, that the Gospel of our Lord puts a premium upon ignorance." In the heat of the debate over the Higher Criticism he referred approvingly to churchmen who "were unafraid that what commended itself to their reason could be hostile to their faith."[21]

On the other hand, he paid little attention to the intellectual content of the sermons he heard, judging his ministers by the inspirational "power" of their preaching. The Reverend George Jackson, who came to Sherbourne Street from Britain in 1904, became an inflammatory figure in Canadian Methodism because of his modernist scholarship. Flavelle never remarked on his learning, but often admired the "power, grace and charm," "the intensity and strength," of Jackson's sermons. "The gospel pure and simple," he said of one, "as powerful as anything I ever heard" of another. "Well, we have been to church twice, and heard two very helpful sermons," he wrote his son from England. "The one tonight made papa cry, was not that funny? It made him thankful too that we had such men as the minister who spoke to us. . . ."[22]

Of course there was no reason why a powerful sermon should not be delivered in an inspiring setting. When a young university student, W. C. Good, criticized the churches for spending so much money on their buildings, Flavelle replied that it was a way of enhancing worship.

If I were to make my choice deliberately I would worship in a lofty cathedral with beautiful windows, stately arches, with great choirs, with ornate service and under such circumstances would grow in reverance [sic] and in those qualities of mind and heart which become a grace and power to an honest man.... Will I say that it has been all waste of money building stately churches when a room with four walls will do as well? The trouble is it would not do as well. The subtle power of surroundings in worship must be allowed to play their part upon men who are tuned in various keys.

For views like this his friends sometimes called him a good Catholic spoiled. Actually his tolerance stopped at Roman Catholicism, which seemed to him the archetypal example of a priesthood and dogma being inserted between man and God. Some good Catholics spoiled drifted into the Church of England; so did some Nonconformists who acquired wealth and wanted social standing. Flavelle could be severely critical of the Methodist Church, but he never considered leaving it. "I am deeply indebted to her for blessings in my life which will ever make me deeply grateful as well as love her so that I will be loyal to her cause."[23]

Nor did his personal habits change over the years. He neither smoked nor drank, and never served liquor in his home. He did not dance. The Flavelle family and their servants knelt in prayer every morning after breakfast. The family went to church at least once every Sunday whether they were in Toronto, sightseeing abroad, or in the middle of the Atlantic. The Sabbath was kept for worship, Bible study, letter writing, and long walks. Occasionally he proclaimed his Christianity to his new associates, as on the day he overheard Robert Christie mocking a devout employee at the bakery. "Mr. Christie," Flavelle said, "I'm not ashamed to confess that every day before I leave my home, I kneel before God and ask his blessing to rest upon me and my business during the day." "You do surprise me," Christie replied.[24]

The visibility of his faith won him the nickname "Holy Joe." But he usually lived agreeably and quietly with religious differences. He still spoke out now and then on temperance, but was not an active prohibitionist crusader, stressing instead the need for education against drink. When Byron Walker congratulated him on a speech urging Methodists to support higher education, and suggested that he might read Huxley's *Life and Letters*, Flavelle promised to add it to his library and was soon quoting Huxley in speeches.

As a good Protestant, as one who believed human expressions of spiritual experience were open to change, and simply as a man of broader experience, Flavelle sided with those who were suspicious of church organization, doctrine, rules, and regulations. In his Sunday School work he sympathized with young people reacting against the excessive negativism of Methodist morality. "I fear the great body of children in Methodism have grown to believe that the chief characteristic of serving God is to take something out of their lives here," he told his teachers in 1904, "that it consists more in the things of which they are deprived in this life than those which they receive, and that when they come to consider giving their hearts to God and being members of the Church, they feel it necessitates the loss of much and the gain of little, except the gain which will come to them after this life." He wanted the School's children, like his own, taught that "laughter, and play, and joyousness, and games, and all that makes up the optimism of youth, form no barrier between them and God."[25]

He also rejected the old notion that his Sunday School children were original sinners who became estranged from God and had to be brought into the fold through conversion at a revival meeting (as he had been). Surely children could be brought up as practising Christians and then be formally admitted into church membership as the natural outcome of their youthful training. "We emphasize conversion and minimize training. The former is needed for sinful men and women, the latter for little children, and if faithfully performed there will be no need for conversion." So in the mid-1890s the Sherbourne Street Sunday School had begun holding annual Anniversary Services each Easter, at which teenagers from the school who had participated in a special study group were received as members of the church. The order of service was based on the Anglican confirmation service, a rite Flavelle had earlier held in "pharasaical contempt." This new approach to youth seemed a happy reconciliation of the old ways to the new conditions of well-to-do Methodism.[26]

The one aspect of the new Methodism he did not find very helpful was the growth of the Social Gospel, the movement equating practical Christianity with specific social reforms. Flavelle got along with Christian social reformers on the principle of living with honest differences of opinion, but he found them sometimes offensive and intolerant in their refusal to do the same, in their determination to prescribe rules and legislation for the whole of society. Christians had a duty to present the claims of Christianity to others, he thought, but "no right to interpret for that man what his personal application of such principles will be to his own life and conduct." At worst, the Social Gospellers could be uncharitable and arrogant; at best he considered them sincere churchmen, trying to do good, who happened to be misinformed.[27]

Taken to an extreme, Flavelle's tolerance could appear to be a watering-down of the old Methodism into an irrelevant personal mysticism, handy religious baggage for a millionaire businessman to carry. Flavelle did not go this far. As a good Wesleyan he believed faith was nothing if it did not change a person's life. To acknowledge God's rule was to surrender oneself to God. A Christian man had an overwhelming obligation in life to serve God and his fellow men. "All you hold and all you possess you hold for the good of others," he told an audience of young men. "You are a trustee holding time, talents, and equipment for the benefit of your fellows. The only real apology for your existence is the service you will render." The worst sin he could imagine, the worst accusation he could make, was that behaviour was motivated by nothing but selfishness.[28]

Having outgrown the narrow zealotry of his youth, Flavelle believed there were many ways of coming to know and love God, many ways of trying to serve Him. Some were called to serve as ministers, others as missionaries or social workers. In his life Flavelle tried to serve God and his fellow men by being an ethical businessman, through his work at Sherbourne Street and his philanthropies, and through doing good works for the community. He never equated his business life with Christian service, or wrote of his profits as a sign of divine blessing. But neither business nor profits seemed to him incompatible with Christian service. A man could be a millionaire without having done wrong. And only a foolish millionaire would fail to thank God for having so blessed his efforts.

III

His big house was built in Queen's Park. Construction began in the summer of 1901 on the west corner of Avenue Road where it divided and became Queen's Park Crescent. The dirt street was little more than a country road through the rolling, wooded parkland owned by the University of Toronto.

Some of Toronto's wealthy had already moved north or west from the older residential areas onto the fringes of the Park. Byron Walker lived in one of the fine houses along St. George Street. Robert Christie's mansion was one of several gracing the east side of the Crescent. But Flavelle's was the first private house built inside the Park. Needing money, the university was opening the area for partial development. Its trustees readily leased their land to a man of means, already a patron of the university, who could be counted on to erect a suitably stately house. It would have to be stately, for its site was literally in the centre of the province's educational life. The closest neighbouring buildings were Victoria and St. Michael's colleges, McMaster University, University College, and Wycliffe College. Due south through the Park was the centre of the province's political life, the Ontario legislature.

Those who watched the construction soon realized that this was going to be a most unusual private house. Its grand front portico, crowned with a huge pediment resting on four colossal Corinthian columns, overwhelmed the viewer. Surely this was properly the entrance to a public building, say an office of the Bank of Commerce, not the front door of a home. Nor did the house have a private face, for around on the garden side, where most houses had back doors, there was another grand portico, exactly the same size but with *six* Corinthian columns. No matter that the columns were made of good Canadian red brick stuccoed over; they were no less solid or imposing for not having been prohibitively expensive.

The rest of the house was equally grand and solid: from the front door-jamb, rusticated with heavy, square stone blocks, to the flat stone arches over the windows, set with separate pieces to emphasize their permanence. The main wing of the brick house was two storeys high; at its east end it pivoted about its main stairwell, angling into a three-storey service wing, like a Y without its left arm. The two wings looked out onto a forecourt ringed with a circular drive leading from gates at the Avenue Road entrance. A balustraded terrace ran along the garden side of the house from the conservatory to the back portico. The view from the terrace was all trees, lawns, and lush flower beds — what might have been the gardens of a private estate.

Entering the house the visitor passed under an ancient family coat of arms, through a marble-floored vestibule, and into the extraordinary front hall. Its vaulted ceiling was covered with Art Nouveau scrollwork and angelic figures, the raised lines making it resemble stained glass. The walls were panelled in oak, with fluted columns and horizontal channelling matching the exterior. The woodwork and the design of the huge central fireplace were a jumble of Art Nouveau, early-eighteenth-century, and Jacobean detail. "JWF" and "CEF" were carved in stone above the hearth, flanking the date of completion, 1902. Around the mantel Flavelle had had the builders carve lines from the verse he had adopted as a kind of motto: "Two things stand like stone/Kindness in another's trouble/Courage in your own."*

---

* From Adam Lindsay Gordon's *Ye Wearie Wayfarer.* The complete verse is:

> Question not, but live and labour
> Till yon goal be won,
> Helping every feeble neighbour,
> Seeking help from none;
> Life is mostly froth and bubble,
> Two things stand like stone,
> Kindness in another's trouble,
> Courage in your own.

The main living rooms flowed into one another along the south side of the ground floor. At the Avenue Road end the conservatory was a phantasmagoria of glass, sunlight, and flowers. It opened into the large, elegant drawing room, then the more formal dining room, and finally the living room, where the panelled ceiling and heavy woodwork reflected the original plan to make it a library. The living room also contained the first pipe organ installed in a Toronto house; beautifully done in grained oak, it reached almost to the ceiling. French doors from the drawing, dining, and living rooms opened onto the terrace; on a summer evening the rooms and terrace merged into a splendid open piazza for hundreds of guests.

Flavelle's study in the service wing was all bookshelves and cedar panelling. He worked at an old oak desk, perhaps the one he had bought for $5.50 in 1887. The panelled billiard room in the basement was not at all the same, of course, as a corrupting public "poolroom." The rest of the cellars were unfinished and used for storage. There was no wine cellar.

Having shivered through every night he spent at Wheeler-Bennett's home in England, Flavelle had central heating installed in this house. But a room centred on its hearth, so all the rooms, including the upstairs morning room, the seven bedrooms, and the master bathroom, had a fireplace. All the upper rooms were spacious: a linen closet would one day see new duty as a history professor's office. The rooms in the servants' quarters were smaller and furnished directly from Simpson's. But if the six live-in servants had to use the back staircase, they also had the privacy of their own dining room, not just a scullery table. The house's rambling attics were never finished, but were a wonderful play area for children and grandchildren, and could double as a dormitory for extra servants brought in for special occasions.[29]

Flavelle named his home "Holwood." The original Holwood belonged to the Earl of Derby and was just down the road from Wheeler-Bennett's "Ravensbourne" in Kent. In the park at Holwood William Wilberforce had decided to move the abolition of the slave trade in the days when Pitt the Younger owned the estate.[30] A bust of Pitt was prominently displayed in the front hall of Toronto's Holwood. In 1917 Flavelle carried the house on his books at $75,000.[31] That might have been its original cost in an era when Toronto's new city hall had been built for less than $2 million. A modern Holwood would cost several millions.

It is not clear what Flavelle had in mind when he planned the house. He must have known he was building one of the grandest homes in Toronto, in its location and exterior design the most visible grand house in the city. It probably did not occur to him that others might see Holwood as a model of conspicuous consumption, a crude flaunting of wealth by a *nouveau riche* plutocrat. Flavelle's only surviving comment on the house, aside from constant delight in the lawns and gardens, is a 1929 letter referring to "its beauty, its stately dignity . . . its restraint."[32]

Holwood's architects, the prominent Toronto firm of Darling & Pearson, also worked for the Bank of Commerce. Many of their buildings, including Holwood, were designed on architectural assumptions associated with the École des Beaux Arts in Paris. Like their banks, like such other Toronto Beaux Arts buildings as Union Station and the Central Library, Holwood was an attempt to recreate the permanence and grandeur of the classical tradition. It was heavy and solid, built to last, and built to impress the viewer with its grand scale and dignity. It invited attention and comment, making a contribution to the public architecture of the city.

Flavelle knew even less about architecture than he did about the intricacies of theology. Frank Darling designed Holwood, and Flavelle's only contribution seems to have been his insistence on the initials and motto being carved into the main fireplace. As a public-spirited, turn-of-the-century businessman, though, he would have been impressed by the classical grandeur of Beaux Arts design. It seemed sensible of architects to imitate the best of the past. If the liberal culture of antiquity was the foundation of modern civilization, as most people assumed, it was not at all unseemly for modern buildings to reflect that culture. Banks were a good example. They were vital institutions of modern society. So it was appropriate for their buildings to combine beauty and stateliness with the permanence customers expected. Similarly, a man of wealth like Flavelle had a vital role to play in society. Surely his house should be beautiful and stately, and it should be built to last.

He would have been hurt to think anyone felt he was showing off in a vulgar or common way by building Holwood. He thought it was a restrained and dignified house because it was conservative and classic in design. As British and American millionaires' houses went, it was not overly large—only seventeen rooms plus servants' quarters—and Flavelle had had Darling's original design severely reduced.[33] Nor was its exterior (or interior) a model of bad taste. Holwood is appreciated by modern art historians as a fine Beaux Arts house. Flavelle would have heartily agreed that the vulgar bad taste of the plutocrat was apotheosized a few years later when his fellow millionaire and sometime associate Henry Pellatt built Casa Loma.

Flavelle was probably not bothered to know that a business associate like

William Davies found Holwood appalling.[34] Davies was a retiring man, whose public role was limited to a few philanthropies. So many of the wealthy retired from the community like Davies. Their houses were opulent on the inside and plain on the outside, if they could be seen at all by commoners wandering into Rosedale or Forest Hill Village. Taken to the extreme, this obsession with privacy was a symbol of selfishness, the wealthy taking their money and hiding.

Flavelle intended to play a role in public life and to use his house as the centre of his activities. His model of how a wealthy man should live came partly from his religious beliefs, but also from his British heritage and regular trips to England. Holwood's interior was patterned after Wheeler-Bennett's "Ravensbourne." Much of its artwork, furnishing, and foliage was bought in England, sometimes on Wheeler-Bennett's advice. Holwood was an English country house set in a park in the centre of Toronto.

It was also Flavelle's statement of his membership in a Canadian aristocracy. He had moved up through Canadian society as though class barriers hardly existed, and would always talk and write as though every man could do the same. But all his Methodist training, so effective in increasing his own mobility, had been in the context of a belief that society was layered in classes. Artificial layering based on the accident of birth was wrong; class divisions based on differing natural abilities were not. Once a man broke through the barriers and changed his class he should live and behave in certain ways. Plain Joe Flavvle of Peterborough was now J. W. Flavelle of Toronto, man of affairs and soon to be public servant. He thought it perfectly natural a few months after he moved into Holwood to offer it to Lord Minto, the Governor General, as accommodation for a vice-regal visit to Toronto. The Mintos were despairing of finding a Toronto house suitable for their entertainments. They gratefully accepted the pork-packer's offer, and for several weeks in the spring of 1903 Holwood was the centre of Toronto's social life as the Governor General and his Lady received. Their servants bunked in the attics.[35]

To ordinary democratic Canadians it seemed overdone. They had trouble distinguishing between a tasteful, appropriate home and an American millionaire's swanky show-off house. Even those who understood the fine contribution Holwood made to Beaux Arts Toronto might have wondered why Flavelle had to have his second columned portico, why even a millionaire didn't have a back door like everyone else. Newspaper readers were titillated by the *Star*'s rumours in 1903 that Flavelle could not afford to maintain

Holwood and wanted to sell it to the government as a lieutenant-governor's residence. Flavelle was outraged and hurt that his old pupil in class, Joe Atkinson, would publish such "impudence." Taking note of the source of Flavelle's wealth, Torontonians called Holwood "Porker's Palace."[36]

With their house and servants and carriages the Flavelles lived like millionaires. They travelled first class and stayed in the finest hotels. But Joe had not entirely lost his sense of proportion. He could laugh at his "wounded vanity" when the family had to take second-class passage for their European tour in the spring of 1903. From Rome he wrote Walker describing how he and Clara were not equipped "to even superficially appreciate what this city means or for what its art Treasures stand. And yet we are making a brave show of it. We would awaken your amusement . . . if you saw us at work. I hope it will mean much for the children." (Rome, he mentioned, was teaching him how badly Toronto needed an art museum; Walker could count on his support in the campaign to found one.) In Venice the Flavelles noticed the city's decay—"Palaces turned into hotels to accommodate a modern up-to-date one-generation American millionaire and his family," Joe wrote from his room in the Grand Hôtel d'Italie.[37]

IV

Clara's illness in November 1903 was almost fatal. As soon as she could travel in December Joe took her to Nassau to convalesce in a warm climate. Nineteen-year-old Mina, rather chastened by her father's earnest discussion of her duties, was left in charge of managing Holwood and its staff. Maggie and Will Milner moved into the house to look after young Clara, now thirteen, and eleven-year-old Ellsworth. Coming down from Lindsay, Dorothea Flavelle settled into her special bedroom suite to be on hand as "Mother Superior." Everyone wrote Clara three or four times a week that winter to keep her up-to-date on life in Holwood—the life of a Canadian millionaire's family in the terrible winter of 1903 – 4.[38]

They had a quiet pre-Christmas season, the Milners' little boy, Arthur, recovering from the whooping cough and his mother suffering the worst cold of her life. The streets were too icy for Dorothea to get outside often, so she contentedly wrote letters and read a history of Methodist missions in America. Clara was busy with her schoolwork and violin lessons, practising more faithfully now that she was a member of the Sunday School orchestra.

Ellsworth's "jim" in the attic was finally being outfitted with parallel bars, travelling rings, and a swinging trapeze. The only major social event of the season was Mrs. George Cox's at-home on the eighteenth; the whole staff of the Bank of Commerce—head office and branches—were invited to bring their wives and sweethearts. Mina, the Fudger girls, Dolly Kemp, and other young ladies from the church helped with the serving.

There were not many social events that December because the bad weather—rains followed by freezes—was causing so much sickness. H. H. Fudger's wife, Hannah, found the social peace a relief. "I wonder if you feel as I do about these affairs," she wrote Clara senior, "that it is a waste of time, and so much empty talk, while there are so many hearts that are hungry & sore & sad, and that need to be ministered unto, and how much greater our own satisfaction is. I know *you* feel that it is better to minister than to be ministered unto."

Ellsworth woke the household on Christmas morning by running up and down the upper hall ringing the maid's bell. Assembling in their pyjamas, they trooped into the dining room to see the big tree, the holly and mistletoe, and the presents. The boys unwrapped their wind-up trains, fire-reels, and climbing engines. There was a handsome silver brush and comb for Clara from her parents, a gold-beaded necklace for Mina, an elegant desk-top bookcase for the Milners. Everyone got and gave books—Mina's favourite was on French châteaux, Clara's was *Ten Girls from Dickens*. After breakfast Maggie took the girls to church, but Ellsworth could be excused to play with his toys because Sunday was only two days away.

The Toronto relatives came to six-o'clock tea. Seventeen sat down at the dining-room table, garlanded with holly and roses, for a "tea" of jellied chicken, nut-and-apple salad, pineapple ice cream, and Christmas cake. It was a light meal because Mary, the cook, had the day off. Most servants didn't like to work on Christmas. Up in Rosedale Hannah Fudger had not found a caterer or waitress for the dinner she had planned. "I just made myself believe I was young again, and tucked in and made a success of it," serving dinner for thirty-two.

After tea at Holwood the family gathered in Joe's study. A Union Jack was stretched across one end of the room. Everyone took turns "fishing" behind the flag with a ping-pong-ball lifter for ten-cent presents, attached by Uncle Will Milner. "The crowning joke," Clara wrote her mother, "was when Grandma got a waxed bird in a cage scarcely larger than itself, which when you pressed down the cage made a hideous noise intended for a chirp."

After that we had charades. Uncle Will dressed as a Franciscan monk . . . and said his prayers in Latin. Then Cousin Will [Rundle] came in as a charwoman with Mina's skirt, red eider-down jacket and hat on. He also had a pail and knelt down and started to scrub the floor after which he talked a blue streak in Irish. The next word was "injudicious." "In" taken as "inn" with Mina as bar-maid, Mr. Campbell as bar-man, and Uncle and Cousin Will as drunken men. "Ju" taken as "jew" was Uncle Will and Cousin Ada as husband and wife come into a shop owned by a Jew, namely Cousin Will, and after a good deal of arguing left in disgust. "Dicious" taken as "dishes," was Mina as hostess and Cousin Ada and Mr. Campbell coming in for afternoon tea. Mr. Campbell played the fine English gentleman who jumps up every time you speak to him, to perfection. "Injudicious" taken all as one, was played by the three men, Cousin Ada and Mina, the men insulting Cousin Ada by making fun of her brother, so that she got up and went out; whereupon the rest all began blaming the others for it. Uncle Will nearly upset the actors by saying in his droll way that "punting along the Don, you know, was one of the chief amusements of Canadians in the summer."

We then sang "Hark the Herald Angels Sing" and they all went home.

The weather turned clear and cold after Christmas. Clara and Ellsworth spent the rest of their holidays in Lindsay, skating, tobogganing, and snow-shoeing with their cousins. The Milners were finally getting used to Holwood; "your house grows more beautiful to me every day," Maggie wrote her sister-in-law. "I sometimes think I shall waken up and find it is a dream that I am actually living here." Will commented, though, that "Maggie is just like Joe, she could live up to Windsor Castle." He could find his way around the house without a guide and had remembered to come home to Holwood every night. A notoriously absent-minded professor, Milner had created a family legend as a newlywed by appearing for dinner one evening at his old boarding-house, having forgotten about his wife.

In Nassau the Flavelles received best wishes for a happy New Year from the Sherbourne Street Sunday School. The young assistant minister, Sher-lock Faircloth, was doing a fine job as substitute superintendent. He was also the talk of the congregation because of his sudden marriage to a spinster seven years his senior. Nobody knew much about the mysterious Eva Edgar. There was much peeping through keyholes to catch a glimpse of her at her first class meeting. Hannah Fudger only knew she did not much like Mr. Faircloth anyway—"I often wish I could love everybody but I can't and don't—an old woman like I am ought to have come to that by this time. Hope I will yet." On New Year's Eve everyone went to the Watch Night service at the church. There were sleigh-rides the next day and a New Year's dinner of goose, spinach, and mince pie.

Perfume from the fuchsias in the conservatory filled the whole front of Holwood. The dining-room table was heaped with red tulips to greet Joe when he came home on the tenth. In the bitter cold Toronto's winter headaches and sniffles had turned into a severe epidemic of "la grippe," with many fatalities. Aunt Lydia Dundas's grippe had become pneumonia, but Dorothea could not go to see her dying sister for fear of infection. The children were healthy, though, except for Mina, who had hurt her leg playing hockey on the backyard rink at the home of Peter Larkin, the Salada Tea merchant. "More elegant would it not be, to say, however, *limb*," she teased her mother, who was losing the battle against her daughters' slang. Everything was "swell" to Mina and Clara that winter, sometimes "howling swell." Hannah Fudger wondered why "kiddies" was a frowned-upon word at Holwood. "It seems to be a term of endearment in our household."

Joe thought Holwood should have a rink too, and soon the children were skating on a forty by hundred-foot sheet of ice on the croquet lawn. Will Milner took up skating with surprising ease.

Clara stood first in her class at school, Ellsworth fourth in his. They both went to public schools, and were conscientious about their homework and practising their music. On Saturdays Ellsworth skated, tobogganed, and romped with his dogs "Nigger" and "Lad," before getting his weekly "scouring" from his aunt. Aunt Maggie was just as hard a scrubber as his mother. When she could put down *David Copperfield*, Clara spent her time planning her "Peanut Tea" for the sixteenth. It was to be one of her first entertainments, a tea because of her father's "baby-hours" rule against visitors after 8:30 p.m. until age eighteen.

Hazel Kemp, whom Clara had expected to be deliberately late, was the first to arrive, sharp at four o'clock. Everyone brought scissors and a thimble. When all had assembled, the girls were turned loose in the living room to hunt for peanuts. As soon as each had found twelve peanuts they set to work making dolls. "It was a pretty sight," Maggie wrote, "forty young girls in pretty dresses scattered all over the room, on the chairs, on the sofas, on the table, & in groups *on the floor*, all busy & laughing & chatting merrily
—it was enough to make one wish to be young again. Old Mr. Addison happened in on one of his friendly calls & got as far as the door when he saw what was happening —He just stood & smiled & said to me —'Isn't that

beautiful. It is Angelic — It would be sacrilege for me to enter.' So off he went, happier for having seen so many bright faces."

After the doll-making, nut salad, peanut-butter sandwiches, pink lemonade, and ice cream with hot chocolate sauce were served in the dining room. While the girls were eating Joe came home and slipped into his study — "It was too much to expect me to go in and run the gauntlet of all those staring impish eyes." In the middle of supper young Arthur gave Olive Miller a prize of violets and lilies of the valley for having made the best doll. The party ended at seven; the living room, Joe wrote, looked "as if a cyclone had gone through it, and that a whirlwind of tissue paper and peanuts had centred on it, drawing within its circle all the peanut remains, and tissue paper remains of the entire city."

The rest of January passed more quietly. Joe was as busy as ever at the bacon factory, but did get home for lunch as often as he could. In the evenings he joined in charades and bezique and the game of passing a story around the circle to see how garbled it would become. The servants were getting along well together, and the family knew that no matter how sharply Katie Kilroy scolded them for inviting last-minute supper guests, she and Mary would always manage to scrape up half a ham, some sweet pickles, and a pineapple mould. Mrs. Marks, who came to do the laundry on Mondays and Tuesdays, was less reliable. "We were absolutely helpless" and almost out of clothes when she failed to come for two weeks. She had to be replaced.

By January 24, Ontario was snowbound; hardly any trains were getting through to Toronto. Most of the senior officers at the Davies factory were sick; trainloads of hogs were lost in the drifting snow outside the city. "Everywhere is sickness, discomfort, and death," Joe wrote. "What a merciful preservation has been ours — I think our great rooms, sunlight, and good air has much to do with it." The moment Clara or Ellsworth sniffled or coughed they were sent to bed with quinine and castor oil and the doctor was called. Clara thought it typically silly of her father to spend four dollars on the doctor when she knew she was perfectly healthy. "Oh how the poor people must be suffering," Maggie wrote on February 4. "Never in my recollection have we had such continuous cold & stormy weather."

In early February Joe and Mina left for Nassau to help Clara move to Augusta, Georgia, where she would have the company of the George Coxes and the Timothy Eatons, also in the south to escape the bad weather. It started to rain in Toronto on Friday the fifth and was still raining after midnight on Saturday when furious ringing of Holwood's doorbell awoke the household. Young Clara described the scene from her bedroom window:

Katie went to the serving room window and saw two women on the porch. She asked them what they wanted, and they said that they must see Mr. Flavelle *at once*. Kate said that they couldn't at that time. She didn't want to say that Father was out of town until she saw who they were. But when they insisted on seeing him, she told them that he was away. . . . Then one of them said that her husband had died in the hospital last evening and that he had told her to go to Father. Then we all felt sorry for her, and Uncle went and telephoned to Dr. Smale to ask what we were to do. Dr. Smale said that he didn't want anything to do with them; that a collection had been taken for them down at the factory and that they were a bad lot. Uncle came back and told them that he could not do anything for them. Then didn't they storm. They declared that they would have justice, etc. . . . They went off down through the Park soon after. The man's name who died was Riley. I think he was a fireman down at the factory.

"There did not seem to be any grief about the death of the man," Maggie wrote, "but great indignation at not getting what they came for."

The weather soon turned cold again, reviving Maggie's "wild desire" to skate. One night, with the boys in bed and Will and Clara at a concert, she got to the head of the stairs on her way to get Mina's skates. Then she stopped—"they would never forgive my foolishness if I had a bad fall. So I went and sat in my room." Maggie never skated. Her days were full enough keeping the house running and catching up on her university social obligations. The classics students, the executive of the Victoria College YMCA, and the "classical wives" came to tea. Fifteen friends were invited to dinner. A formal dinner at Holwood in the winter of 1904 consisted of clear soup, halibut steak cut in small pieces and served with potato balls and sauce, roast beef, mashed and baked potatoes, green peas, sweet and sour pickles, asparagus salad with grated cheese, plum pudding, ice cream and cake, fruit, and coffee in the drawing room. Maggie insisted on paying all the costs of her entertaining.

Evenings out were to see a Shakespeare play, attend a concert by the Mendelssohn Choir ("the whole thing didn't seem nearly so automatic as last year," Clara thought), and take in a fine magic show. Maggie worried that two concerts and a dinner party in one week added up to "dissipation" for

Clara, but was pleased that she sensibly went to bed early most nights. Clara was always fresh for classes at the Toronto Model School, where she was just being introduced to domestic science. The first lesson was in washing dishes.

Joe was back by the twenty-third, his train from Niagara Falls having barely gotten through the snow. Toronto's streets were covered by eighteen inches of solid ice. Business was demoralized, he wrote Clara, "and there is very much suffering among the poor everywhere." Dorothea, who seemed to be failing a bit that winter, was delighted to have her son home again leading the family prayers.

His prayer for us all, himself, and for you brought the tears to my eyes. Such faith, such humility, such entreaty to direction for help, in the home, in school, in the College, in business. Ought I not to be a thankful mother for having such a son, as I know you are of being his wife. "Walking together in all the commandments of the Lord blameless." Long long may you be spared to each other to be helpers to build up righteousness in this Canada of ours. How much such are needed, even in our good city of Toronto is needed, if you saw by the papers at present, the low thoughts of some of its inhabitants in questions of morality.

In the middle of March Dorothea decided she was needed back in Lindsay. The Toronto folk begged her to stay longer, but she had concluded it was her duty to go, "and when once that idea gets hold of her," Maggie wrote, "there is no changing."

Spring seemed to be coming when the family could wear light coats to church on February 28. Even though it was raining, 534 Sherbourne Street Methodists turned out for Sunday School. But 1904 was a leap year: on Monday the twenty-ninth a foot of snow fell in seven hours, followed by sleet and thunderstorms. The streetcars could not run; Joe could hardly breathe driving home in his sleigh. "My heart bleeds for the girls and old men who walked home for miles in the terrific storm," he wrote, "with wet heavy snow underfoot and a driving gale of wind with the closest thickest fall of snow I ever encountered. Now the storm roars, our chimneys almost terrify you. The sleet rattles off the windows, and the flashes of lightning add wierdness to the scene—When will this dreadful winter go?"

More rain Tuesday night turned Toronto into a lake of slush. Twenty-four hours later the temperature was near zero Fahrenheit. It was a busy social week at Holwood anyway. The annual Sunday School tea was held on

Tuesday, highlighted by Frank Yeigh's illustrated lecture on the British Empire. On Thursday, twenty-six prominent Methodist, Presbyterian, and Congregational ministers and laymen came to lunch. Afterwards, they informally discussed the possibility of organically uniting their denominations. Flavelle was one of several speakers in favour of union, and they resolved to hold further meetings. "I was greatly moved and affected by the spirit of the gathering," Joe wrote Clara, "and am wondering if it is possible such a wonder can take place." The meeting eventually led to the formation of the United Church of Canada.[39]

On Friday evening the Reverends Solomon Cleaver and Sherlock Faircloth brought their wives to tea. The new Mrs. Faircloth impressed Joe as bright and rather attractive, an important impression to make on Flavelle because there had been criticism at the church of Faircloth's having married on his salary. The Ministerial Supply Committee was already petitioning the Conference to replace him with a single man. Maggie Milner thought Mrs. Faircloth had led too sheltered a life and was not strong enough to be a minister's wife.

Saturday night Will Milner had a group of students in from the university, but fewer than expected came and Katie complained there would be sandwiches on hand for days. "We made a big hole in the pile last night & there was no bad taste in them," Maggie wrote her sister-in-law. All week down at the factory Joe had been worrying how to get the hogs through that were snowbound in Owen Sound, Lucknow, and Kincardine.

In March Joe went back to Georgia to help move Clara to another hotel in Virginia. He missed the largest gathering at Holwood that winter, more than three hundred church people invited to meet a visiting missionary. "They were a very orderly well behaved crowd who did not exhibit that vulgar curiosity you have often witnessed," Maggie told Clara. (The vulgar curiosity broke out one night a few years later when four hundred ladies attending a concert swept through the house investigating the bedrooms, pantries, and bathrooms. "Come through this little bedroom and we can get out through the back of the house. I hear that the maids' quarters are as good as their own"—and Mina found fifty women in a bedroom trying to find a door hidden by a wardrobe.)

Young Clara concocted the most elaborate prank of the winter one evening. Dressed in a skirt, long waterproof, droopy hat, and black-and-white veil, she sat down in the office off the vestibule while Katie went to get Ruth, one of the maids. Saying a suspicious-looking tramp was at the door and she had been ordered to give her a quarter, Katie persuaded Ruth to come along for support.

Katie gave the dark stranger a quarter. "The Lady says this is all she can give you."

"Thank you, miss."

After more conversation Ruth showed her out and then ran to one of the windows to stare again at the tramp. "Why she is coming back again. . . . I'll soon fix her."

Clara kept up the deception until Ruth was ushering her out a second time. Then she dissolved in laughter; the others had been hiding behind a screen doubled over laughing. The trick quite outclassed Uncle Will's attempt to put a turtle in Clara's bed one Sunday morning.

Joe was home by the end of the month. He spent Good Friday with the children, visiting Toronto General Hospital (he was chairman of the Board of Trustees), and going to church. "Yes, my darling this is a time of year we love to spend together and at home—how the love of God comes to us, and how our hearts respond to the message of Easter time — when 2 boys in church in the choir sang this morning 'Just as I am' my eyes filled with tears and I found my heart lifted in thanksgiving for sins forgiven, and for such a wide open door of mercy for reconciliation to God, when I sinned—His Love." On Saturday he worked on the Davies Company's year-end statement. Saturday night relatives came over to play "Pit." It was the new game from Parker Bros. that year, in which the players imitated bidders on the stock exchange. Clara had first played it at Hazel Kemp's "Pit Tea." "Heaps of fun. . . . Father is as bad as the rest of us over it."

Easter Sunday morning was brilliantly sunny and cold. Joe started the day by leading Ellsworth and Clara on a "hippity-hop" up and down the terrace. Before church he dashed off a letter to his wife while Will Milner played the organ. Joe wished he were in a cathedral. "As I write my heart sings to the organ notes, 'Hallelujah' — How shameful my pride, my vanity, my self importance—He 'who was rich yet for our sake became poor'—Why should I a weak man land myself in His Presence — I am grateful darling, deeply grateful, for God's loving kindness and mercy, for His presence in our home, in our hearts, in the lives of our children." He was just telling her of Clara's good sense in deciding it was too cold to wear her new Easter outfit when she came downstairs with it on, announcing that it had got warmer. The family went off to church to hear Bishop Warne from India.

Sunday evenings after church were reserved for hymn-singing and reading. Aunt Maggie was fairly tolerant about keeping the Sabbath—her boy, Arthur, enjoyed building his Spanish boats with blocks so much that he was allowed to continue naval manoeuvres all one Sunday afternoon. Blocks seem to have been the tough marginal case for Edwardian Sabbatarians. At Ravensbourne the Wheeler-Bennetts also let their little boy, Jack, use his blocks on Sunday, but only to build churches.[40]

The snow and ice had melted by the end of the first week in April. Joe was able to wear his light overcoat to the factory. Wisely, he had not yet changed out of his winter flannels. On the night of April 14 another blizzard hit the city. Torontonians were skating at outdoor rinks two weeks after Easter.

The Sunday School Anniversary services were "full of power," Flavelle thought, adding fifty-four members to the congregation. Holwood was thrown open to university wives ("It would greatly delight you to see the appreciation of these ladies," Maggie wrote, "who are not surrounded in their homes with many of the artistic comforts, as they saw for the first time a really beautiful home"), masters from St. Andrew's College, a class from the church, and the members of Mina's boyfriend's men's club. Clara and Ellsworth had their first strawberries when Joe took them to lunch at McConkey's, Toronto's finest restaurant. He also had lunch with the Duke of Sutherland, Britain's largest landowner, who was in Toronto sounding out Canadian businessmen's reactions to Joseph Chamberlain's campaign for tariff reform. There was a memorable family evening around the fire one night building rhymes, with everybody adding a line. There were minor catastrophes — when Clara spilled her ink bottle over her major school project, a map of the world; when Joe walked into a brick wall and appeared in Sunday School with a bandage on his bald spot.

H. H. Fudger was in temporary disgrace with Hannah for forgetting to pick her up one night after prayer meeting; she had to walk home through the slush. Dickson, one of the gardeners, quit when Flavelle changed him to another job at a smaller wage—"to my comfort as he was not an efficient man." Aunt Lydia Dundas survived the winter, barely. Sherlock Faircloth's appointment at Sherbourne Street was renewed for one more year. On Tuesday, April 19, the heart of Toronto's commercial district burned down. Katie, Clara, Will Milner, and Johnnie Flavelle went down by Union Station to watch the fire. Joe stayed downtown till after three, though the Davies' factory was never in danger.

By the end of April everyone in Holwood was down with "la grippe." But the snow and ice had gone. The country roads were open. The gardeners were repairing the winter's damage to the lawns and hedges. Clara could come home.

On the first of June Joe left for England on the *Oceanic*. Tossing in his berth on a Sabbath morning he reviewed his life—his headstrong youth, the joy of marriage, the struggle to save the children's lives, his business anxieties and triumph, Clara's recovery from the edge of death. "I thought of all the mercies which have been mine, dear — how wonderful was the review of them all — and now came the query — why? my Lord — why? Again and again I remembered a prayer Mother so often used at family worship and which always seemed to me to imply favoritism—which could not be right—'Not more than others have we deserved—but thou hast given us more.' "[41]

CHAPTER FIVE

METHODIST MANAGEMENT

It was about five miles from the teas and formal dinners at Holwood to the killing rooms at the bacon factory. Flavelle moved easily between his worlds, unconcerned about other people's disdain of pork-packing as a messy business. There was no stigma to serving the public by processing and distributing high-quality meats at fair prices. In his drab, undecorated office at the William Davies Company, Flavelle was just the "plain business man" he had always been, dictating endless memos and letters on high strategy in a fascinating industrial situation.

The business had been almost too good in the late 1890s. Only Davies' shareholders knew exactly how good, but the low price of hogs in Canada, the high price of bacon in England, and soaring Canadian bacon exports spoke for themselves. By 1900 competition in the industry had become intense: the older factories had expanded, British provision agents had opened new Canadian factories, and ambitious Ontario farmers were trying to get a slice of the trade by launching cooperative packing houses patterned vaguely after Danish co-ops. When the cooperatives at Brantford, Palmerston, and Harriston all opened within a few months in 1900 there was a full one hundred per cent excess capacity in the industry —facilities to kill 50,000 hogs a week, a supply in 1899 of only 25,000.[1]

In his optimistic moments Flavelle thought Canadian bacon might come to dominate the whole British market, hog production rise accordingly, and the surplus-capacity problem work itself out.[2] Then, again, that might not happen, and no prudent businessman could assume a perpetual boom. Even if supply and marketing conditions stayed favourable, the competition was bound to be sharper than ever. The great days of cheap raw materials, a wide-open market, and little effective competition, were probably over. "We are assailed on every side in Canada and England," Flavelle wrote Davies in 1901. He urged his board to get ready for "the more earnest struggle which is before us. . . . It will be the duty of this Company to spare no trouble and no reasonable expense to hold the present premier position as the recognized leader in the Canadian trade."[3]

I

A company specializing in the sale of one product—Wiltshire sides—on one market—London's Smithfield—was obviously vulnerable. Flavelle determined to diversify his business to make it flexible in the face of competition. He would conservatively buttress his shareholders' investment by aggressively exploiting opportunities flowing from the primary enterprise.

William Davies had begun diversifying almost unconsciously by opening his two retail stores in Toronto as outlets for by-products. Flavelle had added a store or two each year through the 1890s, thinking of them mainly as a way of helping the factory outbid other packers for hogs because they provided a high return on edible offal. There was no real idea how each new store would be received by the public, and often considerable grumbling from the "foremen" managing the existing stores that expansion would simply spread the customers more thinly.

By 1900 Flavelle realized that his fifteen stores were significant profit-earners in their own right. In 1899 they had netted $33,000, small pickings compared to the earnings from the export trade, but a thirteen-per-cent return on the original investment in the company. To everyone's surprise each store's business had kept growing during expansion. "It is no longer a matter of conjecture what support will be given us in any part of the City," Flavelle wrote, "the volume of business at every branch steadily increases year by year." The firm had a "genius" for carrying on a retail provision business, he concluded, and urged his conservative board (i.e. William Davies) to take more vigorous advantage of their opportunity.[4]

The word was not yet used, but Flavelle had created a "chain" of retail food stores in Toronto, one of the first significant chains anywhere in Canada.* Sales were increasing at each store because the expansion of the

---

* At almost exactly the same time and rate of development Pat Burns was creating a chain of meat markets in British Columbia and Alberta to serve as outlets for his beef. Burns and Flavelle seem to have had no contacts at all. Burns was an Irish Catholic and disliked hogs.

system increased Davies' reputation as a purveyor of quality products; the sum of the whole was increasing faster than the sum of its parts, a principle fundamental to successful chain and franchise growth today. Retail chains—"multiple stores" — had developed in England in the 1880s and 1890s. Flavelle had not consciously copied them before, but now he began to study them on his visits as models of what might be done in Canada. "The whole trend of the trade," he reported in 1901, "is toward individual firms controlling a large number of stores. . . . We have a permanent asset in our stores if we do all our work in a first-class way." His observations of how newer rivals had already outdistanced some of the earliest English chains also reminded him of the need to maintain leadership: "We must not fall into the error of wakening up to the necessity for greater excellence after someone comes into competition with us, and whips us into it."[5]

Confident that they knew what they were doing, seeing the stores as a source of important profits in themselves, Davies' men in the early 1900s were investigating every point in Toronto where a useful retail provision business could be done. Flavelle determined that the only competition Davies stores should face would be from other Davies stores. In 1903 there were twenty-four stores in the city and new sites were being bought in the suburbs along the new streetcar lines. "Where the trolley goes it is fair to assume we shall shortly follow," Flavelle wrote.[6]

The logical next step was outside the city. When a test store in Oshawa worked satisfactorily in 1902, Flavelle immediately opened stores in London, Brantford, Brockville, Kingston, and Belleville. In 1903 he noted that the Matthews Packing Company, which had gone into retailing in Peterborough and Ottawa (where its factories were located), would likely try to open stores in the Brantford area, where they had just purchased another factory. "Because of this I am desirous of occupying all points of importance which are reasonably near to Brantford before he is ready to locate in them, and once we occupy the ground I fancy he will hesitate to compete with us at the same points." So he presented plans to open in St. Catharines, St. Thomas, Windsor, Chatham, Woodstock, London East, Galt, Guelph, Hamilton, and Collingwood. "We will probably proceed to occupy the important towns in the Province as rapidly as we develop men," he wrote Wheeler-Bennett. "All this is being done for the purpose of pre-empting the ground and establishing the fact that the retail provision business of the country, as far as it may be operated by packers, will be done by this Company—at least as far as Ontario is concerned."[7]

Why stop at Ontario's borders? With forty stores in the province at the end of 1904, Flavelle decided to build a chain of retail stores around a small packing house in Montreal. "Our ability to serve a great body of people so that they are pleased with the service, has been demonstrated beyond doubt," he argued. "No company in America possesses a similar asset developed to as great a degree. In Montreal, with 350,000 people, even if the great majority are French, is it not reasonable to believe we can use this asset to our profit?" The Montreal factory might also develop an export trade in Wiltshires, but if it did not there was probably enough local business to turn a useful manufacturing profit. In 1905 the packing house was built on land leased from the Montreal Stock Yards Company. The first Montreal store was already open for business; more opened every few months. Eventually there were eighteen stores in Montreal.[8]

It was not unthinkable to operate outside Canada. Suppose the Liberal government some day returned to its old free-trade principles and negotiated a reciprocity agreement with the United States? If hogs could move freely across the border, American packers might drive prices too high for the Wiltshire trade to England to be profitable. In that case the company's retail business might be its salvation. "If we had the right to cross the line with our products I know of no reason why we should not be able to operate thirty stores in Buffalo or twenty in Detroit," Flavelle wrote in 1903. By 1905 he had begun an experiment in Buffalo with three stores and a small canning factory under the ownership of an American "branch plant," the William Davies Company, Buffalo. No Americans had yet founded similar stores in that city. Flavelle was not sure his expansion into the United States would work. If it did, the potential would be practically unlimited; if it did not, the losses would be insignificant.[9]

The retail operations raised an important point of business ethics. Davies' retail stores disrupted the normal channel of distribution, manufacturer through wholesaler to retailer. Like department stores, the company was generating economies by eliminating middlemen and their profits. How could the independent retailer, short of capital and wedded to the established order, compete with integrated operations like these? Flavelle may also have had critics of Eaton's and Simpson's in mind when he meditated on his chain's effect on its small competitors:

I would like to face frankly the possible charge that we are grasping and over-reaching and desirous of carrying out our own ends no matter how much harm we do to small traders who are making an earnest effort to make a living from their moderate sized businesses. I think I would not be the last to call halt if in the conduct of our affairs there was any attempt to crowd out any existing traders by doing our business in a grasping and unscrupulous manner for the purpose of getting rid of our opponents, and then after they were gone, reaping the benefit by charging a higher price for our goods. No such charge even by implication can be made against us. We are simply laying out the line for the successful operation of a great business, alike beneficial to us and of proved worth to the people who buy our products. We refuse to cut prices in anything, but claim support from the purchasing public on the general excellence of our services and the good quality of our products. It has to be, and to all of us regrettable, that in accomplishing this and establishing the provision business . . . on permanently better lines for everybody, small traders suffer. Any hesitation, however, to go on organizing this important business for its most efficient service because in the doing of it someone may be injured, would mean if carried out to its final conclusion, the stoppage of all development and healthy enlargement.[10]

Just as Flavelle had stressed service and quality rather than price in his Peterborough store, so the Davies stores would best their competitors by the superior appearance and quality of their products rather than with cutthroat price competition. This was one of the ways a "high-minded" business operated. It would have been difficult for the stores to do a price-cutting business in any case, for Flavelle's accounting allowed them no price advantage in buying from the factory; they were charged the full market price for all their purchases. In the years before the First World War Davies stores were distinguished by smartness of display, cleanliness, and clear labelling of prices. Flavelle was delighted with their success and obviously proud to have created this thriving, innovative subsidiary enterprise in his own right.[11]

II

In the early 1890s the stores had begun to sell beef as well as pork products, buying the beef wholesale at the St. Lawrence Market. This posed the logical question of factory expansion: should the pork-packing company build its own abattoir to slaughter cattle? Davies' experiments with shipments of chilled beef to Britain in the 1880s had failed, and while Flavelle was eager to try again he did not want to saddle himself with an expensive slaughtering facility only to find he had no outlets for beef beyond Davies' own stores. Rather than take this risk he encouraged his principal hog-buyer on the Toronto market, William Harris, to go ahead with his plans for an abattoir. Davies would buy its beef from him. Harris established his first plant in 1896.

By 1900 Flavelle's officers had persuaded him it was time for Davies to slaughter its own cattle. Plans for a new beef-and-pork-packing house were drawn up. Arrangements to buy land south of the Don site were complete, except for the disposition of a small cemetery, when Harris learned of the project and asked Flavelle to reconsider. Negotiations led to the Davies company investing $75,000 in a fifty-per-cent interest in the Harris Abattoir Company, incorporated in 1901. Flavelle was president of the company, Harris and his sons were the active managers. Davies was to stay out of beef and Harris out of hogs. Flavelle had made sure his company would have half the profits if beef-packing out of Toronto could make money. But only the accident of a graveyard in the way had kept the Davies company from becoming an all-round packing house.

Harris's hope of repeating Davies' success with exports soon failed. Canadian chilled and frozen beef simply could not find a market in Britain. So the Abattoir concentrated on developing a wholesale trade in Canada. By 1905 it was making healthy profits, although not paying dividends while it built up reserves. Flavelle thought the Harris officers had "emerged from a state of raw traders into business men of moderate to fair capacity," and was satisfied with the wisdom of his investment.[12]

The only non-member of the Harris family prominent in the company was James Stanley McLean. A Port Hope boy, who graduated from the University of Toronto with first-class honours in Mathematics and Physics in 1896, McLean had drifted into high-school teaching (including a year or two at the Lindsay Collegiate), tried selling life insurance in British Columbia, and finally drifted back to Lindsay out of work. In 1902 Flavelle offered him a job as bookkeeper at Harris, which he accepted *faute de mieux*. Dorothea Flavelle, according to her son, had brought McLean's suitability for a job to his attention. "I am sure you will never regret it," Joe remembered her saying.[13]

III

The retail stores led the packing houses into one line of manufacture after another. In 1896 a Davies man was sent to study the beef business in

Chicago, including canning. He had trouble getting to see the canning operations there, and suggested the Americans were so secretive because "the
quality is usually so bad they do not want it to be seen." "I am tolerably
certain that no piece of the animal ever goes into the can that will sell for
more money fresh," he reported. Considering that the quality of the Davies
meat "exceeds by far what is put up in the United States," he was ready to
recommend entry into canning on a small scale. It would not be hard to turn
out a better product than the Americans.[14]

The Cook Room Department was soon followed by a Sausage Room
Department, a Pie Room Department, a Tea Department, and a Pickle Department. Most of the goods were manufactured for sale in the stores under
Davies' own brand, another anticipation of later chain-store methods. The
stores were charged full prices by the factory though, for each department of
the business was expected to make its own profit.

Our vague image of the quality of meat sold by packing houses in the
early 1900s probably still reflects Upton Sinclair's 1906 exposé of Chicago's
packingtown. In *The Jungle*, diseased meat, rats, rusty wires, dirt, and the
occasional worker all found their way into the cooking tanks and out into
the world as lard, cooked ham, and potted chicken. A commission appointed by Theodore Roosevelt in response to consumers' nausea on
reading *The Jungle* confirmed many of its charges, particularly those about
deplorable sanitation in the packing houses.

Reacting as usual to American problems, Canadians worried about their
own meat. Immediately after the publication of the American commission's
report, the Canadian Department of Agriculture ordered a special, unan-
nounced investigation of all Canadian packing houses by W. W. Moore, an
official in the department. Moore's report was never made public because it
found some problems in a few of the houses, but its overall conclusions were
favourable:

For a number of years the different packers have been striving to build up a trade
through the excellence of their goods, and most of them fully realize that it would be
a suicidal policy on their part to indulge in doubtful practices or to attempt to carry
on a meat packing business except under the best possible sanitary conditions. At
present the largest Canadian packing house [Davies] is small enough to permit of a
personal supervision by the manager, which would not be possible in a mammoth
concern employing from eight to ten thousand hands. A good class of labor is employed and in nearly every plant I visited I found men who had been working for

their present employer for periods ranging from 5 to 20 years, according to the length of time the plant had been established.

On the whole I found conditions in the meat packing establishments to be reasonably satisfactory. A few of the plants are insanitary in some respects, but the majority are clean, bright and well ventilated. . . .

The William Davies factories in Montreal and Toronto were found to be spotlessly clean and up-to-date in every way; they received no criticism. Not even in wartime, when everything else the company did was under public criticism, were there attacks on the quality of its products. Unlike the American packers, who were producing for mass consumption and did a heavy trade in cheap meats, Davies and most other Canadian houses were producing premium bacon for export markets where quality was all-important. Similarly, the business of the Davies retail stores, where prices were not low, rested on consumer faith in the quality of fresh and canned goods sold under the firm's own name.

The reputation of Canadian packers emerged largely unscathed from the storm over *The Jungle*. Just to make sure, and particularly to protect the good odour of Canadian meats abroad, the federal government in 1907 began inspecting all meat-packing plants engaged in exporting. The packers welcomed the added security government inspection gave their reputations. It was an interesting example of state regulation being favoured by everyone as a way of ensuring that Canada would not repeat American mistakes.[15]

IV

The Moore Report's comments about the quality and stability of Canadian packers' work force were in marked contrast to the wretched working conditions and semi-starvation wages endured by unskilled immigrants in Chicago's packingtown. The Toronto factory of the William Davies Company employed about three hundred workers. None of its records suggest there was any trouble securing or retaining help. Nor were there strikes or attempts to unionize the factory while Flavelle was in charge.

Like Davies before him, Flavelle was a classic paternalist employer. He paid going wages: a typical Davies hand would make $400 to $500 in 1900. But the profit-sharing Davies had begun, and Flavelle had continued, could make an important difference in a worker's annual income. A minimum of

7½ per cent of each year's profits was set aside for cash bonuses, payable partly according to salary and partly on merit. The huge profits of the late 1890s and the comparatively small payroll (as against the cost of raw materials) meant the workers were receiving bonuses of upwards of 25 per cent of their wages, a powerful incentive to stay with Davies.[16]

The company also kept worker loyalty by voluntarily granting wage increases in good times and doing its best to keep wages up and minimize layoffs in hard times. Its working conditions were excellent as packing houses went: its safety record enabled it to get accident insurance at one-third the standard rate for packing factories.[17] In 1900 Flavelle argued that the cooking and canning rooms had to be enlarged to protect the health of the men—"it will be a relief to them and a satisfaction to us all when we can give them better accommodation." The same year he had a separate building erected for employees' lunch and rest rooms (with special rooms for non-smokers), stating simply that "the accommodation we have for our men is not creditable and deserves attention." No other Canadian packer provided similar facilities. Perhaps unusually good working conditions were to be expected from an employer who could write to his wife, "The whistles are just blowing for seven o'clock . . . all meaning thousands of men & women going to work, and to many of them it is a cheerless affair."[18]

Paternal concern for the workers was matched by rigid insistence on hard work and refusal to tolerate insubordination. Discipline was very strict—a man who came out of the bathroom without washing his hands would be fired. Flavelle was fair with his workers, but quick to dress down incompetence. "He'd put on his cap, would go out to the plant, and we'd know someone would get it."[19] In 1902 deputations of workers asked Flavelle for an increase in wages and an extension of the summer Saturday half-holiday through the year. The managing director's response to this extraordinary unrest was recorded in full in the *Minutes*:

At the annual meeting for bonus distribution Mr. Flavelle . . . explained that in the past the policy of the company had been to advance wages without any demand when the conditions of business warranted it, and that at times when other manufacturers had been reducing the wages of their people we had increased those of ours as we found the business justified this. He explained that what these people had been doing recently under pressure we have voluntarily done in the past, and that it was not in order then for pressure to be brought to bear upon us, and especially at a time when business was anything but satisfactory. The managing director asked the workpeople to accept his frank statement that the business was not then in a condition to warrant any advance, which they apparently did, although quite a number of men drifted away. . . .

At the same time he repeated to them what he had before stated, that he was a believer in shorter hours for labour where possible, and pointed out that in many cases workpeople were responsible for the failure to secure shorter hours by their failure to respond by increased energy—and by their endeavours to limit achievement by unwise regulations.

Mr. F. pointed out that in our own case we not only lost the half day, but that the first half of the day was gone through in a relaxed holiday fashion, and that a large part of it was taken up in cleaning up.

At the same time he expressed his feeling strongly that the hours of labour were too long, and hoped at some early time to be able to announce the company's decision to make the Saturday half-holiday an all the year round concession with the distinct understanding that whenever the company found it necessary to call for a full day's work on Saturday, such service must be rendered without any extra pay.[20]

v

The idea of accountability, of a constant concern for exactly where things stood, was deeply ingrained in Methodism. Flavelle made it a central principle of his business life to always have the most complete, accurate statistical portrayal of his company's affairs that could be produced. Most of his accounting methods at Davies—the development of detailed cost breakdowns,* his insistence on interdepartmental sales being charged at market value, his later habit of allowing for full depreciation on all his equipment, his introduction of monthly "budgeting" or forecasting about 1910—were among the most advanced practices of the time in any industry in either Canada or the United States. So advanced that leading chartered accountants balked at his use of methods which have since become conventional.[21]

The aim of his accounting techniques was to increase the degree of individual responsibility within the company. He deliberately departmentalized his business, for example, keeping separate accounts for each department and each store. (Fudger used the same system at Simpson's, and

---

*This was no easy calculation when the raw material was a live pig; how much did one ham cost on the hoof? How much did one hoof cost?

Senator Cox had advised another young Methodist, Joe Atkinson, to keep separate budgets for the departments at the *Toronto Star*, so the profits of one would not hide the losses of another. About the same time the Bank of Commerce similarly departmentalized its operations.)[22] The aim of decentralization was to strengthen executive accountability in the large organization. A big company could overwhelm even its own management when the performance of its components got lost in the work of the whole. Under departmentalization the men at the top could study the health of the parts one at a time, accurately pinpointing trouble spots. Similarly, each of the subordinate managers, now literally accountable for the performance of his department, could be held personally responsible for success or failure. The first important innovation in management since the rise of the large corporation, departmentalization was an attempt to counter the organization's stifling effects on the individual.[23]

Outsiders who interpreted sophisticated accounting procedures as evidence of organizational genius sometimes failed to understand how deeply Flavelle and businessmen like him were committed to individualism. They were tempering and adjusting the new wineskin of the corporation to make it a suitable carrier for the old wine of individual initiative and enterprise. Years later, Flavelle and other big businessmen, who seemed to be the fathers of bureaucratic organizations, confused observers by condemning the erosion of personal initiative in Canadian society. The first principle of management in their generation was to prevent the individual from becoming lost in the organization.

Believing so strongly that individuals made the difference in business, Flavelle spent much of his time recruiting bright young men and studying their performance. He did not make the mistake of strong leaders who surround themselves with sycophants. A key ingredient in his success, he felt, was his ability to choose good men and give them a high degree of autonomy in running their departments. "It never occurs to me that I am any less Chief, or on the last analysis absolutely in command, because I delegate much responsibility to others. I am afraid that my bump of self-confidence would refuse to consider for a moment that there was any one in the business who was dividing with me the supreme authority."[24]

Because Flavelle believed he was indispensable to the business, it seemed urgent to have someone trained to take over if he died or were disabled. Otherwise the organization might fall apart. He found his heir apparent in the Chemistry Department at the University of Toronto. A farmer's son from the Lindsay area, Fred Smale had taken a first-class BA in Chemistry at Toronto in 1892 and a PH D from Leipzig in 1895. He was immediately hired back as a lecturer at Toronto, but Flavelle convinced him that business offered a wider sphere of opportunity for an ambitious, talented young man. In 1898 Smale took up work as a chemist in the laboratory of the packing house. His improvements in Davies' lard were a great success and within two years Flavelle had promoted him to assistant manager. Like Flavelle, Smale was a high-minded Methodist, interested in "the higher life of consecrated Christian work." The two pork-packers were kindred spirits, in perfect agreement on questions of business, public service, and religion.[25]

When Flavelle came into the firm he had insisted on a substantial share-holding. He thought it sensible for a company's senior officers to have a stake in its profits as an incentive to achievement and loyalty. From the mid-1890s he pressed William Davies on the succession problem and the need to bring along other "strong men" by giving them financial incentives. Not wanting to see the ownership diluted, Davies resisted, pointing out how he had been able to find Flavelle—not such a bad choice—on short notice.

In 1900 the disagreement came to a head over Smale. Davies put to Flavelle that the only solution to their impasse would be for him to buy the control-ling interest in the company. In 1901 Flavelle bought 870 shares from the Davies family at $400 a share. He now had 67-per-cent ownership, enough to undergo substantial dilution without disturbing his control. He immedi-ately introduced a new policy of alloting shares to encourage "greater zeal in the service of the Company." Smale got the right to buy 50 shares, John Porter, the manager of the retail stores, an option on 20 shares, both at $175. The company loaned them the purchase price at normal rates of interest. Smale was brought on the board. Through the years there were other stock allotments to senior officers on similar terms.[26]

They had to earn their rewards. Another cliché applying to Flavelle is that he expected as much from his subordinates as he put into the business him-self. The Methodist class leader was given to holding earnest discussions with his officers about the state of their business souls. He once had a frank conversation in London with young Sheed, the man he hoped might suc-ceed Wheeler-Bennett in the agency:

I said, "I am a good deal disturbed lest you are one of that type of man who can talk well and convincingly, but who cannot close business, and if this be true it will be a very sore disappointment to me. . . . If I am wrong," I explained, "if I have misread your sales and your business, no one will be more pleased than myself, but I cannot disguise the fact that if I had been placed in the position in which you have been placed, I do not care what might have been the disabilities under which I labored, or how much or how little freedom I received, I would have made the business go anyway. The greater the disabilities under which I worked the more determined I would be to win, and when the time came for me to talk to my Chief, there would be no uncertain sound in my approach to him.... I would have compelled his respect and an altered course by reason of the actual results secured notwithstanding the difficulties under which I labored." I said, "Sheed, the man I have been looking for, and I am sure the man Mr. Wheeler Bennett had been looking for is the 'plus' man. There are any amount of the ordinary sort about, who cannot struggle against difficulties and win. The man I wanted for the future safety of the Wm. Davies Company was one who was bigger than any difficulty which was presented to him, and who would leave his mark no matter how difficult his post might be."

While all this was said with a frankness that could hardly be anything else than trying, the whole spirit of the interview was admirable. He took his punishment very manfully, listened to the whole matter without temper and with serious respect and gravity, admitted the soundness of many of the things I said. . . .[27]

Sheed survived this kind of treatment; many of the officers of the Davies Company thrived on it, were devoted to their leader, and served the company splendidly. Others undoubtedly rebelled against Methodist management, hating Flavelle's sanctimony. He fired few men because those who found the atmosphere of a Methodist class suffocating resigned first.

Constantly evaluating the work of his men, always looking for new talent, Flavelle became an astute judge of personal capacity. "Flavelle's young men" at Davies and his other companies were an outstanding group of executives. Their most striking characteristic was educational attainment. Smale, a PH D in Chemistry, became a pork-packer. J. S. McLean, Honour BA in Maths and Physics, worked for an abattoir. T. A. Russell, BA in Political Economy, was hired to manage a bicycle company. National Trust was staffed with university graduates, most notably the classicist lawyer, W. T. White. E. R. Peacock, double gold medallist at Queen's in Political Science and English, class of '94, was about to join the staff of Dominion Securities. There were more to come. In the 1890s many businessmen still disdained university graduates—too old and too conceited to begin at the bottom and work their way up — and seldom worried much about recruiting at all so long as there were sons to take over. With his only son still in grade school Flavelle had to recruit; deeply deferential towards the highly educated, he and others in the Cox "family" were among the first Canadian businessmen to seek out university graduates. The later careers of these bright young men who drifted or were enticed into business spectacularly justified the choices.

A man Flavelle trusted was given as much responsibility as he could handle. In 1913, for example, Flavelle sent twenty-two-year-old W. E. Bosnell to Winnipeg to buy hogs, authorizing him to spend up to $50,000 a day. Sixty years later Bosnell still marvelled at this expression of confidence. He was devoted to Flavelle and the company.

The next step was to bring men into the "round-the-table" conferences Flavelle held to discuss company strategy:

It is our practice here to call our men together for counsel. If we are going to enlarge or improve the factory we ask the Foreman of the House, the Heads of Departments, the Engineer, the Chief Carpenter, or any one else who may be of service, to make suggestions which will cause the finished work to be more useful for day to day service. In our store business we bring all the Foremen together, juniors and seniors alike, that we may benefit from their suggestions, and that we may benefit by reason of the association. In the weightier matters of the business we frequently counsel together—yourself [William Davies], Mr. Adie, Mr. Smale, Mr. Porter, Mr. Bert and myself—in couples, in groups, or as a body, going over various plans and suggestions that we may get the benefit of varied opinions. This we have found to not only improve the final plans upon which our decisions may fix, but it makes each man who is brought into counsel more efficient and capable to assume responsibility if it be thrust upon him, or even if he continues in a subordinate position, to make him more efficient in that subordinate position.[28]

This was the coordination that kept a departmentalized organization from becoming fragmented, the cooperative element counterbalancing Flavelle's individualism. He wanted his officers to develop the capacity to run the business in his absence, to be ready to take over when he retired. His aim was to make himself superfluous.

By 1905 he felt he had gone most of the way: "notwithstanding the divided character of our operations, there has been no time during the history of the Company when I could cease to be identified with the Company with as little disturbance as at present."[29] Smale was handling almost all the day-to-day business, and Flavelle was devoting much of his time to public service. He intended to retire from active management in another two or three years.

VI

Equal attention was paid to strengthening and diversifying the British end of the business.

Much of it rested, of course, on the quality of the bacon. The existence of a laboratory in a Canadian company in 1900 is remarkable in itself; Flavelle's may have been the first Canadian manufacturing business to carry out its own research and development. One of the results of the research, combined with Wheeler-Bennett's intelligence work, was the introduction of a new curing method in 1902 that cut slaughter-to-sale time in half. The bacon was still in cure when it was shipped, was further cured in transit, and landed just as the cure finished. Fifteen years later this was still one of the fastest cures used by a North American packer, surprising even experts from Chicago.[30] The laboratory also developed one of the first artificial sausage casings (replacing casings made of intestines, the preparation of which was the single most unpleasant job in meat-packing). Considerable royalties were expected from the patent rights, particularly in the German market, on the eve of the First World War. An American patent was also taken out on the cellulose casing, but apparently was later sold very cheaply.[31]

As early as the mid-1890s Flavelle was trying to reduce his dependence on the Wiltshire trade to Smithfield market by invading Ireland and the American-dominated northern-England market for shoulders, bellies, and other "North Country" or "American" cuts. To tie customers more securely to Davies bacon an advertising campaign was launched to promote the brand. Flavelle and Wheeler-Bennett also decided in the early 1900s to begin bypassing the wholesalers who dominated the Produce Exchange and sell directly to large retailers. "I have been in mortal grips lately with the wholesale men," Wheeler-Bennett wrote, ". . . I believe I shall yet fly the flag of liberty . . . and serve whom I like." The wholesalers nearly succeeded in having him drummed off the Produce Exchange and Davies bacon boycotted. In one of the epochal struggles in the history of the bacon trade, taking on even the great Denny himself, Wheeler-Bennett finally won the right to serve any customer who would take five boxes of bacon a week.[32]

The costs of the English business were unusually high. Wheeler-Bennett charged the highest commission of any agent, four per cent on sales rather than the normal three per cent. As well, some of the new Canadian packing houses had been financed by English agents or had set up their own sales agencies in England; in either case the transatlantic business had to earn only one profit. The Davies business, by contrast, had to support both Wheeler-Bennett and the Canadian company.

Discussions in the 1890s about amalgamating the two houses "and as a united concern stand together to meet a common enemy" had broken down in disagreement about the division of the assets.[33] Flavelle believed Wheeler-Bennett was a great salesman, but his success ultimately depended on the excellence of Davies bacon. Wheeler-Bennett believed Flavelle was a good manufacturer (in no small part due to Wheeler-Bennett's lessons in curing), but salesmanship made the difference between ordinary and out-standing results. Unwilling or unable to buy Wheeler-Bennett out, afraid to lose the best agent in London, Flavelle continued with the not too satisfactory *status quo*.

He did put as much pressure as he dared on Wheeler-Bennett to improve the efficiency of his organization. Like other diplomats or salesmen, the Bismarck of the Bacon Trade would not delegate responsibility. "It is no reflection upon the magnificent capacity of Mr. Wheeler-Bennett to say that [his office] is not the best place in which to grow self-reliant men. Personally he is a man of such dominant force that it is difficult for men of capacity to grow up under him. . . . He knows he can do his work better than any one around him; therefore he is naturally reluctant to divide the responsibility with any one else." Pleading with Wheeler-Bennett to expand his organization and bring along competent young men, Flavelle also tried to protect his company by taking out a $100,000 policy on the salesman's life. By 1903 Wheeler-Bennett had agreed to open a Liverpool office to handle the northern business and Flavelle believed he was starting to give more respon-sibility to his staff. Still, Wheeler-Bennett's agency was the least satisfactory part of the operation.[34]

VII

Expansion and improvement cost money. It was remarkable that the Davies business had grown so much in the 1890s without requiring more capital from the shareholders or more than twenty-five per cent of the profits to be reinvested. It could not last. Between 1899 and 1902 the shareholders had to invest another $250,000 to finance enlargements of the factory and the growth of the store system.

The board was very conservative, reflecting William Davies' contentment in his old age. Flavelle got his way on expansion only after overwhelming his directors with exhaustively detailed memoranda justifying each expenditure of a few thousand dollars. Discussions in board meetings were always earnest and probably often heated—though Davies' deafness no doubt explains the length of some of Flavelle's written communications. Back from his European holiday in 1903, Flavelle read in the *Minutes* of the annual meeting William Davies' expression of regret that the younger businessman had not been present "to hear his confession that he was now convinced that his reluctant assent to store extension, to canning, and general expansion had been all wrong, and that the expansive policy of the Managing Director had been amply vindicated."[35]

VIII

The improvements in the organization took place in the midst of fierce competition. The surplus capacity in the industry meant too many packers chasing too few hogs. Davies' buyers, trying to get hogs for four or five cents a pound, were scoffed at by the aggressive agents for the farmers' co-ops and for the new Collingwood house, who offered six, seven, and eight cents a pound. They went further: instead of paying drovers who delivered at the packing house, the Collingwood people started sending buyers into the country, purchasing hogs at local railway stations and absorbing the costs of shipping themselves. Partly because it was hard to grade hogs outside the yard, partly to persuade drovers to switch their business, they also started paying premium prices for all hogs offered, over-thins and over-fats along with the premium Yorks and Tams. They got the hogs.[36]

Then they sold them cheaply in England. Wheeler-Bennett reported that the "mushroom agents . . . never ceased pelting the buyers" with their product, falling over each other and under each other's prices to get sales. Scorning his feeble competitors, he gloried in the fight. Week after week he cleared every side Flavelle sent at a premium over the other Canadians and cabled for larger shipments.[37]

Flavelle could not enlarge the shipments. The price of hogs that cost him

126

an average of 4.66 cents a pound in 1900 swelled to a record 6.21 cents in 1901 and a new record 6.76 cents in 1902. Disapproving of the new buyers' failure to discriminate in favour of quality, he insisted on taking only graded hogs at the factory. Naturally, the hogs went to competitors. Davies' killings fell from 439,000 in 1901 to 332,000 in 1902, something under 60 per cent of capacity. By then Flavelle had given in and was sending his buyers to country stations. He still felt he could not send Wheeler-Bennett 7-cent hogs and make money.

The farmers' co-ops published their statements, but no one else in the industry disclosed anything. Most of the opposition talked a good line, saying they were running to capacity, making money, and urging the old-fashioned Davies house to join them in the Twentieth Century. Looking at his own half-idle workers and unbelievably high cost-sheets, Flavelle worried that they might be telling the truth. His methods worked well enough through the year ending in March 1901—the company paid out $240,000 in a 60 per cent dividend. Still, it was a sharp decline from the last four years' earnings, and as competition became particularly fierce through the rest of 1901 Flavelle thought the export business might earn nothing at all that year.

Bluster and high hopes aside, by the beginning of 1902 several packers had had enough. The competition was hurting everybody but the farmers (whose co-ops, however, were hurting worst of all). Having fought harder than anyone else, the Collingwood house seemed ready to give up; its owners were making feelers to sell. In Toronto, Charlie Blackwell decided Flavelle had beaten him again and came to discuss his concern—"not I think in any cowardly sense," Flavelle noted, "but rather in the sense of a strong, aggressive young man who has too much good sense to want to spend four or five years in a bitter struggling campaign without any profit resulting to him from it."[38]

Blackwell saw a bleak future for all the packers, locked into years of excess capacity. The only way out would be an amalgamation creating a firm powerful enough to establish "a wise buying price" for hogs. He suggested a merger of Davies, Parke Blackwell, and the Matthews Company, followed by purchase of the Collingwood house. The new firm would normally have its way in hog buying in Canada and would probably also set the market price for Canadian bacon in England.

Flavelle presented Blackwell with a proposition he was sure would be rejected. The three firms' assets would be turned over to a holding company in which Davies would own two-thirds of the stock, the other third to be divided between Matthews and Blackwell. The new company would then buy Collingwood. Each of the old companies would continue to operate as a separate unit with a separate board, "and as far as the public was concerned would be separate and distinct in its own identity." But the William Davies Company (i.e. Joe Flavelle) would control and direct all their operations. To Flavelle's surprise Blackwell was interested and brought the Matthews family into the discussions. By February 1902 there was general agreement to merge according to Flavelle's plan; after a few details were cleared up the deal would go forward for shareholders' approval.[39]

Flavelle gradually realized that Blackwell and the Matthewses had received his proposal so favourably because they were doing so poorly. They both lost money in the year ending March 31, 1902, while the Davies Company, unduly conservative in its estimates, finished about $150,000 in the black—a lot less than previous years but enough to support a 27½-per-cent dividend in a supposedly unprofitable industry. Flavelle had assumed the Matthews retail stores were making money like his own stores; in fact their retailing was a barely profitable shoestring operation. When he and Smale inspected the Matthews plants in Peterborough and Hull they found the managers "without the first instinct of good curing. It is simply incredible to me that their bacon should have had any sort of standing in Great Britain." On another occasion he commented, "We have led these people in every respect. They have been a lot of school boys working alongside of trained men." Davies' earning power, he estimated, would justify an eighty-per-cent interest in the new company, although it was only contributing sixty per cent of the assets.* Having the other houses "at our mercy," he several times considered the option of going on alone. He could continue to pay his shareholders a modest dividend while competitors slid into bankruptcy.

On the other hand the merger looked intriguing. The new company would almost certainly exercise enough buying power to bring down the price of hogs in Canada, enough market power to bring up the price of Canadian bacon in England. The earning power of Matthews' and Black-

---

* He did not try to renegotiate the division because he was certain the others would balk. But it is an interesting reflection of his withdrawal from corporate finance at almost exactly the same time that he did not consider dividing the stock in the proposed new company into preferred and common. The preferred shares could have been distributed according to the real assets each firm contributed, the common according to their past earning power. In failing to make use of this relatively easy way of reconciling conflicting viewpoints Flavelle was being excessively conservative. He had overreacted to his problems with CCM and the Carter—Crume Company.

well's assets could be increased by incorporating "the Davies' methods of thoroughness and excellence" into the other two houses. The supply of Davies bacon going onto the English market could be increased almost at will. George Matthews' six sons would be a fine pool of executive ability for the future; they would use their energies in the service of the Davies shareholders rather than as dangerous competitors. In general, the merger would give the Davies group "a commanding position everywhere."[40]

The William Davies Company shareholders approved the merger agreement on April 30, 1902. Blackwell and George Matthews were to meet Flavelle to sign it on May 2. The only important figure who had not taken a clear position for or against the deal was Wheeler-Bennett. He had wavered: now advising non-cooperation with competitors whose products and agents were contemptible, now attracted by the idea of having unlimited bacon to sell and advising Flavelle to strike while the iron was hot. A Wheeler-Bennett cable arrived on the morning of May 1, urging delay: "Fear you will pay too dearly for houses which may prove deadweight bringing no equivalent but lifting poor competitors to splendid position. . . . Cannot you hold matters in abeyance till you see real strength and position this side and confer with me?" That afternoon Flavelle replied that he was going ahead anyway. Later that evening, overcome by irresolution, he decided to postpone the signing until he had more word from Wheeler-Bennett.

Wheeler-Bennett's follow-up letter stressed his belief that Flavelle was giving a third interest in the company to businessmen who didn't know their bacon. Flavelle decided that Wheeler-Bennett, his "running mate," was too important to the organization for any merger to go through unless it carried his judgment. Hastily booking passage on the *Saxonia*, he set out for England to see his agent.[41]

After the most serious, most searching conversations he had ever had with Wheeler-Bennett, Flavelle got his consent to the merger. He cabled his secretary-treasurer, Edward Adie, to sign the agreement if he thought it necessary. "I did this half hoping he would say, 'I will leave the matter over until your return.'" The decision thrown into his hands, Adie replied that he would leave it over unless instructed otherwise. Flavelle did not instruct otherwise.

During an unusually cold and rough passage home Flavelle decided to postpone the merger for at least a year. "Practically through the entire period of the discussion over this matter," he explained to Davies, "I have lacked the assurance of an intangible sort of judgment that has helped me in nearly all my business considerations, which for want of a better term I have sometimes called an 'instinctive judgment' — a sort of judgment which has become to me a final court of decision . . . when it was impossible to demonstrate that any particular course was the right one." More concretely, very large deliveries of hogs in the last twelve months had convinced his officers that the supply crisis had eased. Flavelle was unsure just how much demand there really was for Davies bacon in Britain, and worried about destroying his premium if he flooded the market. The new company might be overwhelmed with hogs, unable to increase its returns in Britain, and poorly placed to meet new competition. By contrast, the Davies Company now knew how strong it was compared to its competitors — it was in excellent shape to fight on single-handed. "We have our premium in England; we have an excellent organization here, a profitable retail business, a growing canning industry; and therefore if fight it is, we ought to be better equipped for it than any one else."

Flavelle knew he might be missing "what may be the big opportunity for the future of the Company." He was also aware of his apparent weakness as a managing director "who wavers, hesitates, and finally decides against an immediate completion of a transaction which has been brought to its present point through negotiations which have been carried on by himself." He accepted responsibility for this, and wrote Blackwell and the Matthewses asking for a twelve-month postponement.[42]

During that year the three farmers' co-ops became hopelessly insolvent, having lost more than $200,000 in only two years' operation. Most of the other packers were still talking merger, but Flavelle kept dwelling on Davies' strength and the poor earning power of others' assets. Davies' growing retail business alone was worth more than the whole business of the Collingwood factory, worth more than Blackwell's business, would soon be worth as much as the trade done by Matthews' two houses. Despite Davies' old-fashioned ways of doing business, its high costs, poor methods of buying, etc., etc., its *workmen* received more in profit-sharing bonuses than the Collingwood or Parke Blackwell shareholders received in dividends. Davies was probably making more money out of the export business than all the other packers combined. Smale and others on the staff were developing into businessmen of fine promise. Flavelle thought Davies could profitably continue on its lone course, even against an amalgamation of its existing competitors.

The real problem in 1902 was a new competitor. The biggest American packer, Swift's, had finally invaded Canada by buying the small Fowler house in Hamilton. It immediately began aggressive buying, running at full capacity while Flavelle and the other Canadian packers laid low because the export trade seemed unprofitable. Wheeler-Bennett reported that Swift's had to be losing thirty to forty shillings on every box they sold. Did the Americans really not know the business, Flavelle wondered? Did any businessmen work "with feverish haste" to lose money?[43]

By March 1903 Flavelle realized that Swift's had successfully broken into the expanding northern-England trade, a business Wheeler-Bennett had not cultivated because he lacked a competent man in Liverpool. "I am chagrined, disturbed, and humiliated over the character of the campaign during the last four months," Flavelle wrote Wheeler-Bennett.

I have been the officer responsible for the conduct of a business which has been brought into competition for the first time with a large American house, who, asking no favors, seeking no confidences, doing no scolding—organized, carried on, and successfully completed a campaign in which they nearly drove us to a standstill, only to have me waken up and find that they had scored handsomely against us. . . . we were "weighed in the balance and found wanting," . . . we have made "a poor fist of it," and have given to the newcomer an appetite for the Canadian market which will not be satisfied with the house in which he is working. . . .[44]

In response to this challenge Flavelle forgot about merging with the weak houses and concentrated on strengthening the Davies organization. He roasted Wheeler-Bennett for keeping his Liverpool agency "in short frocks and hair done in ringlets when the boy ought to have trousers and short hair." Wheeler-Bennett promised to strengthen the Liverpool business and reduced his commission to three per cent. Store expansion at home was speeded up and the first plans laid for going into Montreal and Buffalo. The bankrupt cooperative packing house at Harriston was bought from receivers, its investors apparently receiving twenty cents on the dollar. Harriston stood at the gateway of an important hog-producing area, and Flavelle bought the factory to protect his supply.[45]

Despite Swift's competition the Davies Company seemed to be having no serious trouble going on its own way. Profits fell again in the year ending March 31, 1903, reflecting the fierce competition of 1902, and the dividend had to be cut to 15 per cent, the lowest yet. Most packing-house owners got no dividends. Then in 1903 and 1904 the high prices of preceding years were reflected in increased hog production while the failure of the farmer co-ops had removed some of the reckless competition in buying. Prices in England held up satisfactorily. Davies' profits from the stores, canning, and cooking were becoming increasingly important in the annual returns. The company held 25 to 35 per cent of the export trade, which had stabilized at a $12 to $15 million annual business. Dividends bounced back to 30 per cent for 1904 and 41 per cent for 1905.* Davies' future in an industry apparently heading for stability after a storm of competition seemed very secure.

It was secure because J. W. Flavelle was a brilliant manager. Unlike businessmen who took the profits of the moment and ran—"traders" he scornfully called them—he had built for the future. In diversifying his business, he had developed the first significant chain of retail stores in Canada. His firm's laboratory was conducting pioneering research in his industry. He had worked out highly advanced accounting techniques to help drive his executives to greater efficiency and achievement. By careful recruiting he had found a successor. He had mastered his business, and operated it so well that he had made money in a wide-open competitive situation. Most of his competitors had not.

IX

If the Davies directors were happy, the Ontario farmers who grew their hogs were not. In the years of frantic competition farmers who had taken packers' advice to produce only prime swine were annoyed when buyers started paying top prices for animals that were nothing but a lump of fat. Why should the poor hog-raiser get as much for his animal as the good one? Surely this failure of drovers and packers to grade the animals could only hurt the quality of Canadian bacon. Still, the packers pleaded that competition was so stiff that the house which tried to keep grading—as Davies had tried—was losing its hog supply. And when hogs were going at record prices of 6½ to 7½ cents a pound no one was kicking very much.[46]

A few years later, when prices were back under 6 cents, sometimes under 5

* Of course they were a return of about half that on the company's total assets, which by now were close to $1 million because of the reserves of undistributed profits it had accumulated over the years. For that part of his holdings he had bought at $400 a share, Flavelle's dividend income was only one-quarter of the nominal rate.

cents, it was time to start asking the confident, well-dressed fellows from Toronto some tough questions. At the 1904 Guelph Winter Fair's bacon session—always a highlight of the Fair—Dr. Smale turned out to be the slickest, smoothest-talking packer sent down yet ("and Bro. Flavelle is a fairly smooth one too"). But here he was still complaining about quality while saying that packers couldn't grade their hogs. Should farmers produce high-quality hogs out of the goodness of their hearts, with no cash incentive at all?

And if competition among the packers was so fierce, why wasn't it driving prices up? Why were prices low all across the province—or, at least, lowest just when most farmers were ready to bring their hogs to market? Maybe the packers were getting together and agreeing to pay the same price. Maybe there was a packers' combine—a pork trust—growing fat on the sweat of the farmers. If there was a trust, everyone knew which company must be behind it. Then, in the summer of 1905, some packers, including the William Davies Company, began importing American hogs in bond for the first time since 1892, shipping the product to England as Canadian-cured American bacon. More evidence, it seemed, of a conspiracy to hold Canadian prices down.[47]

Smale defended the packers before hundreds of angry farmers at Guelph in December 1905. That "inexorable autocrat — the law of supply and demand," fixed the price of hogs, he argued. Prices fluctuated because the English market was volatile, and it was always depressed over Christmas, just when the largest shipments from Canada arrived, because farmers marketed so many hogs in November. Why not market hogs at other times of the year when prices were higher? The packers were importing American hogs to keep their workers busy in the summer when Canadian farmers weren't shipping. The private houses had not deliberately driven the cooperatives out of business.[48] As for grading, the farmers couldn't have their cake and eat it too — they were getting premium prices for all hogs, good or bad; no packer could offer a premium on a premium.[49]

Unconvinced, farmers successfully pressured the federal Minister of Agriculture to stop the American imports. The muckraking *Toronto World* picked up the agitation, bringing the notion of a pork trust to an urban audience beginning to worry about high food prices. North American newspapers were already full of sensational revelations about American trusts; a plumbers' ring was on trial in Toronto for conspiring to fix prices. The discovery of a packers' combine was in tune with the spirit of the time.

The William Davies Company's killings fell by almost 100,000 in the calendar year 1905. Smale, Flavelle, and Davies decided that the agitation was the main cause of the decline. Their responses to critics became increasingly indignant, the outrage of the moralist charged with immorality, the temperance worker accused of being a drunk:

This company does not desire, and has not sought to control the bacon or beef business, either by direct or indirect measures. It has sought to bring all the intelligence it could command to bear upon the business with which it was identified. It has sought for and desires no artificial aid from any source whatsoever. It has believed that industry and intelligence applied to the day to day operations of the company were more useful and more self-respecting, and the results secured from such efforts more satisfying than the same money results secured through combination. We have been guilty of the crime of playing lone hand. . . .

. . . It is vital to the continuance of the bacon industry that a spirit of confidence exists between the breeder and feeder who raises hogs and the curer who ships the finished product to the English market. Where criticisms . . . are founded on actual knowledge, useful and necessary public service is performed in making criticisms. Where they are founded on conjecture and there is refusal to accept as truthful the statements of those who are cognizant of the facts a cruel wrong is done not only to an important industry in which the farmers of the Province are interested, but to business men who have invested large sums of money in buildings and plant. . . .[50]

Flavelle invited his critics to study the William Davies business for themselves. On January 22, 1906, the provincial Minister of Agriculture, the former Minister of Agriculture, representatives of farmers' organizations, and the editors of the *Farmer's Advocate*, the *Weekly Sun*, and the *World* gathered in the Davies lunchroom with Flavelle, Smale, and William Davies. For five and a half hours they discussed the company's affairs. Flavelle read long extracts from the firm's correspondence with Wheeler-Bennett, proving time and time again Davies' anxiety at the way competitors were bidding up prices. He let the outsiders go through the letterbooks themselves, gave them all his data on costs and prices, explained his methods of buying (competitors had once learned Davies' prices in advance when a rival house bribed a telegraph operator; now the company used the telephone), offered to make public anything except the company's profit-and-loss record. Flavelle's great bacon conference was unique in a business world where secrecy was still the norm. The editors of the *World* agreed with his claim that no other private business in Canada would so willingly expose its innermost workings to its severest critics. "The blessed gospel of candor has in Mr. Flavelle its most notable and most successful exponent." It printed a six-thousand-line verbatim transcript of the conference over eight days, and the crusading editors and farm leaders withdrew their charges. Flavelle seemed to have scored a fine victory.[51] All along he and Smale had urged farmers to stop complaining and concentrate on raising hogs efficiently and profitably, had even subsidized cost-keeping experiments to prove that farmers made money at recent prices.[52] The fact that prices were high through most of 1906 bolstered his case and put an end to most producers' grumbling.

But the incident was important. Nothing like this falling-out with the farmers had happened before to Flavelle (except, perhaps, for the CCM affair when he knew he was at fault). He was thoroughly angry at criticism of his business methods by people who were ignorant of the business. He attributed the wrong-headed, untruthful agitation to a desire to destroy the business by disrupting the constructive relationship packers had long enjoyed with farmers. The industry's main problem, he felt, was the danger that farmers would be deflected from their main job of raising good hogs efficiently. Certainly the Davies Company would go on its lone way with even less regard for competitors' behaviour. There would be no consultation in the industry, nothing but wide-open competition.

In reacting this way Flavelle misread the problem beginning to develop in his industry. The cost of raising hogs was gradually rising with the cost of feed, and farmers' margins of profit were shrinking.[53] Despite competition at home, packers were limited in the prices they could offer by the need to compete with other suppliers in Britain. In the 1890s the Canadian bacon trade had boomed because prices on two unrelated markets had been moving apart. Now the reverse was happening as prices fitfully moved closer, diminishing everyone's profits. Farmer attacks on packers were a search for an identifiable villain to explain baffling and complex market movements. Instead of realizing the real meaning of the outcry against the old devil packers, Flavelle tended to take the criticism personally and respond in kind, finding his own black-hearted villains among the critics. This meant that no one understood the long-run problem just starting to appear in the bacon business.

Had he grasped the underlying situation, Flavelle might have tried new strategies. Restoration of the grading system, for example, was badly needed. Unrestrained competition in an industry with excess capacity was lowering quality and annoying producers. The William Davies Company could have improved its reputation with the farmer by at least trying to restore the premiums for quality hogs. If this failed, as it probably would,*[54] it might have called for either packer cooperation or government intervention to restore grading. Someone had to re-establish the rules of the game which the war of individual companies had destroyed. The more determined Flavelle was to operate on his individualist principles—newly sharpened by the pork-trust agitation — the less he understood the limits of individual competitiveness. Had he given the situation more thought, uncoloured by his past phenomenal success, his present resentment at his critics, and short-term favourable prices and profits, he might have understood that pork-packers and pig-farmers, no matter how earnestly they struggled, could not stand up indefinitely against great market forces.

The 1902 merger that never was might have helped for a while. It probably would have enabled the Davies Company to control the buying price of hogs and restore the system of grading. Wider use of Davies' first-class methods would have resulted in some improvement in packer efficiency, and, if Flavelle handled a semi-monopoly position sensibly, in slightly higher returns to the farmer. In the hands of a certain kind of businessman the merger would have begun a serious thrust for monopoly — meeting competition by buying or absorbing competitors to create a giant packing company. It would have produced other advantages for the Davies Company which only became apparent several years later. The merger could have created Canada Packers twenty-five years before it was created. Even if it would not have provided a lasting solution to the long-term struggle to keep Canadian bacon on the British breakfast table, it was worth a try.

One non-economic consideration affected Flavelle's decisions. He expressed it in a 1902 letter to Wheeler-Bennett, explaining his disinterest in further merger discussions:

My views as to the conduct of business differ materially from the views of very many of the gentlemen with whom I would be associated. My present relations with

---

* "Such a course might be very heroic," Flavelle commented, "but we would find ourselves ultimately in the class of business failures, without reputation, without profit, and without capital."

the active spirits in the Davies Company are happy. We have a common standard as to what constitutes an honorable and high-minded conduct of affairs, and generally speaking we have no irritating conditions. I have reached a point where I do not want to take on a large order and become responsible for the organization of an important amalgamation, when in the nature of the case I would have to be associated with many people whose company would not be desirable. I have other channels for exercising any surplus energy I may possess under more congenial conditions.[55]

If Flavelle had been a pure businessman, interested in maximizing his profits, or if he had been the most common variant of the profit-maximizer, an empire-builder, he would have taken the risk of the 1902 amalgamation. But he wanted to pick and choose his business associates. Giving up his freedom to surround himself with such like-minded businessmen as Walker of the Commerce, Fudger of Simpson's, and Smale of the Davies Company was not worth the mere money to be made. He also had "other channels" for exercising his surplus energy. These flowed increasingly in non-business directions. Although he was proud of his company's record of serving its customers, he wanted to serve his community in other ways. And he wanted to spend more time with his family.

After the 1902 merger discussions, Flavelle gave the business on the Don only part of his time. His other world, centring on Queen's Park and its institutions, was at least as "congenial" as the rough and tumble of the packing industry. Moving remarkably smoothly back and forth between the two worlds, he was unwilling to make a complete commitment to either.

CHAPTER SIX

PROGRESSIVE CONSERVATIVE

The Christian citizen had a duty to serve his community. He should leave it "better and purer" Flavelle had prayed the day he decided to make Toronto his home. Managing a good business was a service to the community. But was it enough service and was it visibly unselfish service when it so handsomely enriched the man who served? What about other kinds of service that brought no return except the satisfaction of a job well done?

If businessmen stuck only to business, or only to business and Sunday School, who would undertake the civic obligations? Who would create the modern institutions a community needed to complement its great industries? Who would build the great hospitals, organize the great universities, pay attention to the need for good, honest government? Surely a businessman ought to give part of his time to public service.

Public service was a particular duty for someone who thought of himself as a progressive. Progressive businessmen were modernizing private industries. The public sector needed to make comparable progress. Old, unprogressive ways of doing things and stale, self-interested politicians should give way or be thrust aside so the nation could take its place as a leader in science, culture, and good government. Was this not what modern progress was about? In the early years of the new century few Canadians offered more public service, were more "progressive" in this sense, than Joe Flavelle, as he spent time and money hoping to create public institutions and politics worthy of a twentieth-century nation.

I

For almost eighty years Toronto General Hospital had served the poor of the city, with minimal support from citizens or city council—so minimal that in

1868 the hospital had briefly closed its doors for want of money. It had an endowment of land in the city and occasionally a benefactor like John Macdonald or the Gooderhams gave money for more bricks and mortar. But for the most part the hospital lived, like its patients, as a pauper.

By 1900 the heating and plumbing systems in the ivy-covered buildings at Gerrard and Parliament streets were in a state of near collapse. Lack of heat in the out-patients' building was a menace to *their* health, doctors complained, let alone to the patients'. Cats chased the mice that roamed the wards and patients' beds were spread with "tanglefoot" to catch the flies welcomed in through unscreened windows. It was hard to tell what menaced the patients, though, for the hospital could not afford the staff to keep proper records of cases. For years income from its property had been falling short of current expenses, no matter how low these had been kept.

Most patients—about two hundred and fifty of them at any one time— were still the poor who had nowhere else to go. Doctors worked without fees; in return, physicians affiliated with a medical school could use their patients for teaching demonstrations. But with two medical schools in the city (at the University of Toronto and Trinity University), plus private physicians who demanded open access to a civic institution, no professor had enough patient beds for proper teaching or research. And while the overstaffing of the hospital may have compensated for its out-of-date facilities, every doctor was effectively a law unto himself. The house staff of nurses and resident doctors was disorganized, undisciplined, overworked, and evidently in the habit of collecting under-the-table fees from both patients and doctors.

The hospital's Board of Trustees was composed of the mayor, three provincial appointees, and one benefactors' representative. The mayor paid little attention to the hospital; in 1902 the youngest of the other trustees was sixty-six, their average age was seventy-five. Their meetings, like the life of the hospital, were somnolent. Torontonians still thought of their largest and oldest hospital as an unpleasant place where the poor went to die.[1]

In other European and American cities great hospitals were being built in which the best principles of modern medicine and surgery were used to save lives. Doctors were carefully screened, exact records kept, precise chains of authority established, and the best in laboratories and equipment was provided. Some of the best new hospitals, such as Johns Hopkins in Baltimore, where Canada's own William Osler was physician-in-chief (why did talented Canadians keep leaving the country?), were intimately associated with universities and were becoming great centres of research, the cutting-edge of the advance of modern medicine. In Toronto's one major hospital, by contrast, a progressive businessman touring the wards and talking with patients and staff was struck, Flavelle noted, by "the disinclination of anyone who was associated with the Hospital, either as ministering to its needs or being ministered to by it, to say a good word for it." Was this a credit to the premier city in Canada's premier province?[2]

The same question was being asked about the University of Toronto. The provincial university had evolved in its first seventy years into a crazy-quilt federation of church-controlled arts and theology colleges (including the Methodists' own Victoria College), the non-denominational University College, and the University itself as examining body for arts while providing instruction in the natural sciences and other subjects. Toronto's thirteen hundred students were concentrated in arts; the Faculty of Medicine was only a few years old, the Faculty of Law existed only on paper. Agricultural and engineering education were carried on at provincial schools only loosely affiliated with Toronto. The Queen's Park campus was huge and beautifully adorned by University College; but U.C. was overcrowded, and only a handful of other buildings existed to handle the overflow. Out-of-town students, for example, had to spend their college years wrestling with the geometry of boarding houses. Convocations were held in the gymnasium.

A Board of Trustees managed the university's property, perhaps without proper legal authority; a Senate made academic policy; all appointments were made and salaries set by the Ontario Minister of Education. The chancellor, vice-chancellor, and president of the university had ill-defined, conflicting responsibilities, and it was not clear whether University College had special status within the federation or was just another college. Like the hospital, the university had long since found that expenses outran its income from tuition and its endowment. The province made up each year's deficit. But the Liberal politicians who had been running Ontario for decades often wondered why taxpayers' hard-earned money should be spent educating a small and arrogant elite of college students. Politicians' one firm belief about higher education was that those who paid the professors should choose who and how much to pay. So faculty appointments were made by order-in-council, not always on academic merit—not often on academic merit some thought — and not necessarily on the advice of anyone at the university. Toronto's president, James Loudon, learned of one appointment to his staff by reading about it in the newspaper.

Loudon made a difficult situation worse by being a weak administrator, unsociable, and unbending on the smallest matters. His unpublished memoirs in the University Archives are a vitriolic, nearly paranoiac attack on almost everyone else who held office in the university during his presidency. One of the lowest points in his tenure came in 1895 when student dissatisfaction with professorial incompetence, apparent nepotism in appointments, and the administration's distaste for free speech erupted in the only student strike in the history of the university. Severe repression and a Royal Commission glossed over the incident without anything being settled. As the University of Toronto entered the twentieth century, student morale was low, the faculty was dispirited, there was little money for expansion, and no one had much sympathy for the institution. In the legislature Opposition leader J. P. Whitney spoke openly of "blight and mildew" at the province's premier educational institution.[3]

George Ross's Liberal government poured most of the money it was willing to provide for higher education into Queen's University at Kingston. Queen's was the Presbyterian arts college which had refused to follow Victoria into the federation in 1889. Most Torontonians felt it should have been left to survive on prayer. But by getting the province to finance its secular School of Mining, Queen's dynamic principal, George Grant, had found a way of bypassing the restriction on subsidies to denominational colleges. He seemed to be preparing to turn Queen's into a second provincial university to rival Toronto.

Grant of Queen's, like Dawson of McGill and the presidents of leading American universities (including the Canadian president of nearby Cornell, which attracted many Canadian students — why did talented Canadians keep leaving the country?), seemed to have the executive ability and the awareness of modern educational needs to advance their institutions to national and international prominence. The University of Toronto, by contrast, was in danger of falling behind even a little Presbyterian college in stagnant Kingston. To progressive Toronto businessmen like Flavelle and Byron Walker this was disgraceful.[4]

II

Flavelle became involved in educational work when the Methodist General Conference in 1898 appointed him to the Board of Regents of Victoria

College. Always a generous donor to the Church's Educational Society, he had probably always been interested in its Ontario college. Founded in the late 1830s, Victoria had struggled along at Cobourg until John Macdonald and George Cox (the latter as bursar of the college) led the 1880s campaign to move it to Toronto. Vic was woefully underfinanced, they realized, and could never flourish without the resources of the University of Toronto, particularly for instruction in the sciences. Federated with Toronto, though, Victoria would preserve its distinctive courses in arts and theology, let the University teach science and other new subjects, and perhaps also benefit financially from having moved to the centre of Methodist wealth.[5]

Macdonald, the Masseys, Cox, and the estate of a Gooderham who had renounced drink supplied the money to establish Victoria in its handsome redstone building in Queen's Park and create a small endowment to supplement students' fees and the annual grant from the church. Income from the three sources in the 1890s did not meet the expenses of running a college for two to three hundred students, and the endowment was gradually eroded. The Reverend Doctor John Potts, a sort of one-man bureaucracy for the college and the Methodist Church, persistently dunned leading laymen for help.

Getting Flavelle appointed to the Board of Regents may have been designed to loosen his pocketbook. Ames and Cox were also on the board; Kemp would soon join them. Victoria did become a prime beneficiary of the Sherbourne Street group's philanthropy in 1899 when most of the $90,000 they contributed to the Twentieth Century Thanksgiving Fund was earmarked for the college. Another $150,000 soon followed from the Massey family. For years Potts had prayed for money; "at last God has raised up members of the Board of Regents who are at once liberal and intelligent in their interest in Victoria College," he rejoiced.[6]

The money had to be handled wisely. In 1902 Flavelle moved, seconded by Cox, that the college stop using its endowment to meet current expenses. A finance committee of the laymen invested the endowment in bonds, debentures, and mortgages. Not surprisingly, Cox "family" companies did the business: Victoria banked at the Central Canada, invested through National Trust, and owned securities in Cox-controlled companies. Victoria received a good return on most of its investments; when a less than satisfactory return was likely its patrons twice bought back securities at a premium. Even Ames, whose Twentieth Century Fund donation of $10,000 in Carter—Crume preferred fell rapidly in value, finally bought back the shares in 1919 at par plus five per cent compounded interest. When Potts died in 1907, National Trust became Victoria's treasurer.[7]

The college was now in fairly good financial health. Professors' salaries were raised — though not without the businessmen on the board, particularly Flavelle, insisting on better evidence of effective teaching.[8] The quality of instruction now easily matched that at University College, and Victoria finally stopped losing able Methodist youth (Will Milner, a Methodist minister's son, had himself gone to University College, now taught there, and as late as 1895 predicted that Vic would never turn out a first-class honour graduate in classics). The few Methodists who still avoided the college, President Burwash reported in 1902, were "mostly lovers of sport or persons to whom the high moral tone of the College is not an attraction."[9] Continuing deficits of a few thousand a year were met by Flavelle and the other wealthy members of the board — "our noble group in Toronto," Potts wrote. The college was able to help one of the noble group in a small way for a year or two after 1903 by finding the sixty dollars annually to keep on awarding the A. E. Ames Scholarship while its donor was temporarily distressed.[10]

The Methodist nobility was not popular with James Loudon because they were determined to buy from the university a site for a Vic women's residence. Loudon saw it as a scheme to advance Victoria at the expense of University College (which did not have a women's residence), and part of a broader conspiracy to oust him from the presidency. The two-year fight over the residence lot featured "insulting remarks," abrupt departures from Trustees' meetings, and an ill-concealed attempt to replace Loudon. Flavelle's role in the residence struggle angered enough university people that Walker hesitated to put his name up for the Board of Trustees for fear he would not be elected.[11]

Partly to heal the breach between Victoria and the university, Flavelle founded a university fellowship in 1901, $1500 awarded semi-annually to an outstanding graduate for two years studying modern history at Oxford. The Flavelle Fellowship was well received as a much-needed gesture of support for the university (few other businessmen had made donations; the Rhodes scholarships had not yet been founded).[12] But Flavelle's relations with Loudon did not improve when they got into a dispute with each other and the Minister of Education over the terms on which the first Flavelle fellow, Edward Kylie, would be hired by the university on his return from Oxford. Kylie's rank and salary became a matter of protracted interviews between Flavelle and Loudon, Flavelle and the Minister, Loudon and the

Minister, Flavelle and Kylie, before going to the cabinet for final approval.[13] Such were the politics of university appointments. At least Kylie had not had to follow the older practice of having his credentials and testimonials printed and publicly distributed.

Living literally on university property, Flavelle also had many friends active in its affairs. Milner, of course, was an old hand at university politics. Walker was the most prominent businessman associated with the university. As graduates, both W. T. White and T. A. Russell were leaders in the Alumni Association Loudon had formed in 1900 to lobby for more money. Dr. Smale at the bacon factory retained an interest in the institution from his years in the Chemistry Department. As the university drifted without the spirit or leadership which now characterized Victoria College, the "friends" of Varsity agreed that reform was necessary. There would have to be less political control of its affairs, more scope for presidential leadership. To get anything done there would first have to be a change in the attitude — or personnel—of the provincial government.

III

It was easier to begin to reform the situation at the hospital. In 1902 the Gooderhams asked Flavelle to join the Board of Trustees as the benefactors' representative. He took a year to get his bearings and then began to take the situation in hand. "Mr. Flavelle requested that a tabulated list be prepared of all alterations or additions to the hospital buildings; that the cost of each work be ascertained, and the whole matter of these works be considered collectively before the board embarks on any of them. It was ordered that this be done." The board received its first detailed statements of the hospital's financial position. Finding the accounts unsatisfactory — no depreciation was allowed on houses the hospital owned, for example — Flavelle undertook to advise the secretary on accounting. He handled negotiations with the province leading to increases in rates and subsidies. On his initiative a committee of the professional staff was formed to advise the board on needed improvements. Explaining this apparently novel attempt to involve the doctors in hospital planning, Flavelle wrote in 1903 that it could be "perhaps the first step in setting in force a movement which would ultimately result in the establishing of a very great Hospital with modern buildings and appliances, and administered by a Board composed of gentlemen who were qualified by experience to efficiently direct its operations."[14]

As the older members of the board retired, their most notable replacement was Peter Larkin, another successful businessman devoting his free time to public service. When John Blaikie, Chairman of the Board, retired in 1904, George Gooderham and Larkin nominated Flavelle as chairman. Protesting that Gooderham should take the office, Flavelle agreed to do his duty "anyway for the residue of the current year." [15]

His accession to the chairmanship produced another burst of activity—a thorough reorganization of the house staff, the first appointments of registrars and paid anaesthetists, plumbing repairs, a new accounting system. The chairman also handled routine details of administration: settling doctors' feuds over patients and service, trying to reduce theft in the nurses' residence and from patients in the emergency branch, and carrying on discreet negotiations with the MP for Algoma, who blamed the hospital for his having contracted gonorrhea as a private patient. [16]

The first step towards a new hospital was taken to forestall the corrupting effects of wealth. Twenty-year-old Cawthra Mulock was the heir to the Cawthra family fortune. Already rich on the income from trusts, he would soon inherit the incredible sum of eight million dollars. Unlike Toronto's self-made wealthy, young Mulock would never have to work for his daily bread. Would he ever do anything worth while? In the summer of 1904 someone close to Mulock — perhaps his father, Sir William Mulock — approached Flavelle: "Flavelle, you are in direction of the Toronto General Hospital. Cawthra Mulock is coming into manhood. I am very anxious he should make something out of his life. He has enough money to spoil him if he does not have some serious work to do, and I think if he were to go into the Hospital, and you could get him to go to work, it might be of benefit."

Flavelle suggested the young man's service begin with a donation of $100,000 to build a new out-patients' building. Mulock duly pledged the $100,000, specifying on Flavelle's suggestion that a general plan for gradually rebuilding the whole hospital be drawn up. Flavelle had him appointed to the board. [17]

The prospect of the new out-patients' building brought university doctors' longstanding dissatisfaction with the hospital's east-end location to a head. It was too far to travel for their clinics. They urged the board not to pour Mulock's money into the old site, but to make a clean break and move the hospital nearer the university. Flavelle wanted a closer connection with the university to stimulate research, an idea which was more practical since the 1902 federation of Trinity with the University of Toronto had created a single medical faculty in the city. By the end of 1904 Flavelle had enlisted the support of the university's Board of Trustees for an approach to the provincial government. Mulock's money was pledged and other philanthropists would contribute, but the efforts of private citizens would have to be supplemented by government aid. Once that was guaranteed, a new hospital trust could be formed in association with the university to build a new Toronto General Hospital.[18]

The Ross government agreed to help the hospital if the City of Toronto also helped. But its promise was made only a few days before the dissolution of the legislature for the provincial election of January 15, 1905. For Flavelle there were much more serious issues in that election than his hospital plans.

IV

Heeding his mother's advice, he felt a keen obligation to help improve his community's political life.

In the years after John A. Macdonald's death Flavelle was distressed to see the federal Conservative administration dissolve in a muck of scandal and incompetence. He thought Sir Charles Tupper deserved to be beaten by Laurier in 1896, and was more distressed when prominent Conservatives blamed the defeat on bad luck and smugly predicted a return to power at the next election. Flavelle thought the party under Tupper was ineffective and stale, weakly led and without constructive ability. Unless it changed, the Liberals would govern for at least two Parliaments.

He invited four prominent Toronto Conservatives—E. B. Osler, Charles Cockshutt, W. R. Brock, and Frederic Nicholls—to a luncheon shortly after the 1896 election, told them of his dissatisfaction, and suggested they join him in creating a $50,000 fund to help "mend our fences, enter into new constructive plans, win the big boys and young men who were the sons of Conservatives, or who had no party affiliations, as well as the incoming immigrants." As he remembered the meeting, "these gentlemen were too generous towards the novice to laugh at him; hence in a gracious way they turned down the proposal."[19] They might have taken him more seriously, for it is arguable that the Conservative party never recovered from the defeat of 1896.

He continued to work actively in his local riding association and was an important contributor to party funds, but almost no records of his political donations survive. As he became a visibly public-spirited businessman, both federal and provincial Conservatives tried to interest him in standing for election. The Ontario leader, James Pliny Whitney, was the most insistent; according to Flavelle, Whitney told him the 1902 election would hinge on Flavelle's candidacy in his Toronto riding because his prominence would swing several marginal constituencies to the Conservatives. Whitney was either appealing to his vanity or believed his name would attract much-needed Methodist and temperance votes. After wrestling with his conscience, however, Flavelle declined to run, pleading his business obligations. He did endorse Whitney's cautious temperance platform and contributed substantially to a special Tory fund for that election.[20]

His conscience still bothered him, perhaps more keenly when Whitney narrowly lost the election. Deeply interested in politics, always eager to offer political advice—usually critical—he hardly seemed to be doing his duty by observing from the sidelines while making money in business. So in the summer of 1902 he decided to contribute to Canadian political life by buying or founding a daily newspaper and using it to champion good government and high ideals of public service.

He probably hit upon the idea after learning that the country's most prominent English-language journalist, John S. Willison, was restless as editor of its most prominent newspaper, the *Globe*. Like most newspapers, the *Globe* was owned by men with substantial political interests, in this case a group of Liberals centring on Robert Jaffray and Senator Cox. The paper was expected to advance Liberal policies in both its editorial and news columns. But since 1896 Willison had found it increasingly distasteful to defend either the federal or the Ontario Liberal governments, and had resented having the party whip cracked by his owners. Political subservience offended his growing sense of professionalism as a journalist and his desire to criticize bad men and bad policies wherever they might be found.[21]

Willison had to feed his children, though, and it seemed impossible for a serious Canadian newspaper to survive without the money and advertising patronage flowing from a political connection. A few newspapers — the *Montreal Star*, the *Toronto World*, and the *Evening Telegram* —had developed a kind of independence as "people's papers," cheap, simple, and sensational. This did not appeal to a writer interested in sophisticated commentary on complex political issues. Other papers had been bought by corporations like the CPR or by wealthy businessmen like Frederic Nicholls to advance their business and political interests. That was no answer either.[22]

Flavelle shared Willison's disappointment with the captive press. Also disappointed at the low calibre of Conservative political ideas and leadership (the new federal leader, Robert Borden, was untested and had few able followers), thinking of himself as an Independent Conservative, he hoped to see serious, disinterested, non-partisan discussion of public issues. High-toned independent newspapers existed in other countries — *The Times* of London, the *New York Post*, the *Springfield Republican* — and it might be a notable public service to provide one for Canada. Flavelle had evidently been impressed by Willison's work at the *Globe* through the 1890s. In the last few years Willison had increasingly attacked political corruption, had talked about the journalist as a professional public servant, and was raising important questions about the conflict between corporations and the public. Flavelle did not know him well, but he seemed to be the right man to edit the new paper.

In the summer of 1902 Flavelle made this offer to a surprised Willison:

If I furnish the capital, will you join me in the production of a paper in which you can give expression to your views upon public matters without being interfered with in the interests of party, church, corporation, or any interests which will seek to influence your judgment to cause you to be partisan?

I shall appreciate discussing with you any question affecting public interests upon which we differ, but when we have so discussed the subject, the view as finally determined by you to be truest to the public interest, is the one which will find expession in the paper.

I will at no time ask you to write a line, or to make reference in any way favourable to any interests with which I am identified, whether of a business, corporate or church character.

I do not desire to be known as a newspaper proprietor, or to secure advantage of any sort for myself. I only desire to be of some service to the community in which I live, and shall be grateful if you give me the opportunity, by permitting me to join with you in such an enterprise.

From you, Mr. Willison, I want no pledge other than that you will say you will seek to express your honest opinions upon public matters, undeterred by personal, party or other influences which will keep you from saying what you think ought to be said in the public interest.[23]

Sir Wilfrid Laurier generously advised Willison to follow the obvious bent of his interests. Through the autumn of 1902 Flavelle and Willison shopped for a Toronto newspaper. Plans to buy either the *World* or the *Mail and Empire* fell through and they had to settle for what Flavelle called "a low grade evening paper," the *News*, which was on the market at a bargain $150,000.[24] "I will not attempt to deny how much I am moved," Flavelle wrote his editor about the partnership-to-be. "This decision you have made means so much to you, may mean so much to the country . . . let me say how deeply I prize your confidence, and how much I am indebted to you for giving me the opportunity of working with you."[25] He stopped attending Conservative-party meetings and also wrote Senator Cox asking to be released from his commitment to join the board of the new Grand Trunk Pacific project:

Not because I have any idea that the independence of the journal would be affected by my identity with the Company, or that I would seek to influence Mr. Willison, nor that the Grand Trunk will ask for anything that does not carry my approval; but instinctively I have the feeling that I would be doing an injustice to the high minded-ness of the new effort if I permitted it to be assailed at the very commencement of its career with the statement that it was launched for the purpose of helping on this railway enterprise, and that the alleged independence ascribed as the cause of its creation was a fake and a humbug.[26]

On January 19, 1903, the new management published their first edition of the *News*, "An Independent Journal devoted to Politics, Education, Litera-ture, the presentation of current news and the diffusion of useful informa-tion."

Flavelle reserved the right to discuss issues with his editor—"to think out loud to you upon any question upon which I may have an opinion"[27]—and the two were often together late into the night at Holwood. Willison was the first man of letters Flavelle had known; the businessman took an obvious delight in their discussions. He was often deferential to Willison, sometimes sickeningly fawning, but also ready to criticize editorials that displeased him.[28]

Flavelle often suspected that Willison favoured organized labour in indus-trial disputes. Upset at one balanced leader on trade-union corruption, he chastised Willison for the "inane statement" and "curious morality" of the editorial. "In nine cases out of ten your criticisms carry my judgment, while in this case I am not convinced nor even impressed," Willison replied. Flavelle apologized for having given offence, telling him the response was "only as it should be."[29] All the evidence from Flavelle's letters, Willison's letters, and the *News* itself suggests that Willison did have the final voice in editorial policy.

News editorials caused more friction between Flavelle and his friends than between owner and editor. Almost immediately, for example, *News* attacks on the arrogant incompetence with which William Mackenzie's Toronto Railway Company ran the city's streetcars alarmed the group at the Commerce, who did so much business with Mackenzie. "You must not forget that the primary object of the *News* is to perform public service," Flavelle lectured Byron Walker.

The men [like Mackenzie] to whom society is greatly indebted for many acts of large courage through which the whole community is better, being selfish, grasping, and often mean, the journal which attempts to serve the community has to express itself in vigorous language concerning the crooked relations between such men and governments, as well as to say very vigorous things in condemnation of the administrative quality of such men as regards the general public. I cannot therefore hope that the *News* will do other than very often irritate you and lead you to think that it is unfair.[30]

Flavelle ordered the business editor not to consult him about market reports and to pay no attention to their implication for his companies.[31] If anything the paper's social columns understated the social life at Holwood. Pressure from the owner's church friends could also be a problem: in 1906 S. D. Chown, Secretary of the Temperance, Prohibition and Moral Reform Board of the Methodist Church, complained to Flavelle that the daily racing column, "Three Best Bets," incited readers to gamble. "I hesitate to think that you would feel satisfied to have a journal with which your name is commonly identified become a means of promoting breaches of the law," he wrote. Flavelle replied that it was Willison's decision to make.[32] The *News* followed normal newspaper policies; it carried as many ads for patent medicine and fly-by-night stock promotions as any of its competitors. Only its editorials were intended to be different.

Aside from Willison's normal desire to please his publisher, the two got on well because Flavelle's independent Conservatism and Willison's independent Liberalism came together to bring them into agreement on most public issues. Like other Canadian business and intellectual leaders who had been shocked by the scandals of the 1890s, they both believed that excessive "partyism," expressed in machine politics, was stifling real political debate and corrupting voters. Above all, they wanted to raise the moral tone of political life, injecting ideas and ideals into politics and purging both parties of hacks and heelers.

Flavelle had been particularly concerned about the grimy role money played in politics. He had helped organize the 1902 Ontario Conservative campaign fund as an experiment in openly collecting and openly spending party funds to avoid the stigma of corruption—the Liberals responded by bringing 120 charges of illegal use of the fund in one riding alone.[33] Greed's other main way of undermining good government, he thought, was through politicians giving favours to companies with which they were connected. Flavelle took an austere view—fully shared by Willison—of the need for arm's-length relationships:

The men who are Members of the Government in this country should be absolutely free from any form of business identification with stocks, with bonds, with underwriting contracts, or money interest in any of the several enterprises which are more or less dependent upon Parliament for support and for help. Nor should their private investments be taken in semi-public companies whose interests may in any way be involved in the decision which Parliament will reach in relation to a rival enterprise. . . . One of the sore spots at the moment is the freedom with which Members of the Government identify themselves with all sorts of enterprises, and they are, consciously or unconsciously, bought and sold by designing persons.[34]

This was high idealism for a businessman in 1903, an uncompromising attack on conflict of interest. Although he had severed his own connection with the Grand Trunk Pacific, and the William Davies Company had stopped tendering to supply provisions to Toronto General Hospital, Flavelle had not yet realized how many complications there would be in putting what he preached into practice.

Willison and Flavelle also agreed on most specific issues. Like many Liberals after 1896, including Laurier, Willison had abandoned free-trade principles to support moderate protection for Canadian industries. Flavelle had believed in the National Policy from the day Macdonald announced it, and worked actively against all proposals for reciprocal free trade with the United States. Both were imperialists, looking forward to closer military and political ties between Britain and her Dominions, but neither wanted Canadian industries sacrificed on the altar of imperial preferential tariffs (although these could have enormously helped the export business of the William Davies Company). Flavelle defined their common position to

Wheeler-Bennett: "The loyalty of this country to the Crown will not take the form of jeopardizing the material interests of Canada for the sake of Great Britain. It has not the least intention of allowing England or any one else to manufacture goods for it, if by the placing of reasonable tariffs such service can be accomplished by itself."[35]

The most surprising idea in the first statement of principles of a newspaper owned by a wealthy businessman was that the *News* hoped to be "a good soldier in the 'irrepressible conflict' between private and public interests, and to have an honourable part in the enduring struggle between the unorganized people and the organized corporations."[36] Why should the *News* take on the corporations? Why should Flavelle want it to?

Liberals, of course, had historically hated special privilege. By the end of the nineteenth century in Canada it seemed that oppressive corporations were special privilege in new clothes: the CPR had emerged as a parallel power to the federal government *a mari usque ad mare*; railway, mining, and pulp-and-paper companies whose owners were often politically connected received a steady flow of cash and resource subsidies; utility companies with monopoly franchises had total control over the vital services of modern cities. To someone like Willison it was natural to demand that governments regulate the railways, limit the giveaways, and consider municipal ownership as an alternative to private-utility empires. He was a fairly typical North American "progressive" in seeing private greed versus public welfare as a key social issue of the new century.

Flavelle seems to have reached a similar position through his belief that public service was the only justification for private enterprise. He did not object to businessmen and companies accumulating wealth so long as they did useful things. The *News* should always be "on the side of those who were fighting in the strenuous way of progress and courageous optimism," he wrote his editor:

I would have no fear of supporting men or measures that brought to syndicates, or groups, or cliques if you like, important possibilities of wealth. It might indeed be possible to charge that certain men had received undue favours, but that would not deter me in supporting the measure. I would not be desirous of driving too hard a bargain with men who had the capacity to work out a big problem.

He immediately added a key qualification:

But I would exercise all my force, ingenuity, and determination to get in return for my money, spent with a free and generous hand, a service measured by the need of the country, not by the selfish narrowness of the corporation, or individual, and I would be absolutely ruthless in taking their property from them, even if it beggared them, if they tried any game of living at the public crib without honestly discharging the full measure of service agreed upon.[37]

Distinguishing between responsible and irresponsible business behaviour, perhaps hypercritical of much business practice because he was such a good businessman, Flavelle had little trouble living with Willison's interest in state regulation or ownership when private enterprise did not live up to its promises. This was often enough in the early years of the twentieth century for the *News* to favour public ownership of municipal utilities, the telephone network (Ma Bell came closest to nationalization in the early 1900s), the telegraph system, and a large chunk of the country's railways.

v

Railway policy dominated national politics in the *News*'s first two years. Canada had to have more railways to serve the exploding prairie wheat economy. No one wanted the CPR to be allowed to maintain its monopoly on transcontinental rail traffic, least of all impatient entrepreneurs like Flavelle for whom its periodic inability to move the grain crop efficiently proved its incompetence. The Laurier government had no special brief either for a company that had long been the Conservative engine in election campaigns. Hoping to create a countervailing political as well as transportation power, Laurier decided to support the Grand Trunk Railway's ambitions to build Canada's second transcontinental.

He announced his policy in the summer of 1903. The government would give bond guarantees to help the Grand Trunk Pacific, a Grand Trunk subsidiary, build a line from Winnipeg to the Pacific Coast. The government itself would build the eastern section from Moncton to Winnipeg and then lease it to the Grand Trunk Pacific. The National Transcontinental, as the whole line was to be called, would improve on Macdonald's old CPR deal in every way—the aid would be much less (little cash and no land grants), and the public would own the eastern section. Brushing aside objections in the cabinet (including those of his Minister of Railways, who resigned), Laurier camouflaged the weaknesses of his policy in thickets of his emotional rhetoric.

Flavelle became personally involved in transportation discussions when Robert Borden asked for his advice on the Conservative response to Laurier's policy. In several letters to Borden, Flavelle said much the same as Willison was writing in the *News*. The agreement with the Grand Trunk Pacific for the western section was excellent, and the Conservative party must not oppose it "by being dolorous and repeating the error of the small-spirited men who antagonized the Canadian Pacific Railway." The Moncton to Winnipeg section, though, would be going through unknown territory, looked as though it would be expensive, and would promptly be leased to a private company. Flavelle did not object to the money being spent — he wanted railways — but wondered if there were better ways to spend it.

The eastern division would cost $75 million he estimated. At the current market price of CPR stock, $75 million would purchase a 75-per-cent interest in the CPR. " 'If I were King,' " Flavelle wrote Borden, "I would buy control CPR stock (but not operate now) and hold it as a magnificent asset for the country, both in its earning power and its relation for ever in this country to its transportation problems." If that seemed too strong, he would extend the government-owned Intercolonial Railway from Quebec City to the Great Lakes to provide a publicly-owned trunk line that would make the eastern section of the National Transcontinental unnecessary. Above all, he wrote, the party must adopt a policy "which whether accepted by Parliament or not tells the country in the coming elections that the Conservative Party are equal to the country's hope, courage and requirements, the requirements as seen by men with 'vision.' "[38]

Mackenzie and Mann's Canadian Northern Railway, backed by Bank of Commerce funds, ran across all the railway discussions. They controlled a thousand miles of track in the West and had made clear their intention of eventually going transcontinental. When the Grand Trunk Pacific was being planned, with Cox and Flavelle to be on the Board of Directors, the group at the Commerce had tried to engineer a merger with the Canadian Northern to avoid unnecessary duplication of lines. Thinking Mackenzie and Mann were building too slowly, and apparently placing a low dollar value on their system, Flavelle had urged Walker to pressure Mackenzie into selling and urged Cox to pressure Hays of the Grand Trunk into buying. Pressure was exerted, but discussions broke down on Mackenzie's and Hays's wildly conflicting estimates of the worth of each other's properties. Flavelle seems to have agreed that Mackenzie expected far too much,[39] and was not particularly concerned that Mackenzie and Mann were left out of the National Transcontinental deal. "My respect for Mr. Mackenzie's ability increases," he wrote Willison. "My confidence in him, however, as a type of man to conduct a great railway system after construction is finished, grows less. He is hard, mean, and selfish. His only conception in relation to a transaction seems to be what he can get out of it for himself, and he is not the type of man to whom the transportation interests of a community can be safely committed." He urged Borden to take no account of the Canadian Northern, "having regard to the well known ability of these particular Canadian Northern gentlemen to take care of themselves." He thought they would never finish their line past Edmonton.[40]

Borden's policy reflected Flavelle's advice. He did not particularly oppose the idea of the Grand Trunk Pacific. His alternative in the East was extension of the Intercolonial to the Great Lakes, combined with nationalization of the North Bay—Fort William section of the CPR as a national highway to be used by all systems. Flavelle, Willison, and the News were pleased with Borden's position, and also supported his revised plan of a completely government-owned transcontinental. His correspondence and meetings with Borden left Flavelle impressed with the leader as "a highminded, scholarly gentleman, sane and rational in all his views and public utterances."[41] In the 1904 federal election, however, the News maintained its independence, believing that neither party's railway policy would be very harmful.

Flavelle's notion of having the government buy control of the CPR would have changed the future of Canadian transportation had it been taken seriously. On the other hand, he utterly misjudged the future of the Canadian Northern Railway. When the thought did cross his mind that Mackenzie and Mann might press on to create a third transcontinental line, he was so sure of the country's future progress that, like Laurier, he could not conceive of its railways being overbuilt. Like almost all of his associates, and like Laurier, he was tragically wrong. Thirty years later, when most of the other principals were dead, Flavelle would still be trying to untangle the mess they had all created.

VI

There was a more immediate mess to be cleaned up in Ontario. Most of the scandals of the 1890s had centred on Ottawa or Quebec City. But since the 1898 Ontario election there had been repeated exposures of corruption and raw patronage as the Ontario Liberals, lost without Oliver Mowat, struggled to stay in office. In the aftermath of the hard-fought 1902 election it was widely believed that the Ross government ran a tight, unprincipled political "machine," similar to the "machines" American muckrakers were writing about in their cities. Thoughtful outsiders were appalled at how partisanship seemed to blind citizens to the machinations of corruptionists. Flavelle had founded the new *News* precisely to mobilize high-minded "independent" opinion against what he called "the curse of political trickery & trimming."[42]

Two months after Flavelle and Willison took over the *News* they were handed an issue tailored to their prejudices. The sometimes Conservative MLA for Manitoulin, R. R. Gamey, stunned the legislature by announcing that his switch to the Liberals two months earlier had been in return for a bribe of two thousand dollars, the deal arranged by Provincial Secretary J. R. Stratton. Gamey had gone along with it solely to get the goods on the Liberals. The "Gamey Affair" was Ontario's most sensational scandal since Confederation.

Willison had defended the Ross government with gathering unease at the *Globe*, but he was, after all, a lifelong Liberal. When the Gamey case broke, Willison and Flavelle "reached the common judgment that he [Willison] should declare himself before the matter was discussed with me, so . . . it could not be said that he was influenced by my Conservative tendencies." Willison hardly needed influencing, for he immediately decided that the affair was "A SHAMEFUL STORY," Stratton was guilty, and the Ross government beyond redemption. He said so in the *News* without counting the cost in broken Liberal friendships.[43]

Not surprised at his editor's indignation—"I have felt from the first that there could be no peace between you [and the Liberals] as long as crookedness was in evidence" —Flavelle had to urge Willison to temper his anger with fairness. Both of them actually prejudged the case. When a Royal Commission exonerated Stratton (Gamey had played a devious game, lied to almost everyone, and temporarily fled to Buffalo in the middle of the investigation), they ignored its findings. The *News* fought on against Ontario's "carnival of corruption."[44] A letter accusing his paper of unfounded bias prompted Flavelle's clearest statement of what he was trying to do with the *News*:

If the *News* as owned and edited is not ideal in its relations so as to make it absolutely independent of every sort or kind of influence except that which is defined by the capacity, judgment, honesty, and knowledge of the Managing Editor, then no paper in the history of the world ever can or will be independent.

In the great fight of right against wrong, of decency against indecency, there is no one straight and narrow path which alone has all virtue. Thank God there is room enough for every honest man according to his own light to participate in the struggle in his own way. The *News* exists to be in this fight. It will try to fight with vigor and honesty. It will neither ask for nor grant favors. It will claim no monopoly of sense, highmindedness or virtue; but, please God, it will expose political rascality wherever found and will excuse it by no technical or academic reasoning.[45]

The Ross government had more serious problems than some of its supporters' enthusiasm for handing out bribes. Over the years the Ontario Liberals had lost touch with the growing urban centres in the province. Their policies reflected an agrarian bias towards small government, plus, perhaps, obsolete memories of the need for pennypinching in the 1890s. Ross hesitated to aid the University of Toronto, for example, because rural taxpayers resented paying for the education of middle- and upper-class city dwellers. He also resisted pressure welling up from the municipalities for a government role in the transmission of electricity from Niagara Falls so that manufacturers throughout the province could get cheap electrical power.

Flavelle and his friends were typical of the new generation of progressive men of affairs who had emerged from the hard times of the 1890s. They knew government revenues were increasing; they had no fear of government spending for good causes like universities or hospitals, or of honest, efficient government involvement in industrial development. The Conservative leader, J. P. Whitney, attracted them as a man who would clean up corruption in Ontario, and then work actively to advance the educational and economic interests of the province. As others have noted, Whitney and his supporters were a new breed of *progressive* Conservatives.[46]

The Ross government's record was never as bad as its opponents charged. It did respond to pressures to begin public involvement in hydro-electric development. By 1902 it was freeing money for new buildings at the university and beginning to reform the administration of the institution. The Liberal "machine" was probably not as black as the Opposition painted it; the Opposition was not as white as it painted itself.

The *News* was suitably grateful for evidence of Liberal enlightenment.

But the record of corruption was writ larger after every by-election — by such incidents as the cruise of the steamer *Minnie M* bringing a gang of Americans paid to impersonate Liberal voters across Lake Superior (with a steamer full of Conservative scrutineers in hot pursuit). Whatever Ross did, Flavelle, Willison, and the *News* were determined that good government and political purity should triumph in Ontario. Even repentant sinners should be punished as a deterrent.

Willison's editorials in the *News* were judged a major factor in shifting the independent vote to Whitney in the January 1905 election.[47] The Conservatives won 69 seats in the legislature to the Liberals' 29 and became the dominant party in the province for generations. Progressive Conservatism had come to Ontario.

CHAPTER SEVEN

"DOING ALL THE GOOD HE CAN"

Flavelle had ready access to the new premier. Whitney favoured the hospital project and, after a Royal Commission investigation, reform of the University of Toronto. Wanting him to go ahead with a building programme for the campus, including the new hospital, Flavelle suggested practical reasons for not postponing everything until the Royal Commission had reported:

To have a Convocation Hall, a new Physics Building, a new Museum, four Residence houses for men, an addition to the Residence for women, and a great Hospital building all under construction at the one time as a result of the decision of your Government upon University matters at the first meeting of the Legislature after your Government was formed, is so striking a program that I cannot but think . . . you will show political sagacity which will be well rewarded. . . . The business judgment of your Government will show in such excellent form that you will add to the confusion of your earlier critics who stated there would be lack of business capacity in your administration.[1]

Whitney agreed. In the first session of the new legislature he gave the university everything Flavelle suggested plus a grant of $300,000 towards the new hospital ($50,000 of which would come from the university's endowment as its contribution). In his major speech on the university he relied heavily on Flavelle's letter outlining the projects—omitting, of course, the political calculations.[2] The new government's support for his hospital plan and university reform launched Flavelle on two of the busiest years of his life.

I

National Trust's real-estate experts were already studying possible locations for the new hospital. A large property fronting on Wellesley and Church was one possibility, Goldwin Smith's "Grange" and its park at Dundas and Beverley streets another. But Flavelle was most taken with the thought of snuggling the hospital up to both the legislature and the university. "There is an appeal to the imagination in the corner of the [University] Avenue and College Street which perhaps has no counterpart anywhere else in the city," he wrote Walker. It would be a large and very expensive site because eight acres of slum houses would have to be expropriated and demolished; but, after all, "We are planning for a permanent home of the one commanding hospital in the City of Toronto, probably for all time to come, and I do not believe that eight acres will contain a foot too much property for the true scale of the transaction, and for the ultimate good of the work being performed."[3]

After delicate negotiations with city council—he wanted money granted without crippling conditions and also without a ratepayers' vote in which the jealousies of rival doctors and hospitals might come into play—Flavelle got his request for a $200,000 grant toward the new hospital passed in July 1905. He had promises of $500,000 from governments, $100,000 from Cawthra Mulock, and another $100,000 from the estate of two philanthropic sisters. He needed a further $600,000 or more from private sources, and set out immediately to raise it.

Torontonians had never been asked for so much money. "We have as yet only a moderate amount of wealth available for so heavy an enterprise," Flavelle worried. The general public, he thought, would give about $100,000, but only if prominent businessmen had already shown their support. He singled out five key men—George Cox, Timothy Eaton, Chester Massey as trustee of Hart Massey's estate, E. B. Osler (the millionaire stockbroker in the Osler family), and William Mackenzie—hoping to get $50,000 to $75,000 from each. He planned to name sections or wings of the hospital after each large donor to establish a basis for similar future gifts.[4]

Cox, whom Flavelle thought might concentrate his givings on Grace Hospital because he was a member of its board, pledged $100,000 for a wing in memory of his late wife. The Masseys also gave $100,000 to build a Hart Massey memorial wing. Flavelle had become a friend of Timothy Eaton's over the years; when he put the scheme to Eaton, asking for $50,000, the response was simply, " 'Do you mean to do it well, Joseph?'—I said we did and he replied, 'I will give you the $50,000.' " Osler, already connected with Sick Children's and Toronto Western Hospital, promised $25,000. With Walker's help Flavelle arranged an interview with Mackenzie, letting the hospital's good take precedence over his personal feelings. Characteristically, Mackenzie put him off, but promised a decision in the near future.[5]

His own contribution was $25,000. E. R. Wood, also a trustee of Grace Hospital, surprised him with $25,000. The same amount was pledged from the estate of George Gooderham. Walker, Lash, and Peter Larkin each added $10,000. Much of the money was pledged at a special meeting Walker arranged, enabling the hospital board to proclaim that more than a quarter of a million dollars had been raised in two and a half hours. This set off the appeal to the general public, managed by a Citizens' Committee chaired by Will Rundle of National Trust. Rundle exceeded his $100,000 target by more than 20 per cent. National Trust's $5,000 was the largest of several corporate donations; most companies, including Simpson's and the Davies Company, encouraged their officers to contribute as individuals. Flavelle had hoped for $50,000 from the Toronto banks, but got almost nothing. Also noticeably missing were significant donations from Toronto's doctors. Flavelle had hoped the medical faculty of the university alone could raise $50,000. They raised very little.[6]

The campaign fell short by almost exactly the contribution Flavelle expected from Mackenzie. Assuming Mackenzie and perhaps others would contribute later, Flavelle decided he had enough money to build a new hospital. The work had been "more wearing than I have ever confessed to myself," he wrote Clara in the summer of 1905 while she was holidaying at Sturgeon Point, "but if out of it all comes a great institution that will mean permanent and lasting betterment I will feel that a great privilege has been extended to me."[7]

II

He also had privileges of a sort in all of Toronto's bars. In early April, 1905, Whitney appointed Flavelle to the Board of License Commissioners for Toronto along with John A. Murray, a retired carpet manufacturer, and Lt.-Col. John I. Davidson, a wholesale grocer and municipal reformer. Serving a year's term without pay, the commissioners supervised the granting and renewal of all liquor licences in the city and the inspectors who enforced the liquor laws. Flavelle had been a leading Methodist supporter of Whitney's drink policy, standing for restriction of licences and "the fearless administration of the law" rather than total prohibition. The temperance people were pleased with his appointment and the public generally saw the new board as an example of the Whitney government's high-mindedness. These were not run-of-the-mill patronage appointees, who would bask in their status and do nothing. Arming themselves with Whitney's personal assurance of support plus a written statement from the Provincial Secretary endorsing "a fair, fearless and non-partisan administration of the License Act," the new commissioners proved unusually earnest by actually inspecting the drinking places under their jurisdiction.[8]

All of them were supposed to be hotels. Many were nothing more than saloons disguised as hotels, providing no lodgings or meals, located nowhere near travel routes. The Caerhowell Hotel near Queen's Park catered to university students and MLA's. Flavelle found it "wholly bad" for students and politicians alike. One Saturday afternoon he and Colonel Davidson inspected another hotel at the corner of Bathurst and Bloor: "We found the bar literally crowded with men, many of them in almost every state of drunkenness. We found the halls leading from the bar to the drinking rooms, the drinking rooms themselves, and the private office of the proprietor, all filled with men drinking, many of whom were in the stages of drunkenness. . . . I have never at any time seen such concentration of wretched drunkenness as in this hotel that afternoon." Residents of the area complained bitterly "as to the cruel manner in which sensitive women were treated by these blackguards, who, after drinking, hung around the corner."

Downtown drinking places were not rowdy; instead they had become too fashionable. The commissioners received disturbing evidence about Toronto's most famous restaurant, McConkey's:

. . . as to the demoralization of young women, married and unmarried. . . . Young girls have frequently been brought home in carriages intoxicated, to the distress and heart-breaking trouble of the parents. In one case a daughter of one of the most respected citizens of Toronto was brought home in a cab and the driver carried her into the house and upstairs without the knowledge of her parents, he having been paid liberally to arrange with the servants to bring the young girl in quietly. . . . With the increasing wealth which has come to many homes, and the increasing desire to be a bit smart on the part of many young girls whose heads have been turned,

McConkey's has grown into a place where they can play the smart and defy ordinary conventionalities.[9]

At the end of April the commissioners released a sensational statement describing the fraudulent licensing system, the difficulty their inspectors had getting into drinking spots after hours (while drinkers scrambled out the back way), the striking number of women "served through side-door entrances," and the keepers' refusal to stop serving drunks. The law would be enforced, they announced. Two licences were cancelled, three businesses ordered to be sold, and some forty "hotels" given notice to become real hotels in the next twelve months or lose their licences. According to Walker, Flavelle was "much troubled in mind" about licensing in Toronto. After doing his bacon business in England that summer he made a special study of English pubs, urged on by the Governor General, Earl Grey, who bombarded him with reports and advice on the drink question.[10]

III

Demoralization at the University of Toronto nearly matched that at the corner of Bathurst and Bloor. In 1904 and 1905 the sorry state of education in Queen's Park became standard editorial fare. The *Globe*, for example, published a series of editorials attacking the "deadwood," "fossilism," "indolence," and "inefficiency" of the faculty. When Loudon complained to the editor, he was presented with specific examples of incompetence, freeloading, and drunkenness. He was able to disprove most of the charges, but the papers continued their blanket condemnations. *Saturday Night* was the university's most vitriolic critic: "With few exceptions they [the faculty] are regarded as mediocrities, a bunch of cheap men whose manners, methods, and appearance would hardly pass the inspection of a High School Board in a country village. . . . You would find more dignified and better groomed men, with better carriage and deportment and more intellectual faces amongst the same number of policemen or firemen than you would amongst the professors and fellows and tutors who run the educational mill up in the Park.[11]

The students were said to be ready to strike as they had in '95 except for their fear of reprisals. One student finally did speak out in *Saturday Night*, making sensational charges implicating Loudon of favouritism in awarding scholarships. Accuser and accused were represented by counsel at hearings of a Senate committee investigating the charges, and through March, 1905, Torontonians were spectators at an item-by-item display of the university's dirty linen. The committee exonerated Loudon, but not without implying that the administration of the university was a mess. Loudon thought the affair had been orchestrated by the registrar, James Brebner, who in turn refused to administer the final exams that year under Loudon's direction. By June the president of the University of Toronto was pleading with the Premier of Ontario to fire the registrar. As ever, of course, the exams went on.[12]

Whitney appointed the long-awaited Royal Commission to inquire into the affairs of the university in early October. Its members were Goldwin Smith, who had sat on the Royal Commission that reformed Oxford fifty-six years earlier; Sir William Meredith, chancellor of the university and former Ontario Conservative leader; Rev. H. J. Cody, an outstanding young Anglican preacher and scholar; Rev. D. Bruce Macdonald, a Toronto graduate and principal of St. Andrew's College for boys; A. H. U. Colquhoun, news editor of the *News*, to serve as secretary; Byron Walker; and J. W. Flavelle. Hoping that Goldwin Smith would consent to serve, Whitney delayed naming a chairman.

The Rev. M. L. Pearson of Berkeley Street Methodist Church publicly criticized the selection of only one Methodist layman — Flavelle — for the commission, when both the Anglicans and the Presbyterians were represented by a layman and a minister. The next day, Smith having declined to serve, Whitney announced that Flavelle would be chairman. He denied that religion had anything to do with his choice of commissioners or of the chairman. Whitney may have had more confidence in Flavelle, a supporter whose ideas and ability he knew fairly well, than in several of the other commissioners, but his choice did effectively cut off Methodist complaints about discrimination against their denomination.[13] The appointments were generally well received and the commission settled down to work.

On November 28 Flavelle, Davidson, and Murray suddenly resigned as License Commissioners for Toronto, charging that the Whitney government had made it impossible to carry on their duties. The Provincial Secretary had fired their hard-working, cooperative staff of inspectors simply because they were Liberal appointees; the replacements, Conservatives all, were apparently chosen by a local MLA, Dr. Beattie Nesbitt. The commissioners and the Liberal press interpreted the action as an attempt to undermine their tough-minded, non-partisan enforcement of the Act, serving the interests of party patronage, or the hotelkeepers, or, most likely, both. The resignation caused a storm of press criticism of the Whitney government for what the *Telegram* described as "striking the flag to the spoilsmen."

It was one of the worst setbacks in Whitney's first year in office (and does seem to have been caused by a backbenchers' revolt against the Premier's attempt to limit traditional patronage). Flavelle nearly made the situation worse by resigning from the University Royal Commission. In a ninety-minute interview Whitney convinced Flavelle it was his duty to stay on the commission. The Premier was not pleased by the incident, believing it had occurred only because the government had lifted Flavelle "up so high that the lighter atmosphere may possibly have affected him." The saloon sensation soon died down and the university commissioners carried on with their work.[14]

They met more than seventy times at Goldwin Smith's Grange during the winter of 1905–6, canvassed other universities on their systems of government and financing, visited leading American universities (Flavelle went to Harvard, Yale, and Princeton), and received deputations and briefs from dozens of interested university people and outsiders. With practically unlimited terms of reference, they carried out the most thorough investigation the university had known, though tactfully avoiding a direct inquiry into the most recent incidents and conflicts of personalities.

There was confusion about the main purpose of a university in the early 1900s because of public suspicion that the traditional classical arts curriculum was impractical and irrelevant. Why teach students Greek and Latin and philosophy, give them a BA and inflated notions of their self-importance, and then turn them out with no visible skills to earn their living? Why not instead emphasize the sciences and applied sciences, practical subjects which would equip graduates to take a useful place in the province's economic life? A developing country needed engineers, foresters, agricultural experts, and skilled business leaders more than it needed theologians, classicists, or Shakespearians. The Ontario legislature had been reflecting this sense of priorities by channelling support to the practical sciences, and many felt the pendulum should swing still further. Perhaps it would if the legislature continued to call the tune in university affairs.

The common sense of democracy seemed to suggest that the provincial government should continue to keep a firm hand on the university. It was the state institution, owned and largely paid for by the state; surely the people's elected representatives should continue to control the spending of their money. On the other hand, no one thought the legislature had done a very good job with the provincial university, and many believed that elected politicians were incompetent or unwilling to administer a modern educational institution efficiently or disinterestedly. Political control of appointments seemed to breed patronage and professorial incompetence; the need to come to the legislature for annual subsidies meant perpetual austerity and complete inability to plan for the long term. Progressive educators and businessmen wanted the university run by competent administrators whose only interest would be in educational excellence. Legislatures, they thought, were no more competent to direct the day-to-day affairs of universities than they were to run railroads, hydro-electric companies, or any other complex organizations. They should delegate their authority over university education to an appointed body of experts, just as they were delegating their responsibility for other complex functions, such as the regulation of railways and the supervision of municipal bond issues, to appointed commissions.

Because everyone felt that press coverage of the university's disputes had hurt the institution all the Royal Commission's meetings were private. But, in one last act of spectacular yellow journalism, two *Toronto World* reporters stole a draft of the commission's report from a messenger boy. On March 12 the *World* scooped the province on the future of its university. Those who read beyond the follow-up stories of the reporters' flight to Buffalo, their arrest and indictment on charges of theft, and their lawyers' defence that the report was worth only the paper it was printed on (i.e. less than ten dollars) would have noticed that the draft recommendations were well received as a sensible solution to the university's problems.[15]

The final report, released early in April, was a fine statement of progressive views on the future of the university. The commissioners agreed that it had to "minister, in ways hitherto deemed to lie beyond its domain, to the practical as well as to the intellectual and moral needs of the country," going so far as to assign it a role in training Canada's sons to become her "captains of industry." The report called for a strengthening of all the practical disciplines, expansion into technical education, forestry, and household science, and more emphasis on practical research. The college system was to be preserved, however, not only for the colleges' contribution to religious and moral education, but to "maintain the importance of liberal culture in the face of commercial and industrial development, and the growth of scientific activity." The commissioners found it natural that most of the recent subsidies had gone into practical subjects, but warned against undue practical emphasis. Their ideal University of Toronto combined culture and science, "under the same academic roof, uniting them as far as possible, yet leaving each in its way untrammelled by the union."

The report affirmed the legislature's responsibility for the "efficient management and support" of the provincial university. But everywhere else in North America and Great Britain the state had delegated its responsibility to trustees or agents, so there was no hesitation in condemning Ontario's unique non-system. "To administer the affairs of a State university by a political government, occupied with different matters, constantly changing its party character, and gifted with no special talent for the management of universities, has not commended itself to a practical and progressive people. We see no ground for the belief that this plan of direct State control, rejected abroad and in ill-repute at home, can be made a success in this Province." Criticizing the divided control within the university, the "comparative impotence" of the president, and the way the university had become "the sport of acrimonious party disputes," the commissioners called for a strong central authority which would devote itself "without ulterior interests and motives to the single purpose entrusted to it."

The Ontario legislature, they urged, should follow the American practice of appointing a Board of Governors and making it responsible for the management of the university's money and properties as well as appointments. A suggestion that alumni elect some of the members of the board was rejected as weakening full state control. Academic affairs would remain in the hands of the Senate. The president would be appointed by and responsible to the Board of Governors, but would have much more authority, including the sole right of recommending appointments and dismissals; generally he would give to the university administration "that directing executive quality which in every department of effort in the modern world is regarded as indispensable."

Instead of directly criticizing past provincial financial support, the commissioners simply listed the university's future needs and compared its likely income with that available to American state universities, challenging Ontario to be as generous as Nebraska, Iowa, and Kansas, let alone Michigan, Wisconsin, or California. To fix income on a definite basis they recommended a statutory grant to the university of a percentage of the revenue from succession duties, a figure almost certain to rise as the province grew wealthier. They also thought the university should be provided with a new endowment of at least one million acres of land in Northern Ontario. Running through the report was an unstated assumption that Toronto was to be Ontario's one state university (not a word was said about Queen's or Western), and an explicit hope that it would soon become a great national institution.[16]

There was no significant press or public criticism of the recommendations. Whitney had been kept informed of the direction of the commissioners' work; they, in turn, had been confident enough of his government's approval to include a detailed draft of a new University Act in their report. Less than a month after the commission reported, Whitney introduced legislation following their draft in almost every particular (the land-grant endowment was rejected). It was given final reading on May 11, passed without opposition, and came into effect on June 15. Few Royal Commission reports in Canadian history have been adopted so quickly and completely.

Flavelle had privately made clear to Whitney his belief that the beginning of the new era at Varsity should be symbolized by the retirement of the old president. At Flavelle's instigation Whitney met with Loudon and apparently suggested that Loudon announce his intention of resigning as soon as a new president was chosen. He did so, but negotiations with the new Board of Governors on the terms of his lame-duck tenure broke down when he insisted that Brebner, the registrar, must go. When the board refused to fire Brebner, Loudon's presidency ended in character, with his abrupt resignation and long letters of recrimination. Principal Hutton of University College became acting president while the board searched for a new man to lead the university.[17]

There were few regrets at Loudon's departure. On the whole the friends of the university were delighted with a job well done, a laying of the foundation for a potentially great institution.

Flavelle was appointed to the new Board of Governors. The university decided to recognize his work on the Royal Commission by making him an Honorary Doctor of Law. Believing he did not deserve any kind of university degree, critical of businessmen who took such honours, he considered declining the award. Burwash and Goldwin Smith convinced him that it would be discourteous to the university and to the other commissioners, all of whom were being given degrees. At spring convocation, 1906, Joe Flavelle became J. W. Flavelle, LL D. He seldom used the title.[18]

IV

University affairs had gone smoothly compared to the problems Flavelle was having with the hospital. That winter he had brought the question of staff organization at the old hospital to a head when he learned that a poor old lady had fallen in her room and suffered for weeks with a broken thigh before her doctor examined her; another doctor had not given proper attention to one of Holwood's servants, who died in hospital. As Chairman of the Board, Flavelle insisted on dismissing both doctors from the staff. "There was a tremendous row," he recalled. Unfortunately no Minutes survive of the special board meeting which discussed the cases. Two days later, however, the board established committees to plan the most efficient organization for an up-to-date hospital.[19]

Getting the legislation passed to make possible the building of an up-to-date hospital proved even more difficult in the spring of 1906. Now that the money had been raised, a new hospital Trust had to be created; the old trustees were to give way to a board with a broader membership of provincial, municipal, university, and subscribers' appointees.

Flavelle's plan to make Toronto General an exclusive teaching hospital for the university met with strong objections from city councillors, who thought patients should be free to choose their private physicians, and from private physicians in the city, who agreed. On their part, the staff of the Faculty of Medicine wanted the hospital to contain nothing but free public wards controlled by them. "I cannot remember ever having had such a difficult lot to fight for," Flavelle wrote of the university doctors. "They have few friends, they have many enemies, and they are self-satisfied, or at least the reputed clique who lead them are." There were many rounds of hearings, negotiations, threats, and counter-threats. "I will be much gratified when the long struggle is over and the hospital can go on trying to administer its affairs independent of councils, and groups of doctors and newspaper writers who do not know, and of legislators," Flavelle wrote wearily to Willison.[20]

The struggle ended in June, after compromises had been made to mollify private practitioners without crippling the hospital's teaching functions. National Trust was already at work on expropriation proceedings for the new site. The new Board of Trustees was appointed in July. Flavelle was immediately elected chairman.

V

In the meantime at the *News*, Willison had barely recovered from the good government fight against the Ontario Liberals when he threw himself into a crusade against the federal Liberal government. In the spring of 1905 Laurier's draft legislation establishing Alberta and Saskatchewan as provinces contained clauses apparently restoring Roman Catholics' right to separate schools. There had been no more sensitive issue since Confederation than the role of religion in schools, and Laurier's Autonomy Bills instantly revived deep Protestant hostility to what seemed to be aggressive Catholic ambitions to subvert the ideal of public education. Clifford Sifton, Laurier's Western chieftain, resigned from the cabinet in protest. Many Protestants thought the Catholic Laurier was acting on orders from his church.

Catholic "aggression" was the one issue that could excite Willison and Flavelle more than political corruption. The *News* savagely attacked the Autonomy Bills as a cleric-inspired attempt to fetter Western Canadians with the chains of sectarian education. For two months it carried a banner across its front page: "A FREE WEST, A COMMON SCHOOL, PROVINCIAL RIGHTS, AND RELIGIOUS EQUALITY." When Laurier retreated, Willison still interpreted the watered-down legislation as a surrender to Catholicism. After it was passed he changed his banner to read: "A FETTERED WEST, A DUAL SCHOOL SYSTEM, FEDERAL USURPATION, AND DENOMINATIONAL ASCENDENCY." Willison's twenty-year friendship with Laurier came to an end; he never again supported the Liberal party either federally or provincially. On issues of high politics the *News* became an independent paper in name only.[21]

Many of Willison's friends, including some on the *News*'s staff, thought he had lost all perspective on the autonomy question in refusing to see that Laurier had actually been defeated. His violent continuing attacks on Laurier and the federal Liberals were a mockery of the paper's self-proclaimed high-minded sobriety, were indeed hard to distinguish from sensational yellow journalism. A main reason why Willison was not brought back to reality was that Flavelle exactly shared his opinions on the schools question. In the midst of the fight he defined his position to Borden: "To stand by passively, or to express one's opinion under one's breath at a time when a Church, arrogant with the sense of its power, and operating through a Prime Minister her own son, seeks—and unfortunately seeks successfully—

to lay claim for herself upon the West in opposition to the whole spirit of a free people, is so gross a thing that, much as I dislike discord, much as I dislike race and sectarian agitation, I would set the country aflame, if I could, to render this thing impossible." No other issue so clearly aroused his old Methodist distrust of popery, shattering his pretensions to tolerance.[22]

After the autonomy controversy the *News* seldom varied from the Conservative political line. But Flavelle's friends found its views on some economic questions still disconcerting. Willison had continued his attacks on William Mackenzie's Toronto Railway Company and finally in December 1906 began naming Mackenzie himself as the cause of the problem, calling for his resignation as president of the company. "He is an arrogant, tyrannical man," Willison wrote in a typical editorial, "who permits neither advice nor criticism, nor any questioning of his peculiar system of management, that is really not a system but a disjointed, spasmodic and intermittent jumble."[23]

Mackenzie was furious at the attacks. He and his companies did a tremendous volume of business with the Bank of Commerce and National Trust. A director of the one company, president of the other, Flavelle was using his newspaper to attack the firms' best customer! Alarmed at the situation, Lash, Walker, and E. R. Wood apparently delegated W. T. White to persuade Flavelle to curb his editor. They probably thought Willison had just gone off half-cocked and a word from his owner would suffice. In fact Flavelle himself was "immediately and directly responsible" for the attacks on Mackenzie:

I intimated to Mr. Willison that I could see no way out of the present unfortunate Street Railway situation while Mr. Mackenzie retained his position as President of the Company. I explained that I believed the character of his administration meant inefficiency in the service of the Street Railway Company, and would lead to the continuance of the unsatisfactory condition of affairs, which in my judgment has become scandalous. For these reasons I thought the time had come when Mr. McKenzie [*sic*] should be named as being directly and personally responsible for a condition of affairs which imposed a grievous burden upon thousands of working people daily. . . .

When there is a dogged and unreasoning retention of a position by Mr. Mackenzie (or any one else) in which he uses his power, to check, stop, or render impossible, improvements greatly needed in the public interest, I will allow no admiration of him, and no association that I have to interfere with the free, and if necessary personal, criticism in the *News* of Mr. Mackenzie, in the particular position in which the offence has been identified.

This was set out in a blistering six-page letter to Lash, copy to Walker. Flavelle then laid the whole situation earnestly before his friends:

My connection with the NEWS may be pedantic, may not carry the judgment of many of my friends—indeed it does not. I may have had when it was established, and I may still hold, absurd views of the importance of the work it may accomplish, and be foolishly vain in what I think it may do in the public interest. Yet it still remains true that I undertook the enterprise seriously and deliberately, have assumed a financial burden almost too heavy to bear, and continue to assume it, all that the Editor of the NEWS should be enabled to say, without fear or favour, what he thought ought to be said about public men and public affairs, as he might judge necessary in the public interest. . . .

I have no desire to retain the Presidency of the National Trust Company, or Directorship in the Canadian Bank of Commerce, if by reason of my identification with the NEWS, and general responsibility for its utterances, I bring embarrassment to the Officers of the Trust Company or the Bank, or injuriously affect the interests of the Shareholders of either institution. . . .

He invited Lash and White to meet with him to discuss whether it was necessary for him to resign. The day after he wrote the letter his newspaper referred to Mackenzie as "imperious," "arrogant," "bullying," and "callous." The *News* was not silenced. Flavelle did not resign. The group at the Commerce and the Trust Company decided they could somehow live with an associate a friend once characterized as "troubled by ideals."[24]

The *News* was also troubled by deficits. When he came into the venture Flavelle was prepared to lose money in a good cause, but nothing like the $50,000 a year he found himself contributing to the paper's "Betterment" account. The general problem was his attempt to keep an elite evening newspaper afloat at a time when popular appeal was becoming necessary to attract advertising revenue to meet mounting wage and paper costs. Understanding this, John Ross Robertson of the *Telegram* and Joe Atkinson of the *Star* published lively papers featuring big headlines, heavy concentration on Toronto news, sensationalism, and easy-to-digest editorials. By comparison, the *News* was conservative, dull, and preachy.

Flavelle and Willison did try to modernize the *News* to keep up in the circulation race, and were able to match their competitors at about 35,000 daily sales. Too much of the circulation was outside Toronto, though, which did not make the paper attractive for Toronto advertisers—so its advertising revenue fell far behind its competitors. Flavelle seems to have left management in the hands of Willison and the business manager, neither of whom was particularly competent. His own business judgment was coloured by the way his high-cost pork-packing operation catered to a premium market. He appears to have believed that the *News*, like the Davies Company, could absorb higher costs than its competitors because it would be an elite newspaper. Willison's editorials, unlike Davies bacon, did not convince either readers or advertisers to pay premium prices for the *News*. [25]

In 1906 Flavelle was still answering critics of the *News* by arguing that "a newspaper proprietor has some other duty to the public than to make money, and some other responsibility to society than seeking to inflame prejudice and passion." [26] By the end of 1907, though, Flavelle may have felt finally beaten by the inflamers of prejudice and passion. The issue of hydro-electric development in Ontario, simmering for years, had finally come to a boil in Toronto. The *News* had not only been unable to influence opinion on the question, but had taken an editorial line so paralleling Flavelle's apparent financial interest that it had seriously damaged its reputation for independence.

The *News* supported the general idea of state control of Ontario's electric future. Niagara's power was too important to the economic future of the province to be monopolized by private companies. Willison and the *News* had favoured government regulation of rates as a minimal control and complete public ownership as the ideal solution. The key private companies planning to bring power to Toronto and distribute it there were the Electrical Development Company and the Toronto Electric Light Company, both controlled by William Mackenzie, Frederic Nicholls, and Henry Pellatt. This group was so adept at finding its way round and through agreements with governments, Flavelle advised Whitney in 1905, that only public ownership could prevent them from subverting mere rate control. He urged the Premier to seize the strategic moment and take over the whole power development at Niagara Falls "because of the interests of generations yet unborn, because of enterprises yet to be conceived, and of power demands yet unthought of." [27]

The catch was that Flavelle wanted Whitney to buy out or expropriate the private companies, paying them a fair return on the assets they had created. Over the years a complex series of negotiations between the private power interests, Whitney, and Adam Beck's Hydro-Electric Power Commission (the forerunner of Ontario Hydro) floundered on disagreements over the value of the private companies. In Toronto the city decided that the asking price for the Toronto Electric Light company was exorbitant; better to build its own distribution plant, buy power from Beck's HEPC, and drive the private companies into the ground with superior service and lower rates.

The issue had wider significance, for the Toronto situation would make or break the HEPC and the public power movement in the whole province. The fate of the private companies, the Electrical Development Company as well as the Toronto Electric Light company, also seemed to rest in the balance. In the January 1, 1908, municipal election Toronto's ratepayers were to vote on a by-law authorizing the public facility.

Wanting to see the private companies bought out, Flavelle and Willison balked at the idea of public ownership in competition with private enterprise. It would mean senseless duplication of facilities and inherently unfair competition because the public enterprises had the backing of the provincial treasury. The private companies would almost certainly go under. While Mackenzie, Pellatt, Nicholls, *et al.*, were skilled enough at looking out for themselves, most of their companies' bonds had been taken by British investors on good faith in the government of Ontario. This government had encouraged them to risk their money, apparently promised that it would not compete with these enterprises, and now seemed to be doing its best to destroy their investment. What would the effects of this kind of behaviour be on investors' confidence in Ontario?

So, although Flavelle, Willison, and the *News* wanted public power for Ontario, they found themselves backed into the private power camp on the question of how to go about achieving public ownership. As the issue polarized, they endorsed the private companies' charges that Ontario's Conservative Premier, J. P. Whitney, was sanctioning a quasi-socialist attack on innocent investors, destroying Ontario's standing on world money markets. The policy of building a competing distribution plant in Toronto, the *News* charged in the fight against the by-law, was "neither British, honourable, nor decent." It was a policy unworthy of a South American republic, and communities treating investors this way were sinking "to the level of outlaw states." Flavelle again tried to moderate Willison's passion, urging him to conduct a campaign marked by "character and singleness of purpose." But he shared the belief that the Whitney government was unjustly and stupidly attacking British investors in Canada.

The public power advocates tarred all their opponents as self-interested buccaneers. By 1907 there was no middle ground between public power and the public interest on one side and private power and capitalist self-interest on the other. Exasperated at the failure of his own long-suffering attempts at compromise, Whitney came to share their view, and thought the *News*'s editorials were protecting "the pocket of Mr. Flavelle." Willison, it seemed, had truly been bought.[28]

National Trust acted as trustee for the bondholders in the Electrical Development Company, so Flavelle did have a certain interest in the welfare of the private power companies. But he had no personal investments in the private companies. In the past he had encouraged Willison's attacks on Mackenzie whatever the consequences for the Commerce and National Trust, and until the hydro debate polarized in 1906−7 the newspaper had been anything but a true friend of private power. The *News*'s position on the hydro by-law was, as usual, a reflection of its editor's and owner's convictions. In this case the convictions and the apparent financial interests coincided. To those who refused to make a distinction the paper's high-minded independence was compromised. It seemed to have become another tool of big business.

And it was ineffective. Toronto manufacturers and homeowners lusted after cheap power and saw no reason to worry overmuch about wealthy power barons or faceless English investors. The by-law authorizing public competition with private enterprise in Toronto was approved by an overwhelming majority on Jan. 1, 1908. The sense of accomplishment when the *News* did something useful and influential, as in helping topple the Ross government, may have consoled Flavelle each time he wrote a cheque to cover the paper's deficits. Now it was losing money without having compensating influence. Should he continue an experiment which showed no promise of financial success and increasingly less promise of performing useful public service?

VI

There was much more satisfaction (and no financial penalty) in reflecting on the services Flavelle had performed for the university and the hospital. By mid-1907 the Board of Governors of the university had found their new president. Flavelle was on the committee which had carried out a painstaking search in North America and England, complicated by university factionalism, resentment at any outsider being chosen, and nativist opinion that no Englishman — let alone an American — should be president of Canada's most important university. The governors finally satisfied themselves and most of their critics with their choice of Robert Falconer, a young Presbyterian divine who had been principal of Pine Hill College in Halifax. A good classical scholar, an excellent public speaker, tactful, and appropriately high-minded, Falconer fitted smoothly into his new position at Toronto. With the new organizational structure, rising revenue from the succession duties, and excellent leadership from Falconer, the University of Toronto began its golden age.

Flavelle had played an important but not decisive role in the modernization of the University of Toronto. University reform had been in the air for years before the Royal Commission. The direction reform should take had been talked about for years, most particularly by Goldwin Smith and Sir William Meredith; both served on the Royal Commission and were probably more influential than Flavelle in the drafting of its report. The chairmanship had involved Flavelle not so much in innovation as in exhaustive discussion and negotiation.

It was sometimes said afterwards (perhaps by those who resented the Board of Governors of the University of Toronto meeting in the boardroom of the Bank of Commerce, as it did occasionally in its first year) that the new university structure reflected the influence of powerful businessmen like Flavelle and Walker, whose concern for business efficiency and practicality had overridden the academic interests of mere professors and politicians' concern for accountability. True, the university was going to be governed more efficiently, the practical sciences were going to be given more attention, and the Board of Governors and president were not going to let politicians run the university as they had in the past. But these were changes almost everyone within and without the university had supported, and it did not require any special business presence to articulate them. University reform would have taken much the same course if neither Flavelle nor Walker had been on the Royal Commission.

If anything, these least anti-intellectual of businessmen wanted to prevent business and science from dominating the world of education. All his work on the commission, Flavelle later claimed, was directed to strengthening "the Life" of the university as against the attempt to give it a business-like structure. At the time he wrote Goldwin Smith of his doubts about a man trained in the sciences as a prospective president because "the struggle for the culture subjects (in this commercial and practical community) to hold their own in the University, and the danger that on the scientific side energy may be chiefly centred, seems to call for a president whose interests have been on the culture rather than the scientific side, and whose sympathies for such subjects will be one of the important standards for holding true to the standards of sound education." Walker held the same view.[29]

Flavelle's deepest feeling about his work on the Royal Commission was of the honour and privilege it had been. "You can but guess what it meant to the plain man of affairs, denied University training, to meet almost daily for months with a select body of men of wide culture and to share with them in their consideration and ultimate decisions," he wrote Bruce Macdonald. To Goldwin Smith he added, "the memories of the afternoons and evenings spent at the Grange will be among the most highly cherished of my life."[30] The Grange was the longest possible distance from Peterborough and the office of the William Davies Company.

Flavelle began the movement to rebuild Toronto General Hospital. He did most of the work arranging for government support of the plan and raising the key private donations. In the next few years he made most of the decisions affecting construction, and when the hospital was finished he raised the rest of the money to pay its deficit, much of it from his own pocket. The rebuilding of one hospital in one city hardly seems impressive today when hospitals rise or fall by the score according to the whims of civil servants. It was recognized at the time, though, that Flavelle's work on behalf of medicine in Ontario and particularly on behalf of Toronto's poor was his finest public service, what the *Telegram* called "giant's work."[31] No one else had come forward to do it (least of all Toronto's doctors); it took an extraordinary amount of his time; and there were no rewards for service to the hospital, neither the delights of conversation at the Grange nor the formal recognition of an honorary degree.

There was satisfaction in doing one's duty, in useful service well performed. This was how a Christian man should go through life. "Joe is I suppose as busy as ever," Dorothea Flavelle wrote in 1906, "doing all the good he can." She had always expected he would, whether he became rich or poor in worldly possessions. Young Clara, though, was learning about how other rich people lived from observing the family life of the girls at finishing school in Paris. "I just never knew how much I loved him till I came over here," she wrote about her father. "I am glad to think I have a father who does a few things in life besides play the gentleman. These English girls with their high and mighty ideas do get on my nerves. A man who can hunt is all very well but I prefer a pork-packer and the chairman of a hospital board."[32]

John and Dorothea Flavelle:
a weak father, a very strong
mother.

Joe Flavelle, about seventeen
years old; about to be in business
on his own.

Methodists abroad. Ed Cox, Johnnie Flavelle, and Joe, England, 1881.

J. W. Flavelle, about 1890, thirty-two years old and about to make his first million.

Clara Ellsworth Flavelle, about 1890, thirty-two years old.

Clara, Ellsworth, and Mina Flavelle, about 1896. A fourth child, Josie, died a few months after birth.

The Anglicization of the North
American hog, before and after.
Lighter, leaner hogs were the key
to Davies' premium bacon.
Canada Packers Ltd.

J. Wheeler–Bennett, Flavelle's
British agent and the Bismarck
of the bacon trade.

William Davies, the patriarch of
Canadian pork-packing.

The William Davies Company's factory, about 1914.

Cutting Wiltshire sides for export to England at the Davies
Toronto factory.

A William Davies retail store, Queen Street, Toronto. One of the first chain stores in Canada.

Interior of a William Davies retail store. Cleanliness and high-quality meat compensated for fairly high prices.

George Albertus Cox, godfather of the "family" of Peterborough expatriates who dominated Toronto's business.
Archives of Ontario

E. R. Wood. Started in Cox's telegraph office; became Canada's greatest bond salesman.

H. H. Fudger, President of Simpson's and Superintendent of the Infant Class at Sherbourne Street Church.
United Church Archives

A. E. Ames, the prodigal son-in-law of George Cox.

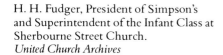

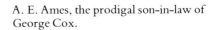

Simpson's, about 1910. Owned by Fudger, Flavelle, and the Coxes. *Archives of Ontario*

Sherbourne Street Methodist Church. Financed by Fudger, Flavelle, A. E. Kemp, and the Coxes. *United Church Archives*

CHAPTER EIGHT

TRYING TO RETIRE

January 1, 1908. Flavelle had New Year's dinner with Fred Smale and his wife. It was anything but a celebration. They were in Rochester, Minnesota, having come to consult the continent's most famous surgeons, the Mayo brothers, on Smale's debilitating gall-bladder illness. Toronto doctors had operated six weeks earlier, but had failed to find the trouble; the wound was still open and draining bile. The Doctors Mayo gave Smale a choice between minor surgery, which would correct the immediate problem but leave him incapacitated, and a major operation that would cure or kill him. Smale chose the latter. "Noble fellow, he is a fine soldier and a good man," Joe wrote Clara that night from his boarding-house room near the Mayos' private hospital.

Smale regained consciousness from the long operation the next morning. For a few hours he seemed to have a chance of pulling through. But he began to weaken at nine that night, his wife and Flavelle at his bedside. The struggle ended in the early hours of the morning. "There was not even a moment's mental perturbation at the last, nor was there physical suffering— his mind was clear, his hand grasp firm, his smile cheery, his voice strong and when his strength failed, without a struggle he closed his eyes and died." Flavelle and Mrs. Smale brought his body back to Toronto.

By all accounts Frederick Smale was a man of extraordinary character and promise, a young man for whom everyone predicted a brilliant future. His death at age thirty-six filled students and faculty at the university with "a sense of desperate loss," the *Varsity* wrote. Flavelle's grief was tempered by his own and Smale's belief in death as a transition to another life, but he could not have helped deeply mourning the friend and associate who most perfectly shared his ideals. By character and temperament Smale might have been Flavelle's son. He seems to have achieved in personal living the combination of humility, grace and self-control that was Flavelle's idea of personal perfection.[1]

Smale's death also created a practical problem in the William Davies Company. Flavelle had lost his heir, the "strong man" he had brought into the business, taught the business, and to whom he had turned over day-to-day managerial responsibility. Having no one else in the company of Smale's calibre, Flavelle was thrown back into active management while having to begin again the search for a successor.

I

It was a special strain to take up Davies' problems again because Flavelle had been trying to reduce his committments to at last have more time with his family. Smale had not only taken over much of his work on the Don, but had replaced him on the Board of Regents of Victoria College in 1906 and the next year had become superintendent of Sherbourne Street Sunday School when Flavelle retired after sixteen years' service.

Flavelle's sense of duty often frustrated his inclination to reduce his responsibilities. "Where duty drives we must be guided," he wrote Clara. Leaving the Sunday School was not "running away from duty," though, because the change would be good for the church. When he tried to resign from the university's Board of Governors about the same time, however, Whitney convinced him that his duty lay in continuing to support the institution until it was well started on its new course. So he stayed on the Board of Governors for another thirty years.[2]

His sense of duty also kept him from insisting that his resignation from the board of the Canada Life, first submitted in 1906, be finally accepted. That was the year of the hearings of the Royal Commission on Life Insurance, and Flavelle allowed himself to be persuaded to stay on the board to help the company and Senator Cox ride out the storm.

It turned out to be a rough passage, not just because of the bad publicity the company received, but also because the facts brought out raised serious questions about the competence of the Canada Life's management. The worried directors decided to investigate for themselves.[3] A committee of them, which included Flavelle, was not particularly critical of the investments in other Cox-controlled companies—if anything these had worked to the policyholders' advantage — but found the company's high cost of doing business alarming. All costs had risen dramatically during the Cox regime; the new business in the United States and abroad had been achieved at excessively high expense; and Canada Life's head-office costs were much higher than its leading Canadian and American competitors. These expenses, of course, directly reduced profits, ninety per cent of which went to the policyholders.

The directors' conclusion — "the improvement sought for can only be secured by such Managerial direction as will lead to the operations of the Company coming constantly under able and wise supervision" — was a veiled request for Ed Cox's resignation. They were too discreet to mention the general manager's personal weakness (referred to in other letters as his "bad habit" or "unfortunate habit"—it was most likely drink) which periodically unsuited him for his duties. But it was in the back of everyone's mind.[4]

A majority of the board were prepared to insist on Ed Cox's resignation. After a private personal appeal from George Cox they agreed to experiment with a joint general managership of Ed Cox and the company's highly regarded actuary, Frank Sanderson. Canada Life would get its new management, but the Cox family would save face.[5]

With the Canada Life apparently reformed, Flavelle left the board in March 1908. In a characteristic farewell letter he explained to Ed Cox why the young man should not feel "hardly dealt with" by the directors. The life-insurance investigations in North America may have been hysterical and unwise, he argued, but they had proven that the men running life-insurance companies had "departed from wise measures and become extravagant and personally selfish in administration." Flavelle made this the text for an extraordinary business sermon:

In its very essence life insurance differs from all commercial business, and from banking and other financial operations. The patrons of a life company must be permanent. The great body of them cannot change from one company to another as they can from one bank to another if they are dissatisfied. Hence to all of us who are identified with the direction of affairs of such companies should come the dignity and responsibility of a great trust.

. . . You will know, perhaps better than anyone else, how, for your own sake, for your mother's and father's sake, I hope that the unfortunate habit that became the immediate cause of the action of the Board, may be overcome and never reestablished. But let me say, you will entirely miss the mark if you feel that this is all.

Consider what it would have meant if during this time of unrest and storm, the General Manager of the Canada Life, and his administration, could have been pointed out as conspicuous for high moral force, and for a grave sense of responsibility to the highest position of trust in life insurance circles in Canada. Believe me, my dear Ed, it is this quality which you must develop if you are to honor the position which you hold and earn the confidence which must come from merit if it comes at all. It has been the absence of high moral purpose in your administration which has constituted the gravity of the criticisms passed upon it. You have had little or no appreciation of the distress which has been felt, not among goody-goody people, but among men of solid worth, men identified with your own agency staff, directors of your own Company, men who occupy positions of responsibility in the community (and all with no selfish ends to serve) that a position of high trust such as that with which you were honored, was held without adequate sense of dignity and responsibility, and with an almost flippant disregard of trustee relationship.

If you read into this episode the hasty act of a few unreasonable people, in place of reading into it the necessity of a deep searching of your own heart and your own standards, resulting in a complete change in your conception of the serious duties attached to your position, you will have thrown away your final chance to earn for yourself a position of honour in the community.

Admitting his own responsibility as a director for the problems of the Canada Life, Flavelle concluded by pointing out that if his letter angered Cox, "your own good sense will on a final reading come to the rescue and tell you that it is not unfair." He sent copies to Walker and to George Cox.[6]

II

Money markets in New York and London temporarily collapsed in the "rich man's panic" of late 1907. Money was tight through the winter of 1907−8 and Flavelle's letters hint of financial problems for the first time in his career since the late 1880s. At the least he could no longer afford to subsidize a newspaper which had no prospect of breaking even and seemed to have declining influence. In the spring of 1908 he was trying to sell the *News*; by October control of the paper had passed to a syndicate of active Conservatives led by Frank Cochrane, Whitney's Minister of Lands, Forests and Mines. The phrase "independent journal" on its masthead was changed to "daily journal." The *News* had again become a party newspaper, Willison a kept party journalist, having changed his parties.[7]

Flavelle later estimated that his adventure with the *News* had cost him from $350,000 to $400,000. He thought it was worth it to have known Willison—who remained a close friend—but in the fulness of his retirement wrote of the venture as "an effort to discharge a somewhat stilted sense of public duty." There were few mourners, least of all the politicians it had been trying to uplift, for the independent *News*. Its impecunious but brilliant competitor, the *World*, supplied an appropriate epitaph to this unique experiment in public service: "The conversion of pigs into pork is one thing, but the slaying of the dragon that waylays the body politic is another. Mr. Flavelle retires leaving the dragon still in possession of the road."[8]

III

Concentrating on the packing business for the first time in several years, Flavelle found the William Davies Company's situation "more pressing than I have ever known."[9] The combination of surplus capacity and shrinking margins on hog production continued to harass the industry. Vocal farmer agitation against the packers did not resume, only because many farmers had simply switched out of hog-raising. Shipments of hogs to Ontario packers were consistently below the levels of earlier years and the volume of sales to Britain began to decline absolutely.

One morning in 1907 Flavelle had been startled to read in his newspaper the complete record of the William Davies Company's dividends since its incorporation in 1892. One of William Davies' surviving sons had introduced these most secret figures as evidence in a minor court case involving the transfer of some shares, and an alert reporter had picked them up. Despite scattered comment about "hoggish" packers, the reaction in the farmers' press to the realization that the leading company in the industry had been paying dividends averaging fifty-one per cent on its share capital was surprisingly mild. Both the *Weekly Sun* and the *Farmer's Advocate* mentioned the company's pioneer work in the industry, and the latter journal pointed out how high profits were achieved by small margins and a large volume. Still, the emperor had been shown to be wearing fine silk under his simple workingman's coat; Flavelle thought the disclosure was a crippling blow to his company's influence in the industry.[10]

As exports declined, the collateral enterprises provided most of the company's income. Here, too, though, the years of one success after another had ended. In 1906 the Buffalo experiment fell apart when *The Jungle* destroyed Americans' taste for meat; the Davies stores there never recovered from the abrupt loss of half their business and were closed out at a loss in 1909, ending what might have been a great opening into the American market. The Montreal and Harriston branch factories also lost money in 1906, the former because of a breakdown in managerial competence. Flavelle reorganized and stayed with both operations, but Montreal remained a trouble spot, barely profitable at best, while Harriston made a profit only once before it was reduced to a storage house in 1912.[11] In some of the stores, particularly outside Toronto, it proved difficult to keep a satisfactory profit margin on the company's traditional high costs. Continuing to opt for a high-priced, high-profit retail business, Flavelle urged his men to "have the courage to charge a sufficient price to give returns for our expensively organized establishments."[12] This strategy may have been wrong.

The company was still able to afford mistakes. Profits were less than a third of those in the great years of the 1890s, and much less as a percentage of capital, but the company made money, paying 15-, 14½-, and 17½-per-cent dividends from 1907 through 1909. However trying the business was, Flavelle wrote as he worked on the 1908 year-end figures, "it is a good old friend and comrade now — it has a fine capacity to do us credit before each year passes. . . . If it were not for the disturbance created by Smale's death it would be first rate. I cannot be easy or comfortable until we can fix up some substitute."[13]

The simplest way to replace Smale was to bring in another strong man. Flavelle's first choice was T. A. Russell, the university graduate he had hired several years before to solve CCM's troubles. Russell, he wrote, "has fulfilled all my expectations, has proved an able business man and fighter with good courage. . . . I know of no man that I would more gladly choose to be associated with me, or in whose general common sense ability I have more confidence." But Russell had an important financial interest in CCM, and its fortunes were riding nicely on sales of the Russell automobile. Having no knowledge of the packing business, possibly wondering if it had as fine a future as automobiles, Russell chose to stay with CCM.

Charlie Blackwell was still talking merger. With Smale gone, Flavelle realized how rich in manpower he would be had the six Matthews sons come into the business through the 1902 merger. Looking back, he realized that he had "destroyed what was undoubtedly the greatest business opportunity of my life" in backing out of it. But now it seemed too late to merge

—the other companies were no stronger, there was aggressive American competition in Canada from Swift's, and a merger would force him to stay active for many more years until he could be satisfied with his successors. So Blackwell was put off again.

The most promising solution seemed to be through Harris Abattoir, the beef-packing house in which Davies' interest now stood at forty per cent. Both James Harris, a son of the founder, and J. S. McLean, now a director and important shareholder, were proving themselves able businessmen. Flavelle was particularly impressed with McLean, who shared Flavelle's passion for accounting and had gradually mastered the other elements of the business. "McLean has proved to be strong, creative and efficient," Flavelle wrote Wheeler-Bennett. "He lacks the delightful gentleness of Smale. He is without the evenness of temper. Indeed he is rather a difficult man in his temper. [But] he would serve me with great loyalty." If McLean came to the Don as general manager of Davies, Harris could stay with the Abattoir and both companies would have first-class management.

Flavelle proposed a fusion of the companies, with each principal taking shares in a holding company. But Harris and McLean, not unhappy controlling their own company and at least as tough-minded as Flavelle, balked at becoming minority shareholders. The three apparently could not agree on the terms by which Harris and McLean might eventually acquire Flavelle's controlling interest, and several rounds of intermittent discussions led nowhere.

In the meantime Flavelle had one promising young man coming along in the company. Edward Carey Fox, a grandson of William Davies, had come into the business directly after graduating from McMaster University with a Gold Medal in Mathematics in 1906. He immediately impressed Flavelle, who by 1908 had him picked as a successor if he continued to develop. But it would take time: "I know something now of what it means to grow men. I know how they can come on rapidly up to a certain point and then cease to develop. I must have time to prove Fox."

He seemed to have no time to achieve anything. Hard on the heels of the succession problem in Canada came word that Wheeler-Bennett intended to retire at the end of 1908. "At one stroke . . . or if you like two strokes twelve months apart, I have met with the loss of the leader in this business, and am asked to release the commanding figure and leader in the London business." It was surprising that Wheeler-Bennett should want to retire at age fifty-two. Still, there could have been a smooth transition in the British agency if he had trained a successor. He had not. None of the efforts to bring young men along in the London office had worked. Flavelle's contingency plan had been to send Fox to London to become Wheeler-Bennett's second-in-command. Now he was needed in Canada. So there was no successor in sight to the Bismarck of the Bacon Trade, not even a Caprivi.[14]

As well, the English business was more sorely pressed than ever. The trouble was Danish competition. Having effectively driven the private packers out of their industry, the efficient Danish cooperatives had formed their own selling agency in England, which operated on a low commission and bypassed middlemen at every opportunity. Buyers, especially retailers, were switching to Danish bacon in droves. In the spring of 1908 Wheeler-Bennett had encouraged Flavelle to fortify himself for "the earnest struggle in which we are engaged, the toughest job you and I have ever been called upon to face, it is going to be 'the survival of the fittest' . . . the men who are most alert, and who have the best balanced judgment will come out on top." Six months later the old campaigner seemed to be leaving the field in the middle of the battle.[15]

The crisis in the English agency strained relations between Flavelle and Wheeler-Bennett to the breaking point. Flavelle pleaded with his agent to postpone retirement, claiming that this was a reasonable request in view of Flavelle's having missed the business opportunity of a lifetime in turning down the 1902 merger "solely and only out of deference to your wishes." That, of course, was not true, although Flavelle may have come to remember it that way. Perhaps knowing he was not arguing on strong ground (though he also thought he had a promise from Wheeler-Bennett to bring along a successor before retiring), Flavelle decided to confront Wheeler-Bennett in person. Equipped with the hot-water bottle Clara had thoughtfully sent along, he had an anxious midwinter passage on the *Baltic*. "I go to I know not what."[16]

Clara had never liked Wheeler-Bennett. Flavelle's conversations with him at the office seemed to confirm her judgment: "Every view you have held dear of the native selfishness of the respected gentleman is true. When I get below the surface I am distressed as well as disturbed. I will be still more so at Ravensbourne. I shrink from going there. . . . I found affairs much worse than I had any idea of."

Wheeler-Bennett's income depended only on the volume of his sales—so long as he had bacon to sell he made money, a very handsome income, whether or not the Davies Company made any profit. The luxury of Rav-

ensbourne now seemed to Flavelle to symbolize Wheeler-Bennett's unfair treatment of the Canadian company. When he went down there the
Wheeler-Bennetts were very kind to him: "There was a warm cozy fire in
my bedroom, a hot water bottle in bed, a blazing wood fire in the dining
room and every thought shown for my comfort—but dear heart with it all
my heart chilled over it all."[17]

The strong-minded businessmen tended to blame each other for the
difficulties of the bacon business. Fully aware of the inroads the Danes were
making — by 1909 he considered the Canadian trade "in a state of liquidation" — Flavelle thought most of the trouble was weak marketing of
Canadian bacon in England. Danish was being sold aggressively and imagi-
natively by agents working on a low margin and under intense pressure
from their shippers. The agents for Canadian, by contrast, were hanging on
in complacent lethargy as their trade withered away. Wheeler-Bennett, for
example, had failed to cultivate the business of the small buyers, the retail
men he had fought so hard to serve in the early 1900s, but whose accounts he
had let lapse. His only outlets for Davies bacon were the few large wholesalers still at Smithfield, men whose market power in competitive conditions enabled them to drive down the price of Canadian almost at will, while
still providing Wheeler-Bennett with a good income from his three-per-
cent commission on their large orders. Wheeler-Bennett's self-interest reinforced this conservatism, Flavelle thought:

As the owner . . . of the London business, and having in himself a great earning
power, notwithstanding his unique loyalty to his shipper, his first consideration naturally continued to be the profits which he would make out of the London business
for Wheeler-Bennett. His commanding strength, his extraordinary capacity to sell,
his power with difficult buyers, enabled him personally, and largely unaided, to clear
the most of the product to large buyers. He did not find it necessary to cultivate an
interest in or patience with small buyers. He is not the type of man who naturally
organizes for the development of a business serving a large number of small accounts, with the accompanying irritation and worry of dealing with small people. It
was not naturally in him to plan, and to be patient in working out the only type of
organization which would secure such results. It was more in accord with his capacity, it was making better use of his earning power, to dispose of our shipments to
buyers whom he could personally handle, than to restrict such buyers and substitute
an accumulation of business which would come from small purchasers secured at an
increased cost by sharing the commission with agents, and paying for travellers. . . .

The course which has been followed therefore has been the one which was profitable to the shipper, but not for the permanent advantage of the shipper. There has been no steady accumulation of small buyers. There has been no intelligent development of new markets or new centres. There has been no enthusiastic force behind the agency organization.

These criticisms were a small part of a forty-six-page memo Flavelle presented to his board on his return from England. A copy sent to Wheeler-Bennett produced a vigorous response in kind, with the blame thrown back on Canada:

The theory that you have set up that a good deal of Canadian bacon can be sold to small retailers green is absolutely unpractical until you get the farmers to join hands with you. . . . you have not the product suitable for the type of trader you are trying to cultivate. . . . We have scores and scores and scores of retailers to call upon, but we have not the product to fit them with. . . . What are you going to do with the product which can only be dealt with by men who have a large and varied clientele? If you "cut the painter" with the wholesale houses, you will find your craft will go down headfirst. . . . The prejudice of the retailer towards Canadian bacon today is simply appalling. . . . How can you expect Canadian sides to have any other than a secondary position when you have allowed the Danish farmers to do their business so much better than the Canadian farmers have done it? . . .

You have referred to the Danish Bacon Agency, which everybody admits is a sink of corruption. . . . everyone of the Directors of these Cooperative curing houses is suborned and corrupted. . . . If your business was done on the lines that this Danish Cooperative business is done upon, it would turn your hair grey. . . . The whole of the Danish business is instinct with life, because it has caught on to public favour, simply because the Danish farmers have produced the article that is demanded, and given hogs reared and fed on the lines that the Danish farmers have done them, there is no reason in the wide, wide world why the Canadian bacon trade should not be abounding with life, vigor, and success.

It is not a fact and it is not true that the first consideration of Wheeler-Bennett was profit in his business; while as a businessman he had an eye to success in this way, his whole time, life, and best efforts have been given for the promotion and success of the William Davies Company . . . risks were taken of which your Managing Director has no idea, and never will. . . .

There is another feature that presses heavily upon us, and which must be ever present with your good self, and that is the out of proportion cost of making Canadian bacon to the making of Danish. Until you can right matters in this direction it is like ploughing the sand to hope for any success or profit or comfort in working the Canadian trade this side, no matter what the ability or what the organization may be.[18]

The partners accepted enough of each other's criticisms to be able to work out a compromise. Wheeler-Bennett agreed to stay on for another year or two as head of the firm and leader in the battle with the wholesalers, but would give two of his young men, Triggs and Hughes, a free hand and a generous share in the profits as they courted the retailers with an eye to developing a large volume in small sales. Partly to salve his pride, Wheeler-Bennett threw himself into the business with his old vigour in the early months of 1909, set his young men to work with high spirits, and completely turned around morale in his office. Flavelle was delighted at the fine display of salesmanship, and for the time being was satisfied.[19]

While it had been vital to keep Wheeler-Bennett in harness, the founder and still president of the company, William Davies, was expendable. Davies had maintained an active interest in the business, attended board and annual meetings, and spoke his mind. As often as not he opposed Flavelle's ideas, giving him a particularly difficult time in 1906 when the expansion into Buffalo and Montreal went sour. Davies was over seventy-five, but still in good health despite his deafness; he remarried in 1908. He was an imposing figure in a certain way: young Jack Wheeler-Bennett thought the white-bearded visitor to Ravensbourne, who received such unusual deference from his father, could only be God—except that it was odd for God to eat so many peppermint candies.[20]

Flavelle, too, had always been properly polite to Davies in spite of his growing belief that Davies habitually put his personal and family interests above those of the company. He was quietly furious when Davies' son released the dividend figures in 1907 without consulting anyone else in the company. Two years later, also without telling anyone, Davies sold the property at Yonge and Queen where the company had an important retail store. Flavelle finally broke his silence with a bitter letter accusing Davies of repeatedly ignoring the company's interests and advising the Davies family to resign from executive positions. At the 1909 annual meeting Flavelle became president as well as managing director and Edward Adie moved up to the vice-presidency. William Davies played no further role in the William

Davies Company except as a minority shareholder. According to Flavelle he accepted his final retirement "philosophically."[21]

Flavelle also wanted to retire, and E. C. Fox was quickly given most of his managerial duties. Learning of Flavelle's restlessness, several outsiders approached him with a view to buying his shares. His first inclination, however, was to pass the company on to the young men who had grown up in the industry. In a proposed 1911 scheme, Harris and McLean of the Abattoir would join Fox to buy control from Flavelle. The deal came unstuck when Harris and McLean, who had little use for Fox (a feeling he reciprocated), insisted that Flavelle agree to sell the two of them a controlling interest at some future date. The negotiations broke down with some ill-feeling.[22]

Worrying about the future of the business if the Taft—Fielding reciprocity agreement was accepted in Canada*—at the least the company would need more working capital—Flavelle finally engineered his own reorganization in June 1911. A new William Davies Company was incorporated to acquire all the assets of the old company and its subsidiaries. These assets were appraised at $2,400,000, reflecting substantial reserves and the growing value of Davies' real estate. The old company's capitalization was $1 million, so each $100-par-value share was actually worth at least $240. The shareholders were given $25 cash plus 1½ shares in the new company for each share in the old company. In view of its assets ($2,150,000 after the cash dividend), the new company's capitalization of $1,500,000 was very conservative, in marked contrast to the fictitious capitalizations of many companies being reorganized or merged about the same time. To raise more working capital the new company also floated (through Dominion Securities) a $1,250,000 issue of sinking fund bonds.[23]

Through sales to the young men in the company Flavelle's Davies holding had fallen to just over 50 per cent, worth $1,200,000 before the reorganization. Taking cash and stock dividends and increases in capitalization into account, and valuing his holdings at $400 a share in 1901, Flavelle had been getting a 6- to 8-per-cent annual return on his investment, not much more than he could have made by selling out in 1901 and investing in good securities. But it was undoubtedly much more than any other pork-packer had made.

The threat of reciprocity passed in 1911, not without Flavelle's assistance. The reorganized William Davies Company used its new capital to finance a

---

* For that agreement and Flavelle's role in it, see Chapter Nine.

major expansion of its cold storage and warehouse facilities and of the Montreal stores. Fox moved up to the general managership in 1912, Flavelle remaining as president. Fox was eager for major expansion into Western Canada, but for the time being the company preferred to ship its Western hogs live to the Toronto factory. It also remained satisfied with the old factory on the Don, although Flavelle knew it was out of date, and the construction of the Union Stockyards at Toronto Junction suggested there would be a new centre for livestock marketing in Toronto. Harris Abattoir, by contrast, decided to move to Keele and St. Clair; moreover, its new factory there, opened in 1913, included facilities to slaughter hogs. The plans to fuse the companies having failed, Harris and McLean were ready to go into competition with Davies in pork. In general, the Davies Company seems to have been excessively conservative in not looking even to relocation in Toronto, let alone expansion into the Canadian West.[24]

The company may have neglected its Canadian opportunities because Flavelle believed the British market still held the key to the future. If only, that is, there was proper selling. Wheeler-Bennett's commission was down now to 2½ per cent, and Triggs and Hughes were busy cultivating new customers, but by 1911 the company was making little or no profit on its exports. "If only the English market had some life in it, if it would only let us out with a whole skin," Fox lamented. "But every box shipped to England means a big sore blister to us. . . . I feel good and sore when I think of the export conditions. Here is Bennett living like a lord out of us, with a population of thirty to thirty-five millions of people to feed and he has no more power of distribution, hardly, than Puddy Bros. He lives in a circle and his business is done in a circle." Flavelle had the grace to remind Fox of Wheeler-Bennett's magnificent work in years past.[25]

Wheeler-Bennett finally retired in 1912. By the end he was doing little selling himself, but it was grossly unfair of Flavelle to refer to his "personal service grown stale" when he was just carrying out his commitment to bring along successors. The long partnership apparently ended with some bad feeling, for Flavelle could not get over paying a large commission on profitless sales. The William Davies Company bought Wheeler-Bennett's fixed assets (nothing extra for goodwill), fired Triggs and Hughes, and brought back A. F. Sheed — who had earlier failed to satisfy either Wheeler-Bennett or Flavelle — to head a new firm, Sheed & Thomson, in which Davies had a 60-per-cent interest. The agency's commission was cut to 2 per cent, and 60 per cent of its profits would come back to Canada.

Sheed & Thomson's explicit strategy was to cultivate many small, regular customers in order to minimize the need for the flamboyant open-market selling of Wheeler-Bennett's days.[26]

Most Canadian companies had given up the British trade—Davies' sales of about $4 million a year in England were approximately 70 per cent of Canada's bacon exports. Flavelle still believed his competitors had failed because they did not understand the trade. Now that new men had taken over in Canada and England he enjoyed "robust faith" in the future of the business.[27]

The faith was not justified in the two years before the war. Canadian bacon exports continued to fall 35 per cent per year: in 1913 the Canadian trade was one-tenth of the Danish. In the year ending March 31, 1914, the William Davies Company lost $103,768 on its English exports, recouping only a fraction of that in dividends from Sheed & Thomson. The company stayed modestly profitable thanks to the retail stores and dividends from Harris Abattoir. But its shareholders received only a 5-per-cent, a 7½-per-cent, and a lowest ever 3-per-cent return on their capital in the years 1912—14.[28] With the English market virtually gone, the store system beginning to decline, and Harris Abattoir the more aggressive company in Canada, the William Davies Company seemed to be living on its past.

Flavelle had stubbornly refused to accept defeat in Britain. He failed to recognize what lesser packers understood—that movements of costs and prices had made Canadian bacon exports across the Atlantic uneconomic under normal circumstances. Believing individual effort could conquer any obstacles, he continued a strategy which amounted, as Wheeler-Bennett had warned, to "ploughing the sand." As Wheeler-Bennett had also realized, the panacea of a reorganization in England achieved nothing. The William Davies Company's real opportunities by 1914 lay in expansion into the Canadian West as a packer and across Canada as a retailer. Not realizing this himself, Flavelle had compounded problems for the future by failing to bring J. S. McLean, who might have realized it, into the firm as his successor. Documents are scarce for these years, but Flavelle's leadership of Davies seems to have become conservative and unimaginative, perhaps as he had said about Wheeler-Bennett, a "personal service grown stale." Had Smale not died, of course, Flavelle would have been able to do what he had most wanted in the business—retire from it several years earlier.

IV

Flavelle's other business interests had developed very satisfactorily, giving him considerably less anxiety than the William Davies Company. Pork-packing had been one of the few industries in any trouble during the Laurier years. The rush of settlers into Western Canada after 1900 was soon followed by the last great rush of British capital to Canada. Millions of people and billions of dollars poured into the country, creating a business climate in which it was hard not to do well. Except in the short, sharp downturns of 1902−3 and 1907−8, speeches at annual meetings were an almost tiresome litany of self-congratulation on continuing national prosperity and record company earnings. The capital requirements of Western homesteaders, municipalities, and the railway builders gave financiers a ready outlet for their money, allowing them to settle down to more normal business after the heady promotions around the turn of the century. Not until 1909−12 did another surfeit of capital, mostly foreign, tempt financiers and promoters, led by upstarts like young Max Aitken, into another wave of mergers and flotations to create paper to sell to eager investors. The bust finally came late in 1913 when foreign capital markets dried up. By mid-1914 the Canadian economy was in serious depression. But a lot of money had been made by then.

National Trust grew quietly and smoothly, feeding on the Western mortgage market, Canadians' growing use of institutional executors, and fees for trusteeship services. Zebulon Lash literally loved the company, Will Rundle remembered; after each board meeting Lash would "put his hand in his pocket and take out one, two, three and sometimes more little slips of paper upon all of which would be given the particulars of new trusteeships of one kind or another which between meetings he had secured for the Company." Flavelle left daily affairs in the hands of W. T. White, who had developed, he wrote, from "a free lance and a gambler" into a "man of affairs."[29] When White developed further in 1911, into a Conservative Minister of Finance, Will Rundle moved easily into his job. By 1914 the trust company was administering total assets of $44.5 million and for several years had been paying a 10-per-cent dividend on its capital. It had yet to lose money on a mortgage, and, probably reflecting its president's advice, had carefully chosen which of the securities issued by Mackenzie & Mann it would handle or invest in.[30] The trust company's earnings were never spectacular—trust companies didn't (and don't) work that way—but it had been a good investment, financially satisfactory to Flavelle as well as providing him with congenial associates.

He enjoyed the association with Fudger at Simpson's both personally and materially. His $117,000 investment in $167,000 par value of Simpson's shares in 1902 had grown by 1913 to a holding of 1,567 preferred and 8,562 common shares, carrying a par value of $1,012,900 on which the company was paying a steady 6-per-cent dividend. He had reinvested only $5,700 in 1907, rather more than balanced by the $250,000-plus in dividends he received through 1913.

The Simpson's investment grew so remarkably because the partners limited themselves to a 6-per-cent annual dividend. The rest of the profits each year were added to the firm's capital, the owners taking stock dividends. The big store and mail-order system was able to earn a consistent 20 to 25 per cent per annum on the owners' capital, so their investment was growing by about 17 per cent compounded annually, a rate at which money doubles every four years. A total investment in Simpson's of $500,000 in 1902 had become $1 million by 1906, $2 million by 1910, and $3 million by 1912. By 1913 Flavelle was making more from Simpson's dividends than he was from the William Davies Company.[31]

The department store seemed to run exceptionally smoothly under H. H. Fudger's management, the key to its progress being constant expansion. Reinvested earnings financed regular additions to the Toronto store and a major entry into Montreal in 1905 (the same year the William Davies Company went into Montreal). C. L. Burton, who bought Simpson's in the late 1920s, implies in his memoirs that the company was not being well managed and its financial condition was precarious in the prewar years.[32] True, Simpson's was having to raise more working capital by 1912, and its internal organization may not have been as efficient as that of the William Davies Company (Burton's portrait of Fudger suggests he was more conservative than Flavelle, less skilled at accounting, and unwilling to pay high wages; he also seems to have been more interested in theology than business problems). Perhaps, too, Eaton's was even more successful in the same years. Like the Davies Company, Simpson's was surprisingly conservative in not having begun major operations in the West. Eaton's had.

In fact, though, the business had been a marvellous success by any normal standards. Its Methodist owners, not single-mindedly devoted to creating a department-store empire, were not at all dissatisfied with its progress. If there were serious internal problems, Fudger was astutely hiring a man who could solve them when he brought Burton into the store in 1911. Nothing in Flavelle's papers suggests that Simpson's gave him a moment's anxiety.

The other silent partner in Simpson's was Senator Cox. In his late sixties now, Cox was beginning to fade from active business life, perhaps more quickly after the bad publicity he received during the life-insurance investigations. In 1907 Walker replaced him as president of the Bank of Commerce. It was a natural change of leadership for the bank, but coincided so closely with the insurance mess that some wondered if the Senator's resignation had been voluntary.[33]

Whether or not he had been eased out of the bank's presidency, George Cox was also on the defensive as the directors of the Canada Life reviewed his family's stewardship of that company. Round one had seen the directors' investigation leading to the near ousting of Ed Cox from the general managership in 1908. At that point Flavelle had resigned from the board. But he could not avoid involvement a year later when round two began with the Senator's decision that his salary as president should be raised from $15,000 to $25,000 to stay in line with the salaries of the heads of other prominent banks and insurance companies.

Since Cox and his family had absolute control of the company there should have been no problem about his salary—except for the consciences of his friends and associates on the board. This time Zebulon Lash, solicitor for Cox, the Commerce, and the Canadian Northern, acknowledged as Canada's finest corporation lawyer, took the lead. As a policyholder from an American company when the insurance scandals had broken there, Lash had always been sympathetic to the policyholders' point of view. He had served on the directors' committee investigating the affairs of the Canada Life in 1907 and was uneasy about his position as director of a life-insurance company absolutely controlled by one family. It had not seemed to matter earlier, for Cox had encouraged the directors to exercise their independent judgment. Now, hard on the heels of well-deserved criticisms of the Cox family's role in the Canada Life, including criticisms of the salaries Cox and his sons drew, the Senator wanted more money. It was Lash's turn to write a business sermon to the Cox family:

The undertaking of any life insurance Company is a public trust. The undertaking of the Canada Life is one of the most important and far reaching of the public trusts in Canada. . . . The opinion has been gradually forcing itself upon me that no life insurance Company like the Canada Life should continue to be controlled by one man or by a few with common interests, . . . At the present time whenever there is an opportunity of discussing the affairs of the Canada Life in public it is treated by the enemy as belonging to you and as practically existing for the benefit of your family, and it is attacked for that reason; and the great services which you have rendered to the Company and the fact that its Board of Directors comprise some of the most prominent and independent and successful business men in Canada are to a great extent lost sight of. . . . In view of what I have said and of what you know has been said about the amounts you and your sons are receiving from the Company and about your using your control in connection with your own and your sons' position, I think that the present is an inopportune time for you to urge your application.[34]

Opposition from several of the directors forced Cox to back off from his "salary grab." Lash hoped he would go further and give up family control of the company, though retaining the presidency. Asked for advice by Lash, Flavelle was even more disillusioned. "He is not sensitive to shock in relation to his own conduct," Flavelle wrote of Cox, "and is peculiarly lacking in appreciation of the reasons for the criticisms so freely pressed upon him." The public's distrust of the Senator was sometimes ignorant and unfair, Flavelle thought, but it was extraordinarily widespread, even—perhaps especially—among Cox's political friends. And after almost forty years' association with the Cox family, Flavelle had finally decided that the distrust was justified:

I have grown to believe that Mr. Cox does not possess the moral qualities which enable him to understand trustee relationships, . . . I do not therefore believe the public mind would show any appreciable change which would reflect greater confidence in the administration of the Canada Life, if the control of the share capital were no longer vested in him, while he still was at the head of its administration.

Flavelle had come to believe that the only way to protect policyholders was through mutualization of life-insurance companies—ownership by the policyholders themselves. If the Coxes were forced out of Canada Life, control might just pass to another man or group of men. Flavelle's memo to Lash veered between urging him to force the issue all the way to mutualization or not at all, and the middle course of breaking the family's control of the company so it would not dictate the presidency after George Cox's death. In any case the struggle would not be easy:

You will ask a man to set aside the thing which he has desired more than all else in life
—the right and power to control the affairs of the Canada Life. . . . He will be
intensely reluctant to yield to any pressure, no matter how serious, which will take
from him that which he has coveted, worked for and paid to secure.[35]

Lash pressed the matter with Cox, charging that the company's interests
came second when they conflicted with Cox family interests. Then an investigation of the Eastern Ontario branch, managed by Bert Cox, disclosed
minor financial irregularities which had been reported to only one of the
two general managers, Ed Cox. The Senator came away from a stormy
interview with Lash believing that the lawyer was accusing one of his sons
of embezzlement and the other of suppressing embezzlement. At the least,
Lash was accusing the father of serious nepotism. He wrung from Cox a
proposal, no less nepotistic, to acquire control of the Dunlop Tire & Rubber
Goods Company for Ed to manage. That fell through when the British
Dunlop company decided to take control itself.[36]

Then Cox agreed to appoint a new vice-president, J. H. Plummer, to act
as a buffer between himself and his sons. That failed when Ed Cox's bad
habit again overcame and incapacitated him. The Senator refused to fire his
son, and Lash resigned from the board in disgust. He withdrew the resignation when, among other concessions, George Cox agreed in writing that
Ed's fate would be in Plummer's hands if such an incident happened again.

The climax came in the spring of 1911 when Sanderson, the other general
manager, suddenly announced his resignation. It turned out that George
Cox (perhaps emboldened by the celebration of his fiftieth anniversary with
the company) had promised Sanderson a retainer of five thousand dollars a
year for seven years as consulting actuary to the company if he resigned.
Cox claimed the joint general managership had not worked. Lash was
incensed, labelling the deal with Sanderson illegal and immoral, and the
Senator's manoeuvring on behalf of his son "the most glaring and objectionable case of nepotism I have ever met with."

On April 24, 1911, the board met to receive Sanderson's resignation. The
Coxes and Sanderson were absent. On a deciding vote cast by Plummer,
Lash and his supporters lost. In June, Lash, Walker, Walker's brother, and
another director resigned from the board of the Canada Life.[37]

George Cox's business methods and business morals had been repudiated
by his most high-minded associates—Lash, Walker, and Flavelle. Cox's personal, dynastic approach to his affairs—the normal way of doing business

in the 1890s — was now anachronistic to men who had been shaken by the public demand for higher, more impersonal standards of trusteeship. Even so, the ties of business and friendship were strong enough to prevent the dissidents from making their quarrel public. Canada Life's policyholders never knew of the long, futile struggle to reduce the Cox family's control of the company. There was some bitterness immediately after the resignation and considerable gossip about a falling out of the big Toronto interests. Perhaps because Cox was slipping into virtual retirement, tempers cooled and nobody resigned from anyone else's boards.[38]

George Cox died in January 1914. Ed Cox inherited the presidency of Canada Life. He died a few months later, never having lived free from his father's shadow. Bert Cox became the next president of the Canada Life.

V

Flavelle seldom invested in new ventures after his experiences with underwriting and stock promotion at the turn of the century. He occasionally supported a relative or friend in a business—guaranteeing, for example, the credit of the Imperial Paint & Varnish Company, which was managed by a nephew. Or a few thousand might be earmarked for an interesting proposition—in 1907 Flavelle and White were the active spirits in a small syndicate backing a timber-staking expedition in British Columbia. He kept a small interest in John and William's thriving businesses in Lindsay, but the Flavelle brothers were not close business associates after the 1890s. Johnnie and Will, prosperous and prominent local businessmen, but not really operating in Joe's league, financed their own timber expedition to B.C. in 1907 (employing a young forestry student named H. R. MacMillan), which eventually led to Will's son, Aird Flavelle, establishing himself as a sawmill owner on the Coast. Aird turned to his Uncle Joe for regular advice on business strategy.[39]

There was also a senior role in a new bank. Flavelle was vice-president of the Penny Bank of Toronto, federally chartered in 1905 to receive savings from school children for deposit in the Post Office Savings Bank. Operating in schools across Toronto, the Penny Bank taught children the habit of thrift and the uses of interest. It was a popular institution with bankers and other businessmen, especially Methodists. It proved its usefulness almost immediately — during the hard winter of 1907–8 in Toronto, it was reported, "the bank accounts of many children, small though they were, saved the day for almost destitute families."[40]

The Penny Bank was one of several semi-charitable organizations in which Flavelle was more or less active. Usually less rather than more, for official positions as Councillor of the British Red Cross Society, Director of the Toronto Working Boys' Home, or Governor of the Toronto branch of the Victorian Order of Nurses usually only signified that he was expected to (and did) favour them with substantial donations. He gave money to almost every charity in Toronto and most outside Toronto, but saved his free time for his church, the university, and Toronto General Hospital.

VI

After retiring as superintendent of the Sherbourne Street Sunday School Flavelle became a class leader again, meeting weekly with his class into the war years. By now the class was a dying institution in Canadian Methodism, and it was one of the "old-fashioned" characteristics of Flavelle's faith that he remained a class leader so long. Class meetings were a form of weekly devotion and mutual self-help, however, offering the personal moral and spiritual succour Flavelle saw as the essence of Christianity. In all other affairs of the church he sided with the forces of modernization.

From 1903 until the formation of the United Church of Canada in 1926 he was a member of various Methodist and joint committees on Church Union, always supporting Union, never playing a leadership role. In 1902 he was appointed to the General Board of Missions of the Methodist Church, which supervised missionary work stretching from downtown Toronto to western China. Again he tended to let others take the lead, although he would occasionally offer important support for reforms. At the Methodist General Conference in 1906 Newton Rowell, an idealistic corporation lawyer active in church affairs and Liberal politics, spearheaded a movement to divide the mission organization into home and foreign divisions and bring in younger men to replace seventy-two-year-old Dr. Alexander Sutherland, who had been Mission Secretary for more than thirty years. Attending his first General Conference, Flavelle strongly supported Rowell's plan. "J. W. Flavelle, LL D, then arose with a bishop's mace and bludgeoned the game old warrior in approved ecclesiastical fashion," the *World* reported. "He drew no blood, but you could hear the dull thuds."

Christian businessmen were sometimes thought to be intent on turning churches into corporations. At this conference it was Sutherland who complained that the plan to divide the Mission Board was unbusinesslike. Flavelle argued to the Conference that business models were inappropriate for a church. The aim of business was "to get everything you can out of your fellow man," that of the church was "to help other men." If the delegates must take examples from business, he suggested they think of the model of a partnership rather than a joint stock company with its single executive authority. The Conference agreed to the reorganization. Apparently Flavelle, Fudger, and Rowell had also hoped to see other aging administrators, including Dr. Potts, eased into retirement, but could not gather enough support to force the issue. Their small attempt to stir up the old bureaucracy stemmed from a feeling that the church was inadequately responding to the need for vigorous work in Western Canada.[41]

A more serious division in Methodism had been developing for years over basic theological beliefs, centring on the validity of the Higher Criticism of Scripture. As the young and well-educated increasingly doubted the literal truth of the Bible, the old guard saw the fundamentals of their faith being eroded in parallel with the whittling away of their power in the church's organization. An evangelical Anglican offensive against the Higher Critics at the University of Toronto in 1908 stirred Dr. Albert Carman, then seventy-five years old and General Superintendent of the Methodist Church since 1884, to launch his own campaign against heresy at Victoria College.

In February 1909 Carman publicly attacked the Reverend George Jackson's interpretation of the early chapters of Genesis, charging him not only with teaching heresy but with having contravened Methodist discipline by his very presence in Canada. Here was the General Superintendent of the Church in open dispute with one of the most popular professors at its leading college—not about angels and pinheads, but about whether a Methodist might dare to disbelieve in angels or dare to think that creation had taken longer than 144 hours.[42]

Jackson, who had moved to Victoria from Sherbourne Street, was a member of the British Wesleyan Connection. In attacking the arrangement under which Jackson had come to Sherbourne Street in 1906, Dr. Carman had forgotten that he had suggested it, and had also ignored the fact that Jackson could not join the Canadian church without forfeiting his pension rights in England.[43] More seriously, Carman's attack on Jackson's scriptural views was based on distortions of what Jackson had said, bypassed the normal disciplinary channels of the church, and generally seemed to be a voice from the past rejecting widely held new views.

Jackson's polite defence of his position coincided with a statement from the Pulpit Supply Committee of Sherbourne Street Church explaining the circumstances of his first appointment. Flavelle had been on the committee, had found Jackson one of the most powerful and moving preachers he had ever known, and had become a close friend of the gentle, scholarly minister. He saw in Carman's attack the personification of everything he most disliked in his church — intolerance, rudeness, authoritarianism. He leaped to Jackson's defence with an open letter to Carman, published in all the Toronto papers:

. . . You assail a brother minister in a manner from which a man in the ordinary walk of life, among those whom you would term Godless people, would be protected by the instinct of good breeding, untempered by the grace of religious profession. You have shocked and distressed men of every communion in the spirit of cruel spite displayed, and the bitter spirit of the heresy-hunter which is found in every part of your communication.

It is not for a layman to pass upon what constitutes a sound or unsound interpretation of Scripture, but he will carry the approval of all sensible men, in asking that, where differences of opinion exist, a spirit of tolerance be shown to every man who honestly seeks to know the truth. . . .

There are many men who are not members of Christian churches who walk softly in the presence of the problems of sin and misery, with which they are confronted every day, and there is an ever-increasing body of men identified with every branch of the Christian Church who profoundly sympathize with them in their anxious inquiry as to how the teachings of the New Testament can be applied to these problems, and how the baneful influence of intolerant ecclesiasticism and churchly pretension can be minimized.[44]

The Jackson — Carman dispute was a major airing of the issues of freedom of thought and speech within the Methodist Church. To Carman and some of his defenders it was also a confrontation with the wealthy laity of Sherbourne Street Church. Learning of the manoeuvres to replace Dr. Potts at the 1906 General Conference, Carman interpreted that action, along with the defence of Jackson, as evidence of "who set up to rule the Methodist Church." At the 1910 General Conference he openly attacked the Sherbourne Street laymen, arguing from Wesley's warning not to make rich men a necessity to the church. Flavelle, Fudger, Kemp, and the Masseys were the rich men Carman and his supporters had in mind. Flavelle had in fact retired from the dispute after his open letter; Newton Rowell, Fudger, and Principal Burwash handled the negotiations and drafted the compromise resolutions on which Jackson and Carman agreed in 1909, only to have the fundamentalists reopen the issue a few months later.[45]

Both sides tried to use money as a weapon. Carman's supporters claimed that Methodists would not give to an Education Fund which supported the teachings of "a negative rationalistic Unitarian preacher." Chester Massey made clear that there would be no more Massey money for Victoria if the policy of padlocking up-to-date professors was allowed to succeed. Not particularly interested in the arcane theological issues at stake, the laymen only wished to get on with the church's practical work. "I believe the great mass of men to-day are sick of theological controversies," Rowell wrote, summing up their viewpoint, "and desire more and more less theology and more practical Christian living—more preaching and teaching such as our Lord Himself gave."[46]

It was not laymen's money that finally triumphed when an anti-Jackson resolution was defeated at the 1910 General Conference, but rather the realization that the attacks on Jackson were a direct threat to freedom at Victoria and within the denomination generally. As Principal Burwash testified in a private letter, Methodism's wealthy laymen had not, on the whole, thrown their weight around behind their dollars. "There is little fear of men of wealth running the Methodist Church," one of the most prominent Social Gospellers argued in the *Christian Guardian*. "Our only danger of autocracy lies in an entirely different direction. Panic and storms of devout prejudice threaten us more seriously than does the influence of mere wealth." Jackson stayed at Victoria, Carman gradually slipped into semi-retirement, and Flavelle continued to teach the young men in his class that Christianity was not about theology or ecclesiastical organization, but about prayer and service.[47]

Having agreed to stay on as a member of the university's Board of Governors, Flavelle remained in the background, leaving leadership to men like Walker, White, and president Falconer. In 1908 he refused to become chairman of the board, pleading the strain on his time caused by Smale's death.[48] He did his share of committee work and was also active in the social life of the university; he particularly enjoyed his turn as host to the Historical Club when Holwood's living room witnessed debates on topics ranging from old-age pensions to the religious situation in France.

Flavelle and Falconer became close friends and the president often informally asked the businessman's advice on university problems. In 1911, for example, Falconer was in a dilemma about the next appointment to the History Department. Should it be the sound young Anglo-Saxon, Gilbert Jackson, or the brilliant Jew, Lewis Namier, both students at Oxford? Reviewing the file, Flavelle did not approve of a second-class-honours man, Jackson, holding an important appointment at Toronto. "Nor do I like the choice of a Polish Jew as an interpreter of history, and I presume constitutional history to our young men," he wrote about Namier. "The selection of a man, distinctly a foreigner, who by his broken accent constantly proclaims it, for such a position disturbs me and makes me uncomfortable. Moreover I am not sure that a foreigner understands British institutions. He may have an intellectual perception of them yet not understand them." In view of Namier's high recommendations, though, he favoured the appointment for at least a trial year. But Jackson got the job, largely, it seems, because of the casual anti-Semitism of the leaders of the university. He was adequate. Namier, later Sir Lewis Namier, became one of the greatest British historians of the century.[49]

Under Falconer's leadership the reorganized university ran smoothly, well lubricated by its fixed percentage of the fast-rising succession duties. Its problems practically disappeared from public view, not least because the Board of Governors met *in camera* and told the press little about its decisions. Most of the unfavourable publicity the university did receive came from journalists and Liberal politicians who wondered why the people's university was being run so secretively, with not even its budget being discussed in the annual estimates. Why weren't the people of Ontario or their representatives even being informed about the work of the university, the Liberal Opposition leader wrote Flavelle. Why had the Royal Commission suggested, and Whitney gone along with, the view that "the people's representatives should not be trusted to vote ample funds wherewith to carry on the work of Toronto University? I don't understand that point of view at all."

Flavelle explained that the Board of Governors dealt with many "delicate" questions, "the wise solution of which . . . will be almost impossible if the discussions and considerations are subject to the hysteria peculiarly present at the moment, in newspapers which feel themselves possessed of ability to offhand settle all questions of public, and indeed frequently private interest." Politicians were about as bad; it would damage the university to be "subject to the ordinary rules of political controversy." Above all, the institution needed "a period of rest from criticism in high places," particularly the Ontario legislature. At the same time, Flavelle hoped the board would deter criticism by improving its public relations and spending its money responsibly. He supported "democratizing" the university by opening its labs and classrooms for post-secondary education, but also wanted entrance standards raised to weed out students unsuited for full-time work at a university. The university had a dual role: serving the ordinary people of Ontario while training an elite for the nation. How else could excellence be maintained in a democracy?[50]

The new hospital would have a similar role: ministering to ordinary sick people while advancing the frontiers of medical science. Like the university, it would be administered by appointed trustees doing their business quietly and efficiently. At one of the first meetings of the new hospital board a proposal to admit reporters was overwhelmingly defeated.[51]

The board was simultaneously running the old hospital and planning the new one. Neither job was easy. Costs at the old building were rising sharply, from $1.34 per patient day in 1907 to $1.53 in 1908. Flavelle resisted cutting standards of care to save money, but had no objection to achieving "economy in wages" by hiring women to replace the male kitchen staff. The main building's leaking roof had to be patched and a concrete floor installed in the nurses' residence to keep out the rats. Otherwise maintenance was cut to a minimum. In the meantime it proved a mistake to work with a single firm of architects—Darling & Pearson, chosen by secret ballot—rather than to hold a design competition. The architects worked slowly, came up with a design the board could not possibly afford, had to be sent back to their drawing boards, and did not produce an acceptable plan until 1909.[52]

There were also important running disputes over staff reorganization. In 1908 the board implemented new regulations putting the first limits on outside activities of the staff, setting up an age of retirement, and organizing "services" in the departments. In the final arrangement, Flavelle's and the other businessmen's desire to install strong executive leadership in the departments was partially frustrated by the doctors' insistence on a wide degree of individual autonomy.[53] Then, when the trustees announced their appointments to the new positions, they created a storm of protest in the university by bypassing some of the senior professors of medicine in favour of younger men. Ex-president Loudon and the bypassed senior professors led the protest. The *Telegram* aired their grievances, muttering editorially about "the over-weening confidence and self-sufficiency of 'the business man.'" Loudon and his supporters assumed that by having given $50,000 from its endowment to the new hospital the university had gained control of staff appointments. Flavelle eventually worked out another compromise through a joint committee. The incident confirmed his belief that the Faculty of Medicine had been "mischievous and troublesome in almost all matters having to do with the hospital."[54]

By 1909 inflation was becoming a noticeable phenomenon for the first time in modern Canadian history. Even Darling & Pearson's scaled down plans required far more money than Flavelle had anticipated, forcing him into another round of fund raising. Not hesitating at a little manipulation in a good cause, the board had already begun buying unnecessary advertising space in the Toronto papers to keep the goodwill of newspaper proprietors inclined to slant editorials against non-advertisers. In 1910 Flavelle turned himself briefly into a political organizer when a ratepayers' vote was needed to enable the city to double its grant. The board hired a special staff to run its campaign; Flavelle made each trustee — Falconer, Sir William Mackenzie, Cawthra Mulock, *et al.* —personally responsible for delivering twenty-five votes, each doctor responsible for ten. The by-law carried.[55]

The university also doubled its contribution. Flavelle raised his gift from $25,000 to $75,000 and then to $100,000, and went through another series of interviews with his wealthy friends and acquaintances to induce them to raise their subscriptions. He was elated at his success with John Eaton, principal heir to the store that Timothy built. Flavelle wanted the Eaton donation raised from $50,000 to $250,000:

I asked him for an appointment today. When I went in and laid before him some photographs showing the wards of the surgical side, he said, "Do you know what you are showing me? You are showing me the wards of the surgical wing of the hospital which will be erected in memory of my father." Having said this he passed to other matters as though it were a mere incident. You may be sure that it did not seem a mere incident to me, and that I was not very sure whether I was head up or feet up, as I had prepared myself for a long struggle, and found that I had no part to play at all except to listen to his statement.

Eaton's donation eventually totalled $360,000. (Asked his opinion, Flavelle had once reluctantly told Timothy Eaton that young Jack was leading too high, wide, and handsome a life to be entrusted with responsibility. "You will live to see you are wrong and I am right," the old man had told him.)[56]

There was harder bargaining with William Mackenzie, who finally agreed to give the $100,000 he had originally been asked for, only to find Flavelle now wanting $250,000. Flavelle's account of their interview is a rare statement of his approach to fund raising. When Mackenzie balked,

I replied that I hoped he would allow his friends, who whether they were sometimes critical like myself, or whether they occupied a less critical relation, all were alike interested in every move which he took and in the position which he filled in the public eye, to support the larger sum. I indicated that we would all be grateful if the scale of his giving would be such that we could feel proud of it. . . . I feel that if we can all co-operate together and secure Mr. Mackenzie's subscription for $250,000 it will settle the hospital matter . . . I think, moreover, that it will put the giving of Mr. Mackenzie on a proper basis, and one which we can all look at with pride in contrast to what is being done in Montreal by men who hold representative positions such as Mr. Mackenzie holds here.

The records do not show whether Mackenzie ever committed himself. In 1911 an anonymous donor — was it Mackenzie himself? — pledged the $250,000 expected of the railway magnate.[57]

Two hundred slum dwellings in Toronto's "Ward" area were demolished to clear the eight-acre site; after clearing, the ground was disinfected. The Governor General laid a cornerstone in April 1911. During construction, the board's Building and Finance committees met almost every week. Four men —Flavelle, P. C. Larkin, Will Rundle, and a public-spirited insurance agent named Mark Irish—chaired all the committees, handling all the problems with the contractors, the design of the refrigeration plant, incineration, fencing, and a thousand other minutiae. On December 6, 1911, City Council's request that Canadian-made doors be used for the new buildings was rejected because the contractors could not find any suitable Canadian doors; the cooling system for the drinking water was approved on May 9, 1912; on January 6, 1913, the architects were told to put closets in the private rooms; on January 20 it was decided to use swinging doors in the pantries. Earlier, the Building Committee agreed to spend an extra $75,000 on the special beige-coloured hardened brick Darling & Pearson had designed—cut stone or terra-cotta would cost too much, white brick would make the hospital look cold, and red brick would make it look like a factory complex. On the other hand no money was allotted for special ornamentation or other architectural frills.[58] The main building's beautiful cupola was only a vestige of what might have been.

1911 was a particularly good year for the economy and Toronto's business prospects were specially bright after the defeat of Laurier and reciprocity in September. The trustees decided to go ahead with Private Patients' and Obstetrical buildings, adding another $500,000 to their costs. In addition to the main building containing an administration section and major surgical and medical wings, the complex now included the Shields Emergency Hospital, the Cawthra Mulock Out-Patients Building, a Pathological Building (being built by the university), a nurses' residence, a servants' building, a power house, and the Obstetrical and Private Patients' buildings. Planned at 400 beds and a cost of $1,300,000, the final complex had 670 beds, costing $3,450,000.

With some patients already in place, the hospital's doors were opened on June 19, 1913. Even though Flavelle had spent several weeks doing nothing but raising money, and had pried a further $210,000 out of City Council (to cover the total cost of the site), the building fund was still about $800,000 short. In his speech to the two thousand guests at the opening ceremonies Flavelle paid tribute to the unselfish work of the doctors and nurses and asked the public for more money.[59]

There were hundreds of small details to tidy up — Flavelle was given authority to handle them all — but the thirty thousand visitors to Toronto General Hospital that day saw the most modern, best equipped hospital in Canada, one of the best in the world. More than half its cost and all the planning and fund raising had been provided by private citizens working under Flavelle's direction. Just after the laying of the cornerstone in 1911, the Governor General had recommended that Flavelle be made a Knight of Grace of the Order of the Hospital of St. John of Jerusalem. He declined the honour, writing that he desired no recognition "for the very moderate service I am able to perform in the field covered by the objects and purposes of the Order." After the hospital was opened in 1913 the Governor General again tried to recommend him for a knighthood. He agreed to accept, but then asked that his name be withdrawn. It was.[60]

CHAPTER NINE

PUBLIC BUSINESSMAN

People who met Flavelle in these middle years of his life remarked on his extraordinary gentleness and self-control. Immaculately but never showily dressed, he was invariably soft-spoken, quiet, and courteous. He never got excited, never showed temper or dismay, never stopped quietly smiling as he talked. "He could go hungry and lean and half sick if need be through the turmoil of life and smile and smile." He did not seem to be a prepossessing man and was reluctant to talk about himself:

An obviously passionless man, he placidly leans back in his chair, opens a casual letter, gazes out of the window at a box-car bumping along a siding; back into the office where it looks as though everybody works but father. And he takes a long period of extremely valuable time to convince the interviewer that there is nothing in his personality worth any one's while to investigate, nothing in his career that ought to interest anybody as a spectacle, but if people choose to take an interest in whatever it has been his privilege to do, why there's no real reason why they shouldn't have at least the plain facts of the case.[1]

He had no apparent personal magnetism, was sometimes thought colour-less, but seemed to have unusual powers of persuasion. "His strength lies in his sweet reasonableness," an editor wrote, "he is all candor and quietness, and his face shines with the certainty that you are a sensible man and will agree with him in a moment. Farmers who come to him to kick and com-plain retire hushed and awed."[2] He seemed to go directly to the heart of the matter, explaining the crux of a complex business problem with a lucidity seldom found in captains of industry. He handled a crippling workload without visible strain. Altogether in his unassuming way a formidable man to do business with or disagree with. Also a man hardly anyone thought they really understood.

Under the surface he had always been impulsive, passionate, quick-tempered, and proud. Some of the same tendencies had destroyed his father, who never learned to curb the urge to find momentary release in drink. All of Joe's training, however, by Dorothea and the church, had been aimed at instilling self-control, self-discipline, total mastery of emotional drives. All the while he was mastering his business, organizing other people, or raising money for good causes, he was also intent on mastering himself to the point where no one, including himself, could fault the impression he made. By middle age he had achieved an impressive outward demeanour. No one saw Flavelle lose control in any normally offensive way. No one was insulted by him, shouted at, or snubbed. Those who disliked him never claimed he was rude or boorish or ill-tempered.

Because he was a perfectionist Flavelle was never entirely free from self-doubt, a sense of inadequacy and failure. It was a personal failure to argue a point badly before a church committee and antagonize some of its members: "Your husband is not a wise man dear, and yet I so desire to be." It was a personal failure to be only *respected* by his employees — the servants *loved* Clara. It was a personal failure not to succeed in life, but also a sin to be ambitious and to be proud of success. It was even a sign of weakness to have to work at being strong, for the virtuousness of the truly good man should emerge effortlessly. "What a poor affair I have made of so much of my life," Flavelle wrote in his fifty-first year; "I feel as though there had been a thread of insincerity running through it that has been hollow and unsound for years."[3]

His mother would have understood her son's restless dissatisfaction, except that she had faded into senility. Even that, to this saintly Methodist woman, was an indication of failure. "She knows something is the matter and conceives it is badness on her part—she thinks it is something for which it would be right to find fault with her," Joe wrote.[4] Dorothea died in the spring of 1908 in her eighty-fifth year.

Flavelle knew he was the product of a particular upbringing (in speeches to young men he often dwelt on the malleability of character and the importance of good habits in moulding behaviour, sometimes using a ball of putty to illustrate his points), and understood how his neo-puritanism was becoming suspect in the new century. In Cairo, Egypt, in 1912 he read in the *News* about a mass meeting in Toronto, chaired by Willison, to protest the closing of the toboggan slides on Sundays. The protest seemed rational and sensible, he wrote. But he was still puzzled,

as to the restraints which should be exercised if we are to retain a serious sense of our duty to matters other than those of mere pleasure and gratification. No one would want puritan conditions re-established—but what the puritans stood for in moral purpose and courage is what the present generation requires.

If left to personal initiative the line of least resistance will likely be followed. The automobile, the Sunday game, the late Saturday night (into Sunday morning) ball claims attention, and the desire to worship God seems to wane if attendance at public worship is any index. A dance here last night (Saturday) which was attended by the military officers broke up at four this morning. . . . This morning at "All Saints" (English Church) many privates but practically no officers were present at the morning service. . . .[5]

Sometimes he seemed almost to envy people free from continuous self-repression. The members of a theatrical troupe travelling on the *Oceanic* in 1907 fascinated him: "Their life is so different from ours . . . their treatment of one another, the absence of shy modesty in their women, the perfectly natural manner in which the men, now one again another chuck the women and girls under the chin, lay their hands upon their shoulder & head familiarly and innocently, practising their daily habits, strike one as at least singular." Watching them reminded him to be tolerant — "for how little we know of others' environment and training"—but also finally to fall back on his own training—"how thankful we ought to be for our pure wholesome surroundings, so full of comfort and so replete with safety."[6]

In his youth one of the Methodist safety devices was to shun actors and the theatre as dangerously corrupting. Flavelle had grown out of that and heartily enjoyed a good play. But he still judged the stage by Methodist standards. Cyril Maude, whom he had just seen in *A Flag Lieutenant*, was one of his favourite actors, he wrote Clara, because he "always makes me desire to do better after hearing him. Is this not a useful test for a play and an actor?"[7]

Romantic thoughts and romance literature often moved him to tears. So did inspiring sermons and hymns. He loved choral and religious music, and was thrilled when his daughters became members of Toronto's Mendelssohn Choir. He followed the choir on its first American tour in 1907. "That darling Father wept like a baby all the way through," Mina wrote her mother after the New York debut. "Never, he says, did he hear such singing, never expected to hear anything like the symphony in Heaven. The entire choir have lost their hearts to him, and have made him father confessor, medical advisor, information bureau; and in fact he is loved by all. Clara thought he would go wild last night in Buffalo but tonight he sobbed and clapped." On their return to Toronto the singers were his guests for an evening's entertainment at Holwood.[8]

There was more time for relaxation and travel as he gradually reduced his business commitments. By 1906 he had become a motoring enthusiast, having switched from an electric automobile to a Russell —which he was taught to drive by Russell himself. He spent more summer weekends at the Sturgeon Point cottage colony, and in 1907 built his own cottage, "Swannanoa," on the site of the old resort hotel. Not so much a cottage as a summer mansion — servants' quarters, gardens, tennis courts and lawn-bowling pitch, set back from the lake in a grove of towering oaks—"Swan" was the grandest of half a dozen cottages owned by Flavelle brothers, cousins, aunts, and in-laws, including J. S. McLean, who had married one of Johnnie Flavelle's daughters. McLean and Joe became arch-competitors for Sturgeon Lake's muskies. Johnnie Flavelle and Will Milner introduced Joe to golf, his favourite relaxation for the rest of his life.

The trips to England always turned into holidays after business was done. In 1912 the family spent four weeks on the Nile, followed by a motor tour of northern Italy and the Riviera. The next year the Flavelles, following the Fudgers and E. R. Woods, discovered California's climate, its golf courses, and its unlimited opportunities for sightseeing and "automobiling."

Flavelle encouraged his children to learn "the art of taking pleasure out of every experience and every surrounding." He was usually fascinated by his travels and was a tireless sightseer. His letters from Egypt include meditations on similarities with biblical times, comments on the Nile as a modern transportation network, and reflections on the future of British power in the country. During Atlantic crossings he tended to keep to himself, fighting seasickness, catching up on his sleep and reading, and observing his fellow passengers. A Japanese writing letters would catch his attention—"I cannot but be struck with the beauty of it." He would like to talk with Dr. Wilfred Grenfell, the famous Labrador missionary, but was too shy—"I can see no natural way of talking to him." So he would make friends with other Toronto businessmen and linger after dinner talking religion, business, and public affairs.[9]

He was not without the prejudices of his upbringing and nationality. "By George! Think of all this for the Royal Family. I don't wonder there was a revolution," the North American democrat commented on seeing the Louvre. Holwood notwithstanding, he fancied himself as among the retiring wealthy, and appreciated an Atlantic crossing where an obviously select company (judging by the number of ladies' maids on board) went their way without swagger or ostentation. And, he added, where there was "almost a complete removal of the Jew. I do not know for what reason—but to me it is highly satisfactory. They are disturbingly disagreeable to me."*[10]

One or more of the children came on most of the trips. Clara was his favourite, bright, cheerful, interested, "a companion of companions." Mina, the first to be married, had an erratic temperament and often quarrelled with her parents. As Ellsworth grew up, Joe tried much too earnestly to mould his character, forcing the lad to carry an impossible burden of his father's expectations. Ellsworth, who did not enjoy good health, reacted by becoming very close to his mother; he developed very few interests in common with his father and had little taste or aptitude for following in his father's footsteps. Flavelle's disappointment with his son was the consequence of having expected too much. Instead of blaming himself, he seemed to believe that Ellsworth had been spoiled by wealth, by not having been forced to fend for himself from an early age. To one of his ministers Flavelle gave the self-made man's classic explanation of his son's failure to "achieve" as much as he had in life: "I wish my boy had my chance."[11]

If Clara junior had been male, Joe would have had his business heir. She inherited his ability and temperament and had thriven on her parents' strict upbringing. She was an excellent and popular student at finishing school in Paris in 1908–9, but worried endlessly about spending too much money, not making the most of her opportunities, not being a credit to her parents. With Mina about to marry Wallace Barrett (and never to fulfil her ambition to be an opera singer), and her mother a semi-invalid, Clara dutifully came home to be second mistress of Holwood rather than continue her education. She, too, would spend her life as wife, mother, and doer of good works,

---

*There are only two anti-Semitic references in Flavelle's papers, both in shipboard letters. It was a casual prejudice widely held among WASPs of the time. It was probably carried into his business affairs as an unconscious matter of course. There is no evidence of active prejudice and what there was did not stand in the way of Flavelle's relationship with the few prominent Jewish businessmen he came to know during the war.

becoming a member of the Order of the British Empire for her work with the Red Cross in the Second World War. Businessmen who knew Clara in later life found her executive ability remarkable; if genuine women's liberation had happened half a century earlier, one of them suggested, Clara could have stepped into her father's position. At the time, her father would have been among the first to consider it unseemly of her to try.

I

The failure of the *News* experiment did not lessen Flavelle's interest in politics. As he cut back on his business responsibilities he had more time to follow and comment on public affairs. His position in the Hydro fight after his independence as a License Commissioner had dissipated most of the influence he had enjoyed with J. P. Whitney at Queen's Park. But the federal Conservative leader, Robert Borden, continued to seek his advice fairly regularly.

Borden was another idealistic and high-minded "progressive" Conservative. He shared the businessman's interest in clean and efficient government and in the need to make Conservatism relevant to modern industrial issues, particularly the debate on public versus private ownership. Although they were not close personal friends, Borden and Flavelle often thought alike, and the party leader seems to have valued the advice of his sympathetic Toronto follower.

Not that Flavelle was a particularly partisan Conservative. As Tories went, he was unusually loyal to Borden as leader, but like many other businessmen, he was not displeased with the Laurier Liberals' moderate protectionism and expansive immigration and transportation policies. He sometimes gave money to deserving Liberals—idealistic young Mackenzie King, fighting his first election campaign in 1908 (earlier Flavelle had offered him the job of superintendent of Toronto General Hospital), fellow churchman Newton Rowell, who became leader of the Ontario Liberals in 1911. Nor was Flavelle immune to Sir Wilfrid Laurier's considerable charm, at least on social occasions. In 1910 he enjoyed a half-hour conversation with Laurier after dinner at Government House, and was even more pleased when the Prime Minister asked to meet Clara. "When I introduced him to Mrs. Flavelle he said, 'You know, Mrs. Flavelle, Mr. Flavelle and I have been friends for many years.' My common sense told me the whole thing was humbug and yet with the perversity of human nature I was gratified." [12]

Flavelle's moderate goodwill towards the Liberal government evaporated literally overnight on January 26, 1911, when he read the terms of the trade agreement just negotiated with the United States. If Parliament and Congress ratified it there would be free trade in natural products across the border, plus reciprocal tariff reductions on selected manufactured goods. This would be the first major reduction in Canadian/American tariffs since the Reciprocity Treaty of 1854.

Most farmers had always wanted reciprocity, of course, and even Sir John A. had given the Americans a standing offer of free trade in natural products. The catch had always been the National Policy of protecting Canadian manufacturers from foreign competition. Now Laurier seemed to have succeeded where Macdonald had failed, by getting an agreement which did not seriously affect the tariffs on most manufactured products. Reciprocity and the National Policy were not incompatible. To most Liberals, some of them worried that the party was ossifying after fifteen years in power, the agreement seemed likely to give their party a new lease on Parliament Hill. Many Conservatives thought so too.

Flavelle spent the evening of the twenty-sixth drafting a long open letter on the implications of reciprocity for his industry. The *Star* gave it front-page coverage the next day, for Flavelle's letter was the first sign of important business opposition to the agreement.

Free trade in livestock and other foodstuffs, Flavelle claimed, would give the whole Western Canadian market to Chicago packers because of their locational advantage. Cheap American barrelled and salt pork would overwhelm the Canadian article in the lumber and mining camps of Ontario, Quebec, and the Maritimes. Canadian packers would be left with only their local markets for fresh and high-quality cured meats. As well, American prices would inevitably set the level of the hog market if it were placed on a continental basis. As prices fluctuated it would sometimes be possible for Canadian packers to continue buying for export, but at other times it would be much too expensive. With the export demand no longer determining prices for Canadian hogs there would be no regularity of supplies for the export trade. Flavelle foresaw the gradual, perhaps even the rapid extinction of Canadian capacity to sell meat in Britain and Europe.

Knowing his special pleading would be ignored if the agreement seemed to be in the national interest, Flavelle argued that it was not. Most Canadians were doing very well after more than a decade of sustained economic progress (except, he noted, some of the lower-paid urban wage-earners and salaried men with moderate fixed incomes). Farmers in particular were enjoying unprecedented prosperity; yet the reciprocity agreement would be "solely in the interests of these prosperous farmers." An agreement which would seriously upset important industries, hurt interprovincial trade, and threaten exports, was being introduced "in favor of the most highly prosperous class at present in Canada."

Finally, Flavelle thought more than money was at stake. At any time in the preceding fifty years, a commitment to "mere material prosperity" would have led Canadians to cast their lot with the United States. "We have had other ideas than mere material prosperity. Why surrender these in our time of success and enlargement for what is represented as added material gain, when a possible penalty is the ultimate loss of political independence?" Flavelle had immediately seen reciprocity as a threat to the political as well as the economic integrity of the nation.[13]

He did his best to mobilize opposition to the agreement. Taken off guard, Willison at the *News* was inclined toward a middle-of-the-road position. Flavelle urged his former associate to call on the Conservative party to rise above its "poor halting policy" of balancing sectional interests, "and boldly declare for National pride, solidarity and the continued adherence to that policy of Canadian nationalism which had so great an exponent in Sir John McDonald [*sic*]." "Willison, we are at the parting of the ways," he urged. "No man stands in the breach, no prophet stands to warn and encourage the people—you have the power. . . . Who knows, yours may be the voice and pen which arouse men to a sense of their responsibility and be influential in determining the political future of the northern half of the continent."[14] Whether as a result of Flavelle's advice or his own inclinations, Willison soon swung into line. The *News* eventually opposed reciprocity to the point of hysteria.

Byron Walker, now Sir Edmund Byron Walker, was also hesitating to speak out against reciprocity, fearing he might offend some customers of the Commerce. Flavelle urged him to speak out anyway, to exercise his "commanding influence" because of the grave political significance of the proposals. He admitted to Walker that his material interests probably influenced his judgment despite his "most earnest effort to set them aside as a controlling factor." But having publicly opposed the Liberal party's proposal for unrestricted reciprocity in the 1891 election, and having been just as critical of reciprocity in 1903 as he was now, he felt justified by consistency. Whether or not his financial interests were involved, Flavelle simply did not want Canada to have closer economic ties with the United States.[15]

Early in February Flavelle led a packers' delegation to Ottawa to present Laurier, Finance Minister Fielding, and Customs Minister Paterson with a detailed memorandum predicting the collapse of their industry under reciprocity. The packers received no satisfaction from the Liberal ministers.

By now Walker had decided to come out against the agreement. At a special meeting of the Toronto Board of Trade Flavelle seconded Walker's resolution opposing reciprocity. Many Toronto manufacturers and businessmen had come to share their alarm; the resolution passed by a vote of 289 to 13.[16]

In the meantime Zebulon Lash, a lifelong Liberal, had been organizing a movement of prominent Toronto Liberal businessmen against reciprocity. On February 20 the "Toronto Eighteen" released their manifesto, opposing the agreement as a threat to Canada's economic and political stability. White of National Trust and E. R. Wood of Dominion Securities were close associates of Flavelle's who signed the manifesto along with Lash and Walker. Lash had consulted with Flavelle in organizing the Liberal revolt. The day after their manifesto was released the Toronto Eighteen met at Holwood to plan their campaign.[17]

Willison apparently became the dissident Liberals' chief liaison with Borden. Within a few days Lash, Willison, Clifford Sifton (Laurier's ex-Minister of the Interior, who had independently come out against reciprocity), and Lloyd Harris, the Liberal MP for Brantford, had worked out an agreement with Borden to cooperate with the Conservatives in the next election. Among other things Borden promised the renegade Liberals representation in any ministry he might form and agreed to consult Lash and Walker on such appointments. Dropping behind the scenes now that Lash and Sifton had assumed leadership of the Liberal revolt, Flavelle thought Laurier could be in trouble if he had to take reciprocity to the voters.[18]

Conservative filibustering on the agreement through the spring of 1911 did force Laurier to go to the people. Flavelle tried to avoid any part in the election, but he undoubtedly contributed heavily to Conservative party funds (his fellow trustee at Sherbourne Street, A. E. Kemp, was the chief Tory organizer for Toronto) and the propaganda organizations of dissenting Liberals. And he became unpleasantly involved towards the end of the campaign when the Liberals dragged forward J. W. Flavelle and the William Davies Company as good reasons why Canada needed reciprocity.

The Liberal candidate in West Toronto, Gordon Waldron, had been involved in the *Weekly Sun* when it had raised the charge of a packers' monopoly several years earlier. Now he centred his campaign on the high cost of food and the low prices of hogs, blaming both on monopolists like Flavelle. In pamphlets and posters he republished the William Davies Company's dividend record through 1906, suggesting that Mr. Flavelle had had enough prosperity to keep him satisfied for a while. Reciprocity would free consumers and farmers from "the clutches of Flavelle" and the other millionaires who specialized in exploiting the public.[19] The Reverend J. A. Macdonald, editor of the *Globe*, also attacked the Davies Company at election meetings, charging that a packers' monopoly kept the price of hogs in Canada below American prices. Joe Atkinson had the *Star* building's front window turned into a refrigerated showcase and filled it with meats bought in Buffalo and at Davies' stores in Toronto; the consumer could see for himself, the *Star* claimed, how much cheaper meat was in Buffalo—and would be in Toronto under reciprocity.

Flavelle replied with angry letters to Macdonald and the papers and through full-page advertisements taken out by the company. Both Department of Agriculture and press reports of hog prices were misleading, he argued, and again offered to open his books to his critics to prove it. The *Star*'s food buyers had purchased low-grade and dissimilar American cuts to compare with first-class Davies meats (an American cooked ham with the bone in and rind on was being compared with a Davies boneless skinned cooked ham; Davies pork bologna was being compared with American beef bologna). They had also bought an ounce or two more than a pound of each Davies product and then listed the total price as the price per pound. A William Davies buyer was sent to Buffalo to obtain truly comparable products. In the company's display, set up in the window of the Queen-and-Yonge store, the comparisons all favoured the Toronto consumer. Willison's *News* also mounted an anti-reciprocity food exhibit, which the *Star* promptly labelled unfair, biased, and partisan.[20]

The nationalism (and self-interest) of Flavelle, Walker, Lash, Sifton, and the Conservatives crushed the mild continentalism (and self-interest) of the Liberals in the election of September 21, 1911. 134 Conservatives would face only 87 Liberals in the next Parliament. Gordon Waldron and all other Liberal candidates in Toronto were defeated. After ten years as Opposition leader Robert Borden had become Prime Minister. As one of the first and most energetic Toronto opponents of reciprocity, Flavelle had done more than his share to bring Borden's "progressive" Conservatism to Ottawa, as he had done earlier in bringing Whitney to power in Ontario.

II

Flavelle was not a candidate for office or appointment, but now had intimate Ottawa connections. There was not only his long-standing support for Borden, but also his friendship with Willison, who became the Prime Minister's closest adviser among Conservative journalists. A. E. Kemp was a minister without portfolio in the new government. Best of all, Borden paid his debt to the Toronto Eighteen by making W. T. White Minister of Finance. White was popular and prominent among Toronto businessmen, and had just proven himself an excellent political campaigner. But his whole business career had been at National Trust under Flavelle. His most prominent community work had been for the university in association with Flavelle. He had originally been thought of as one of Flavelle's young men, a protégé of the older businessman. The appointment gave Flavelle great satisfaction.

He was not so impressed with some of Borden's other choices, and thought the cabinet consisted largely of "men of ordinary parts." For all his good instincts Borden seemed a little too inclined to compromise with old-fashioned machine politics and machine politicians, men like Manitoba's Bob Rogers, the new federal Minister of the Interior, whose "immoral" methods Flavelle thought "offensive to so many right-thinking people."[21] During the next few years Flavelle several times reminded Borden of the need for the highest idealism in public life and the least possible role for Robert Rogers.

Regardless of Rogers, the Borden government was a fairly progressive reforming administration. Flavelle was generally enthusiastic about its policies, and on several issues, notably the problems of the West and imperial relations, his views were typical of the mentality underlying the new Conservatism.

Western farmers interpreted the reciprocity election as a kick in the teeth from Eastern big business. For the first time since the Métis resistance of the 1880s, Western "alienation" became a major factor in Canadian politics as dissident agrarians began to talk up the idea of a third party to break the grip of the big shots of Bay and St. James streets. As one of the bigger big shots Westerners were complaining about, Flavelle decided soon after the 1911 election to see what had happened on the prairies since his last visit in 1901.

He spent several weeks in the autumn of 1911 visiting Winnipeg, Regina, Saskatoon, Edmonton, and Calgary, talking with other businessmen, educationists, churchmen, and farmers. The recent growth and future prospects of the West dazzled him. Since his last trip the population of Winnipeg had grown from 40,000 to 140,000, Saskatoon from nothing to 15,000, Calgary from a few thousand to 45,000, he wrote. A million dollars' worth of beautiful buildings were already in place on the three-hundred-acre Saskatoon campus of the University of Saskatchewan. The new Winnipeg offices of the Commerce and the Bank of Montreal were worthy of being set beside the Royal Exchange in London. The value of the fertile land in the three provinces had increased by two billion dollars in five years. Flavelle saw farmers working the land with gasoline-driven traction engines drawing gang ploughs that could break thirty acres a day and even keep going at night with "head lights." He saw the domain of a Swedish immigrant who had brought $100 with him to Saskatchewan in 1904 and now owned 25,000 acres, needed 36 binders to work them, and had just grossed $150,000 on his flaxseed alone. Flavelle's letters about the trip are sprinkled with adjectives like "astonishing," "staggering," "spectacular."

Few Westerners were more optimistic about the region's future than this visiting Eastern capitalist. He expected the banking business in Winnipeg to outstrip Toronto's within five years, Vancouver to become Canada's largest city within twenty years of the opening of the Panama Canal. Predicting "astounding growth" in Western crops, he brushed aside all talk of hail, frosts, drought, or other disasters—"you may dismiss them all as having no considerable bearing on the longer future of the country. It will bear any or all of these misfortunes."[22]

It was the Westerners, not the West, that alarmed him. He found "restless anger and irritation" on the prairies, a belief that Easterners like himself were holding the West in bondage as a market for their manufactured goods. Much of this spirit, he thought, reflected the heightened self-importance emigrants from the East developed when they found out how easy it was to make money in the West. "The wealth which has come to them without effort on their own part, they attribute to their cleverness. . . . They are and will be an impatient people, restless under restraint, and ready on what they consider sufficient provocation to assert their right to follow their own course. . . ."

However unfounded in reality, the Western sense of grievance, along with the tens of thousands of immigrants' ignorance of things Canadian or British, convinced Flavelle that national unity was Canada's most urgent political problem. Always a believer in personal contact, he naturally thought Easterners should go West more often. He also wanted political action on certain Western grievances, particularly the shortage of railway facilities (for which he blamed the CPR). He suggested the federal government might honour the 1915 centennial of John A. Macdonald's birth by endowing Canadian Studies departments at Toronto and McGill; their scholarship programmes could bring students together from across the country. For the first time he began to question some of his assumptions about the tariff, suggesting tough treatment of manufacturers who failed to see that protection had to serve the national interest as well as their own.[23]

Flavelle would have liked the Borden government to have gone further than it did in attempting to conciliate Western opinion (it passed important legislation regulating the grain trade and increased federal assistance to agricultural research), but like many Eastern Conservatives he was not interested in substantial alterations of national policies in the interests of Western Canada. The West was doing so well, had so much promise, that it didn't need further government favours. Most Western grievances could be dismissed as inconsequential; the best advice to give Westerners was to work hard and cultivate their large gardens. Flavelle's most characteristic comments on national unity were to urge Willison to continue writing articles "making a claim for patience and fairness in the West, with an honest examination of what has been done and accomplished for and on behalf of the Western man and the success and wealth that has come to those who have chosen the West for their home." If only Westerners could be made to realize that they had never had it so good.[24]

III

Flavelle was a fairly typical Canadian imperialist. An anglophile by birth, he had made his fortune as a hog butcher for the Empire, read English literature and history almost exclusively, and criss-crossed the British Isles on his holidays. His Canadian "identity" was a British identity, and he never doubted that Canada would one day take her place at Britain's side as a full-fledged member of the family of British nations. Some day there might even be a super-imperial government ruling a federation of self-governing British nations.

He was interested enough in visions of the Empire's future to become associated with Willison, Edward Kylie, Arthur Glazebrook (a Toronto banker), Walker, and others, in the Toronto branch of the Round Table movement. It was organized in 1901 by Lionel Curtis, the most zealous of the group of young imperialists in England who launched the movement to spread the dream of imperial unity they had developed while working under Lord Milner to unify South Africa after the Boer War. Milner's "Kindergarten" group in England saw themselves as the centre of an Empire-wide web of Round Table groups, all promoting imperial federation through study, propaganda, and the use of personal influence in high places.

Like many Canadian imperialists, however, Flavelle was a less than zealous Round Tabler. He did not believe the Empire could be more closely united until the Dominions had grown out of their colonial status to maturity. Nor was he interested in imperial economic devices like preferential tariffs (which would have enormously helped his bacon business if they crippled Danish competition) that might impede Canada's progress to industrial nationhood. As a progressive colonial businessman, and as the partner of J. Wheeler-Bennett, he knew a lot about British condescension towards colonials and the deep conservatism of British business. The supercilious English too often tried to further their own interests at the expense of their colonies. Closer imperial unity could develop *after* the British learned to accept Canadians as equal partners in the life, mission, and business of the Empire.[25]

But history was barely giving Canada time to grow up. By the end of the first decade of the twentieth century Britain's inability to compete economically and militarily with the dynamic German Empire (Flavelle himself had been very impressed with German enterprise and progress during his 1903 visit) was becoming apparent. Ready or not, the Dominions would have to help the Mother Country if British hegemony, particularly over the world's oceans, was to be maintained.

In the first round of Canadian debate on military aid to Great Britain in 1908–9, the Laurier government decided the most appropriate Canadian contribution to imperial defence would be to build a national navy. The alternative of financing more Dreadnoughts for the British navy, which was favoured by many Conservatives, seemed to smack of colonial subservience.

Flavelle was not unhappy with the 1909 policy, but by 1912 he shared imperialists' concern that the naval crisis was now too severe to waste time and money fiddling with long-range Canadian schemes. Britain badly needed help; Canada was surely rich and mature enough to give generously. The very act of contributing to imperial defence, Flavelle thought, would symbolize "the measure and the dignity of the young community entering into manhood and assuming a share of the burden long borne by the senior." While Borden was in England in the summer of 1912 being briefed on imperial defence requirements, Flavelle helped found a non-partisan movement calling for an emergency contribution to British naval defence within the framework of a long-term commitment to a Canadian navy.[26]

Largely because of French Canadian resistance to imperialism in any shape or form, the Liberals fiercely opposed paying what seemed to be colonial tribute. The Borden government's Naval Aid Bill — authorizing a $35-million contribution to build three Dreadnoughts for the Royal Navy — passed the House of Commons in the spring of 1913 only after the Conservatives used closure for the first time in Canadian parliamentary history. In retaliation the Liberal-dominated Senate promptly rejected the bill, causing a major political crisis and leaving the country with no naval policy.

"No single event in public affairs in Canada during my lifetime so deeply moved me as the action of the Liberal party in relation to your naval proposals," Flavelle wrote Borden. Rejection seemed to him a shameful, spiteful, partisan act, an attack on Canadian dignity and manhood. Laurier's position, he decided, was simple opportunism. "I am not sure but personally I would prefer the morals of an out and out vagabond to this type of high-sounding, phrase-making public man, who seems to be as successful in humbugging himself as those who surround him." Among those who surrounded Laurier he singled out supposed Christian idealists like Mackenzie King and Rev. J. A. Macdonald of the *Globe* as practising a transparently dishonest brand of partisan Christianity, a kind of religious life "which brings religious profession into disrepute with manly men."[27]

He urged Borden to go to the country on the naval question. Perhaps a solid French Canadian anti-imperialist vote would bring the Liberals back into power, but the Conservatives would at least have retained their self-respect. Borden's vacillation on the naval issue — he was not sure he could win an election in 1913 or early 1914 — confirmed the businessman's earlier suspicion that Borden was temperamentally unsuited to take bold initiatives. "Associated with the many excellencies of which the Premier is possessed, there is the handicap in the lack of firm decision, which promptly deals with matters with the courage and grasp belonging to a man who makes up his mind in a reasonable length of time the course which he will pursue, and then presses it to a conclusion."[28]

Flavelle and others would repeat this criticism of Borden many times in the next few years. Borden was a cautious leader. But Flavelle's impatience also reflected the confident businessman's belief that politicians should act with the despatch of a chief executive—and, perhaps, an idealist's belief that it was better to take a losing stand on principle than no stand at all.

IV

Stands had to be taken on another problem much closer to Flavelle, White, and their circle than issues of imperial defence or relations with the prairie provinces.

Laurier's railway legacy to the Conservatives was two transcontinental systems struggling to be born. The National Transcontinental and the Canadian Northern were racing to finish their main lines and branch systems, each company bringing thousands of miles of new track into operation every year. Both faced rising construction costs. Both, but particularly the Canadian Northern, could raise fresh capital only as long as foreign investors were willing to swallow new issues of Canadian railway securities. By 1912 the portfolios of foreign investors were stuffed with Canadian bonds and debentures. In 1913 and 1914 their appetite dried up completely. There was a general feeling in foreign money markets that Canada and "Canadians" were overdone — a feeling also reflected at home, where the frantic pace of development, peaking in 1911–12, began to coast to a standstill. By the winter of 1913–14 the nation was in a serious depression and the unfinished railways were in desperate straits.

They naturally turned to the public teat. The Canadian Northern needed the most help, and needed it urgently to avoid defaulting on its bond interest. In 1913 and again in 1914 the Borden government had to balance the political unpopularity of giving more aid to Mackenzie and Mann's private railway against the economic (and political) consequences of a Canadian Northern default and collapse. Mackenzie and Mann's major creditor, the

Bank of Commerce, was vitally interested in the government's decisions. Many thought National Trust had a similar interest. To political outsiders it looked as though the Minister of Finance, W. T. White, was also all too interested in the decision—although he had resigned his business positions, he had been so closely associated with the Canadian Northern/Bank of Commerce/National Trust group in Toronto that it was not unnatural to assume he was their man in Ottawa, ready and willing to bail out his friends.

In fact, National Trust had been very careful with its Canadian Northern business, never tying itself too closely to promoters whom Flavelle—and by reasonable inference, White—suspected. Far from being "friends" of Mackenzie and Mann, the trust company's officers were among their severest critics in the inner circles of Toronto business. Shortly after a long conversation with White in the spring of 1914 Flavelle was probably reflecting their joint views when he wrote of Mackenzie, "He has no friends other than those he acquired by purchase in one way or another during the course of his career." The Canadian Northern's supposed friend in Ottawa, W. T. White, was in fact one of its harshest critics, and at several points in the 1913–14 discussions was ready to let the railway default and go into receivership.[29]

Other ministers and businessmen did not share White's confidence that a Canadian Northern collapse could be contained. It could destroy the already shaky credit rating of all Canadian securities in foreign money markets. Provincial and federal governments would have to honour guarantees on Canadian Northern bonds; some provinces might be strained to the financial breaking-point. Other companies, including possibly the Bank of Commerce, could be pushed towards collapse. The cabinet decided to keep the entrepreneurs going, but not without demanding compensation. By the spring of 1914 forty per cent of the common stock of the Canadian Northern was owned by the Dominion government in return for new bond guarantees; if the Canadian Northern still could not meet its obligations, the government could take over the rest of the common stock. The Canadian Northern/Commerce group were immensely relieved when the uncertainty of the situation seemed to have eased. But they all felt, according to Flavelle, that the terms were tough and White had "acted badly" in supporting the exaction of the common stock.[30]

Flavelle, by contrast, saw nothing wrong with the agreement. In 1903 he had suggested government purchase of a controlling interest in the CPR. In 1909 he had advised Borden that further aid to the Grand Trunk Pacific should be conditional on the government taking a controlling interest in its common stock. Because Mackenzie and Mann were the men most likely to finish the Canadian Northern, he supported letting them go on, but thought it only reasonable of the Canadian people to demand a share of their profits in return for further aid. The prospect of more trouble, leading to total government ownership of the Canadian Northern, did not unduly bother him.[31]

He was more concerned about the judgment his friends at the Commerce had exercised in their involvement with Mackenzie and Mann. The sources are obscure, but Flavelle, acting on his own or with other directors, seems to have insisted on a full statement of the Bank of Commerce's relations with Mackenzie and Mann being placed before the Board of Directors at the end of 1913. From it he concluded that for several years the executive officers of the bank had been making advances to Mackenzie and Mann companies, which they had deliberately avoided bringing before the board. He euphemistically labelled these actions "a departure from sound practice" and held Sir Edmund Walker — "your own good self (to whom we have all been indebted for high standards)" —personally responsible. When the strain of negotiations with Ottawa was eased at the end of April 1914, he drafted a pained letter to Walker resigning from the board of the Bank of Commerce.[32]

Nothing happened. Flavelle did not resign. The letter may never have been sent. Flavelle must have been persuaded to stay on because he had his facts wrong, or had exaggerated their significance, or because he would be a useful watchdog in the future. All the actors—Flavelle, Walker, Wood, Mackenzie and Mann, Lash, White, and Borden—would take railway finance more seriously in the future. The years of boundless optimism, bold ventures, and easy credits were over.

V

As his support for a tough railway policy showed, Flavelle still seemed to be a "progressive" Conservative, suspicious of the abuse of private corporate power, interested in state regulation and even public ownership of basic utilities. He still believed Toronto would never get good streetcar service until the city owned its own transit system. He was a patron of the Toronto Housing Company, one of the earliest efforts to provide low-cost housing to Canadian workers. He earnestly believed that campaign contributions

225

gave large corporations undue influence over politicians, and supported full disclosure of campaign contributions and expenditures as a way of breaking "the partnership between public men and corporations." He worried generally about the lack of idealism in Canadian life. The central task of leadership, he thought, was to challenge Canadians to rise above mere materialism.³³

These elements of continuity masked fundamental changes taking place in Flavelle's thought in the years from about 1909 to 1914. Reacting most obviously to criticisms of his own industry, he was gradually becoming less eager for many kinds of reform, much more conservative than progressive.

Under Flavelle's management the William Davies Company had played by all the rules of the game. It had minded its business, produced the best products it could, bought and sold openly on competitive markets. More intense competition had spurred Flavelle and his officers to greater effort, efficiency, and excellence. The company had not combined with other packers to exploit farmers or with other sellers to exploit consumers. Anyone could come into the industry and try to do a better job of serving the public. Until someone did that successfully it seemed fair to assume that the Davies Company and its competitors were doing their work reasonably well. Moreover, in the quarter-century Flavelle had been in the meat-packing industry, it had developed from the era of farmer slaughter and local distribution, with almost complete wastage of by-products, to its present state of mass processing, world-wide distribution, and intensive use of by-products. Driven by the profit motive and competition, the leading packers had turned a primitive, inefficient system of production into a giant modern industry serving the public in ways hardly conceivable a generation before. It was not a bad record.

Yet by 1910–11 Flavelle and his industry were under repeated attack. The belief that a packers' combine controlled the buying price of livestock had not died out among farmers and journalists, and in Ontario was often being used to account for the apparent unprofitability of some kinds of farming. At the same time the rising cost of living was starting to create consumer restlessness about high food prices. Why was the food industry charging so much? Middlemen like the packers were starting to be attacked at both ends: by producers for buying low, by consumers for selling high. Farmers in a troubled industry needed a villain; so did consumers suffering from inflation. In 1910 the federal Minister of Labour, Mackenzie King, was quoted as saying that trusts and combines were undoubtedly the most important cause of high food prices. He was drafting anti-combines legislation to put a stop to it. In the 1911 election the villains were called by name—J. W. Flavelle and the William Davies Company.

Flavelle denied, denied, and denied again that anything improper was taking place. In letters and speeches he tried to explain how the industry really worked, earning its profits by taking a small mark-up on large volumes, the competitors driving each other into greater efficiency. He could not see how packers could fairly be criticized, indeed he thought they should be credited for their "rare capacity" in becoming the most efficient of all workers in the food industry.[34]

When criticism persisted no matter what he said, Flavelle concluded that his industry was being used as a scapegoat by people unwilling to face up to their own shortcomings. He criticized consumers who complained about high food prices, for example, asking how much they knew about comparative shopping, the efficient preparation of food, the use of cheap nutritious cuts, and the other arts of household science. Most of his attention, however, centred on the other end of the industry. He had been buying farm products for more than forty years and believed he was considerably more informed about the business of farming than most farmers were about packing. As early as 1883 he had addressed the Peterborough YMCA on "Opportunities Abused: The Husbandman." He had always been interested in agricultural science and in 1909 had spent considerable time with agricultural experts while serving on an International Commission on Bovine Tuberculosis. Now, as criticisms of the packers melded with general complaints about the plight of Ontario farming, Flavelle acted as a kind of elder statesman of the packing industry in writing and speaking about the real causes of the agricultural problem.

The trouble was simply the failure of farmers to rise to their opportunities, he argued. They were not very efficient — certainly nothing like as efficient as packers. In 1910, just as in 1880, too many of them made do with poorly drained and fertilized land, poor seed, poor breeding stock, and poorly paid help. They did not reinvest their profits. Agricultural colleges and experimental farms (the real origins of "research and development" in Canadian industry) had shown how intensive, efficient methods could create incredible productivity gains. But the average Ontario farmer was lucky to achieve half the productivity of the scientific farmers at the Ontario Agricultural College, and in his methods lagged far behind the ordinary farmers in a progressive little country like Denmark. Many Ontario farmers, Flavelle thought, lacked the enterprise, the courage, the hope, "that grasp and vision which are dominant in every other field of activity in the country."

Farming seemed to him an occupation peculiarly sheltered from the stimulus of competition. Farmers would always survive; there were so many of them that a neighbour's efficiency and productivity had no adverse effect on any individual farmer's returns. Then, too, rural areas tended to conservatism because they missed "the intellectual stimulus and quickening" of city life. It could only be provided by such institutions as the farm press, rural schools and agricultural colleges, and government departments of agriculture. These supportive agencies should encourage farmers to be more productive, pay higher wages, provide better housing and conveniences to keep farming attractive for their families. Agitation against other people was no solution. The rural press, educators, Ministers of Agriculture, had to realize and then tell farmers the truth: "The farmer, like everyone else in the community, can, on the last analysis, secure results only from his own effort, supported by intelligence, sound sense and industry."[35]

Flavelle was urging farmers to try harder, just as he and his company had tried harder when it was threatened by more competition. Hard work and self-reliance had been an effective prescription for business troubles in his own career and should work for others. Ironically, of course, trying harder in the face of adversity was no longer working in the Canadian bacon trade to Britain. Similarly, it probably would not have worked for many Ontario farmers for whom the gains from increased efficiency would not balance the gains from leaving the land. Most farmers, like most businessmen, could not rise to the level of excellence of the best in their industries no matter how hard they tried. A whole industry, whether farming or meat-packing, could be in serious trouble even though a few farmers or packers were still doing well. It was unrealistic and arrogant of Flavelle to attribute these troubles to personal incompetence, as he did in his comments on fellow packers and farmers alike. He failed to see the point at which the determined individual's effort amounted to ploughing the sand.

He was also preaching from a remote and suspect pulpit, a millionaire's perch far removed from the realities of ordinary people's lives. In his own eyes he was an ordinary businessman who had made good, now advising others to adopt the simple methods he had used. To others it was not obvious that a multimillionaire could possibly have done it all by hard work, sobriety, and thrift. No one could amass that much money without exploiting somebody, if only Dame Fortune. It was cheap talk for a millionaire to tell poor folk whose lives were hard enough already that the main thing to do was stop complaining and work harder. More than cheap talk, it was a convenient way of ducking hard questions about how a millionaire had earned his money and what ought to be done with it. Even as he was giving them, Flavelle realized that his sermons defending his industry were having little impact.[36]

He kept trying, for anti-corporate sentiment was starting to have serious consequences. Other businessmen (such as the owners of street-railway companies) had sensed it earlier. Flavelle had begun to realize it in the life-insurance investigation and the fight over Ontario Hydro. It was Mackenzie King's Combines Investigation Bill of 1910, however, that opened his eyes most clearly. Under the terms of the proposed legislation an allegation from any six citizens that a trust or monopoly was at work could set a major government investigation in motion. The William Davies Company was liable to be swooped down upon, put to immense trouble, and perhaps have all its operations publicized for competitors to see, the moment any six farmers decided that the old packers' combine was oppressing them. This would be an intolerable interference in the affairs of an innocent business.

He wrote King several long complaining letters. Yes, some businessmen (mostly Americans) did combine to exploit the public. Governments should stop them. Yes, good men should attack evil, and, if necessary, use legislation to help equalize wealth. But surely "agitation" against corporations had gone far enough. The agitation against his own company was utterly wrong, had been exhaustively denied, but still persisted. Now things had reached the stage where a successful businessman "is practically told that he is a criminal and that he is to prove to the contrary."[37]

Another instance of success being penalized was workmen's-compensation legislation, pending in Ontario by 1914. An excellent safety record had won the William Davies Company a two-thirds reduction in its accident-insurance premiums from the private companies. Under the Ontario government's scheme it would be lumped in with all other packing houses, including feeble, fly-by-night concerns that paid little attention to safety. Flavelle saw no more reason why his company should pay for accidents in butchering shops than that Sir John Willison should pay for them.[38]

Anti-business, anti-corporation agitation in North America, Flavelle felt, had passed the limits of its usefulness. The critics of big business, like the critics of his company, were looking for a victim to punish for all kinds of social problems. They were intolerant, impatient, shrill, and potentially very dangerous. He still insisted in his speeches that he was conscious of and opposed to unfair business practices — "the predatory actions of unscrupulous men" — and he held to this position where real buccaneers like William Mackenzie were concerned.*[39] But it was time for the public to remember the positive contribution businessmen made to society. Most business was carried out honestly; most businessmen were working diligently, without seeking special favours.

It has been forgotten that the community owes much to the creative force of men with constructive capacity who, while accumulating power and wealth for their personal gain, have been leaders in movements which have brought great benefit to the general community. At a later period when society through experience learns to organize more wisely, much wealth which now comes to the individual or to the small group of individuals, will be more widely distributed through the benefits derived from co-operation or co-partnership or some form of voluntary association. It will still be true, however, even under such circumstances, that capacity to organize, supported by intelligent industry, will bring wealth to individuals and corporations. It will still be true that the public will owe a debt of obligation to the men of vision, courage and purpose who inaugurate and assume the responsibility for movements of vital interest to the public, which smaller and more critical men will not undertake. In undertaking such work these men will not be possessed of a spirit of philanthropy. They none the less, however, serve the community at large while so generously taking care of themselves.[40]

The Ontario Hydro fight seemed to him to show how thoughtless agitation interfered with real social priorities. Toronto voters had approved a by-law to spend millions on a power plant to serve manufacturers who should be able to fend for themselves on the open market and to light the homes of the comfortable (who could afford electricity). In the meantime, Torontonians tolerated the continued pollution of the city's water supply,

---

* Mackenzie was almost certainly the businessman Flavelle described as having 'in a very emphatic way asked me what I had against him. I said—'Nothing, my dear Sir, except that you take advantage of all the safeguards that society has established for the purpose of making possible the orderly conduct of affairs, with protection to you and others who are interested in property and in carrying on great enterprises, and having participated in these you undertake on your own account to be a buccaneer, going to the limit of the law, and sometimes beyond it to further your own ends.' "

shamefully poor housing conditions in the city, insufficient playgrounds for the poor, and inadequate hospital facilities for the treatment of contagious diseases. While the middle and upper classes and the self-interested agitators benefited, not much was done for the ordinary people.[41]

In speeches to Canadian Clubs, church groups, and business organizations, Flavelle suggested that social unrest based on attitudes of envy, scolding, and class agitation, give way to a new spirit of cooperation. Not the usual concrete forms of cooperation, like marketing schemes or stores, for these could not be much more efficient than existing systems of marketing (unless, like combines, they got special privileges). By cooperation he meant "an increased sense of responsibility which each man should bear to his fellow, that what he undertakes to do will be well done — a cooperation which claims from those observing it an obligation to raise the standard of efficiency by personally well done and well considered work." If everyone recognized his duty to do his job well, both the individual and the community would profit. Minding one's own business in the fullest sense was the best way to contribute to the community and create real social harmony. The unity and cohesion of society could best be preserved if people stopped trying to blame others for their faults, stopped trying to secure redress by burdening others with legislation, and did their work well.[42]

Working out his ideas in response to specific situations—he was much too busy to think systematically about social problems—Flavelle was beginning to articulate a thorough-going individualism, amounting to a pronounced social conservatism, in the years before the Great War. As more reformers proposed collectivist solutions to social problems, Flavelle became less interested in their kinds of social reform. As reformers came to centre on the abuses of capitalism as a system, Flavelle became less a critic of his fellow businessmen, more their defender. He had seemed to be an up-to-date twentieth-century "progressive" Conservative; now he increasingly sounded like a nineteenth-century liberal individualist, one of a type historians have dismissed as largely irrelevant to the new Canada taking shape by 1914.[43]

Actually, it was the issues Flavelle worried about that were largely irrelevant before 1914. The flurry of farmer and consumer concern about monopolies and the special problems of the packing industry in the prewar years did not add up to a significant challenge to the economic system. Canada had no "trust-busters" comparable to Theodore Roosevelt or Woodrow Wilson. King's Combines Investigation Act, which so distressed Flavelle, turned out to be ceremonial legislation which threatened no one.

Flurries of public concern about the powers of the "big interests" in the Laurier years produced little change beyond the establishment of Ontario Hydro and a smattering of other public utilities. Canada's few radical reformers were not taken seriously. Companies did their business without important government interference (except to help them). Employers looked after the social welfare of workers who did their jobs properly. Philanthropists like Flavelle looked after the welfare of those unable to work. The deserving were looked after, the undeserving were undeserving.

VI

Flavelle was easing into retirement, enjoying the good things of life after his years of hard work. Politics and reading and small acts of public service could fill most of his time, travel the rest. The long summers of golf, fishing, picnics, and Sunday walks at Sturgeon Point were particularly relaxing. For the summer of 1914, though, the family decided to pass up the Point and instead take a motor trip through England and Wales.

Joe, Clara, Ellsworth, and young Clara boarded the ten o'clock train for Montreal at North Toronto station on the evening of June 18. Amy and Lily Dundas, Will and Ada Rundle, Mina and Wallace Barrett, Stanley and Edith McLean all came to the station to see them off. It was still swelteringly hot when they boarded the *Calgarian* at Quebec City the next day. But the decks were soon swept by cool sea breezes and, except for two or three days of fog, the passage was uneventful.[44]

CHAPTER TEN

THE BUSINESS OF WAR

The family's tour of England in the warm and sunny summer of 1914 was suddenly broken off early in July when Clara took sick and had to be rushed to London for surgery. While she recovered in a nursing home Joe saw old friends, attended to business (National Trust was opening a London office) and church affairs, and followed the downward course of European diplomacy.

Like most people in England he did not realize that a European war was imminent until the last days of July. On Wednesday the twenty-ninth, when Austria declared war on Serbia, he was at Oxford as the guest of A. J. Smith, the Master of Balliol. Several members of the English Round Table were also visiting the college, including Lionel Hichens, a former member of Milner's Kindergarten, who now ran the giant steel and shipbuilding firm of Cammel Laird. Late into the night the dons and businessmen discussed the international situation, groping to understand what a war would mean and whether Britain could see one through. They still hoped fighting could somehow be avoided.[1]

Flavelle went back to London for the August Bank Holiday weekend. "My mind fails in its attempt to grasp the significance of all this terrible war situation," he wrote Willison on Saturday, the day Germany declared war on Russia. "Yesterday was calm with little or no hint of the Storm. Today anxiety, concern, trouble covers the face of the civilized Globe — it is as though one were in some horrid nightmare and that it would pass. . . . The gloom and anxiety over financial London cannot be comprehended."

No one feared the outbreak of war more than businessmen active in international trade. War would be a knife slicing through the intricate web of world trade and finance. Markets and sources of supply would instantly disappear; millions in debts would be uncollectable. For a week stock exchanges everywhere had been engulfed by panic selling; no one knew what would happen when they reopened, if they reopened, after the weekend. No one knew whether London's great banks and acceptance houses would be able to meet obligations maturing in the next week, for millions in remittances from the Continent would never arrive. International finance was a house of cards resting on the City of London, and it seemed about to collapse. "Men are staggered and stunned," Flavelle wrote, ". . . uncertainty of what may occur makes brave men quake."

The holiday crowds thronged around Westminster and Downing Street as governors met to prepare for the worst. In his room at the Welbeck Palace Hotel the Canadian visitor was deeply pessimistic:

The dislocation of trade and commerce means untold thousands of idle workers whose limited resources will speedily disappear, particularly with the necessities of life at war prices. The possible suffering on this score of women and little children here and in every continental country beggars description. One draws the veil over what the actual war will mean for women, for children, for homes where the actual struggle takes place, and the heart-broken who lose loved ones, who may yet be spared the actual contact with conditions immediately in the line of moving or fighting troops. Will the Good God stay the hand of man, or will cruelty be given full license, and this awful struggle go on?[2]

I

His despair was already passing by the time England declared war on Tuesday, August 4. "I cannot compass or comprehend this happening. The greatness in the leaders in finance, in Government, in the press, in parliament, in the man on the street. The reserve, the power, the poise, the capacity. . . ." He was specially impressed by the vigour with which Lloyd George, Chancellor of the Exchequer, rushed through an emergency programme of war insurance, debt moratoria, and other measures to prop up business morale. The effect on businessmen had been "electric," Flavelle wrote on the thirteenth. "The City wears a different face — perplexity, anxiety, staleness has given way to vigor, courage and hopefulness."

Clara's convalescence proceeded smoothly and the family went home on the *Adriatic* late in the month. Joe was full of inspiration at the way the English had responded to war:

I have always been pro British, I have long admired this people, but their conduct during these two weeks fills me with amazement. The quiet calm way they have faced a new and terrible situation, their resource, their deep human sympathy, their poise and self possession, their determination to see this thing through, and the willingness of the young men to enlist and for all to ask, what can I do, is inspiring. This people did not want war, they had no idea it would come . . . they took on this dreadful burden and no one murmurs or finds fault with his fellow. A decadent race? A dying people?—the truth is that this people were never so great.[3]

Like most English-speaking Canadians Flavelle assumed the war was being fought to defeat aggressive German militarism. He never doubted Germany's responsibility for the war or Canada's obligation to go into battle at Britain's side. As a Christian idealist he soon came to believe in the war as a holy crusade to free the world from tyranny.

But that response developed only later. After the tide of financial panic Flavelle had seen in London had ebbed, public opinion in both Britain and Canada swung round to the idea of carrying on "business as usual." The troops would go to France, beat the Germans, and be home again in a few months. That would be the end of the war.

Flavelle's life went on as usual through 1914 and early 1915. He had never taken any interest in the militia or military affairs, and in any case at fifty-six he was far too old to enlist. Of course there were special contributions to be made to the Patriotic Fund, which supported the families of Canadian soldiers abroad, and to the Red Cross. But there were no significant war taxes (in August Thomas White had estimated Canada's war needs at less than fifty million dollars; he raised the money by borrowing and slightly higher tariffs on coffee, sugar, spirits, and tobacco), no shortages of goods, and no serious restrictions on most people's movements or liberty. Flavelle spent some of his time at the hospital arranging to fill vacancies created by staff who had volunteered for service and helping to work out accommodation for the victims of the outbreak of cerebrospinal meningitis among the troops quartered in the Toronto Exhibition buildings. He also spent a lot of time in 1914 and 1915 corresponding with the Toronto Conference circuits of the Methodist Church about the need to give more money toward ministers' salaries.

In the autumn and winter months he spoke to Canadian Clubs in Toronto, Hamilton, Ottawa, and Winnipeg, describing the financial crisis on the eve of war and the British government's resolution of it. In Canada, he pointed out, Finance Minister White had acted just as decisively. Governments generally had responded well to the emergency and kept the gossamer threads of credit, finance, and trade from beginning to separate.

Flavelle did worry about how certain Canadians were trying to use the war to avoid their responsibilities. This had nothing to do with recruiting or war service but was a product of the depression. Hard times were still causing more anxiety and more real suffering in the country than the fighting in France, where Canadians were not yet in combat (the author of the *Canadian Annual Review* for 1914 tried to be optimistic in writing that "after the first temporary dislocation of the War period and the fear of the unknown which affected all business, recovery was steady until a condition almost normal to a time of depression was reached").[4] The idea of a moratorium on debts, something like the British August moratorium, appealed to many mortgagees who were having trouble meeting their payments, as well as to a number of Canadian municipalities whose bonded debt was becoming intolerable with the collapse of real-estate values.

It was inconceivable to Flavelle—and all other financiers—that Canadians should use the excuse of war to avoid paying their debts. Comparisons with the temporary British moratorium on debts owed internally were silly for a debtor country whose very "lifeblood" was its credit rating abroad. If foreign investors found they could not collect the interest due them, when it was due them, there would be no more money loaned to Canada, and the depression would become far worse. Flavelle urged his business audiences to stop scolding bankers for insisting on financial responsibility and to realize that the long overdue economic readjustment had nothing to do with the war. Their job was to "play the game," keep their heads up, and "take your punishment."

Going further, he suggested that employers should remember the good years they had had and make a special effort to help their workmen through the depression by running their factories at a loss if necessary:

Suppose you have a year when you lose five percent upon your capital in place of making twenty? We have a supreme duty towards the working people of this community, and there will be anxiety to know how to keep people at work. And might I suggest . . . that the way to relieve the burden we have on ourselves is to consider somebody else who has a bigger burden than we have to bear. There is a statement in that Good Book which says: "He was rich, yet for our sakes became poor, that we, through his poverty, might be made rich."

He also urged provincial governments to organize public works for the unemployed, and privately criticized White and Borden for failing to call provincial treasurers and bankers together to insist that Canadian resources be brought to bear to fight unemployment.[5] The leadership he felt the country needed that fall was not to deal with the war but to do something about unemployment.

II

The war was starting to have its own impact on unemployment. It is thought that a fair number of the thirty thousand Canadians who sailed for England in September with the First Contingent of the Canadian Expeditionary Force had nothing better to do than volunteer and be assured of decent clothes, food, and housing—after a fashion. The business generated by the need to feed, clothe, house, and arm the men gave jobs to thousands more workers filling the war orders which poured out of Major-General the Honourable Sam Hughes's Militia Department. The military needed boots, tents, belts, harnesses, saddles, horses (the horses needed hay), rifles, ammunition, trucks, underwear, and a thousand and one other items. Almost all of them had to be provided by private contractors.

A few million dollars' worth of Canadian war orders, though, was hardly significant. The big money was being spent by the countries raising the big armies—Great Britain, Russia, France. If Canadian industries could get a share of that huge business the war might usefully end unemployment and restore profits to satisfactory prewar levels. This idea may already have been in Flavelle's mind in London the day after war broke out when he met Henry Denny, a younger member of the great Anglo-Irish packing family, who was about to become a purchasing agent for the War Office, and told him that the William Davies Company would be glad to serve in any way it could.[6]

The William Davies Company was particularly well situated to develop opportunities opened up by the war. The soldiers not only needed to be fed, but war conditions soon crippled Denmark's ability to dominate the British market. Suddenly Canadian bacon was in demand again in England. Davies' exports of hog products, running at a $3-million annual rate in the last peacetime year, swelled to $6 million in the twelve months ending March 31, 1915. The bacon was sold as usual on the open market in London, in competition

237

with all other packers, but with the War Office, acting through Denny, as an important new buyer.

The War Office was also a major buyer of canned food for the armies in France, and by the end of September the William Davies Company had secured an order for 46,000 cases of tinned corned beef ("bully" to the men in the trenches). In the confusion of the early months of war, when every company with anything to sell was besieging governments for orders, this first contract was secured "by bringing ourselves to the notice of the War Office and bringing pressure to bear," E. C. Fox wrote. By the end of the year, through tendering in competition with other suppliers, the company had secured British and French orders for 63,000 more cases. The corned-beef business alone was worth $320,000 in extra sales through the end of 1914; by September 1915 it had more than quadrupled and the company was employing an extra four to five hundred hands, practically all of them taken from the ranks of the unemployed.[7]

Davies' profits for the year ending in March 1915 were $580,751, compared with $154,605 the year before. The dividend was raised from 3 per cent to 15 per cent and the surplus ploughed back into increasing capacity. Through the spring and summer of 1915 the company's shipments to England continued to surpass anything in its experience.

Other Canadian manufacturers were not so well placed as a firm that had been exporting to England for years. Most Canadian manufacturers, coddled for decades by the tariff, served only the domestic market and could not compete abroad even in such ordinary lines as clothing and footwear. Canadians had virtually no experience producing armaments. The only factory in the country where heavy ammunition had been made in peacetime was the Dominion Arsenal in Quebec City. The private "munitions" factories in the country, including Sir Charles Ross's rifle works, could be counted on the fingers of one hand. Canadian manufacturers thought the major part of the wartime business would consist simply of replacing German products on the Canadian and American markets. The Canadian Manufacturers' Association's major response to the war was another "Made in Canada" campaign. Through much of 1915 Canada was exporting workers in search of war jobs — some railwaymen went to Russia; about two thousand skilled mechanics went back to England to work in munitions plants there.[8]

The war pushed Canadians into munitions manufacturing in spite of themselves. Late in August 1914, when it became clear that the Germans were not going to be beaten in a few weeks' fighting — if they could be beaten at all—the British War Office began dimly to realize that huge supplies of armaments were needed. The existing capacity of British munitions firms was soon fully booked, and inquiries were made about possible supplies from North America. With its huge industrial potential, the United States was the most promising shipper; but it seemed worth while to find out whether Canadian manufacturers could produce some of the simple shells in high demand by the artillery.

When he received the first inquiry into Canada's capacity to produce shells for field guns—Britain needed fifteen- and eighteen-pounder shrapnel shells —Sam Hughes, the Minister of Militia and Defence, called some of his manufacturing friends to Ottawa to see if they could fill orders. None of them had ever made a shell, but they assured Hughes that with a few weeks' time to retool, Canadian industry could turn out four thousand shrapnel shells a week. Hughes relayed their request for a firm order to England and formally constituted a Shell Committee to handle any orders he obtained. Colonel Alexander Bertram, head of John Bertram & Sons of Dundas, Ontario, was chairman of the Shell Committee; the other manufacturing members were Thomas Cantley of the Nova Scotia Steel and Coal Company, George Watts of Canadian General Electric, and Ebenezer Carnegie of the Electric Steel & Sheet Metals Company of Welland. Three military advisers were also appointed. On October 1, 1914, the Shell Committee contracted to supply the War Office with 200,000 fifteen-pounder and eighteen-pounder shells, the first 20,000 to be delivered by the end of that month. The contract price was $8.30 per shell for the fifteen-pounders, $8.55 for the eighteen-pounders. The order was to be completed by May 31, 1915. At its prewar capacity it would have taken the Dominion Arsenal twelve years to produce these shells.[9]

Shells were not the same as complete rounds of ammunition. The *shell* was simply the steel body of the projectile, launched from the gun by the explosive in its *cartridge case* and exploded by the *fuze* which was its nose. Neither cartridge cases nor fuzes were included in this first order. Filling the order would be difficult enough for Canadian manufacturers quite unused to the standards of precision required to make a finished shell body from a forged-steel block. Most of the machinery for the work had to be bought in the United States. There was hardly anyone in Canada with any technical knowledge of ammunition; as its Ordnance Adviser the Shell Committee appointed Ebenezer Carnegie's brother, David, who had been trained at Britain's Woolwich Arsenal and happened to be visiting Canada on business when the war broke out. Only ten manufacturers could start work on the contract in October because there were only ten sets of gauges suitable for the job in the country.

In Britain and the United States orders for complete rounds of ammunition were given to large experienced firms. In Canada there were no large experienced firms, but very many small firms across the country desperate for business and employment for their men. Encouraged by the Borden government, and perhaps having no alternative, the Shell Committee decided to spread the work around by parcelling out the various operations involved in shell production (forging, machining, assembling) to a number of manufacturers, providing each with his raw material and taking delivery of the finished product. New orders were received from England long before any shells had been made under the first contract. By the end of December the Shell Committee had orders for another 2,050,000 shells and 1,900,000 cartridge cases, to a total value of close to $25 million; seventy-two companies were at work machining and assembling shells, sixty-seven were manufacturing components. The first few thousand shells from Canada were shipped in December, more than a month behind schedule. But David Carnegie was already in England, on behalf of the Shell Committee, soliciting still more orders. Canadian manufacturers, he claimed, could produce high-explosive as well as shrapnel shells and could now produce the complete fixed round of ammunition.[10]

Making his rounds at the War Office, Carnegie was given priority treatment as the representative of a committee of genuine manufacturers working with the Canadian Department of Militia and Defence. He was ushered into offices ahead of crowds of other businessmen waiting to see government purchasing agents who did not want to see them at all. These were an extraordinary group of mostly unknown men, who descended on London from North America in the winter of 1914–15, purporting to be able to supply everything from TNT to aeroplane propellers. They often presented impressive letters of introduction from prominent politicians and claimed to represent American or Canadian manufacturers with unlimited resources.

In fact almost all of them were brokers, middlemen who specialized in making contracts for manufacturers. The idea was to negotiate an option on a manufacturer's output and then place it with a purchaser—or, vice versa, to secure a contract from a purchaser and place it with a manufacturer — in either case taking a substantial percentage commission. There was nothing disreputable about the brokerage function on markets where many small buyers and small sellers needed middlemen to bring them together; but with their huge buying power governments hardly needed to negotiate multi-million-dollar war contracts through brokers. Realizing this, many brokers tended to stay out of the business and many "high-minded" manufacturers avoided using brokers (the use of middlemen to obtain government business was a practice "repellant to honorable Houses," Flavelle wrote in 1915).[11] The field was left open to men who came from the seedier fringes of commerce where they were used to wheeling and dealing at breathtaking speed, putting little on paper, and often misrepresenting their resources and opportunities. The British purchasing staff did their best to avoid this "singular collection of sharks and adventurers," but were often misled or confused by their apparently solid credentials.[12]

Who was the Canadian "Colonel," J. Wesley Allison, for example, who arrived at the War Office in October claiming that Hughes of Canada had authorized him take all orders the British wanted to place through the Canadian Department of Militia? What did it mean when he used letterheads marked "Canadian Committee for Supply of Allied Armies with Arms and Ammunition," and at the same time claimed he was the sole purchasing agent of the Russian government in Britain acting in association with one Mackie in Petrograd? Who were his other associates, "Colonel" William McBain and George Washington Stephens, living with Allison at the Savoy Hotel and also claiming they were backed by Hughes? The group was bombarding the War Office with offers of "deals" on rifles, aeroplanes, horses, life preservers, gun cotton, dried meat, shells, blankets, nickel, horseshoes, anything at all the Allies needed.

British officials made one inquiry after another to the Canadian High Commissioner, Sir George Perley, who denied again and again that Allison's "Syndicate at the Savoy" had standing with anyone in Canada—only to find out to his embarrassment and anger that Hughes had cabled Lord Kitchener in September nominating Allison to handle purchasing on his behalf. Hughes lamely explained to Borden that he had given this authorization to his old friend, Allison, in the rush of the moment, had forgotten about it, and had made other arrangements since. In any case their wild claims utterly discredited Allison and his syndicate with the British.[13]

British purchasing was increasingly being done through authorized and reputable channels: the Shell Committee and the Canadian Pacific Railway in Canada, and, from January 1915, J. P. Morgan and Company in the

United States. The Allison group moved on to Belgium, France, and Italy. In Rome Allison represented himself as a purchasing agent for the British and French governments and had to be explicitly disowned by the British foreign secretary. None of Allison's "deals" were taken up, but his friend, "Colonel" H. J. Mackie in Petrograd, did obtain a Russian order for several million shells and placed it with the Canadian Car and Foundry Company, Senator Nathaniel Curry president. The order was the syndicate's greatest success and was paraded as one of the largest war orders placed in Canada in early 1915. Almost all the work was promptly sublet in the United States. Nothing else materializing for his group in Europe, J. Wesley Allison went back to New York in February to drum up any war business he could find in the States.[14]

In contrast to the disappointments suffered by brokers and speculators like the Allison gang, David Carnegie found the War Office highly receptive to his claims that Canadian manufacturers could handle much larger orders. Canada was promised "any amount of work" if her manufacturers could produce the complete round. In February large new orders were placed for sixty-pounder shells and the still larger 4.5-inch shells. In April 1915, after considerable Canadian pressure, the War Office contracted with the Shell Committee for five million complete rounds of ammunition — shells, cartridge cases, and fuzes. The April and May orders were worth more than $100 million. War was becoming very big business for Canadian manufacturers.[15]

III

By the end of 1914 Canadians were learning that the war was also going to be deadly serious business. There would be no quick victory; the armies were dug in across France and Belgium for the winter. Recruiting for a Second Contingent of the CEF was almost complete; a Third Contingent would be announced before the year's end. In Britain, Kitchener's "New Army" was being recruited to replace the old professionals of the British Expeditionary Force, who had been slaughtered at First Ypres. At Christmas, 1914, some of the troops fraternized across No Man's Land, but on the home fronts English and Canadian civilians began to loathe all things German.

The new spirit hit home to Flavelle when the German-professor issue threw the University of Toronto into a crisis. The controversy started when Professor Mueller of the German Department supported his sons' protest against an anti-German speech by their high-school principal. The young Muellers were suspended from school, and the Toronto Board of Education urged the governors of the university to inquire into the conduct of Mueller senior and his professorial supporters. Whipped up by the *Telegram* and the *World*, the affair soon turned into a demand that the university fire its German-born professors because they could not avoid bias, could possibly pass valuable information to the enemy, and should not be paid from public funds in wartime.

A majority of the Board of Governors agreed with public opinion. The last letter written before his death by D. R. Wilkie, a governor of the university and president of the Imperial Bank, was a demand that President Falconer fire the three University of Toronto professors thought to be German citizens. The *Telegram* thought the Board of Governors could be prosecuted for trading with the King's enemies. Students and staff of the university pleaded for reason and respect for academic freedom — and for that were accused by the *World* of having been corrupted by the German professors. Falconer was rumoured to be ready to resign if the board dismissed the Germans against his recommendation.[16]

The board met on December 3 and 4 to decide the fate of Professors Mueller, Benzinger, and Topper. In a detailed report Falconer showed that the professors had kept their pledge to remain silent on the rights and wrongs of the war, explained that the wireless set in Professor Mueller's home had been dismantled before war broke out, and concluded there was no cause for dismissal. His position was also in accordance with the Governor General's proclamation of August 7 declaring that law-abiding German and Austrian citizens in Canada should not be interfered with. Ignoring Falconer's report, E. B. Osler moved that the three professors be asked to resign or suffer dismissal. Zebulon Lash moved an amendment, seconded by Flavelle, that in view of the Governor General's proclamation no action be taken. Supported only by Lash, Flavelle, Walker, and Macdonald of the *Globe*, the amendment lost, nine to four. Falconer did not vote. Another amendment, requiring the professors to take leave of absence, was carried. Both Flavelle and Walker supported it, but Falconer had his dissent recorded in the minutes. Osler also opposed the amendment—for the reverse reason —and resigned from the board in protest after the meeting.

Mueller, Benzinger, and Topper were placed on paid leave of absence.

Within a year all had resigned or retired from the staff. In the interim the university weathered a storm of criticism for paying public funds to German citizens (T. L. Church pledged that as mayor he would move to suspend the teaching of German throughout Ontario; Thomas Hook, MPP, was reported to have said, "If we can't get university professors of British blood to train our youth, then let us close the university"). Flavelle continued to support Falconer against what he called the "danger in this somewhat hysterical City from an excess of zeal without knowledge." He agreed with the Governor General's proclamation and viewed "with singular satisfaction the courage, and the wisdom, and the firmness of purpose" of Falconer in standing against the hysteria whipped up by the press and politicians. At the same time he hinted to Falconer that it was too bad students had been permitted to form political clubs, for politics on campus were apt to alienate Ontario's Conservative politicians, upon whom the university was so dependent for freedom and money.[17]

IV

In September 1914 there had been occasional grumbles about the shoddy supplies given to the Canadian soldiers assembled at Valcartier. By the end of the year these had turned into insistent charges of profiteering and corruption in the provision of war materials. As the CEF trained on Salisbury Plain in England it became clear that the men were equipped with boots that became a mass of soggy pulp in wet weather, inferior uniforms that had to be replaced by British cloth, utterly useless trenching shovels (of a design patented by Sam Hughes's secretary), and increasingly suspect Ross rifles. Although the boot scandal became obscured in charges and countercharges, and the Ross rifle was permitted to go forward into battle, the investigations led to two Conservative MP's being drummed out of the party for profiteering on war contracts. Several other instances of profiteering and unnecessary middlemen's commissions were uncovered. Much, perhaps most, of the trouble with equipment was caused by haste and inefficiency in the early purchasing operations rather than by outright corruption. On the other hand, an unduly large number of the more suspect transactions, as well as the work of the Syndicate at the Savoy, could be traced to people who happened to be old friends of the responsible minister, Sam Hughes.[18]

These minor problems with Canadian supplies paled by comparison with public outrage in England at the shell shortage Sir John French used to explain the failure of his army's Flanders campaign in the spring of 1915. By mid-May public dissatisfaction with the shell scandal, plus the growing belief that Churchill had bungled Gallipoli, forced Asquith to bring the Conservatives into a coalition government. The most important ministerial change was Lloyd George's move from the Exchequer to the new Ministry of Munitions, where he was determined to get shell supplies moving.

The staff of the new Ministry found the shell-supply situation appalling. "When we had made all the most generous allowance that we could," the Under-Secretary of Munitions wrote, "the conclusion was inevitable that if a statement of the arrears of some of the great armament firms had been published, and the grotesque disproportion between their undertakings and their performances revealed, their reputations would have been destroyed for ever." [19] It was hard to tell whether the companies were most to blame for having undertaken far more than they could carry out, or whether the War Office had been incompetent in loading them with work far beyond their capacity. Whatever the case, Lloyd George's new brooms, usually wielded by private businessmen brought into government for war service, swept through red tape and civil-service procedures to revolutionize the supply situation.

Canadian manufacturers had contributed at least their share to the 1915 shell shortage. Almost without exception they were behind in their deliveries. By the end of May the Shell Committee had accepted orders worth $170,000,000, but had delivered supplies worth only just over $5,500,000. Only two per cent of the shells it had agreed to produce were going forward to Britain on time. As in Britain, there was an enormous supply of shell bodies, which were useless without the cartridge cases manufacturers had been unable to deliver on schedule. [20]

Some Canadian manufacturers were also starting to complain about the allotment of contracts. It was said that large and thoroughly reputable concerns could not get orders, that mushroom companies of no standing had been given orders and then either failed to deliver or made millions on the shells they did produce. There were rumours that the Shell Committee had allocated contracts as political patronage. Most disturbing was the known fact that the manufacturing members of the Shell Committee — Bertram, Watts, Cantley, and Ebenezer Carnegie — had given out large contracts to their own firms. They hardly seemed disinterested enough to preside over Canadian munitions manufacture in the best interests of either the British government or Canadian manufacturers as a whole. [21]

As some manufacturers finished their contracts that spring and summer, and as other manufacturers became interested in getting a share of the shell business, there were also complaints about the lack of new British orders. Huge new orders were being placed in the United States. Hardly anything was coming to the North American Dominion whose boys were fighting at Britain's side. The Borden government was worrried about the employment situation in the coming winter, and in any case had felt from the beginning of the war that Canadians deserved British orders roughly proportionate to their share of the fighting. It was galling to see the Americans prospering in their neutrality.

By letter, by cable, and in person, Borden, Perley, and several Canadian ministers pressed the British for more Canadian orders. By June 1915 the government had sent more than two hundred communications to Britain advancing Canada's claims. The Prime Minister was not at all happy in his dual role of war leader and chief procurer for Canada. By the time he sailed for England at the end of June he was fed up with the Shell Committee, not because of the allegations of corruption, which he did not believe, but because it was so inefficient. "I find it almost impossible to get the Shell Committee to give a plain clear statement of the facts which will make the situation so clear that the manufacturers and general public will understand the difficulties," he wrote. "Even when they do move their proceedings are so slow and ineffectual that the best results are not produced. I have had to undertake the dictation for them of statements and interviews and it is, of course, absurd that any such duty should be cast upon the Prime Minister."[22]

The Ministry of Munitions had independently decided that the Shell Committee was useless. It was "utterly inefficient" for its job, the Under-Secretary noted in his diary, and no matter how loudly the Canadians complained there would be no more orders until it was reorganized. Earlier, the War Office had been considering schemes for reorganizing Canadian production; one suggestion that spring was the establishment of a Canadian Supplies Department whose chairman in Canada would be J. W. Flavelle. The Ministry of Munitions decided to delay action, however, until D. A. Thomas, MP, a Welsh coal magnate, went to Canada and reported on the situation.[23]

V

Flavelle had been going on with his usual round of business, university, church, and hospital activities. But, like others, he had become increasingly worried about the war. Holidaying with Clara in the southern United States in March 1915, he had been depressed and disappointed by American disinterest: "I heard no discussion at all concerning the wrong done to the Belgiums [sic], or any manifestation of acute interest in the fact that the Allies stood for liberty and freedom, as against the blighting influence of militarism. . . . I have come home with the feeling that sooner or later the American people will have to pass through a great sorrow or a great struggle which will turn their attention away from material things and pleasures. . . ." Alarming news was also coming from Will Rundle, now general manager of National Trust, who was in London on business. Jim Macdonnell, a Rhodes Scholar they had hired in 1911, had described to Rundle the "hell let loose" he had gone through at Second Ypres. The gas attack at Ypres and the sinking of the *Lusitania* had finally ended the City's mood of business as usual. The British were talking of practically nothing but the war. "The average man of high standing is prepared to use gas or anything else with which to destroy the Germans," Rundle wrote. He passed on news of the shell shortage, the terrific casualty rate of officers at the front, and businessmen's fears that no nation could stand the rate of spending Lloyd George was proposing for 1915. National Trust was losing one fine officer after another to the army—Percy Molson, the "very life" of the Montreal office was the latest to go—but Rundle and Flavelle decided not to try to persuade anyone to stay. "The Empire is going to need all the men it can get to save itself, and anything less than the salvation of the Empire sinks into utter insignificance in comparison."[24]

Flavelle chafed at the lack of opportunity to do something useful. "There is a growing feeling among those of us who must stay at Home that we should strive to be worthy of the men who have gone to the Front," he wrote Rundle. "Many a man is seeking to perform his ordinary duties more seriously and more efficiently in answer to this call, but all that we may do seems commonplace in contrast to the service of the brave fellows who are giving their all."[25]

Aside from delivering the occasional speech to farmers on the need to increase food production, the only outlet he could find was to give advice to politicians. In June he corresponded with Borden, Kemp, and Sir George Foster, the Minister of Trade and Commerce, on the need to organize the manufacturers to secure new war orders. He knew little of the inside story of shell production in Canada, but felt the manufacturers must have failed in initiative and organizing ability. Perhaps manufacturers who had been childishly hanging around Ottawa looking for business should be called together and told "some plain earnest things" about the need to cooperate in informing the British of their exact capacity to handle new orders. In urging this, Flavelle was more worried about the Canadian employment problem than British war needs. "Our manufacturers should feel a pressure resting upon them not only to make money for themselves but also to bring business to the country which will provide employment and add to our resources against the heavy days which are inevitably ahead of us," he wrote Kemp.[26]

Kemp and Borden explained to him some of the problems of Canadian shell manufacture. Flavelle's advice was not particularly useful to them because he knew so little about the situation, but he had made them aware of his belief that new initiatives were necessary in munitions supply. He was also writing in the context of the William Davies Company's considerable success at obtaining and filling war orders. There were not many other Canadian businessmen with the same record who showed the same earnest concern for the war business as a whole. In October 1915, Borden asked him to serve as a representative of business on an Economic and Development Commission he was appointing to investigate ways of stimulating production in Canada.[27]

VI

Through the summer of 1915, while Borden spent much of his time in England trying to get more orders for Canada, D. A. Thomas was in Canada investigating the Shell Committee. He worked closely with Sir George Foster, and they concluded that the committee was hopelessly inadequate. As an administrative organization, supervising the work of hundreds of manufacturers, it was totally inefficient. Its only executive officers — Bertram, the chairman, and David Carnegie, the ordnance adviser — were snowed under by details that should have been delegated to others. The corridors and staircases outside their Ottawa offices were jammed with manufacturers sitting on shell boxes waiting to see one or the other about orders.[28]

Bertram and the other manufacturers on the committee had a hopeless conflict of interest. "They are themselves deeply interested parties in securing contracts for themselves & those with whom they have affiliations," Foster reported to Borden. "The dual interest vitiates equal dealing & the knowledge that it exists destroys confidence & causes great dissatisfaction among the manufacturing interests." None of the contracts had been let by tender, and Thomas became convinced that Britain had been paying inflated prices for Canadian shells. He also criticized the Shell Committee's policy of spreading its work around to a large number of manufacturers, many of them small and inefficient, when the job should have been centralized in a few large factories. It may have made political sense to ship forgings from Ontario to be machined into shells in British Columbia and then shipped back again—incurring the highest labour costs in Canada and four thousand miles' worth of freight charges—but there was no economic justification for placing these orders.[29]

It was not even clear what the Shell Committee was. It had been appointed by Sam Hughes, a Canadian minister. Did this mean the Shell Committee was controlled by and responsible to Hughes, and thus the Government of Canada? Apparently not, for Hughes had appointed the committee in some vague capacity of his as agent of the British Secretary of State for War, so it was apparently responsible directly to Britain. But then again, what had the committee been appointed to do? Was it authorized to act as agent for the War Office in distributing British contracts in Canada? Apparently not, for each British order took the form of a contract between Hughes, on the one hand, and the four manufacturing members of the Shell Committee—Bertram, Watts, Carnegie, and Cantley—on the other, to supply the War Office. So instead of being agents in a trustee relationship with the War Office, the Shell Committee seemed to be an organization of four manufacturers who had secured all the British shell orders and were subletting them to other Canadian manufacturers (albeit on the understanding that any profits they made would be returned to the War Office). General Bertram took this line in his disputes with Thomas, arguing that so long as the committee filled its contracts at the price accepted by the War Office nobody had any business criticizing any of the prices it paid for components or any of its methods of allocating orders.[30] That kind of statement sealed the fate of his organization.

There was some talk of the Canadian government taking the situation in hand by forming its own Ministry of Munitions. But most members of the cabinet, including the Prime Minister, wanted nothing to do with the administration of British munitions purchases in Canada. Borden favoured a reorganization of the Shell Committee to make it directly and clearly responsible to the British Ministry. Sam Hughes violently objected to any change that would sever the committee's relation with him and his department. It was his "baby," he put it, "a model to the whole world."[31] By the end of September, four months after it had been decided that the Shell Committee was incompetent, nothing had been done to change it. Nor was Canada getting any more business—Thomas had authority to place huge new orders for large-size shells but refused until the Shell Committee agreed to let contracts by tender.

By now Borden was besieged with protests, increasingly specific, about the Shell Committee. T. A. Russell of the Russell Motor Car Company (which had evolved out of CCM) came to see him about fuze contracts. Despite his firm's willingness to bid competitively for the five million fuzes for the fixed rounds ordered in the spring, the contracts had been let to two American companies. The whole point of the Shell Committee's work, of course, was supposed to be to generate business in Canada. F. P. Jones of the Canada Cement Company (as capable of making shells as any other firm, for none had experience) came to Ottawa complaining about his six-month effort to get contracts: it had reached a climax when he told David Carnegie the committee's methods were crooked—and got invited to tender the next day (the Shell Committee did experiment with tenders under Thomas's pressure). Then Jones was told his tender was absurdly low, even though he judged it would clear him a million dollars' profit in twelve months on an investment of $700,000.[32] Others charged that manufacturers with orders had sublet them at fat profits, that Cantley's and Bertram's own companies made the fattest profits of all, and that some manufacturers, particularly those who were Conservative MP's, had obtained sweet contracts through political influence. "Rumours and gossip of a most serious character are afloat," White wrote Borden in mid-October. "The situation . . . is becoming intolerable and this I know is the view of nearly all the other Ministers." Except Hughes, of course.[33]

None of the principals—Borden, Thomas, Hughes, and the members of the Shell Committee—were getting on with any of the others by now, so the British government decided to start afresh by sending out Lionel Hichens, the businessman-imperialist Flavelle had met in July 1914, on a special mission to clear up the Canadian mess. He was to get the new orders placed, get a new organization going, and find competent Canadians to run it. While Hichens was *en route* to Canada, accompanied by another Round Tabler and former Kindergarten colleague, Robert L. Brand, Borden did his best to have the charges against the Shell Committee investigated.

The trouble was, and to an extent still is, to find out exactly what the Shell Committee had been doing. Its records and statistics were a mess; Bertram and David Carnegie had made many oral promises of contracts, leading to bitter misunderstandings and no records. Some of the charges against their organization were sour grapes; others, like Jones's charges against Carnegie, were a combination of misunderstanding and inexperience. A special investigation of the most serious accusations against Bertram and Cantley cleared them of all but errors of judgment committed under trying circumstances. A Conservative who later looked into the charges of partisan letting of contracts was "astounded," and evidently a bit sorry, to find that Bertram had not taken any interest in the politics of the firms getting his orders. Convincing explanations were provided for Russell not getting the original contracts for fuzes. They were let to American firms because no Canadian company would take them; Russell's firmed-up bid had appeared just after the eleventh hour had expired.[34]

In passing, Borden did learn that the Shell Committee had first made contact with one of its American fuze contractors in April 1915, when Sam Hughes advised David Carnegie to approach J. Wesley Allison in New York to inquire about the U.S. fuze situation. Asked to explain, Carnegie wrote Borden that although he had heard some suspicious things about Allison from War Office officials during his trip to England, "General Hughes has always spoken most highly of him to me and that was enough to satisfy me that Col. Allison was a worthy man." Claiming that Allison had helped the committee get in touch with low-cost manufacturers at no personal gain to himself, Carnegie added, "I should feel horribly taken in if it were proved that he was not a straightforward man." Borden knew rather more about the deal than Carnegie, but let the matter rest, for the time being.[35]

There is little doubt that the manufacturers on the Shell Committee were personally honest. They had taken on an enormous and complex job with no precedents, no guidelines, and no idea of how difficult it would become. They had distributed the first orders at extremely high prices, but argued with some justice that these were necessary to induce manufacturers into a new and uncertain kind of business with very heavy start-up costs. British and American experience, as well as Canadian, showed that it was next to impossible to let munitions contracts by tender in a situation where the tenderers, because inexperienced, would have to set their bids on little more than guesses. The business had been spread widely among small Canadian firms because there were no large Canadian firms capable of handling big contracts. It had been spread across the country in response to government pressure to provide jobs in the West; the West's claim for war orders was based on the high percentage of men it was sending to the front, not on economics. Finally, all prices paid by the Shell Committee had been approved by the British War Office, and the Canadians felt it unjust to blame them for expenditures approved by the home government itself.[36]

That said, the Shell Committee was also clearly inept at administration, had no way of pressuring manufacturers into efficient, prompt fulfilment of contracts, and was publicly compromised by its leading members' conflict of interest. Also, there were huge profits being made on many of its contracts. Manufacturers who got contracts a few months after the earliest ones, or who took their time starting their work, found how astonishingly quickly costs fell after the first bottlenecks to Canadian munitions manufacture were broken. With falling costs, a few months' delay on a contract could mean many thousands of dollars' profit — a positive incentive not to get work done on time. Similar windfall gains were being made by British and American manufacturers, but the Canadian situation seems to have been a bit worse because of the Shell Committee's incompetence.

And there were still rumours floating around Ottawa about big profits on that American fuze contract, the one arranged through Allison, in whom Carnegie had put such trust. Insiders knew that the transaction could not stand public scrutiny and that the trouble ultimately stemmed from Sam Hughes's friendship with Allison. If only to stop Hughes from using war purchasing as an opportunity to give more business to his shady friends, the Shell Committee had to go.[37]

VII

Even in 1915 there was still more pressing business than getting on with the war. Or, rather, the war was bringing old business problems to a head. Canada's railways were clogged with new war traffic, but governments were forcing them to carry it at old rates despite soaring operating and repair costs. European money markets were effectively closed for the duration, so there was little prospect of borrowing any new money. The situation was too much for the already staggering Canadian Northern: by the winter of 1915 it was ready simultaneously to have its last spike driven and to default on its securities. The greatest business failure in Canadian history seemed at hand.

By the spring of 1915 the Bank of Commerce was advancing money to the Canadian Northern to meet its interest obligations. Unknown to anyone but the bank's directors and Sir Thomas White, the advances were guaranteed by letters to the bank from Borden, in effect pledging the Government of Canada's credit to keep the railway going.[38] The government did not know what it wanted to do about the railways. Borden and White did not think they could face a collapse, especially in wartime; yet they were not ready to bring the issue before Parliament. So the private arrangement was made to postpone what was now inevitable — for the Grand Trunk Pacific was also going down, dragging with it the Grand Trunk.

Privy to the full extent of the trouble through his Commerce directorship, Flavelle urged Borden to face the inevitable and take over all the faltering railways — the Canadian Northern, the Grand Trunk Pacific, and the Grand Trunk. "Do not the very difficulties of the situation create an opportunity for the establishment of a state-controlled national railway system under circumstances of exceptional advantage," he wrote the Prime Minister in June, "in which the country . . . out of the crippled position of the railway corporations can enter into possession of great properties and for all time control the railway policy of Canada?" Very little of the public's cash needed to be spent on the transaction, for the stock and bondholders of the private railway companies would "cheerfully" exchange their securities for equivalent Government of Canada bonds. It was just the kind of bold, imaginative proposal, Flavelle suggested, to take to the country in a general election.[39]

(Since the war began he had been speculating on how the Liberals could be crushed, for his belief that they were a Quebec-dominated, fundamentally disloyal and dishonest party had deepened. In September 1915, he was still urging Borden to go to the people on a policy combining railway nationalization with "a National call to sacrifice and duty," so the nation could be saved from "the calamity of having Canada represented in the Empire's conferences which must follow the war, by a Government dependent on non-British votes for its power.")[40]

Borden had already considered and rejected holding an election on the issue of railway nationalization. One factor in postponing action was White's perception of the flaws in a scheme like Flavelle's. As usual when he was advocating public ownership, Flavelle wanted private investors to be bought out in transactions that would have left them satisfied with the purchase price. "The question at once arises as to what it has to sell," White wrote, referring to the Canadian Northern. Why should the government negotiate with the investors in companies "desiring to sell liabilities as assets"? He saw no reason why the faltering railways should not eventually be permitted to go into receivership and their properties then be sold, probably to the government, without tiresome and expensive bargaining with individual investors. In any case, the government was facing too many other obligations — more troubles than were likely to be resolved "for years to come and possibly not in your life-time or mine," White wrote Flavelle—to leap blindly into any policy.[41]

He would have denied it as a motive underlying his suggestion, but Flavelle's scheme for nationalization would also have helped resolve the Bank of Commerce's problems with the Canadian Northern. Before Borden had come to the rescue the bank had extended tens of millions in credit to Mackenzie and Mann and their enterprises over the years—many of those millions backed by stocks and bonds whose value was declining almost daily. Sorrows were starting to come in battalions too, for one Mackenzie and Mann company after another was slipping towards insolvency: the Mexican utilities were threatened by revolution; their other Latin American ventures, made with a consortia of Canadian investors backed by the Commerce, were suddenly up in the air because the utility genius, Dr. F. S. Pearson, had happened to sail on the *Lusitania*. Through the summer and fall of 1915 the directors of the Commerce spent long hours reviewing troublesome accounts, almost all of them relating to Mackenzie and Mann.

In the midst of this turmoil, in September, Sir Edmund Walker resigned as chief executive officer of the bank (though retaining the presidency), and Alexander Laird resigned as general manager. The new general manager, John Aird, put before the directors a memorandum outlining strict new guidelines regarding information to come before the board. It would include "the presentation to the Board at the same time of all credits to individuals or concerns which are directly or indirectly connected, in order that the Board may have knowledge of the aggregate advances to any particular interest."[42]

The circumstances of the change in leadership at the Commerce suggest it had not come without pressure from some of the directors. Flavelle had been very concerned about management's relations with the Canadian Northern in 1913 – 14. Through these months in 1915 he was one of only two directors in continuous attendance at the meetings. He probably did as much as anyone to press Laird and Walker for an accounting, and may have been instrumental in bringing about the change of management leading to Aird's reforms.

The directors were also obviously worried about the bank's stability. Despite later stories about Aird having kept a pistol in his desk so he could go too,[43] it was not so much a matter of cliff-hanging as the erosion of confidence that might take place if and when an accounting had to be made public. Too much erosion, of course, could prove disastrous, or at least force the bank into drastic retrenchment at a time when its lending power was vitally necessary to war finance. Even with the change in management the problem was still extremely grave. Flavelle must have been anxious that fall. To Borden, the Canadian Northern/Bank of Commerce problem was a "nightmare."[44]

VIII

Having had his own troubles with munitions work at Cammel Laird, Lionel Hichens was more tolerant than D. A. Thomas of the Shell Committee's failings. "I am entirely satisfied that the Shell Committee have carried out their work well," Hichens wrote Borden.[45] But he never doubted that it would have to be replaced, particularly when he, too, found himself besieged by manufacturers seeking orders and complaining about the Shell Committee's inefficiency. Hichens and Brand spent much of November considering who should be entrusted with the new responsibility. After preliminary talks with the CPR in Montreal about securing Edward Fitzgerald, the railway's brilliant assistant head of purchasing, they went to Toronto for further discussions, including a session with Sir Edmund Walker, to talk over possible names. They returned to Ottawa with their minds made up. Borden and Hughes both approved their recommendation to the Minister of Munitions, Lloyd George.*[46]

Flavelle was playing golf on November 23 when he received a telephone message asking him to meet the Governor General in Ottawa the next day. He assumed the Duke of Connaught wanted his help with some charity. He was "confused and perplexed" when Connaught asked him to accept the chairmanship of the Imperial Munitions Board, the new organization to have full responsibility for British munitions purchasing in Canada.

---

* In Hughes's case, Brand wrote later, "it was like getting a bull into a box and shutting the door on him before he knew where he was."

His own business interests were very pressing. Clara was not well. He had no experience with munitions manufacture, no way of knowing what would be expected of him or for how long. There was no comparison with the semi-honorific appointment to the Economic and Development Commission. Taking on the new organization, handling the quarter-billion dollars' worth of orders already placed, would be undertaking one of the biggest jobs ever in Canada. He accepted the offer almost immediately, for this was his opportunity to serve his country and the Empire in wartime.[47]

Why Flavelle? Walker may have recommended him. Hichens, an idealistic Christian like Flavelle, had met him in 1914, if not earlier, and probably had been impressed. Brand may have known him through the Round Table groups—to which all four of them belonged—or through his partnership in Lazard Brothers, an investment bank which had become deeply involved in Canadian Northern financing. Flavelle's name had been mentioned in England earlier. The Canadian government does not appear to have suggested him, but had no objection to him. He had an admirable record as a very successful businessman who also believed in public service. This more than countered his inexperience at munitions manufacture. Flavelle's appointment was welcomed by the press as the sign of a new departure in Canada's troubled munitions business.

CHAPTER ELEVEN

THE SHELL GAME

Having decided to take the job, Flavelle immediately went to Montreal to ask the president of the CPR, Sir Thomas Shaughnessy, to release Edward Fitzgerald for service in Ottawa. Knowing of his brilliance as a purchasing agent, the British had particularly wanted Fitzgerald for the new organization. Shaughnessy asked Flavelle when he wanted Fitzgerald on duty. Flavelle pulled out his watch and said there was still time to catch the afternoon train. Fitzgerald missed it, but was in Ottawa the next day with his staff.[1]

Another Montrealer who had been singled out in advance to serve on the IMB was Charles Blair Gordon, the forty-eight-year-old president of Dominion Textiles Limited. J. F. (Peter) Perry, an Englishman and former Kindergarten colleague of Brand and Hichens, who was working as Canadian agent for the investment banking firm of Lazard Brothers, was asked to handle the Board's finances. David Carnegie of the old Shell Committee was kept on as the technical expert; so were Alexander Bertram and Sam Hughes, the latter as honorary president, to maintain the appearance of continuity. The other appointees — E. R. Wood of Toronto, G. H. Dawson, Surveyor General of British Columbia, and J. A. Vaillancourt, President of the Hochelaga Bank — were regional window-dressing.

Flavelle, Gordon, and Perry, the full-time members of the Board, worked without pay. Flavelle at first balked at accepting even expense money. Board employees, like Fitzgerald, were paid regular salaries. The other members received small honoraria for attendance at meetings. The Board's formation was officially announced on November 30, 1915.

Flavelle had asked for and been given full executive authority as Chairman of the Imperial Munitions Board, making the organization very much a one-man show. He answered not so much to his fellow Board members —

after the first few months the Board seldom met—as to the British Ministry of Munitions. The Government of Canada had no formal links with or control over the Imperial Munitions Board, which was simply an agency of the Ministry of Munitions carrying on business in Canada. Flavelle also determined that Canadian politicians would not be allowed to meddle in the Board's affairs; its work would be done on a thoroughly businesslike basis. Some of the Board members themselves had to be told this—at their first meeting Vaillancourt told Flavelle he would get a room and come to town a few days a week to look after his French-Canadian friends. "I told him I did not think it necessary to tax himself in this way, as we were all approaching our duties from the standpoint that we had no friends; our business would be let by tender and would go through the Purchasing Department, and hence he could probably relieve himself of this obligation."[2]

Leaving Clara at Holwood, Flavelle took a room at the Château Laurier for the duration of the war. The Shell Committee offices were a few blocks away in the Union Bank Building. On December 1 the whole organization was turned over to the IMB and Flavelle began work as the czar of the Canadian munitions industry. Hichens and Brand stayed on for the first week to help out.

I

His first visitors were manufacturers begging for contracts. His first mail was a flood of letters from members of Parliament naming manufacturers in their constituencies who should receive contracts the Board would soon be letting for shell boxes. As Flavelle began to study existing contracts and orders pending, he naturally wanted to know how the prices paid in Canada compared with British and American. None of the Shell Committee people knew! Nor did the Government of Canada, which could only pass on a Hamilton steel manufacturer's opinion that Canadian prices were the lowest. The Ministry of Munitions must have known the prices, but was too disorganized to be able to supply the information on short notice. It took weeks, in some cases months, before the IMB got accurate estimates of the cost of munitions manufacture in other countries.[3]

Flavelle also learned that all the while it had been operating in ignorance of comparative prices the Shell Committee had given Canadian manufacturers an open invitation to collusion by sending out uncoded price figures over open telegraph lines. A number of manufacturers, most notably the steel companies, seemed, in fact, to have been quoting common prices. "The waste and extravagance in the securing of supplies for War is appalling and must run into fabulous figures," the Chairman concluded after ten days on his job.[4]

War business could not wait for Flavelle to break in his new organization. Hichens had warned him that new fuze orders had to be placed immediately so Canada could ship complete rounds instead of the unfuzed shells already in oversupply. Otherwise there could be no new orders for Canada. In its first week, without calling for tenders, the Board let contracts for two million time fuzes: the Williams Manufacturing Company of Montreal were to produce one million, T. A. Russell's automobile company of Toronto the other. An American firm, the R. W. Phillips Company of Worcester, Massachusetts, was also expressing interest in fuzes, offering to make millions of them at a lower price than anything the Canadian firms would accept. But Brand had information from New York warning the Board to learn more about Phillips. So nothing was done immediately about his offer.[5]

The fuze decision enraged the honorary president of the IMB, General Sir Sam Hughes. The Phillips fuze offer had been arranged at Hughes's request through his great friend, Colonel J. Wesley Allison. Dealing with Phillips rather than Russell, Hughes claimed in letters to Flavelle and the Prime Minister, would save the Board $670,000 on a million fuzes.

Flavelle saw Borden on December 9, explained his belief that Phillips was a promoter trying to get a contract to float a new company (taking his profit on the underwriting), and got assurance of the Prime Minister's support in this and any other dispute he might have with Hughes. "I do not anticipate any misunderstandings with the General," Flavelle wrote Hichens that afternoon. That evening he had a two-hour meeting with Hughes in which there was complete misunderstanding — the minister was outraged at Flavelle's aspersions against Phillips and Allison. The next day, Friday, December 10, while Flavelle was absent from the IMB's first meeting, Hughes delivered an impassioned speech on fuzes, Phillips, Allison, and Flavelle, charging that the real "promoters" were Russell and Flavelle, that the Phillips Company was "infinitely" the strongest in the business, and that Flavelle had awarded the contract on the basis of past friendship with Russell. The General threatened to resign from the Board and let the world know the true story about fuzes.[6]

While Hughes was attacking him at the Board's meeting, Flavelle was in the Prime Minister's office where Borden and his Minister of Labour, T. W. Crothers, were trying to persuade him to do something for the manufacturers of eighteen-pounder shells who were out of orders and about to lay off workers. Particularly in the West, the recruiting effort would suffer if it seemed that war needs were not serious enough to keep the shops going and men employed.

They also raised the general question of munitions wages. In all public-works contracts let since 1900 the Government of Canada had stipulated the payment of "fair wages" (prevailing wages, sometimes determined by union scales). The British government had fair wage provisions in its munitions contracts at home, as well as elaborate limits on munitions profits plus privileges for unions arranged by Lloyd George in the spring of 1915. Canadian trade unions wanted contracts let in Canada to contain some kind of wage protection, and had been petitioning both the British and Canadian governments ever since the first contracts had been let. The British had said they would write a Fair Wage clause into their contracts if the Canadian government would enforce it. Under pressure from labour, Borden seemed willing to accept this if the IMB thought it would work.

Realizing he had so many large manufacturers in default on shipments that he could reallocate some of their orders, Flavelle agreed to find more business for the small manufacturers. On the Fair Wage matter, though, he was not helpful. As Hichens had concluded earlier, Flavelle did not believe there was serious unrest over wages in the munitions plants, and he predicted "great confusion" and endless disputes if manufacturers suddenly had to pay higher wages for new war work while still being able to pay the old rates for old and non-war work. He urged Borden not to press the issue, committing the IMB instead to cooperate with the Department of Labour in cases of unfair treatment of workers; it could discipline uncooperative manufacturers by withholding contracts.[7]

There were also serious business-political problems unrelated to the IMB. Borden called Flavelle in the next day, Saturday the eleventh, to discuss the railway situation. The Bank of Commerce was insisting that Mackenzie and Mann turn over their remaining shares in the Canadian Northern as further collateral. Facing the year's-end accounting, Aird was insisting on this as the only alternative to announcing large losses on the various Mackenzie & Mann accounts. Mackenzie had complained to Borden about being stripped of his shares. The Prime Minister and cabinet were afraid he might give up in despair, letting the Canadian Northern crash. Could Flavelle help?

En route to Toronto that night, Flavelle discussed the situation with Mackenzie, trying among other things to disabuse him of the (quite accurate)
notion that he, Flavelle, was antagonistic to him. He soothed the entrepreneur's feelings about the transfer, paving the way for the shares being turned
over the next day while they were all in Toronto. That kept the Commerce
and Mackenzie & Mann going on together for another few months.[8]

II

The fuze issue continued to sizzle through December. Phillips came to
Ottawa, but his interview with Flavelle began and ended with questions
about why Phillips was behind on subcontracting he was doing for one of
the American companies working on the June 1915 fuze contracts. A few
days later Phillips telegraphed, offering to make fuzes cheaper than anyone
had ever suggested, and Hughes wrote Flavelle to draw his attention to the
telegram. Flavelle now believed Hughes was trying to build up a case against
the Board to make public; if he did, he would probably have the support of a
fair number of the MP's who had been receiving cool, noncommital replies
to their requests for contracts for manufacturers in their constituencies.

He had thought this kind of thing might happen in Ottawa. "There has
been no time for the conventional forces to assert themselves," he wrote
Clara,

but they have no intention of yielding to some new upstart, and I can see signs of
gathering clouds. . . . If I fall I will have a hungry lot after me. . . . I must not only be
right, which is not difficult, but I must learn how to drive hard and true and yet not
offend those in official life who are less anxious to drive true than they are to secure
advantage for themselves or their friends. I am fortified by the great assurance that I
was chosen for my work and that if I keep my heart true in its simple obedience to my
Heavenly Father, He will bring it to pass—so I am full of hope and courage and am
keen every morning to start and loth [*sic*] every evening to stop.[9]

The reports on Phillips Flavelle was starting to get more than strengthened his case. Carnegie visited the Worcester factory and advised against any
contracts. Gordon reported that the American Ammunition Company,
whose graze-fuze order Phillips had taken on subcontract, was threatening
to put him into receivership, and the banks were refusing him any further

loans. At some point Hughes himself showed Flavelle a draft of Phillips' prospectus for a twenty-million-dollar company — the prospective Canadian fuze contract figured prominently in the calculation of future profits. Other information confirmed Flavelle's view of Phillips as an undependable enthusiast, incapable of carrying out his promises. Finally, Gordon came up with startling news in New York: the IMB was paying the American Ammunition Company $3.72½ each for 1,666,666 graze fuzes under the Shell Committee's June 1915 contract. This contract had been let at a time when Morgan's had been contracting for fuzes at something between $1.45 and $1.75 each. After getting the contract, American Ammunition had sublet it to Phillips at $1.40, meaning that it would take $4 million off the top. Even if Phillips' involvement in this deal was innocent, it looked as though the Shell Committee—IMB had been skinned for $4 million thanks to Sam Hughes, J. Wesley Allison, *et al*.[10]

Fortified with this information, Flavelle could disregard Hughes, who was now trying to interest him in another friend of Allison's who was offering to build a small-arms factory in Canada. The General "only wants counsel with me that I may agree to some scheme or plan whereby Colonel Allison and his associates may have contract relations," he wrote Hichens. It must have been particularly galling to Hughes to be cold-shouldered by Flavelle. Years before, as a newspaper editor in Lindsay, he had resented the business and social prominence of J. R. Dundas and John and Will Flavelle. Now young Joe had taken the war business out of his hands.[11]

III

As comparative price information was assembled, Flavelle found that the Shell Committee's prices had been slightly higher than American prices in almost every instance, invariably much higher than British prices.[12] Because costs had fallen so drastically in the last few months, manufacturers who were still filling their first orders were making unconscionable profits. The Dominion Bridge Company of Montreal, for example, was working on its early order for eighteen-pounder high-explosive shells at $5.70 each at a time when new orders were being placed at $1.75. The Steel Company of Canada was behind on a contract for 50,000 sixty-pounders at $6.00; the price for new orders had dropped to $3.55. And so on through a depressingly long list that included General Bertram's own company and the Welland plant of Ebenezer Carnegie. True, it was common policy to permit manufacturers to recoup their investment in plant and machinery on their first contract, so no matter when the first order was filled, its price would have to be high to cover these costs. Even so, the profits could be too high. The Collingwood Shipbuilding Company, for example, stood to make $120,000 on a $300,000 order after all costs had been met.[13]

With the help of Alan McAvity, a young Nova Scotia manufacturer who had volunteered for service with the Board, Flavelle worked through much of the Christmas season reviewing the Shell Committee's contracts. On Saturday the twenty-fifth they worked all day before Flavelle took a night train home to Toronto.[14] Because so many manufacturers were in default on their delivery schedules, Flavelle was able to impose price reductions on them and/or to cancel parts of their orders. He did this with Dominion Bridge, Stelco, Massey—Harris, Bertram & Sons, and Ebenezer Carnegie's Electric Steel & Sheet Metals Company. Manufacturers grumbled, offered many excuses for their delays, and refused to believe their prices were out of line with American prices (almost always they had heard about the highest American prices in the earliest days of the war). Most realized, though, that they could be worse off than dealing with Flavelle. As a businessman who deeply believed fair profits were justified, he met his manufacturers at least halfway and was able to work out agreements with almost everyone. Dominion Bridge's scaled-down prices would still return 30 per cent profit on their turnover, and the Collingwood Shipbuilding Company would clear at least $40,000 on what was now a $200,000 contract. One of the few firms that did not voluntarily consent to the reductions — but was forced to — was Bertram & Sons, the company owned by the former head of the Shell Committee.[15]

There were some manufacturers or would-be manufacturers who never should have been near the business. One promoter from Northern Ontario had a shell contract but not even a site for a factory; his order was cancelled. An Ottawa man was complaining to politicians that he probably wasn't getting orders because he refused to offer kickbacks to members of the IMB. Investigators from the IMB found his jobbing shop had nine lathes and no heat. All the machinery was frozen solid. And there was an American firm, the Edwards Valve Company of Chicago, whose executives came to Flavelle complaining that the Shell Committee had unfairly cancelled an order for

500,000 cartridge cases arranged the summer before through Colonel J. Wesley Allison. By the date the last case was to have been delivered, the Edwards Company had yet to ship its first case. Pleading trouble in their plant from German sympathizers, the Americans begged Flavelle for reconsideration. He gave them two more extensions, but apparently never received a case.[16]

Asked later why he bent so far to help an inept contractor like the Edwards Company, Flavelle gave a clear statement of his approach to these difficult situations: "the policy the Board has had in mind is that the Crown had no right to take advantage of people who made an honest effort, and where the conditions under which they operated were severe, that they were not in the position of traders to punish, but rather to interpret what was the just and fair relationship towards a contractor who had tried to do as well as he could and had a difficult time." Almost invariably Flavelle gave his manufacturers some benefit of the doubt, not always to the Board's profit. "I think I am rather easily humbugged," he admitted a few months after these negotiations.[17]

Flavelle's reductions saved the Board about two million dollars. He was also able to give some of the cancelled orders to small firms needing business. All the new business would be at "the lowest price consistent with a fair profit."[18] Where costs were uncertain, the best British and American experience would guide price-setting. Contracts would go only to firms likely to live up to commitments.

The new policies caused more grumbling, as well as attempts to bypass the IMB. Colonel J. J. Carrick, MP, for example, turned up in New York soliciting business from Morgan's for his Winnipeg factory, saying the IMB had no new orders for him. Flavelle explained to the Morgan people that Carrick "is a characteristic promoter; now it is land, now it is mining stock, or again it is shell contracts. He turns up at every period of excitement. He is unbalanced and unsteady. . . . The work he has undertaken for this Board [under a Shell Committee order] will be tardily performed, and is quite as much as he should undertake."[19] Senator Frederic Nicholls had originally resisted having his two companies, Canadian General Electric and Canadian Allis–Chalmers, try to make fuzes. Then he had complained repeatedly to Borden and the Ministry of Munitions about the lack of orders. Like several other manufacturers, he balked at the IMB's new prices and turned to everyone's dupe, the Russians, in the hope of getting orders on a cost–plus basis. Flavelle warned the purchasing agents for the Russians that Nicholls' companies were poorly organized and constantly behind in their work.[20] Cooperation like this among Allied purchasing agencies, combined with shared information about prices, would save millions for the home governments.

Because of the fuze shortage, Canada's bad record generally, and the growing need for larger shells, Britain was placing no more orders for the small eighteen-pounders. Even with the reallocations there were not enough orders to go around. Having just decided to recruit a total of 500,000 Canadians, the Borden government became increasingly desperate for orders for the Western factories — not on their merits, but solely to help the recruiting drive. Responding to pressure from the Prime Minister (the kind of high-level political pressure no agency, no matter how "businesslike" its affairs, could ignore), Flavelle joined the government in urging more British orders for the Western provinces. He was able to get a subcontract to machine and assemble 250,000 shells from the Canadian Car Company—it was far, far behind on its big Russian order—and also managed to get authorization from Britain for another 100,000 eighteen-pounders.[21] He was not impressed, however, with the way manufacturers in places like Moose Jaw were begging their MP's to get them more orders when they were still behind on existing contracts. The first response of a dissatisfied manufacturer always seemed to be to complain to his MP — or, if the manufacturer were already an MP or Senator, to the Prime Minister. Flavelle wrote countless letters to politicians, patiently explaining his methods and his decisions. Privately he became more than a little impatient with their constant interference in his business.

There were also ominous signs that the IMB might be drawn into labour disputes. Some Toronto and Hamilton metal workers were pressing their bosses to bring in the nine-hour day, long established in many other industries; and in his plants Senator Frederic Nicholls (whose wage policies in 1914−15 had been at the root of much of labour's interest in a Fair Wage clause) was refusing to talk to his men about their many grievances. In Medicine Hat, Alberta, the three firms on shell contracts decided to cut wages when Flavelle cut their prices. They were still getting twenty-five cents a shell more than Eastern manufacturers and had orders only as a make-work project. When one firm ignored warnings to maintain wages and provoked a strike, Flavelle cancelled its contract. The pressure worked: the owners replaced their managers, settled with the workers at the old rates, and got their contract back. In tactful letters and personal interviews with the Toronto and Hamilton manufacturers, Flavelle argued that this was no time to "split hairs" with labour and that it would be wise to pay extra for the tenth hour of the working day to avoid any outbreak of the "strike fever." Some manufacturers responded well to this gentle interference. Others, like Senator Nicholls, resented it, storing up problems for the future. In these early attempts to quiet troubled waters the IMB worked closely with officials from the Department of Labour, as Flavelle had promised.[22]

By midwinter Flavelle was reasonably satisfied with the IMB's development. It was still being shaped as an organization, but he was delighted with the work done by Fitzgerald in purchasing, by McAvity in relations with the manufacturers, by Gordon on the fuze problem, and by George Edwards, a prominent Toronto accountant, who was helping to improve the book-keeping. New men were being recruited every week from private industry to strengthen head office's ability to administer contracts engaging more than 400 factories and some 175,000 workers. Flavelle did not yet feel, however, that contractors had responded as well as they might have to the new organization:

I find that, unconsciously, manufacturers and public men think of this shell business primarily for the advantage it may be to Canada and unconsciously place in a secondary position the need of the Imperial authorities. . . . At the moment there is considerable outcry here for more orders. Some of the noisiest and most ill-tempered are those who have filled their contracts in the most slovenly way, or are still deplorably behind in their deliveries. . . . We have not . . . a good name for keeping our promises. Manufacturers have been more content to secure orders than they have been to exercise energy and capacity in executing them.[23]

The single most pressing problem was still the fuze mess inherited from the Shell Committee. By placing their original orders in the United States (in the hope of getting quicker production), the Shell Committee had put off beginning to develop any Canadian fuze capacity. The trickiest part of fuze production was loading powder into the fuzes under rigidly controlled conditions. None of the Canadian manufacturers, including T. A. Russell, who first thought he could, was able to set up satisfactory loading facilities. So Flavelle decided to imitate methods used by Lloyd George in England and have the IMB do the fuze loading itself. C. B. Gordon was at work launching an IMB-owned "National Factory" to do the loading. But it would not come into production until the summer.

IV

On January 20, 1916, Flavelle was surprised to receive a letter from Sam Hughes dated December 13, 1915. Written just after their first conflict over fuzes, it was Hughes at his most typical. Rambling through the fuze question, he raged at Flavelle as a novice in munitions, as "the most 'sanctimonious promoter' " Sir William Van Horne had ever encountered,* as a man "of a peculiar turn of mind." He brought up the CCM affair and accused T. A. Russell of having profiteered on contracts with the Militia Department in 1914. J. Wesley Allison, Hughes wrote, was "the friend of every honest man . . . his one desire to keep prices down . . . to produce the best possible article for the least possible money without any profit whatever to himself." Flavelle replied coolly, telling Hughes of the "rake-off " on the fuze contract Allison had helped to negotiate, and stating his readiness to lay the Phillips case before an impartial tribunal. They had no more correspondence on the matter.[24]

About the same time, the press and *Saturday Night* began to print rumours about trouble at the IMB. Members of the Board were said to be disaffected by Flavelle's autocratic methods — first Gordon, then Vaillancourt were reported (falsely) to be on the brink of resignation. Flavelle was forcing contracts on manufacturers at ridiculously low prices; he had given a fuze contract to a Canadian automobile concern with which he was friendly at a considerably higher price than other reputable companies would have asked; the Chairman's domineering, unsympathetic attitude was causing manufacturers to refuse orders; and so on. There were a number of suggestions that the IMB had failed and should be replaced by a Canadian Ministry of Munitions.[25]

The *Globe's* Ottawa correspondent told Flavelle that Sam Hughes was his source for the stories. John Ross Robertson of the *Telegram* told him he had seen all the correspondence between Hughes and Flavelle. Other malignant rumours circulating privately around Ottawa could be traced back to Hughes and his cronies, Flavelle thought. He was sure the Hughes crowd was supported in their attacks on him by other people who had been offended by the Board.

---

* The letter referred in a confused way to some business deal in Chicago years before in which Hughes claimed Flavelle, Van Horne, and later Allison were all involved. There is no reference anywhere in the rest of Flavelle's papers to such an unlikely incident.

... we have aroused considerable criticism. Men who found it easy to secure contracts; men who directed contracts for their own advantage, or men who took contracts for larger amounts than they could complete within a reasonable time, do not like the firmness with which we deal with all such situations. Politicians who were in the habit of securing favours are outraged at our method of allotting the business to firms of good standing, at the lowest prices. The middle-men and hangers-on, who had such an influential position, are left stranded under the new conditions. They have had powerful associations and connections. All of these are hungry as wolves, and as savage. In addition, there has been a carefully and persistently worked plan for bringing discredit to the new Board by our active friend, the Minister. Some fresh story is circulated each day, and about once a week there is a quickener, in the form of a newspaper statement with flaring headlines.[26]

Flavelle thought, probably correctly, that the campaign for a Ministry of Munitions was launched by people who wanted the war business turned back over to the politicians and political manufacturers. It would recreate the days of the Shell Committee, a group Flavelle considered to have been "children in the hands of a dominant Minister." As for Sam Hughes, "he was either a child, a fool, or a corrupt man, in the hands of a corrupt gang, on the one side, and powerful, greedy men, on the other."

For several weeks in late January and early February Flavelle worried that the campaign would succeed and he would be displaced. If it happened, he told his friends, he would at least have made the one abrupt departure from normal methods of carrying on public business, would have "effectively stopped for the time being as bad a gang of vagabonds as could be found in any country."[27]

In fact he had little to worry about. Another reason for the whispering campaign against the IMB may have been to try to deflect mounting Liberal criticism of the Shell Committee in the House of Commons.* Knowing they were on to something, but not quite sure what, Opposition MP's first hurled general charges of profiteering, conflict of interest, and corruption at the Shell Committee. Soon they began to narrow in on Hughes, Allison, and the June 1915 fuze contract. They did not rise to the planted bait about the IMB; its operations, including Flavelle's fuze fight with Hughes, re-

* Flavelle received Hughes's December 13 letter on fuzes on January 20, two days after the first major attack on the Shell Committee in the House of Commons. The two possible explanations of the delay are a breakdown in government postal delivery or an attempt by Hughes to cover his tracks by attacking Flavelle.

mained free from parliamentary discussion. The Prime Minister, who had reprimanded Hughes for his letter to Flavelle, had no desire to let his erratic minister get his finger back in the contract pie. As well, Hichens reported from England that the Ministry was very pleased with the IMB's work, now had complete confidence in the Canadian operation, and was about to place much-needed orders.[28]

V

The British were now long on confidence, but were starting to run short of cash to pay for Canadian munitions. As early as the autumn of 1915 Britain began to suffer from shortages of foreign currency, and for a time in November the Shell Committee was unable to pay its bills.[29] In December the situation eased when Thomas White, astonished that his appeal to Canadians for a $50-million war loan had been subscribed twice over (having always assumed the home money market was insignificant, the Canadian government had never before tried to borrow domestically), lent the extra $50 million to the imperial government to pay for munitions purchases in Canada.

By February 1916, the IMB's spending was approaching $5 million a week. By spring the credit would be exhausted. With the foreign-exchange situation worse than ever, the British Treasury opposed placing new orders in Canada unless new credits could be arranged to cover most of the cost. Flavelle found himself becoming a fund-raiser as well as a munitions-maker.

He approached White about another loan from Canada. White refused, citing his own heavy war expenses plus the continuing need to support the railways. Nor did he want the IMB to try to raise money on the American market, where he was planning to float a big Canadian loan. Instead he recommended an approach to the chartered banks.

Flavelle was dubious at first, for the banks had played little part in this kind of large-scale finance, had a generally defensive mentality, and were trying to keep liquid that winter because of their fear of a railway bust. His one high card was the prospect of most of the money being spent in Canada and so coming right back to the banks to swell their deposits. No loan would mean no new orders, a drastic shrinkage in the munitions business, and, consequently, a drastic shrinkage in the banks' business. He thought the argument might be telling enough that he advised White to urge the banks to lend $75 million rather than $50 million—"the money would speedily go into circulation and find its way back again into their vaults."[30]

White agreed to present the Board's case to a committee of the Canadian Bankers' Association at a meeting on March 1. Flavelle and Gordon were also present. Before the conference the businessmen had done "missionary work" with the bankers individually, and White—by now an adroit politician—leaked to the press the news that the banks were considering supplying credits for new munitions orders in Canada. The meeting went well, Flavelle reported, except for resistance from Frederick Williams Taylor of the Bank of Montreal, who wanted manufacturers to take pay in British Treasury Bills, which could then be discounted by the banks. This would enable the banks to rediscount the paper in the United States, a scheme unacceptable to the Treasury, which was also preparing to borrow there. The bankers finally agreed to advance $50 to $75 million on the strength of Treasury Bills to be held in London (i.e., not to be resold in the United States) and on condition that new British orders approximated the amount of the loan.[31]

It took several weeks to work out the details. Flavelle had to struggle to get the new orders authorized from England and technically failed to meet the condition. The Bank of Montreal balked at going up to $75 million and only contributed its share of the increase when the CPR deposited a special $5 million for the duration of the loan. The banks wanted to be able to call the loan after a year, and the interest would be stiff. When the deal was finally closed, Flavelle saw it as "an Epoch in the financial life of the Empire . . . evidence of our developing manhood among the nations." It marked Canada's passage from a dependent of Britain, always borrowing abroad, to a nation whose private banks were now lending money back to England. "The transformation seems almost a miracle."[32]

VI

There would never be a month or even a week when the IMB had no problems on its hands. In March 1916, Flavelle had to deal with all the complaints from manufacturers and MP's over the awarding of the box contracts: there had been 1500 tenderers and a spread in the bids of 500 per cent. A number of the higher bidders and their MP's saw no reason why that should disqualify them from contracts. Other MP's thought the IMB's staff, especially its large corps of inspectors, should be hired through the usual Ottawa channels (i.e. on recommendation from local MP's). Flavelle refused to let politicians even see the names of his inspectors.[33] Out in British Columbia there seemed to be one minor problem after another: first it was manufacturers' resentment at having some of their production allotment diverted to the "prosperous grain-growing area" of Moose Jaw; then it was the inspection staff's resentment at the indignity of having their time spent in factories recorded; then it was the great varnish fight, when ten thousand B.C. shells were rejected by the IMB's Winnipeg assay office because of too much lead in their varnish — much more favourable assays had been produced on the spot in British Columbia.[34] More serious was the occasional discovery of fraud by a manufacturer: the deliberate erasure of inspection marks on some shells at the Sorel Steel Foundries; the use of fraudulent inspectors' stamps at the Jenckes Machine Company in Sherbrooke. Fraud was not common, but it had to be watched for.[35]

Organized labour had been pressing all winter for a Fair Wage clause in IMB contracts. At another meeting with Borden and Crothers early in March Flavelle again opposed the idea, arguing that a number of manufacturers would probably refuse contracts, leading to delays in war production. Instead, he agreed to have the Industrial Disputes Investigation Act applied to munitions factories; on application from either management or labour there would be conciliation before any strike could take place. Crothers also thought this was a better step than introducing the Fair Wage clause.[36]

The new machinery failed to stop Senator Frederic Nicholls from locking out the machinists at his Allis—Chalmers plant over the issue of the nine-hour day. The International Association of Machinists threatened to retaliate by pulling out all its Toronto workers. A Royal Commission had to be appointed to investigate. "There is at the present time a shifting about of labour from factory to factory and a general restlessness, due to the feeling of labour that there is an opportunity to secure concessions in regard to hours and wages that was not [sic] offered for many years," one of Flavelle's friends reported. He thought the Royal Commission might only bring the unrest to a head.[37]

These relatively minor problems did not interfere with Flavelle's satisfaction at the IMB's progress through the spring of 1916. He had new orders and the money to pay for them. He had a first-rate team of businessmen and seemed to have won his struggle against political interference in general and Sam Hughes's interference in particular. His staff was still growing to handle a business now spending about a million dollars a day. New executives were brought in to straighten out transportation problems, the gauge problem, the distribution of components, and a dozen other problems as they arose. Flavelle was delighted with his men's conscientiousness and predicted that the IMB was on its way to becoming "one of the most efficient working organizations in Canada."[38]

VII

Having avoided being dragged down to their level, Flavelle began to chafe at politicians' failure to rise to his own standards of efficiency and service. So many of them seemed to spend so much time in his own office, seeking favours for constituents. In Parliament they wasted days rehashing the past, with the Opposition in an "impudently disrespectful" mood. "All the active members of the Government are greatly over-worked and over-wrought. They have very little opportunity for quiet reflection and almost no oppor-tunity to come in contact with the real spirit in the country."[39]

He thought the real spirit was good, at least if the grace with which the business community had accepted White's war-profits tax in February was any example. No other group in the country had been affected by extra taxation and yet businessmen had not complained except on a few points of detail. (The lack of complaining had surprised him personally, for although he had congratulated White on the budget, he had himself objected to several aspects of the new tax. He was probably ashamed of himself when White refused to moderate it in any detail "at a time when mothers and wives are giving up their sons and husbands . . . men are offering their lives to save the industries of the Empire." And perhaps more ashamed when Will Rundle wrote that National Trust would deem it "a privilege to pay its full share" of war taxes, and complained that White should have gone on to levy an income tax and been tougher on companies with watered stock.)[40]

The Canadian people were ahead of their leaders in facing up to the impli-cations of the war, Flavelle thought. If only the politicians would even follow the public, let alone offer leadership:

There has been response to every call. We have furnished men, we have given money, our women have asked what can we do? Our business and corporate interests known to be selfish in their training and practice, accept without protest, many with actual approval and satisfaction, the imposition of taxes hitherto unthought of. We are developing character with our new experience. . . . I am troubled in the lack of response at the national capital. The desire to secure party advantage, the sordid desire for the help that comes through patronage—the almost complete absence of the Spiritual and the ever insistent presence of the personal occasions surprise and concern. The surprise of the uninitiated is increased in his wonder why there should be such servility to the commonplace and small, why success should be sought or temporarily accepted by leaders through the acceptance of standards of men deficient in calibre and vulgar in morals. . . . There would doubtless develop a good deal of contempt for the straight laced who was only critical . . . but I cannot believe the courageous leader who simply did right and continued to do it each day would suffer —He would have opposition, and personal discomfort and there would be an outcry from the common place party trickster . . . but there would come support from the country . . . I do not believe I am wrong in saying that the exhibition of Parliament is unedifying, and the general atmosphere unworthy of the times.[41]

The atmosphere became more highly charged when the Liberals finally detonated the fuze scandal late in March. Thanks to the work of private detectives in New York, they were able to produce agreements made by the promoters of the American Ammunition Company to divide $1 million in commissions on the Shell Committee contract. $220,000 was to go to J. Wesley Allison. The revelations caused a sensation in Parliament, forcing Borden to recall Hughes from England and set up a Royal Commission to investigate.

Flavelle had apparently not known about the commissions on that fuze contract, but did know it had been sublet and had himself gone through round two on fuzes with Hughes, Allison, and Phillips. He had also learned, as had the cabinet (but not the Opposition), of another transaction early in the war in which Hughes allowed surplus small-arms ammunition from the Dominion Arsenal to be sold through a third party to the imperial government, the third party taking a healthy profit. The new revelations caused his opinion of Hughes to harden into conviction:

I believe him to be mentally unbalanced, with the low cunning and cleverness often associated with the insane; possessed of remarkable physical energy and love of the spectacular. He has commanded wide attention, notwithstanding his vulgar brutality and coarse language. I have reluctantly reached the conclusion that the body of crooked men he has had about him have been there through design, and that he has shared in the profits which have arisen out of the various transactions engineered by them. Everywhere I have turned there has been the same disturbing and disastrous connection. I am inclined to think he is without moral appreciation of his conduct, and is not fully responsible.[42]

Flavelle sympathized with the anger of backbench Tories, who found their party and the government endangered by Hughes and the wretched fuzes. His sources in the cabinet—probably White or Kemp—told him the ministers all wanted Hughes to go. However, "the Prime Minister has not only been a good friend, and therefore reluctant to remove him, but he dislikes anything disagreeable, and shrinks from it to such an extent that he lives in a perpetual atmosphere of the disagreeable rather than deal decisively with the troublesome factor." To Flavelle, who also hoped Hughes would be removed, the old issue of Borden's leadership capacity was coming to the surface again. "It is probably true that the Prime Minister commands the affection of his party to a greater degree than at any previous time; he is possessed of such high character, is so modest in demeanour, is so patient with everyone, that the party warms to him in his period of difficulty and trial." But there was his failure to offer robust leadership. "Under normal circumstances the indecision of the Prime Minister is an element of weakness; in the present abnormal state of affairs it is probably a fatal weakness."[43]

The railways added to everyone's troubles. The Grand Trunk Pacific and the Canadian Northern were effectively broke and had to be bailed out by the government or collapse. The public, press, and many MP's saw no reason why the roads should continue to bleed the Treasury. But Borden, White, and the bankers knew how severe the consequences of a bankruptcy could be. Indeed, Borden had promised the Bank of Commerce that it would not suffer losses on its advances to the Canadian Northern. On Sundays in Toronto Flavelle often met with Aird and Walker. They agreed "that the Bank should not consent or yield to pressure to abate from the full under-taking provided in the letters." White seemed to accept the obligation and, according to Flavelle in April 1916, was ready to "cross the bridge with a bold announcement that they will take over the [Canadian Northern] road," presumably through purchase of the outstanding common stock.[44]

As usual, Flavelle had been urging a takeover on Borden and White. Perhaps unjustly, he thought Borden would naturally resist a policy requiring "vision and imagination . . . infinite courage and firmness." He expected more of White and found it intensely frustrating when the Finance Minister would talk boldly one day, hesitantly the next. His vacillation on railways, Flavelle thought, was typical of his erratic personality:

White is efficient, but uncertain in his daily judgment. It is difficult to recognize him as the same man from one day to another. It is no discredit to be perplexed during the time a man is reaching a decision as to the course which ought to be followed, but it is not easy to understand a strong man, full of creative force and vigour one day, and in the depths the next. By right, White should be the right hand supporter of the Prime Minister, and give robustness to the administration, and become easily the commanding figure in it. He has earned, and is entitled to the respect of all for his brilliant administration in his own department, but I fear he is of little strength for team play. A time like this accentuates his difficulty in losing sight of himself.

The only other minister for whom Flavelle had significant respect was Arthur Meighen, who was still a junior member of the cabinet. "They are a wobbly lot," he wrote of the cabinet as a whole.[45]

The ministers decided to continue to wobble along on the railway question. Parliament was asked and grudgingly agreed to provide money for the railways, including the Canadian Northern's past and future interest obligations (although it was not told about the private commitments to the Commerce). A Royal Commission was to be appointed to recommend what should be done next. The roads would keep running, the country would keep paying, and the bankers would keep worrying.

In the meantime the Royal Commission on Shell Contracts had been taking millions of words of testimony about the Shell Committee, fuzes, Allison, and Sam Hughes, while another investigation probed the small-arms ammunition deal. No one could show any ties between Hughes and Allison except friendship, or any malfeasance by Carnegie and the Shell Committee beyond a naive mistake (Flavelle thought it a stupid mistake) made under pressure in letting the fuze contracts at unnecessarily high prices to friends of Allison. Flavelle testified briefly before the Royal Commission in May, talking generally about the IMB's methods. The commissioners knew there had been correspondence between Flavelle and Hughes over Phillips and the December 1915 fuze contract. The Liberals wanted it made public; counsel for the government did not. The commissioners decided it could not be used as evidence because the imperial government did not want IMB correspondence made public.[46] That saved Sam Hughes's job, for the time being, because the additional circumstantial evidence against Hughes in the Phillips affair would surely have made it impossible for Borden to keep him in the cabinet. Deliberate corruption still would not have been proven—Flavelle's own assumption that Hughes had stood to profit on the Phillips deal, among others, was never backed up by solid evidence—and it has never been proven.

Hughes defended J. Wesley Allison to the last as "the biggest and best man in Canada — and the cleanest too." As he meditated on the imperatives of war, the sorry state of Canadian politics, and the indecisiveness of the government, nothing upset Flavelle more than Hughes's praise of Allison. "We are sharers in a world struggle," Flavelle wrote Willison,

we have sent our young men with pride; we have borne our sorrows with restraint . . . we are surprised that we have been able to bear as well as we have a man's burdens . . . .

What is to be said under such circumstances, when no voice is raised, no pen writes, of the humiliation and shame incident to J. Wesley Allison, et al., and the vulgar, coarse Minister who shames us by parading them as paragons of virtue and excellence? Who fills the chief place in our daily press? Allison! Has our sense of proportion deserted us; has our perspective utterly failed?

A Minister of the Crown can say, unrebuked, that there is more decency in Allison's little toe than in the Auditor General's carcass. He can continue being brutal to his staff; he can go on using violent, profane language; he can take his comrades and companions and force them upon our notice—men who can secure no recognition in self-respecting circles. Is there no call for recovery of our sanity, and is there no one who will make a claim on behalf of our dignity and self-respect? . . .

The world is in travail; there is great sorrow; there are the refining influences of suffering—how can we ignore all these and allow the common, the sordid and the impudent to go filling chief places, unashamed and unrebuked? . . . If in these surroundings, we can not appeal to ideals, when will we?[47]

Allison was rebuked by the Royal Commission for taking a commission on the fuze contract. The Government of Canada punished him by removing his name from the list of Honorary Colonels. While the investigation was on, C. B. Gordon of the IMB had been renegotiating the fuze contract with the American Ammunition Company (it was in default on deliveries, but the IMB decided to negotiate rather than cancel because no one else could supply the fuzes faster). He was eventually able to save the IMB $1 million— $1,500,000 on the contract. The Phillips Company of Worcester, Massachusetts, had gone bankrupt shortly after failing to get a contract from Flavelle.

Sam Hughes remained as Minister of Militia, the minister in charge of Canada's fighting men. But the shell scandal, on top of the formation of the IMB, had destroyed his influence in everything to do with war purchasing. Hughes himself had once hoped to strike it rich in business by being an agent in big "deals," by inventing something, or by being in on promotions.[48] He was one of a large group of get-rich-quickers, including Allison, who were constantly chasing rainbows around the fringes of established business, relying heavily on their friends and contacts to show them the way to the pot of gold. Denied riches and prominence in business, they often found social status in the militia and useful connections in politics. They were not necessarily dishonest men, but neither were they reliable or competent, particularly in carrying out business undertakings. Allison was the semi-respectable broker who seemed to have found his pot of gold during the war thanks to his friendship with the Canadian Minister of Militia. If he had been a friend of Sir John A. Macdonald or one of his cronies in the 1880s it all might have worked then. As war moved from supplying harnesses and horses to an old-fashioned militia to spending hundreds of millions equipping modern armies, the old-fashioned businessmen *cum* politicians, like Hughes and Allison, proved inadequate or worse, and were replaced by experienced professional businessmen like Flavelle. It remained to be seen how much better the new men could do, and whether they could remain beyond criticism.

CHAPTER TWELVE

TO HELL WITH PROFITS

"We have failed in a good deal of our work . . . lack of perspective and lack of understanding . . . delay of delivery of materials of every kind . . . promises which we have made for shells to be shipped have not been carried out . . . the Ministry are anxious . . . physical defects in the shell." [1]

Flavelle had been carried away by pride in the IMB's early success. As the spring of 1916 turned into a long, hot summer, shell production proved a trickier business than he had imagined. Deliveries increased, but the programme was still far behind schedule. British and American producers had solved most of their problems and were starting to meet their commitments. Canadian manufacturers had not and were not. Far worse than that, the quality of the Canadian product was poor. A small matter for manufacturers of bacon or widgets, deadly business for gunners trying to fire Canadian-made 4.5-inch shells that too often exploded in their faces.

I

Making munitions in Canada was such a decentralized and complex business that there were bound to be delays. No factories produced complete shells, let alone complete rounds. The IMB bought steel to be forged, delivered shell forgings to machiners and then assemblers, sometimes thousands of miles away, shipped shells to loading depots, sometimes thousands of miles away, coordinated the supply of shells with the production of cartridge cases and fuzes, and worked into the process dozens of parts handled by suppliers scattered from Vancouver to Georgia. Any factory's failure to meet deadlines affected a dozen other factories. Any factory with problems had excuses: supplies had not arrived on time, someone else had failed to meet standards, the IMB was being unreasonable, and so on. "Whatever may have been the advantage to Canada to have the work widely distributed in the hands of a number of unimportant people," Flavelle wrote in April 1916, "it has been a mistake from the standpoint of production . . . . The main fact is we undertook more business than we planned intelligently to complete . . . . Viewed from the standpoint of normal operations, what Canada has done is remarkable; viewed from the standpoint of an emergency, what Canada has done is unsatisfactory." He gradually realized that attempts to mesh precisely his system's operations were bound to fail. The solution was to allow manufacturers greater lead time while also overordering to create a margin for inefficiency and delays.[2]

No Canadian manufacturing operations had ever been carried out with so much concern for quality. The shells had to be checked, rechecked, and checked again to ensure uniformity and reliability (they were probably the first truly interchangeable "parts" made in Canada). The Shell Committee had borrowed officers from the Dominion Arsenal to organize a staff of inspectors to perform the necessary checks on manufacturers' work. The IMB inherited this organization, headed by Lieutenant-Colonel G. Ogilvie. The inspectors were administratively under the Board's control, but received their instructions from Britain, where the quality standards were set.

Inspectors had absolute power to reject faulty work. The manufacturer would have to take the losses involved. Complaints from manufacturers that inspectors were applying absurdly high standards became commonplace. Flavelle just as commonly ignored them. In the spring of 1916, however, he had to bring all his sweet reasonableness to bear on David Carnegie, his Board's own technical expert, to stop him from siding with steel manufacturers who were charging Ogilvie with enforcing unreasonably high standards. "Carnegie has such a generous mind," Hichens wrote from England, "that it never occurs to him that some people are only too ready with mean motives." Fortunately Carnegie's energies were soon taken up proving his innocence—precisely Hichens' point—in the fuze scandal.[3]

The real inspection problem was poor standards and poor performance. As soon as it was realized that Canadian 4.5-inch shells were not reliable (more than one in every thirty thousand rounds was damaging its gun by exploding prematurely; this was about thirty times the rate for eighteen-pounders), the British began to reinspect Canadian products. They isolated the 4.5-inch problem in the quality of steel used, quality so far below standard that they wondered if another kind of steel had been accidentally used as shell steel.[4] The first "Made in Canada" fuzes were also starting to arrive in England from T. A. Russell's Toronto factory. Woolwich Arsenal inspectors threw out fifty to seventy-five per cent of the first shipment; on the second shipment the failure rate was higher. With adequate inspection in Canada the fuzes would never have been shipped.[5]

When the Board abruptly changed the specifications for 4.5-inch steel late in June, manufacturers were thrown into confusion and anger. Every shell forging in production had to be reinspected and turned back if it failed to meet the new standards. All the steel companies, already complaining about ultra-rigid inspection, were behind on deliveries, forcing the Board to order extra steel in the United States. It, too, failed to arrive on time. Meanwhile, it took weeks for Flavelle to convince Ogilvie to move his headquarters from Quebec City to Ottawa. Flavelle hoped that closer coordination between the Board and the inspectorate would prevent repetition of these problems. He admitted having foolishly given Ogilvie too much independence.[6]

The likelihood of labour troubles increased as war needs sopped up the country's surplus manpower. By the spring of 1916 there were no more unemployed, but both the army and the economy needed more hands. Told to get men for the armies, recruiters went to where the men were—in the munitions factories. Complaints poured in to the Board about workers and inspectors leaving their jobs to volunteer. Himself dubious about Canada's commitment to put half a million men in khaki, Flavelle had urged the government to make plans for regulating the labour supply. Nothing was done. Even his request for a system of badges to distinguish workers in essential industries was blocked by Sam Hughes. Without some identification, an able-bodied male in civilian clothes was apt to be taunted on the streets as a coward and a slacker. In desperation some firms issued their own badges; these were ignored by recruiting officers.[7]

Manufacturers gave unskilled men crash courses in operating complicated machinery. French Canadians and immigrants of all nationalities were imported into Toronto to take over some of the heavier jobs. Women first began to volunteer for munitions work in the spring of 1916, but manufacturers hesitated to use them. Afraid of accidents, they were reluctant to put women on machine work; complaining of their inexperience, they refused to offer women wages equal to men. There were immediate complaints from the women, many of whom were soldiers' wives from the middle class, others who were used to working for wages in domestic service or offices. The manufacturers, they thought, were trying to make a profit out of women's patriotism.

Unprepared himself for such a drastic evolution in the relations of the sexes, the IMB's Chairman tried to steer a middle course on wages, pleading for mutual tolerance:

I do not think it is a time to argue over details. I think it is the duty of all to ask: "What service can I render?" If manufacturers are greedy, and are unreasonable, efforts should be made to develop in them a sounder spirit.

If women, who of necessity are inexperienced, and who are physically unfit day after day to perform men's service, seek to bargain before they commence work what their pay will be, or seek to establish some theory of equality of payment for equality of service, I think they too should be reasoned with.

. . . It would appear to me that the thing to do is to get to work, and to prove to men in public positions that there is a real service which can be performed by women. . . .[8]

One of Flavelle's investigators pinpointed a relationship between labour shortages and labour unrest. "It is the intelligent and patriotic workman who has enlisted," he wrote. "Those of the opposite type have now the opportunity, and in many instances make use of it, to demand exorbitant and immediate raises in wages and other unreasonable conditions. So independent have workers become, that the employer has no assurance that his organization will not be impaired at a moment's notice by the loss of certain operators." Observations like these, fairly common among IMB officials, may or may not have been founded in reality. There was no doubt that labour was becoming restless, in no mood to be left out of the profits in munition-making.[9]

The Royal Commission appointed in April to investigate problems in the Toronto and Hamilton plants led to more problems. Two of the three commissioners recommended adoption of the nine-hour day, with the tenth hour, obviously necessary in wartime, paid for as overtime. The third commissioner objected that the recommendation would disrupt non-war work and become a precedent for peacetime. The International Association of Machinists threatened a general strike of machinists in the area early in June if the majority recommendation was not implemented. "It is a time when we all seek to be wise as well as firm," Flavelle wrote the general manager of Stelco, urging him to begin negotiations to avoid a strike. Instead of cooperating, the Hamilton manufacturers sought refuge in patriotism: "In view of the fact that so many of our Canadians have offered their services and are willing to risk their lives Overseas, we feel that it is incumbent and not unreasonable to ask those who remain behind and who, at present, are earning abnormally high wages, to extend, rather than seek to curtail their activities in the production of munitions." Flavelle persisted with an open letter to the affected manufacturers, urging them either to accept the Commission report or to negotiate until an agreement had been reached to avoid a strike.[10]

Some manufacturers cooperated. "We are determined not to permit any trouble to arise on any minor matter that would affect the delivery of our munitions," T. A. Russell wrote. His company granted the nine-hour day, as did several Toronto firms. So did Frank Baillie's Canadian Cartridge Company in Hamilton, which was at work on a large cartridge-case contract. More typically, the vice-president of Canadian Westinghouse denied that any unrest existed in his factory, claimed the Royal Commission should never have been appointed, and refused to do anything. "We believe our employees . . . are true and loyal subjects, with the good of the Empire held far above the question of whether they shall work 50 or 55 hours per week, and if left undisturbed by labor agitators will continue to demonstrate their loyalty and patriotism by a sustained production of munitions as earnestly as those who have gone to the front in defence of their King and Country."[11]

The Hamilton machinists and tool-makers struck on June 11. The Employers' Association of Hamilton published violent denunciations of the workers as the dupes of alien labour agitators who were crippling the cause of Great Britain and her Allies. Crothers, the Minister of Labour, asked Flavelle to threaten to cancel the manufacturers' orders. Flavelle would not go that far:

Much as I am disturbed over the possibility of labour troubles, I would not be warranted in suggesting to the Board that they take such action. I am, as you know, a believer in the nine hour day. I would like to see the shorter hours established. I do not, however, consider that the Board should take sides in a matter upon which there is so serious a difference of opinion. The question of fairness or unfairness to employees is not involved, nor is it a matter of an employer endeavouring to unduly reduce wages.[12]

He did go to Hamilton at the mayor's request and spent several days trying to reason with the employers. The negotiations, he commented, were "somewhat discreditable to all concerned."[13] A negotiated settlement collapsed, and the strike dragged into July before the machinists drifted back to work, beaten.

With labour conditions starting to become tense across the country, someone in Ottawa — perhaps Flavelle, perhaps Crothers, perhaps both — decided to have the Press Censor limit news of the strike to the Hamilton papers.[14] Tactics like that, if known about, would have reinforced labour's doubts about a Board whose Chairman objected to the Fair Wage clause. On the other hand, Flavelle's repeated attempts to persuade manufacturers to be reasonable were not publicized either. "You will remember that every labour difficulty adds to the danger of labour trouble somewhere else," he wrote the manager of Winnipeg's Vulcan Iron Works in September. "Therefore, there is the more reason for the employer—who, of necessity should take a broader view of the situation than the employee—to recognize the possible bearing that his troubles have upon the production of munitions in factories other than his own." One of Winnipeg's most anti-union firms retorted, "This is a free country, and as long as we live and remain in the manufacturing business, we are going to do our small share of keeping it free . . . the day will never come when we will have to take orders from any Union."[15]

As the summer dragged on, labour unrest diminished, but manpower shortages did not. Flavelle shared the belief that recruiting of the "men of conscience" seriously reduced efficiency in the plants. As well, much of the heaviest and most unpleasant work had been done by foreigners. Some of the Central Europeans had left Canada to fight for their countries, some had been interned as enemy aliens. Everyone suffered terribly from a prolonged heat wave in the summer of 1916. In August the factories were depleted as thousands of workers quit to go West on the annual harvest excursion. Rail fares West were so low, wages so high, that Colonel Cantley's Nova Scotia Steel plant, in which labour relations were never very good, lost 250 men in three days. Flavelle complained repeatedly about the government's failure to implement any plan for controlling labour, even the obvious expedient of importing Americans for the harvest.[16]

He was continually adding to his own staff, now almost five hundred in the IMB's new quarters in the Transportation Building. Flavelle often remarked on the unselfish devotion of his staff, the best he had ever worked with, but nothing seemed to ease the burden of work. "We are gathering men about us as fast as we find them, only to disappear as a stone disappears as a child tosses it into the lake." Peter Perry, who would always be the most forthright of Flavelle's friends, gently suggested to him that the Board might also be short-staffed at the top. "I take it he means, in substance, a shortage at the very top. This can not be changed now; it is easily possible, but it would not be wise."[17]

II

There were occasional bright spots. A few manufacturers were doing splendid work. F. P. Jones of Canada Cement, for example, who had complained so bitterly about the Shell Committee, had made good on his promises to install a plant in record time for making big 9.2-inch shells. Within three months he had a production line ready, "probably the smartest thing that has ever been done in Canada," Flavelle thought. The extra steel forgings from the United States were ordered to keep Jones supplied; it would be months before any of the other heavy-shell contractors had finished installing their machinery.[18]

Russell was having trouble with his fuzes, but at least was eager to learn. His partner, Lloyd Harris, had rushed to England to get advice on the problem. And he did avoid labour troubles. So did the management of the Algoma Steel Company, which raised wages fifty per cent in twelve months in 1915–16 rather than slow down production.[19] Then in July the IMB received a cheque for $758,248.03 from Frank Baillie of the Canadian Cartridge Company. Baillie was returning half the profits on a contract for two million eighteen-pounder cartridge cases he had taken from the Shell Committee in August 1915 at the going rate of $1.75 a case. A stockbroker, who had begun his career with Dominion Securities, Baillie had had no experience in manufacturing. He had won the contract for his new company by offering to return any profits he made on the second million cases. When Flavelle and Hichens had originally reviewed the contracts, they questioned the deal, thinking Baillie would pad his costs. He did not, submitting cost figures showing only wages, raw materials, and the cost of power; he made no charge for plant amortization, and had returned $300,000 more than he had predicted because he got his manufacturing cost for the second million down to forty per cent of his original estimate. Flavelle was delighted with Baillie's work. Other manufacturers were reported to have been "very disturbed" by his gesture. None of them followed his lead.[20]

To round out the summer's troubles, the Board was running out of money again. The $75-million loan from the Canadian banks had lasted through June. To finance July work Flavelle negotiated a further $24-million loan from the banks. He hoped for $50 million, but was frustrated by the Bank of Montreal's determination to remain liquid. "Taylor is timid to a degree," Flavelle wrote bitterly, "and seems to have almost a miser's satisfaction in the great volume of liquid resources which he has available." White, who wanted the banks to underwrite his next war loan, supported Taylor. He assured Flavelle, however, that the IMB could expect a credit of $50 million from the proceeds of that loan; there would be no cause for alarm.[21]

All planning was upset when the expected breakout on the Somme turned into a massacre of British soldiers. The war was not going to end in 1916. It would consume more men, more shells, more money. By the middle of July White had turned pessimistic about his ability to finance the Canadian war effort. He warned Flavelle that Britain should be ready to pay for its Canadian purchases from its own resources for the rest of the year. But Brand in England, now working as the IMB's representative at the Ministry, also warned Flavelle that the Somme fighting was forcing everything to be reconsidered. Britain had planned to stop buying munitions in the United States, expecting domestic and Canadian capacity to be adequate. Now large new American orders would have to be placed. "I do not know whether anyone knows actually what financial methods will have to be adopted to meet all these claims upon us," Brand wrote, trying to explain why Canada should lend more money even if White had to levy severe new taxes to raise it. Brand and Flavelle agreed that White should be invited to England to see at first hand the seriousness of the situation.[22]

With White still postponing his domestic loan until the strategic moment (an annoyed Flavelle felt he had missed his chance in June), and the British Treasury having no idea how it would find the dollars to keep on meeting its North American commitments, the IMB's bank credit melted through the July heat. On the twenty-eighth Flavelle had to cable frantically to England for funds; otherwise the IMB would have been out of money the next day.[23]

He got money to keep going for one week, to August 5. Without telling him, the Treasury sent two cables to White asking him to come to England and requesting that Canada look after all of the IMB's financial needs after August 5. This extraordinary request that he effectively double his war spending reached White on the morning of August 4! He told Flavelle "in unmistakeable terms" that he would have nothing to do with either request. "I will not undertake it as an obligation, either actual or implied. I have no doubt the Imperial Chancellor is heavily burdened; he may consider that I am not heavily burdened. I can not allow his judgment to prevail; I will only be governed by my own judgment. . . ." Flavelle agreed that White had no obligation to pay for munitions Britain had ordered in Canada, thought the British pressure had been unwise, and cabled the Ministry for more money. The Treasury found it, for the time being.[24]

Although Brand was faithfully putting the Board's case to the Treasury — pointing out the oddity of placing millions of dollars' worth of orders in Canada and then announcing that Canada should foot the bill — he was also exasperated at Canada's lack of cooperation. "What I sometimes feel, as I think you do with some of your bankers and financial people," he wrote Flavelle, "is they forget that to lose the War is still worse than to inflate their currency. . . . Inflation brings many evils, but in War it may be absolutely unavoidable. . . . It is no longer a question of sound finance, or anything like it, and if we were all financial purists like the Bank of Montreal, we should have all stopped fighting months ago." Perry was in England and learned that Reginald McKenna, the Chancellor of the Exchequer, was sleepless with worry, expecting a financial collapse between June and October 1917. Perry thought White was being petty in refusing to come over simply because he had (correctly) interpreted the invitation as an attempt to pressure him—". . . I had hoped for better things from White." All Flavelle could do in Ottawa was try to stay on good terms with White and advise the British on how to do the same.[25]

He also blamed mistakes in the American operations for much of Britain's exchange problem. The British had placed huge orders in the United States, pouring money into that country, without requiring the Americans to lend some of it back. Flavelle thought one reason why Britain had not bargained hard to protect its exchange stemmed from the ambiguous position of J. P. Morgan & Company as the American purchasing agency. "I find it difficult to discover any essential difference between your own agents and those who supply your war materials. The interchange of interests between the big Financial Corporations and the large industrial corporations has been too close to make it possible for independent service to be rendered to the Crown." When Britain did float a major loan in New York in September he thought Morgan's interest in satisfying its banking allies had led to the terms being far harsher than necessary.[26]

White again underestimated the amount of money Canadians had available to lend to their government. His September war loan was oversubscribed by more than eighty per cent. At the end of the month he had no trouble lending the IMB $50 million. He had also agreed to go to England for discussions about financial planning for 1917.

IV

Finance was almost the only problem under control by September. All the big 8-inch and 9.2-inch shell production was far behind schedule. Canadian Fairbanks, for example, had just started production on their November 1915 contract, having had to rebuild completely the plant they had originally installed. Ingersoll Rand was still installing equipment. Jones of Canada Cement had his production up to 700 shells a day, but was on the brink of a nervous breakdown and was still not on schedule. Cantley's Nova Scotia Steel Company, an organization Flavelle found "trying," had delivered less than 10,000 of the 250,000 4.5-inch forgings it had promised over the summer, only 60 per cent of the steel promised.[27]

Russell was shipping more Canadian fuzes, but in England they were still being reinspected and thrown out "by the bucketful." Then Canada's reputation reached its nadir when a shipment arrived of 18,000 6-inch shells from the Montreal Locomotive Works. Even a layman could see their faults, could stick pins into holes in the steel which had been filled with paint. Ninety per cent of the shells were rejected. "I found all the soldiers and people from Woolwich buzzing around like angry bees, and expressing their opinion of Canadian methods in unmeasured terms," Perry reported. "I never felt so ashamed in my life. There was absolutely nothing to say when they pointed out that if our shells had gone to the Front as we sent them out—and after all they are not supposed to be re-examined here — they would have killed hundreds of our own men, and destroyed every gun in which they were used." Ministry officials were doubting Canada's capacity to produce anything bigger than the small eighteen-pounders.[28]

Ogilvie had failed to measure up to his job as head of inspection. His organization was understaffed, poorly trained, and badly supervised. Russell's defective fuzes apparently got through inspection because of the failings of one Browne, a senior inspector, ex-inmate of an insane asylum, who had taken to drink. Himself overworked, Ogilvie had made disastrous snap decisions; an investigation finally revealed that the 4.5-inch shells' steel defects had been caused by his assigning from memory a testing tolerance exactly twice what it should have been. By the end of September the Ministry had decided to reorganize the Canadian inspection system. Lieutenant-Colonel W. E. Edwards was sent out to make the necessary recommendations.[29] About the same time, probably at Flavelle's request, another specialist came out to advise on methods of "diluting" labour in the factories through more reliance on unskilled men and women. He was to work with Mark Irish, the insurance broker and Ontario MPP, who had been active with Flavelle in hospital affairs and had helped in the early months with the IMB's insurance programme.

As early as June 1916, Brand had suggested that Flavelle come to England for discussions about the future of Canadian production. The Ministry had then expected to reduce Canadian orders because war requirements would diminish.[30] Now the financial problem made it imperative to reconsider the whole programme, still with a view to reducing Canadian orders. It would be particularly useful to have Flavelle in London while White was there. Finally, although it was not said openly, the British must have wanted some reassurance that Canadian manufacturers really could fulfil their commitments. So far they had not seen much evidence.

Late in September Flavelle spent a few days in Toronto. They were highlighted by Clara's wedding to Captain Frank McEachren, and then saddened by the need to console Sir John Willison over the loss of a son in France. Flavelle's own son, Ellsworth, was also in uniform, but had been incapacitated by pleurisy and was not permitted to continue serving. To implement doctor's orders that Ellsworth lead an outdoor life, Flavelle bought a two-hundred-acre farm for him outside Oakville, where he expected Ellsworth to become a professional farmer.[31]

After several days back in Ottawa settling the terms of White's loan—and learning that White could not get away to travel with him as they had planned—Flavelle sailed from New York on the *Nieuw Amsterdam* on October 5. As he prepared to leave he was still frustrated at Canadians' failure to commit themselves to total war: "We are so prosperous; there is so much money in circulation; labour is so actively employed, and the re-action from the earlier apprehensions of misfortune to business so great, we are in further danger of misunderstanding our obligation and duty. We are without leadership in the Press, or from men in the Government at Ottawa or any of the Provinces."[32]

V

In the old days he had been just another colonial come to London on business. He was there on business now, but had come a long way from the bacon trade. A dinner party on his first night in London included Margot and H. L. Tennant, Winston Churchill, and Edwin Montague, the Minister of Munitions. Flavelle felt totally out of his depth at this level of English society:

The conversation was brilliant. Small talk with remarkable repartee, but so foreign to all I know or all I meet in ordinary conditions that I am sure I sat with a vacuous smile which was inane to a degree. They all simply went on and except for my immediate table companions it was as though I were not there. After dinner with my whole person I found as much difficulty as a boy has with his red hands or the girl for the first time self conscious has with her appearance. I felt the vacuity of my countenance increasing.

He "escaped" from the evening at 11:30, whistled vainly for a cab, and finally got a lift back to Brand and Perry's quarters in a "swell car" driven by a chauffeur. "I was a fish out of water," he wrote home.[33]

In the business discussions at the Ministry he was on familiar ground and impressed the British with his grasp of the situation, his earnestness, and his confidence in Canadian production. The failure on the Somme had caused the Ministry to increase its estimated requirements much more than he had realized. Huge new orders for 1917 were going to be placed in North America for ammunition, steel, explosives, and aeroplanes. Canada could get a lot of this business if Flavelle could convince the Ministry that the IMB could do as good a job as the Americans. One factor in Canada's favour was unexpected: because of Flavelle's extra steel purchases in the summer, the IMB had secure supplies at a time of mounting American shortages. "I fancy they gave us credit for more forethought than we really possessed in having such a quantity," he wrote to Gordon. He also learned that the Americans had had quality and inspection problems that summer similar to his own.

He argued vigorously to Ministry officials that part of the inspection trouble was simply a product of distance—North Americans could not get on the phone to Woolwich to clear up disputes and technical problems the way British manufacturers could. When he was taken to the warehouses to see the rejected Canadian shells he was buoyed a bit to see just as many British and American rejects.[34]

As he received queries about Canada's ability to expand production into this or that new area, he cabled Gordon several times a day for information, and used this as the basis for his promises. He was a servant of the imperial government, but that did not stop him from being an enthusiastic salesman for Canadian industry, out to get all the business his country could handle.[35]

British purchasing would surely be tilted in Canada's favour if White pledged Canadian loans to pay for the orders. White was in London now, and through conversation and formal letters Flavelle tried to persuade him to make some commitment. Arguing that the shell business had already put the Canadian steel industry into a sound financial position and established many other companies on a profitable basis, Flavelle urged the Finance Minister to help Canada seize this "great opportunity" from the Americans. If the war dragged on, all Canada's resources would eventually go "into the pot." There was nothing to lose in going all out to secure useful business now. He was sure that the Canadian banks could do more, perhaps through borrowing in the United States. If this caused liquidity problems in Canada, the banks could be given advances from the Canadian government.

White was preparing to spend three times as much money in 1917 as Ottawa had spent in 1913. He believed that the kind of borrowing Flavelle wanted the banks to undertake would either impair their liquidity at the worst possible time ("I must also bear in mind the railway situation which is a great menace") or force the government to sanction very harmful inflation. A better way to raise money was to tap the real savings of the Canadian people by selling them bonds.

Unfortunately it is difficult to bring home to the Canadian people the importance of thrift [he wrote Flavelle], and I find a wide-spread desire on the part of the business community to make investments abroad or wherever else they may obtain a high rate of interest. If we could make available the national savings of the Canadian people, there would be little difficulty in providing for our war expenditures and for credits. . . . The proper way of meeting the situation is to make the industrial and business community and indeed all the citizens of Canada realize that our ability to finance depends upon national saving.

He continued to refuse to make commitments, promising only to extend aid from time to time as the banks' situation and his own permitted.

Despite White's apparent financial purity (his reliance on borrowing rather than taxation caused inflation anyway), Flavelle got his orders. When he sailed for home at the end of November he had authorization to supply almost a quarter-billion dollars' worth of shells, explosives, propellants, fuzes, and steel in the first half of 1917. It was still undecided how the orders would be paid for.[36]

VI

The discussions at the Ministry, plus a few days' work on his own affairs, took up almost six weeks. The round of social and semi-social engagements continued: a private dinner with Reginald McKenna, the Chancellor of the Exchequer; lunch with the Duke of Devonshire, who had just become Canada's new Governor General; dinner with Dr. Jameson of South African fame; weekends at All Souls and Balliol; a visit to the Wheeler-Bennetts at Ravensbourne; and a weekend at Cliveden as a guest of the Astors. The future Lady Astor astonished him — "not still a moment, superabundant energy . . . unlike anyone I have ever met, brilliant, vivacious, clever and human to a degree. She sets aside conventions and is almost daring in her frankness."[37]

One of the greatest honours in his life came when George v summoned him to Buckingham Palace. He was ushered in without formality and had twenty minutes alone with the King. "I was surprised and impressed by the King's somewhat intimate knowledge of Canadian affairs and of Canadian public men and public questions. When I rose to leave, he shook hands and bade me good-bye and safe voyage to Canada. The simple dignity, yet informality of the whole procedure, has left a grateful and lasting memory." He was still the poor Methodist boy from Peterborough writing a memorandum about his visit to the King for his children and grandchildren. Back at Holwood Clara read about her husband's honour in the Canadian papers. "It sort of made me feel queer all over."[38]

He stayed with Brand, Hichens, and Philip Kerr in their bachelors' quarters at 23 Cambridge Square. During the weeks he established what would be a lifelong friendship with the group of Round Tablers. Flavelle thought they represented "a new type of man; they practice good works in the most unassuming manner and are consumed with the desire to render public ser-

291

vice."[39] Hichens, who employed over fifty thousand men at the Cammel Laird shipbuilding works, particularly impressed him. He never forgot a discussion about the social role of businessmen in which Hichens talked of the businessman's first duty as being to the well-being of his employees, the second duty to the consumer, and the third to himself. This discussion helped Flavelle come to express his own view of profit as a by-product of service in business.

Until his visit he had not grasped the scope of the British war effort. The Ministry of Munitions was ten times the size of the IMB. Flavelle saw multi-million-dollar factories owned by the Ministry which were more efficient than he had believed possible in any factory anywhere. He saw the giant explosives establishment at Gretna, spreading over nine thousand acres and employing some twenty thousand workers. Fourteen months earlier the area had been nothing but a moor. The Ministry was probably the greatest business enterprise in history, he wrote Walker. The men working in it, he thought, were worthy of the best in any nation. He, Flavelle, had been taken into that group as an equal. On the whole they had praised the work of the IMB.[40]

Impressed as he was, Flavelle still kept his critical judgment of the British effort. He urged the Ministry to plan for the longer term and to overorder to protect against new shortages. He was still dubious about their reliance on Morgan's for the American business, believing the bankers would not give disinterested advice. He shared the growing British disgust with the uncertainty and aimlessness of the coalition government's war policy, remarking to Brand that the country had to get rid of Asquith or face disaster. And to Gordon he described how "the cumbrous equipment of the public service" retarded efficiency in the Ministry:

You have practically a lot of water-tight compartments . . . no system of inter-change which would lead to promptness and despatch. . . . The trouble is to get a co-ordinating mind or a co-ordinating body. . . . Always congestion at the top as well as delay all along the line. . . . The Treasury must be consulted. . . . The system inevitably hardens into inflexible routine and it is wholly inadequate for the emergency conditions of war, and yet as it is the only organization at hand . . . there is nothing for it but to follow in the procession, hoping that through alertness one may see a break in the ranks occasionally and succeed in getting through where others have failed.[41]

He probably thought his own organization was more efficient than its parent. But he had no illusions about the differences in the war efforts of the two countries. British manufacturers were now paying sixty to eighty per cent of their profits back in taxes. Government control of their operations was increasing daily; soon their balance of war to non-war production would be set by fiat. Meanwhile, Gordon reported that Canadian manufacturers were grumbling about war production interfering with their booming non-war business; some were even talking about cutting back on their munitions production. One cabled inquiry about late deliveries of a vital product brought back the contractor's explanation that he could not get enough electricity for his plant because of a power shortage caused by the Christmas rush in Toronto.[42]

Flavelle's trip climaxed in two visits to the fighting men. On the night of November 11 (during which most Canadians in London were getting drunk to celebrate Sam Hughes's resignation), Flavelle, White, Sir George Perley, and Waldorf Astor boarded a destroyer to visit the Grand Fleet at Scapa Flow. The visitors were given a privileged place on the bridge as the destroyer ploughed through heavy seas. It rendezvoused with the fleet at night under the light of a full moon. Flavelle was awed to see the endless rows of silent warships, the course of history resting on their strength. On the deck of Vice-Admiral Sturdee's flagship the next morning they joined in morning prayers. "What struck me was the absence of cast or place in the whole service. Men who but a few moments before had stood at attention in the presence of senior officers, joined with these same officers on equal terms in the presence of Him whom they worshipped." The experience seemed a dream to him. He wrote his daughter that night, "Can I have seen this fleet? Can I have met these men—. . . I do not think I can ever forget it."[43]

The next weekend he and Brand left for France to see the front, a privilege increasingly difficult to obtain. They spent November 17 and 18 in and around Albert on the Somme where the Canadian Corps had been in battle since early September. The Canadians had taken Courcelette on September 15. On November 11, some 17,000 casualties later, they had taken the Regina Trench, a mile beyond Courcelette. Flavelle and Brand arrived at the front during the artillery barrage of the seventeenth, building up to an attack on the eighteenth. From an artillery observation post they watched the big shells dropping on the German lines. They watched German planes driven off by anti-aircraft fire over the British lines. And they visited a forward dressing station where a party of 250 wounded men brought back from Beaumont Hamel were being treated (some of these, it appears, must have been from Bartholomew Bandy's company[44]).

Ordinary experiences for visitors to the front, except that this was the end of one of the greatest battles—greatest slaughters—in history. On the first day of the battle, July 1, the British forces had suffered 60,000 casualties. Now, in November, the Somme battlefield was a sea of frozen mud and corpses, its villages blown literally to pieces, its roads tracks between shell holes, and its air rotten with death. Flavelle saw men returning from the trenches plastered with mud from the tops of their helmets to their heels, many of them dozing as they marched. He saw the horses and ammunition carts caked with slime. He saw the fresh platoons marching crisply to the front. He thought of the conditions under which the men served—wet, cold, sleepless, under fire—"and as I looked at them, tens of thousands of them, guns booming on every side and shells whistling over my head as they went on their dread message to the other side, this one thing came back to me again and again and again: My God! What have these men done? What have these men done that they must be punished in this way?"[45]

The last Allied attack on the Somme took place the second day they were there. The Canadian Fourth Division took Desire Trench. The Canadians had suffered 25,000 casualties in seven weeks on the Somme. Since July 1 more than a million men had been killed or wounded in the battle. Flavelle had seen the uses of his shells.

On his last day in England Flavelle visited a former employee, a lad who had attended the Sherbourne Street Sunday School, and who Flavelle had last seen when he came into the Davies office to shake hands and say good-bye. He was now lying in hospital, one leg amputated at the thigh, the other at the ankle. "What do you think the lad said? 'It makes me proud to have you come and see me, sir.' . . . And what else do you think he told me? Of the nurses and doctors and of kind friends, and of the fight—'It was a great fight, sir.' "[46]

VII

The American liner *Finland* took eleven days to cross the Atlantic. It moved slowly, fully lit at night, spotlights playing on the American flag to show its nationality to submarines. Flavelle's travelling companions included White, Lord Shaughnessy of the CPR, W. M. Acworth, who was on his way to Canada to serve on the Royal Commission looking into the railway mess, and J. P. Morgan. There are no records of the businessmen's discussions every evening in the smoking room, only of Flavelle's promise to tell Rundle about them in person. For the first three or four days White chattered incessantly to him during the daytime, changing his views on the financial situation every few hours to the point where Flavelle feared he would have to tell him to stop. Perhaps in defence, he got to know Lord Shaughnessy well for the first time.[47]

They landed in New York on December 6. Flavelle gave a brief interview to reporters, saying his trip had taught him that "war is the first and last thing." He went straight to Ottawa for a weekend's work, then shared a private car with Kemp and White on the Canadian Northern's 11:00 p.m. Sunday-night train to Toronto. On the way White again worried about the need to make his position on IMB finance clear to the British.[48]

On Tuesday the twelfth Flavelle, Fitzgerald, and Gordon held a private meeting with some two hundred manufacturers in Toronto. It started with a number of them complaining about thin profit margins on their contracts. Flavelle listened, and thought of the men in the trenches he had seen, of the mud, the rats, the cold, the wet, the wounds, the suffering and death. He thought of the comfort and security and home life of the men he was listening to, and of the failure of many of them to make their promised deliveries.[49]

When it was his turn to speak he described what he had seen in France. He talked, too, about the defective Canadian shells he had seen in England and what happened when a shell exploded prematurely. "If any of you here are responsible for such a shell I could almost wish that it would explode right here in our midst instead of in the ranks of our own gunners." As always, he spoke in his quiet monotone; but, according to a *Star* reporter who had found his way in, his speech carried "terrible conviction in its every word." Occasionally he stopped to rub his eyes. The audience was silent. Reminding the manufacturers of their late deliveries, he asked them why they were not back at their plants urging and planning for more production. Instead here they were coming to the IMB to ask for more profits. "Profits!" he exclaimed, his voice not rising, "I have come straight from the seat of a nation where they are sweating blood to win this war, and I stand before you stripped of many ideas. Profits! Send profits to the hell where they belong."[50]

VIII

On December 10 Lloyd George had replaced Asquith as British Prime Minister, his popular support resting on hope that he would end the drift and confusion of the Asquith regime and win the war. Fresh from Britain and the battlefields, Flavelle understood the need for the new Prime Minister. Yet if Britain needed new leadership, how much greater was the need in Canada where it still seemed to be business as usual, profits as usual, political games as usual, and fewer recruits every month, particularly among the French Canadians? A number of Flavelle's friends and acquaintances now favoured some kind of win-the-war coalition government for Canada to end the political squabbling and get on with the job, perhaps by bringing a number of dynamic businessmen into the cabinet to give the country efficient administration.

Joseph Atkinson's Toronto *Star* was in favour of a National Government for Canada. Professors George Wrong and C. B. Sissons of the University of Toronto were advocating it. Liberal businessmen like A. E. Ames and Will Rundle were also supporting the movement. They knew Flavelle was sympathetic. When he was in Toronto on December 12, Arthur Hawkes, a *Star* reporter, met with him to ask his support. The next day Hawkes met with Colonel Reuben Wells Leonard, another National Government enthusiast, Wrong, and A. E. Ames. When Wrong suggested Flavelle as the logical man to lead an open movement for National Government, Hawkes decided to try to get Flavelle to speak to a small dinner party of "knowing dependable men" the next weekend in Toronto.[51]

Flavelle was to speak at Canadian Club luncheons in Ottawa on Saturday the sixteenth and in Toronto on Monday the eighteenth. Whether or not as a result of his conversation with Hawkes, he decided, on the thirteenth, to appeal for a coalition government in his Ottawa speech. Thinking it proper to warn the Prime Minister, who was in British Columbia, he wired that afternoon:

I return from England deeply impressed with the absence of party spirit in the conduct of public business in Great Britain. This results not only from the gravity of the issues which have caused men to rise above party, but because the government is made up of men from both parties. . . .

The grave character of present conditions, the serious nature of the French Canadian attitude, and the magnitude of our obligations have caused me to believe that a Coalition Government should be formed now. . . .

I am of the opinion that if a general election on party lines is held shortly it will mean setting the heather on fire, English versus French, with long years of bitterness to follow.

I am of the opinion if the Liberal Party is returned to power, with or without

Laurier for leader, they will owe their election to the French Canadian who refused to fight, and to German and Austrian voters who will undoubtedly vote against the Government.

I am of the opinion that when a Government thus elected undertook to determine in conference the future relations of the country to the Empire we should have cruel strife.

. . . I desire to express my belief. I do not wish to commit you to any position by this wire, but in view of your consistent support and consideration in the discharge of my duties as Chairman of the Imperial Munitions Board, I feel I owe it to you to send you this message.

He also showed the telegram to White. Appalled, the Finance Minister pleaded with him not to speak out. Later that day White met with Borden's secretary, A. E. Blount, and dictated a telegram for Borden describing his interview with Flavelle. White told Blount that a coalition would mean the ruin of the Conservative party. White got his own position on the record because he knew that some of the coalition talk envisaged his replacing Borden.

Borden wired Flavelle the next day urging delay. "I am confident that you are not fully seized of the situation as it presents itself to me. There could be no object in your making such a statement except for the purpose of influencing public opinion and your official position would lend an unusual importance and significance to your views." He noted in his diary a suggestion that Flavelle be appointed Director General of National Conscience.[52]

For the next few days Flavelle agonized over his speech, worrying about how far he could go in view of his official position as a representative of the imperial government. He wrote Hawkes and Wrong, making clear that because of his job he could not lead the movement they were hoping to organize. On the other hand, his impatience was anything but cooled when White again warned him that Canada would make no commitments to pay for British-ordered munitions. And some time in that week Colonel J. J. Carrick, MP, one of the manufacturers at his speech in Toronto, told him that it had been "a very nice Sunday School talk." Flavelle had known Carrick for years as a real-estate promoter, and during the war as an unreliable munitions-maker. He considered Carrick to be a liar, immoral in both business and politics. When Carrick made the comment Flavelle had to stop himself from punching him.[53]

His Ottawa speech on the sixteenth began as a routine description of the

IMB's work. Press reports of what was called his "To hell with profits" speech had implied that Canadian manufacturers had failed and were a horde of profiteers. Flavelle tried to explain that he had not accused them of failure generally; rather, he had called for impeccably high standards of production. It was not enough to produce only 999 good shells out of 1000. Every shell had to be perfect and on time. Any failure by worker or manufacturer, he said, "is a crime against the state." It was easy to become angry with manufacturers for profiteering or politicians for dithering:

But why at this time? This much must be said for the manufacturer: he at least is devoting his energy and his time to the production of something that is absolutely necessary for the state. Why have anger towards the manufacturer when you have none towards yourselves? What has been our position in Canada? Am I saying too much if I indicate that, on the whole, we have looked upon the war as an extra? Am I stating it too strongly if I say we are almost drunk with the prosperity which comes to us through the expenditure of immense sums of borrowed money? . . . Is there evidence in this country of national sorrow and concern? God knows, some of you have paid, and some of your sons have paid the final penalty, and they are lying over in France or in Flanders. But, speaking broadly, as a people, is there sorrow? Is there any deep arousal of moral earnestness? Is it not "Business as usual," and profits larger than usual?

He talked about the front, how as he had watched the soldiers he wondered how people back in Canada could ever be worthy of them. "I ask you, gentlemen, I ask you in this Capital city, you who are judges of the Supreme Court, you who are Cabinet Ministers, you who hold responsible positions, you business men and others, I ask you, do you mean to play a worthy part —to be worthy of these men?"

Toward the end of the speech he turned to party politics in Ottawa.

I could not conceive of any condition where party politics were more bitter or insistent . . . as if it were a horse race that was on in place of a great war in which the very life of the nation is in peril.

We have to live together in this country. We have one-third of our community who are French Canadian people. We of British birth and British aspiration and British temper cannot sink them in the St. Lawrence and have them disappear. Nor can they —notwithstanding their viewpoint—nor can they live in a country other than with us. And God forgive us for either party strife or sectionalism or any other fault whereby we fail to help one another, to understand our mutual point of view and work one with the other for the common good of the state. . . . If a general election is held shortly, a racial cry will be inevitable and English will be pitted against French and French against English, and there will follow years of bitterness. Moreover, remember when the struggle of the war is over, the group of men who will sit around the table in council with the representatives from other Dominions to determine what will be the future of this Empire will have to be a group of men chosen from this Dominion not by party guidance or by party methods, for it is inconceivable to me that a Government sustained by a vote of a section of this Dominion which, no matter for what reason or conscience, were unwilling to do their share in this struggle would be permitted without civil strife to determine what part Canada should take in the Imperial Council which must follow the war.

I bring to you, to whatever extent you will permit it, as serious a note as I am capable of indicating, that this great struggle, all the things that are involved in it, all the sacrifices that are being made by your sons and your brothers and your fathers, all that this Empire stands for, all that these people at home are suffering, call upon us to burn up the dross and to pray God that we may be wise and patriotic and truthful and heart-searching in our relations to ourselves, and that we seek above all to be right.

Flavelle thought he had held back, but he had not. The audience, astounded by the earnest passion of his speech, understood him perfectly.[54]

He was scheduled for a repeat performance in Toronto on Monday noon. White was also to speak in Toronto in the evening. That Monday morning the *Globe* carried a lead article claiming Flavelle's speech was part of a conspiracy to replace Borden with White. The reporter knew of the Flavelle–Borden telegrams and claimed White had encouraged Flavelle to call for a coalition anyway. Except for the facts about the telegrams, the article was wholly incorrect. It seemed to have been planted by someone in the Conservative party hoping to blunt the effect of Flavelle's Toronto speech, perhaps also worried that White's speech might hint at a coalition. To some in Ottawa there did seem to be circumstantial evidence that the two businessmen were working to create a "National Trust" government.[55] There was no truth in the supposition.

Flavelle began his Toronto speech with an unqualified denial of any intrigue to advance White or interfere with the affairs of the government of Canada. Any telegrams he might have sent were his own business. But he repeated his comments on the political situation, warning of the possibility of racial and civil strife, and urging his audience to consider how to avoid it. He described the Board's work and again explained that he had been urging manufacturers towards perfection. Yes, they made profits, but at least they were supplying necessary war materials. "During this time when you have been somewhat censorious or cross against the profiteer or angry with the Government, what have you done? How far have you served the state . . . ?"

He told them what he had seen in Britain, how much of their cherished freedom the English were giving up, and of the cable he had received about power shortages and Christmas business.

My God, Christmas trading! What difference does it make whether my friend Ryrie sells a dollar's worth of jewelry or not during this time? What difference does it make whether my friend Fox closes up the William Davies Stores so as to sell goods only in daylight? What odds is it if my friend Fudger finds his profit and loss sheet affected because there is not light enough to spare to light people who come to trade?

Why do we do this? We are not mean. We are anxious to respond to any call made upon us, but why expect that the call will only come from some Government circle? Why do you not call yourself? Is this Canadian Club to be a place where men will come to have their fancy tickled by an address every few weeks and fail to assume responsiblity for activity which will cost something? . . . Things are too comfortable with us. We rather pride ourselves in saying it is business as usual. We are gratified in finding our balance sheets, and our profit and loss sheets, the best in our record, and we have the spirit, although we are not quite so honest in stating it as the good woman I heard of in Earlscourt yesterday who said, "This war do bring a lot of good cheer."

He tried to tell the comfortable Toronto businessmen what he had seen on the Somme, what it was like for their own boys in the trenches—"there is no Christmas trading there, gentlemen!"—what it was like to meet that young lad in England and to wonder whether he was fit to be in the same room with a man like that, what he had felt when he was complimented on his "Sunday School" talk. He tried to stop, but the audience urged him to go on as long as he wanted. He concluded that the problem was like the biblical devil, who could only be cast forth by prayer and fasting. Also, that if Canadians failed to develop character from the war they would miss the only asset war could bring.[56]

These were the best speeches Flavelle ever gave. His trip to England and the front had been one of the most moving experiences of his life. He had come home with his feelings about the need for service and sacrifice, the beat of his moral pulse, feverishly heightened. He desperately wanted to preach a revival, to convert his audiences to total dedication to the war.*[57] He wanted to tap in their souls all the power and fervour and spiritual force that Methodism drew on and brought out in himself. It was not coincidental that many of the other prominent Canadians urging coalition and an all-out war effort in 1916 were also Methodists.

Although nothing came of it that winter, Flavelle's speeches probably strengthened the agitation for a coalition government. His own name was mentioned fairly often as a possible minister in a coalition government.[58] White, in his Toronto speech, had summarily dismissed the *Globe*'s story as "odious beyond contempt," and had gone on to deliver a bland plea for more wartime saving. There was no doubt of White's loyalty to Borden. And far from hoping his friend would lead a coalition, Flavelle thought he was failing to offer sensible financial leadership.

Flavelle might have been able to bring down the Borden government. He was at the peak of his prestige as a businessman and public servant. He had first-hand knowledge of the situation in England and France. He also had first-hand knowledge of what had gone on in the shell business and never been revealed, notably the Phillips affair. Some of his friends still hoped he would lead the movement for a National Government. Had he agreed, or had he made more speeches like those in Ottawa and Toronto, he might have created enough public concern to force a change in leadership at the top, perhaps a coalition, perhaps with himself in the cabinet. "Toronto is seething with discontent with the government and so is the whole country," George Wrong wrote him toward the end of the month. "I should like to see a government with not a politician in it! I hope and pray that you may see your

---

*It is notable, however, that he said nothing about conscription in these speeches or at any other time. His special role in the war economy seems to have led him to be hesitant about military conscription because of the need for labour at home. Instead, he seems to have favoured a more drastic total conscription for war service at home and abroad, including conscription of wealth. His concern about French Canadians and loyalty stemmed as much from the prewar naval debates as it did from wartime recruiting.

way to giving us a hand. My heart is heavy hardly less for my country than for myself." Wrong had learned that his son, Harold, a former Flavelle scholar, who had been missing in action since July 1, was dead.

Flavelle would go no further. He wished he could supply real leadership to the National Government movement, but he had to carry out his duty to the imperial government. He had been told at the beginning to maintain good relations with the Canadian government. In his speeches he had interfered in Canadian domestic politics and seriously annoyed both Borden and White. He had either to stop or resign from the IMB. As for the future, and the prospect of cabinet service, "I do not deceive myself; we must not confuse the aroused feeling which I possess at the moment because of what I experienced in England to throw us out of the perspective as to the service I may be able to perform. The limits of my capacity are fairly clearly defined, and I must have the good sense to work within these limits."[59]

CHAPTER THIRTEEN

PLOUGHSHARES INTO SHELLS

When Flavelle left for England in the fall of 1916 his factories were supplying about 400,000 shells a week, ranging from the staple eighteen-pounder shrapnel through the huge 9.2-inch calibre, three-hundred-pound howitzer ammunition. The orders for 1917 called for a seventy-five-per-cent increase to about 700,000 shells a week, most to be loaded, fuzed, and shipped as complete rounds. There was to be a vast expansion of Canadian production of explosives and propellants; including cordite, nitro-cellulose powder, and TNT. The Chairman of the IMB was authorized to push some of Canada's pioneer aviators aside and get on with the business of mass-producing aeroplanes and pilots. Flavelle was also expected to continue applying his friendly pressure on Sir Thomas White to get Canada to pay for most of these British orders, because it was obvious to almost everyone on the inside that Britain could not.

I

The IMB was reasonably well structured to handle the new orders. Like the companies Flavelle had been running for years, it was a decentralized, departmentalized operation, whose executives worked with a high degree of autonomy subject to the Chairman's final authority. "The Chairman told us it was up to us to get Shells and he did not care how we got them," one of his department heads remembered.[1] Flavelle remarked often that he paid no attention to the details of the IMB's structure, only being concerned with his men getting the job done.

As head of the Purchasing Department, Edward Fitzgerald, "Fitz," had the most demanding administrative job. He was responsible for buying all of the Board's materials and negotiating all the contracts with manufacturers. The old days of verbal contracts at sweetheart prices had long passed. Whenever possible—as soon as manufacturers had enough experience with a job that it could be costed—the Board let contracts by tender, and then only after investigating to ensure contractors could live up to their promises.[2] The standard contract, devised by Zebulon Lash, set strict delivery schedules and protected the Board's interest in the event of termination. IMB staff had compiled detailed information on the costs of all manufacturing operations, along with comparative British and American prices. For normal work, governments no longer absent-mindedly tossed windfall profits to manufacturers. In late 1916, for example, manufacturers of 4.5-inch shell forgings were allowed about twenty-per-cent profit on each forging, machiners about twenty per cent for both profits and general plant maintenance. After 1916 there were almost no complaints about profiteering on shell contracts. By the summer of 1917 there was considerable grumbling by manufacturers that profits were too low.[3]

Fitzgerald was a superbly efficient, even-tempered administrator, with none of the abrasiveness Flavelle could sometimes transmit when he was excessively angry or excessively righteous (or both). A bit more the man of the world than Flavelle, at least in preferring bars in Hull after work to cider at the Rideau Club, Fitzgerald nonetheless came fully under the Chairman's influence. "It is given to few men the faculty of securing the real affection we all have for your husband," he wrote Clara while Joe was in London. "As for myself there is a deeper feeling. His counsel and guidance and unwavering confidence. His fearlessness to do that which he considers right. His open heart and kindliness have made me love him as a son loves his father."[4]

The Distribution and Transportation departments coordinated the flow of supplies from plant to plant up and down and across the continent. At any one time some $50 to $100 million worth of goods were in the hands of manufacturers or in transit between factories. Day-to-day relations with the manufacturers were looked after by the Production Department, whose experts toured the plants advising on machinery, methods, factory organization, and possible new contractors.

The departmental lines of authority, their executives, and even the names of the departments fluctuated as Flavelle moved to cut one log jam after another. Charles Gordon was his normal second-in-command and all-purpose trouble-shooter. When production was lagging in the spring of 1916,

Flavelle began to bring in other businessmen to take charge of special problems. James Wood, a Simpson's executive, and Frank Baillie, the cartridge-case manufacturer who had given back half his profits, reorganized shrapnel. Fred Southam of the publishing family handled sixty-pounders and 4.5-inch shells. W. A. Peterson of the CPR's Mechanical Department took the large shells in hand; and Tom Russell, by the autumn of 1916 a successful fuze manufacturer, organized other fuze factories to increase their output. Using time-and-motion studies, comparative production ratings, and roving trouble-shooters, the IMB's production staff standardized shell-making at levels of efficiency far beyond anything that individual manufacturers working in isolation and secretive competition could have hoped to attain.[5]

The first effect of Lieutenant-Colonel W. E. Edwards' arrival from England in October 1916 to take over the disorganized inspection operation was further confusion. Worried inspectors overreacted by raising their standards impossibly high, forcing scores of manufacturers to bring work to a standstill until the inspectors got their standards and methods straightened out. Manufacturers' bitterness about inspection was a major factor underlying the unrest Flavelle attacked in his "To hell with profits" speech in December.[6] It was well into the new year before inspection, now formally incorporated as a department of the Board, began to run smoothly. Even then there was often friction between Edwards and Flavelle as the Britisher determined to guard the autonomy of his department (its orders and specifications always came directly from England) and preserve proper hierarchical channels of communication and coordination with the rest of the IMB. "Form counts a great deal with him," Flavelle wrote of Edwards, "and from time to time I have to see him to make amends for some slip which I have made. . . . I really do not care whether I sign a letter as Chairman or whether I sweep the office if I can only get the work done, and I have therefore sometimes rather scandalized the Colonel by my failure to recognize the importance of his position." The good effect of Edwards' work was the rapid decline of complaints about defective Canadian shells getting across to England. By early 1917 Canadian shrapnel was going directly to the front and by the end of the year the British had stopped reinspecting any Canadian products.[7]

While Flavelle had been in England, Mark Irish had been pouring his considerable nervous energy into organizing a Labour Department of the IMB to encourage manufacturers to accept "dilution" of their workforces with unskilled men and women. Irish concentrated on recruiting women, but soon realized that his department's propaganda—newspaper ads ("Are You Doing a Man's Work?"), illustrated booklets, a motion picture, and a model factory at St. Catharines, Ontario, staffed entirely by women—had to be aimed at the manufacturers too. "We met opposition from every shop superintendent," Flavelle wrote in 1917. "He was having plenty of worry as it was and did not relish the idea of adding to his discomfort by introducing women into metal work where they had never been in Canada before. The manufacturer hesitated at the outlay necessary to accommodate women operators, and generally what has been accomplished was achieved with considerable difficulty."[8]

Most levels of government cooperated with the Labour Department: the provinces, except Quebec, obligingly bent their Factory Acts to permit the use of women on night shifts; the federal government agreed to suppress reports of assaults on women going to and from night work. But there was a major stumbling block in the person of R. B. Bennett, MP, who, as Director of National Service, might have been expected to have encouraged the use of women workers in industry. "He is extremely emphatic that the employment of women will create a female industrial army doing the work of men at a lower wage," Irish reported of Bennett, "which, when the Overseas Forces return, will be opposed by a male army of unemployed. He conceives that the women, once engaged in factory work will never give it up." Bennett's disinclination to set the stage for sexual industrial warfare meant there was little coordination between the IMB and the National Service Commission.[9]

Irish, who put a bubbling, extroverted mask on a deeply insecure personality—and who also saw Flavelle as a father figure to whom he felt profoundly obliged ("I believe I should pick pockets if you asked me to do so")—was also more than a little unsettled by the requirements of his job. His daughter, who drove him from meeting to meeting, remembered that Canada's chief recruiter of women workers in the Great War was terrified at having to speak before female audiences. After three months of sixteen-hour days on the job, Irish was at the point of a nervous breakdown. He refused to take a rest for fear of being considered a "quitter" and "disloyal" to Flavelle. At Mrs. Irish's request, Flavelle finally ordered him to take a rest.[10]

The IMB's money flowed out under the supervision of George Edwards, the dean of Toronto's chartered accountants, who came to help in the early days and then volunteered for the duration. The Shell Committee's account-

Holwood; the main entrance to the public house of a man in public life.

The Governor General and his wife, Lord and Lady Minto, leaving Holwood for the races, 1902. They had borrowed the house while Flavelle was abroad.
Art Gallery of Ontario

Holwood, south side: an English country house set in a Toronto park.

Front hall, Holwood.

Dining room, Holwood.

The Royal Commission on the University of Toronto, 1905-6. *L. to R.*: the Rev. D.
Bruce Macdonald, the Rev. H. J. Cody, Sir William Meredith, Flavelle (Chairman),
Dr. A. H. Colquhoun, Goldwin Smith, B. E. Walker. *Archives of Ontario*

Packing and lacquering shells, Canadian Fairbanks–Morse, Toronto. The Imperial Munitions Board spent over a billion dollars on war orders. *Public Archives of Canada*

Working on fuze parts, Russell Motor Car Company, Toronto. Women did almost all the men's jobs, but most went back to housekeeping or cleaning after the war. *Public Archives of Canada*

Shell shop, Medicine Hat Pump and Brass Manufacturing Company, Medicine Hat.
Public Archives of Canada

Assembling JN-4 aircraft, Canadian Aeroplanes Limited, Toronto. Canada's first and finest aeroplane factory.
Public Archives of Canada

ing methods had been defective in not recording where supplies were at any given time, making it impossible to compile inventories from the accounts. Edwards created a totally new accounting system designed to stress the responsibility of each contractor for the materials in his possession. The IMB always knew who owed it what and how much. Edwards also fashioned a daily system of auditing the books, so that within twenty-four hours of the end of a day's business the Board had a fully audited picture of its finances. These procedures almost entirely stopped wastage of material by contractors; they so impressed the British that Edwards was asked to help set up their accounting system in New York after the United States entered the war.[11] Sharing a passion for up-to-the-minute accounting stressing individual responsibility, Flavelle and George Edwards held each other in considerable mutual respect.

The Chairman himself was accountable to the Ministry of Munitions. Flavelle and Bob Brand, the IMB's agent in London, were in constant cable communication as Brand coordinated the IMB's reports and requests to the various departments of the Ministry. The IMB was not independent — its programme was subject to Ministry approval of both quantities and costs, sometimes broken down into quite small parcels. The IMB had considerable leeway in placing orders and setting prices, much more than Morgan's in the United States, but always within limits. Flavelle occasionally acted on his own responsibility, clearing with London afterwards, but he never forgot or could forget that he was a trustee for the imperial government.

He had no formal connection with the Government of Canada. The IMB was a *British* organization, staffed by Canadians, operating in Canada as independently of the Canadian government as good sense and growing financial dependence permitted. In December Flavelle had come close to forgetting the need to stay on good terms with Borden and White. He did not forget again. Canadian politicians continued to pester the Board over minor patronage matters; Flavelle continued to send them away disappointed as graciously as he could, often reflecting to friends that the Board was "skating on thin ice" in its relations with the government.[12]

II

There were a number of jobs private industry could not carry out for the IMB. In early 1916 the Board had established a Canadian "National Factory,"

British Munitions Limited, at Verdun, Quebec, to handle the tricky business of loading fuzes. It was inspired by Lloyd George's National Factories in England, one of his typically unconventional responses to the shell shortages of 1915. In general, the British war effort was characterized by earlier and more vigorous use of government power to regulate or replace the free operation of markets than Canadians dared to undertake. In IMB operations through most of 1916 Flavelle did not seem particularly interested in emulating the more direct British methods. His only other National Factory—the British had scores of them — was created in mid-year when Albert Gooderham volunteered to turn his Toronto distillery over to the IMB to manufacture acetone (essential in the production of cordite) from grain by a special process developed in England. As British Acetones Toronto Limited, managed by Gooderham for a token rental, the liquor factory became the Empire's principal supplier of acetone. Teetotallers like Flavelle might have reflected that the distillery was now producing lethal chemicals in a good cause.

The vastly expanded requirements for 1917, the increased sense of urgency about war production, and what he had seen in England dissolved Flavelle's hesitations about founding more National Factories. Within a month of his return in December 1916, five more IMB-owned enterprises had been launched and more were being considered.

The British needed more explosives and propellants. Several private companies were already producing cordite, TNT, and nitro-cellulose powder for the Board, but were having trouble fulfilling old contracts, let alone taking on new ones. M. J. O'Brien of Renfrew, Ontario, the mine owner, railway contractor, and hockey grandee, was particularly inept at meeting his obligations, proving himself, according to Gordon, "an impossible man to deal with."[13] To get him out of the way and get his nitro-cellulose plant working effectively, the Board leased it, putting their own men in to run it as a National Factory, British Explosives Limited. The other private nitro-cellulose plant, Aetna Explosives of Drummondville, Quebec, was losing money for its American owners. They wanted the Board to take it over on a lease or cost-plus deal. Flavelle considered the factory an expensive, poorly designed white elephant. The Board allowed Aetna to slide into receivership and eventually be closed down when the demand for nitro-cellulose eased.[14]

While Flavelle was in London arranging the new business, Gordon was approached by another American firm, the Davis Durkin Corporation, with an offer to construct and operate a major explosives complex for the IMB. He cabled details to Flavelle, who found the British explosives experts "frightened to death" of Davis Durkin because of previous experience in the States. But they were also attracted by the terms of the Americans' proposal. On Flavelle's assurance that Gordon's business judgment was impeccable, the Ministry authorized the IMB to contract with Davis Durkin for the immediate construction of an extensive plant at Trenton, Ontario. Davis Durkin would then manage it for the Board as the British Chemical Company.[15] Another agreement was made with Canadian Explosives Limited to construct and manage a parallel complex at Nobel, Ontario, to be known as British Cordite Limited. Outdoor construction was not normally undertaken in the Canadian winter; workers at the Trenton and Nobel sites suffered cruelly from inadequate housing and frostbite as they raced to get the plants up and in production by the next summer.

Flavelle never believed he had the full cooperation of the steel companies, with the outstanding exception of Algoma Steel. The other companies — controlled, he felt, by "a body of Buccaneers . . . treating these businesses as stock exploiting schemes, rather than sound commercial enterprises" — were continually late in deliveries, often reluctant to divert material from their non-war business, and hesitant to reinvest their considerable profits in increased capacity. The Board needed every pound of steel it could get, and yet forty-five per cent of the steel used in making shell forgings was discarded as turnings. Unable to convince the private companies to install electric furnaces to melt scrap turnings, Flavelle decided to have the IMB go into the steel business. In late January, 1917, British Forgings Limited broke ground on a site at Ashbridge's Bay, Toronto. By summer its furnaces were in production.[16]

These six National Factories had developed logically from the pressure of munitions requirements and the limitations of private enterprise. The seventh National Factory, Canadian Aeroplanes Limited, grew out of a strange combination of the IMB's interest in establishing a new industry in Canada and the Canadian government's disinterest in having its own air force, especially one run by Sam Hughes and his cronies.

From the beginning of the war, various aviation enthusiasts, some of them personally interested in manufacturing aeroplanes, had been urging the creation of a flying school in Canada to train Canadian pilots in Canadian-made planes. Neither the British nor the Canadian governments was particularly interested at first. Brought in as intermediaries in the discussions, Perry and Brand of the IMB did become enthusiastic at the thought of creating a new Canadian industry; through the spring and summer of 1916 they promoted the idea of an IMB-managed aircraft factory and IMB involvement in a training scheme. Complicated dickering over which government would pay for what ended that autumn in the context of waning British air strength at the front. There was an urgent need to expand the Royal Flying Corps. By December the British had agreed to finance and operate a training school in Canada, the Canadians to underwrite the costs of an IMB aeroplane factory.[17]

Having no war orders, the Americans were not yet mass-producing what in peacetime were still expensive toys. There was some reason for Flavelle's belief that the new programme would "easily make Canada the centre of the airplane industry on the continent." His factory would produce fifteen flying-machines a week. Perhaps their engines could also be made in Canada. An Aviation Department of the Board had been formed in November under E. R. Wood and Frank Baillie. Before the programme had been finally approved it had bought Canada's one aeroplane factory, the tiny Curtiss Aeroplanes Limited branch plant in Toronto.[18] The Curtiss company had been turning out a handful of planes to service a private training school operated by Curtiss's friend and manager, J. A. D. McCurdy. McCurdy, the British Empire's premier aviator in the *Silver Dart*, had been energetically lobbying for a Canadian production-and-training programme, but was partly compromised by his personal interest in getting contracts for the Curtiss factory and school. When the IMB bought Curtiss Aeroplanes, its promoters—McCurdy, Sir Henry Pellatt, and others—received by Flavelle's reckoning a profit of $80,000 to $100,000 on a cash investment of $10,000.

There was a sharp disagreement over the price to be paid for the six planes and the spare parts the company had on hand. McCurdy was further upset to find there was no place for him in the IMB's Aviation Department. When McCurdy complained to Borden, Flavelle explained that the asking price for the equipment had been grossly unreasonable, and dismissed the pilot as "a disappointed promoter . . . under the impression he would succeed in working out a situation greatly to his own profit. He is now seeking to command sympathy by making representations that he was badly used. He would be more worthy of respect if he offered to go to France and get into the fighting line."[19] McCurdy did not serve in France.

Established American engine-makers refused to either manufacture in Canada or go into partnership with Canadian Aeroplanes Limited, the IMB's aeroplane factory. So the Hispano-Suiza engines for CAL's JN-4 trainers had to be supplied from the United States. John Willys of the Willys – Overland Motor Car Company, however, which had recently established a Toronto plant in a joint venture with T. A. Russell and his associates, offered to go into the aircraft-engine business in Canada. Negotiations with Willys led to a contract to build Sunbeam "Arab" engines in the Toronto plant. It would take time to retool: Willys thought he could manufacture by late summer, 1917; Flavelle suspected it would be 1918 at the earliest. In the meantime Frank Baillie, as Managing Director of CAL, had contractors working round the clock putting up a million-dollar, six-acre aircraft factory in Toronto. He had machinery running while construction was still going on, and produced his first nine JN-4's in April. By July CAL was turning out more than twenty-five planes a week, by November more than fifty.[20]

IMB contractors were also at work twenty-four hours a day creating the bases where Royal Flying Corps officers sent from England would train Canadian boys for the air war in France. In less than seven weeks in the dead of winter some two thousand workers turned seven hundred acres of stump-ridden wasteland at Camp Borden into a fully equipped training camp, complete with barracks, hangars, paved landing strips, running water and sewage, electricity, and telephones. Recruiting for the RFC, Canada, was already under way at the Long Branch camp outside Toronto (one of the first rejects is said to have been a white beagle already outfitted with helmet and goggles); men were at work on other sites at Leaside, Armour Heights, Mohawk, and Rathbun, Ontario. E. R. Wood's health had given way in January — he and Irish were the first of several of Flavelle's friends to break down in 1917 — and he was replaced as Director of the Aviation Department by George Morrow, another Peterboroughnian who had worked up through the old Cox family of companies. The combination of Morrow, the commonsense administrator, and Baillie, the dynamic entrepreneur, was impressive — "The driving force which they have put into this matter exceeds anything I have ever met," Flavelle wrote Brand in March.[21]

The National Factories were regularly incorporated companies, each with a Board of Directors appointed by its sole shareholder, the IMB. The managers were given almost as much autonomy as private companies had and were expected to price their products to amortize their investment. Flavelle did not want this first experiment in government-owned manufacturing in Canada — British government-owned — to waste public funds. Referring to his National Factories generally, Flavelle wrote that the Board had avoided private ownership because "we felt it was a situation in which, time being of the essence, we wanted no restriction in the interest of private advantage to stop pushing the work to a definite completion."[22]

There could have been more expansion of IMB operations that winter. In December the British asked about Canada's ability to contribute merchant shipping for the Atlantic lifeline. Flavelle commissioned a report from J. W. Norcross, General Manager of Canada Steamship Lines, which recommended a takeover of all ships being built in Canada and organization of all the shipyards to produce new tonnage. Flavelle was prepared to act, apparently intending to standardize Canadian shipbuilding under direct IMB control. As with the aviation programme, he looked forward to postwar dividends if the industry could be developed to support a Canadian merchant-marine fleet. But the British decided to delay action while they sent out a shipping expert to organize the purchase of new tonnage in North America.[23]

Flavelle soon realized that his shell contractors could not expand production as readily as they and the IMB had assumed. Machinery was beginning to wear out and could not easily be replaced; manufacturers proved unable to reach the rated capacity of their factories. "We suffer under the penalty of a great number of small plants administered by men of small calibre," Flavelle wrote Borden in January. The Board, he felt, should have set up National Factories to machine and forge shells. Had he known the limits of private enterprise in advance, Flavelle probably would have made National Factories the backbone of the industrial effort in Canada, as they were in England. But now it was too late to get into the business. No new National Factories would be created. The structure was in place, the orders had been given, and there was nothing to do but get on with the job. "We go on day after day and again the next day and day after. These young men who are in senior places fill me with wonder and admiration. I do not quite make out how they stand it — it is work, work, heavy work, and late hours. I am deeply grateful to them — they have served the State with great efficiency and have remarkable capacity."[24]

III

Would that others had the same capacity. The Board was struggling to increase output in the face of one problem after another beyond its control. By late December, 1916, unusually severe winter weather was playing havoc with railway schedules, and shortages of locomotives prevented urgently needed coke getting through to IMB plants. By February thousands of loaded cars were lying idle on sidings across the country, some of them literally buried in snow, waiting for engines to get them through. The first load of gun-cotton consigned to British Explosives at Renfrew was so solidly frozen that it was almost impossible to unload. Then none came at all. Then it came but the plant had no coal. On one day old shell boxes had to be burned to keep the frost out of the building. As February turned into March, forging plants in Montreal were shutting down for want of steel because 250 carloads shipped from Sydney two months earlier were lost somewhere on the Intercolonial. Machining and assembling plants were about to close too. Finished shells were piling up at the factories because there were no cars to get them to the seaboard. The Ministry was complaining.[25]

No one seemed to be doing anything. The railways were short of locomotives, partly because they were still offering duplicate and triplicate passenger service between major cities. Flavelle wanted the government to work them "in common for national service" and hoped the government would buy its own cars and locomotives in the United States. He blamed the coal shortage on the big steel companies that owned the Cape Breton coal mines and were content to take profits on shortages. Here, too, government should intervene. "I am increasingly impressed with the importance of a firm hand being exercised over a good deal of production. I do not think the remedy is in Government control, but I do think it is in Government direction. . . . The whole situation should be dealt with in a strong, forcible way."[26]

But where was the strong man to take charge, a man with the vision and drive to cut through red tape and the trivia of politics, to bring in outsiders and get the job done? Where was the man with "a prophet's vision or a prophet's inspiration"? Where, at least, was Canada's equivalent to Lloyd George? "The simple and direct way in which he sets aside party and takes over the burdens for the State quickens one's blood and makes one long for something of the kind in this country," Flavelle wrote Willison in January. "If it could have been possible to have had a Prime Minister—or a very able second to the present Prime Minister, who could gather about him a small company of men and give them ample power and call upon the nation to respond!"[27]

But no, the politicians seemed to drift on with their endless partisan bickering, their endless discussions of whether or not elections should be held, whether a National Government should be formed, on what dates by-elections should be held, why the IMB should give their constituents contracts, and so on. Late in February Borden left for England to sit in the Imperial War Cabinet — a noble enough mission, except that Flavelle and other high-minded citizens found it morally offensive for Borden to take with him Robert Rogers, the quintessential Conservative machine politician, whose reputation was diminishing weekly with reports of kickbacks and payoffs in his Manitoba fiefdom. Flavelle saw the Rogers incident as a sign of Borden's "extraordinary absence of political sense . . . another evidence of his fatuous adherence to the renegade in politics." "How can any man be expected to understand his obligation to the State who will carry the Minister of Public Works to England with him as worthily representing Canada in this momentous time?" he asked in another letter, and also wrote Borden complaining about his choice of travelling companions.[28]

In February and March Flavelle found Ottawa a "wretched place . . . so unworthy of this time of trial and anxiety that one either wants to run away from it or to go into the fight and say freely what he thinks of it all." He complained often about the "ball and chain on my leg" and warned Brand he might resign if things did not improve on the Prime Minister's return. "I could and should set the country on fire with indignation," he wrote about the supply shortages.[29]

He had no personal desire for public office, he told his friends. Some of them still insisted on mentioning him as a Canadian equivalent to the strong businessmen Lloyd George had brought into his cabinet. In a *News* editorial Willison even hinted at Flavelle as a candidate for Prime Minister, a suggestion his old employer dismissed as "silly." Some politicians, however, were not so sure of Flavelle's motives. He was powerful, rich, impatient, severely critical of the government. Rumours of his plots to have White replace Borden changed during the winter to whispers that he was working through Will Rundle, Newton Rowell, and other Toronto Liberals to get into a Laurier cabinet after an election. "Yesterday with unashamed frankness, a leading member of Parliament and government supporter told me I was in league with the Liberals, that I had been at a meeting in Laurier's house and was conspiring against the Government. I was advised that I possessed the stink of intrigue, etc. How curious — the politician is a strange mixture of knave and fool, and cannot understand that straightforward action may be truthful and sincere and means nothing more than it says."[30]

Flavelle had not visited Laurier, was not conspiring on anyone's behalf, and was not spreading his views outside his circle of close friends. He did have strong views. He was disillusioned with the Borden government that spring; he believed it, or any reformed Conservative government, would be deservedly beaten in an election. Laurier, he thought, just might respond by bringing in outsiders to form a truly National Government.[31] As in England, the new blood in a National Government might provide the vision and executive ability, perhaps even "the prophet spirit." Flavelle had made his discontent public in his December speeches, and, of course, he so obviously fitted his own and others' description of the ideal businessman to bring in to get the job done that it was hard for insecure politicians not to assume that he was up to something. He was a British civil servant, all too interested in Canadian politics, all too strategically placed to change jobs easily.

IV

The one minister omitted from Flavelle's criticisms that winter was White. The reason was not Flavelle's satisfaction with the Finance Minister — he thought White was too cautious in the timing of his loans, too reluctant to start tapping ordinary Canadians' savings, and too vacillating in everything. "White seems to centre finally about the right place, but in the process of getting to that point he is a sore tax upon those who have to live with him."[32] Nonetheless, he had to be lived with as amicably as possible because the IMB could not come close to paying for its supplies without a constant flow of cash from the Canadian treasury.

The programme called for more than $250 million worth of shipments from January through June 1917. The British Ministry of Munitions had placed these orders without any assurance from the British Treasury, or anyone else, of funds being available to pay for them. Canada was expected to help. Canada had to help. But the one thing Sir Thomas White would not do was firmly commit the Canadian government to help. Flavelle's tactlessness at the end of 1916 did not help either. In the week in December when his speeches so embarrassed Borden and White, he compounded the error by writing the Finance Minister a letter harshly critical of "this body of timid, fearful financial men," the Canadian bankers. That same day White got the banks' agreement to lend the IMB $50 to $75 million to keep it going through March. He passed the news to Flavelle along with a severe dressing-down for questioning the bankers' financial judgment. Flavelle ate humble pie and never again wrote so sharply to his ex-employee, now very much his own man.[33]

The banks partly confirmed Flavelle's doubts by holding to the lower figure of $50 million. White had to make up the difference and the British Treasury found the remaining millions to cover IMB expenditures of just over $35 million monthly through March. In that month White's first 1917 Victory Loan was hugely oversubscribed and he promised the IMB a further $25 million in each of April and May. But the IMB's monthly spending had jumped to about $50 million and the British could not make up the shortfall. By April White was again being asked for extra help and the Canadian banks were beginning to lend the IMB money on two- to four-week terms while the Treasury scrambled to find dollars.[34]

Ten million dollars of White's extra aid was earmarked for the IMB's ship-building programme. Apparently stillborn in December, it had been suddenly revived in early April as the submarine menace reached its peak. Through the winter Flavelle had watched and worried as the British Ministry of Shipping's North American agent, James Esplen, scattered orders broadside in the United States at prices ten to thirty per cent higher than tonnage was going for in Canada, while ignoring IMB offers to help. Dealing through New York middlemen, Esplen wound up paying twenty-five per cent more for Canadian ships at the end of March than the IMB could have had them for at the beginning of March. Flavelle saw Esplen only once to discuss the situation — while the Englishman was changing trains in Ottawa. "John Bull is being bled by every smart trader, and everyone who touches him. I feel sore over the whole situation," Flavelle wrote of British purchasing generally. He described the shipping mess as the most uncomfortable and distasteful business the Board had been involved in.[35]

Early in April the British finally authorized the IMB to let contracts for the total steel-vessel capacity of Canadian shipyards. Flavelle asked Colonel William Gear, Vice-President of the Robert Redford shipping company, to act as the Board's Director of Steel Shipbuilding. Within weeks the Ministry of Shipping agreed to an IMB proposal to also have 2,500-ton wooden ships built in Canada. This scheme had been developed by Perry as a way of funnelling more business to British Columbia;[36] the British approved it despite doubts about the programme's practicality. To implement it Flavelle created a new Shipbuilding Department for British Columbia under the direction of R. P. Butchart, the cement magnate and gardener. Flavelle would soon learn just how uncomfortable and distasteful the shipping business could be.

V

Much of Flavelle's impatience that winter flowed from his fear that the war was going badly. He knew the seriousness of the submarine menace and of Britain's financial problems. He had always known that the Empire's only sure salvation was American help.

I cannot let my haunting fear of this submarine peril unduly possess me. All that British liberty stands for, all that it means to the rest of the world—brutish coarseness versus justice hang in the balance. Can the United States stay out and see all that the world cherishes of tenderness and charity and truthfulness, ruthlessly cut down? How can I ever think well of that people?[37]

For one of the few times in his life he felt the strain of work and worry and had to take aspirin to help him sleep. His bedtime reading was H. G. Wells's uplifting war novel, *Mr. Britling Sees It Through*.

The Americans finally joined the war in April. With their power thrown into the balance Flavelle could not understand how or why Germany would carry on. Perhaps the German armies would follow the Russian example and overthrow the Kaiser. The immediate job, of course, was to work the Americans into the war effort. Flavelle went to Washington in mid–April and again at the end of the month to participate in the first round of Anglo-American planning. Aside from getting assurance from American munitions organizers that American raw materials would still flow freely to the IMB, he stayed in the background, giving advice to the British and Canadian diplomats and ministers when asked. He wondered whether the Americans' "free loose democracy" could produce an efficient war machine, but was thrilled at the significance of the new alliance. "I filled up and could not have spoken if I had been addressed," he wrote about one of the ceremonies—"a really great occasion under 3 flags at Washington's tomb."[38]

The United States came into the war just as Canadian industry, like the Canadian army, was making its maximum contribution to the Allied effort. The men in France took Vimy Ridge in April, advancing after the German lines had been shredded by the artillery. At home more than 600 factories, more than 250,000 workers, were turning out shells for the 1917 campaigns, producing almost 100,000 rounds a day. In 1917, 23,786,206 shells were shipped, something between one-quarter and one-third of all the ammunition used by the British artillery in France, more than one-half the shrapnel.[39]

The Imperial Munitions Board was the umbrella agency organizing and supervising Canadian production. In a sense, Flavelle was running the biggest business that had ever existed in Canada, indeed, by mid-1917, the biggest business in North America. He had more men working on his contracts than any Canadian businessman had ever supervised, and was spending far more money—over $2 million a day for some weeks that spring—than any Canadian businessman had ever spent. The production network for the IMB covered far more territory than the old empires of the fur trade; the factories employed far more men than the CPR; the Board spent far more money than the Government of Canada had ever spent before the war.

Since 1914 there had been all sorts of false starts, delays, missed opportunities, and simple mistakes in creating a Canadian munitions industry from nothing. There were more problems to come. At best, too, Canada's manufacturing contribution to the war was primitive by British and American standards — Canadians made ammunition; others made guns, tanks, and fighting aircraft. The long-term benefits of war industries to Canada in terms of new processes and methods were shared by other industrial countries, resulting in a treadmill situation and no comparative advantage. Contrary to the common notion that wars have been good for the Canadian economy, the country would probably have been richer in both the short and long terms if the war had not happened. There were few, if any, great economic benefits to Canada flowing from the Great War.

Still, the IMB's achievement was impressive. Canadian manufacturers had been pushed into reaching higher standards of precision and efficiency and a far higher volume of production than anyone had thought possible. Charges of corruption, incompetence, profiteering (in munitions), and political meddling had virtually disappeared. The British, who had been saved millions since the days of the Shell Committee, were entirely satisfied with Flavelle's work and doubted they could have found anyone in Canada to do a better job.[40] Flavelle and his men were doing their job about as well as it could be done. None of them seems to have reflected on the destruction and carnage their products were causing; they were convinced they were working in a good cause, the highest cause, putting tyranny to death.

Their work was the Dominion of Canada's industrial contribution to the war effort — munitions made in Canada by Canadians, and, increasingly, paid for with Canadian money. But Flavelle's organization was the *Imperial* Munitions Board. To some Canadians, certainly to some Ottawa politicians, it must have seemed anomalous that the umbrella agency organizing and supervising Canadian munitions production was appointed by and responsible to the government of Great Britain. To Flavelle and his British associates on the IMB, their organization was a model of practical imperialism. It transcended national interests, even national governments, in helping mould the Canadian and British economies into one war-making unit. The IMB, Robert Brand wrote, "has in the sphere of munitions to a great extent overcome the weaknesses of the Imperial constitution. . . . If the British Government had not developed the munitions resources of Canada through the Imperial Munitions Board and had left it to the Canadian Government, and if the financial responsibility had rested on that Government, not very much, I think, would have been done."

As graduates of Lord Milner's South African Kindergarten, and as members of the Round Table, Brand, Perry, and Hichens had wanted to create supranational organizations for the Empire. The war gave them their chance, and because of their desire to build up the Empire's industrial capacity the Englishmen sometimes fought harder to develop Canadian industries, such as aeroplane manufacture, than the Canadian government did itself. They also came to believe, as did Flavelle, that the IMB could be a model for the future. In Round Table discussions before the war, Flavelle had urged caution and the slow, voluntary development of closer imperial ties. The war, the IMB, and his British friends convinced him that the process should be speeded up. In speeches in London in November 1916, and Toronto in April 1917, he instanced the IMB as a model imperial tie and called for a centralized British Empire governed by an Imperial Parliament as the only postwar alternative to "the vainglorious standards of an extreme Nationalism."[41]

Neither Canadian nor British politicians paid much attention to the dreams of the little band of imperialists. Like many other aspects of the Canadian war effort, the IMB's work was taken for granted back in England. It was usually forgotten about, for example, when staff lists and descriptions of the Ministry of Munitions were drawn up. Lloyd George, the first Minister of Munitions, forgot about it completely in his *War Memoirs*. Even as Flavelle and the other Round Tablers in England and Canada were calling for imperial centralization in 1917, the politicians who ran the Empire were laying the foundation (through Resolution Nine of the Imperial War Conference) for Dominion autonomy leading to complete independence.

No one in England hesitated, however, when Brand suggested that Flavelle should be honoured for his work. Flavelle and Gordon between them,

Brand wrote, "have probably saved the British Government more money in the last twelve months than any other persons." There was some discussion about which title a colonial holding an imperial job should take, and whether the Canadian government should be consulted. When the British could not agree among themselves which order of knighthood to confer upon Flavelle, it was decided to accept Brand's suggestion of a baronetcy. Gordon got a knighthood.[42]

Quite a few Canadians, including several of Flavelle's friends, were not sure that citizens of a North American democracy should accept any titles, particularly hereditary ones. In turning down the two offers of a knighthood before the war Flavelle may have shared that opinion. He had "a hard struggle," he claimed, over this offer. Perhaps he was influenced by the thought that his appointment and service had been to the Empire, not just to Canada. At bottom, too, the owner of Holwood, with its coat of arms carved in stone over the front door, believed in an aristocracy of ability in democratic Canada. So long as poor boys had the opportunity to climb the ladder it was not wrong to have those top rungs. In a maudlin letter to Sir John Willison (who had accepted his title years earlier and was just then lobbying for a Senatorship), he tried to explain how he was of the people, but not one of them:

The barrier between me and the men who worked with me in cellar and packing house has been growing. I am out of their lives, and I have lost much. This puts me further away from them. Yet the reasons for, led me to accept and thus put aside those against it. I think in my heart I look back to my life from which I came with longing. The simple people are so true and so genuine, and they were kind to me and in those days of struggle and victory, believed in me.[43]

VI

If they had ever believed in him, the men who claimed to speak for the "simple people" no longer did. In the same week that Joe Flavelle became Sir Joseph Flavelle, Bart., a special conference of trade unionists, called by the executive of the Trades and Labor Congress, attacked the IMB as being hostile to organized labour, negligent of workers' welfare, and unwilling to negotiate in good faith. Flavelle and Gordon were called "absolutely unfair and antagonistic" to munitions workers, their public attitudes described as "cant and hypocrisy." Union leaders muttered about the possibility of a general strike if action was not taken to reorganize the IMB and/or if the Borden government proceeded with its recently announced policy of conscription. In effect, the trade unionists were calling for Flavelle's resignation because of the IMB's labour policies.[44]

The crash programmes to build the Trenton and Nobel explosives plants and to create the bases for the Royal Flying Corps had involved the Board in major outdoor construction in winter — something almost never done in Canada. Even with hundreds of thousands of men in khaki and the munitions factories running at full capacity, there was still enough surplus labour in winter that IMB contractors found they could get men to work at less than union rates. There were disputes about some of the contractors' relations with unions, and particular confusion at Trenton when the Davis Durkin Company had to fire its first contractor for criminal incompetence. Working conditions in freezing temperatures were anything but normal. Taking his usual position that it was not up to the IMB to tell contractors what wages to pay, Flavelle had politely rejected a request from the Minister of Labour that the Board enforce union rates on these projects.[45]

As spring turned into summer and all of Canada's surplus labour was absorbed on the farms and construction, the normal bidding-up of wages was not the boon to existing trade unions that it seemed to be. The hectic pace of activity, particularly in the munitions industry, was undermining the usual hierarchy of skills, wage differentials, and authority among workers. Most of the new munitions workers were unskilled "operatives," working on piece-rates at which they were soon able to earn more than skilled "mechanics," who still tended to be on hourly rates. The new men and women workers were not organized and were therefore unresponsive to trade-union leaders' attempts to remedy the problem.[46]

Conditions of work and wages on IMB contracts, then, offended organized labour in both winter and summer. In times of both labour shortages and labour surpluses trade-union leaders found established wage scales and differentials eroded by rapid change and innovation in the war economy. On top of it all, inflation had begun to threaten the incomes of some of their members and conscription for military service loomed as the ultimate in state coercion.

The June attack on Flavelle and the IMB at the special conference was a lashing out at the several problems union leaders were facing in 1917. The complaints about the IMB were based partly on wages and working conditions at its construction sites, partly on the use of female and unskilled labour in the munitions plants without more consultation with unions. One of the most prominent grievances of 1915 and 1916 was also revived—the Board's refusal to insert a Fair Wage clause in its contracts. Since the attack on the IMB was coupled with an attack on conscription and a challenge to the government to do something about the high cost of living (say, by nationalizing all cold-storage plants, abattoirs, and canneries), and since the Liberals promptly raised the issues in the House of Commons, the Borden government took the protests seriously.

It was more a political question of pacifying union leaders than it was a serious threat to industrial activity. The special labour conference was secret and by invitation only. It was attended by the leaders of only some of the unions affiliated with the Trades and Labor Congress; a number of these— tailors, garment workers, bookbinders—had nothing to do with munitions work. In any case, according to Department of Labour estimates, there were about four times as many hands at work in IMB factories as there were in all of the trade unions affiliated with the TLC. There had been no formal complaints to the Department of Labour about working conditions on the construction sites, nor in recent months about conditions in any of the factories. Since the Industrial Disputes Investigation Act had been extended to munitions industries in March 1916, there had been no applications for a conciliation board from any munitions workers. A confidential memorandum prepared by the Deputy Minister of Labour concluded that "the allegations with respect to dissatisfaction and unrest among the munitions workers and statements made as to evil working conditions among them are largely without foundation." The memorandum reinforced Flavelle's belief that the attack on the IMB had developed in response to left-wing pressure on the labour establishment, what he called the growth of the "demagogue" or "socialist" element in the labour movement.[47]

Nobody thought a Fair Wage clause in IMB contracts would have any tangible effect on workers. Wages were so high, Mark Irish pointed out, that in no case would the formal institution of union wage scales force a wage increase. Crothers, the Minister of Labour, reported to Borden that the IMB had been generally faithful in carrying out its promise of cooperation and there was no substantial ground for complaint by reason of the absence of the Fair Wage clause. Flavelle summed up his position in a despatch to England:

The root of the matter is, as far as the Trade Unions are concerned, that they are aggrieved that the Board will not allow itself to be used as a lever for imposing recognition of the Trade Unions on employers. . . . The position of the Trade Unions in Canada is by no means so well established as in Great Britain and no doubt (and not unnaturally) they see in the conditions created by the war an opportunity for improving it. It is our view, however, that the Board should not allow itself to be used for this purpose especially in view of the temporary nature of its functions.[48]

His public response to the criticisms was a general statement deploring the possibility of production being held up by industrial disputes. Comparing the conditions of men at the front to those working at home, he suggested it would be a crime for either workpeople or manufacturers to force work stoppages in the munitions industry. In a separate circular letter to all munitions manufacturers he appealed to them to give personal attention to avoiding labour problems.[49]

When employers were not able to avoid labour problems, they tended to take them to the IMB. The Consolidated Mining and Smelting Company in British Columbia, for example, was facing a concerted drive to unionize its mines and smelter. Rather than accept a union check-off, its general manager, J. J. Warren, urged Flavelle to pay higher prices so the company could give a greater wage increase. Flavelle refused. Anticipating trouble, Warren asked for a doubling or tripling of the guard on the smelter. Flavelle non-committally passed the request to the military, who also refused to act. Warren fought a strike, fulminated about the country going to the dogs, and continued to press fruitlessly for higher prices and troops. Further west, Butchart complained that strikes were destroying the IMB's wooden-ship-building plans and called for the conscription of all men of military age who refused to work. Flavelle told him that contractors would have to solve their troubles themselves, that there were procedures to follow using the Industrial Disputes Investigation Act, and that the Minister of Labour was sincere in handling his "most unenviable position." He added, correctly, that on the whole Canada had managed to get through the war with much less labour trouble than other countries.[50]

That was true through 1917 in the munitions plants, largely because wages kept up easily with the cost of living; with overtime, incomes must have considerably outpaced it.*[51] Neither the employees nor the employers who

---

* There are no statistics on wages paid by IMB contractors. From 1914 to 1917 wage rates in metal trades across Canada rose approximately twenty-eight per cent; wage rates for machinists in Toronto, Hamilton, and Montreal, the cities that had the most IMB work, rose by approximately fifty per cent. The weekly cost of living on a "family-budget" basis, averaged for sixty cities, rose thirty per cent from July 1914 to July 1917. Overtime, at higher rates, was normal in all the munitions plants.

worked for the IMB had to pay a price for their patriotism in the way that the men at the front did.

The root of most of Flavelle's labour troubles was his determination to keep the IMB at arm's length from contractors' labour disputes. Because the IMB wanted its orders filled on time, its experts would help manufacturers get their jobs done. The Production Department, for example, gave free advice on plant organization and manufacturing technique. Irish's Labour Department had also helped manufacturers ease labour shortages by recruiting women workers. As part of that programme it encouraged manufacturers to provide special facilities for the ladies' comfort, including lunchrooms, first-aid stations, and recreation rooms. This was the one significant improvement in factory working conditions sponsored by the Board. It also strongly encouraged a policy of paying women equal wages, but it is not clear that manufacturers followed this advice. Flavelle's men would advise, but except in abnormal circumstances would not require. "My position from the first has been," Flavelle repeated in the winter of 1917, " 'We are in the country to observe the conditions which are present in the country and not to attempt to interpret for manufacturers what their duty is to organized labour. Our duty ends when we co-operate with the Minister of Labor for the country in which we are found in assisting to redress any injustice which he tells us work people are suffering in factories where we have contracts.' "[52]

The spectre, of course, was of becoming directly responsible for fixing the wages and working conditions of a quarter of a million workers, over the heads of their nominal employers. The Board would be bound to offend either the workers or their bosses. Either group might respond by refusing to produce. They could not be coerced unless the Canadian government was willing to move to a fully controlled economy, conscripting workers and employers alike for industrial service. It was not willing, and Flavelle continued to draw fine lines in his policy of attempting to keep both workers and employers satisfied by not rocking the boat too strongly. Flavelle warned Mark Irish not to turn the Labour Department into a hiring agency to procure skilled workers for manufacturers, because labour would probably be offended. On the other side, he would not issue a statement disapproving of employers who cut piecework rates because he thought there could be irrationally high piecework rates as well as unfairly low ones.[53]

He also clung to his opposition to the Fair Wage clause after most others had decided to give in. By the June 1917 discussions of labour policy, Crothers had decided it would do no harm to put the Fair Wage clause into contracts to pacify the labour leaders. Irish concurred, suggesting that with their sense of status re-established the labour leaders would "take a holiday from agitation." He had also decided it would be morally right for the IMB to subscribe formally to fair wages at a time when men were fighting and dying for that right. The Chairman was not convinced by Irish or Crothers (he still felt, as he had argued for some time, that the clause would be useless unless the Canadian government set up an enforcement mechanism, which it would not do), but finally agreed not to stand in the way of a Fair Wage clause if the Canadian and British governments wanted to put it in. They seemed to want to.[54]

There the matter stood. Nobody did anything more about a Fair Wage clause, and, after the June steam-letting, organized labour left the IMB alone. Flavelle had worried that the labour leaders might attempt to tie up the munitions plants, but there were only a couple of isolated strikes over local issues in June. One of these Irish arbitrated:

I listened to a presentation of the case from both sides together, then I separated them and gave the employer a frank, candid, opinion . . . of where I thought he had not acted wisely. I then got Labour and I told Labour in no qualified terms of what I thought of their action and I must have made some impression because two of the men cried and they are not weaklings. . . . Be it said for Labour they conceded my request first and with a grace that did them proud. The manufacturer kept his bristles up until the last moment but finally came to the scratch.

Flavelle remarked that in his limited experience with labour problems he too had found the workers more reasonable than their employers.[55]

VII

The real threat to the well-being of both employers and workers, and to the war effort itself, had nothing to do with relations in the shops. It revolved around finance and Britain's growing inability to find the money to keep the IMB going.

Uncle Sam's belligerence included taking a tough line on his allies' use of American money. Almost immediately after coming into the war the Americans began pressing the British to stop spending borrowed U.S.

dollars anywhere but in the United States. Without access to this money Britain could not provide the millions over and above White's loans that were necessary to keep paying the Canadian bills. Through May and June 1917 the IMB lived from hand to mouth as Flavelle juggled short-term bank loans, always getting the most generous help from the Commerce. Pending Treasury approval, the Ministry of Munitions was ready to increase its Canadian orders to eight hundred thousand shells a week from July through December. The Treasury never approved—it insisted that all the new money spent in Canada had to come from Canadian sources. But, as usual, White would make no long-term commitment. He was worrying about how to pay his own bills because he, too, was being cut off from U.S. money markets.[56]

Brand came out to join in the discussions. In June, he, Flavelle, Perry, and Gordon were all in New York trying to work out the problem with Lord Northcliffe and Sir Hardman Lever, the heads of special British missions in the United States. For a few days in June it seems that the IMB had no money it could draw on and was kiting cheques to keep going. One cable after another from London insisted that Canadian purchases had to be paid for with Canadians' money or the programme would be cut back.

More than the shell programme would be cut back. The British were also short of money to pay for Canadian foodstuffs — all the wheat, cheese, bacon, hay, oats, and flour they were buying to feed the civilian population, the armies, and the armies' useless horses. After frantic conferences in early July, another makeshift was worked out to keep the Board going to the end of the month. It involved more bank loans, deferred interest payments, and a $15-million advance by White on his August commitments.[57] In a few weeks everything would be up in the air again — British and Canadian financial solvency, the future of the munitions programme, the jobs of a quarter-million munitions workers.

VIII

There was breathing space in the second week in July for Flavelle to clear his desk of business and slip away for a few days' rest. He had just promoted Fitzgerald to Assistant to the Chairman and had no qualms about leaving the organization in his hands. The July finances had been settled; nothing more could be done until White found out whether he could get permission to float a big loan in the United States. The labour scene was quiet except for a mildly bothersome impending street-railway strike in Toronto which might keep a few munitions workers away from work. There would be no problem with the Russell Motor Car Company's plant, for it had elaborate plans to get its men to the plant; but by hiring every rentable truck and car in Toronto it had cornered the transportation system. Still, when the strike began on Wednesday the eleventh, E. C. Fox reported that every single man had got to work on time at the Davies plant, so there was not likely to be much trouble in the munitions factories. "The agitators of the present strike are a lot of new people with no sense of obligation or sense of decency," Fox reported.[58]

In spare moments Flavelle had also been conferring with Fox about how the Davies Company might respond to public concern about the high cost of food. There were rumours, even questions in the House of Commons, that food-processing companies were holding huge supplies in cold storage to create artificial shortages and drive up prices. Fox had publicly replied to these and Flavelle had written a long letter to an MP explaining how cold storage worked in a modern economy. Will Rundle had suggested that the government's newly appointed Food Controller, W. J. Hanna, might investigate the cold-storage business to reassure the public. Flavelle had passed the advice on to Fox, but the general manager pointed out that W. F. O'Connor, the Cost-of-Living Commissioner appointed nine months earlier, was doing just that. "As he has [knowledge of] the cold-storage situation for the last five years, he told me that he was able to refute the newspaper and public talk about the accumulation of supplies," Fox wrote on Tuesday the tenth.[59]

No progress in the war. More death and destruction, brought home to Flavelle that week by news that Percy Molson, the National Trust employee they had valued so highly, was dead in battle.

Some progress toward more leadership at home. White's news that he was going to reduce Canadians' excessive purchasing power by levying an income tax encouraged Flavelle. The Prime Minister had returned from England in May convinced that conscription was necessary to keep up the reserves, and a coalition government necessary to carry conscription. Negotiations towards a coalition might conclude successfully at any time. On the tenth, Flavelle wrote Rundle, who as a prominent Toronto Liberal was fairly close to both Laurier and the Ontario party leader, Newton Rowell, urging that someone high in the Liberal party "with imagination, and vision, and courage" assert the necessary leadership to break the deadlock and bring about a National Government. He hoped it might be Rowell.

He saw Borden that day on another private matter—the wretched railway mess. Because the aid authorized by Parliament had long since run out, the Commerce was again relying on private letters from Borden to justify its loans to the Canadian Northern, and was understandably anxious that the situation be resolved. In May the Drayton–Acworth Royal Commission had recommended a government takeover of the faltered transcontinentals. Flavelle thought that a CPR proposal to buy the Canadian Northern was very attractive and had given some time to acting as a go-between on the matter. His war experience had led him to question his earlier belief that a government could run a railway efficiently. But the government had blocked the CPR attempt, at least for the time being, for fear of a private railway monopoly. Borden was still hoping to get his coalition before facing up to a takeover of the Canadian Northern. At the meeting on the tenth, Aird, E. R. Wood, Lash, Flavelle, and Borden agreed to keep the situation "in statu quo" until the end of the month.[60]

Through these weeks Flavelle had been mentioned occasionally as a possible minister in a coalition government. There is little evidence that any of the politicians were seriously thinking of him as cabinet material, but he was highly enough placed and the rumours were persistent enough (the politicians were considering bringing in a businessman from the IMB, but it was Gordon, not Flavelle) that he had half expected to be sounded out. After a long discussion with White on Monday the ninth he realized it would not happen. "I will have no ordeal of decision to face," he wrote Clara on the tenth. "I realize how concerned I was, now that the anxiety has passed."[61]

His public and private business dealt with, Flavelle left Ottawa on July 11 to spend a few days with his family at Swannanoa, his Sturgeon Point cottage. Two days later, on Friday the 13th, an ordeal he had never expected began.

CHAPTER FOURTEEN

HIS LARDSHIP

When he went to Ottawa in December 1915 it never occurred to Flavelle that his continuing role in the affairs of Simpson's, The National Trust, the Bank of Commerce, or the William Davies Company could be questioned. They did not do any work for the IMB and he had no interest in any company that did. So the Chairman of the IMB maintained his private business interests. He was often in Toronto on weekends to confer with Aird and Walker about railways, attend Simpson's board meetings (which were switched to Saturdays for his convenience), consult with the senior officers of National Trust, and—keeping up public obligations—spend an hour or so at Toronto General Hospital. As always, the first business claim on his spare time was the William Davies Company. E. C. Fox, the general manager, kept him closely informed and consulted him often about the remarkable effects the war was having on the company's fortunes.

I

Rank on rank the hogs were gathered up the ramps to the killing-rooms at the William Davies factories. Most were finally served in the trenches in four-ounce portions of bacon, part of an imperial soldier's daily rations.

The war had revived the dying Canadian bacon trade with Britain beyond anyone's expectations. Neutral Denmark found it profitable (and perhaps prudent) to divert much of its bacon to Germany. English and Irish farmers could not make up the shortfall of supplies for Britain's home population, let alone feed the armies. Huge shipments of Canadian bacon were required. Having kept its faith in the British market, the Davies Company was ideally placed to exploit the breakthrough. Its corned-beef sales continued in the millions of tins, but were only a sideline to the manufacture and sale of Wiltshire sides. When Flavelle left for Ottawa in the fall of 1915 to make shells, his employees at the Don and Montreal, not unlike soldiers at the front, were slaughtering at a faster rate than they had ever thought possible.

Operations had already expanded into the United States. As it had done twice before in its history when Canadian hog supplies were inadequate, the Davies Company had begun to purchase American hogs in Chicago. They were slaughtered, singed, and trimmed there, then brought to Canada for curing and re-export. This Canadian-cured American bacon did not command the same premium price in Britain as Canadian Wiltshires, but apparently yielded a better profit margin than the all-Canadian product.[1] The Davies people were intrigued to realize they could get U.S. hogs in competition with American packers, then sell American bacon in Britain in competition with American packers, and do as well as or better than they could in Canada. Perhaps these American operations held out real opportunities for the future.

For the moment it was difficult enough to make the most of wartime opportunities. By the winter of 1915 – 16, for example, Fox was on the brink of having to cut back shipments because it was so difficult to get space on Atlantic steamers. There was never a problem involving losses at sea — insurance covered that hazard — but it was necessary to get Davies' highly perishable product, cured for quick sale and consumption, across on a tight timetable.[2]

An eye had to be kept on competitors, of course, because the company's products were still being bought and sold on open markets. Even the War Office made its huge weekly purchases on the floor of the Produce Exchange through Henry Denny. The Matthews – Blackwell Company had also stayed in the British bacon trade during the lean years, and its sales ballooned in the first years of the war. Other companies leapt into exporting when they realized the profits to be had. One of the most aggressive newcomers was Harris Abattoir, forty per cent owned by the William Davies Company.

By late 1915 both Matthews and the Abattoir had followed Davies into the United States to buy hogs. Although J. S. McLean of the Abattoir agreed to buy in Indianapolis rather than compete with Davies for Chicago hogs, his new English sales agency did compete directly with the older firm. E. C.

Fox resented competing with a company of which he was a vice-president, representing the Davies minority interest! "While we are on their Board we must advise soundly and freely," he complained, "yet they are securing the benefit of our experience and we are securing nothing from their experience." Then he was outraged when the Abattoir's British agent tried to use his interlockage with Davies as an entrée to War Office business. "These people resent our interest in their business and yet they are only too glad to grasp the name of the Davies Company if they think it will help them get a little more business, and they are not very particular whether they truthfully state their case or not. . . . I never come across these men in business that I do not find something that raises the hair on one's back."

Flavelle shared Fox's view that Harris and McLean's business ethics were "flexible," and agreed that something had to be done about the ownership situation. He ruled out fusion of the companies because he would not work with Harris and McLean. The likely solution would be for the Harris people to buy out the Davies interest when they could raise the money.[3]

The war did things like this to longstanding business relations. Another of Fox's problems was friction with Davies' banker, the Commerce. There were running disputes about practically every aspect of financing, most stemming from Fox's discovery that other banks offered better terms than the Commerce. He and Flavelle were ready to reconsider that relation when the war ended.*[4]

They did not want the war to change the quality of their bacon, which had always been the key to Davies' reputation and its premium prices. Transportation tie-ups, however, were a constant threat to a perishable product. Flavelle advised Fox to adjust his cure, and, when signs of taint appeared, warned him to tighten up on cellar procedures. In the winter of 1916 he saw samples of pork-and-beans submitted to the CPR's Purchasing Department

---

* The disagreements, too complex to go into, showed a fascinating interplay of change and conservatism. As their operations grew into a very big, continent-wide business, the Davies men began to shop carefully for the best financing for each aspect of their transactions. The Commerce complained that it was traditional and proper for a firm to do all its business with its principal banker, any extra costs being made up by the general benefit of the relationship to the client. When he ran the company Flavelle had accepted this custom and never thought to shop around. In these disputes, however, he did not let his directorship in the Commerce prevent him from supporting Fox. Under pressure from its aggressive customer, the Commerce was forced to make concessions. On the whole, Canadian banks did not surrender the idea of exclusive relationships with clients until after the Second World War.

as part of tenders for a British contract and wrote Fox about the inferior appearance of their own product. The contract had gone to the Simcoe Canning Company, which had offered better quality at a low price.[5]

Corned beef for the War Office also had to meet quality standards. According to Flavelle there were no complaints about Davies quality. There was one moment of alarm in the spring of 1916 when muckraking French newspapers published rumours about steel hooks, like fishhooks, being discovered in tins of Davies corned beef. It looked like sabotage. Flavelle and Fox could not believe it. They speculated that a very rare tin might have had a drop of excess solder curved into a hook-like shape; or, perhaps the odd pin used to attach labels to quarters of beef had gotten into a can. Nothing was heard of the matter except for more French newspaper charges against other packers.[6]

Davies' annual statement at the end of March 1916 was very satisfactory. Sales had increased from $19,800,000 to just over $27,700,000. Profits, including dividends from Harris Abattoir and Sheed Thomson, had risen from $580,000 to $1,539,473. About $500,000 would go out in the new taxes levied as a temporary wartime measure. The shareholders received $300,000 in a 20-per-cent cash dividend. A further $500,000 was formally reinvested through a 33 ⅓-per-cent stock dividend. The rest was added to reserves. The returns on shareholders' capital were almost as good as they had been in the salad days of the bacon trade in the nineties.[7]

Packing-house workers were also receiving record wages as Fox struggled to keep his factories fully manned. "We are constantly short of labour and we cannot even get a foreigner today under twelve or thirteen dollars [a week]," Fox reported in the spring of 1916. On the other hand, "there is not restlessness among our regular people. They inherently recognize that during periods of depression we have never as yet taken advantage of that to reduce their own standards of living." To keep the workers satisfied he raised the 1916 bonus and regularly advanced wages when he anticipated restlessness. By the end of the summer Davies and Harris were the only packers, he calculated, whose capacity was not being limited by labour shortages. Continuing to anticipate restlessness, in 1917 the company set aside $50,000 to launch one of the earliest pension programmes in Canadian manufacturing.

The enlightened paternalism pleased Flavelle, who twice wrote Fox during the summer of 1916 worrying about the effects of the heat wave on their workers. "Do not think me intruding, I am sure, if I remind you of the importance of making these people as comfortable as possible. I wonder if you could spare time for a quiet hour to take a survey of the works and determine what minor improvements could be made forthwith that would add to the comfort of the work people." It seems to have been in this heat wave that a morning bath caused Joe to remember how far he had come from his origins. "What a luxury a bath is a morning like this," he wrote in a note to his wife. "One remembers the army of working men and women who must put on the same underwear as yesterday, and are denied the comfort of a bath. I wonder if we all unconsciously lose our touch with the less fortunate and are failing in the consideration that matters."[8]

II

Fox expected the next year's profits to fall to the 1915 level or lower. His main problem was a short supply of hogs. Rising grain prices through the winter of 1915 – 16 had discouraged farmers from converting cereals to pork. With the company's raw-material costs rising sharply, and a huge volume of meat being cured and in transit at any time, a break in the British price could lead to severe losses. Unwilling to take the extra risk, Fox decided in the spring of 1916 to cut his British shipments thirty to fifty per cent. "There is no use being obsessed with volume at the present prices when we know that our cost is above any possible clearance considering the amount of product that has to be sold," he wrote Flavelle in March. "I think, therefore, we should make volume secondary to profit."[9]

Traditional business practices were starting to crumble under the artificial conditions of war. In June 1916, the British government began subsidizing Dutch packers to help deflect their bacon to England rather than Germany. The Canadians found themselves having to compete on the market with subsidized producers. Then the William Davies Company was caught locked into long-term high-priced contracts for shipping space when the shortage eased and rates dropped sharply, giving an advantage to new shippers. With Denny at the War Office continuing to urge an expansion of Davies shipments, the company insisted on some protection against loss. Among other suggestions it offered to turn the business over to the British, working the factories under instructions for a fee based on the turnover.[10]

Denny preferred to begin dealing on a negotiated-price basis, offering protection against losses to induce the company to expand volume. "Conditions now are such that you will not be expected to take the whole risk of market on business of this size," Sheed cabled in July, 1916,

Would think it necessary that some arrangement be made on basis of cost in Canada and States which could be cabled from week to week that would allow Denny to reduce quantity if prices get excessive or if necessary instruct you to take more hogs. Whole position is that Denny wants you do their business in preference to any other packers, but you must not expect too much out of it and they do not want you to lose money by doing it.

After agreeing to sell to Denny at a fixed price during July, Fox and Sheed got the British purchaser to agree to take future shipments at either a price to cover costs or the market price if it were higher. Fox considered the arrangement "one of the best strokes of business" Sheed had done. "Of course it is a perfectly fair basis, but it is contrary to the custom of the bacon trade. You can depend upon it that we will not adopt an attitude of bargaining in this thing because of this arrangement." [11]

For the next six months the company shipped its War Office bacon knowing it could not lose money. It could not make limitless profits on high market prices either, though, for Denny had kept his option to fix quantities. He could also change the deal if the situation seemed to be getting out of hand. As well, the knowledge that he could get all the supplies he wanted from his largest Canadian shipper at a low fixed price, plus his preponderant influence on the market, enabled him to hold the market price for Canadian bacon below the level it would otherwise have reached, helping hold down bacon prices generally. The British were far from disadvantaged by the arrangement. Each party was giving up the possibility of extreme profit in return for protection against extreme loss.

At the same time as he made his arrangement with Davies, Denny (and other British purchasers) was beginning to make "forward" agreements with American packers, stipulating the price to be paid for bacon not yet shipped. [12] This was the first step towards the development of a futures market in hog products. It would have been just as easy—and have saved a lot of grief later—to have put the Davies business on a forward basis in the summer of 1916. In February of 1917 that happened, in effect, when the War Office stopped open-market purchases of bacon and began taking tenders for forward contracts. For the rest of the war the William Davies Company continued to sell large quantities of bacon under the new system.

Even after February 1917 bacon for the British civilian population was still being bought on the open market. Prices had risen gradually through 1916; they soared in the winter and spring of 1917. Fox and Flavelle found it bewildering to sell on a market like this. All their experience suggested that high prices induced new supplies leading to lower prices. Flavelle had thought Denny, acting for the War Office, was probably driving prices higher than necessary and wondered if the British had not blundered in their choice of a purchasing agent. When Denny came off the market in February and prices kept rising, Flavelle could not believe they were rational. He favoured a purchasing organization in North America to buy all the meat for the European Allies just as the IMB bought munitions in Canada and other agencies bought sugar and grain. It would save an enormous amount of money. "In the meantime," he noted in March 1917, "the unfortunate consumer is being badly punished."[13]

III

Consumers knew it in both Britain and Canada, where meat prices were one of the more visible symptoms of serious wartime inflation. Politicians naturally bowed to consumer pressure to try to hold lids on prices. By the end of 1916 the British had appointed a Food Controller with powers to fix prices. In Canada the Borden government had made it a criminal offence to raise unduly the price of necessities and had authorized the Minister of Labour to investigate trading in these goods. In December 1916 W. F. O'Connor, a Halifax lawyer whom Borden used as a troubleshooter for various wartime jobs (he had helped draft the War Measures Act), was appointed acting Cost-of-Living Commissioner to conduct the investigations. He began studies of sugar, coal, and cold storage, the last of these because it was popularly believed that cold-storage facilities allowed middlemen to hoard food in speculation against higher prices.

Packing houses fell under O'Connor's cold-storage inquiry because they all had refrigeration facilities. In January 1917 the Davies Company received a long questionnaire asking about its costs and sales. The categories used differed sharply from normal packing-house accounting systems (most simply, for example, the questionnaire required information based on the calendar year rather than a firm's accounting year), and Fox replied that it would be difficult to return the form on time. He invited O'Connor's office to send in its own people to do the work if they wanted to, and repeated the invitation in a second letter. "You are welcome to all the information we can give you. It is a fact, however, the information you ask for is in a form the

William Davies Company do not keep, and we doubt whether many other concerns keep their records in that form. . . . You can send a whole staff down here to investigate, but if you do not choose to do that I would ask you to wait for a few days longer until we can get these figures prepared."

While O'Connor was investigating, Fox was making his own suggestions for bringing prices under control. In April he twice wrote Sir Thomas White, urging action to help the consumer: ". . . a consumer is compelled to pay a price for meat which is not only practically prohibitive to the poor person but is becoming impossible to those of moderate means." It might help in Canada to import American meat duty-free as a war measure. As for Britain, where the Food Controller was trying to freeze retail prices at levels that would simply stop foreign suppliers from shipping, Fox suggested joint Canadian–American fixing of wholesale meat prices as the only effective solution. "There is no ulterior motive in suggesting this policy," Fox argued. "We cannot be benefited — we may not do as well as if conditions were free, but we are in unusual times where nothing counts if either the Germans win or if because of improper foresight the masses of our people face starvation." By June Flavelle and Fox were considering breaking one of their company's oldest traditions and approaching American packers to discuss joint action to bring down the buying price of hogs. There was no other way to lower significantly the price to the consumer. Side bacon was selling in Toronto for about fifty cents a pound, the equivalent of five dollars a pound sixty years later.[14]

Despite the price-fixing agreement with Denny, the company did not maintain profits in the year ending March 27, 1917. Sales increased by another 50 per cent to more than $40 million; profits shrank slightly to $1,379,904. Higher war taxes would take about $650,000 of this, and major reinvestments were planned to prepare for postwar competition. So only $250,000 was paid out to the shareholders in a 12½-per-cent dividend.[15] Assuming that the company was not making money from April through July 1914, its dividends from wartime earnings had totalled $775,000. Flavelle's share of these was $390,096.

IV

W. F. O'Connor's report on cold-storage conditions in Canada was submitted to the Minister of Labour, Thomas Crothers, on July 9, 1917. It was to be reviewed in cabinet before release, but Crothers gave James Muir, a reporter for the *Ottawa Journal*, an advance view.[16] Instead of waiting for the report's official release, the *Journal* published Muir's story on the morning of Friday, July 13.

HUGE MARGINS SHOWN ON BACON TRADE
Flavelles Ltd Made 5.05 Cents A Pound
on 100 Million Pounds
Profit Only 3.67 in Year Previous

A startling revelation of profit-taking in food, during last year particularly, when prices rose so spectacularly, was made yesterday by Mr. W. F. O'Connor, K.C., the Cost of Living Commissioner.... Tremendous profits have been taken by two Canadian firms, Flavelles Ltd., and Matthews – Blackwell, Ltd. The "margins" run into millions of dollars. They run into millions on one article....

Members of Parliament were in a commotion last night, and drastic action was promised. It is understood that action will be taken to demand for the public treasury the immense profits made out of the war woe of the country....

The Canadian Press sent out the same story. It was front-page news across Canada, usually under heads implying a five-cent-a-pound/five-million-dollar profit on bacon.

Once they realized that their target was the William Davies Company, not Flavelles Limited of Lindsay (Johnnie Flavelle got in the first rebuttal of the story as "outrageous" and "damnable"), reporters got through to Sturgeon Point by telephone. Caught totally by surprise (if anything, he had thought O'Connor's report would reassure the public about cold storage), Flavelle dashed off a public telegram to Borden. He labelled the charges "grotesquely untruthful both in the mass and in detail," claimed they evidenced "a curious mixture of ignorance and malice," and demanded an inquiry into what he thought were Department of Labour accusations that his company had taken a five-million-dollar profit on bacon.[17]

It was the journalists rather than anyone in the government who had grossly distorted Davies' and Matthews – Blackwell's profits. O'Connor's report*[18] avoided using the word "profit." Instead it used "margin" to des-

---

* Actually compiled and written by a strikingly good-looking young MA in economics from the University of Toronto, Miss E. J. McKenna, whose graduate work had been financed by a Flavelle Scholarship.

ignate the difference between the cost to cold-storage companies of the goods they stored and their final selling price. The 5.05-cents-per-pound "margin" the Davies Company had made on 98 million pounds of bacon in the calendar year 1916 (which by rough calculation produced a $5 million "profit") actually included all of the company's costs of curing, overhead, shipping, insurance, and sales. This was evident on a careful reading of the report.

But there was enough criticism of the Davies Company in the report to have made a semi-sensational story without the distortion. In some ways the report was a vindication of the cold-storage industry as a whole, for it found utterly groundless the "weird stories" of food being destroyed to limit supplies or hoarded in cold storage to create scarcities and high prices. There was no such thing as a "food trust" in Canada. Instead there was, generally, lively competition and small, reasonable profits. High food prices were caused by huge wartime demand at home and abroad.

In the case of bacon exports, however, the report held that "no more striking example of a monopoly of any one commodity can be cited from the trade records of any country supplying the Allies with food." Companies "v" and "ix" (easily identifiable as Matthews—Blackwell and William Davies) had handled 83 per cent of all the bacon exported from Canada in 1916, up from just over 50 per cent in 1914. There was no special criticism of Matthews—Blackwell, but company ix's "margin" on its bacon had risen from 3.67 cents per pound in 1915 to 5.05 cents in 1916. "The margin of 3.67 was sufficient, satisfactory and profitable in 1915. Why not in 1916?"

O'Connor made no recommendations, claiming action was up to the new Canadian Food Controller. He did note that if the "profiteering" (his report's one use of the word) he had uncovered in bacon had taken place under new legislation affecting 1917 he would have urged the proper Attorney General to prosecute. "Aside from the matter of illegality, is this sort of thing to be considered respectable?" O'Connor's report concluded. "Mine may be the voice of one crying in the wilderness, but I have to register in the negative."[19]

Some newspapers, not all, quickly corrected the confusion of "margin" with "profits." It was also realized that O'Connor had found Matthews — Blackwell's "margin" to be reasonable. The report's accusations against the William Davies Company stood. The company had obviously been making a lot of money selling bacon. It seemed to have captured a spread between buying and selling costs greater than any other company's —such as Mat-thews—Blackwell's. Some newspapers had already prejudged the issue edi-torially: on July 14 the *Winnipeg Free Press*, for example, wrote of "extortion and deliberate profiteering . . . illicit profits . . . the systematic movement to enhance food and other prices . . . the nefarious schemes of heartless profiteers." Other papers demanded a full investigation. As the other Winnipeg paper, the *Tribune*, noted, there seemed to be "A Hog Somewhere" in the bacon business.

v

The Prime Minister wrote Flavelle on the fourteenth regretting the release of the O'Connor report without his knowledge. "It must be at once admitted that the report should not have been made public without submitting it to you and giving you an opportunity of explaining it and of showing the Company's version of the transactions therein set forth. Mr. Crothers . . . made a grave mistake." A. E. Kemp told Flavelle he had never seen Borden so angry with a minister as he was with Crothers in cabinet that day. Borden had immediately decided to have an inquiry. Flavelle met him a few days later to discuss the situation. "He is very sore," the Prime Minister noted in his diary.[20]

Flavelle's friends were outraged. To Will Rundle the report was "obvi-ously either incompetent or malicious, while the spirit in which the news-papers have presented it is nothing short of vicious. Whither is the press leading us?" George Allan, a Winnipeg businessman, thought the coverage illustrated the tendency of the press "to hang men connected with the Cor-porations of the country and try them afterwards." Edward Adie, the gentle former secretary of the Davies Company, now semi-retired, was incensed at the firm being held up to "the obliquy [*sic*] of the Empire" by a man "utterly incapable of co-ordination of factors, analysis & deduction." Flavelle him-self was thoroughly angry and hurt, but found comfort in his innocence. "Of course I feel the matter," he wrote Clara on Monday the sixteenth, "but how dreadful if it had been true. There can be no permanent scar on one's own consciousness under the circumstances." He realized, though, that the damage to his reputation might be permanent. "It will remain long with the public—very long."[21]

Flavelle and Fox were determined to fight back. In many ways the

O'Connor report was a misleading, in fact stupid, document. Its fundamental premise, that the meat-packing companies were basically "cold-storage" companies, was silly. True cold-storage companies simply held products in refrigeration until they were ready for market or consumption. Packing houses, which developed long before refrigeration, stored their products for a time in coolers, but to say this made them "cold-storage" companies was like describing a kitchen as a refrigeration room. And then to compare packers' "margin" on operations, which included all their manufacturing costs, with the much smaller "margin" of true cold-storage companies was absurd.

As the Davies Company had pointed out in January, the questionnaires were next to impossible to apply to packing houses. The packers were asked for their costs and selling prices of pork, bacon, and hams, for example. Were all their raw pigs to be entered as pork? Or were they to be "broken down" into the intended final product? Davies' returns did break them down because the company's accounting system had been finely tuned to do just that. Other packers, whose accounting was much less sophisticated, answered the questions on a completely different basis. Asked for its costs of "bacon," the William Davies Company had given its cost of that part of the hog carcass destined to become bacon; Matthews—Blackwell, Fox thought, had stated the cost after the bacon had actually been cured. So Davies' "margin" included curing costs, while Matthews—Blackwell's did not.

The companies had also interpreted "cold storage" differently. Some had given returns on only their frozen meats, others on only the goods they were holding specifically in cold storage, the William Davies Company on all its products. Matthews—Blackwell had submitted returns on four different bases for four of their five plants; the fifth factory had not reported at all! At a meeting of the packers in August the manager of the Ingersoll house mentioned that his company's Wiltshire sides had been reported to O'Connor under pork, rather than bacon. Fox casually remarked that a good many packers seemed to have submitted their cold-storage rather than their general packing-house stocks —"and a grin of assent went around the room." The comparisons attempted in the O'Connor report were wildly invalid. Had the Davies Company not tried to answer the questions fully and honestly, had its accounting system not been the best in its industry, it might have avoided any criticism.[22]

The company tried to explain some of these points to the public in a full-page advertisement over Fox's signature published in the leading newspapers on Tuesday, July 17. Taking the 5.05-cents-a-pound "margin" as a rough working figure, Fox explained how 1.2 cents was the cost of manufacture and a further 2.9 cents the cost of transportation, insurance, and selling. On O'Connor's figures, the actual profit per pound on Davies bacon had been 0.95 cents, less than a penny a pound. Davies' own figures for the year ending March 27, 1917, showed profits of 0.67 cents per pound on all meats, 1.04 cents on butter and cheese, 1.04 cents per dozen on eggs, just under half a cent per tin on canned goods. The average purchase in its retail stores was 35 cents, on which the profit was 0.62 cents. Total profit on sales had been 3.45 per cent before tax, an estimated 1.69 per cent after tax. The "margin" had increased from an alleged 3.47 cents per pound to 5.05 cents because of higher ocean-freight rates and war-risk insurance.

The company offered to cooperate fully in another investigation. It "has not now—nor at any time during the fifty years of its operation—anything to conceal in method or practice of carrying on its business," Fox stated. "It does, however, claim the right to conduct its export business without abusive comment from Government civil servants — especially when the conclusions drawn from the data asked for are improper and false." After mentioning the 1916 offer to work for the British government at fixed returns, he concluded,

If the passing out of existence of a corporation such as the William Davies Company, or if nationalization of packing houses would materially and permanently reduce food prices, then in view of the present world tragedy it ought to be consummated without delay. The fact of the matter is, however, that with millions of people in Europe turning from producers into consumers because of war, and the tremendous destruction of food products incident to war, there is no remedy for the high prices of food while such conditions last, except the remedy of thrift and increase of production.[23]

To Flavelle's friends the ad seemed a conclusive answer to the O'Connor report. Rundle and Fred Southam urged him to have it published across the country. Flavelle worried about the expense, but then decided to go on, "striking this thing hard now that we have committed ourselves to it." The ad was published in every newspaper and magazine, English and French, in Canada.

Readers were not impressed. Why take the word of a self-interested private company over the report of an officially commissioned, reputable government investigator with no axe to grind? It was all very complicated, but surely something was fishy in the bacon business when that 5.05 cents got magically turned into only 0.67 cents. Then again, even on Fox's figures (take 0.67 and multiply it more than a hundred million times) the William Davies Company seemed to have been making a lot of money out of the war, well over a million dollars in 1916 alone. It hadn't made anything like this in peacetime. Why should any company be allowed to make a fortune in war, especially through dealing in the necessities of life? What about the head of the company, the new baronet, so visible in public life, so pious and oh-so-moral, who had told everybody else that profits should go to hell? What about practising what he was preaching? Why not? The Methodist Church's own journal, the *Christian Guardian*, spoke directly to Flavelle: "There is a feeling abroad in Canada today . . . which declares without any circumlocution that the man or the corporation which comes out of this war richer than when they went into it have missed a magnificent opportunity and have failed to exhibit true patriotism."[24]

Public feeling about food profits and prices was intense. Journalists and MP's remarked publicly and privately that they had never seen such anger. The man on the street and at his breakfast table had been grumbling for months about food prices, sure that someone was raking in money somewhere. Now he knew who. It was the packers' trust, led by the hypocrite millionaire Flavelle. "A great big hypocrite," according to J. C. Watters, president of the Trades and Labor Congress; a "blatant" hypocrite who should have his title withdrawn, according to Toronto labour leader Jimmy Simpson. A Conservative MP urged Borden to be doubly careful handling the question: "having been engaged in recording Canadian political events for the past quarter century I can truly say that I never before met with such wide spread *rage* over any other scandal."[25]

Why buy from the profiteers? The public spontaneously boycotted William Davies retail stores. Even Davies' wholesale customers demanded that Davies products arrive in unmarked trucks so they would not be seen to be dealing with the food trust.[26]

In Ottawa the Liberals tried to direct some of the public's rage against the government. Why was it appointing a commission to investigate a Commissioner? Maybe to apply a coat of whitewash? What qualifications did George Henderson, K.C., have for heading up the new commission? His experience defending J. Wesley Allison, another profiteer, at the Shell Commission a year or so ago? Why weren't workers or consumers going to be represented on the commission? Why hadn't the government done something about food prices two years ago when the Liberals first asked for price control? Why weren't they doing something about the O'Connor report now? Was there something special about Sir Joseph Flavelle, say his utility as a supplier of Conservative campaign funds, that let him off O'Connor's hook?

What about Flavelle's job as head of the IMB? George Kyte, a Liberal backbencher who specialized in sniffing out corruption, wondered aloud how the Davies Company got shipping space for so much bacon. It was said that Davies bacon was going to England on ships carrying the IMB's munitions. He had no authority for the rumour, Kyte told the House, but the Davies Company could always deny it. Superb character assassination: since February the War Office had taken its bacon delivered at seaboard and the Ministry of Shipping had allocated space to get it across. Some bacon probably did go on munitions ships. All Flavelle could do was deny using influence. Since this was not a denial of his allegation, Kyte refused to withdraw it.

W. F. O'Connor said nothing in public. At Crothers' request he wrote a supplement to his report blaming the press for misinterpreting it and the Davies Company for not having filled in the questionnaire properly. He had asked them about overhead and shipping costs and they had not given him the figures. Their accounting had been so bad that, yes, a new investigation was obviously necessary. He would not retract the charge of profiteering. Profits of well over a million dollars in wartime were obviously excessive, a bad example, and inconsistent with a spirit of sacrifice and service. "These are not the times for money making, and I can see good cause and good reason for so urging."[27]

Explaining the need for a second inquiry to the House of Commons, Crothers stressed the company's failure to give O'Connor complete cost figures. The implication of having withheld information (only to produce it in their advertisement) became another item in the popular indictment of the Davies Company. Why the deceit? What were they hiding?

The bacon scandal was prime fare for editorial writers. The *Globe* was glad to see that the O'Connor report had generated too much heat to be put in cold storage. The *Star* thought the order of Baronets needed to be supplemented by a class for Baconets; the Ottawa *Citizen* accused the packers of having hogged everything but the squeal. The Regina *Leader*, one of the most bitter Liberal papers, wrote of "price hogs" and the need to treat profiteers as traitors. The *Edmonton Bulletin* commented on a certain profiteer's idea "that the public should fast while he preys."

The harshest attacks were in *Saturday Night*, the Toronto weekly which had criticized the IMB early in 1916. Then it had written of Flavelle's incompetence and the need for a Canadian Ministry of Munitions. Now it demanded the immediate resignation of a man charged with "the most sordid and despicable trafficking, namely, the accumulation of great wealth out of the blood and agony of those who fight in the trenches and of their women and children who are now living scantily on the pittance of a soldier's pay." Accusing the company of trying to buy publicity, *Saturday Night* refused to print the Davies ad (or summarize it as news), and announced in advance that any finding in Flavelle's favour by the Henderson Commission would be disbelieved.[28]

Saturday Night's leading political columnist was H. M. Gadsby, who specialized in inside dope, superb invective, and passionate hatred of Christian "Uplifters" like Newton Rowell ("the little tin Jesus"), Joe Atkinson ("a human catfish"), and Joe Flavelle.* Gadsby's "Joseph Discovered by His Brethren" in the August 18 *Saturday Night* was an elaborate retelling of Joseph's monopoly of Egypt's food supply and his being caught out. The modern Sir Joseph was

. . . known far and wide as a righteous man, who went about sighing because there were not more commandments to keep. . . . No one suspected for a moment that he would over.look the most important commandment of all—the eleventh commandment—thou shalt not be found out. . . .

Sir Joseph has denied everything. Wherever public opinion showed a sore spot Sir Joseph plastered it with a page advertisement in a daily newspaper. . . . If Sir Joseph had used one more column he would have proved that he was giving his bacon away, and that we actually owed him money for it. . . . For fifty-two cents a pound Sir Joseph ought to stamp every rasher with his coat-of-arms. . . .

Over at the Munitions Board they express anxiety about the dear man's health, and wonder if nothing can be done to stop these coarse allusions in the press. Ridicule, too, is bad for Sir Joseph—he withers under it like a flower in the noonday sun. A chastened Sir Joseph pervades the lobby of the Chateau Laurier. No longer does he shake hands moistly with the visiting brethren. No longer does he stroke one's coat

---

* He also disliked modern art. In 1913 Gadsby had coined the term, "Hot Mush School," to describe early Group of Seven works.

and breathe moral reform in one's face. . . . Never have I seen so bedraggled a martyr as Sir Joseph. . . .

They've all got their eyes on Sir Joseph. Even the Chateau Laurier orchestra senses the change. Formerly when Sir Joseph strolled along Peacock Alley it would play "He's the Lily of the Valley, the Bright and Morning Star." Now it plays "Old Black Joe."

Old Black Joe's mood actually swung between anger and calm acceptance. After the first few days he tried to stop reading the critical editorials, many of which came to him in the mail anonymously. "I will not pretend that I do not care," he wrote one of the company's officers, "because I do care a great deal. On the other hand, there are the daily duties to be performed and I mean to go on discharging them to the best of my ability." To Clara, who was terribly upset at what was being done to him, he noted that the public was even angrier at him than at the company. "This is a new experience. Why should I be exempt from what better men have suffered? I am not lowering my colours to anyone, but am doing my work day by day and neither making nor seeking explanation. . . . What trouble we would be in if the charge were true. I am thankful, so thankful, to be without a shadow of reproach in myself. I am often wrong, but not in this."[29]

He could not easily understand being singled out for vilification by the newspapers and politicians. He considered O'Connor an incompetent place-hunter, who should never have been given important responsibilities. Crothers' release of the report and the use of it by the press, especially Liberal newspapers, seemed to Flavelle and his friends an obvious political ploy. Perhaps it was retaliation against the apolitical IMB; perhaps it was a campaign to destroy a leading supporter and possible member of a National Government; perhaps it was both. "It has been decreed that your father is to be killed politically," Joe wrote his daughter, "hence the punishment in the press and the publicity widely spread that I am a vulgar profiteer while professing virtue. The attacks have been singularly violent — result — exit Flavelle as a political possibility — Poor people, if they only could have believed that not only did I not plan political recognition, but that they could not have dragged me into it with a pair of horses."[30]

He considered attempting to cut off some of the criticism by taking action for libel. He had a clear case in law when the *Globe* published a Liberal riding association's charge that the IMB purchased millions' worth of supplies from companies Flavelle controlled. But it would have to be a jury trial, and his lawyer warned "that in view of the attitude of the local public in Toronto and vicinity, from whom the jury would be drawn, it would be impossible to count upon a fair trial by jury." Either that, or the *Globe* would use a formal retraction as a text for a further attack. Rather than get into the courts or any kind of prolonged public dialogue, Flavelle decided to put his case once and for all before the Henderson Commission.[31]

In the meantime he carried on at the IMB, where the financial crisis was disrupting everything. He was under more strain than he had ever faced, and perhaps Gadsby was right in mentioning fears for his health. Many of his friends — Rundle, Gordon, Brand, Newton Rowell, Flora Eaton, P. C. Larkin, and others—rallied to his support with notes and calls; the Governor General, the Duke of Devonshire, made a point of inviting him to lunch and assuring him that he, Devonshire, knew the stories were untrue. There were a few fine days at the Point with Clara, the Milners, the McLeans, good fishing, and long Sunday walks (and all-night train rides getting there and back). And there was his faith to take him outside himself:

I read such an exhilarating chapter in a little book this morning on the joy of Jesus in life. His joy in service, His joy to do His Father's will, His joy in bringing help to others and His joy in bearing burdens. These weeks find me too full of myself, too concerned in what is being said of me, too much troubled because much that is said is untrue. It is of you dear, of our children, of those who are outside in the great world of suffering and Pain, it is of these I should think, not of myself.[32]

VI

A. G. Brodie of Price, Waterhouse and Company, and G. T. Clarkson of Clarkson, Gordon, and Dilworth, were the expert accountants appointed to the investigating commission chaired by Henderson. By the end of July teams of auditors from their firms were poring over Davies' and Matthews – Blackwell's records back to 1913. Fox was distressed at the way they descended on his office, determined not to talk with anyone, determined to apply their preconceived notions of accounting to the company's unusual business. "I must confess a terrible disappointment at the mental calibre of these chaps," he told Flavelle. "The head auditor today asked me 'if smoking bacon was not the same as curing it' . . . it was Brodie who challenged our big hog clearance sheet and stated that everything should be at the same cost because it did not cost us any more to make a belly than it did a foot."

Flavelle urged his manager to be patient. "Remember if they should get a wrong view of the business, nothing would save the reputation of the business or the officers connected with it, if the auditors make an adverse report, or if they fail to support our view of the transaction."[33] Knowing it would take them forever to recast the company's accounts their way, Fox waited until the auditors gave up and came to him to talk it over. They finally accepted the Davies system and worked from there. It took fifteen to twenty auditors about six weeks to complete their study.

Young, idealistic, and dedicated to his business, E. C. Fox was deeply disillusioned at what was happening to the company. He alternated between anxiety at the prospect of being cross-examined on a witness stand and determination to fight the issue out. "It has been a pretty big shock to my beliefs in democracy and the relationships that should exist between men." Flavelle reassured him every few days:

We would be in genuine trouble if we were in the wrong. At bottom there is no real trouble when we know we are right. It is disagreeable and unpleasant for one's self and particularly for one's friends; the scar can never be wholly removed as far as the public is concerned. The knowledge, however, that we know there is no part of the business which cannot be examined to the bottom, and that we have been guilty of no misconduct either in commercial ethics or commercial morality, is the thing that will abide.[34]

Fox was specially puzzled by the accusation that they had withheld information from O'Connor. He had his treasurer and accountant check the records and sent Flavelle copies of all the correspondence. On August 2 he wrote Flavelle that Crothers' statement to the House was "an absolute lie: there is no correspondence nor conversations that directly or indirectly bear upon this; there has been no asking or suggestion, or any inquiry that would hint at anything whatsoever other than the sheets that were submitted, which merely ask for—costs and selling prices. I hope I cannot make this too clear to you, for we are being maligned. . . ."

Four days later he had two sheepish company executives in his office. In checking the copies of the questionnaire, they had looked at only one side of the sheet—"the reverse side, which was supposed to be a re-cap, had a small column for 'storage, delivery and overhead charges,' and, in typewriting the re-cap in, the columns were so small the figures pretty well overlapped into the other column—and it got missed." A silly error, which probably would not have changed O'Connor's use of "margin," though it might have meliorated his conclusions, had got the company accused of withholding information. Flavelle thought Fox was marvellously restrained in so coolly describing this "inexcusable blunder."[35]

How about seizing the initiative, Fox wondered, by offering the Davies plant to the Canadian government for the duration of the war on the basis of a specified return to the shareholders? It might be both morally right and economically sound. Flavelle rejected the proposal; it would be seen as "an act of weakness, in which, having been soundly hammered, we undertake to do now what we should have done before." His inclination, pending the formal hearings, was "to adopt the advice of Mother Cottontail to the little rabbit: 'Lie low and say nothing.' "[36]

VII

Clara senior came to Ottawa in September. They had a lovely week, breakfasting in their room at the Château and always finding time for lunch together. They tried not to talk much about the investigation, but it kept cropping up.

The Patriotic Hog

Fair ladies, lords and gentles, here's a line
Which blushes not to eulogize the swine:
The "Ex" or "Fair" displays the varied charms,
Which brains and beauty cultivate on farms;
Of all attractions in the catalog,
There's none to match the patriotic hog.

Why titter at this unpoetic theme?
Just saunter thru the pens to muse and dream.
See all these porkers, happy, full, content,
Who snore and grunt in pious ravishment; . . .

He swallows all the food that he can hold—
When presto! change! the meal is turned to gold;
No doubt his pride will swell when he has found
That bacon sells for fifty cents a pound.

What was the argument we tried to chew?
Oh, yes—as patriots, hogs to trough are true;
Their country needs their pork, their death is dure,
And nabobs wait, their sides and hams to cure;
In short, they shame our mouthey demagogs,
And are, par excellence, real titled hogs.

William Henry Taylor,
Toronto World, Sept. 6, 1917.

"Here I am in a very important position, going up to be tried as a drunken man or a felon might be—yes it bites deep," Joe said to her one day. If only the truth could get out, Clara thought, there would be no harm. "But for a man as full of integrity and good service as Father is, to be dragged through the mire in this form, is really asking a man to bear a good deal."[37]

By mid-September Flavelle was deeply pessimistic. There would be a minute investigation of the company's business—not just by the commission and its counsel, but also by a lawyer for *Saturday Night*, Gordon Waldron. Waldron, a very partisan Liberal, had been the author of many of the attacks on the packing trust back in 1906, and had bitterly attacked Flavelle in the 1911 election. For no obvious reason, except perhaps to blunt accusations of a whitewash, Henderson had accorded him semi-official status at the hearings. Flavelle assured his family that he had nothing to hide, nothing to fear from any question about anything his company had ever done: "Through all these days of bitter attack my heart has sung the one song— There has been no wrong." But now he was certain that whatever he and Fox tried to say would be misunderstood—"some reference to dividends, some catch phrase, will set the public and newspapers going again. . . . Every household where bacon is used finds in this wickedness of the Davies Company the reason for the dreadful price of bacon. They do not understand. . . ."[38]

The hearing opened in the Council Chamber of Toronto's City Hall on September 17. It was even worse than Flavelle expected. The auditors submitted all the details of the company's ownership, sales, profits, dividends, and holdings in other businesses. Testifying for the company, Fox spent hours in the first two days trying to explain why certain write-offs in 1916 and 1917 for depreciation and bad investments were justifiable charges against profits rather than attempts to evade war taxes. Waldron accused him of trying to suppress information. Henderson found it hard to believe that

349

Davies and Harris Abattoir, each company owning shares in the other, could be fierce competitors. On the third day the public learned of the no-loss agreement with the War Office, learned how Davies had been selling bacon for six months in 1916 on a no-risk basis.

As the third day's hearing was concluding, to be followed by a three-week adjournment so the accountants could finish their work, Henderson started asking Fox unusual questions about how the company cured its bacon. Did it use a "post-curing" process? What was the aim of that post-cure? Had Fox ever instructed his officers to have War Office bacon post-cured?

"Not to my knowledge."

"I would suggest that you make a very careful investigation and go over your correspondence carefully. . . . You know we want to be perfectly fair to you."

The *Globe* headed that day's story, "Bacon Given Extra Weight by Post-Curing."[39]

In June an employee in the Montreal factory, John Wardle, had written Lloyd George charging that the War Office was being defrauded on Davies bacon because it was being kept an extra fourteen days in salt water to gain more weight. Wardle thought this was "Trickery and nothing else but Daylight Robbery and Fraud," compounded by most of the company's shipments being underweight when they arrived in England. Writing again after the O'Connor report, Wardle offered to quit the company and expose it if Lloyd George would pay him $35 a week. To prepare for the exposure he took certain letters from the company's files.[40]

Lloyd George's office passed Wardle's letters to Sir Robert Borden's office. Without telling Flavelle or the Davies Company about the new charges, Borden or one of his secretaries passed the letters on to Henderson. His questions about the post-cure took Fox completely by surprise. Henderson's investigators then decided to examine all the company's correspondence about its export trade, the thousands of letters and cables between Montreal, Toronto, and London. When the hearings resumed in October the company would be on trial not only for profiteering, but also for selling salt and water to the military as part of a Wiltshire side—giving both the product and the purchaser an extra soaking.

The revelations of the first three days had been damning enough for most people. Here was a company that had been making eighty- or ninety-percent profit on its capital during the war (maybe a little less if it could get away with its tricky write-offs). Through dividends, Sir Joseph had been getting a "wage" of $53.00 an hour from pork-packing in 1917. Canada's fighting men were paid $1.10 a day. Flavelle was "The Baron," making millions out of poor Canadians. A Conservative returned soldier suggested he would be dealt with by the men when they came home from the trenches; a Liberal paper commented that profiteers should face a firing squad. In his widely circulated column, H. M. Gadsby wrote about Flavelle's "pernicious activities . . . pious Sir Joseph, who deplores everybody's profits but his own . . . associated with hogs so long that he caught some of their manners . . . long known as one who had all his feet in the trough at once. . . . him and his Toronto group of looters." Red Cross canvassers in Toronto were told time and time again that the profiteers should pay, not the public.

Even the Ottawa *Citizen*, a Southam paper friendly to Flavelle and the IMB, called the profiteering policy which had made him a war millionaire "barbarous," and could only excuse him as the scapegoat of a rotten system generally. It was a final, stunning blow to learn that one of his superiors, Lord Northcliffe, chairman of the British War Mission to the United States, had remarked in August that Flavelle would have to resign if the scandal got worse. Then Northcliffe's comments on a visit to Toronto were paraphrased to Flavelle as, "I can tell you how we deal with profiteers in England, we lock them up, no matter how high their position may be."[41]

Now he considered resigning. He wrote Brand on September 28 asking advice. Despite the traditions of the William Davies Company, despite its reputation for integrity and aloofness from the trade, despite his willingness to have the company's business honestly examined, there was no hope of vindication at the next round of hearings. He had seen the letters Wardle had stolen and knew the sillier statements in them would be lifted out of context. It was inevitable that hostile investigators would find other phrases and expressions to use against the company. Flavelle wanted to be free to reply and wanted to relieve the Ministry of Munitions from criticism for keeping him on. On the other hand he hated the thought of giving in to what he was sure was a campaign orchestrated by a group of "political thugs":

The political machines on both sides—and particularly the Government side—desire this very thing to happen, and it is for this purpose the campaign is designed.

You are to remember that this effort to discredit me has support from more or less influential members of the Government Party, including men of Cabinet rank. They chafe under conditions in which our work is carried on: We are spending huge sums

351

of money—no inconsiderable portion of it Canadian money; we are of no assistance to them politically; we have refused to recognize the claims of patronage on us; we have carried on the business independently with the object of securing efficient service. They do not claim that we have been unfriendly to the Government—one of the reasons for their anger is that they have been unable to locate anything definite against us. . . .

If I met these conditions in my private life, in business or financial circles, the course would be clear. I should look for and receive, the support of my associates against the whole pack of clamouring wolves. I am, however, in a position of public trust. I have no previous experience to guide me, and I am perplexed as to my course.[42]

Brand would not hear of his resignation. He was convinced of Flavelle's innocence and enraged at "the foul newspapers and still fouler men" pursuing the IMB's Chairman. He, Hichens, and Perry would all defend him at the Ministry if necessary. Brand was also ready to speak out in Canada on Flavelle's behalf and poured scorn on Borden and White for not coming to his defence. A few days after Flavelle proposed to resign, Brand, Gordon, Lord Northcliffe, and Lord Reading were in Ottawa to talk him out of it. Northcliffe's misunderstanding had been cleared up.*[43] Flavelle agreed to stay on at least until the Henderson Commission reported. No one in Ottawa knew he had gone through this anguished consideration, he wrote his daughter, "I cannot allow anyone to see that the thing hurts. . . . I carry on as though twas all Sunshine."[44]

VIII

The hearings resumed on October 11. Flavelle came to Toronto to be with Fox, who was on the verge of a nervous breakdown. After each day's testimony a doctor put him to bed with an opiate. Worrying about Joe had also driven Clara Flavelle to the brink of collapse.[45]

---

* Northcliffe may have thought Flavelle was using his position as an employee of the Ministry to make big profits on bacon contracts with the War Office. According to Brand, some people did think that Flavelle should not have been connected with a company taking contracts from a government he was serving. Brand's counter-arguments were: (1) there were no connections between munitions and meat; (2) many of the businessmen working for the Ministry of Munitions were far more vulnerable than Flavelle, having a more direct conflict of interest; (3) strict application of the principle would mean that "business in war time must plainly come to a stop."

It took two days of testimony by Fox plus a tough cross-examination of Wardle to clear up the post-cure confusion. Since introducing its "new cure" in 1902, the Davies Company had been able to get bacon to England almost twice as quickly as any other packer, Canadian or American. But it had to be shipped and sold quickly for smoking. By 1917 transportation conditions were too uncertain to continue with the rapid, light curing of the bacon; some of it had to be "post-cured" to preserve it longer. Use of the post-cure simply meant that the company reverted to the normal curing methods and times used by other packers. Davies bacon did gain weight in the post-cure, but no more than and possibly not as much as any other packer's bacon. Every purchaser knew there was a weight gain in curing, just as there was a weight loss between killing and curing. It was impossible to ship underweight bacon because the boxes were weighed on arrival and short-weights debited from the purchase price.

This was made clear in the commission's final report, which was not widely read. As Flavelle had expected, the press was most interested in statements taken out of context ("this will mean many dollars to us" in a letter ordering more post-curing — an obvious reference to losses if lightly cured bacon deteriorated), and Wardle's hearsay statements ("take care of your pickle, it is worth from 25 to 28 cents a pound . . . the British government know no better than to pay that price for salt water"), which were denied under oath by the people alleged to have made them. The public and press were also curious to know why Canadian bacon cost more in Toronto than it did in England (the answer was greater retail volume and lower retail costs in Britain), and were disconcerted when a leading retail merchant announced that in preparing to testify before the commission he had realized he was selling bacon at a loss — he was going to raise his price to sixty cents a pound![46] The most avid readers of the post-cure testimony were probably Flavelle's competitors, learning for the first time about one of the most advanced curing methods in North America (later, in the final report, they also learned a lot about accounting).

J. T. Matthews spent two days defending Matthews – Blackwell's profits —large, but not so large as Davies' —and defending both companies from charges of collusion in their buying. Even when he had wanted to talk prices with Fox, he testified, Fox had refused. Matthews used considerable patience in convincing Chairman Henderson that it was a natural economic process, not exploitation of the consumer, for British demand to drive up the price of bacon in Canada. Fox was back on the stand the next day going cable by cable through the origins of the minimum/market price agreement with Denny. Certain facts—it had been a no-loss proposition for Davies; no other packer enjoyed such a deal—stood out like two sore thumbs.[47]

Watching his wife, his manager, his company's reputation, and his own good name all collapse, Flavelle saw the investigation as "indescribably cruel." Then he thought about his bitterness and decided it was unworthy. There was a war on.

There is sorrow and sacrifice and anxiety and loss everywhere. Men and women are torn and bleeding and asking How long, Oh Lord, how long? . . . Why should I fail or complain or be cheaply heroic? Is injustice, and wrong and cruelty, which bring their blighting influence upon ten times ten thousand of homes, innocent of any wrong doing or conduct, to miss me who have had a return in profit as well as loss in this dread business? Down deep somewhere in my subconscious feelings, I have a hint, that to the worthy man there may come the experience "In the fellowship of His Sufferings"—I can make no such claim. In His presence I can but cry with bowed head and heart "unclean," "unclean"—but if I might follow afar off unseen and unknown I might know the blessing.[48]

IX

On Saturday, October 20, His Lardship, the Bacon Baron, finally took the stand. A columnist went down to City Hall expecting to see "a bull-necked gentleman with a purple face, a plaid vest, a diamond stick-pin, and a permanent hole in the corner of his mouth where he stuck his cigar." Instead he found a mild-mannered old gentleman dressed in a grey coat, a semi-clerical collar, and a black bow-tie, who talked for hours in a monotone while fingering the Bible on which he had taken his oath. "Who ever heard of a millionaire pork-packer looking like a rural dean at a church picnic?" The scene in the Council Chamber seemed more like a prayer meeting than a showdown with the pork trust. Even the reporters looked subdued and reverent.

Flavelle had asked the Prime Minister to intercede with Henderson so his own lawyer could examine him first. After all the attacks and the latitude both Waldron (who never should have been there at all) and the commission's counsel had enjoyed, Flavelle thought it only fair to let him state his case before being cross-examined. "We are not criminals or cheats, or frauds.

We have been decent people minding our own business." Borden went along with the request.[49]

It was pretty dull all morning, as Flavelle droned on over familiar ground. The write-offs were legitimate, there had been no IMB influence used in securing contracts, there had never been any collusion with other packers, and so on. The Denny agreement was "a perfectly natural transaction" under the circumstances. Consider the after-tax profits this way: if they were all given back, the farmer could get an extra one-eighth of a cent per pound for his hogs, the consumer a rebate of one-sixth of a cent per pound on his bacon. If the farmer got nothing extra, bacon could sell for two-fifths of a cent less per pound.

He wanted to answer the charge that he had consigned everyone's profits except his own to a dreadful place. He explained the context of the December outburst. "And, sir, I would say just the same today if it became a question as to whether a manufacturer would carry on his obligation to complete his munitions in accordance with his contract, or whether he would hesitate to make the necessary expenditure because he hesitated about the profits that he had." Canada should thank the munitions manufacturers for the courage and resourcefulness with which they had developed the business. "In place of the Chairman of the Munitions Board believing the manufacturers of Canada should not have a profit on the production of munitions, he has sincerely and earnestly believed from the first that it was a proper and natural thing, and if they did not make a profit they could not have the courage to put in the necessary plant, and the munitions could not be produced." He concluded by saying publicly what he had been saying privately for months: no transaction in the twenty-five-year history of the company could embarrass him.

After lunch he sparred briefly with the commission's counsel, James Bain, about whether the 1916 profits had been greater or less than in 1917.

"Even at that they were very large?" Bain asked.

"Very."

"Beyond the dreams of the ordinary person, anyway?"

"They are very large profits. You must not forget—"

Bain interrupted—"And greater still, Sir Joseph, in 1917, and I am wondering if—"

Flavelle interrupted—"If I had any qualms of conscience?"

"I will put it that way if you want me to."

"None whatever."

Gordon Waldron took him back through all the suspicious details, trying to cast them in the worst light, until he got rebuked by Henderson. How much richer had Flavelle become during the war? He did not know exactly because he did not know the market value of his investments. "I am poorer than I was before the war if you use the word poorer in a sense of a disbursement of money." He disclosed his holdings in Simpson's, National Trust, and the Commerce. "I have not anything to conceal in the world" was his last comment on the witness stand.[50]

X

The Henderson report was released in late November. It was only twenty-seven pages long, much of it an account of Davies' methods of determining costs and profits. There was no monopoly among the packers; indeed their aggressive competition for hogs to meet wartime demand had driven up prices. The Denny contract enjoyed by Davies was unique, but it was a "business negotiation influenced only by business considerations," having nothing to do with Flavelle's public position. Davies and Matthews—Blackwell had made exceptionally high profits during the war because of an extraordinary expansion of volume plus a higher percentage of profits on sales. As well, consumer taste during the war had moved further towards choicer cuts of meat, such as bacon, lessening packers' returns on other cuts and so forcing up the prices of those in greatest demand.

Some $270,000 of Davies' write-offs against profits were ruled out on strict accounting principles and disregarded by the commission's accountants — the practice itself was commended as "evidence of good business judgment" (as usual, Flavelle's organization was anticipating losses that other companies had not thought of facing). O'Connor's concept of "margin" was ignored as the auditors restated Davies' profits in several different ways: on sales (excluding retail operations) the company had made 2.87-per-cent profit in the year ending March 1915, 5.32 per cent the next year, and 3.99 per cent the next. Retail-store profits averaged about 3 per cent on sales. The profit on pork products sold in Canada had been 0.62 cents per pound in 1916 and 0.37 cents in 1917; on Canadian bacon exported to England 1.19 and 0.90 cents; on American bacon exported to England 2.37 and 1.58 cents; and so on. As a return on capital, after deducting interest on borrowed money, profits had been 43.32 per cent in 1915, 80.02 per cent in 1916, and 57.48 per cent in 1917. These, of course, became the damning figures.[51]

Flavelle saw the report as vindication:

. . . it seems to me an astonishing thing that I should have been scarified over the Continent and our Company called every bad name, when after these weeks of bitterness the report can only say we made a great deal of money out of a small return upon a big turnover. I do not know what fresh bitter thing the papers will say to save their face, hence I am not sure what will occur, but this much is plain, no breath of wrong conduct is suggested.[52]

Outside the business world, which understood the notion of turning over capital to accumulate big returns (the *Financial Post* supported the Davies Company throughout the affair), almost no one shared Flavelle's views. There were those who always believed the worst about the company and the sanctimonious baronet. The transformation of the post-cure issue into a spoiled-meat myth which lasted for generations is a remarkable example of wartime hysteria reinforcing everyman's suspicion of wealth, delight at exposing hypocrisy, and fear of being poisoned. Perhaps, too, the myth was perpetuated by veterans' remembrance that meals eaten in a world of corpses were nauseating.

The more interesting disagreement with Flavelle's position was that voiced by those who accepted his view of the company's integrity, agreed that he had done excellent work at the IMB without conflict of interest, and profoundly shared his attitude to the war. After all the confusion and distortion had been cleared up, the salt-and-water story exploded, the Denny contract explained, the "margins" understood, and so on, there remained the "great deal of money" out of a small return upon a big turnover.* Eighty-per-cent return on investment in one year, fifty-seven per cent the next. Should Flavelle have had no qualms of conscience about earnings like these?

Where was the courage in risking money to make more money at a time when soldiers were risking and losing their lives at $1.10 a day? Surely it was wrong to believe that normal commercial ethics — honest profit-making, business as usual — were good enough. Real business service in war would disregard profit and loss. Real patriots would not be enriched by the war, except spiritually. Flavelle had appeared to send munitions profits to hell—

---

* Or, as the *Mail and Empire* put it, "It has been made plain the bacon profits were not those of the speculator; they were built up by the little rake-off on every rasher."

357

where they did belong in wartime—but his own company had done nothing to limit its own profits. To several commentators Flavelle seemed to represent "the spirit of modern commercialism," a spirit profoundly out of touch with the suffering and sorrow and longing for a better future of a people at war. If Flavelle *had not* meant what he seemed to say in his "To Hell with Profits" speech, it was too bad, for he had seemed to be challenging business to rise to a higher morality. If he *had* meant what he said, he had failed to live up to his own standards. In an editorial on the Monday after his testimony, the Toronto *Telegram* summed up this widespread feeling:

The evidence of Sir Joseph Flavelle is appalling in its revelation of Sir Joseph's inability to recognize that the ordinary standards of commercial prudence and business integrity are superseded by other and higher standards in wartime.

Sir Joseph is described as a hypocrite and arch-conspirator against the public welfare. Sir Joseph Flavelle is neither a hypocrite nor a conspirator. Conscience dictates all the paths in which Sir Joseph Flavelle travels. Conscience divorced from the power of self-criticism is worth nothing as the governor of conduct. . . .

Sir Joseph Flavelle does not under-estimate the services of [the William Davies Company]. Nor does Sir Joseph over-estimate these services. Sir Joseph does underestimate the truth that in these times the mother who offers her son, the wife who offers her husband, the boy or man who offers his life does not get a war profit on the volume of his exertions in defence of liberty. . . .

Sir Joseph Flavelle did not fail in his duty to the Imperial Munitions Board. The work of Sir Joseph in the chairmanship of the Munitions Board was of enormous national value. Sir Joseph Flavelle failed in his duty to his country. All that was asked of Sir Joseph Flavelle was to lay the treasures of business efficiency on the altar of his country. The worst that could happen to Sir Joseph was to carry his business through the years of war with no greater profit than the same business earned in peace.

The truth that Sir Joseph Flavelle cannot realize and does not understand is the truth recorded in the question that comes from the hearts of wives and mothers. WHY? WHY? WHY? should war restrict the earning power of our husbands and our sons to $1.10 a day, and that same war enlarge the earning power of Sir Joseph Flavelle, Bart., to $3000 per working day? The question that speaks in the eloquence of sacrifice was not silenced by the evidence of Sir Joseph Flavelle. . . . The ideals that Sir Joseph Flavelle accepts, the procedure that Sir Joseph follows, are honestly and sincerely followed. God forbid that Canada in war time should publicly accept such ideals or approve of such procedure![53]

Flavelle was too proud to reply. He did not believe that men should enrich themselves out of the war. He did believe in profit-and-loss accounting as a test of commercial efficiency. In free competition a company like his own made money because it offered better service than its competitors. Its profits were a legitimate return to the *company* for that service. After the war it was as certain as sunrise that there would be a fierce international competition for business, perhaps a terrible economic crisis. If Canadian business was going to weather that crisis, and maintain jobs and earnings for Canadians, Flavelle believed it had to have wartime profits to be reinvested in new plants and new ventures. It would be shortsighted in the extreme if Canada's postwar industrial capacity were "crippled" through the confiscation of profits.[54]

What *individuals* did with the money they made in war was another matter altogether. Flavelle had no objection to income taxes in war. In fact he had wanted White to act faster than he did to reduce consumer spending on non-essentials.[55] Critics went to the heart of the matter when they asked how much Flavelle had made personally during the war. At the Henderson inquiry he stated that in terms of cash income he was poorer than when the war began. He did not elaborate, nor was he asked to, but he was obviously referring to money he had given away. Later I describe his philanthropies in the 1920s and 1930s. Most of his papers for the years before 1920 were destroyed in a flood at the Davies Company. The "donations" listed on three surviving monthly statements of his assets and liabilities (June and October 1917, November 1918) total $70,106.[56] His average monthly income from dividends during the war was about $11,000. There is no doubt in my mind that he gave away more than he earned. On this point he could have satisfied his critics in 1917 by producing a list of donations since the war began. To do so would have been an intolerable blow to his pride, to his sense of propriety.

Perhaps he—or, at least, his company—was still vulnerable. Through the war the William Davies Company had brilliantly expanded its business without gouging anyone and without playing fast and loose with commercial ethics. All the charges against it, except the final criticism of its profits, were unfounded. Like other officers of the company, Edward Adie thought its contribution to the war effort was splendid: "our Company could not have done Britain a greater service than it has, if it had sent a brigade of men to the front, instead of the almost superhuman efforts it has made to supply them with Commissariat!"[57]

359

But always at a profit. And always in a business relationship. In the Flavelle—Fox business correspondence through 1915, 1916, and 1917, it is hard
to tell there is a war on, hard to find instances where the company wants to
do much more than work overtime for the sake of the war. Fox decided in
March 1916 to make volume "secondary to profit"; the company was not
ready to take extra risks to maintain supplies, not ready to go out into a
commercial No Man's Land. Similarly, there were no direct corporate donations to patriotic causes (nothing comparable to Simpson's $100,000
donation in 1914), only dividends and reinvestments to prepare for peace.
Flavelle did not want the war to cripple companies, but it crippled a lot of
men.

The critics sometimes seemed to want businesses to commit economic
suicide during the war, and perhaps there was no reason to expect the Davies
Company to behave suicidally. Soldiers at the front did not normally do
that. Some soldiers did win medals for bravery by taking unusual, some
times suicidal, risks. Superb industrial soldier that it could be, the William
Davies Company did not deserve medals for corporate bravery. Nor did
most Canadian businesses or most trade unions during the Great War.

XI

Three days after Flavelle's testimony, Winston Churchill, the Minister of
Munitions, cabled an expression of confidence and instructions to carry
on.[58] Flavelle no longer considered resigning. Several journalists and politicians thought he ought to resign, not least because he was a major political
liability to the Borden government.

It was now the Union Government, for Borden had finally put together a
coalition in October. It was to go to the people on December 17. The main
issue would be conscription, but the Liberals would try to capitalize on all of
the old government's sins. Before releasing Henderson's report the cabinet
had tried to defuze the profiteering issue by announcing strict limits on
packers' profits. Any earnings beyond eleven per cent on capital would be
taxed away. But there was still Sir Joseph Flavelle, Bart., the guilty profiteer,
clinging to office in Ottawa, still one of the most powerful men in Canada.
"Very strong feeling everywhere against Flavelle and urgent request that he
retire from Chairmanship of Munitions Board," Borden noted in his diary
on November 22. Three days later, after a conference with several ministers,

he recorded "great fear that Flavelle's retention in office will injure government" (though adding one opinion that Flavelle would not hurt them among the farmers, an obvious reflection of record hog prices).

The politicians wondered what to do about Flavelle. He told Willison that several editorials in the *Ottawa Journal* urging his resignation were planted by members of the government. "The word had gone forth that I was to be appealed to to get out of the way as I was an embarrassment to the government. They did not succeed in getting the member of the government who was to 'Bell the Cat' to do so, so chose the newspaper method." [59] Whether or not this was true, the Prime Minister did not choose the straightforward recourse of asking the British to dismiss Flavelle.

Although he understood why the man on the street hated him (along with the man in the trenches; a story is told of Canadian soldiers circulating a coat of arms for the new baronet showing him earnestly sucking the teats of a huge sow), Flavelle persisted in his belief that the agitation had been "set on foot" and supported by interested politicians, a number of them Conservatives. He was never precise in naming his enemies or their motives, veering between a notion that the old party machines were destroying him for having advocated a coalition government and the thought that he was a victim of a conspiracy of grafters and place-seekers, perhaps the old Hughes gang, who were striking back at the IMB.

He had annoyed so many people in Ottawa that his near-conspiracy theory was not implausible. Machine politicians in both parties hated the sanctimonious millionaire who had been condemning their methods for years and had openly called for a coalition. In those 1916 speeches he had also attacked French Canadians and caused serious trouble for Borden and White. Most Liberals, particularly Roman Catholics, had long distrusted the prominent Methodist Conservative who had been involved in their 1911 defeat. Their Ontario leader, Newton Rowell—a close friend of Flavelle's— had destroyed their party by going into the Union Government.

Gordon Waldron, *Saturday Night*'s counsel at the investigation, was a Laurier Liberal whose animosity to Flavelle went back a decade. H. M. Gadsby's acid pen was paid for by the Liberal party at $3,000 a year for his weekly syndicated column. When the Liberals split in October, Gadsby's attacks on Flavelle suddenly stopped because the Unionists offered him more money. [60] Some people thought Flavelle had bought him off. Flavelle in turn thought *Saturday Night*'s campaign was inspired by its proprietor, A. W. Gagnier, who had been bitterly offended in one of his business deals by the IMB. [61]

Saturday Night's record of trying to get Flavelle out of office seems to support this suspicion, as does the lavish publicity the journal gave to certain ship-building operations in British Columbia.

As for the rest — Flavelle's belief that Crothers was deliberately malevolent, his references to cabinet-level opposition, his claim that the PM's own secretary, A. E. Blount, had leaked the telegrams and the Flavelle – White conspiracy story in 1916 — there is no supporting evidence. The bacon scandal began in a tragicomedy of errors and ignorance. It might never have happened had O'Connor and his researchers known what they were doing, or had the Davies Company not been so honest, or had its officers read their questionnaires more carefully. Once it was out in the open it was sustained by the press and by Canadians' dislike of high prices, profiteers, and over-righteous millionaires. The politicians did not need to set Flavelle up as a scapegoat. Few of them were sorry to see him in that role.

XII

He would have been one of the most active Unionist supporters in the general election of 1917. The Union Government was the coalition, win-the-war, reform administration he had desperately wanted. All his business friends actively supported it. Flavelle probably gave money. He dared not offer a word of support, for he was one of the government's greatest liabilities. "Flavelle, pork, and profits" was a major side-issue to conscription in the campaign, as the Liberal rump tried to refocus public sentiment into an attack on greedy corporations and profiteers and plutocrats like Flavelle. They were resoundingly defeated, but no thanks to Flavelle. In the post-mortem a Toronto campaign worker reported that Flavelle had been the Union Government's greatest handicap.[62]

At last the critics seemed to have exhausted themselves. "Shall we close this chapter," he wrote his daughter on December 19, "it is all over except the unfortunate remembrance in every part of Canada that I am to be remembered after the war as a profiteer."[63]

CHAPTER FIFTEEN

SEEING IT THROUGH

September 1917. The war was literally bogged down in the mud of Passchendaele. The Russian front had collapsed. The French army had been destroyed as an offensive force. Britain was on the edge of bankruptcy. The Americans had not yet begun to fight. The Canadian people were bitterly divided over conscription and intensely angry at inflation and the activities of profiteers like Sir Joseph Flavelle. Munitions plants were beginning to close down—not because their products were not needed, but because no one had the money to pay for them. At the Imperial Munitions Board Flavelle spent his time pleading with financiers for more millions, calculating how to break contracts at the least cost in dollars and jobs, and, in the hours left over, fighting for the survival of his company and his reputation in the bacon scandal. "How I wish wish wish it was all over." [1]

I

There was no more British money to buy munitions in Canada. The Treasury had drawn the line and stood on it: not a shell was to be bought that could not be paid for from Canadian loans or dollars raised in the United States. The financing might have worked out on that basis: White could have kept on lending $25 million a month; the Americans would have allowed $15 million a month from their loans to Britain to be used to pay for IMB purchases in the United States, mostly of raw materials. By phasing out work on shells larger than six inches, an action which had already been anticipated, Flavelle could have gotten the IMB's monthly spending down to the $40 million level without disrupting the hundreds of plants at work on the smaller shells. Also, as some of the big shell manufacturers were starting to realize, it might have been worth sounding out Washington to see if the Americans, bound to need a lot of ammunition, might be interested in placing orders with well-equipped, experienced Canadian manufacturers.[2]

The trouble with this scheme was that it almost literally put guns before butter—or bacon or cheese. Great Britain had to have Canadian foodstuffs and could not pay for them either. If the $40 million was the upper limit for spending in Canada, most of it—as much as $30 million in some estimates—would have to be diverted from munitions to pay for food and other essential Canadian goods. For a few weeks in late August it looked as though the IMB would be cut back to a starvation ration of $10 to $15 million a month. To emphasize their predicament, on August 23 the British abruptly suspended all purchases of meat in Canada. It turned out to be only a temporary freeze, but it happened to add to Flavelle's personal troubles because the public interpreted it as a reaction to the bacon scandal.[3]

In earlier financial crises Flavelle had tended to agree with London's view that Canada ought to shoulder more of the burden. Now he inclined the other way—Canada did not have the liquid resources to do much more than maintain its proposed level of aid. If the Treasury's ukase were carried out there would be a Canadian liquidity crisis in attempting to finance the raw-materials exports, combined with an acute industrial crisis as the IMB closed down munitions factories. There would be political repercussions, too, if Canadians found out that Britain wouldn't spend a shilling in Canada and the Americans wouldn't lend a cent to be spent outside their country. How could the Borden government, which in August and September looked as though it would face a straight party fight, survive this revolutionary dislocation of the Canadian economy? No matter that Flavelle now felt Borden had failed and should resign. Britain's rigid position, dictated, he thought, by orthodox, apolitical Treasury officials, was indefensible and would greatly damage Canada's overall war effort.[4]

The negotiations, conferences, cables, and letters flowed on, battering against absolute deadlines for paying bills, placing orders, extending or cancelling contracts. No conclusions . . . no instructions . . . "drift" . . . "an impossible position" . . . "like the Hebrews of old, being asked to make bricks without straw" . . . all the while being pilloried across Canada as the Methodist bacon bandit.

By the end of September finances were finally worked out. The IMB would get upwards of $25 million a month from the $40-million pool. To live within its means it would severely trim the shell programme: no more 8-inch and 9.2-inch orders, no more fuzes, no more complete rounds; instead, just the shell bodies — 120,000 eighteen-pounders a week, 100,000 4.5-inch, 140,000 6-inch. For want of money Canada's munitions industry was being crippled—cut to less than half its capacity—just as it had come of age. The shipbuilding, aviation, and explosives programmes, however, were not cut back. And, in a typical war paradox, an urgent new programme had to be mounted in British Columbia to procure supplies of spruce for aeroplane manufacture.

The axe fell at the right time in one crucial way. Just beginning to mount their war effort, the Americans were about to spend billions on munitions. They appeared to be offering characteristically generous prices. Could Canadian manufacturers, with fully amortized plants and two or three years' experience making munitions, tender for some of the American business? If that ran afoul of Congress's interest in America-first purchasing policies, there was at least a sellers' market in machinery. A machining or forging plant could be sold as a unit, shipped across the border, and reassembled. The Canadian manufacturer who had already written off his plant could make a fine windfall profit selling out to Americans. Or, if he could get a contract to manufacture in the United States, he could simply move his equipment south and become an American manufacturer himself. By October 1917, a number of Canadian manufacturers had sold out or moved, others were flocking to Washington hunting for orders, and Americans were flocking to Canada hunting for plants to buy.[5]

At the IMB there were mixed feelings about this tilting of the munitions axis from an imperial toward a continental orientation. It would be all right for Canadians to take American business, so long as it did not interfere with the remaining British contracts. But the thought of Canadian capacity literally emigrating to the United States was another matter: British orders had paid for these plants; surely they should be kept in Canada as insurance against some new desperate need for more shells. Flavelle countered the lure of American money by having Ottawa pass an order-in-council forbidding the export of munitions plants or machinery without a licence. He also sent Carnegie and James Wood to Washington to see if the IMB could play a role in procuring and administering American orders in Canada. Perhaps the IMB could act as a Canadian agent for the U.S. Ordnance Department in much the same way as it acted for the British Ministry, and so coordinate the flow of business from both Allies.

The American purchasers were willing to do business if the Canadians could offer lower prices. Because of their experience and liquidity Canadian manufacturers could significantly underbid Americans, at least on small shells. They would machine and assemble U.S. 75-millimetre shells for $2.00 each, for example, when the average American tender was for $2.15. As a businessman Flavelle was disgusted at American insistence on getting markedly lower prices in Canada. As Chairman of the IMB he was a bit relieved that the American orders would not be too much more profitable to his manufacturers than their British business. Privately he thought American government purchasers were much too liberal with American manufacturers — "When the business is made too easy, it robs it of the virility that comes through care and attention and struggle."[6]

The arrangement was settled early in November. The U.S. Ordnance Department would place orders in Canada if Canadians could come in at least seven per cent below the American price. The IMB would allocate the orders, supervise production, and make payments on behalf of the Ordnance Department. The first American contracts for 75-mm shells almost completely absorbed the surplus eighteen-pounder capacity created by the British cutbacks.[7]

Flavelle was bemused and a bit uncomfortable at finding his Imperial organization serving the United States in Canada. He had argued, however, and the Ministry had agreed, that this was the best way to guarantee that British interests would still have first priority. Besides, it was good business for Canada. As Flavelle summarized the IMB's new relationship:

... the practical position is—that because we are Canadians and deeply interested in everything that affects Canada, we are unable to hold ourselves exclusively to our technical position. We have, therefore, used the Official Organization of the Ministry of Munitions to secure business for Canada. . . . We have been the most efficient agency in Canada during the war (indeed practically the only agency) in bringing war business to Canada.[8]

The Ordnance agreement also symbolized the new reality of the American presence in the war. Just as the Americans held the trump cards in the financial game, so their industrial effort would determine the continuing prosperity of Canada's factories. For both Britain and Canada the centres of economic decision-making had moved to New York and Washington. C. B. Gordon of the IMB had left Ottawa in June to become vice-chairman of the

British War Mission to the United States. Brand of the IMB left London to become the mission's financial adviser. As early as May, Flavelle had wanted direct IMB representation in Washington to handle Canadian financial problems. In November he picked T. A. Russell's partner, Lloyd Harris, for the job. In February 1918, Harris was appointed chairman of the Canadian War Mission in Washington, the first distinct, independent Canadian diplomat stationed in the United States. Such were the ironies of the struggle for the British Empire's survival.[9]

II

There was now almost constant grumbling by manufacturers that British prices were impossibly low or British inspection impossibly strict. Maritime and British Columbia shell-makers, for example, both nicely timed protests to coincide with the 1917 general election. In a showdown with the Maritime manufacturers, who were led by his former right-hand man, Alan McAvity, Flavelle told them their problems sprang from their own lack of ability. He did worry, however, about causing a storm of protest as the IMB tried to allocate the high-priced American business among Canadian manufacturers. To keep manufacturers as happy as possible, he promised on his own responsibility to extend certain British contracts, getting authorization from London later. A group of 4.5-inch-shell makers was pacified with promises of bonuses for delivering shells on time. Very few earned their bonuses.[10]

The one clear instance of profiteering Flavelle discovered in 1917 was in one of his own National Factories. Canadian Aeroplanes Limited was still selling its JN-4's at $5,000 each, although the cost of production had fallen from $4,100 to $3,200. Flavelle did not mind Frank Baillie's charging the Americans all the market would bear (he had a small U.S. contract), but drew the line at one agency of the British government making money at the expense of another. He ordered an immediate price cut in sales to the IMB. Baillie finally had to cut his American price too, but still cleared $1,000 a plane. He had already amortized the CAL plant from profits and built up a $500,000 reserve. By early 1918 he was offering to build bombers or scout planes or both for the American government. In turn, the Americans wanted Flavelle to free Baillie to manage the John Willys aircraft factory in Buffalo, which was far behind on a $50-million order. Flavelle and Baillie declined.[11]

367

Operating exactly as though he were running a private business, Baillie made the aeroplane experiment easily the most successful of the National Factories. James Wood at British Forgings and Albert Gooderham at British Acetones operated the same way—to the point where IMB officers, such as Irish and even George Edwards, the chief accountant, were considered outsiders and meddlers.[12] But, like Baillie, Wood and Gooderham did their job and did not waste money. The Montreal fuze plant, British Munitions, had also paid for itself and generated a million-dollar surplus; when the fuze programme was cut back it was turned into a machining factory. The training programme for Canadian pilots, administered by Royal Flying Corps officers, was another outstanding success, producing almost as many pilots by the end of 1917 as were being trained in Britain.*

There had been tremendous cost overruns in putting up the Renfrew and Trenton explosives plants. The Renfrew operation was never very satisfactory—IMB officers did not get on with Canadian Explosives Limited, which managed the company very profitably for itself while resenting even inquiries about safety standards.[13] British Chemicals at Trenton, however, became the IMB's nightmare operation. The Davis—Durkin Company had estimated its cost at $1,900,000. By the end of 1917 more than $5,200,000 had been spent and the complex was nowhere near being competitive with private enterprise. Davis—Durkin had bungled every aspect of the operation. By the end of 1917 the IMB realized that Messrs. Davis and Durkin were personally responsible for Trenton's problems and that it had been a mistake to deal with them at all. A fire in November, caused by lack of elementary safety precautions, cost five lives. In its aftermath Flavelle brought the complex under direct IMB management. The ultimate responsibility for the mess, of course, lay with Gordon and himself for having let it begin despite British warnings about Davis—Durkin. Their defence was the urgency of war.[14]

Almost every transaction the IMB had in British Columbia was disrupted by misunderstandings, grievances, breakdowns in communication, strikes, and other problems. Shell manufacture on the Coast never ran smoothly. The steel shipyards were continually embroiled in labour troubles. Every carpenter in the province seemed to think he should be in on the contracts for wooden ships, every machinist should be manufacturing engines and

* Actually the Royal Flying Corps, Canada, was located in Texas in the winter of 1917–18, having migrated south in search of better flying conditions.

fittings for the ships. "Our friends in British Columbia are hard to please," Flavelle wrote in July 1917 (when his troubles were just beginning). "If it is not one trouble it is another. If they do not secure contracts to satisfy them, they find fault; when they do secure contracts, they find fault with either material or some other supplies. The one thing that they seem to find no fault with is themselves."[15]

Three weeks before the 1917 election, for example, H. H. Stevens, MP for Vancouver, wired Borden to protest the IMB's choice of an American firm to supply masts, spars, and derrick posts for the wooden ships. It was a typical complaint by Stevens, who had already had at least one sharp quarrel with Flavelle over boiler contracts for his constituents. Alerted by Flavelle, Butchart phoned Stevens to point out to him that the American price for the equipment was $14,535, the lowest British Columbia bid $25,347. Stevens told Butchart he had too many complaints about the IMB to bother checking the accuracy of each.[16]

Austin Taylor of the Montreal Locomotive Works was sent West in November 1917 to organize emergency procurement of Sitka spruce for aeroplane construction. There was no existing organization capable of getting out high-quality spruce, normally used only for pulp, from the Queen Charlotte Islands and the fjords of the northern coast. On his arrival, Taylor was deluged with offers of spruce from timber-brokers and limit-holders. The B.C. Loggers Association promised full cooperation at "no profit of any kind . . . other than the amounts which they shall receive as the rental charges and depreciation allowances on the equipment furnished" — on donkey engines they were asking a modest rental of 100 per cent per year plus 120 per cent depreciation, and wanted comparable rates for other supplies. When Taylor rejected these offers there was a wave of public protest directed at the IMB and its incompetent Eastern agents early in 1918. The favourite tactic was to charge IMB people with corruption—profiteers taking their lead from Flavelle, the Bacon Baron, men "so low and debased as to allow poor bleeding Britain to be fleeced in this great hour of her trial." The matter was smoothed over, temporarily, by the Vancouver Board of Trade.[17]

Then labour unrest surfaced in shipyard workers' demands for wage increases to maintain parity with American West Coast shipyards. Yard owners expected the IMB to meet the extra costs of wage increases. As usual Flavelle wanted to avoid responsibility for setting any wage rates. His man on the spot, W. P. Butchart, shared employers' disgust at people who could not see the need to fight it out with the workers, whom he thought should be treated as "industrial soldiers" threatening desertion. "For Gods sake you will keep entirely away from commissions and the like and the ships will be delivered to you on time," he wired Flavelle. Over Butchart's protests Flavelle asked for a Royal Commission to smooth over the situation. It did, temporarily.[18]

Flavelle could not easily understand why British Columbia was a perpetual trouble spot. He shared most Eastern and Western businessmen's opinion that the province was plagued by trouble-making unions increasingly influenced by extreme left-wing "agitators." But he was not much happier with British Columbia businessmen and politicians, who did not seem to appreciate the Board's generosity in spending more than $50 million in a province which had little economic justification for being in war business at all:

They are like a hungry pack of wolves and appear to be without any reasonable sense of balance or proportion. The business which the Board has given to British Columbia has changed the Province from being in great anxiety and trouble concerning business, into prosperous activity. Not only do they exact these excessive wages and charges, but all sorts of people seem to delight in representing that there is graft everywhere in the operations of the Board. It is difficult to understand where these stories arise or why sensible people support them. Nothing seems to be too bad to be repeated; no one seems to care whether they have personal knowledge of it or not— the fact that someone says it is sufficient reason to repeat it.[19]

This fairly common Easterner's conclusion about British Columbia did not give enough weight to sheer distance as a catalyst of misunderstanding. Had Flavelle and his other officers been on the spot, their conciliatory attitudes might have eased some of the criticism. And stories about IMB graft must have seemed plausible at a time when the whole country was reading stories about Flavelle's profiteering.

Another not totally successful IMB project was the formation of an Inventions Committee to consider proposals for advances in technology. There was considerable technological progress in Canadian manufacturing during the war (Baillie's aeroplane factory was particularly innovative in its assembly methods and in improving the design of its products; the IMB was also involved in the discussions leading to the founding of the National Research Council), but none thanks to the Inventions Committee. Its correspondence consists wholly of polite rejections of proposals for perpetual-motion machines, electric-arc rays, and the use of cayenne pepper to make the enemy sneeze. One inventor thought aeroplanes would fly faster if their wings were covered with feathers, another thought fighter pilots would lose their bearings if exploding anti-aircraft shells filled the sky with ribbons. There were several proposals for the invention of the machine gun, and one suggestion that "shrieking" shells would wear down the morale of the enemy. The IMB's technical adviser thought the shells might be filled with mouth organs so the enemy could shatter his own nerves.*[20]

III

The strain of wartime business was having a real effect on the nerves of several of Flavelle's associates. During 1917 Will Rundle, J. S. McLean and Will Flavelle suffered nervous breakdowns. In Ottawa Sir Thomas White had been complaining for a year that his job was destroying his health. By early 1918 he was trying to resign. Borden would not acept his resignation. White finally left for California so abruptly that the Prime Minister did not have a forwarding address for his Minister of Finance. A. K. McLean, the former Liberal financial critic, became acting Minister of Finance while White tried to pull himself together and consider his future.

Canadian war finance had been so completely in White's hands that no one in the cabinet, including McLean, really understood its intricacies. White had advised McLean to ask for Flavelle's help in drawing up his forecasts for 1918. When Borden found McLean's work inadequate, Flavelle quickly became Ottawa's senior financial expert, drafting new estimates himself and presenting them to Borden, who was impressed. He asked Flavelle to come to Washington with him the last week in February for conferences with the British and Americans on the financial outlook. Flavelle was Borden's chief financial adviser during the Washington talks, putting Canada's case "very ably" to Lords Reading and Lever, Borden noted, and also helping Borden prepare for his meeting with Woodrow Wilson.[21]

The chief problem between the countries was Canada's inability to handle its trade deficit with the United States in 1918 if Britain could not cover the costs of any of its Canadian purchases. Flavelle's role was to argue as persua-

---

* In the 1939–45 war the Germans equipped their dive-bombers with sirens whose shrieking did affect the morale of their victims.

sively as he could for large American loans to Britain to pay for Canadian goods, while at the same time pressing the British to at least put up sterling credits to cover Canadian obligations maturing in London. The Americans also had to be urged to keep placing orders in Canada to help the balance of payments.

The February discussions were not conclusive, but Allied financing for 1918 eventually worked out roughly along the lines anticipated by the Canadians. American and Canadian loans covered all Britain's purchases in Canada. The American component of the loans, plus heavy U.S. purchasing in Canada, made it possible to cover the deficit in Canadian–American trade. The IMB itself had no financial problems after the summer of 1917. With the reduced British programme Flavelle got along easily on about thirty million a month, even building up surpluses. Through the spring of 1918 he continued to advise McLean on Anglo-Canadian finance, particularly how to overcome the objections of British Treasury officials, including J. M. Keynes, to granting certain sterling credits in London. The Treasury officials had their way.[22]

During the Washington meetings Lord Reading privately asked Borden about the Canadian government's attitude to Flavelle. It was the only indication that the British ever worried about the effects of the scandal. "Told him very appreciative," Borden wrote in his diary. With the election out of the way Flavelle's value as an administrator more than outweighed his liability as a public figure.[23]

IV

In March E. R. Wood, visiting White in California, found Canada's Minister of Finance sitting in bed reading a book on pessimism.[24] It was appropriate reading for the spring of 1918, for the fourth year of the war seemed to be ending in disaster. In France Ludendorff's offensives brought Germany to the edge of victory. At home, machine guns had to be trained on anti-conscription rioters in Quebec City on Easter weekend. Labour was more restless than ever, profiteers like J. W. Flavelle in more disrepute than ever. Morale, such as it was, was being sustained only by ever more extravagant talk of social reform when peace came. Flavelle, restless and distraught by worries, found his own sustenance in prayer.

The obsessive worry through March and April was the prospect of defeat in battle. The British were retreating toward the Channel ports, the French toward Paris. Any day the Germans might make the final, catastrophic breakthrough. The events of these weeks seemed to Flavelle the most stupendous in history—"the fate of Christian Civilization as we understand it trembles in the balance. . . . the Sun of our British Empire may now be setting. The scale is so huge, the issues so momentous, the mind cannot grasp the significance of it all." Everyone at the IMB went about their duties under a shadow, he wrote, waiting for reports from the front. "We eat and work and sleep, and rise to the task again the next morning to repeat the operations in a dull, dazed sort of way and have almost lost the power of acute feeling or shock."[25]

His pessimism was starting to go beyond day-to-day anxiety. He had thought occasionally about the course of imperial relations after the war, had sometimes worried about the need for government and business to be ready to weather temporary economic hardship at war's end. Now he also began to wonder how people's growing expectation of sweeping peacetime reform could possibly be met in a world devastated by the conflict. The costs of the war would be terrible, perhaps unendurable. Even if the war could be won it was not obvious that real benefits could be obtained.

I am unable to forget how whole communities of men fail to understand that there is always a reaction from the abnormal. Plans predicated upon a continuance of prosperity; of sustained business; of sustained land values through the boom period, etc. etc., look strangely out of balance when the bubble is pricked, or the volume of business becomes greatly restricted, or the lands are unsalable. I do not want to be one to say "Let well enough alone" and do nothing, but let matters work out their own end. I do believe, however, that . . . there will be a long morning after: everyone looking for business and wondering how they will get it. A good many of the rosy plans now advanced for a new earth, and new relations, will look strangely out of proportion. Many of these proposals of working men arise out of their belief that high wages can continue; that steady work can be secured through help of the State. Well—perhaps they can!

I wonder when it is all over, and we take up our tasks, and resume our individual relations, and again become business-getters against the rest of the world, will we have the resource; will we have the money; will we have the willingness to pay through taxes for minimum wages, for sustained labor for every man who wants to work, in the production of goods which will be sold at less than cost to Nations outside?

So many of these plans savour more or less of the German method. So many of them assume that the State can perform for the individual what, it seems to me, the individual must perform for himself, that I am perplexed. . . .[26]

It was clear that he, personally, would have no role to play in after-war service. As he had sensed but perhaps not fully understood, the scandal would not die out; his profits would not be forgotten or forgiven. One incident after another that spring kept the public's awareness of his "crimes" alive. On the third day of the parliamentary session Charles Murphy poured out all of the Laurier Liberals' bitterness in a violent attack on Newton *Wesley* Rowell, indicting him, among other things, for his association with the "cult of commercialized Christianity" practised by those other high-minded Methodists, John *Wesley* Allison and Joseph *Wesley* Flavelle. The speech coincided with more publicity about William Davies' operations, this time a revelation that the company's Winnipeg branch had incinerated 8,500 pounds of spoiled chicken, part of 50,000 pounds it had been holding in cold storage for almost a year and a half, apparently to obtain higher prices.* The chicken scandal then became part of D. D. McKenzie's attack in the House of Commons in early May, in the course of which Flavelle was identified as a leech, parasite, liar, hoarder, plutocrat, and "political god-father" of the Minister of Finance.[29]

---

* "I'm utterly ashamed of the whole thing," Fox wrote Flavelle. The Winnipeg manager had been acting on his own, without telling head office, and going directly contrary to instructions to get out of poultry that the other managers had followed. Flavelle explained the incident to Borden, admitting that it was "indefensible throughout" and "unfortunate to a degree." In August the company received still more bad publicity when its Montreal licence to deal in eggs was suspended because of a violation of local regulations. Again Fox had to admit carelessness and humiliation: "There isn't a shadow of excuse for it."[27]

Flavelle did not learn until years later that Fitzgerald of the IMB was involved in a real food scandal that spring. Fitzgerald had discovered that the Simcoe Canning Company, victors over Davies in the bidding for the 1916 pork-and-beans contract (let by Fitzgerald's former purchasing office at the CPR), had shipped millions of tins containing beans only, covering up the lack of pork with falsified documents. Neither the Borden government nor the War Office would take up Fitzgerald's suggestions of a public inquiry. He thought it was because of the presence of several prominent Conservative politicians on the Board of Simcoe Canning's parent company. They were the same politicians who came to his office one evening and offered to make restitution in the form of a $14,000 cheque made out to Fitzgerald personally. Fitzgerald crushed the cheque, threw it on the floor, pointed at the politicians, and said, "You have stolen the soldiers' food. If I had the power I would unhesitatingly have some of you shot. There is nothing you can do to rectify such damnable action. Get out!" He told Flavelle about the incident in 1935.[28]

Members of Parliament passed another kind of judgment on Flavelle and other titled plutocrats when they endorsed an order-in-council effectively disbarring Canadians from receiving hereditary titles. Flavelle thus became the last Canadian domiciled in Canada to receive an hereditary title. Titles might have been restricted to appease Canadians' war-born egalitarianism, but sensitivity to special privilege had become specially heightened by the case of the baronet and his bacon. His reaction to the titles debate was mild contempt at yet another sign of public hysteria. "If the tragedy of the world were not being enacted, one would laugh."[30]

It was harder to be amused at the effects of the scandal on his private life. Clara had been deeply depressed and a virtual recluse all winter. She rallied a bit in the spring, but Joe had to give her all the time he could spare and decided to have her join him in Ottawa for the winter of 1918–19. On their weekends in Toronto, Clara wrote her daughter, "Of course we keep much to ourselves and really go to no place where we are not quite sure regarding our comfort there, with the result that we go no place." Holwood's one social function that winter and spring was a dinner for the officers of the William Davies Company to celebrate the annual meeting. "Who could have thought that an idealistically honorable business would have passed into such a trial and have caused bitterness and hatred and evil speaking and heartless criticism," Joe wrote.[31]

The criticism that most affected him came from his fellow Methodists. He had been condemned in the *Christian Guardian*, referred to critically from pulpits, and ridiculed at church conferences. Many Methodist friends had written offering their support, but others he had known all his life had found the revelations a terrible disappointment. It was difficult to defend him — Fudger described how hard it was even in closed committees to counter "the half-baked socialism" prevalent in the church: "any taking up of the cudgels by myself or others who I know feel about it as I do is discounted or misinterpreted because of relationships or community of interest."[32]

The war was radicalizing many Methodist leaders, turning them for a time into almost doctrinaire socialists in their search for social salvation and disdain of profits. The Methodist General Conference in October accepted what is still the most radical social and political platform endorsed by a Christian church in Canada. Flavelle, who had been narrowly elected as a delegate from the Toronto Conference (creating still more adverse press comment), had insisted on having an alternate take his place.

"I think the trying experience for me is that I cannot share in good work or be identified with Church activities or fill my place as a Christian man," he wrote his daughter, ". . . the Christian fellowships of a life time are gone." He resolved to give up formal participation in the general affairs of the church, partly to save Methodists from the embarrassment of his presence, partly, I suspect, to make clear his resentment at those who had shown so little faith in him. He never considered leaving the church, criticizing it publicly for its social doctrines, or cutting back on his donations. His letters to his family often ended with the thought that he still had "the never failing, never failing opportunity of laying all before Him with whom there is no misunderstanding."[33]

By May he again wanted to resign from the IMB:

I feel the cumulative effect of these attacks in many quarters. It is impossible to overlook the complete absence of defence from any official quarter and the actual support given to the public clamor by men holding high positions. I hold the unusual position of being responsible to a Minister Overseas, and therefore am denied what usually comes to servants of the Crown: the defence of their actions by a responsible Minister.[34]

Flavelle overlooked the fact that he was under attack mainly because of the meat business; no minister, overseas or at home, could defend his private affairs very effectively. Special British eulogies on the good work of the IMB and its Chairman could seem to be an unnecessary interference in Canadian affairs, while at the same time none of the Canadian ministers had any responsibility for this British agency.

Flavelle seems to have been particularly annoyed that Borden did not speak in his defence. "No one acted towards me personally as badly as Sir Robert," he wrote just after the war.[35] Borden, of course, had many more things on his mind than Flavelle's predicament. He had little reason to defend an unpopular man whose favours for the government were easily balanced by the troubles he had caused politicians. He may personally have disapproved of Flavelle's business operations, as Arthur Meighen seems to have.[36] At the least, he was only being true to the form Flavelle well understood in letting this minor matter take care of itself. In his moods of self-pity Flavelle occasionally thought Canada's future hinged on his being vindicated in the bacon scandal.

V

In its third year of operations, and with a considerably reduced programme, the IMB should have run smoothly through 1918. It did not. The war had gone on too long, strains and tensions had become too serious, for there to be a period of normality in the Board's work.

In a re-enactment of the 1916 quarrel, the steel manufacturers, supported by David Carnegie, were in a complicated, acrimonious dispute with Colonel Edwards over inspection. The British Columbia shipbuilding and spruce programmes were both in chaos, also because of disputes with inspectors. Fitzgerald had to be sent out on an emergency mission to unravel the tangle. As the Royal Commission on shipbuilders' wages in British Columbia finished its work, another round of labour troubles developed over its recommendations. With workers on strike and Butchart wanting to conscript every able-bodied man from eighteen to sixty for industrial work, Senator Gideon Robertson, a respected unionist, had to be sent West to find a compromise.[37] In Ontario there was a wave of public agitation against alien workers in the munitions plants—why not replace the foreigners with deserving veterans? Mark Irish found it impossible to convince the press and public that the aliens did work shunned by Canadians and that few veterans were in any shape for heavy physical labour.[38] Maritimers led the manufacturers' background chorus of complaints about the Board's allocation of the American orders. At Willys—Overland in Toronto, Tom Russell was having technical problems trying to make the Sunbeam "Arab" aeroplane engine. At Canadian Aeroplanes, Baillie had to lay off twelve hundred workers when he did not get an American bomber contract; then he took most of them back when the Americans placed an order for F5 four-engine flying boats, one of the largest aircraft yet built. Baillie delivered his first F5 in June, before Washington had sent him the final blueprints.[39]

More disturbing, supplies of steel and pig-iron essential to the shell programme were not getting through from the United States. The Americans seemed impossible to deal with. Washington was a jungle of uncoordinated departments, boards, and agencies, all spending huge sums of money on grandiose schemes which were not working. "They had some sort of an idea that by stamping the Stars and Stripes on an enterprise success was assured," Flavelle wrote E. R. Wood. "They must travel over the old road of intelligent effort and concentrated attention."[40]

Flavelle finally got a chance to strike back at a critic when the president of the Vancouver Liberal Association wrote the Minister of Public Works accusing IMB officials of taking bribes. When he refused to substantiate or retract his charges, Flavelle directed Butchart to "leave no stone unturned" in prosecuting him for libel. The hapless Liberal was harrassed for months by

IMB lawyers, until even they thought it was vindictive to pursue the matter beyond his several retractions. Flavelle let it drop on November 12.[41]

More or less recovered, Sir Thomas White returned to Ottawa at the end of May. At his first meeting with Flavelle he criticized the IMB for spending its excess money on war materials other than munitions and ships. "The interview left the impression that the same somewhat captious Minister returned that went away," a weary Flavelle wrote. And added, "It is a bit trying to those who have stayed on duty to be lectured and admonished by a Cabinet Minister who has been away from his duties for some months." The day before, in a note to his daughter, he admitted the strain: "I have all day felt I wanted to cry out if any one else bothered me, and only held myself in because I must. . . ."[42]

VI

By summer the fear of defeat had given way to a sense that the war could be won in another two years or so. Most of the IMB's production problems had been worked out — as they usually were — with a little experience. Not so with labour problems, for unions across the country were more militant than ever. They were enjoying spectacular growth as workers looked to organizations to protect them from inflation and/or to win wage increases which for once might put them ahead of the game. In a very tight labour market, in a war-weary country fed up with sacrifice and profiteers, in a year when the old order was collapsing and the new just starting to emerge, perhaps in Russia, socialists and syndicalists were given more attention in labour circles than ever before. Their talk about bringing capital to its knees through a general strike was taken seriously. To some, labour's millennium seemed at hand. To others, it was at least time to do something about long hours and lousy pay and the high cost of living. 1918 was the worst year of the war for strikes: miners went out in Nova Scotia, Alberta, and British Columbia; police struck in Montreal and Toronto; Winnipeg had a dress rehearsal for the 1919 general strike; Canadians endured their first national postal strike in July; the railways were kept going only because the men got parity with American railway workers.

Munitions plants were not singled out for special attention, and probably suffered less disruption than other industries. Wages seem to have stayed high and overtime was always available. The issue of the Fair Wage clause was completely forgotten. Even so, production in the plants had fallen off about thirty per cent, Irish reported in June: "All the enthusiasm and all the ideas that munitions are vitally essential has gone out of the minds of the workpeople. . . . Today they take the War, and the work related to it, as they take the sunrise—an incident of the day." A few days later he remarked that he had been involved in mediating almost as many strikes in May and June as Flavelle had let contracts. "I have had the cupidity of the manufacturer and the stupidity of the workman to deal with until I am pretty well fed up. . . . The situation is rotten and I feel certain that if once one single good strike of large proportions gets a fair start, we shall have the whole bally thing tied up."[43]

Flavelle tended to share employers' prejudices about the causes of the labour unrest. He echoed their view that recruiting and then conscription had taken the best men. With these gone, "the spirit of bitterness and criticism which has been abroad in the country has made ignorant workpeople restless and inclined to disbelieve their employers. There is some apprehension that we may have somewhat widespread labour disturbances. . . . Meantime, the scale of wages rises, which in itself is not a mischievous thing if there was good spirit in connection with it."

Whatever his private feelings, he had to urge concessions to maintain production. Early in July, for example, Toronto toolmakers threatened to tie up all the munitions plants unless a dispute at T. A. Russell's works was solved in their favour. "You have served well and efficiently during the war," Flavelle wrote Russell. "I know of few men who are more entitled to respect and support. Is this a case where you and your associates will have to render one more service and accept the miserable position of having to do what you believe is unjust so as to avert a general tie-up? . . . Sometimes a fight is the only way out. Sometimes, however, nothing is gained by a fight even when the case is a just one. I know you will not forget that the issues are of far-reaching importance." Russell gave in graciously.[44]

British Columbia employers were less willing to compromise, more certain they were fighting a principled resistance to lazy idlers and Bolsheviks. Butchart shared their view and found Flavelle's conciliatory attitude incomprehensible. In June Flavelle had to order him to cooperate with Senator Robertson in the effort to find a *modus vivendi* with the shipyard workers. Robertson worked out a settlement based on continued parity with American workers, but not with much help from Butchart, who wrote Flavelle that the Senator was a liar, unprincipled and worthless. Butchart's was the employer's point of view at its most primitive:

Senator Robertson went over the top with the labour leaders, partly composed of radical sociologists [*sic*] and I firmly believe German sympathizers, and aided by the big guns of the Ottawa Government. . . . we looked to Ottawa for some support and were given the mailed fist. . . . The tactics he used here were contemptible and dirty. . . . Why do they pander to organized labour as they do? . . . cheap and splendid labour is available from China in unlimited quantities; we have the land to place them on, and can return them to China when we please. They should do us immense good at this time in producing food and reducing the cost of living. It would be a great economic advantage to import Chinese by the thousands at this time; this is recognized, but the coward streak in our legislators blocks the way.[45]

Flavelle mustered all his patience in persuading Butchart to accept Robertson's settlement rather than resign. Yes, the settlement was one-sided, a surrender to the workers. But, no, he did not think Robertson would deliberately lie, and the labour leader was in fact held in marked respect by most people in Ottawa. Having asked him to go to the Coast, the IMB had to accept his decisions. Besides, the ships had to be built. "We are in a period of national stress, hence we must all sink our individuality and accept the bitter things as they pass with as good grace and sense as we can command."[46]

That was in June. By the end of July Butchart had broken the Robertson agreement in a dispute with caulkers and the process of calming him down had to be repeated. Meanwhile, Robertson had to go to Toronto to settle a blacksmith's strike which affected every machine shop in the city. To Irish's disgust, one of the most obstinate firms refusing to take back strikers was the IMB's own steel plant, British Forgings. Flavelle was out of town when that problem was dealt with. He had earlier written Fox at the Davies Company urging him to do all he could to avert a strike by keeping up wages and looking to the workpeople's comfort. "The danger of the present situation is that men will let matters run to the breaking point and then give a good deal of attention which could more wisely have been exercised over a considerable period in advance." Intelligent paternalism in labour relations could still go a long way; the Davies Company remained strike-free.[47]

The IMB contributed to pressure on the government to take stronger action to head off the unrest. In July an order-in-council seemed to outlaw strikes during the war. It turned out to be only hortatory, for it lacked a penalty clause. The reaction to it, Flavelle wrote, was "irritation on the one side and amused contempt on the other." His own respect for the government, never very high, was eroded still further. Strikes continued to break out here and there through the summer. Irish counselled against special appeals for extra effort because workers would not respond. Extra time off had to be granted Toronto workers on Civic Holiday weekend, and for the first time in several years some of the plants observed a Labour Day holiday. Holidays were not so disastrous as previously, Irish thought, for since national prohibition had been introduced most plants had their full labour force the morning after.[48]

VII

Early in August 1918, Flavelle learned that the best British opinion saw war going on indefinitely. Will Rundle thought the Allies would be lucky if they won by the end of 1920. On October 1, 1918, the Flavelles moved into the Rockcliffe Park apartment they had leased for a year. Most of Joe's time in September was spent negotiating the 1919 programme.

The British would need little help from Canada. They had the shell capacity and Canada was not able to manufacture the tanks or many of the aeroplanes which had become the instruments of modern war. Over Flavelle's sharp protests, the Ministry of Munitions intended to cut further its Canadian spending.

Canadian industry's salvation in 1919 would be American orders, for shell production south of the border was lagging disastrously. American troops at the front were being supplied with British and French ammunition. Sixty per cent of the first 75-mm shells received by the U.S. Ordnance Department came from the IMB's Canadian contractors, who had sixteen per cent of the orders. Flavelle spent ten days in Washington in September, coming home with promises of large American orders through 1919. He found it incredible that the Americans had achieved so little, and sent Winston Churchill a long commentary on the chaos in the American programme caused by the lack of effective coordination. He had to be careful not to publicize the superior performance of Canadian manufacturers, however, for fear that any boasting about the business having come to Canada would raise protectionist hackles among American businessmen. He had never much liked Americans as a people or as businessmen. His wartime visits reinforced his biases — his Imperial organization and its Canadian contractors, he was sure, had done a better job than the Americans.[49]

About seven o'clock in the evening of October 14 a fire broke out in

British Explosives' TNT plant outside Trenton. The first explosion came soon afterwards. Men dashed through the streets of Trenton yelling at townsfolk to flee for their lives. The seven thousand citizens fled in cars, carriages, and on foot. Women and children fell by the wayside exhausted. The town's police force and firefighters also fled. C. N. Barclay, the young manager of the plant, organized his men to bring up the fire engines from the town to try to contain the damage. They got carloads of TNT out of the yards, cut the connections to the other plants in the complex, and kept fighting the fire until the military guard drove them away. There was a new explosion almost every hour through the night, the last coming at 6:20 a.m. when ten tons of TNT in the drier house went off.

By morning there was only a crater where the TNT plant had been, but the power plant and acid lines had been saved. Flavelle was immensely relieved to learn that no one had been killed and the only damage in Trenton was broken windows. The first reports he had heard, on a train to Ottawa, had Trenton on fire, large numbers of dead and injured, and damage as far away as Belleville. The first press reports estimated a hundred deaths. The Board's investigation located the fire's cause in an error by one of the most experienced hands.[50]

It was only at the end of that week, about the eighteenth of October, that Canadians began planning for an early end to the war. On the twenty-first Flavelle thought it might be over in as little as three months. There was a flurry of cables and meetings in London and Ottawa to figure out how to end munitions work in some four hundred factories employing two hundred thousand men and women without creating an employment crisis. There was also time to work out the last production problem — a power shortage in Ontario caused by Ontario Hydro's inability to satisfy both war needs and consumers' taste for homeheaters and Tuesday electric ironing.[51]

Flavelle complained to his friends that neither manufacturers nor the government had any sensible plans for postwar reconstruction. The government was particularly poorly equipped to undertake the job:

No member in the Government has shown talent or appetite for the work. There is a ripple of excitement at the moment because events at the Front seem to indicate that there may be immediate necessity for action. The plain fact is, the Government as constituted provides no training, capacity, and no previous experience for this duty. The Prime Minister is a lawyer, the President of the Council is a lawyer, the Minister of Labour is a lawyer, the Minister of Justice is a lawyer, the Minister of Trade and

Commerce is an academic man, the Minister of Finance is a lawyer, the Minister of the Interior is a lawyer, the Solicitor General is a lawyer, the Minister of Colonization is a lawyer, the Minister of Militia is a lawyer. How can you expect affairs to be dealt with by this group of men, no matter how honest their intentions are?[52]

As in the spring, he had trouble grasping the enormity of the drama the world was living through. "What of Germany?" he wrote young Clara: "1914, prosperous, proud, efficient . . . now in 1918 facing calamity, a crushing burden of reparation, a loss of territory, a change of government, with deep humiliation not only for the present but in the records of history for all time. . . . She carries the hatred of millions of the human family. Hers is a weary burden taken up by an unchastened people who as yet know no repentance and for whom, until repentance comes there can be no salvation."

He was thrilled to have been permitted to share in the destruction of German arrogance and tyranny, helping the old world give birth to the new. He thought the future would be wonderful and envied his children their share in making it. He saw no role for himself in postwar public life. "My activity will largely pass with my duties here. I can have no effective voice in any activity following the war—the great body of the press—of the public —of my own church, know me as a convicted profiteer—selfish, greedy and pressing burdens on the poor. Of course it hurts sweetheart. . . ."

The war ended at three in the morning, Ottawa time, on the eleventh. Factory whistles awakened the city. Flavelle could not keep back his tears. Instead of joining the crowds celebrating in the streets he stayed in his apartment and quietly gave thanks.[53]

CHAPTER SIXTEEN

NEW WINESKIN, OLD WINE

Flavelle was sixty years old in 1918. During the war he had performed his most important public service. The bacon scandal, he thought, ensured that there would be no more public service. Before the war he had effectively retired from active business management. Now he expected to resume his retirement—to live quietly with Clara, travel, read, gradually get his financial affairs in order, and enjoy his grandchildren. Although he was not showing or feeling his age (his only physical ailment during the war had been toothaches), he thought of himself as an old man now and believed age should step aside gracefully.

In fact Flavelle lived for another twenty years and did not resign the last of his major directorships until the year before his death. His "retirement" in the 1920s and 1930s was more active than many other people's prime of life. He remained prominent in business, was back in government service by 1921, became an articulate, prolific spokesman for economic conservatism between the wars, spent more time giving money away than making it, and in the 1930s was again pilloried as a grasping profiteer. He grew up in a world of Methodist pieties, Queen Victoria, John A. Macdonald, Benjamin Disraeli, railways and potatoes and salt pork. By his death, his activities and interests had compassed insulin, Chinese Communism, Keynesian economics, television, and the need for a new Imperial Munitions Board to help make war on Hitler.

I

The eighty senior officers of the IMB met formally for the first and last time on November 25, 1918, at the Château Laurier for a victory banquet. Nine courses, including hors d'oeuvres américains, consommé à la victoire, salade Beatty, and coupe canadienne, were followed by four hours of congratulatory speeches, presentations, and toasts (imbibed, Perry explained, "out of respect for our Chairman's feelings, and for the laws of the Province of Ontario, in cups that cheer but do not inebriate"). Lloyd George and Churchill had cabled their appreciation of the Board's work and Flavelle's personal service. Everyone testified to the Chairman's good work. He thanked everyone else, and tried to express his "deep sense of humble gratitude that in this the greatest of world struggles, when the fate of the future hung in the balance, you and I, some of us born on farms, in country villages, in towns or cities, doing humble work and growing up in struggle, should be spoken of as having made a valued contribution." Zebulon Lash recited William Henry Drummond's poem, "Johnny's First Moose." Fred Southam sang "Loch Lomond." They closed the evening with "Auld Lang Syne."[1]

Later, Flavelle personally thanked his associates with gifts of engraved sterling.* He spent many hours writing letters to business and political acquaintances, trying to find jobs for those who could not return to their old employment.

These were the pleasant tasks. There was much more work to be done after November 11 as the IMB shifted into reverse. The organization had to self-destruct as quickly as possible, but with a minimum of waste and demoralization of the labour market. Hundreds of half-finished contracts had to be terminated; tens of thousands of munitions workers had to be reabsorbed into the peacetime economy; millions of half-finished shells, spruce logs, aeroplane parts, and other articles had to be sold as war surplus. Flavelle could have left the job to someone else, but decided it was his duty to see the work through to the end. As official liquidators for the British Treasury, Flavelle and George Edwards spent the better part of the next year dismantling the IMB.

It seemed absurd to go on making shells, but the IMB simply could not throw one to two hundred thousand men on the labour market by abruptly suspending all work. Even a few weeks' severance pay, Flavelle thought,

---

* Some of them had been honoured by the King in 1917 with membership in the Order of the British Empire. Frank Baillie was knighted for his gesture in returning profits. Flavelle's list of recommendations for 1918, including knighthoods for Fitzgerald and George Edwards, was never implemented because of the Canadian government's reluctance to let Canadians take any titles after the resentment caused by Flavelle's and other wartime honours.

would not adequately cushion workers against the demoralization of sudden unemployment. After urgent intergovernmental consultations on the eve of peace, and a promise of subsidies from the Canadian government, it was decided to let manufacturers keep working for up to four more weeks while they made plans to convert to peacetime business and their surplus employees found other work. All the shells produced in that month, of course, would be sold for scrap. Half-finished ships, on the other hand, would probably be worth more if the work were completed, so shipbuilding carried on into 1919. So did repairs to the already finished wooden ships, which, on November 11, were scattered in Atlantic and Pacific ports from Acapulco to Newport News, stranded by defects in their boilers. At Willys—Overland T. A. Russell, who had finally manufactured a Sunbeam "Arab" aeroplane engine that would pass inspection, a few days after the armistice, was allowed to finish those in production.[2]

The termination clauses in IMB contracts required the Board to compensate manufacturers for work done on a contract; its own men took inventories at the plants to form a basis for settlement. Flavelle had considerable latitude to deal with special cases. Where a contractor could not recover his outlay on plant and machinery, for example, the Board agreed to make up the difference and take possession of the equipment. Manufacturers who were behind on deliveries at war's end were dealt with personally by Flavelle. In deserving cases he apparently helped a few "lame people." But where Flavelle blamed the manufacturer for his troubles he took a firm line:

I am not unmindful of the difficult position in which your transaction at Montmagny has placed you. You must not forget, however, that as trustees of the Imperial Government, we are bound to have regard to their position as well as the position of the contractor. You will remember, too, that your Company has had some years of operations which, if wisely conducted, would have given you the same results as were secured by others who were given contracts at the same or a later time. We cannot, therefore, in justice take care of the inefficiency of administration which has been the occasion of the Company being in the present unfortunate condition.

He reminded Austin Taylor to be particularly careful settling the spruce contracts in British Columbia because of that province's tendency to demand special consideration—"you will need all your sanity and good sense to hold true to the Ministry's position."[3]

There was the usual wrangling, but all claims from the Canadian contracts were settled fairly quickly without anyone resorting to legal action. The U.S. Ordnance Department was much stickier about the contracts it had placed in Canada through the IMB, and there were serious delays in getting the Americans to recognize the existence of some of the IMB's contracts, let alone compensate the manufacturers. The American side of the business dragged on well into 1919, reconfirming Flavelle's belief that the American political system and bureaucracy could not do anything efficiently.[4]

Shipbuilding had been the most disagreeable of the IMB operations. The programme was far behind schedule and very expensive. Most of the ships, ordered in 1917, were not finished until the summer of 1919. Labour troubles continued into peacetime, with British Columbians objecting to the Chinese crews the IMB imported to sail finished ships to England. The last ship, the *War Magic*, built by a syndicate headed by Senator Frederic Nicholls, was delivered on January 31, 1920. Flavelle's post-mortem on this failed programme blamed everyone from the British Ministry through the IMB's own officials.[5]

Flavelle and Edwards had to dispose of huge quantities of IMB-owned material and equipment on markets that were "dragging to dead." There were 411 fully equipped aeroplanes from the aviation programme, for example. Flavelle wanted to sell them in Canada to promote civil aviation, but was worried about safety hazards if they were sold for "promiscuous flying" in the absence of any federal regulation. The overworked government was not ready to act. Flavelle finally set aside fifty JN-4's to give to the government, and sold $4 million worth of planes, engines, and spare parts to an American syndicate for $75,000. His only alternative would have been to burn them.[6]

The linen used to cover aeroplane wings was sold to Eaton's for sheeting. The special streamlined wire was sold for fencing. All of the Royal Flying Corps quartermaster stores were shipped to England, as were the thousands of gallons of castor oil used to lubricate rotary engines—after the oil was found too impure for human consumption. Flavelle got into a prolonged quarrel with the Government of Canada over the price it would pay for the RFC bases, finally refusing to negotiate further because bickering was "beneath the dignity" of the Ministry of Munitions. The final indignity was an attempt by the Department of Public Works to expropriate the Beamsville base. Outraged that Canada would dare expropriate imperial property,

Flavelle was preparing to go to court when White finally arranged a compromise.[7]

Canadian Aeroplanes Limited's huge factory in Toronto was sold to the Columbia Gramophone Company for $600,000. The undamaged buildings at Trenton, which had cost about $3 million, were sold to an American fertilizer company for $200,000. Sir Charles Gordon, now back at Dominion Textile, offered the Board $400,000 for the British Munitions plant at Verdun, Quebec; Flavelle held out for $500,000.[8] British Forgings was apparently sold to a British firm, Baldwins Limited, interested in taking up steel production in Canada. Neither Flavelle nor the Canadian government considered continued government ownership or operation of any of the National Factories. There seemed to be no market for any of their products, no reason not to wind up a generally successful venture that had paid for itself and made a million dollars profit (almost all of it from British Munitions and Canadian Aeroplanes) for the imperial government. Like many Canadian firms and industries whose production underwent hothouse growth in wartime, the National Factories represented more capacity than the peacetime Canadian economy needed.

Flavelle, Edwards, and the IMB moved to Toronto in early March 1919. The exit from Ottawa coincided with another attack in Parliament on March 3, a wild, rambling, self-justifying speech by Sam Hughes in which he accused Flavelle of being "the owner of the government," having conspired to overthrow first the Shell Committee and then Borden, and having made $100 million on American contracts through the IMB. Flavelle issued a formal, point-by-point denial of Hughes's charges. On the next day Hughes began his campaign of vilification against Sir Arthur Currie. Flavelle's only regret at leaving Ottawa was at having forgotten his golf clubs.

A small IMB office and skeleton staff in Toronto carried the liquidation on into 1920. By November, with the last American contracts settled, the last half-finished shells shipped to England (where there was a better market for scrap), the last surplus gunpowder destroyed, and only the Russian freight-car order and the dispute over the car ferry Leonard's spare propeller to be settled, the IMB closed its doors. Including the Shell Committee, the organization had spent $1,250 million in producing 65 million shells, 49 million cartridge cases, 30 million fuzes, 35 million primers, 112 million pounds of explosives, 2,900 aeroplanes, 88 ships, and other assorted supplies.[9] After a final British audit of IMB accounts showed no irregularities, the destruction of its records was permitted. Flavelle kept his correspondence as Chairman. He resigned on August 17, 1921.

There were ambitious plans for the peacetime future of the William Davies Company. During the war Fox and Flavelle had agreed that their American operations offered the best prospects for the long term. As early as 1916 they had declined to take an interest in Western Canada's largest packing operations, Pat Burns' companies, in order to develop their Chicago business. In 1918 they spent about $750,000 on a packing house of their own in Chicago. At the same time they sold Davies' interest in Harris Abattoir to J. S. McLean and Jim Harris for $827,000 ($235 a share), ending a relationship that had soured years earlier. Even before the bacon scandal, there seems to have been a decision to contract the retail-store operations; the public's distaste for Davies' products after the scandal broke must have confirmed their belief that retailing should have a low priority.[10]

Fox and Flavelle expected exports to remain the basis of the business. Davies would dominate the English market for premium bacon, and, particularly through their American house, would penetrate the entire European market in pork and beef. Urging Fox to send agents into Germany in September 1919, Flavelle reflected that a year ago he had thought trade with Germany would not resume during his lifetime. He was not generally optimistic about postwar business prospects, but Flavelle did believe the Davies Company would do well. "It has a great future. It is ably managed; thoroughly well organized, with highly efficient men at all points. . . . I believe the business in Chicago will grow into great proportions, and will ultimately quite over-top the Canadian business."[11]

Fox wanted a bigger stake in the company's future than the fifteen-percent interest he had gradually acquired. Flavelle had always believed that ownership should naturally pass to the active officers of a company (in his will he had directed his executors to sell his shares to Davies' officers on a favourable basis, absolving them from liability if they turned down a higher offer from outsiders), and was not surprised when Fox and two associates offered to buy his shares in late 1918. He was willing to sell 7,500 shares, half his holdings, at $150 each. Much to his surprise the Bank of Commerce would loan the Fox group only $250,000 of the $562,500 they needed to give Flavelle the fifty-per-cent down-payment he wanted. Despite his letters explaining the deal and expressing full confidence in Fox and the company's future, the transaction floundered on the bank's failure to loan more money. The fact that Flavelle had been a director of the Commerce for twenty-three years had no influence on the Toronto manager's judgment.[12]

Nobody was very happy with the situation. During a European trip in the spring of 1919 Flavelle decided to get out of the packing industry entirely if Fox could give him a good price for all his shares.* He offered all 15,000 shares to Fox at $200. Fox had new financial backing. An old classmate at McMaster, Cyrus Eaton, had gone into investment banking in Cleveland and had met Flavelle during the war. Possibly at Flavelle's suggestion, Eaton was able to arrange American underwriting commitments for a reorganization and stock issue that would allow Fox to buy out Flavelle and take control of the company.

The Chicago subsidiary, William Davies Incorporated, was reorganized to buy out its Canadian parent, William Davies Limited. Sale of non-voting preference shares in Davies Incorporated provided the cash to buy out Flavelle and any small shareholders in Davies Limited who wished to sell. The remaining Davies Limited shareholders, mainly Fox and his associates, exchanged their holdings for common shares in Davies Incorporated which carried voting rights. It was an interesting transaction — creating an American company, most of its capital provided by Americans, which was fully controlled by Canadians. The press annoyed Flavelle by incorrectly calling the deal a sellout to Americans.[13]

William Davies, still hearty in his eighty-ninth year, came to the shareholders' meeting which discussed the sale of the company he had founded to a group led by his grandson. Motoring in the American South a few months later, William Davies was butted by a goat while relieving himself at the roadside. He never recovered from the injuries and died in 1921.

On December 15, 1919, Flavelle sold his 15,250 shares in William Davies Limited to William Davies Incorporated at $200 plus $7.08 interest since April 1 — a total of $3,157,970. Considering that his holdings in 1911 had been worth $1,200,000, he had done very well in his last eight years in the packing business. This was a reasonable price on the basis of the firm's real assets, though, was not swollen by a goodwill factor, and was much less than a simple extrapolation from wartime earnings would have justified (as well as a lot less per share than the Matthews — Blackwell group received when they sold out to Americans in the same year for $9 million). Flavelle resigned as president of William Davies Limited on December 29, 1919, leaving the

---

* I cannot find an explanation of this change of heart, which is important in view of the Davies Company's later fortunes. Flavelle might have changed his mind about the future of the company, but a few months later he again expressed great confidence in its earning power and claimed he would rather keep his shares than reduce his asking price.

packing industry for good. He expected Fox to carry on the business successfully.[14]

III

After relatively lean years from 1912 through 1915, Simpson's had resumed
its normal growth rate during the war. The shareholders' assets, worth
about $3 million in 1912, had doubled again by 1919. A reorganization of the
mail-order business, establishing major offices in Regina and Halifax, had
been completed. In March 1919 each Simpson's employee received an extra
week's salary to celebrate the twenty-first anniversary of the Sunday School
teachers' purchase of the business from the Simpson estate.[15]

But H. H. Fudger was sunk in existential despair. His life's dream of
passing his fortune and position to his brilliant son, Dick, was shattered
when the young man's health, never robust, gave out in 1918. In his late
sixties, no longer very interested in anything but searching for the meaning
of life in religion and philosophy, Fudger decided to put his estate in a more
liquid condition. In 1919 he offered Flavelle most of his Simpson's stock at
$150 a share. In January 1920 Flavelle used $1,053,600 of the proceeds from
his sale of Davies stock to buy 7,024 shares of Simpson's common from
Fudger. He bought another 1,000 shares from Bert Cox (whose main interest in life had become horses and hunts in England), bringing his Simpson's
holdings to about 18,500 shares, just over a 60-per-cent interest.[16] That
spring he moved his headquarters from the IMB's Toronto office to the executive floor of Simpson's. But he had no desire to take over management of
the store from Fudger and remained in the background as vice-president,
counsellor, and general strategist. The two aging businessmen agreed to
give their senior executives more responsibility, and expected to sell out
completely in about five years.[17]

Flavelle's desire for a fairly quiet life and fairly liquid assets explains a
course not taken in Canadian retailing. In 1920 the Hudson's Bay Company
approached him with a merger offer, looking towards the consolidation of
the two businesses in a new organization to be brought about through stock
transfers. "If I were a younger man," Flavelle wrote Sir Augustus Nanton of
the Bay, "the scale of the enterprise would be attractive, and the responsibilities stimulating." But there would be too much work and worry, too
much uncertainty in the early years of the venture for an old man to under-

take. With the Hudson's Bay Company evidently unable to make a good cash offer for control of Simpson's, the discussion ended.[18]

IV

Herbert Hoover's hog policies alerted Flavelle to the passing of the business world he had known before the war. As United States Food Administrator in 1918, Hoover was able to control both the flow and prices of foodstuffs going to Allied purchasing agents. To increase U.S. swine production for 1918 he had indirectly guaranteed record prices to farmers. By the end of 1918 packers were being overwhelmed by the bumper crop of pigs. The law of supply and demand should have dictated a dramatic decrease in the price of all pork products. But Hoover was continuing to force packers, and through them Allied purchasers, to pay high fixed prices that no longer made economic sense. Artificially high prices were also being maintained by government purchasing agencies for wheat; in December 1918, Flavelle estimated that the free play of supply and demand would bring the price of North American wheat down from $2.20 a bushel to at least $1.75 and probably $1.25 for the 1919 crop.[19]

During the war, governments had taken control of food marketing when laissez-faire policies seemed to lead to excessively high prices. Now the situation was reversed. Governments were holding prices at high levels when the free operation of market forces would drive them down. The consumer was paying the cost, most particularly the poor and hungry consumers in Europe. "There is a strange inconsistency in our action—a struggle for the liberties of the World coupled with official action to make starving peoples and bankrupt Governments pay the highest price for food stuffs that can be exacted from them," Flavelle wrote scornfully. In their anxiety to protect producers from deflation governments were surely "playing with fire . . . the destructive forces of revolution will be incomparably greater in their reaction upon North America than any profit which they may secure from sustaining food products at extreme values."[20]

Moreover, high food prices kept the cost of living absurdly high, triggering large wage demands as workers tried to keep up. But how were record wages going to be paid? Canada's wartime prosperity had rested on artificial demand for munitions and foodstuffs. How could prosperity be maintained with the munitions business gone and Europe about to return to full food production? At the least, a fierce international competition for trade was going to develop. Oversupplies on world markets were bound to bring about a deflation, a return to more normal conditions, and the sooner the Canadian economy got in shape for this the better. In the meantime starving Europe was still being forced to pay "terrible" prices for food "so as to add to the already swelled wealth of Canada and the United States," and people on fixed incomes at home were suffering grievously from inflation.[21]

Flavelle was deeply pessimistic in the first winter of peace, sure that an economic reckoning for the war was about to come due. The costs of the war had to be paid. By interfering with natural market forces to avoid paying them for as long as possible, governments were only making a menacing situation worse.

His diagnosis of imminent deflation was incorrect at first. The unemployment crisis he predicted for the winter of 1918 — 19 did not materialize. Suppressed wartime demand in both North America and Europe, combined with easy credits and high government spending, created a hectic postwar boom. The capacity of Canadian industry and agriculture was at least as strained through 1919 as it had been during the war. Soldiers and munitions workers were absorbed into the peacetime economy surprisingly easily (so were women war workers, most of whom went back to housework). On the other hand, inflation caused by overheating of the economy in an atmosphere of heightened postwar expectations created more social unrest in 1919 than Canadians had experienced since 1837.

Industrial relations dissolved into something like open class war, symbolized by the Winnipeg General Strike. Organized farmers struck through the ballot box as the United Farmers of Ontario smashed the two-party system and, incredibly, formed a provincial government after the October 1919 election. Western farmers were organizing to do the same in their provinces and then to break the two-party system at Ottawa. Unprecedented prices, unprecedented wages, unprecedented strikes, and an unprecedented collapse of political stability accompanied the otherwise easy transition to peace.

It confounded his gloomy predictions, but the chaotic postwar boom was no more welcome to Flavelle. Artificial prosperity and high expectations at a time when sacrifice and hard work should have been the order of the day offended his deep conservative instincts. Now he criticized not just governments but all classes in society for putting their selfish interests before the imperative need for frugality and service. "We continue to have business prosperity," he wrote Brand in September 1919:

The same general conditions are present with us as with you—the prodigal expenditure of money on all forms of luxury, whether the cheap jewelry, gramophones and cheap motor cars of the work people or the expensive extravagance of the richer classes. Wages and salaries continue advancing—the range of industries with shorter hours of work increases weekly. The almost universal statement of employers of labor is that efficiency per workman per hour has been much impaired. Costs of all commodities are at extreme figures. Abnormal conditions are everywhere in evidence. We have not yet developed a constructive and sober leadership. Nor does the community show any temper to respond to such guidance if it were available.[22]

Labour's demands for higher wages and shorter hours were of a piece with farmers' insistence on high food prices, he thought; both producer groups were organizing to make unrealistic, unsustainable demands on the community's wealth. Then they were institutionalizing their organized selfishness by entering politics as special-interest groups, cutting across normal party lines. The unity and cooperation Flavelle thought had characterized the Canadian community during the war (like most English Canadians he forgot about French Canadians), had given way to class conflict and the loss of any sense of the public interest.

Class differences are being magnified and groups are being organized for the benefit of the members of the group, with but little regard to the community as a whole. . . . There is a grave danger to the state when sections of the community organize almost wholly for their own benefit, and, with increasing power, undertake to dictate to the community and to frighten politicians, that the thing which they consider best for themselves must be given, or they will exercise the power of their organization to bring such discomfort to the community and politicians that they will secure what they demand.[23]

This was the most common theme of his reflections on Canadian society in the early postwar years. His distrust of organizations and the demands of interest groups became the key to his conservatism for the rest of his life. It was an unusually clear blending of nineteenth-century individualism and economic liberalism with a more traditional Tory concern for the organic well-being of communities. The national interest, Flavelle thought, rested on each individual doing his duty to society. The community was the sum of its individual parts. Its cement was not institutional or organizational, but rather the spirit of service, goodwill, and self-denial arising whenever men worked hard, played the game, and accepted their lot in life. When they formed organizations to pressure others into doing for them what they should be doing themselves, cooperation gave way to conflict, and unity and harmony in a community disappeared. He increasingly used the metaphor of the family to describe communities, and saw class and group action as the equivalent of personal rebellion against the spirit of self-sacrifice binding a family together. To argue this way was to make the old small-"l" liberalism the basis of a twentieth-century conservatism.

V

Flavelle knew the general economic break was coming when, in the spring of 1920, he observed how department stores gradually slipped into price-cutting to reduce inventories. By summer he saw tight money ahead, and accurately forecast the serious liquidation which set in that fall.[24] By winter commodity prices had collapsed, business and trade had fallen off, and emergency relief was being given to hundreds of thousands of unemployed.

He had expected it for so long that Flavelle was almost relieved by the recession and deflation. He had little sympathy with those caught unprepared, and was particularly annoyed when some governments still tried to hold up commodity prices in the interests of businessmen and other producers. In October 1920, for example, the Board of Commerce, originally set up by the Dominion government to protect the consumer from profiteering, tried to fix a *minimum* retail price for sugar to protect refiners caught with expensive stocks. Flavelle wrote Arthur Meighen complaining about this reversal of the board's function:

All who produced, manufactured and distributed commodities during the war secured the advantage of advancing markets; the consumer paid the penalty. When the situation is reversed, how can an agency of the Government intervene to protect from loss, and keep the burden on the consumer? I have held the view that no Profit and Loss account could properly be closed out during the war, until all concerned faced the debits of declining prices. I cannot reconcile this protection of long stock on declining markets, whether held as the result of speculation, or simply in the ordinary way of business.

The government gave way in the face of this and similar protests, and the sugar refiners took heavy losses — to the consumer's benefit.[25]

395

Complaints about hard times in 1920 and 1921 did not impress the austere businessman. Almost everyone, farmers and workers especially, had done well during the war. Canadians had carried on into peacetime in a fool's paradise, expecting to earn more and more for doing less and less, drunk on prosperity and high expectations. Now they were having to sober up, a necessary and beneficial experience.

. . . it is a common condition of society that men must accept loss as well as gain. The greater the gain, the greater the swing to the other side and consequent loss. It is a very sound thing that we should get the values of great commodities on the lower basis. No one need spend undue sympathy upon the great body in the community, comprised of agriculturalists, business men and labour, which has had so much profit, and now is confronted with loss. We need a revival of the spirit of service in the community. There has been almost an abandon to a spirit of money spending for personal pleasure and satisfaction, and a general disinclination to work hard. Do as little as possible, and get as much as possible, has been too common. The old-fashioned discipline incident to suffering will do good on the whole rather than harm.[26]

Flavelle thought there was little that governments could do to meliorate the postwar confusion. As the issue of commodity prices showed, the main effect of using emergency war powers in peacetime was to delay the return to normality and further distort the economy for the benefit of special interests. To someone who had seen how politics and politicians interfered with business during the war, and who had also begun to understand that democracy was necessarily and rightly unbusinesslike and inefficient, it was natural to doubt the capacity of the state to engineer the peacetime adjustment. "So many think you can remedy, by legislation, by Commission, by Controllers," he had written in early 1918. "These, when they set to work, throw into force regulations and directions and make new ills, they did not realize, greater than the ills they seek to correct. . . . Society has a curious way of accommodating its activities without too much interference."[27]

The best kind of leadership Flavelle thought governments could offer would be to help private business deal with the problems of production, marketing, and employment. He favoured and helped plan an aggressive drive to expand Canadian exports immediately after the war — it proved unnecessary in the 1919 boom. Beyond that, he rejected the idea of applying to peacetime any of the methods of state control used during the war. Public ownership, he thought, killed initiative and the impulse to efficiency. Most state regulation of business was unwise interference with its freedom, also leading to inefficiency and waste. Social reform by legislation, well-intentioned as it was, usually had unforeseen harmful consequences.

He was particularly interested, for example, in Ontario's experiment with a minimum-wage law. A friend and relative by marriage, Rev. J. W. MacMillan of Victoria College, was the first chairman of the Minimum Wage Board. When the law went into effect in 1922, Will Flavelle described how the Lindsay stores were laying off salesgirls who were not experienced or efficient enough to give ten dollars a week worth of service—"we will have to weed out the ordinary and conduct the business strictly on business lines with little sentimental thought." The unemployment created by the minimum-wage law confirmed Joe's suspicion that "the superimposed thing which comes from legislation urged by earnest people seems frequently to throw something else out of balance, which was not anticipated, or understood. . . . I am becoming increasingly conservative that we cannot correct these difficulties by legislation." To MacMillan he spelled out his objections in more detail:

If you could standardize men as you standardize machinery, you would have no difficulty in securing support for many theories which are held, of which the minimum wage is one. There can be no such standardization. A living wage for one man, or one family, is not a living wage for another man, or another family. One is thrifty and has married a thrifty wife. Another is drunken or shiftless, or has married a wife who cannot manage, and trouble follows. Moreover, you cannot standardize the conditions under which the product which the man is to sell will be marketed.

I will not only not challenge but will support the position that society must learn how to give a reasonable standard of comfort in response for honest labour honestly performed. This result, however, is contingent upon much that should first be effective, and primary to your standard must come the teaching of the individual, and the development of a sense of responsibility on the part of the individual. All your minimum wages, and all your other regulations, are only make-believe while stern serious effort is absent to produce individual character, and individual responsibility and capacity. I believe that a great deal of the propaganda of the past three years of well intentioned good people, declaring that a new era had dawned in the world and justice and fair play was to take the place of privileges, has been largely mischievous and has been injurious to the people it sought to help. If all the world would develop character and sense of individual responsibility, there would not be much need of the doctrinaire who has but little experience in the actual conditions associated with production, transportation and markets.[28]

He had no use either for unemployment insurance, which was being widely advocated in the early 1920s as a way of providing some security to the worker. Always in close touch with economic conditions in England, he shared the belief of many businessmen there that the great postwar expansion of unemployment benefits, particularly reliance on the "dole," was creating additional unemployment by giving a disincentive to work. "I wonder if State aid in housing is a sound measure?" he asked in another letter. ". . . It is not so much the house in which a man lives that matters, as the kind of man who lives in the house. I suppose it would be said that without better housing you will fail in improving the character of the people who are housed. I am not sure that I accept the affirmative side of it—that by the State providing better houses you will have a better quality of people to live in them."[29]

Many of the social reformers Flavelle distrusted were Methodist ministers. His church's quasi-official commitment to the Social Gospel and social reform did not affect his loyalty or his donations, but he felt little in common with clergymen whose views he considered naive, mischievous, and even revolutionary. One of the most prominent Methodist Social Gospellers, the Reverend Ernest Thomas, suggested to him in 1921 some kind of conference between conservatives and radicals in the church to clear up misunderstandings and search for common ground. Flavelle was not interested, believing that the differences were fundamental:

I have no quarrel with the spirit or purpose of the men who believe the type of teaching which they are promulgating as the remedy for the world's ills. I have a distinct quarrel with the teaching. I believe it to be pernicious and mischievous. I think we had an example of it in Winnipeg. I believe we have a further example of it in Russia. I believe with equal sincerity, that there is much about the method of the operation of the present system which is cruel and crushing. I do not believe that the remedy is to change to another system which is not only cruel and crushing in its effects, but is inevitably, in my judgment, bound to be cruel and crushing as a system. I would rather remedy the ills of a thing which I believe to be sound, than take the ills along with a thing which I believe is unsound. In the latter case, I multiply the ills by as many times as the theory is fundamentally unsound. I do not hope for you to agree with this view because you honestly hold a different opinion. I do not think we do wise to humbug ourselves with terms, or think of a situation relieved by compromise through negotiation. You cannot mix oil and water.[30]

His views could seem ridiculous. Here was a millionaire, not a material worry in the world, opposing social reform, claiming other people thought too much about getting wealthy, and urging them to work hard and accept their lot in life. Another spokesman for privilege who was trying to deny justice to everyone else. "So you see," Flavelle concluded one of his sermon-letters just before leaving for California, "I can preach the virtue of hard work, and more of it, and long hours, and more of them, for others, but can go off and have freedom from worry, and freedom from care, on my own account. How we love to be virtuous at other peoples' expense."[31] He sometimes remembered not to take himself too seriously.

But he was serious, and he was more than a mouthpiece for established wealth. He was obviously troubled in the 1920s at signs that his values, the values of Peterborough Methodism in the 1870s, were being abandoned in the postwar world. He fell in love with California's climate in the early 1920s, but was appalled at the Californians—Hollywood's "painted women," open Sundays, the high divorce rate, "these people always aiming at the extravagant, the ultra, . . . one wonders what it all means." Even Methodists from the old days seemed to be forgetting their roots in the new society: when the Flavelles took tea at the E. R. Woods' lavish mansion outside Los Angeles Joe was depressed by the splendour of the house and gardens.[32]

Other symbols of bigness and wealth, especially those featuring a high degree of organization, also bothered him. Henry Ford's automobile plants were the epitome of modern industrial organization. Flavelle thought a Ford factory must be "the most dis-spiriting place possible. . . . This organization of repeat work kills the development of the craftsman. He is simply a cog in a huge operating machine, and we are in danger of forgetting that a man is a man, and has a right for all round development."[33] Reflecting on his own career, he invariably recalled how little attention he gave to organization, how much effort he spent cultivating individual performance. Had he been reminded that the modern assembly line developed from pork-packers' dis-assembly lines, he would have argued that this was the least important aspect of the work.

In 1922 Flavelle was a delegate to the Methodist General Conference and was active on committees working out the structure of the new church soon to emerge from union with the Presbyterians and Congregationalists. But he was not very optimistic about the church's future in a hedonistic society:

In a somewhat confused way, I wonder what all this organization means. The machine and machinery representing church organization is better than ever it has been, but so many of our churches are empty, or nearly so. An ever increasing body of people grow careless regarding worship. Many of the better classes using the golf links, or weekend automobile trips, and tens of thousands of workpeople and their families spending the Sunday picnicing, or out of doors in their Ford or other cheap cars. Back of it all, is the restless desire of each group or class to compel the community to give an increasing share of what is going to them, and to their class. . . .
I do not know what it all means. I suppose the sound thing is for each of us to do the best we can each day.[34]

VI

He paid little attention to early postwar politics. He did not want governments to be very active, did not believe Borden's Union Government had the capacity to give much leadership to the country. The only cabinet minister whose ability he genuinely respected (whatever he thought about his temperament) was White. Almost his only contact with politics in 1919 and 1920 revolved around White's future plans.

The Finance Minister wanted to get out of public life. His years in Ottawa had eaten up his savings, forced him into debt, and made it impossible for him to provide for his wife if he died. If White did return to private life, Flavelle hoped he would come back into National Trust. As the businessmen discussed this prospect in late 1918, though, they realized its unseemliness. "The whole country would at once jump to the conclusion that he had been sent to Ottawa to put through the Ry. business & having delivered the goods he was going back to his job," E. R. Wood wrote. "Rundle is tremendously strong on this & says the move contemplated would, in his view, ruin White & bring great discredit on all the Institutions concerned & those identified with them."

As Rundle had anticipated, White "flopped over" and decided to stay on a bit longer. Although Flavelle thought his petulance told against him, he saw White as "head and shoulders" above his colleagues, the Prime Minister included. As the Union Government struggled through the turmoil of 1919, semi-leaderless because of Borden's absence at the Peace Conference, no one knowing whether to keep the coalition going or return to old party lines, Flavelle became more and more convinced that White was the only minister who could succeed Borden and eventually go to the people with any hope of success. "I do not consider that businessmen in the country have any adequate realization of the seriousness of the situation," Flavelle wrote Sir Charles Gordon in December 1919.

If an appeal is made to the country in a general election, I think, undoubtedly, we would have a farmer Government. We have in Ontario. There would follow legislation of the type which Crerar is advocating, and industrial and financial operations in the country would pass through a period of strain and anxiety and trial. It occurs to me that men should sink all their differences at the moment and realize that they must come together and urge the only man who has a possibility of success, to assume this responsibility.[35]

Peter Perry suggested that White might stay in public life if his friends raised a subscription to alleviate the financial hardship. It was a fairly common practice in British and Canadian politics. Over Rundle's objection that it would be worse than bringing White back into National Trust, Flavelle took up the idea. He apparently enlisted Gordon and Wood's support in offering White an annuity of at least fifteen thousand dollars to stay in politics ("As it would almost certainly be misunderstood and misinterpreted, it might be wise to leave a definite commitment on the matter until after the new Government appealed for re-election," he wrote Gordon). White would not consider the proposal. Although Borden and a majority of the cabinet wanted him to take over as Prime Minister, he finally refused in the spring of 1920 and the succession passed to Arthur Meighen in July. White resumed his directorships and became a vice-president of the Bank of Commerce, but did not become a full-time businessman again. "I have believed of White," Flavelle wrote in a kind of epitaph to his friend's political career, "that, if he had the religious conviction which, whether he liked it or not, forced him to assume obligations, he would have the last element necessary for a truly great man."[36]

Flavelle had not worked closely with Arthur Meighen during the war; indeed, Meighen seems to have been one of the ministers who took most seriously the criticisms of Flavelle. When Meighen became Prime Minister,

Flavelle hoped he could marshal the same forces in Canada and the same desire for normality that had swept Warren Harding to victory in the United States. "Meighen has the intellectual capacity, and the platform ability," he wrote Willison. "Whether he has at bottom the character necessary for such leadership I do not know." He sent Meighen a routine congratulatory note and must have been a bit puzzled when, in reply, Meighen wrote that Flavelle was "in a position by reason of your gifts and standing to be of exceptional assistance to me and of exceptional service to the country at this time."[37]

VII

It was the railway situation again. The effort and money poured into salvaging the CPR's insolvent competitors during the war had been only the beginning. Fundamental decisions had been made: the Canadian Northern nationalized, the Grand Trunk Pacific thrown into receivership and taken over, a decision reached to take over the bankrupt Grand Trunk. Private enterprise in railways, save for the CPR, had been superseded. But what would the next step be? What would public enterprise in railways look like?

In the spring of 1921 the sprawling government-owned system—the old Intercolonial, the new National Transcontinental, the Canadian Northern, the Grand Trunk Pacific—was being administered by a Board of Management which was still formally the Canadian Northern Board of Directors. Negotiations for settlement with the Grand Trunk were still in progress. The trains were running on all the tracks, but not very often on time and at a staggering cost to the public purse. In his 1921 budget speech, Finance Minister Sir Henry Drayton estimated that some $160 million of the taxpayer's money would have to be spent that year to cover operating losses, interest payments, and capital improvements. The government railways were costing Canadians more than the whole Government of Canada had cost in any year before 1913.

No permanent administration had been set up. The system was being called the Canadian National Railways, but legislation creating it as a legal entity was in limbo until proclaimed by order-in-council. The main reason for the government's delay in issuing the proclamation was its need to find executives able and willing to run the new railway. "This Government owned system of railways is the biggest business enterprise this country will ever have," Flavelle commented to Willison in 1920. "The chief figure in the Government owned system should be a man of affairs, with proved judgment, capacity and large grasp, rather than the railway man, no matter how expert he might be in that field. . . . He should not be more than forty-five or at the most fifty years of age. This would give him a clear ten or fifteen years for service at top capacity."[38] This was a casual letter, for Flavelle had paid little attention to the railways since 1917.

The Prime Minister came to Flavelle in Toronto in late March, 1921, to ask him to become chief executive officer of the Canadian National Railways system. Meighen told him the cabinet unanimously wanted him for the job. He would be the foremost of a group of three appointees, with as much executive authority as he wanted—in effect he could write his own terms for the job. The job, of course, was to run "the biggest business enterprise this country will ever have," a railway system half again larger than the CPR, larger than any single railway in the world. For a businessman who believed in putting his talents to public service, it would be hard to imagine a greater opportunity.

His first reaction to Meighen's offer was intense satisfaction that the cloud over his character had lifted. The Ottawa politicians, a number of whom had not been unhappy at the destruction of his reputation, had been forced to recognize his ability and integrity. They had come to him as the man best fitted for the top business position in Canada. "I am grateful in a degree I cannot express for this evidence of your confidence in my character for an important public office," he wrote Meighen.

Should he take the job? He was sixty-three years old, no longer believed in public ownership in principle, and was scarred from his wartime public service. White and Rundle, the only friends he consulted, both thought he should decline; one of them commented, Flavelle wrote, "that if the appointment were made, both the Government and myself would find it has been a mistake, and that through an impossible idealism in administration, I would render myself unhappy and bring embarrassment to the Government."[39] On the other hand, what did duty dictate? "I have sometimes thought I would go to hell if it were necessary, if it were a duty," Flavelle said later, referring to this offer.[40] His age did not matter, he thought, for, if he broke under the strain, "it did not make any difference if I died sooner or not, if I did the thing I ought to do." His distaste for public ownership could not be a factor either, for public ownership of the railways was a fact; someone had to make it work. And however much had gone wrong in Ottawa during the war, no one else knew as much as he did about running a public enterprise while keeping politicians at arm's length.

There was one overriding duty. To Clara. She had supported him in his busy-ness, his absences from home, his fights with the press and politicians, for almost forty years. Now he was about to start it all over again and go on for the rest of their lives. She would not come right out and say what she thought, but her "quietly accumulating distress as the days passed, and the crushing weight of it upon her," finally caused Joe to make up his mind to refuse. "At our age," he wrote Will Flavelle, "my first duty is to her." He wrote Meighen declining the job.[41]

Meighen persisted. He asked Flavelle to come to Ottawa to advise during negotiations with the Grand Trunk shareholders, then asked him to serve on the interim Board of Directors the government was appointing to manage the Grand Trunk pending formal creation of the CNR, then asked him to be chairman of that board. Flavelle agreed to all three requests, largely so he could study the railway problem from the inside, and on condition that it was clearly understood he would not go on to head the CNR. Everyone, including Meighen, promptly forgot about the condition and urged him to agree to carry on when the new system was launched. The announcement of his chairmanship of the Grand Trunk prompted a French Canadian Liberal MP to make one last attack on his wartime money-making. This time a number of newspapers defended him, and another Liberal, W. C. Edwards, hailed him in the Senate as the finest businessman in the country. The Governor General was very friendly. In Ottawa, at least, the scandal was almost forgotten, the wartime service highly valued. There was considerable sentiment among Conservatives and businessmen that Flavelle was, as Fred Southam put to him, "the Moses who can lead your country out of the railway wilderness."[42]

A Moses had to be found somewhere. The costs to Canadian taxpayers of inefficient, politically influenced management of the giant enterprise would be incalculable. It was unthinkable, of course, to shut down more than half the railways in the country. It was just as unthinkable to turn them back to private owners, if only because the government would literally have to pay anyone to be foolish enough to take on their burden of debt. Nor was there any way of eliminating most of the debt, in the way that receivership did for private companies, without a default on its obligations by the Government of Canada, which was also unthinkable. There was really only one alternative to soldiering on with the CNR—turn everything over to the CPR.

This, in effect, was what the CPR wanted. In April 1921 Lord Shaughnessy, just retired as CP's president, revived a 1917 proposal that the CPR manage all the railways, working the giant system as efficiently as it could, but with Parliament making up the deficits and guaranteeing their existing dividend to CP shareholders. The attraction of the Shaughnessy Plan lay in its exorcism of the spectre of incompetent government management: the railways would be handled by one of the most efficient management teams in the world; surely this was the way to minimize their cost to the Canadian taxpayer. Montreal business in particular, which saw public management of the CNR leading to either ruinous taxes or the ruination of the CPR through unfair competition, or both, applied heavy pressure on Meighen to drop the search for a CNR head and opt for the Shaughnessy solution.

Flavelle would not serve as head of the CNR, but he would offer his best advice on the future of the railways. He was not optimistic. He doubted privately that anyone could withstand the pressure politicians would put on the administrators of a publicly owned railway: "political influences in the various ridings; the strained position of governments having narrow majorities in the House; the ignorance of public men covering the nice problems associated with a great business; the heart-breaking experience through the inevitable errors of judgment . . . being magnified in the press, in Parliament by angry ministers or a captious opposition, or by interested parties. Is it possible, under such difficult circumstances, to carry on successfully the most difficult business enterprise ever undertaken in Canada, and upon a scale greater than anything hitherto attempted in Canada?" He thought not.[43]

But the experiment had to be tried. The Shaughnessy Plan was even more impossible, no matter how many of his business friends saw it as a panacea. Flavelle had often been naive about politics, but on this issue he well understood why Parliament could never give private administrators a free hand running public property. Above all, it could not raise the spectre of a railway monopoly by giving the CPR a free hand. Flavelle had learned over the years to have more respect for the prudent efficiency of the CPR's management, and got on well with Lord Shaughnessy and the new president, Edward Beatty. But he believed that competition, clumsy, cruel, and flawed as it was, was still essential to maintaining excellence in business. More important, the Toronto big businessman agreed with every Western farmer and every radical politician that a CPR monopoly would be a threat to Canadian democracy:

If the Canadian Pacific Railway secures a contract to operate the National System of Railways as well as their own, a small group of men sitting round their board table will make or unmake future Governments of Canada through the use of money and the enormous power which comes through the control of money during an election even for legitimate expense and publicity, and through the influence they can exercise in every constituency in the Dominion by skillfully directed effort through the men who are serving the Corporation.[44]

The CNR's new managers, whoever they might be, would face immense operational problems. Denied recourse to receivership, they could never earn enough money to lift the demoralizing burden of debt lying over the system. The only way to give the CNR's leadership an incentive to compete with the CPR, Flavelle thought, would be for Parliament to agree to start afresh, as it were, by writing off all past government subsidies, and allowing future subsidies to be recorded as interest-free loans covered by common and preferred stock. This would bring the cost of servicing the CNR's debt close to the CPR's interest and dividend obligations, setting the two great railways in competition from a more or less fair start. It would also solve the problem of how to set rates at a level that would not inordinately benefit the CPR.

Flavelle published his assessment and proposals in a long open letter to Meighen in August 1921. It did not contain his private disdain of the Shaughnessy Plan, or a frank expression of his doubts about public ownership. He did warn repeatedly that everything depended on Parliament, the press, and the public all supporting the national railways, so that able managers would come forward and would have the freedom to get their work done. At best, the country would lose hundreds of millions of dollars on the national railway system. The only final solution to the railway problem would be when more immigrants to Canada created more traffic. They had planned the railways in 1903 to serve the people who were coming to Canada. Now they needed the people to make the railways pay. "None of us were wise enough in 1903 to realize the extent of our blunder, . . ." Flavelle confessed.[45]

Gloomy as it was, the Flavelle Plan was a welcome alternative to the Shaughnessy Plan, virtually the only articulate alternative any businessman offered. It represented much-needed support for Arthur Meighen against the political power of the CPR and Montreal business, forces which looked increasingly ready to line up with the Quebec Liberals, get Meighen out of power in the next election, and then muscle Mackenzie King into opting for the Shaughnessy Plan. The open letter also got Flavelle snubbed at the Mount Royal Club a few days after its publication.

Flavelle was still the obvious candidate to head the CNR, more so after his open letter. In a last, well organized effort to change his mind, a delegation of some forty representatives of Ontario Boards of Trade and Chambers of Commerce met with him for three hours on September 14, 1921. Most of his business friends, including E. C. Fox, Sir Edmund Walker, and W. T. White, joined the delegation; nine speakers offered reasons why he should take the job. In reply he gave what must have been a disappointing speech on the job's impossibility—"I have very grave doubts if the angel Gabriel came down that this great property could be administered"—meditated aloud on his sense of duty, and held out no hope that he would reconsider.[46] By now Parliament had been dissolved. When Flavelle refused, the search was suspended until after the December 6 general election.

VIII

As chairman of the Grand Trunk Railway Company of Canada, Flavelle became a director of seventy-nine subsidiary companies and travelled in his private railway car, the *Bonaventure*. But the job seemed likely to be no more than a few months' light housekeeping, pending the Grand Trunk's integration into the CNR. Flavelle knew next to nothing about running railways, and although he was chief executive officer, intended to leave the work to his president, Howard Kelley, and one of the vice-presidents, W. D. Robb. He would make the usual elder statesman's interventions and queries — why didn't the Grand Trunk trains from Lindsay run on time? why did Mark Irish have to call the CPR to find out when the Grand Trunk train from Chicago was arriving? and so on?[47] It turned out that the job was not so easy.

The election campaign in the autumn of 1921 confirmed Flavelle's suspicions about political interference in the management of publicly owned railways. The Grand Trunk loyally complied with the government's decision to have the national railways speed up orders and repairs to alleviate unemployment over the coming winter, but Flavelle resisted when the Ministers of Railways and Finance told a delegation of workers that they would support an abandonment of short-time in the Grand Trunk repair shops. "I do not presume to suggest that any deputation of men have not the right to make representations to members of the Government of Canada upon any subject," he wrote the Minister of Railways, "but I do think that where a body of men are charged by the Government with the responsibility of administering a property, none of their workpeople should be heard without the knowledge of the administrators, and that care should be taken to avoid placing in an awkward position the men whom the Government had charged with the duty of administering the property." He kept short-time as a necessary economy measure.[48]

In 1910 the Grand Trunk had taken away the accumulated pension seniority of striking workers. Mackenzie King, who had arbitrated the strike, was convinced that the company had broken its promise to himself and the men by this action, and was determined to restore the pension entitlement when he got back into office. Prodded by Senator Gideon Robertson, Meighen anticipated King in September by asking Flavelle to reopen the issue. Flavelle considered the request "political interference in the administration of the company's affairs." A special board meeting produced an eight-page statement defending the company's past actions and refusing to reopen the matter. Flavelle probably drafted the key paragraph rebuking the government:

The Board is also impressed with the view that it would prove embarrassing to the operations of the Company, and subversive in a measure of the good discipline of its employees, if it should transpire that the men can succeed by application to the Government to obtain, out of the revenues of the Company, compassionate allowances which the Executive Officers of the Company, in the exercise of their best judgment for the welfare of the general enterprise, have deliberately refused.[49]

There was considerable annoyance in the Maritime provinces at the consequences of the Intercolonial Railway being transferred from direct control by the Minister of Railways to the new CNR system.* In October the Prime Minister's secretary phoned Flavelle in New York to tell him that in three

---

* According to Flavelle the consequences were, "the cancellation of an almost incredible number of passes, the placing of the charges for passenger and freight service under the control of the Board of Railway Commissioners in a manner similar to the other railways . . . the centralized purchasing of supplies and materials in place of the purchases under the old patronage system, and generally, the loss of opportunity of going to a political Minister and urging upon him concessions of one form or another, not based upon merit, but upon political patronage or the fear of political punishment."

days Meighen would announce in Moncton the agreement of the Grand Trunk and Canadian Northern officers to decentralize the new CNR. One of the new divisions, completely staffed and with important local autonomy, would be located in Moncton. Flavelle immediately wired the Prime Minister, refusing to agree. He would not tie the hands of the new executive in advance, and, in any case, believed in centralization. The Prime Minister did not make his proposed promise in Moncton. Flavelle later thought that Maritime resentment at losing control of the Intercolonial was a major reason why Meighen won no seats in Nova Scotia or Prince Edward Island.[50]

The most sensational use of railways was made in the last few days of the 1921 campaign. In November, realizing that integration into the CNR was still months away, Flavelle decided to begin some housecleaning at the Grand Trunk. The company was top-heavy with highly paid senior executives, who would inevitably be asked to retire after amalgamation. Flavelle began to press Kelley and Robb to "cut out the deadwood," both to save money and to help position younger Grand Trunk men favourably for the later competition for the top CN positions. Kelley resisted, however, complaining that it would be disruptive to make major changes in the last months of the Grand Trunk's life. His senior staff were demoralized enough at their uncertain future.

They did have one hope. Lord Shaughnessy's plan would return the Grand Trunk to its shareholders as a separate system. The Grand Trunk would live if the Shaughnessy Plan were implemented. It might be if the Liberals won the election. In late November someone in the Grand Trunk offices leaked the details of Flavelle's deadwood proposals to the *Montreal Star*.[51]

On November 30, six days before the election, the *Star* headlined a "STARTLING RUMOR! REVOLUTIONARY RAILWAY CHANGES SAID TO BE CONTEMPLATED." Montreal was to be deprived of many of its best-railway men in an "autocratic" coup to "facilitate the carrying out of certain dubious plans." The dubious plan, it seemed, was to locate the new CNR head office in Toronto, thus stealing the continent's greatest railway head office from Montreal. "NOMINATED AUTOCRATS . . . A DEADLY BLOW TO THIS CITY, ON THE IMMEDIATE EVE OF VOTING . . . THIS ACT OF RUIN . . . Sir Joseph Flavelle is looked upon as master of the Government on railway policy, but the interests of Montreal cannot be sacrificed to gratify the whims and caprice of one man."

Alerted to the dastardly plan, all the Liberal candidates in Montreal were promising to frustrate the conniving Torontonian. The Liberal Publicity Committee bought full-page ads in the papers: "MONTREAL THREATENED, Destruction of One of its Greatest Assets . . . certain beyond a shadow of doubt. . . . the Government is to blame. . . . Sir Joseph Flavelle is reported to have made millions during the war . . . WE MUST STAND IN OUR OWN DEFENSE." A similar ad in the Maritimes claimed Flavelle's next step would be to move Maritime railway shops and offices to Toronto.[52]

It was a classic roorback, the publishing of an absurd charge too late in the campaign for it to be effectively denied. The owner of the *Montreal Star*, Lord Atholstan (*né* Hugh Graham), had bedevilled Conservative politicians for years with his penchant for political intrigue. In this campaign he had joined the CPR in supporting the Quebec Liberals on the assumption that the Quebec *bloc* in a Mackenzie King government could force the implementation of the Shaughnessy Plan. "Baron Roorback"'s contribution to the campaign cost the Conservatives three or four seats in Montreal, they estimated, the only seats they might have won in a province boiling with hatred of Meighen for his role in introducing conscription.[53]

Flavelle knew that his plan to reduce the deadwood at the Grand Trunk formed the basis of the *Star's* charges. President Kelley, who had stalled about acting on the suggestions, must have gone to the press himself or shown the correspondence to someone who did. Meighen had warned Flavelle that Kelley was too much an old Grand Trunk man to be trusted, and should be replaced; now Kelley had been "disloyal," a new experience for Flavelle in his business life. He considered having Kelley fired, considered resigning himself, but finally decided to carry on until he could discuss the railway's future with Mackenzie King. At a remarkable Grank Trunk board meeting on December 11, he set out his thoughts "with good temper and great frankness" in Kelley's presence, indicating the nature of the disloyalty and his decision that the incident would be forgotten.[54]

The next day he joined Arthur Meighen at a meeting with Atholstan and A. R. Carman, the *Star's* editor. Meighen had demanded to see the "unimpeachable authority" the *Star* had claimed for its "STARTLING RUMOR." Atholstan took the group directly to Kelley's office. Meighen described the scene as "absurd beyond words":

Kelley and Carman cut a sorry figure and looked the part. They asked me what questions I had to ask and I said "None; I was there to be presented with those proofs." After a lot of stupid stammering Kelley pulled out a key and got a sealed envelope from a vault containing [Flavelle's] letters that I had already seen and that referred only to the retirement of a few officials. Not a word even contemplating or suggesting the removal of one man out of Montreal. I took a record of them, told them there was no evidence there that would impress a child out of the cradle. Kelley admitted there never had been a suggestion to move anybody from Montreal. Lord Atholstan was quite debonair but the others looked the part of convicted humbugs. I had the satisfaction of telling them that the entire episode was the most despicable conduct I had ever known in my life.

In his account Flavelle added that Atholstan would have been deeply humiliated if he had had normal human feelings, "while poor Kelley presented a spectacle that made me sorry, rather than angry." [55]

He was sorry, too, that he had been used as a bogeyman to frighten Montrealers about their city's economic future. As in the bacon scandal, he was an excellent symbol, this time of the dominance of Toronto and Torontonians in national business and politics. He and White were insiders in the group that had built the Canadian Northern to compete with the CPR, then used their dominance of the Conservative party to nationalize it (with a $10-million payment to Canadian Northern shareholders that helped get the Bank of Commerce out of serious trouble) and the other non-CPR roads, and were now making sure the CNR would be separate from and hostile to the CPR. The Torontonians had to be watched out for—all the more so when Toronto newspapers like the *Telegram* egged them on by suggesting that, yes, the CN's head offices should be moved away from reactionary, burnt-out Montreal.

Flavelle was not consciously hostile to Montreal on this issue. In believing that the CPR should not get control of the national railways, though, he was personifying old Toronto traditions. The city's opposition to a Montreal-based railway monopoly was as old as George Brown's attacks on the first board of the Grand Trunk. Now the last chairman of the Grand Trunk was a Torontonian, dedicated to having the historic railway swallowed up in a national system to compete with the CPR.

IX

Arthur Meighen and the Conservatives had been crushed at the polls. Flavelle had always been impressed by Mackenzie King's idealism, had even found *Industry and Humanity* an impressive book, but had decided he did not like the Liberal leader. "He is clever, he has many high ideals, he works hard; but, generally speaking, for one reason or another, men do not trust his judgment, and perhaps some of them do not trust his disinterestedness, not in the sense that he is dishonest or dishonourable, but that he is so self-centred that he is unable to lose himself, and all his actions are more or less coloured by the limitations imposed in men possessed of an over supply of self-consciousness." This acute assessment of King was spoiled only by Flavelle's adding, "He does not wear well, either in the House or in the country." [56]

In January Flavelle spent most of a day discussing railways with King and W. C. Kennedy, the new Minister of Railways. King urged him to stay at the Grand Trunk, despite his impasse with Kelley, until the government completed the reorganization. "The interview was most illuminating," King wrote in his diary. "Flavelle was clear, concise, made big problems very simple—showed a fine mastery of the situation, altogether was most helpful." Some newspapers were urging King to renew Meighen's offer to Flavelle; Flavelle told King he would not take the job if it were offered. He did spend several days briefing Kennedy and did all he could to impress the government with the impossibility of the Shaughnessy Plan. He was obviously pleased that the new administration was not going to be in Montreal's pocket and that King was too politically astute to give the national railways to the CPR. [57]

Flavelle's last months at the Grand Trunk were unhappy and unproductive. Relations with Kelley, already impossible, only worsened until the president finally left in August. The Grand Trunk's Toronto chairman managed to annoy Montreal's elite again when, as an economy measure, he tried to cancel plans to build a special station to serve the Royal Montreal Golf Club. A delegation of angry members convinced him that it would be politic to go ahead with the station. The politicians continued to meddle: so long as Flavelle was chairman the Grand Trunk would not agree to have its Central Vermont cars repaired in Canada at an extra cost of $225 per car. Nor would it reopen the 1910 pension issue, even under threat of legislation. Flavelle scolded King for interfering in Grand Trunk affairs contrary to promises made by his own Minister of Railways. [58]

Flavelle got on well with Kennedy, the Minister of Railways, but by the end of the summer he believed that Mackenzie King's main concern was "to play the role as the possessor of superior virtue and knowledge" rather than get constructive jobs done. Whatever the members of the King government were saying, "all their actions seem to show that they unconsciously consider the administration of these railways as part and parcel of the action of Government and that they have a right to act and speak as though they should interfere in management." Meighen urged him to resign and openly criticize the King government's mismanagement. Flavelle decided to stay on and offer constructive criticism in a troubled time for the railways. He had just drafted a long letter to King in early October, 1922, supporting "with such earnestness as deep conviction can command" the need for the new chief executive to be a Canadian, when the government announced that it had found its man, Sir Henry Thornton, an American, who had been managing railways in Great Britain.[59] The Canadian National Railways was brought into full formal existence by order-in-council on October 4, 1922. The Grand Trunk disappeared, ending Flavelle's brief career as a railwayman. One of the first acts of the new regime was to restore the 1910 pension rights.

Had Flavelle taken the CNR job he would either have put an end to political interference in issues like the pensions, or resigned on principle, causing a sensation. He would probably have pressured the government into writing down the CNR's debt as he had suggested in 1921. He would have tried to assemble an executive team to run the CNR like those he had put together for the William Davies Company and the IMB. His letters on railways suggest that he would have tried to reform traditional accounting methods (Canadian railways still did not budget for depreciation, for example, a practice Flavelle considered totally unsound), and that he would have favoured early cooperation with the CPR to consolidate services and lobby governments for rate increases. His methods might or might not have worked; most likely, he would not have lasted a year in office under the King administration. It was important, however, that he had so strongly supported public ownership against the Shaughnessy Plan. He would not try to make the CNR work himself, but he had helped make it possible for Sir Henry Thornton to have the chance.

No one knew much about Thornton, except that he had achieved a reputation as a "superman" in railway management in Britain and in France during the war. Flavelle was one of the principal speakers at the Montreal Board of Trade dinner welcoming Thornton to Canada in December. He wished Thornton well and was genuinely impressed on this first meeting. In his own remarks he stressed the natural wealth of Canada and how the nation and the railways would inevitably prosper if politicians gave them the chance. After insisting so often that the experiment in public ownership had to be tried, he helped launch it by warning that "the reliance placed upon what Government can accomplish is pathetic."[60]

x

In the autumn of 1923 Flavelle was invited to a reunion dinner Winston Churchill was holding for the senior men at the Ministry of Munitions. The work of the IMB had been on Flavelle's mind that year. He was still trying to clear up confusion about a supply of defective small-arms ammunition originating in one of Sam Hughes's discreditable ventures. From England David Carnegie had asked him to help gather material for the history of the IMB he proposed to write. Flavelle had agreed and insisted that he be permitted to underwrite any losses on the book. He was also corresponding with heraldry experts in England about his coat of arms as a baronet. He had a vague memory that his maternal grandmother's family had a crest with an arm reaching for a star, and thought something might be added to this to show his war service, the whole thing being "as moderate as good sense will direct, so as to obviate the appearance of ostentation." The first design, featuring spears, swords, and a flaming cannonball, did not seem to Flavelle to convey a sense of munitions production during the Great War. He was more satisfied with a second effort in which the hand reaching for the star was flanked by two eighteen-pounder shells. This became the Flavelle coat of arms.[61]

Joe and Clara sailed for England on the *Mauretania* on October 30. The reunion dinner at the Trocadero restaurant on November 8 was a fine success, with Churchill making a powerful appeal to his fellow Englishmen not to let political quarrelling dissipate the sense of unity and common purpose they had shared during the war. The night before, Flavelle had also heard an excellent speech by Mackenzie King, in London for the Imperial Conference, at a dinner for families with historic ties with Canada. The group included Lord Durham, Lord Elgin, Lord Grey, the Archbishop of Canterbury, the Duke of Devonshire, the Duke of York, leading politicians, and a score of other peers. It was the most distinguished company Flavelle had ever met and he could not help being proud that Mackenzie King represented Canada so well.

There were more social and semi-social gatherings than Flavelle had time for—the inauguration of Chatham House, the gift of Colonel Reuben Wells Leonard of St. Catharines, Ontario, as the permanent home of the British Institute of International Affairs; the Armistice Day service in Westminster Abbey; dinner and a long confidential talk with Peter Larkin, Canada's High Commissioner; luncheon with Leo Amery at Admiralty House; dinner with Sir Michael Sadler at University College, Oxford; tea with the Master of Balliol; an hour with an old munitions friend who was editing the *Economist*; dinner with Geoffrey Dawson of *The Times*; lunch with the heads of Lloyds, the Westminster, and Barclays banks. Brand and Lionel Curtis gave him opposing views on Stanley Baldwin's capacity to lead the British people. Lionel Hichens and Lord Weir were not too gloomy on prospects for the shipbuilding and steel industries. Flavelle talked over the retail business and conditions among the working class with old friends in the bacon trade and the department stores, and was given a briefing on European agricultural prospects by the resident Massey—Harris manager. In strictest confidence Wheeler-Bennett agreed to do one last study of bacon samples to try to determine why the William Davies Company was having so much trouble with its British exports. From London Flavelle went to Paris and spent several evenings talking European affairs with another wartime acquaintance, who was serving as Secretary of the Reparations Commission. While her husband dined and talked, Clara did more shopping than Joe thought she should ("why shop away from home in damp London?") and suffered through a series of colds.[62]

Montagu Norman, the Governor of the Bank of England, questioned him closely about Canada's economic relations with the United States, wondering if Canadian reliance on Pennsylvania coal and New York money didn't make the Dominion dangerously dependent. Flavelle stressed that Canadian banks had always operated in New York and that Canadians were borrowing American money to finance hydro-electric developments which would free the country from the need to import coal.

I thought that with our increased strength and added sense of importance we would resist [American] pressure and would not lightly or easily be squeezed into the loss of identity as part of the British Empire.... I pointed out ... that in the organisation of Canadian society we were one. To Halifax or to Victoria, to Winnipeg or to Montreal we carried a common spirit on things that really mattered. For instance in church organisation you find no indication of copying American methods in certain sections of the country as against British and Canadian methods.[63]

Most of the conversations were about the condition of England. While Flavelle was there, Stanley Baldwin stunned the country by calling an election on his decision to adopt protective tariffs. It was the only solution to Britain's unemployment, Baldwin argued, massive unemployment caused by imports on the one hand and the inability of the disrupted European countries to buy British goods on the other. Most of Flavelle's friends thought Baldwin had acted rashly, but all of them agreed that Britain was in serious economic trouble. Taxation to pay for the war was crippling British enterprise; high unemployment benefits seemed to be crippling the morale of the work force; the salaried middle class was still suffering badly from inflation. In addition, the rise of the Labour party seemed to have destroyed the traditional two-party system in British politics. Meanwhile, in Europe, Germany was in danger of complete economic collapse from uncontrolled inflation in the wake of France's occupation of the Ruhr. For the first time Flavelle began to wonder what had been won in the war.

He tried to discount his friends' pessimism. "It is always difficult to be assured what importance to attach to bankers' and financial men's views politically," he wrote Willison. "They are so often for what favorably affects comfort and stability, that their annoyance and discomforture does not necessarily indicate they hold a sound public view." Many of Britain's industries seemed to him to be healthier than the financiers thought, and the government's financial problems did not necessarily reflect the overall state of the economy. The extension of unemployment insurance almost certainly caused more people to come forward as unemployed, invalidating comparisons with past totals. It did bother him to reflect on what this support for the "unemployed" did to their will to work:

Private citizens having odd jobs feel they should try to help, and have an "unemployed" looked up. He examines the proposal and finds it is not as good or little better than his dole, and he says no—or he turns down that job as one he does not like. No one can but be concerned when a man is willing to work and cannot find it —and one feels some remedy should be possible—but this dole remedy will not do. . . . I can discern the day coming when men will curse those who established it.[64]

It was in many ways his most interesting trip to England. But try as he might to be optimistic, the times were out of joint. While he was on his way home in December the Labour party gained fifty seats in the British election, enough to make it virtually certain that Britain would soon be governed by a party representing one class. Back in Toronto, Flavelle remarked on the prominent Canadians who had died or left public life while he was away — Lord Shaughnessy, Sir William Mackenzie, W. S. Fielding. His brother, John Flavelle, had died earlier in the year. As 1923 ended, Flavelle pondered how little time was left to the men of his generation, and worried about the future of communities which seemed to have lost their bearings. "I wonder what it all means," he wrote E. C. Fox, "I presume nothing but time will establish new conventions. May we not, however, hope that over the English-speaking world men of sobriety will establish centres of influence whereby young men of unselfish purpose will seek to spread good will, and offer themselves for patient service in whatever field they occupy, that we may become more rational and fairminded." [65]

CHAPTER SEVENTEEN

ELDER STATESMAN

Sir Edmund Walker died suddenly in March 1924. Sir John Aird was appointed president as well as general manager of the Bank of Commerce. Not wanting to concentrate too much authority in one man, the directors created the new office of Chairman of the Board, vested it with responsibility for "the general supervision of the business and affairs of the Bank" at an annual salary of twenty-five thousand dollars, and unanimously invited Flavelle to take the job.[1]

The appointment symbolized his position in Toronto business in the 1920s. With Walker, Zebulon Lash, and Sir William Mackenzie dead, A. E. Ames minding his business carefully, the surviving Cox sons tending to their hounds, and Sir Thomas White in semi-retirement, Flavelle and E. R. Wood were the most prominent survivors of the old Cox family of businessmen. The Cox companies had grown up and apart over the years, of course, and although many of the corporate interlockings persisted, the old relationships were not nearly so important in the 1920s. Flavelle was an elder statesman of Canadian business generally. He was the chairman of Canada's third-largest bank, president of one of the most prominent trust companies, owner of a major national department store, the man who had done Canada's biggest business job in the Great War and turned down an even bigger one at the CNR afterwards. Few of his fellow businessmen had taken the bacon scandal seriously; it had no effect on his standing within the business world. He was in constant demand as a speaker, and his opinions were regularly sought by fellow businessmen, journalists, and politicians.

He almost always obliged, for he was deeply interested in the course of business, public affairs, and the moral health of his community. Next to listening to religious music and the delightful new experience of playing with grandchildren, his favourite pastimes were discussing or writing about current events. He distilled his views from wide reading—history and biography, British and American periodicals, business-news services, several daily papers; conversations with visiting businessmen, politicians, and clergymen; correspondence with old IMB friends at home and abroad; chance encounters and observations on his business and holiday trips; faithful attendance in the boardrooms of the Commerce, National Trust, and Simpson's; and reflection on what he had seen and done in his lifetime. He expressed his opinions to anyone who asked and was willing to listen—other businessmen and visitors at luncheons and dinners, old friends in the evening at Holwood, ambitious young men in the ·Bankers' Educational Association, YMCA groups, Junior Chambers of Commerce, students at St. Andrew's College, and local businessmen gathered for Board of Trade or Canadian Club affairs from Calgary to Halifax.*[2] And to anyone who was willing to read and answer letters. He loved to respond in detail to the slightest query or statement of opinion from a correspondent. Two or three double-spaced pages (dictated to a secretary) was a brief comment on public affairs; four to eight pages the norm; some questions, such as the state of the Conservative party, could not properly be handled in less than twelve to twenty pages. Letters to his regular correspondents—Brand and David Carnegie in England, Rundle, Willison, or White when they or Flavelle were out of town, and Jim Macdonnell, the manager of National Trust's Montreal office—were Flavelle's medium for organizing his thoughts on public issues. He circulated copies of some of his more polished letters and occasionally took the initiative in having copies of a major letter or speech sent to leading editors and politicians.

His speeches were usually well covered by the press, sometimes reprinted in full in the newspapers and/or published as pamphlets. He did not write directly for publication and did not like giving formal interviews to reporters. But his willingness to hold off-the-record talks with journalists and editors, as well as send them copies of his letters, gave him considerable

---

* A hitchhiker could also become an audience. Driving into the city one day in 1923, "I picked up a young fellow, who, I would judge, was a bank clerk, or a man in a broker's office. He asked me—'Do you think business will be better this fall?', and I replied—'I wonder if, on the whole, business is not as good, or better, than we should fairly expect. I wonder how far your enquiry arises from a desire to have business bear heavier burdens than it ever bore before, so as to give better salaries, shorter hours, more time for pleasure, and to produce larger dividends. Would it be worth while asking whether we could not subject business to a lessened strain for personal appetites and pleasures, and personal expenditures. . . .' "

influence with the press. Through J. B. Maclean (founder of Maclean—Hunter), and later Floyd Chalmers, he occasionally influenced the *Financial Post*; in the late 1920s and 1930s he was also close to J. W. Tyson of the *Financial Times*. Through Fred Southam, who had worked for the IMB, he became particularly influential with the Southam newspapers, getting to know and correspond with John M. Imrie of the *Edmonton Journal*, M. E. Nicholls of the *Winnipeg Tribune*, and Charles Bowman of the Ottawa *Citizen*. He knew and sometimes exchanged letters with J. W. Dafoe of the *Winnipeg Free Press* and R. J. Cromie of the *Vancouver Sun*. During a 1925 visit he developed a close friendship with W. H. Dennis, publisher of the *Halifax Herald*, giving him newspaper contacts from coast to coast. Sir John Willison, who continued to write for the London *Times* until his death in 1927, remained a close friend.

In his letters and conversation Flavelle tended to make ten words do the work of five, and seldom missed the appropriate platitude. But he had a rare knack for explanation—breaking a complex business or political problem into its several components, illustrating his points with homely examples and quotations, summing up men and events in sharply turned phrases. Laymen and other businessmen marvelled at the lucidity of his analyses. Some of his correspondents tried to respond to his letters in kind. None of them sustained the effort. Editors sometimes printed his views verbatim, with little or no attribution. Flavelle was pleased at the opportunity to influence public opinion without becoming personally involved in controversy.[3]

I

National Trust and the Commerce were still heavily involved in mortgages and loans in Western Canada, making the region a central concern of the Toronto financiers. Flavelle was particularly anxious to see what the war years had done to the prairie provinces whose growth had so impressed him in 1911. In August 1920 he, Will Rundle, Ellsworth and Guy Flavelle (a nephew), combined business with pleasure by motoring from Winnipeg to Calgary. As his party's two Cadillacs rolled along dirt roads and sometimes over open prairie, Flavelle saw drought-stricken farms expected to yield no more than six bushels of wheat to the acre and lush farms expected to harvest sixty to eighty bushels of oats per acre. He was most impressed by the improvements since his last visit—there were so many farms where the old sod hut or frame shack stood beside or behind brand new homes and barns. As in 1911, he found the general increase in wealth amazing "in a country born but yesterday." At luncheons and dinners in his honour, hosted by old friends or local National Trust or Commerce managers, he preached what became his standard sermon to Western Canadians. "Uncle spoke in his usually fine manner," Guy Flavelle wrote from Regina. "His speeches all try to show the very small differences between Grit and Tory, between east and west, between farmer and manufacturer. He sees Canada working together as a whole to solve its many problems." Flavelle knew that the high prices Westerners were still getting in mid-1920 could not last and that there would be years of low prices, failure, and hardship ahead—"but the unerring crop will come, the increase of wealth will go on . . . the tide of wealth, under the averages which years establish, cannot and will not be stayed." He thought the main problem in the West was simply Westerners' lack of understanding of the Eastern point of view of national problems — misunderstanding fostered by the failure of opinion-leaders across the country to travel, talk, and educate.[4]

Attempting to practise his preaching, Flavelle was often in the West in the 1920s. High prices had disappeared by 1921 and the region suffered considerably in the years of postwar recession. Flavelle repeatedly addressed Westerners' sense of being beset by hard times and hard-nosed Eastern businessmen. Some farmers were suffering hard times, he admitted. But he always warned against exaggerating the long-term problem. Seventy-five to ninety per cent of Western farmers were always able to meet their obligations. As Flavelle told a Winnipeg audience in 1921, how could there be any long-term anxiety in a region where the egg production in Manitoba alone was worth half a million dollars more than Canada had paid for the whole of the North-West during his own lifetime? "Blue-ruin" talk from Westerners seemed to him to come dangerously close to "fouling their own nest," not least because pessimism would discourage investors from risking capital out there. "Of one thing I am sure," Flavelle wrote a Western businessman in 1922, "the condition of the West is better than the West itself knows." Thus the headlines on his 1924 visit: "Former Munitions Board Chairman Urges West to Face Future Undismayed: Little Justification for Grumbling, Much Cause for Thankfulness in Canada, Board of Trade Told"; "Cheerful Note is Sounded by Sir J. Flavelle"; "FLAVELLE STRIKES OPTIMISTIC CHORD ON WEST'S FUTURE. Says Unbounded Confidence in Great West Fully Justified"; "Flavelle Surprised at Sound Position in West"; "Flavelle Talks Individualism to Solve Western Problems."[5]

He saw no political solutions to the West's temporary problems. The Progressive party seemed to him to represent aggressive sectionalism tied to class selfishness. It was bound to do harm because it aimed at dividing Canadians rather than uniting them. In any case the West's problems were mostly psychological, only partly economic, certainly not political. In the worst year, 1923, Aird of the Commerce thought the economic and political problem was serious enough for the Bank to consider supporting government-sponsored debt consolidation in the West. "I supported the view which you already know I hold," Flavelle wrote Rundle, describing the discussion in the Executive Committee, "that what was wanted in the West was not Government interference, but a wholesome return to the conviction on the part of Western men that the manly part was to face their troubles and depend upon their own efforts to see them through. In this process some, perhaps a good many would fall by the way, but a sturdy quality of independence would be established in the remainder (and this remainder should be eighty or ninety per cent of the whole)." The wise farmer, he thought, would stay out of debt, try to diversify his crops, and if necessary reduce his standard of living.[6]

Flavelle's message to the Maritimes was much the same. In 1925 he addressed the Halifax Board of Trade at a time when the region's dissatisfaction with the postwar Confederation was beginning to express itself in the Maritime Rights movement. Flavelle told his audience that all Canadians' duty was to remember the sacrifices of wartime and get on with daily work in a spirit of goodwill. "It's all right, Flavelle, to say that we should work hard ourselves," the president of the Board of Trade told him afterwards. "I don't think anybody works any harder than we do [at this point Flavelle inserted a '?' in his account of the incident]. As to good will, to tell you the truth we are rather tired of hearing people talk about good will. I will ask you a plain question: what are you people in Ontario willing to pay Nova Scotia to remain in Confederation?" Flavelle did not record his answer, but told a correspondent that "at bottom the heart of the [Maritime] people is sound, and not greatly moved by the statements of somewhat cowardly business men who do not relish being uncomfortable. . . ."[7]

On national unity, like most other questions, Flavelle's views could seem absurd—the Toronto plutocrat on safari into the hinterland to tell the natives to work hard and stop grumbling. Of course the importance he placed on developing a proper national spirit in Canada was natural for a Methodist perfectionist who believed anything could be accomplished through effort and will. He wrote about the need to develop "a creative form of good will" in Canada, and eloquently connected that idea with Canada's most persistent national problem:

Good will is perhaps more vital to this country than any other in the world. We are a long narrow strip, stretching from the Atlantic to the Pacific; each section divided by great physical barriers, denying a continuity of population which enables the co-mingling of people with different views. . . . The lines dividing the Maritime Provinces and Quebec are sharply defined; the racial lines between Quebec and Ontario are sharply defined; the physical barrier of one thousand miles of rock and water between Ontario and the Prairie Provinces is sharply defined; as are also the two great ranges dividing the Prairies from the Pacific Coast. Each of these sections has its own peculiar problems. The test of statesmanship, the test of the rank and file of our people, is to learn how wisely to consider one another's point of view, and determine upon such courses as may be possible, where we will be united in a common effort to build up this great country. At the moment, there is not sufficient will for good will. We are magnifying rather our local and sectional points of view, and there is very considerable danger in it.[8]

II

Try as he might, Flavelle could not dismiss Canadians' problems as mostly psychological. By 1924 there was some recovery from the deflation in the West. In Central and Eastern Canada, however, manufacturing activity declined in 1924 and 1925, retail sales stagnated, and unemployment increased. Tens of thousands of talented Canadians, university graduates and skilled craftsmen alike, were emigrating to high wages and steady work in the United States. Immigration, nowhere near prewar figures, did not even compensate for the loss, let alone enlarge Canada's pool of human resources. Taxation to pay for the war debt and the deficits of the CNR was much, much higher than Canadians had thought possible before 1914. The most gloomy prognoses came from businessmen in Montreal, particularly appalled at the railway deficits, out of sorts with the Conservative party, and overcome with a kind of mindless pessimism symbolized by Lord Atholstan's 1923 "Whisper of Death" editorials predicting imminent national collapse. The 1920s seemed to be a stagnant, depressing decade in Canada. "There is a strangely contradictory situation in Canada," Flavelle wrote as 1924 ended,

Montreal is the centre of deeply pessimistic feeling, and quite influential people in their pessimism are predicting that inside of fifteen years we will be absorbed into the United States. Most worthy people in Ottawa . . . are predicting the same thing. . . . they have a feeling that we are without leadership in a constructive policy and broken into units, each section for itself—West, extreme East, and middle—and that we are in danger of desiring affiliation with the United States to ensure a greater share of material prosperity.[9]

He thought the situation was contradictory because Canada's foreign trade was increasing, his own companies were healthy, and Canadians were very wealthy by all prewar standards. He made these points in speeches, attacking the "spirit of whining," wherever it was found, as a discredit to Canadians' manliness. Privately he disdained the Montrealers for their lack of confidence. He thought a line by Robert Louis Stevenson—"When men begin to lie down with the bestial goddess of comfort and respectability"— might explain part of what he called "the rich man's trouble" in Montreal. "With all its size and manliness," he wrote on another occasion, "Montreal has a peculiar provincial atmosphere, and a failure in robustness which seems inseparable from men or communities who think of themselves as being possessed of privilege. The Bank of Montreal has been persistently pessimistic during the past two or three years. . . . faith in the future based upon our development in things which are worth while, is outside the ken of the Canadian Pacific and the Bank of Montreal group. To put it brutally, it is too fine for them." Earlier, he had criticized his own bank's officers for joining the woeful chorus, suggesting that "thankfulness" for Canadians' good fortune was preferable to fault-finding, especially by bankers whose institution was in the happiest state in its fifty-year history.[10]

Still, the business and national problems were real, and Flavelle did at least his share of worrying about them. The burden of postwar taxation on those with high incomes seemed to him a disincentive to Canadian growth. Rich men were salting money away in bonds rather than risk having up to fifty per cent of their profits taken by governments, with no compensation for losses. In 1924 Flavelle called for a fifty-per-cent reduction in the income tax. "You are right in saying that advocacy of such a step would be more effective if it came from one who was less directly affected by the Income Tax," he wrote a critical editor,

Is this, however, a sufficient reason for precluding me from stating my views upon a public matter of much importance to men and women who are dependent for their living upon securing employment? I was careful to say . . . that I was not speaking on behalf of rich men, inasmuch as under emergency conditions arising out of the war, it was just that those who were in possession of means should be required to pay freely; rather I spoke on behalf of workpeople, dependent upon the initiative and leadership of enterprising men, who risked their means and gave their time to the development of new or increased activities. Under the existing system of taxation, men of this class query—Why should I engage in new enterprises? If I lose on them, the Government bears no part of the loss; if I make on them, a very important part of the profit passes over to the Government; under such circumstances, I prefer to invest in Government securities, and for the present, am not interested in new enterprises. —Therefore, as the spirit of enterprise and adventure in business was being seriously affected by the existing system of taxation, I advocated its revision—not in the interest of the tax payer, but in the interest of all the community adversely affected when the spirit of enterprise showed a low state of vitality.[11]

He hoped more intelligent cooperation between the CNR and CPR might reduce the former's deficits, and thought some overall savings in provincial and municipal spending might be possible.*[12] He harped on the urgent need for more immigration—more people to realize Canada's latent wealth, more people to reduce the per capita overhead charges for railways, governments, and war debts. He disbelieved so strongly in organizations and government activities, though, that he tended to discourage friends' interest in grandiose plans to subsidize immigrants. Canada needed hardy, self-reliant newcomers, not people lured by pauperizing government aid. The Sifton campaign of the early 1900s had gone as far as Flavelle thought governments should go. It was unfortunate, he thought, that Western Canada, so adept at complaining, had not produced a constructive, creative successor to Clifford Sifton.[13]

Governments could lead the way. They could cut taxes, advertise for immigrants, improve the climate of enterprise, and generally instill confidence. By 1924 Flavelle was beginning privately to lament the political system's failure to produce men like Macdonald or Laurier, who had led Canada through previous troubled times. Mackenzie King was not a com-

---

* If a solution could be found for the enduring problem that "the tax-payers, who are outraged at the size of their tax bills, continue to want the sort of improvements and expenditures in which they are interested, and to decrease the improvements and expenditures in which other people are interested."

comparable leader. "King . . . is woolly, heavy, dull, in all constructive measures. He talks well; he feels virtuous. After a fashion, he is virtuous. He has
no qualities to arouse men, either in his own party or amongst his opponents." Flavelle thought he had gone down steadily in the public's regard.
"There is not sufficient balance between his sentimental idealism and practical capacity." [14]

The businessman had not much more regard for Arthur Meighen, with
whom he met occasionally to discuss national problems. Flavelle was not
happy with Meighen's tendency as Opposition leader to load the CNR and
the Ministry of Railways with the sins of Liberalism, or in sympathy with
the leader's determination to stress the tariff as Canada's central political
issue. Meighen respected Flavelle's judgment "above that of almost anyone
else," according to his biographer; he did not know Flavelle's judgments
about himself:

Meighen is clever, penetrating in his criticisms, and sometimes makes a rather painful
exhibit of King's duller mind and duller work in Parliament. I do not think, however,
he is winning favour. His cleverness is recognized everywhere. The destructive character of his criticism, however, does not awaken enthusiasm, except with a few
ultra-partisan folk, who are always pleased to have their opponents shown up in a bad
light. Meighen's capacity is that of a first Lieutenant, attached to a big, human,
fine-spirited, constructive leader. . . .

He is the terrier who worries the other fellow, the auditor who discovers mistakes
in the man of constructive imagination.

In what Meighen would have considered the cruellest blow, Flavelle decided
that the Conservative leader's "blue-ruin spirit" paralleled the destructive
views of Sir Richard Cartwright in the 1870s and 1880s. [15]

There were no alternatives in sight. The Montrealers toyed ineffectively
with various schemes for replacing Meighen. Sir Charles Gordon sounded
Flavelle out at least twice on the prospect of White returning to active politics, perhaps in combination with the conservative Liberal, Sir Lomer
Gouin. Flavelle thought White's heart was still in public life, but doubted he
had the patience to wage an uphill fight for the prime-ministership even if
Lady White would agree to his return. [16]

The absence of political leadership particularly bothered Jim Macdonnell
in Montreal. He considered Montreal's wealthy almost totally lacking in a
spirit of public service; Canadian capitalists generally, he thought, fell short

of the standards set by an earlier generation who "with all their faults . . . had minds above money." Flavelle, consciously attempting to be a Canadian aristocrat, agreed:

I fear that the ease and rapidity with which wealth has come to some representative rich people in Canada has occasioned all the danger that was contemplated in the old verse concerning "the camel" and "the eye of a needle." The word "leadership" is rather overworked, and yet, because we have lost in democracy the responsibility of a privileged class, a percentage of whom had definite convictions of their duty to the community, we more than ever need leadership with character, to take the place of the voluntary leadership assumed by the privileged people.

Both Flavelle and Macdonnell began to recall the kind of leadership qualities Canadians had summoned up in wartime, and wondered how it would be possible to revive the courage and dedication of those years.[17]

There was an example of the wealthy trying to provide leadership in young Vincent Massey's decision to enter public life in 1925. Massey went in at the top, as a minister without portfolio, before standing for election. Flavelle wished Massey had not chosen to go into "the feeble Liberal Party, with a feeble leader," and was very upset that Massey should accept a cabinet post without resigning the presidency of Massey–Harris and his other directorships. He put the conflict-of-interest issue to Massey; Massey claimed it was not a problem. Later, when the conflict became an issue in the election campaign and Massey did resign his positions, Flavelle regretted that he and Rundle had not taken a stronger line earlier with Massey in their capacity as trustees for Massey–Harris shareholders. When Massey was defeated in the October general election Flavelle thought the hitherto sheltered young man would ultimately profit from the experience and his mistakes.[18]

The 1925 campaign was one of the least satisfying he had ever seen. He thought Meighen totally failed to attract first-class candidates for the Conservative party, tried to win the election single-handedly, and made far too much of the tariff as the key issue. (In his correspondence with Macdonnell, who believed the Tories were going to have to back down on protection, Flavelle still defended the National Policy he had supported since 1878, but agreed that Tories had been too obsessive about the issue since the war and manufacturers had been too greedy.[19]) He was so openly critical of the Conservative campaign that rumours spread around Toronto that he would support the Liberals.[20]

He loyally supported his party, but was genuinely surprised that it did so well, emerging with a plurality of the seats. Mackenzie King should have been "red-blooded" enough, Flavelle thought, to carry out his original intention of resigning to give Meighen a chance. "It would probably have cost him his leadership, but he would have retained his self-respect." But then Meighen made a transparent appeal for French-Canadian support a few weeks later in a speech in Hamilton in which he advocated the holding of an election before sending Canadian troops abroad in any future war. Flavelle sympathized with Meighen's attempts to overcome the stigma of conscription and shared the common belief that Quebec was naturally conservative on all other issues. He thought it was to the "lasting discredit" of the Conservative party that none of its leaders was fluent in French. This Hamilton suggestion, however, was "clumsy," "foolish," and "stupid to a degree." It confirmed Flavelle's view that Meighen, too much the critical, narrow-minded Westerner, "will never be a sound exponent of Conservative principles." He even questioned Meighen's integrity:

Mr. Meighen is so self-centred a man, and so well satisfied with his own views that one is always at a loss to account for some position which he will take. Notwithstanding this, there has been an underlying conviction that whatever his errors of judgment, he was a sincere, red-blooded man. This particular episode has disturbed many Conservatives, and made it almost impossible to avoid the conviction that this new position was a tricky performance, unworthy of a sincere man.[21]

Flavelle found the political manoeuvring of 1925—6, featuring King's resignation, Meighen's short-lived government, and King's attack on Lord Byng for giving Meighen a dissolution, about what could be expected from the incompetent politicians. The parliamentary sessions, he wrote in July 1926, had ranged from "uncomfortable to discreditable." King's final attempt to avoid defeat in the House was "a shocking, unmanly, wretched business!", a reflection of King's "self-centred egotism." He thought the ensuing general election the least interesting in a generation, but was delighted to see the end of five years of minority government. He had no higher regard for King ("he has not won men's hearts, nor has he succeeded in eliminating a feeling bordering somewhat on contempt on the part of the best men in both the Liberal and Conservative Parties"), and found the thrice-beaten Meighen simply pathetic.[22]

Flavelle's most direct participation in politics in the 1920s was to endorse

Howard Ferguson's liquor policy in the 1926 Ontario election. The Conservative government was proposing to replace provincial prohibition with the private sale of liquor under government permit. Flavelle publicly opposed a further plan to establish beer parlours in hotels. When it was dropped, he told the press he supported the Ferguson policy as "the best obtainable change enforcible under the existing state of public opinion." The Conservatives used this statement by a "Life-Long Temperance Worker and One of the Foremost Laymen of the United Church" prominently in their campaign literature. Reminding him of the great campaigns of years gone by, old friends and clergymen pleaded with Flavelle to say it wasn't so. His family divided, as Will Flavelle left the Conservatives to support total prohibition and invoked the memory of their dead brother, Johnnie, on his side.

Markedly upset at appearing to betray lifelong friends, Flavelle patiently explained his conviction that prohibition was not going to be enforced: "I dislike Government Control as such . . . but I dislike unrebuked law breaking more." He had also come to view coercion as a blunt instrument for attempting to achieve temperance, and although he agreed there had been "revolutionary" effects on working people, he thought that prohibition had to be abandoned until an educational campaign had laid the foundation for a more broadly based renunciation of drink. He knew there would be more drinking and drunkenness under the Ferguson policy, but partly blamed the temperance people for having relaxed their efforts to educate the public. He was troubled, too, by the charge that temperance people were interfering with other people's liberties at no cost to themselves. His acceptance of voluntarism on the drink question—he was soon writing about the need to encourage individuals to take a voluntary pledge of total abstinence —was a practical application of individualism that he would have considered unthinkable in his youth. It also helped the Ontario Conservatives, well on their way to re-establishing their hegemony, to sweep the 1926 election.[23]

The federal Conservatives, Flavelle thought, were about where they had been in 1896. The party had no constructive leaders, no constructive ideas, no dynamic young men, "no prophet of hope and courage." It had fallen back on the old cure-all of the tariff, and the old reliance on manufacturers for campaign funds. It had lacked faith in Canada during hard times and been smashed at the polls. Barring a Liberal blunder it seemed unlikely that the Conservatives would regain power for two or three Parliaments. In all the years since the 1890s, Flavelle thought, the Conservative party had chased after power when it should have been cultivating a sense of national vision and recruiting young men of character. "The Party must learn that its duty is to Canada and to public matters in Canada, rather than to itself and to its members," he wrote an English correspondent. "It will have to win the respect of the country. . . ."[24]

Flavelle did not attend the Conservative party's first national convention in October 1927. He had known the new leader, R. B. Bennett, during the war — they had both stayed in the Château and often chatted in Flavelle's room at night. "He had a passion for a thing which in abler men would be called intrigue," Flavelle wrote of Bennett in those earlier years, "and yet, back of it all, I believe there was a real desire to render public service. . . . His real trouble will not be with the Opposition or with the Party, but with himself." Flavelle noticed how, in his acceptance speech, Bennett swung back to phrases imbued with his early Methodist training, and knew the new leader would seek guidance in prayer. "There is always the wonder of Divine Mercy."[25]

III

Perhaps politics were not so important. By the middle of the decade there were signs of a return to prosperity. The 1925 crops were good all across Canada and got good prices. Interest in Canada as a land to emigrate to seemed to be picking up abroad. In 1926 all the statistics turned upward — railway tonnage, railway earnings, exports, immigration figures, and crops for a second year in a row. Two trips he took that autumn vividly impressed Flavelle: he was one of a party of thirty-five businessmen invited to see Alcan's great power developments and aluminum-reduction works at the company's new town of Arvida on the Saguenay; then, with the other directors of the Commerce, he spent a week in Northern Ontario, visiting Sudbury, the Kirkland Lake–Timmins mining areas (descending to the 3,400-foot level of the McIntyre mine), and the new pulp-and-paper towns of Iroquois Falls and Kapuskasing.

He found it intensely interesting and more than a little surprising to look closely at a country he had only whisked through in the dead of night on westbound trains—"You cannot go to the North country without a sense of shame in your ignorance concerning what has taken place only a night's ride away from home." He had expected to find a frontier not unlike the lumbering and farming frontier north of Peterborough in his boyhood, and marvelled at the good roads, the electrification, the running water, and the fine hospitals in the new company towns. He had never taken any interest in mining ventures and was stunned to realize that the rocks of the Shield really were one of the world's great mineral storehouses. "I must confess to a stupid lack of appreciation of what could be accomplished through the development of water powers in the production of electric energy," he wrote Macdonnell. The northern trips had been an eye-opener to the profit possibilities of hydro. "I suppose I may excuse myself partly for my obtuseness in having been so close to the unfortunate results of the early development of power at Niagara Falls, which finally resulted in ugly losses to private enterprise, and the creation, at the expense of private enterprise, of the Ontario Hydro Electric system, with its subsequent ruthless disregard for the usual decency. . . ."[26]

"Do not misunderstand my letter: there is no boom in Canada," Flavelle could still write in December 1926. Many traditional industries and trades were still depressed, especially in the Maritimes, and there were parts of the West doomed to drought and drift. But Canadians had tended not to notice the positive developments—"the fact is, whether governments are awake or asleep, . . . the latent possibilities of the country are being understood and developed by restless men, with more or less a spirit of adventure, who are risking their own and other people's money in proving the effectiveness of their views concerning certain natural products."

It was a bit disturbing that so much of the new money coming into Canada was American. "One rather longs to put the clock back thirty years in his age, that one could share in an effort to organize Canadian capital to have a more important participating interest in these developments." He did note that the Herbert Holt–J. W. McConnell–Sun Life group in Montreal were active in the expansion, and that Harry Gundy of Wood Gundy had also become deeply involved. " 'A good deal of a plunger' old-fashioned people will say [of Gundy], and their theory will be proved if he comes a cropper. 'A very able man, adjusted to modern conditions,' other people will say, and if he succeeds, he will win the applause of all."[27]

The Holts, the Gundys, and the McConnells aside, Canadians generally seemed to have missed the opportunity to take a commanding share in their country's future. Possibly reflecting conservatism in his own investments, Flavelle thought the burden of taxes had discouraged Canadians from risking their money, and this timidity had been accentuated by the sense of gloom and doom, scolding, growling, and blue ruin after the war, tending to make the Canadian people "temporarily shy of adventure." The new prosperity seemed to confirm his contra-cyclical optimism early in the decade, and to teach again the old lesson that Canada offered unparalleled opportunities for hard-working, courageous, adventuresome businessmen.

When will our people, young and old, come to realize that our danger is not on the material side, but lies in unworthy fear in a northern bred people—to use a vulgar phrase, "the absence of guts." We want an easy time, as short hours of work as possible, as much leisure as we can get. . . . We greatly need the power that comes from character. We need the joy of adventure and the delight in daily toil and daily service, and a mighty belief in the country.[28]

But there was always balance, always the need to temper enthusiasm. In his speeches and letters celebrating the prosperity of 1926–7, Flavelle noted the speculative boom in mining and other stocks in Toronto and forecast an inevitable break with the usual losses to speculators and stock gamblers. Canadians were only beginning to realize how much material betterment they were enjoying, he wrote Lord Byng in January 1927, "and in the realization the revulsion of feeling may lead us into . . . exhilaration which may become as foolish as was the sense of depression."[29]

IV

The companies Flavelle was directly involved with had no special problems in the difficult years of the 1920s. At National Trust, the Bank of Commerce, and Simpson's, company policy mirrored his caution about the first postwar boom. Sitting on heavy reserves and with no long-term commitments, the businesses were all ready when the break came. When National Trust suffered its first net loss on mortgages in 1923, accumulated reserves made the effects inconsequential. At the Commerce, "our own position is sounder than at any time during the twenty-five years of my association with it," Flavelle wrote Rundle in August 1923. "We are entirely comfortable."[30] In 1918, cautious buying policies were instituted at Simpson's; when Flavelle took control in 1920 his accounting reforms pushed buyers into still more care by loading departments with the true costs of their operation. At some time in the early 1920s a tradition of weekly meetings of the senior officers at Simpson's ("somewhat desultory, restless conversations," Flavelle called them) was turned into a formal comparison of weekly results with forecasts and objectives set the week before, completing Simpson's adoption of a system of budgeting. Flavelle urged other businesses, ranging from the Bank of Commerce to his brothers' companies in Lindsay, to adopt a similar system, which was still largely unknown in Canadian business.[31]

Assets and profits declined slightly at the Commerce in the early 1920s, and the number of branches decreased as consolidation began on the prairies. Simpson's sales and profits also declined. But dividends did not have to be cut at either company. At National Trust, profits increased every year, as did the assets the company was administering. The beginnings of government intervention in the Western mortgage market, with the prairie provinces instituting low-cost rural credit programmes, had no effect on the trust company except to cause Will Rundle to devote more space in his annual general manager's address to warnings against "the siren voice of sapping paternalism."[32]

Other businesses were not so fortunate. Canada's chartered banks endured a major crisis in the early 1920s. Several of the smaller banks had to merge with their larger competitors to avoid insolvency. The Home Bank, some seventy branches large, found no one willing to assume its liabilities and failed on August 17, 1923. The Commerce participated in an emergency loan to La Banque Nationale in 1922, announced its absorption of the fifty-one-year-old, 154-branch Bank of Hamilton ten days after the Home Bank failure, and helped the Dominion Bank get through a brief run on its branches in October 1923.[33]

One natural consequence of the Home Bank collapse and the other banks' difficulties was a public demand for government inspection of the banks. Flavelle believed bankers were foolish in blindly refusing to have anything to do with inspection; like Walker, he believed it would have been wise to anticipate public concern by working out a scheme of self-inspection through the Canadian Bankers' Association:

The Bankers should be able to devise some workable plan whereby communities would not be subjected to violent agitation, or commerce to anxiety . . . or the banks to "runs" which may jeopardize their position. It may be the banker can sit tight and say—these are crazy, foolish people, and it is idle to do anything but to allow the temper to burn itself out. I confess I am not convinced that this is a wise course. It seems to me it will be inevitable, if the bankers fail to present a constructive measure, the pressure of crowd opinion, demagogue newspapers, hard-pressed politicians, and people who suffered sore losses will lead to legislation which the banker will angrily dispute, but will be compelled to accept. He will complain, and probably rightly, that the legislation will have mischievous results, and the public will be befooled, but if this is so, and the bankers pay the bill, may not some of the fault of it be laid at their door?[34]

His first action after becoming chairman of the Commerce was to attempt to improve relations between it and the two big Montreal banks. In May 1924 he organized several meetings in Montreal to talk over the general banking situation with Williams-Taylor, Gordon, and Sir Vincent Meredith of the Bank of Montreal, and Sir Herbert Holt of the Royal Bank. He managed to convince Meredith that inspection through the Canadian Bankers' Association would work, but both Holt and the Commerce's own president, Aird, disagreed strongly. The big bankers could not develop a common front for or against bank inspection. Federal inspection was made mandatory later that year. Flavelle thought the discussions had had some utility in establishing friendly relations among the big three banks, which were generally thought to be at daggers drawn.[35]

Flavelle and Aird were in conference with the Montrealers again in 1925 when the premier of Nova Scotia, E. N. Rhodes, appealed to him to intercede with the management of the British Empire Steel Company, the holding company that had acquired virtually all of the Nova Scotia coal, iron, and steel properties in 1920–1. A five-month-long strike by fourteen thousand coal miners had led to rioting, bloodshed, and impending starvation on Cape Breton Island. When it appeared that a government-sponsored settlement was about to be blocked by the intransigence of Roy Wolvin, BESCO's president, Rhodes wired Flavelle asking him to help "save the industry and the province from disaster." Flavelle, who had no use for BESCO's managers and their labour relations, organized the company's bankers, the Commerce and the Bank of Montreal, in "earnest and direct efforts" to influence the BESCO directors. They finally accepted the settlement, thanks largely to the outsiders' intervention. This had been the worst of a long series of strikes against BESCO. "These industries can never succeed under the active direction of Mr. Wolvin," Rhodes wrote Flavelle. "He is one of the most cordially hated men I know."[36]

Flavelle became more involved in the unhappy affairs of BESCO the next year. The first major Canadian trusteeship National Trust had undertaken, agreeing in 1899 to act for the bondholders of the Dominion Iron and Steel

Flavelle as Chairman of the Imperial Munitions Board, the czar of Canadian shell production. Sketched by F. H. Varley. *Public Archives of Canada*

Sir Robert Borden, Prime Minister of Canada. An embattled war leader glad to leave the munitions problem in Flavelle's hands. (Robert Craig Brown)

Trenches: the effects of the shells. Flavelle saw the battlefield in 1916.
Public Archives of Canada

W. T. White. As Minister of Finance,
Flavelle's former protégé at National Trust
provided most of the money to pay for the
shells. *Public Archives of Canada*

General Sir Sam Hughes, an old enemy of
the Flavelles. Hughes and his cronies had
to give way to competent businessmen to
supervise war production. *Public Archives
of Canada*

E. C. Fox, General Manager of the
William Davies Company, who provided
good meat for soldiers in the trenches.

The Pork Baron Illustrated

Addressing a meeting of prominent Canadian manufacturers, in the Board of Trade, Toronto, Sir Jos. Wesley Flavelle, of Wm. Davies Co., pork packers, lifting his spectacles, and wiping the tears from his eyes—a very characteristic pose—said: "As I stood in the trenches beside our brave Canadian boys, I said to myself, "My God, what have I done in return for what these boys are doing for me?" Later, on the same subject, raising his eyes to Heaven, and with uplifted hand, he said: "What have we to do with profits in this war? I WOULD LIKE TO SEND PROFITS TO THE HELL WHERE THEY BELONG."

In 1917 Flavelle was probably the most hated man in Canada, ridiculed and abused because of the William Davies Company's profits.

Who Did You Do In the Great War?

A Flavelle family picnic in the 1920s.

Sir Joseph and Lady Clara Flavelle, the 1920s.

The Flavelle brothers, Johnnie, Will, and Joe, about 1920.

The "Commodore," in his launch at
Sturgeon Point.

"Piscatorial Patriarch"

Two generations: Ellsworth and Muriel Flavelle, Joseph and Clara Flavelle.

PACE·ET BELLO PARATUS

The Armorial Bearings of Sir Joseph Wesley Flavelle,
of Toronto in the Dominion of Canada, Baronet.

Heralds' College.
19th August
1924.

The coat of arms of Sir Joseph Wesley Flavelle, Baronet. The last Canadian domiciled in
Canada to receive an hereditary title.

Company, was still in effect. DISCO was a subsidiary of BESCO. In June 1926 DISCO defaulted on its bond interest, was placed in receivership, and was turned over to National Trust, which acted for the bondholders as receiver and manager. It was a situation apparently unique in the annals of receivership. The BESCO people claimed DISCO was an insolvent property and wanted to sell it off. The National Trust officers decided the property could be run profitably but had no long-term future except as part of the BESCO group. There were hardly any non-BESCO executives to manage DISCO's steel mill and iron mines, but National Trust hesitated to recruit outside executives, who might lose their jobs in a reabsorption. From the summer of 1926, then, the officers of National Trust acted as an executive group for DISCO at its Sydney steel plant and Bell Island iron mines.

DISCO desperately needed sales. Flavelle was instrumental in arranging a major order for 25,000 tons of steel rails from the CPR. Will Rundle made a special trip to Germany to find business there, and both he and Macdonnell worked on special Jamaican and Indian orders in London. Macdonnell also handled labour relations in Cape Breton and Newfoundland. The National Trust people achieved an excellent working relationship with both the men and the local authorities. Edward Fitzgerald, who had retired from the Hudson's Bay Company, was commissioned to do special studies of the steel plant and then was hired full-time to handle sales. After a trip to Newfoundland in 1929 he wrote Flavelle, "I was cautioned that graft was rampant and inevitable. We secured a contract for over $450,000 of rails and not one five cent piece was paid for it. . . . Clean hands are priceless."[37]

Good luck had a hand, too, in helping DISCO earn substantial operating profits under National Trust's management. The receivers took over just as Canada's economy turned the corner, and the company would have been hard-pressed not to make money from 1927 through 1929. Still, Flavelle thought much of the success was due to the efforts and integrity of the trust company's senior officers, of whom he was intensely proud. They were the first people to operate DISCO, he thought, whose main concern was the underlying health of the business rather than the profits to be made through stock-jobbing or dividend-stripping.[38]

The trust company's solicitors were also busy, fighting in the courts an attempt by Wolvin and BESCO to undertake a reorganization that would leave DISCO and its bondholders out in the cold. One result of these complex, unfriendly struggles was that Flavelle again became disgusted with Montreal finance, in this case the Bank of Montreal and the Royal Trust

Company. It was finally an alliance of Toronto and Montreal capitalists, the Holt-Gundy interests, who began to unravel the mess in 1928 by purchasing control of BESCO and beginning to plan a friendly reorganization. Even so, the situation was so complicated, with so many companies and so many classes of securities to be straightened out, that the trust company officers were still running their steel mill and iron mines through 1929. They were being very careful with the Gundy group's new proposals, too. Flavelle noted that he had seen too many "stock-jobbing operations" to take any decisions on behalf of the bondholders until he saw a complete final plan and understood all of its implications.[39]

V

Flavelle had a sentimental interest in another company in serious trouble in the 1920s. The timing of his sale of the William Davies Company could not have been better —just after he sold, everything began to go wrong in the bacon business. The deflation of 1920 – 1 was particularly severe in meat products, and all North American packers took heavy losses selling high-cost inventory at slaughter prices. At the same time the export business became particularly costly to Canadian packers when their sole British customer, the Ministry of Food, began wielding its monopoly power ruthlessly to avoid taking losses on its own mistakes. In one of several incidents, Fox estimated that the Davies Company lost a million dollars in the winter of 1920 – 1 when the Ministry stopped all purchasing in North America on January 1 but did not allow any imports until March 1 while it peddled surplus stocks without competition. Almost all the money invested in American facilities had to be written off, as it became impossible in a depression to compete with the big American packers. Fox estimated that the first six months of his control of the William Davies Company were the worst six months in the history of the industry. When it closed its books in September 1920, William Davies Incorporated had lost $102,150 —the first loss in the history of companies bearing the William Davies name. The next year the loss was $1,235,673. "Have you ever stopped to think how much 'Good Luck' does play in the lives of some people?" Fox asked in a January 1921 note to Flavelle. "Don't think this is a cynical remark of mine or a bitter one. It is just a reflection that I have at the moment."[40]

Things improved, but not much. The company edged a few dollars into the black in 1922, lost $630,000 in 1923, recouped about $425,000 in profits in 1924–5, then lost another $1 million in 1926–7. The net achievement in roughly eight years under William Davies' grandson was a loss of $2,526,000. Holders of Davies Incorporated preferred stock received dividends paid out of reserves in 1920, none afterwards. Flavelle had a token $75,000 worth of Davies preferred, which he had given to members of his family. When the dividends stopped he took the shares back, replacing them with the equivalent value of dividend-paying government bonds.

The company's American operations had been terminated. The retail-store chain had been allowed to run down during and immediately after the war and was apparently never profitable in the 1920s (the stores were sold to a wholly-owned subsidiary, A. Martin & Company in 1921, and finally sold off completely in 1927. Each time he saw the annual reports of food chains like Loblaws, Flavelle wrote J. S. McLean in 1931, he regretted his "folly" in not adding a grocery line to Davies stores and developing the system when he was first in the field).[41] When the mess created by the Ministry of Food finally cleared up in Britain there were only a couple of years of moderate profits before Danish bacon swept the market so completely that Canadian packers could not make any money. Not even the establishment of a national swine policy in Canada, featuring government grading and premium prices, leading to consistently high quality, could overcome the Danes' advantages of distance and time. By 1926 there were not even sporadic profits for Canadian exporters, but Davies Incorporated was still trying to find its lost British market. Particularly with the retail stores in decline, it had no significant Canadian base to fall back on.

One Canadian packing company did not share in the industry's general misfortunes in the early 1920s. As president of Harris Abattoir, J. S. McLean concentrated on building up the domestic business and operated through 1921 and 1922 on minimum inventories with maximum reliance on forward sales. He carried out drastic and ruthless cost-cutting, and refined his accounting still further by working out systems of weekly returns and departmental "return on investment" accounts. During the war Harris Abattoir made money at about one-third the rate of the William Davies Company. In the postwar years when Fox was losing $2,500,000, McLean made $1,949,610 for the Harris Abattoir shareholders.[42]

Although he had encouraged Fox to ask his help at any time, Flavelle saw little of his former protégé in the years after the sale. They occasionally exchanged friendly notes (the sale had left behind "complete good feeling and mutual respect," Fox wrote in January 1920), and Flavelle sometimes gave Fox written advice on difficult questions, but they seldom met and Flavelle never went near the factory on the Don. Flavelle occasionally exchanged letters and visits with Wheeler-Bennett, too, who had become less of a burden to his family in retirement after being appointed High Sheriff of Kent. As early as 1921, Wheeler-Bennett passed back gossip about how Fox was dissipating Davies' splendid reputation in Britain. In 1923 Flavelle asked the old agent to give him one last report on Davies bacon versus the competition. Wheeler-Bennett had not lost his touch or his taste—"Davies' is good product, but it lacks flavour, is insipid to the taste, the lean is too hard and not toothsome. . . . Harris is in much the same category, but is less hard in the lean. . . . Peterboro Matthews was by far the best Canadian product, slightly saltier, with nice flavour, lean, mellow, and softer to the teeth. . . ." "I never thought I should be writing a letter like this any more in my life," he concluded. "I did it . . . to try and help you to a solution of something that seems to press heavily upon your mind."[43]

Fox came to Flavelle for advice in 1925, trying to find out what had gone wrong. " 'Are you sure that the trouble is not within?' " Flavelle asked after listening to Fox's statement. Fox "was deeply hurt by my enquiry, and said he would have expected it last of all to come from me." This was apparently the last conversation they had for many years. E. C. Fox lived into the 1950s; when I asked people who knew him about his attitude to Flavelle the answer was simple: "He hated him." In his hatred and old age Fox also decided that Flavelle had used him as a scapegoat in 1917 and had been unethical in the negotiations leading up to the 1919 sale. That was not true. It was true that Flavelle was totally unsentimental in judging Fox to have failed in the packing business where J. S. McLean had succeeded. "They purchased their raw product on the same market; they sold their finished product on the same market; and, by a strange coincidence, their volume of business was approximately the same," Flavelle wrote in 1927 in language he had habitually used when Davies beat its competitors; "he [Fox] found that he had only been a child in contrast to the judgment of a full-grown man."[44]

Flavelle did not consider how Fox's bitterness must have been sharpened by the fact that he had followed an overall strategy at Davies—American operations and exports—which Flavelle had approved of before he left the company. Flavelle's riposte would have been that the successful businessman knows when to abandon a faulty strategy. Particularly as McLean perfected his accounting, to the point where he was operating a finely-tuned weekly budget system, Flavelle's admiration grew for a former competitor whose methods he had sometimes scorned. In fact and in spirit, J. S. McLean had become Flavelle's real successor in the packing industry.

The last time Flavelle had used the image of children and full-grown men had been in 1902 when he was considering a merger to take over his principal competitors. Conditions in the industry in the 1920s paralleled those of the early 1900s: surplus capacity, heavy losses, one strong house. After several years' discussion, J. S. McLean engineered the merger Flavelle had backed away from a quarter century earlier. In 1927 a new holding company, Canada Packers Limited, acquired control of Harris Abattoir, William Davies Incorporated, the packing house run by Flavelle's first Toronto partners, the Gunn family, and the American firm which had bought out the Matthews — Blackwell business. Although the value of their properties had declined since 1919, the Davies shareholders still contributed a bit more than Harris Abattoir to the physical assets of Canada Packers. Because their assets had much less earning power, they received a much smaller proportion of the common stock. McLean and Harris controlled the new company. McLean was its president, E. C. Fox an unhappy vice-president, soon to leave the packing business.[45]

McLean consulted Flavelle from time to time as he worked out his plans to take over the William Davies Company. Flavelle thoroughly approved of the merger. One Sunday, during a particularly trying time in the discussions, the family at Sturgeon Point were astonished when Flavelle missed church; he was in an earnest business discussion with McLean.[46]

Wheeler-Bennett did not live to see the great merger of the Canadian houses. He would have opposed it because the strong should never deal with the weak. In his last letter to Flavelle he remarked that Britain's General Strike reminded him of his great fight to sell bacon to anyone who would buy, and how he told old Denny then that the two grandest words in the English language were Liberty and Freedom. "Britons never, never, never shall be slaves," he concluded. He died in June 1926, aged seventy.[47]

VI

Flavelle turned down opportunities to become involved in other companies in the 1920s, declining, for example, directorships in Massey—Harris and Canadian General Electric. Nor did he play any significant backroom role, either as strategist or financier, in the mergers, promotions, and company reorganizations that blossomed under the stimulus of easy money. His position, combined with businessmen's passion for gossip, led to other people thinking they saw his fine hand at work everywhere. "I find it is quite a common view that I am mixed up in some way in many of these important mergers and other transactions," he wrote in 1928, "and that the absence of my name in association with them, is a clever way of concealing my hand, which is none the less there. As a matter of fact, I am in none of them." His only role in new companies was to buy "an odd thousand shares of some security that I think is worthwhile."[48]

Old friends did induce him to take an important position in one more company. In 1927 he agreed to Bob Brand's request that he become Chairman of the Board of the Canadian Marconi Company, Limited. It was *the* Canadian wireless company, having grown out of the day in 1901 when Guglielmo Marconi heard through the static on Signal Hill the first transatlantic wireless message, " . . . ". Originally a subsidiary of British Marconi, the Canadian operation was cut adrift during a retrenchment programme in 1927 and offered for sale. Controlling interest was purchased by a holding company in which Brand and Sir Robert Kindersley, acting for Lazard Brothers, were the dominant force, and the Radio Corporation of America, another ex-subsidiary of British Marconi, was a non-voting partner. As Brand put it to Flavelle, their aim was not to make money, but simply to prevent Canadian Marconi from "falling into wrong hands" and "to try & do a service to Canada and the Empire." They wanted Flavelle to act as chairman so that they could have a prominent Canadian on hand to handle high-level negotiations in Canada about the company's future.[49]

Canadian Marconi's marine wireless division, handling ships' wireless and operating coastal stations for the Government of Canada, was steadily profitable. So was its radio broadcasting station, CFCF Montreal, which claimed to have been the world's first. There was less money in the fiercely competitive radio and radio-equipment market. Everyone thought the key to the company's future was going to be the development of long-range wireless telegraphy and telephony. It had a very strong patent position, was operating a reliable short-wave service from England to Canada, and might be in on the ground floor of really spectacular developments if "wireless" replaced cable as the chief means of communication over land. Even though the company was operating only a few thousand dollars out of or in the red each year, it might have an interesting future.

Flavelle's job was to help Brand, Kindersley, and their friends chart a course for the company's future, particularly to work out some stable arrangement with other wireless and telegraph companies in England and America. RCA and the Lazard people wanted a Marconi alliance with the CPR, for example, to forestall the possibility of American telegraph companies joining with Canada's leading telegraph company in a competing wireless venture. Through 1927 and 1928 Flavelle was Marconi's spokesman in an intricate and time-consuming game of threat, bluff, and negotiation with both Thornton of the CNR and Beatty of the CPR. These negotiations finally resulted in the CPR taking a small interest in Canadian Marconi, but not before the company had switched its receiving and distributing contract to the CNR.

In an illuminating exchange of letters with Perry, Lazard's Montreal agent, Flavelle himself suggested another new business relationship for Canadian Marconi:

Flavelle to Perry, August 31, 1927:
By the way, if there is any natural basis for the Canadian Bank of Commerce being the banker for the Marconi Company, it would constitute a reasonable peace-offering to my friends at the Bank, when they criticize me for taking on fresh duties.

Perry to Flavelle, September 26:
If it were anywhere else I would not feel any hesitation, but the account I understand has always been with the Bank of Montreal, & our friend Taylor is very sensitive about their "historical" accounts.

He has not yet got over the giving of part of the Hudson Bay Company account to the Bank of Commerce and he would never forgive you or me if we switched this one—the account I think is of very little commercial value, but it is a name.

Flavelle to Perry, September 26:
I wish our friends in the Bank of Montreal were as considerate in accounts they are associated with as they desire everyone to be in accounts carried by them. They are the most complete representation of the selfishness and narrowness of old-fashioned privilege which we have in Canada.[50]

The British side of the communications picture seemed to sort itself out when a government-encouraged merger united all the transoceanic wireless and cable interests to form Imperial and International Communications.

This ended one of the dangers Flavelle's friends had worried about — that Canadian Marconi might fall into the hands of a hostile cable company. Flavelle wondered why it could not now be sold to I & IC. He must have been a bit disconcerted by Brand's explanations that it was necessary, under Lazard's assurance to RCA, that the American company be satisfied it could get along with anyone who controlled Canadian Marconi. Without quite knowing it, Flavelle the imperialist was helping forestall British control of Canadian wireless, and doing so in the interests of an American company![51]

David Sarnoff and Owen Young of RCA seemed to hope that the little Canadian operation could go a long way on its own. They urged Brand and Perry to find a first-rate manager for the company, and to consider what it could do in developing a wireless network across Canada, expanding its radio-manufacturing business, and beginning to plan to participate in the development of talking movies and television. Flavelle was interested in a friend's suggestion that television broadcasting could be an agent of Canadian unity ("It will be an inspiring experience," C. A. Bowman wrote him, "to sit at home in Ottawa watching, by television, the sailing of a Canadian Pacific liner from Vancouver . . . to see the landing of migrants from passenger ships from Canada's eastern ports; to watch and hear the reapers at work on the prairies . . . or automobiles being turned out in the Oshawa factories."),[52] but he knew he was unequipped to lead a company on the frontiers of electronics. He also knew that the alliance with RCA was probably unnatural. "Do I state the case too strongly," Flavelle wrote Perry, "when I suggest that this isolated Canadian unit, separated from the British merger, and a poor relation of the big American corporation . . . creates the impression that we are an orphan at the door, with no place to go?" Urging his friends to take some resolute action, he offered to resign from the company at any time.[53]

Flavelle was also unhappy at the way Canadian Marconi was being treated as a glamour stock, imbued with the magic of radio and (through RCA) the movies. In 1927, when Canadian Marconi $1-par-value common stock, on which no dividend had ever been paid, was selling at around $3 on the New York Curb Exchange, Flavelle issued a statement saying that the price was unwarranted. In October 1928 the price went over $10; in November it broke through the $20 level and Flavelle heard that normally shrewd investors like Arthur Meighen thought it was a good buy. Flavelle was decidedly uncomfortable as even the nominal head of a company whose stock had become the plaything of "peculiarly impudent" speculators.[54]

VII

He was also uncomfortable with the situation at Simpson's. When he bought the controlling interest in 1920 he had expected to resell it to senior executives in a few years. In the meantime he and Fudger would direct the company's strategy. Except for earnings, which were never disappointing, things did not go well.

One of the key strategic problems involved bringing the senior men along to be ready to take over. Flavelle succeeded in persuading Fudger to devolve authority in a way he never had before, but he was not comfortable with the Fudger protégé who got most of the authority, C. L. Burton. He felt that as a businessman Burton was too narrowly a department-store tactician and that, like Fudger before him, Burton was too disinclined to bring along other strong executives. He may have hoped that Clara's husband, Frank McEachren, and his own son, Ellsworth, would be brought into senior positions. And when Burton approached him in 1925 with a plan for reorganization to give some managing executives greater control in the company, Flavelle felt he was attempting to forestall others in the firm.[55]

After some backing and filling, Flavelle and Fudger accepted an arrangement worked out by J. H. Gundy. A new holding company, Simpson's Limited, bought all the shares in the Robert Simpson companies for $150 a share cash (raised by a bond issue) and $100 worth of Simpson's "no-par" common stock. Flavelle exchanged his shares in the old companies for about $2,500,000 cash and 40,000 shares in the new company. That was about a 40-per-cent interest, still large enough to maintain control. C. L. Burton emerged from the reorganization as the second-largest shareholder with about 15 per cent. Three thousand of his shares were a gift from the company in appreciation of his services, a suggestion made by Fudger. Both Burton and Fudger promised Flavelle that a greater effort would be made to bring along new talent.[56]

After 1925 the situation got worse. In his old age and contra-cyclical conservatism, Flavelle disapproved of the major modernization and expansion programme pushed through by Burton and the other executives. Eaton's had upset the easy department-store duopoly in Toronto by buying land at Yonge and College streets and announcing plans to erect a big new store there. Simpson's decided not to follow Eaton's uptown, but were afraid that someone else — most likely the Hudson's Bay Company — might take up Eaton's offer of the land across from its new College Street store. Members of Flavelle's family were grumbling openly about Burton's autocracy, but Flavelle was worried that a quarrel with Burton might drive him and others into the arms of a competitor. As he turned seventy he dreaded the thought of having to make decisions about Simpson's future on his own if Fudger, now seventy-five, were to die.[57]

There had been at least half a dozen feelers from Americans in the last few years. In 1928 Frank McEachren and Ellsworth Flavelle joined with two of Simpson's senior men to formulate a proposal to buy out Sir Joseph. Burton, asked to come into the group on a twenty-per-cent basis, indicated that no discussions should proceed without Flavelle's knowledge. When Ellsworth refused to tell his father about the discussions, Burton did.[58] Nothing more came of the proposal. Flavelle seldom alluded to his disappointment with his son and his son-in-law, whom he no longer considered competent to keep Simpson's in the family.

Soon afterwards, Flavelle persuaded Fudger to take the American offers seriously, provided that Canadian management of the operation would be retained. Two American department-store organizations came to Toronto in the spring of 1929, studied the company, and offered $135 to $136 a share for Simpson's common stock. While Fudger and Flavelle were considering the offer, J. H. Gundy came to them "entirely unsolicited and unexpected," offering $150 a share on behalf of Wood Gundy and a group of Simpson's senior executives led by Burton. It is not clear whether Burton or Gundy had taken the initiative in forming the group. Flavelle, who seems to have been surprised that the Canadians could raise the money, had no objection to the offer. Although $150 meant roughly a 400-per-cent appreciation on his shares since 1925, Flavelle thought the price was not unreasonable in view of 1928 earnings of more than $15 a share. Burton later estimated that about 35 per cent of the purchase price was paid for intangible assets, including goodwill.

On June 15, 1929, approximately 60,000 shares of Simpson's common, the entire holdings of Flavelle and family, Fudger and family, and the Cox interests, were sold to Wood Gundy. Flavelle received just over $4,800,000 for his shares, and members of his family another $800,000 or more. Wood Gundy immediately proceeded to reorganize Simpson's Limited, with major new issues of bonds, preferred stock, and two classes of common stock. Two months after the sale Flavelle wrote Jim Macdonnell that the price he got "was very reasonable in contrast to transactions of a similar character during recent years." "We had no share in the method of refinancing," he added, "which was carried through in a characteristic manner."[59]

The sale ended his thirty-one-year connection with Simpson's. Flavelle did not reflect on how profitable it had been materially. He deeply missed his daily association with H. H. Fudger. Fudger, the gentle merchant prince, had the same regret. "I am depressed with a sense of loss akin to bereavement," he wrote to Flavelle. "No association or friendship has come into my life which I have prized as highly and nothing can take its place."[60] Fudger died ten months later.

VIII

Through 1928 and 1929, the most prosperous years Canadians had ever known, Flavelle gave frequent speeches on business conditions and wrote his long letters on the state of the nation. He sometimes referred to himself as a member of a past generation—marvelling, for example, at the vast sums of money financiers had to invest these days, professing to be amazed by a conversation about diesel engines with Sir Henry Thornton and the experience of speaking directly to Mexico City by telephone. In fact he had taken on a new job as chairman of the Ontario Research Foundation, a public-private organization created to advance industrial research in Ontario. Most of Flavelle's speeches to businessmen in 1928 and 1929 were sermons on the need to increase efficiency and productivity by paying attention to the best modern methods, supporting research, and being up-to-date in accounting by using a budget system. The refrain of all his talks was to look to the business itself, do it as well as it could be done, and take the profits it produced as a by-product of work well done.

The political scene was quietly satisfactory. Flavelle felt that Mackenzie King—"a much more capable politician than was supposed"—had done a fine job of bringing new blood into the cabinet, making it one of the strongest since the palmy days of Laurier. "Except through some accident," Flavelle wrote at the end of 1928, "it would appear the Liberal Party will be continued in Government for many years to come."[61]

Along with other businessmen, especially railway leaders, he was unhappy at the government's reluctance to launch a great immigration programme; fortunately more people were coming to Canada anyway. Flavelle wished that not quite so many of them were American entrepreneurs and financiers, backed by the "almost irrational faith they have in our future." "I think there is no doubt that it has been American capital, applied to water powers, production of paper & pulp, the necessary investment in timber limits and the investment of American money in the development of our mineral resources that has, in addition to our purely native industry in agriculture, been responsible for the active condition of business in the country today," he wrote in 1928. Although taxes had been reduced, he still believed they were a disincentive to Canadian investments in enterprise.[62]

And it was curious how investors were combining the security of tax-free, low-interest bonds on the one hand, with stock-exchange speculation on the other. Flavelle understood how technical developments in corporate finance—particularly the issuing of low-cost no-par common shares—were feeding the public's appetite for speculation; and he saw how it was in the interests of companies to raise cheap capital without incurring fixed interest obligations. "When the morning after comes in the present speculative fever," he wrote in Feburary 1929, the corporations would benefit from the greater liquidity no matter what happened to the investors.[63]

Investors were surely going to get hurt, for, as White wrote him in the spring of 1928, the stock-buying spree had become a "mania." In the fall of 1928 one of Flavelle's acquaintances became an early "derelict . . . thrown on the shore," having lost $250,000 gambling in mining stocks. Many others were about to lose bundles in Canadian Marconi, J. W. Flavelle Chairman, which reached $28.50 a share in November 1928. At this price the market value of a company with assets of about $5 million and earnings of $00.01 a share, was $129,789,000. Flavelle was starting to be criticized by friends who had *not* invested in Canadian Marconi because he said it was overpriced. In an interview with Floyd Chalmers of the *Financial Post* he finally repeated his statement of a year earlier that Canadian Marconi was overpriced at $3.00. In two days it fell from $28.00 to $8.00. It also helped spark a short, sharp decline on New York markets that cost investors several billions—a portent. "I am afraid a great many people must have lost a lot of money. It really is a heartless kind of robbery," Brand wrote. "It is very bad, too, for the Company, but I do not know how it can be stopped." It did not exactly stop, for the Marconi shares continued to sell in the $9.00-to-$10.00 range, 900 to 1000 times company earnings. The New York markets went on to new highs.[64]

In speeches to the annual meetings of National Trust and Simpson's early in 1929, Flavelle again warned against speculation. He told the Simpson's shareholders about a couple of farmers who had made $500 each in INCO shares a month or so ago. "One of them said, when he could pick up more in a few days on the stock market than he could in a year on the farm, he was not going to waste his time in plowing any more. It is our wager that they will eventually go back to the plow."[65]

In June 1929, when enthusiasm for the future of corporations in North America was at something close to an all-time high, a young man in Colborne, Ontario, wrote Flavelle asking his thoughts on the debating question, "Resolved, that a farmer with $1000 and stock and implements is in a better financial position than a city man receiving a salary of $2000 per year." In a five-page reply Flavelle contrasted the dependence of the clerk in a large organization with the "fine independence" of the farmer. A very few clerks would rise to positions unattainable by any farmer, but most would not. On balance, the farmer's life was better. "In the truest sense of the word 'gentleman,' a farmer occupies a gentleman's position. He is independent, has an opportunity to make the best of his life with the least interference from others, and an opportunity to benefit his industry and his enterprise by the quality of his work, and the intelligence of the direction of the affairs on his farm. He has considerable freedom in time for reflection, and a deliverance from much of the distracting excitement of urban life."[66]

CHAPTER EIGHTEEN

"OPEN HOUSE FOR BEGGARS"

Flavelle had been brought up to give time and money to good causes. All his life he continued to give time and money—to Toronto General Hospital, the University of Toronto, Sherbourne Street Church, and dozens of religious and charitable organizations. As he grew older he gave up some of his responsibilities—and promptly took on new ones. He gave more money away than he had ever done before. He did not like publicity for his work or his donations. They were services the community had a right to expect from its men of wealth and standing, and from anyone who believed in the higher life of service.

I

He ran one last fund-raising campaign for Toronto General Hospital. One of the big subscribers to the building fund had given none of the money he pledged (it was probably the anonymous donor of 1911, who was probably Sir William Mackenzie), and several other pledges had not been met. In 1916 Cawthra Mulock, whose promise had started the fund-raising back in 1904, had still not paid his full $100,000 towards the Cawthra Mulock Out-Patients' Building. Will Rundle nagged and haggled with him, getting an occasional $10,000 instalment after threatening to take him to court.[1] Mulock died in the influenza epidemic of 1918, still owing $26,000. Cases like his, plus the failure to sell the old hospital buildings, plus accumulated interest, left the building fund about $800,000 short by 1918. Anticipating trouble trying to raise money after the war, Flavelle attempted to clear the deficit that year.

"For manifest reasons I must not say anything to munitions contractors," he wrote T. A. Russell, appealing to him and Lloyd Harris as personal friends to give $10,000 from their company. He asked Sir Frank Baillie for $50,000, E. C. Fox for $15,000 from the William Davies Company, and J. S. McLean for $15,000 from the Abattoir. Other friends pledged $50,000. His own contribution, pledged without publicity in February 1918 when he was still Canada's hated profiteer, was $250,000. To protect the hospital from tardiness he asked his friends to agree that five-per-cent interest would accumulate on unpaid pledges from March 1, 1918. After some delay, Will Rundle and H. H. Fudger led a campaign to solicit other Torontonians and approached the province and the city for further grants totalling $250,000. By mid-1920, just before the postwar bust, the money had all been raised and Toronto General Hospital was debt-free. There were even some windfall grants. Charlie Blackwell, Flavelle's old competitor in the packing business, made a sizeable donation for laboratory equipment out of his proceeds from the sale of Matthews – Blackwell. In 1922 the Cawthra Mulock estate gave Toronto General Hospital $45,000 in full settlement of Mulock's pledge plus accumulated interest.[2]

While Flavelle was in Ottawa, Rundle and Peter Larkin saw the hospital through a major wartime operating crisis (in 1917 the trustees threatened to close its doors unless the city and province helped meet the operating deficit). A new superintendent, Horace Brittain, instituted major organizational and accounting reforms.[3] The most significant change was the 1919 decision to centralize the "services" in medicine and surgery under a single head. Favoured by Flavelle in 1908, but opposed by the university doctors, centralization was urged on the hospital by the university, which was reorganizing the Faculty of Medicine. All these changes had taken place by the time Flavelle began to attend board meetings regularly again in 1919.

His routine duties as chairman—trying to get the staff to explain why a lunatic who had jumped out of a window and killed himself had been kept in an unbarred room on a top floor, getting to the bottom of the affair of the Chinaman and the Emergency Department, looking into *Jack Canuck's* (absurd) charges that the new superintendent was a "chicken chaser" and that Flannigan in the Engine Room was bootlegging hospital whisky — were varied but not overwhelmingly demanding. "The big constructive period of the Toronto General is over," he wrote early in 1921. Flavelle, Will Rundle, and Peter Larkin resigned their administrative positions on the board early that year. Charlie Blackwell, who had just come on the board, took over Flavelle's job. At Flavelle's last meeting as chairman of the board there were glowing tributes to his work.[4]

He was a trustee of the hospital for the rest of his life, but seldom attended meetings. He did sit on the committee which established a diabetic clinic following the successful treatment of Leonard Thompson with insulin, and often discussed general hospital policy with Blackwell. Most trustees were always apathetic, he assured the new chairman, and the university people had always been tactless. Flavelle faithfully attended the annual graduation ceremonies for nurses, whose work always appealed to him as a form of public service. In 1927 he pledged $50,000 to the campaign for major new buildings; in 1930 he agreed to give another $25,000 and then $35,000 more.

II

Affairs involving the hospital caused a major threat to the system of university government Flavelle had helped to establish in 1906. It was the modernization of the Faculty of Medicine, partly to meet the terms of large grants from the Eatons and the Rockefeller Foundation, which led to the centralization of clinical services at the hospital. As in 1908, hospital reorganization created a storm of protest inside and outside the university from doctors who lost privileges and prestige. Their complaints to Ontario's farmer premier, E. C. Drury, triggered more general dissatisfaction with the University of Toronto: the Board of Governors was autocratic; the Senate and the alumni were ignored; the system was "a big business machine," designed by an autocratic businessman; there were not enough residences for farmers' sons; distinguished doctors with overseas service were being dismissed because the university wanted "Yankee money"; and so on. Drury himself chaired a select committee to look into the government of the provincial university.

Flavelle testified before the committee and gave a major speech to the Toronto Canadian Club defending the university's administration as both democratic and a demonstrably excellent way of governing the factious academy. He greatly feared a return to the confusion, demoralization, and bad publicity of the years before 1906. The committee agreed with most of the criticisms of the medical and hospital reorganizations and recommended significant changes in university government to weaken the powers of the Board of Governors. Before anything could be done, the Drury government was defeated. Howard Ferguson's Conservative government tinkered a bit, but let the issue simmer and die. The reorganized services at Toronto General worked very well, and the Board of Governors system at the university lasted until 1971.[5]

Flavelle stayed in the background at the university. His only active committee work on the board was to serve on the Insulin Committee, helping develop royalty and licensing policies for the world-wide manufacture and distribution of the miracle drug. Most of his influence in university affairs was exercised in behind-the-scenes conversations with Falconer, other governors, members of the staff, and members of the Ontario legislature. "There is none of my friends with whom I could confer so helpfully as with yourself," Falconer once wrote him; the aging president told others how much he regretted the failure of new businessmen on the Board of Governors to understand and sympathize with the university in the way men like Walker and Flavelle had.[6]

He gave modest amounts of money to the university: $2,500 for the War Memorial Fund, $10,000 for the Banting Research Fund, $5,000 for the Maurice Cody Fellowship Fund, and innumerable smaller donations for portraits, scholarships, special lectures, and the university band. In 1928, for example, he contributed $30 of the $200 fund Pelham Edgar raised to help E. J. Pratt go to New York over the Christmas vacation. Pratt wanted to study a ship and interview the crew. The result was his poem *The Roosevelt and the Antinöe*. In 1925 Flavelle and E. R. Peacock agreed to pay $2,500 a year for five years so the university could strengthen its commercial programme by hiring A. J. Glazebrook (in his spare time the guiding spirit of the Canadian Round Table movement) to teach courses in banking and commerce. They continued the arrangement until Glazebrook retired in 1937, then gave the university $1,500 annually for his pension.[7]

III

In early 1928 Howard Ferguson asked Flavelle to become chairman of the just-created Ontario Research Foundation, a unique public-private venture to undertake and encourage industrial research. In the late 1920s the possibilities of payoffs from industrial research seemed truly great—improved efficiency and greater competitiveness for Ontario industries, less reliance on American know-how and processes, more jobs for young Canadian scientists and technicians, who otherwise left Canada almost automatically. Canadian industry was not doing very much research—private companies were spending a combined total of only about $400,000 year, Flavelle estimated in 1930—and the Dominion-wide organization, the National Research Council, was being kept caged and famished by Mackenzie King. Ferguson took up industrial research as a pet project, put through the legislation setting up the ORF, and personally solicited endowment funds from companies doing business in Ontario (his government matched private contributions, which totalled $1,870,000, dollar for dollar). Flavelle thought Ferguson's scheme was a sign of growing national maturity in Canada, agreed to be chairman of the new organization for a year to help get it launched, and pledged $50,000 to the endowment. His was the only significant donation by an individual.[8]

Through his own pioneering work at the William Davies Company, through the contributions research made to munition development and production during the war, and through his contacts at the university, Flavelle was closely acquainted with the state of industrial research in Canada. He drew on the IMB and the university for the scientist to serve as the ORF's first director: Horace Speakman was a British-born chemist, who had supervised the acetone production in Gooderham's distillery during the war and then taught in the university's Department of Zymology. Flavelle drew on his packing and war experience to help formulate an initial ORF policy of doing contract research for trade associations. Industries could profit from research done on behalf of all their members, he hoped, just as all the packers had always needed to incorporate the most advanced methods in their struggle to survive on the British market and the shell-manufacturers had all profited from the free exchange of information and expertise during the war. J. S. McLean agreed to become the vice-chairman of the ORF, and the packing industry was one of the first to ask for the Foundation's help.

Flavelle spent a considerable amount of time in 1928–9 working with Speakman, meeting with scientists and businessmen to publicize the ORF, and assuring suspicious National Research Council people in Ottawa that his aim was federal-provincial cooperation rather than competition in research. In September 1929 the cornerstone was laid for new laboratories connected with the ORF's Queen's Park offices. Flavelle thought there was bound to be public disappointment when miraculous discoveries (comparable to, say, the discovery of insulin) did not pour forth from the ORF's labs. Well-funded as it was, the ORF still had less money each year than several individual American companies spent on research. Even so, it was surprising and disappointing when manufacturers seemed disinclined to take much interest at all in the ORF, especially in the idea of cooperating to sponsor industry-wide research. More cynically, J. S. McLean had doubted from the first that many Canadian manufacturers had ears to hear the gospel of increased efficiency through research. The trade-association idea was particularly idealistic. As Flavelle might have known from his own experience, competitive manufacturers, even meat-packers, wanted to keep new processes to themselves.

In spite of the disappointments, there was enough work to keep the ORF's staff busy (at Speakman's insistence they also devoted part of their time to pure research), and to raise the possibility of the ORF needing more money than its modest endowment income. Flavelle was persuaded to stay on as chairman. He and Speakman became close friends; particulars of the organization's projects fascinated him, and he was valuable as an articulate and influential figurehead of the ORF.[9]

IV

There was always time for the Church. After the bacon scandal Flavelle was never highly visible or vocal at church events, and was particularly disinclined to renew his old relationship with Victoria College. But his determination to become just another worshipper soon weakened in the face of constant urging from Methodist officials; he seldom turned down a request to serve on committees or give confidential advice on some problem in church organization or finance. As a loyal supporter of Church Union, for example, he sat on half a dozen Methodist and joint committees working out the details of the Union and the structure of the new church. He helped raise a special fund to pay the expenses of the Union campaign and was chairman of a layman's committee which did useful lobbying in Ottawa to support the controversial legislation giving legal substance to the United Church. He was deeply moved by the first ceremonies of the United Church of Canada, held on June 10, 1925. In morning, afternoon, and evening sittings, eight thousand delegates to the General Council, their wives, friends, and other onlookers, worshipped and took communion in Varsity Arena. Flavelle had been worried that it would be undignified to hold a service of worship in anything but a church.

He did not think the Methodists had provided particularly strong leadership in the Church Union movement, and was not sorry to see some of the older generation step aside. He helped raise a $20,000 fund to buy S. D. Chown, the Methodist general superintendent who decided not to stand for election as moderator of the United Church, an annuity to supplement his superannuation. He hoped that T. Albert Moore, another old Methodist, who became the semi-permanent general secretary of the organization, could also be nudged aside before he accumulated too much power—"If he were not a Christian man, and were in New York," Flavelle wrote of Moore, "he would make an excellent lieutenant to a Tammany Chief." [10] The central officers of the Methodist Church, he thought, had been too powerful, their position too antithetical to the democratic spirit of Methodism. As a member of the United Church's Commission on Permanent Organization, he almost certainly cast his influence on the side of decentralization and disorganization. After Union he served on many of the church's central committees and worked very closely with ministerial bureaucrats like James Endicott, Jesse Arnup, and Peter Bryce. But he was always afraid that the church was overorganized. Three years after the formation of the United Church he was asked how it was doing as an organization:

There is in every community, a percentage of men and women who love office. . . . In the church, there is a percentage of the same type who find great satisfaction in office. They are restless for meetings, for Conventions, for conferences, and councils, for inspirational meetings, etc. etc. . . . as they are generally pertinacious, new organizations develop, new secretarial positions are created, and new committees formed. They are hard-working, devoted people; they put the rest of us to shame in many respects. Meantime, men who are immediately next the work are sometimes irritated because they think there is an attempt at domination from the central bureau. . . .

I am one of the old-fashioned sort, who grew up to look to the minister for leadership and counsel. In matters of social reform and moral endeavour, he seemed to me to be in his natural position in leading the members of his congregation in an intelligent sense of responsibility. I fear, however, the tendency of the modern, highly-organized church is to make the minister somewhat less important in initiative and constructive leadership. . . . one instinctively thinks of him as being somewhat overshadowed by the perhaps necessary organization of a great body. How to wisely control the disposition to organize, how to keep in reasonable place those who are ever calling for some fresh exploitation in meetings or other forms of activity, is the problem. . . ." [11]

The United Church did not seem to him to be fulfilling the highest hopes of its founders, hopes expressed at that first luncheon in Holwood in 1904. As a perennial member of central committees handling church funds, Flavelle shared the deep concern in the late 1920s when givings to support missionary and general denominational work fell far short of both budget targets and reasonable expectations. He knew there were explanations for the financial problem — the rise of competing social-service organizations like Rotary and Kinsmen, disillusionment with missionary work, the general postwar determination to enjoy a higher standard of living. Still, he felt that the short-fall in contributions was also a sign of his church's inability to influence its members' lives. "There is a disappointing lack of power in our Christian lives," he wrote in 1929. "This United Church, so successfully merged in all the mechanical processes, has, as far as one can observe, produced no deep consciousness of spiritual character, enlarged and enriched by the new opportunities." The United Church was a merger of religious organizations. Flavelle sometimes wondered whether it was vulnerable just like business mergers—perhaps denominationalism had its good points: "It may be in the order of divine planning that virility and power in human effort have some necessary association with competitive action, and that the competitive spirit is not wholly unlovely." [12]

His personal religious life centred on daily prayer and Sunday worship at Sherbourne Street. Class meetings had died out at the church during the war and Sunday School attendance had declined sharply from the years of Flavelle's superintendency. The Sherbourne–Carlton neighbourhood had changed markedly as the wealthy and their children had left for Rosedale or Forest Hill and their old homes were converted to boarding houses for middle- and lower-middle-class tenants. H. H. Fudger, for example, bought Senator Cox's mansion and turned it into a residence for working-class girls. Few of the new people came to Sherbourne Church. By the late 1920s the congregation was declining and there were not many church activities beyond the Sunday School and Sunday services. Sherbourne still featured some of the best preaching and the finest music anywhere in the United Church, and three of its wealthy pillars, Fudger, A. E. Kemp, and Flavelle, were still among the most regular worshippers. But where was Sherbourne going? Its congregation, like that of so many other downtown Toronto churches, had moved away and was dying.

In 1928 Sherbourne's minister, Richard Roberts, estimated that the United Church needed only three well-equipped churches to serve the eastern downtown area of Toronto. Instead it had ten. Rather than see the "Sherbourne tradition" gradually die out, Roberts suggested the congregation might merge with Metropolitan Church, which was experiencing the same problem much further downtown, to concentrate their resources in making one great United Church cathedral in the heart of Toronto. H. H. Fudger was not unsympathetic to Roberts' scheme. Flavelle, on the other hand, thought the congregation's duty was to stay in the neighbourhood. "We should stand by to assist at least with our means, that the work may go on." They finally decided to raise a fund to modernize the church building, particularly to equip it for more community activities, and to endow Sherbourne Church so there would be a substantial income after the wealthiest layman had died. Flavelle contributed $50,000 to the improvement and endowment fund. He also contributed $50,000 to help rebuild Metropolitan Church—which had been destroyed by fire—on condition that the reconstruction include a centre for social work.[13]

Flavelle had always given his largest donations for missionary work. The one major church-related job he took on in the 1920s involved missionaries working on the other side of the world. On the Chengtu plain in China's Szechuan province, within sight of the mountains of Tibet, there was a North American university, the West China Union University. It had been founded in 1910 as a joint venture of the Society of Friends and the (Anglican) Church Missionary Society in England, the Baptist Church North and the Methodist Episcopal Church in the United States, and the Methodist Church of Canada. As the dominant missionary force in West China (they had one of the largest concentrations of missionaries there of any church anywhere in the world), the Canadian Methodists played the leading role in founding and staffing the university. The aim was to help win West China for Christ by offering a Christian higher education to converted Chinese who would become leaders in community and church. By the early 1920s some 600 students were enrolled in schools on West China's 150-acre campus just outside of the walled city of Chengtu; about 200 of them were taking university courses in arts, science, medicine, and dentistry, while living in western-style dormitories "less ugly than those at the University of Toronto."[14] The university's property was owned and managed by a Board of Governors appointed by the participating mission boards. Flavelle had been a nominal, inactive member of the board for several years, representing the Methodist Church. In 1923 he agreed to succeed Newton Rowell as chairman.[15]

The chairmanship involved quarterly meetings—usually in New York, occasionally in England—and a good deal of prosaic financial work. Flavelle pleaded with the mission boards for more support, held up the admission of women to the university until the women's missionary societies of the churches agreed to help support them, and regularly reminded president Joseph Beech in Chengtu to use his funds only according to the board's allocations. He had difficulty getting a clear accounting of the spending in China, let alone bringing Beech's spending under control, and had to write gentle sermons to Beech on the danger of erecting more buildings than the university could maintain and on the obligations of Christian trusteeship:

I hold such tenacious views concerning trusteeship that I am unable to look upon the aggregate of funds as being available for buildings as long as the money lasts. I believe that the obligation peculiarly rests upon Christian men to strictly observe the conditions under which moneys are advanced, and that we should not borrow, or use without the formality of borrowing, monies which are pledged for one set of buildings, for another set of buildings, . . . I know it is usual in church work to be flexible in this regard, but I also know that the violation of trust relationships carries inevitable penalties. . . . I am seeking support for a sound procedure recognized as binding upon men of affairs, and which should peculiarly apply to the discharge of obligations under the direction of the church.[16]

Flavelle had a simple-minded view of missionaries as "unselfish and devoted people . . . who desire no reward other than being of service in enlarging their [the natives'] view of life and bettering their physical as well as their spiritual condition." There is no evidence that he ever thought in terms of a connection between extending missionary work and extending capitalism. "The only purpose we have in China is that we may extend the knowledge of the Christian religion and faith with its beneficent consequences." He shared the missionaries' belief that their job was to plant the seeds of Christianity in China and then gradually withdraw as a Chinese Christian church grew and flourished. Most of the time he spent on mission business was passed reading the missionaries' long, detailed, and troubled accounts of their work.[17]

They would not admit it, but their work was not succeeding. A few Chinese responded to the new religion, and considerably more were interested in the education and jobs the missionaries offered, but others linked Christianity with foreign domination of their country and saw the missionaries as imperialist agents. At the best of times the Christians were strangers in a

457

strange land, tolerated because of the power of their home governments' gunboats. In the 1920s the outsiders' situation became perilous as China's warlords discovered the uses of xenophobic nationalism. In 1926 a wave of anti-foreign agitation swept China, reaching fever pitch after the British bombardment of Wanhsien. In October the campus of West China University rang with shouts of "down with the foreign dogs, death to the traitors." The university had to be closed. At their governments' urging most foreign missionaries withdrew from the interior of China in the winter of 1926–7.

Flavelle thought that missionaries had volunteered to emulate the early church and suffer all things for Christ. He was not pleased with his church's role in the withdrawal, particularly a cable sent to United Church missionaries urging them not to take any risks. The five Canadians who disobeyed instructions and stayed in Szechuan — the only whites who stayed — impressed him as men willing to take risks for their faith.[18]

Flavelle had trouble understanding missionaries' behaviour generally in China. Why was there apparently never the money available to pay the Chinese who taught at the university salaries equal to the white teachers'? Or to supply them with housing? If the Chinese were to be equals in the work, why did the churches fail to take "the first and natural step of treating the Chinese relatively as well as we treat our own missionaries?" Sometimes Flavelle thought the problem lay with the Anglo-Saxon's "unconscious sense of superiority, with paternalism so irritating to others"; other times he wondered if the missionaries were not falling short of their calling in the way they "require more comforts in these fields than naturally belong to the exponents of the religion which has Jesus for its central figure."* On the other hand, he opposed any policy of rapid transfer of control of the university to local Chinese, arguing that they were still unprepared for administration and unreliable in their faith. As long as Chiang Kai-shek's Nationalists, who were demanding Sinoization of missionary schools, could not establish anything approaching a stable government in China, it was safe to play a waiting game.[19]

West China was generally peaceful in the late 1920s and the work of the university resumed. The missionaries were only occasionally cursed in the

---

* As a small step towards providing better facilities for the Chinese staff at WCUU, Flavelle donated $2,500 to build them residences. The money lay around unused for several years. When he pressed for an accounting, Flavelle was told that the natives would only accept Western-style houses like those built for the missionaries. This would be too expensive. Flavelle concluded from the incident that the mistake had been to build the Western-style houses in the first place.

streets of Chengtu and could easily dismiss the odd campus placard reading "Down with the Foreign Slaves" or "Take Back the University." In good times and bad they had an unlimited capacity to put the best face on events. In 1930 the Canadian dean of the Faculty of Science, Clifford Stubbs, was thrown from his bicycle and stabbed to death on campus by a gang of anti-foreign radicals. White flowers were set up at his funeral to spell out "VICTORY." The funeral orations centred on Christ's prayer, "Father forgive them, for they know not what they do."[20]

v

Flavelle did not make major donations to West China Union University (he gave a token $1,000 for several years, $750 to $1,000 annually for scholarships, and $10,000 in 1929 for hospital beds) because he was already contributing heavily to the missionary funds of the church. His yearly missionary givings through Sherbourne Street rose from $2,500 in 1915 to $10,000 before Union in 1925. He contributed $25,000 to the United Church's new Maintenance and Extension Fund (supporting both home and foreign work) in 1925, then tried to hold his annual contributions at $20,000. When givings fell short of projections, he subscribed an extra $50,000 in 1929 to be spread over the next three years to help meet the deficit. When that was not enough, he added $10,000 more. When he sent large cheques like these to Annie Martin, Sherbourne Street's faithful secretary, he always reminded her to deposit them quickly so the church would not lose a few days' or weeks' interest on the money.[21]

There were any number of smaller donations through Sherbourne Street. Before Union he gave $400 to $600 annually to the Educational Fund, $500 to $1,000 to the Anniversary Fund, about $1,000 for local operating expenses, and $50 to $100 to the Poor Fund. Years earlier, a number of the laymen of Sherbourne Street had agreed to subsidize the salary of the minister of King Street Church, located in a downtown working-class area; Flavelle's share was $400 a year. He paid $50 annually into a fund set up to support one of the old ladies of the congregation in the Bayview Private Hospital. There were dozens of special occasions, like the time he donated $10 to help cover the deficit on the 1923 Sunday School picnic, or the $5 he gave Richard Roberts for the fund to buy a new overcoat for the usher who had his stolen while taking up collection at an evening service. Another time Roberts sent Flavelle a bill for a communion chalice—"if you keep open house for beggars as you do, you have only yourself to blame . . ." he wrote.[22]

Other Methodist and United Church congregations solicited his help for their building funds and their building funds' debts. He thought a congregation should normally be self-supporting, but seldom refused a token $50 or $100. If the congregation obviously needed help he gave more. In 1926, for example, he gave $500 towards the debt of Metropolitan Church in Swift Current, Alberta, $1,000 for Wesley Church in Lethbridge, and $1,000 to the building fund of Woodbine Avenue United Church in Toronto. The next year he refused to contribute to the building fund of Rhodes Avenue United Church in Toronto, but gave $500 to Runnymede United and $1,000 toward a new Sunday School building at George Street Methodist in Peterborough. After learning that the Rhodes Avenue congregation was largely working-class, he relented and gave $200. He almost always declined invitations to lay the cornerstones of new churches.

Wealthy and generous laymen supported a bewildering array of good church causes. Flavelle helped needy theological students through college; helped ministers in debt; paid half the costs of repairing a layman's buggy, damaged when the horse ran away *en route* to a Christian Stewardship meeting; subsidized delegates to the Methodist General Conference and the United Church General Council; gave $500 to $5,000 donations to Albert College, Alma College, Regina College, and Mount Allison University; gave $200 to the Missionary Society's Centenary Celebration Ministers' Railway Fund; helped pay missionaries' passage to China and Chinese students' passage to Canada; gave $500 towards the cost of an organ for Wesley Church in St. John's, Newfoundland; paid for a lighting plant in a hospital run by the United Church's Queen Charlotte Marine Mission in British Columbia; and gave $25 to help a Methodist minister in Northern Ontario oust his town's leading bootlegger from the mayoralty.

Few ministers were well enough paid to save money for holidays or medical bills. When the layman who worked most closely with a minister realized his need, he would contact two or three friends to do something about it. Flavelle and Fudger, for example, helped the Rev. James Endicott cover the costs of his wife's terminal illness in 1925; E. R. Wood, J. H. Gundy, and Flavelle pooled $200 each in 1927 so Rev. and Mrs. Jesse Arnup could have a vacation. In 1928 A. E. Kemp raised $3,000 — $750 from Flavelle — so that W. E. Wilson of King Street Church could take a long holiday from his work with the dregs of Toronto. (Wilson had been doing his job for sixteen years

without a break. Kemp was afraid his health might give way completely —
six years of similar work after he had left Sherbourne Street had destroyed
Sherlock Faircloth's health, leading to his early death.) Flavelle particularly
admired Wilson's work and sent him $100 whenever he learned that the King
Street Poor Fund needed help. He did the same for Rev. J. O. Johnston, who
was also doing inner-city work with the poor at Berkeley Street Church.

A myriad of non-denominational Christian organizations also hoped for
support. Flavelle had been active in YMCA work in Peterborough; it was an
unusual year in the 1920s when he did not give at least $5,000 in response to
appeals from various local, provincial, and national branches of the YMCA,
and another $500 to $1,000 to the YWCA. Despite his waning sympathy for
prohibition, he seldom denied requests for $250 or $500 or $1,000 from the
Ontario Prohibition Union, the Young People's Temperance Movement, the
Dominion Alliance, and other temperance organizations. Local, provincial,
national, and international Sunday School and religious-education councils
hoped for and got $50 or $100 a year. Community social-work agencies
which had grown out of the work of churchmen, such as the Neighbourhood Workers' Association, would rely on Flavelle for $100 to $200 a year,
with extra sums for emergencies and Christmas celebrations. In 1899 Alfred
Fitzpatrick, a Presbyterian minister, founded what came to be known as
Frontier College, an organization sending college students to work with
labourers in lumber, mining, and railway camps. Flavelle helped Fitzpatrick
from the beginning; in the 1920s he gave Frontier College $250 to $500 a
year, much of it in emergency donations when Fitzpatrick ran out of money,
and also guaranteed the college's credit at the Bank of Commerce. Fitzpatrick noted the contrast between Flavelle and the "certain number of wealthy
men [who] hedge themselves about 'with quantities of unavailableness' and
we are unable to get past their secretaries."[23] He was one of the few friends
who vigorously defended Flavelle in 1917.

Then there were all the other charities and good causes. "When any philanthropy or undertaking for the good of the community is discussed and
the matter of finances raised, your name is invariably the first mentioned," a
friend wrote Flavelle in 1933.[24] He was the largest private contributor to
Toronto's combined charities' appeal, the Federation for Community Service, increasing his annual donation from $1,000 in 1921 to $5,000 in 1924.
He gave the Canadian Red Cross $1,000 a year to 1927, $2,000 afterwards.
Amateur athletic organizations, which always needed small sums to send a
team somewhere, pay for prizes, or buy new equipment, were never turned

down. Flavelle made small contributions ($5 to $100) to the Toronto Federation of Catholic Charities, the Jewish Boys' Club Building and Fresh Air Camp, the Bulldog Breeders' Association of Canada, the Women of Mooseheart Legion Kapuskasing Chapter, the American Federation of Labor (to help with expenses for its 1929 convention in Toronto), the Single Tax Association of Canada, the Imperial College of Tropical Agriculture, a fund to support orphaned children in Mesopotamia, the Ontario Motor League for its annual orphans' outing, and hundreds of other organizations.

There were innumerable appeals from friends or other prominent Canadians raising money for their favourite causes. E. R. Wood usually solicited for the "Y." Vincent Massey was a patron of the National Council of Education, and Holt Gurney raised money for the National Boys Work Board. The Royal Ontario Museum was Sir Edmund Walker's special project. Aemilius Jarvis took a consuming interest in the Navy League of Canada. Wives of Governors General carried on the tradition of Lady Aberdeen, who Flavelle had helped, by leading campaigns to raise money for the Victorian Order of Nurses. Sir Robert Borden and Newton Rowell appealed to him on behalf of the League of Nations Society. In his own family Clara senior took a special interest in the Earlscourt Children's Home and the Wimodausis Club, Clara junior specialized in ladies' auxiliary work at Toronto General Hospital, and Mina was interested in the Toronto Symphony Orchestra Association and the Canadian National Institute for the Blind.

Ties of friendship, of course, meant reciprocation in philanthropy. Flavelle could not turn down a request from E. R. Wood, Tom Russell, or Jack Eaton because they had responded so generously to his fund-raising. Many others could not refuse an appeal from him. Occasionally the wealthy joked about the "begging letters" they wrote each other, but, just as in business, a respected friend's connection with a charity guaranteed that it was a worthy cause. "There are many men in Toronto who would not hesitate to double their cheque if your name were associated with the enterprise," an acquaintance wrote Flavelle, asking him to become honorary treasurer of a war-memorial campaign.[25]

A friendship formed years earlier on the University Royal Commission led Flavelle into his most substantial donations of the 1920s. One of the commissioners, D. Bruce Macdonald, was principal of St. Andrew's College, a boys' school founded in the early 1900s. At Macdonald's urging Flavelle joined St. Andrew's Board of Governors in 1912, but was an inactive member until 1924, when plans were afoot to move the school from Rosedale to Aurora, north of Toronto. Flavelle agreed to become Chairman of the Board and pledged $25,000 to the building fund. The next year he subscribed a further $50,000, and when Macdonald insisted, against his wishes, on naming one of the residences Flavelle House, Flavelle then insisted on paying the full cost of any building named after him. Flavelle House at St. Andrew's finally cost $86,580.

There were not enough other donors to pay the full costs of the new buildings, and in 1927 Flavelle proposed that the $250,000 deficit in the building fund by erased by: (a) $50,000 donated by the other governors; (b) $50,000 raised by himself and T. A. Russell; (c) his own contribution of $150,000. Macdonald and the other governors readily agreed. Two years later, on October 25, 1929, Flavelle agreed to pay the $130,000 cost of a Junior School building. Four months later he offered to pay for a chapel for the school at an estimated cost of $70,000. One of his first acts when he made large pledges like these was to amend his will to ensure that the commitment would be honoured if he died.

Flavelle liked to attend and speak at graduation ceremonies and Old Boys' dinners at St. Andrew's, but did not explain his interest in the private school. He appears to have decided that the children of the well-to-do—the Canadian aristocracy-to-be—needed the special training found in English "public" schools,* and hoped he was helping Macdonald create a great new residential school. "We are making history for Canada in improving the foundations on which St. Andrew's College rests," Macdonald wrote him in 1926. "Long after you and I have passed on to another sphere I trust the College will have national importance in its influence on the life of the country."[26]

Large donations for institutional bricks and mortar were complemented

---

* The problem was to overcome the handicap of being rich, with the attendant danger of creating idle sons who never learned the value of work or dollars. The headmaster of Appleby School expressed this concern well in a 1917 letter to Flavelle, who was then a member of the Appleby Board and about to give a talk there on the theme, "To whom much is given": " . . . most of them are the sons of rich men. We have, I think, been quite successful in causing them to forget this in the School. . . . the fact remains that they will all of them succeed to positions of responsibility and influence when they grow up, and we are doing our best to give them the idea of the unselfish life."

There is an oral tradition that St. Andrew's College was founded to accommodate Presbyterians who could not get into Upper Canada College. Training at St. Andrew's was more disciplined, more spartan than at other schools, and the boys were apparently drawn from a wider cross-section of economic and religious backgrounds. These characteristics would have appealed to Flavelle.

by the small sums Flavelle gave quietly to people in need. At home, at his office, by mail, and on the street, he was asked for help by and on behalf of old friends, former Sunday School students, classmates in Peterborough, distant relatives, old employees, and total strangers. The lady who a long time ago had refused to be waited on by a snip of a boy in John Erskine's store in Peterborough came to him for help.[27] Perhaps it was Mrs. O'Beirne, whose hospital bills he paid in 1912, and whom he helped support in the early 1920s until relatives took her in. Or it might have been Mrs. Hartley from Peterborough; Flavelle gave her $10 in 1918 to help buy fuel for the winter, $14 in 1920, and $17 in 1921. In 1929 he gave Fred Irwin, a former member of the George Street Sunday School, $25 for board and passage back to Peterborough. Mrs. Guinn, who had once worked at Davies, wrote him in 1926 about her family's crippled son and her husband's inability to earn very much as a minister because of his deafness. Flavelle helped the Guinns financially that year, and in 1929 gave them $1,100 for medical expenses and their son's education. There is no indication why he helped the Keals, or what happened to them—in 1925 he tried to find Mr. Keal a job; in 1926 he gave them $75 to pay off debts and keep them until Keal started a job; on January 1, 1927, he sent them $25 for rent. At the other end of the spectrum Aemilius Jarvis, scion of a Family Compact family, Commodore of the RCYC, and leader of the Navy League, desperately needed help in 1924−5 when he was fined $60,000 and spent six months in jail after being convicted of conspiracy to defraud the Ontario government in bond transactions. Flavelle gave Jarvis what the latter called "very material assistance which has prevented forced sales, and, in consequence, further loss," and for the next ten years supported Jarvis's vain attempts to get a new trial to clear his name.[28]

Flavelle could not begin to keep track of his givings himself. Nor could he be sure that all the causes and people he was asked to support were worthy. During his years at Davies' the company's secretary-treasurer gave out Flavelle's cheques and kept accounts of his donations. His first private secretary, Frank Hay, often gave him memos on his past donations to an organization and began checking the credentials of some of the new organizations asking for money. Hay's successor, Muriel Gladman (a Peterborough girl, who had practised her stenography by taking down sermons), sometimes visited supplicants herself. By the end of the 1920s Flavelle had Miss Gladman regularly referring some of the smaller requests from down-and-outers to Rev. W. E. Wilson at his new social-work centre, Dixon Hall. In return, Flavelle made sure that Wilson's Poor Fund was kept topped up.

In other cases he might rely on friends to investigate an unusual request. In 1928 Frederick Philip Grove's publisher, H. C. Miller, asked Flavelle to contribute to the $5,000 fund he was raising to pay Grove's debts. Otherwise it seemed that the writer might have to leave Canada for more lucrative contracts in the United States. Knowing nothing about either man, Flavelle asked H. S. Southam for information. Southam asked the parliamentary librarian, Martin Burrell, about Grove. When Burrell opined that Grove was a man of sterling character and a national asset, Flavelle gave the $200 he had been asked for. Southam decided to send a contribution too.[29]

There were fraudulent requests. When Percy Carlton called at the office with a story about having just come out of Toronto General and needing train fare to an aunt's in Windsor, Miss Gladman gave him $10. He wrote for more money a few days later under the name Percy Locke and made the mistake of appearing at the office to pick it up! When Thomas Fox wrote asking for a second $25, Flavelle had him investigated and found he made his living writing begging letters describing the misfortunes of a man whose imaginary three sons had been killed in the war. "It is not easy to 'tighten up,'" Flavelle wrote a friend who had warned him to investigate some of these letters more fully. "I have no doubt I am frequently done when I do not know it. At times I am done quite frequently when I know it, but I do not know any other better way to get out of the situation than to permit myself to be done." The case in question involved a stranger in Lacombe, Alberta, who had persuaded Flavelle to send him $100 to be passed on to the teenage bride of a drunken syphilitic husband.[30]

Flavelle would sometimes refuse a request for money as "unnatural" or "unreasonable." It was unnatural to be asked to support local charities in other cities, for example, or to help pay the salaries of ministers of other congregations. Communities and congregations had to learn to help themselves, to live up to their responsibilities. Because the Terra Cotta Methodist congregation was still small and struggling, Flavelle did agree to help with the minister's salary in 1925. "Be careful this sort of thing does not break the morale of your people more than the thoroughly sound effort to meet their own fair obligations," he warned. In 1920 he refused to contribute to a fund to augment ministers' salaries in the Bay of Quinte Conference, noting that many laymen in the churches which were asking for money had bought $750 to $3,500 automobiles that year. They could afford cars while asking someone else to pay their ministers.[31]

Similarly, he was afraid of demoralizing individuals by allowing them to depend on rich men like himself instead of finding ways of making do

with what they had. With their low salaries ministers posed an almost in-
soluble dilemma. Flavelle was continually being asked for help, sometimes
by troubled ministers themselves, sometimes by other ministers who knew
of their plight, sometimes by other wealthy laymen raising a fund.

There are a great many of our ministers [he wrote in 1919] . . . who find great
difficulty in making ends meet. Their social position, the demands which their own
education have made upon their resources, and the demands which their standards
impose upon them for the education of their children, call for expenditure of a much
more important character than is understood by the Boards who are responsible for
providing their stipend. . . . there are many of our men who have not been out of debt
at any time since they left college. . . .

The sound remedy is an aroused conscience on the part of our people that they
should pay to the ministry a more adequate salary. My experience causes me to be
fearful of gifts, as it also causes me to be fearful of allowing a man to continue to be
burdened with debt which cannot reasonably be discharged by any savings he can
effect out of his current salary. On the one hand, you have the somewhat poor manager who learns to get out of his difficulties by a gift received from some outsider —
the first time it is taken with great reluctance and hesitation; the second time it is
asked for without much hesitation; and the third and further requests grow into a
vested right. I have not found any difference in this respect between preachers and
other men.

The other side is: the burden of debt which can only be discharged through savings
from an already inadequate remuneration imposes such hardship upon wife and
children, and not infrequently breaks the spirit of the man himself.[32]

Instead of turning down a request for help, he would often ask that it be
scaled down, or send a smaller sum. It was not appropriate for one man to
contribute too large a percentage of a fund, he felt, for organizations and
fund-raisers should develop a broad base of support. As well, he wanted to
spread his contributions widely, and often wrote that he was giving less than
asked so that he could meet other requests. He frequently remarked that he
wanted to support all the good people who asked him for money, but simply
could not do it.

He did not meddle in the internal affairs of organizations he supported,
and was inclined to keep on supporting them even when he found their
work disappointing or annoying. Ministers, social workers, nurses, and others who had committed their lives to doing good were models of unselfish

devotion. "You, and men or women actuated by the same motives, who do good work, always put to shame those of us who are mere onlookers," he wrote Alfred Fitzpatrick at a time when he was strongly criticizing Fitzpatrick's attempt to turn Frontier College into a university. In 1929, when he was attempting to get more money out of United Church businessmen to meet deficits in the Missionary and Maintenance Fund, one of them mentioned that he did not approve of a lot of the work. "While I know that a good many laymen who play a large part in affairs, are privately critical of the official work of their Church," Flavelle answered, "I cannot but think that if they had the privilege of observing it at close range, they would be, like myself, humbled in the presence of the men who do it. Their devotion and faithfulness always put me to shame, when I come into close grips with them in attempted critical reflections upon some phase of their activities."[33]

Flavelle gave away more than $100,000 a year during the 1920s. How much more than $100,000 is impossible to reckon because no records survive of a number of his donations. Assistance to close relatives and to business friends in trouble was not recorded on the file cards Miss Gladman kept of routine gifts. Nor were Flavelle's political donations, except for a few hundred dollars annually to Toronto Conservative associations. If Flavelle took his mother's injunction to support his church and his party to mean that they should be supported equally, he might have given as much as $500,000 to help with political campaigns in the 1920s. On the other hand he might have been so estranged from federal politics that the figure would have been substantially smaller. He gave away at least $1 million in the 1920s. That was about sixty to eighty per cent of his income from interest and dividends.

VI

He referred to requests for help as "claims." It had been common in the old Methodist Church to set aside special services in which the "claims" of missionaries, educators, and workers in other special areas would be presented. The congregation responded in the extent to which they recognized the validity of the claim or were moved by the power of the appeal. This still happened occasionally in the 1920s and Flavelle often responded by scribbling an IOU for $100, $500, or $1,000 and dropping it in the collection plate.

He was very annoyed when the Methodist Church, becoming more businesslike in the early 1920s, put congregational givings on a budget system.

467

Members would simply give so much every week and the total would be divided according to the budget allotment. For several years Flavelle insisted on allocating his givings in the old way. As givings fell short after Union, and as he watched givings decline in the American churches supporting West China Union University, his opinion hardened that budget systems in churches led to undue dependence on organization and a failure to develop "the vital force of conviction on the part of the giver that it was a duty to give." The same was true of secular philanthropy, he thought: centralized, once-a-year fund-raising through united appeals, such as Toronto's Federation for Community Service, failed to educate citizens to accept repeated giving as a duty. Perhaps what others saw as a great step forward in organizing philanthropy was actually another instance of an older sense of community and responsibility withering away in the postwar world.[34]

Flavelle's was rapidly becoming an older world—one in which personal donations and personal good works were the duty of a Christian steward and the duty of a gentleman. Flavelle did not want publicity for his donations. He often asked for anonymity and was not interested in achieving either status or a sort of immortality by leaving his name on buildings, hospital beds, or churches. The satisfaction, pleasure enough, came in the act itself—in being virtuous according to God's commandments and in being a responsible man of wealth and title in the community. The Methodist should make perfect his character, enjoy brotherly relations with his fellow men, and minister unto them.

CHAPTER NINETEEN

THE MORNING AFTER

It was a marvellous autumn in most of Canada, with a particularly fine Indian summer, and only some slight concern that the lack of rain might be hurting crops. The one cause for misgiving in the fall of 1929 arose from the determination of the Wheat Pools in Western Canada to get higher prices. The pools' Central Selling Agency had decided not to market the year's wheat, plus the surplus from 1928, until British and European dealers offered better prices. Lake freighters, the railways, and even the banks were starting to suffer from the lack of shipments and sales. "Statistically, it is probable that the grain dealers and pool are right, and that before another crop comes round, wheat will be wanted at higher than the prevailing price," Flavelle wrote; "but in the meantime, it is not altogether easy to excuse this powerful combination who are responsible . . . for the free movement of products being upset, and with it upsetting many other things. . . . Of course, it is a passing incident and has no large bearing on conditions in Canada."[1]

On Tuesday, October 29, the worst day in the history of North American stock exchanges, Flavelle cancelled an engagement so he could be sure to attend the Commerce board meeting that Friday. He thought there would probably be an unusual number of questions about the situation. "I would not have you think there is any anxiety . . . ," he wrote Peter Perry, "except such as you, or other persons identified with financial corporations, would necessarily feel when there is such a disturbance. One of the surprises of the situation is the manner in which additional margins are being given on broker's loans."[2]

He stayed close to home and was often at the bank through the first fortnight in November —"not because we had any anxiety about our own position, as we have at no time in the history of the institution been more comfortable and liquid; but because so many influential customers of the bank were in an anxious state of mind, incident to losses both embarrassing and deeply disturbing." The Commerce stood comfortably through the crash because it had no investments in common stocks and because the brokers to whom it had given credit were able to meet calls for more margin. "Not a penny of loss has been sustained," Flavelle wrote on November 20. He was worried about the future, though, for he thought there were bound to be adjustments. A number of businessmen had impaired their liquidity by diverting cash into speculation, and would soon be in trouble; construction activity was likely to decline, causing a rise in unemployment.[3]

Of course it was only money being lost in the stock market. In most of his speeches for the past several years Flavelle had been emphasizing "higher considerations"—talking about business as service, profit as a by-product, character and spiritual development as the most important things in life. On November 14, 1929, he spoke at the Border Cities Chamber of Commerce Ambassador Bridge Opening Luncheon in Windsor. In the introduction to his standard speech he referred to the unparalleled stock-market losses and the dismay many of his listeners must be enduring:

May I venture to say that whatever may be your losses and your anxiety, the things that matter in life are not those which you have lost. They are the love of home, the laughter of your children and the regard of your friends and neighbours.

And if you have been foolish or unwise and have less money now than a few weeks ago, remember that you'll not be remembered in your community for the money you leave, but by your reputation there.[4]

I

"We have had the poisonous influence of great desire for money and more money," Flavelle wrote Lord Byng in May 1930, trying to explain an era he knew had ended. In familiar language the lifelong teetotaller compared the boom to a drinking-spree, the bust to the "morning after." But he already doubted that it would be a normal sobering up. The stock-market binge was one manifestation of a deeper social malaise, the drunkard's "furred tongue that tells of deeper disarrangements":

We had been accumulating not only inflated credit, and inflated values of commodities, but a spirit of inflation in the public mind, reflected in all sorts of extravagances; personal, speculative, amusement, and the type of excesses that belong to such a period. This led to a heavy building programme, purchases of automobiles in immense numbers, an excitable state of mind, evidenced by excessive style features in clothes, and generally an absence of quiet, sound judgment of sober-minded people.

. . . there has been a period of deflation, and everywhere, in all walks of society, there has been conscious and unconscious decision to buy less, build less, social party and jazz less [sic].[5]

Business was already being hurt. Flavelle expected things would get worse. They got spectacularly worse in Western Canada as the Wheat Pools and thousands of farmers who had speculated on the Grain Exchange found that prices were not going up. By October 1930, wheat prices had broken through their previous low for the century. The coarse-grains market was "impossible." Crops in northern Alberta and Saskatchewan had been rained and frozen out. Thousands of farmers had lost their savings speculating on the wheat exchanges. Commodity prices generally had collapsed.

There was still no special anxiety for the bank at Commerce board meetings, "but we are made aware every few days of impaired positions of people who should have known better." And in Flavelle's office he had more people asking for help finding work than he knew what to do with. "There is no question about the extent of the unemployment, nor of the suffering of a lot of people who will not say much, but who, none the less suffer. . . . " He was depressed and pessimistic when he spoke to students at St. Andrew's College a year after the stock-market crash, blaming his own generation for "maladministration of the trust" it held on behalf of the young. The only consolation seemed to be that, unlike the generation before, his would not need to force the young to go to war to solve the trouble.[6]

No one in Flavelle's circle seemed to know what had caused the collapse or what could be done. Flavelle's binge-hangover theory of the business cycle seemed at least as useful as Sir Thomas White's rhymed musings:

> What made Humpty Dumpty fall?
> Nobody knows for certain at all;
> Some say the cause was the stock market crash,

And the call which the brokers sent out for more cash;
While some say Humpty had started to fall
Before the crash and before the call;
But nobody knows for certain at all.

Some think Humpty was filled up with gas,
And thus it was that it came to pass,
Inflated with credit, high prices and rent,
And call loan interest at twenty per cent.,
With watered stock and no-par shares,
And bull propaganda that frightened the bears,
With high pressure selling throughout the whole nation,
Instalment plan buying and goods saturation,
Humpty, they say, with all his inflation,
Just naturally burst, and fell from the wall;
But nobody knows for certain at all.[7]

Herbert Hoover's administration in the United States had declared war on the Depression and through a myriad of organizations was spending money and spreading propaganda to restore business confidence. Flavelle doubted that any organization could get to the heart of the problem, and particularly scorned the attempts of governments and private organizations to set floors on falling prices. As he studied the plight of Western farmers who could not recoup their costs on grain, he recalled how American and Canadian farmers had done well by converting low-priced barley and other grains to pork half a century earlier. Perhaps the Western farmer was at fault for relying on a single crop, for refusing to commit himself to the year-round work required in diversified farming. If so, Western Canadian farmers were going to pay a terrible price for their reckless improvidence: "machine[ry] debts cannot and will not be paid. Interest on mortgages will not be met. Store bills will not be discharged. Bank credits will be frozen. . . . There is no quick measure of relief. There is nothing that any of us can do by money loans in the West to retrieve the immediate situation." He did not know what could be done beyond the efforts of public and private charities. He did approve of the new Bennett government's programme of public works to give jobs to the unemployed. "Clearly it should be the duty of the State, failing other means, to intervene that men who are willing to work should find employment."[8]

Conditions steadily worsened in the first half of 1931. Companies began passing dividends on common and preferred stock, even defaulting on bond interest. Stock values dropped relentlessly. "Each fresh decline discovers fresh corporate or individual [with] weakened financial resources," Flavelle wrote. He was giving more and more assistance to businessmen who "have violated the law under the pressure of circumstances, and have made use of funds in their possession in an improper way. These have to be taken care of, or much suffering is brought to bear upon innocent people immediately associated with them." Never in his life had the calls for his time and attention been so insistent, "and in many cases so hopeless," he wrote Clara junior. "I am too much in the swirl of it all to feel any sense of authority in my judgment as to how long it will last." But Canadians were deluding themselves in expecting "that some one would wave a magic wand" and it would be all over. When Howard Ferguson asked his opinion of events in Stalin's Russia, he felt competent to guess only that freedom could not be suppressed. On the other hand, "We make such a sorry spectacle at the moment over this Continent in unemployed and hungry people, in contrast to those who have more material things than are good for them, that one cannot think too well of our own basis of civilization."[9]

There were always compensations, even looking out the window on a lovely spring day as he wrote his letters:

Outside the birds are in full song. A beautiful small birch, its silver bark glistening in the sun, the delicate tracery of new growth showing up between me and the blue blue sky; across the hollow is the rich green of the hill side, and the noble skyline of Trinity College satisfies and delights. In it all God is good, and what does He require but that we shall do justly, love mercy and walk humbly with our God.[10]

II

In June 1931, Flavelle spoke to the Canadian Credit Men's Trust Association on the problem of commodity prices. It was the most carefully prepared speech he had ever given, was broadcast across Canada on the CNR's network, and the published text was distributed to all his friends and acquaintances, the editors of every daily paper in Canada, and MLA's in Ontario, British Columbia, Alberta, Saskatchewan, and Manitoba.

He was convinced that prices for primary products would stay low for years. Every organized undertaking to raise commodity prices, even to stop their decline—ranging from Brazil and Egypt's attempts to stockpile coffee and cotton, to the efforts of the U.S. Farm Relief Board and the Canadian Wheat Pools to stabilize wheat prices — had been defeated by irresistible market forces. Farmer agitation for action on prices was a futile and probably harmful diversion from the duty to get on with the job as efficiently as possible.

To spread the burden and prepare the way for recovery, other Canadians were going to have to suffer along with the farmers. Wages and salaries were bound to come down to adjust to the lower commodity prices. Flavelle was worried that they were being held artificially high by labour and capital, especially labour, thus creating more unemployment. "The need is not for limited employment at present rates," he argued, "but full employment at an equitable wage." He pleaded with labour to cooperate and stop fighting the inevitable: "A stricken world, in which the hearts of men are sorely tried, does not call for the exercise of arbitrary power, but for the redeeming qualities of grace and wisdom. Will organized labour in the United States and Canada give the needed leadership, that wages shall be readjusted to the lowered values of commodities?"

The answer, of course, was a resounding no. Businessmen and many editors approved of the speech, but labour leaders damned the proposal as bound to reduce purchasing power. They also damned Flavelle for profiteering in the Great War. If Sir Joseph was really so interested in the unemployed, why didn't he use some of his millions to help them? If he didn't approve of the present system in Canada, why not deport him to Russia? Somebody wrote him that he deserved to be tarred and feathered. It would have been more to the point to notice Flavelle's failure to single out R. B. Bennett's new sky-high tariff as the device that kept both prices and wages in Canadian manufacturing unduly high.

Flavelle thought labour's reaction to his speech was fairly moderate and seemed content that the suggestions got wide publicity, particularly in the West. Lowered wages, lowered standards of living generally, were bound to come. Whether they liked it or not, Canadians were going to endure "the discipline of suffering." It was bound to lead to wiser standards and better conduct.[11]

III

At his most pessimistic, Flavelle had not realized what was coming. The effects of collapsing stock values and commodity prices were almost trivial compared with the possible consequences of the financial collapse set off by the failure of Austria's Kredit Anstalt in the summer of 1931. Central European banking and exchange fell into chaos. When non-confidence crossed the Channel, the Bank of England could not save the pound and Britain's Labour government could not save itself. Britain went off the gold standard on September 19, and a National Government had to be formed to deal with the emergency. On September 21, 1931, securities dealers faced the worst crisis since August 1914; Canadian stock exchanges opened, but would not permit stock sales at lower values. The Canadian dollar followed the pound down, dropping 3 ¼ cents against the American dollar on September 21, 5 ¾ cents the next day. In November and December it went below 80 cents U.S. World money markets were effectively closed in the currency chaos that autumn.

Canadians could not borrow in the United States. The decline of the Canadian dollar had increased the burden of foreign debt and interest obligations by ten to twenty per cent at a time when exports brought in unprecedentedly low prices. Yet governments at every level needed to borrow to service their debts and cover their deficits. Aided by Dominion guarantees, the banks helped municipalities and provinces as best they could; but in the worst of the chaos, in November, it was not even clear how much investor confidence even the Dominion government commanded. "I listened with some dismay yesterday to a conversation between a mixed company of very thoughtful men," Flavelle wrote the acting Minister of Finance in November, "in which the query was raised—'Are you sure the covenant of the Dominion Government is good?' "[12]

The $150 million National Service Loan of November 1931 was advertised and sold as though the country were at war. It was a resounding success. The crisis gradually eased. The fact that it had happened, exposing Canada's terrible vulnerability to its foreign "bankers," reinforced Flavelle's view that Canadians' standard of living had been extravagant. During the war, and again during the 1920s, Canadians had become used to living on borrowed money. Individuals and governments had spent recklessly—on automobiles, highways, railways, radios — and were now over their heads in debt. "We have created too big a machine for economic operation, for a limited population of ten million people," Flavelle wrote Howard Ferguson at the end of 1931. Collectively and individually Canadians were going to have to retrench. "We in Canada must learn to live within our means. We have gone mad on spending, and have accumulated a burden of unproductive debt so formidable that it is a grave national menace. None of us can point the finger of fault-finding at the other. We have all been mixed up in it. . . . Meantime, we must perform as other humans, and carry on the day's work."[13]

His own day's work was starting to lessen a little. In the spring of 1930 the steel and coal reorganization was completed; National Trust returned DISCO to the new company, Dominion Steel and Coal, just in time to get out of the receivership triumphantly. That major piece of work done, Flavelle retired from the presidency of the trust company and became chairman of the board. Will Rundle was National Trust's second president, with Jim Macdonnell moving up to become general manager. They consulted Flavelle on important issues, and he faithfully attended board meetings, but his role in the company's affairs steadily declined.

At the Commerce he was on hand for the urgent meetings about the stock market in 1929, the plight of the Wheat Pools in 1930, and the plight of the dollar in 1931, and was occasionally a member of bankers' delegations to discuss these problems in Ottawa. Again, though, he gradually became less involved in the formation of the bank's general strategy, more the ceremonial chairman. There were no special crises for either the trust company or the bank during the Depression. They cushioned losses from reserves, retrenched, made some money on safe investments and loans, and continued to pay reduced dividends.[14]

The least significant of Flavelle's company chairmanships took up the most time. Negotiations involving Canadian Marconi seemed to go on forever, without any perceptible progress. Flavelle's gesture of goodwill to his British friends cost him days and nights travelling to Ottawa or Montreal, conferring with civil servants and railway or cable-company officials, reading and writing convoluted letters on the problem of the Bell Telephone contract or the latest CPR position on who should handle British cable business. A plan to have I & IC absorb Canadian Marconi ran afoul of "Canadian" nationalism, as expressed by General Sarnoff of RCA ("it seemed to him that from a national point of view the offer of the I & IC was objectionable but that was not his business"), and the arch-imperialist, R. B. Bennett ("Bennett referred with some acidity to the desire which he said appeared to prevail in London to centralize everything there to which he said he was entirely opposed"). "What a curious lot of tangles there are in these partly business, partly friendly, partly public spirited associations," Flavelle commented in the midst of it all. In the meantime the company was going nowhere except further into the red. Flavelle became thoroughly disgusted with everyone involved and agreed to remain as chairman much against his better judgment.[15]

V

In early 1931 Flavelle also became thoroughly disgusted with a large number of the professors at the University of Toronto. For several years there had been growing controversy over the Toronto Police Commission's rigid control, to the point of suppression, of open-air meetings held by communist and communist-front groups. In January the Toronto papers were agog with the publication of an open letter signed by sixty-eight faculty members of the university condemning the commission's interference with freedom of speech and assembly. Public interest in the professorial statement became not unlike the 1914 German-professor situation, except that this time the academics seemed to be defending communism. "Flavelle, what are you Governors going to do about this damn nonsense of the University Professors?" a cabinet minister asked him.

He certainly was not going to approve of it. Flavelle thought the Toronto sixty-eight were "a group of innocents," who had stupidly and irresponsibly helped inflame an already unpleasant situation among the police, demagogue politicians, newspapers, and the communists in Toronto. There was no serious threat to free speech in the city, he believed; he knew there was a very serious threat to the university from the public and members of the legislature who assumed that professors, like civil servants, should not address public issues. By taking a course of action which endangered the university, the professors had abused their position as "trustee[s] for the institution."[16]

Flavelle's idea of academic freedom included protecting German professors from being fired because they were German, but did not encompass giving professors licence to say anything they wanted to about political issues. By now, though, he was one of the more conservative members of the board. A special committee decided that Falconer should meet with the offending professors and remind them of their responsibilities. He did, the board issued a resolution dissociating the university from their action, and the issue faded away. At its next meeting the board turned to the student newspaper, the *Varsity*, which had suggested that U. of T. students and graduates were largely atheists, and that the professors were teaching atheism. The governors unanimously repudiated the article and the university's Caput suspended the *Varsity* for the rest of the year. Flavelle missed the meeting, but would have approved.*[17]

VI

"He is now at the age of 73 one of the youngest men in Canada," a journalist wrote in early 1931.[18] After having gone bald in his forties and having become grey-bearded in his fifties, Flavelle seemed to have stopped aging. Without his beard he would have looked like Daddy Warbucks in his favourite comic strip, *Little Orphan Annie*. People noticed how he walked down University Avenue and Bay Street with the stride of a young man in his twenties. Coming out of the opera or the symphony, the old gent in the long coat and top hat would put two fingers to his lips and whistle for a cab as shrilly as any doorman. He could still snare houseflies in his left hand. He drove his own car, leaving the chauffeur to drive the family. One of his favourite stories, used to illustrate any number of points in speeches, was about the time he and Fudger were talking so earnestly they drove through the red light at King and Bay streets. "If youse two old gents would talk less and look more," said the policeman who stopped them, "it would be good for youse."[19] His cars—a Packard at one time in the twenties, a Pierce-Arrow in the thirties—were always black. He said nothing, but was obviously not pleased when a niece who was living at Holwood started parking her bright yellow roadster in the front drive. On the other hand, he once lent his car for the evening to a couple of U. of T. students and their girlfriends whom he met at a public lecture.

He still played a full eighteen holes of golf, scoring decently. His handicap was probably about fifteen—at least that was the line he drew below which a man was obviously neglecting his business. When he got a hole-in-one in California in 1926 E. R. Wood put up $500 if he could show him how to do it

---

* He must have been a bit dismayed during the 1931 incident when Jim Macdonnell, very much his protégé, strongly disagreed with his narrow view of academic freedom. In 1941, when the university went through a more serious crisis over academic freedom, Macdonnell and J. S. McLean were the two most influential governors defending professors' liberties.

again. He curled occasionally at the Granite Club and skipped a rink that beat the Lieutenant-Governor to open the 1927 season; the next year his rink beat the president of the Ontario Curling Association, with Flavelle "frequently making the shot by superior play on his part."[20] The *Financial Post* called him the "piscatorial patriarch" of Sturgeon Lake, where he still threw back black bass weighing less than 2½ to 3 pounds in an almost fished-out lake. He always cast, never trolled, but shocked highbrow casters by using a plug. J. S. McLean was his favourite fishing companion, except that they were too competitive ever to fish from the same boat. At Holwood the Methodist boy had learned to play billiards. More liberal than his brothers, he enjoyed playing bridge or cribbage in the evenings.

He liked to attend football and hockey games, cheering loudly for Toronto. One night, when an Allan Cup game at the Mutual Street Arena had gone into several overtime periods, Flavelle bought all an apple boy's apples, stood up and tossed them into the crowd. Horace Speakman, who was there, remembered him as "simply a big happy boy" at events like that. His seven grandchildren remembered that Holwood was never gloomy. It was marvellous to play hide-and-seek in the attics and cellars, slide down the grand front stairs on tin trays, and ride up and down on the dumb-waiter. All the children Flavelle knew were invited to Holwood every year to watch the Santa Claus parade go by. And in the evenings the light used to shine from his bald head as the grandchildren sat at his feet, spellbound, while he read stories from Kipling or Uncle Remus or A. A. Milne.

He could be tough and rigid. Nobody was ever late for an appointment with Flavelle. The way to get on with him in conversation, a broker recalled, was to be sure to be better prepared on the subject than he was. A nephew, Stuart Flavelle, never forgot being told to come back at the end of the month with *proper* accounts for one of the Lindsay businesses. A grandson, Frank McEachren, was picked up by the chauffeur at St. Andrew's one day, driven to the Bank of Commerce, and ushered into the boardroom. From the other end of the long table his grandfather expressed grave concern that Frank had overdrawn his account by $3. It was not true, and, when he realized he was wrong, grandfather took the boy to lunch, a movie, and a hockey game.

The Flavelles spent the fall and early winter at Holwood. In the early spring they would holiday for a month or so in California, Hawaii, or Bermuda. May and June were often spent at "Ashburnham," a two-storey, California-style, stucco-and-tile villa Flavelle had built on a farm he bought near Oakville in 1920. His managers grew strawberries on the land, and

Flavelle fancied himself a gentleman farmer. The farm seldom turned a profit. In July and August the whole Flavelle clan gathered at Sturgeon Point, with the busy men driving in and out of the city as affairs dictated. As he got older Flavelle would sometimes pull over to the side of the road for a nap *en route*.

The adults enjoyed lawn bowling and croquet at Swannanoa. The grown-up children and nephews and nieces played tennis and sailed. The grand-children played polo with field-hockey balls and sticks while riding their bicycles, and hunted down Swannanoa's bats with tennis racquets. Everyone went on the inboard launches for the shore parties and picnics—dressed in their summer whites they sat on the ground and dined off linen and fine china in the most formal informality. They played tricks on absent-minded Uncle Will Milner; the best was the time they got him trying to bail out a fish-box in one of the boats that continually refilled itself.

On Sundays the tennis court and lawn-bowling pitch went unused. Long walks were the morning activity for old and young together. Joe would usually have caught a maskinonge the day before, and carved it with loving care for Sunday midday dinner. The only boat taken out was to get the minister, who conducted an afternoon service at the octagonal wooden church Clara had built for the Sturgeon Point community in 1915. Sunday evenings were for hymn-singing, followed by grape juice and ginger ale. Every evening there was time for relaxing on Swannanoa's huge verandah, looking out over the gardens and oak-shaded lawns, chatting about politics or the university or flowers or the grandchildren's progress at school. Thornton Wilder's Theophilus North writes about "my idea that somehow I might penetrate that magic world . . . and glimpse those enchanted late afternoons in Newport when professors played croquet with their children until fireflies hovered over the wickets and a voice called 'Come in, children, and wash your hands before supper.' "[21]

The Flavelles had the best of everything, but no one could think of Sir Joe as extravagant. "That's too showy," he told his children when they urged him to buy a Rolls-Royce. He did not have a large wardrobe, and, no matter what his valet said, insisted on wearing his old grey business suit. The knees got worn and Sir William Mulock once remarked to him at a Board of Governors' meeting that he must have been doing a lot of praying lately. In his talks to young people Flavelle often tried to tell them that the most important thing to develop in life was a "background of repose."[22]

Age caught up with others in the family. Maggie, Minnie, and Johnnie

Flavelle were dead. Will Milner, Joe's brother-in-law and closest friend, died suddenly in 1931. Clara's health was becoming increasingly uncertain as recurring lung problems were added to her kidney weakness. She was the same age as Joe, but very obviously an old lady. In 1927 she nearly died from her lung condition and after that spent more and more of her time in bed. An elevator was installed in Holwood to help her get about. Despite Joe's busy-ness since the war they had not spent so much time together since the first years in Peterborough.

VII

Flavelle was not particularly close to R. B. Bennett. He thought the Conservative leader did a reasonable job as Opposition leader and was not surprised when the Liberals were beaten by Bennett and the Depression in 1930. Canadian Marconi and Bank of Commerce affairs took him to Ottawa fairly often. He shared the common judgment that Bennett's government was a one-man affair whose fate might well hinge on the Prime Minister's physical stamina. He continued to remark on Bennett's links with his Methodist upbringing ("At bottom it is not humbug. After you have made allowances for his egotism and vanity it will be found that the underlying, impelling force is the early religious training in his Mother's home"), and was impressed that Bennett had gone out of his way to be gracious and kind on the occasions they had met.[23] On the other hand, Flavelle's interest in specific policies of governments was falling off. He was old, and he believed no government could solve Canada's economic problems.

Bennett wanted to make some use of the businessman's talents. Citing Clara's health, Flavelle turned down the Prime Minister's request that he serve as Canadian representative on a League of Nations economic commission. He found it less easy to resist Bennett's desire to appoint him to a Royal Commission on railways. The subject had always fascinated him; he had been personally involved with the railways since 1903 and may have felt twinges of responsibility for the unhappy situation they were in twenty-eight years later. Flavelle was one of the first people Bennett contacted about the Royal Commission. They had several meetings to discuss others who might be appointed. On Remembrance Day, 1931, he was in Ottawa waiting to see the Prime Minister, wondering whether he—and Clara—would again find themselves serving the country.[24]

481

Mr. Justice Lyman Duff was appointed chairman of the Royal Commission to Inquire into Railways and Transportation. Lord Ashbridge and L. F. Lorree were outside experts from Britain and the United States. Flavelle, Dr. J. C. Webster from New Brunswick, Walter Murray, president of the University of Saskatchewan, and Beaudry Leman, general manager of the Banque Canadienne Nationale, filled out the membership. Flavelle agreed to serve only after being allowed to veto Bennett's first choice of a Western representative. The Royal Commission was created because both Beatty of the CPR and Thornton of the CNR, faced with staggering declines in freight, passenger traffic, and earnings, had asked for it. It was given sweeping terms of reference to inquire into all forms of transportation relating to the railways. Flavelle worked closely with Duff planning the commission's schedule. It included a tour of the West — out via CN, back via CP — to hear testimony and see the systems.[25]

They travelled straight to Victoria, holding long sessions on the way out with railway executives, "living thinking soaking in railways," Joe wrote Clara. On the way back he had never seen anything like the effects of a fresh fall of snow in the Fraser Valley — "the Glory, beauty, Magnificence of the Mountains seemed a thing impossible. God is good dear. God is great. The Wonders of His love and Power are without measure. He dear has you in His keeping, and He holds me also in safety that we may live and work and love each other, our children, and men and women who are with us and about us."

It was a "horrible nightmare" to be in Toronto without him, Clara wrote. Surely the trip East after Christmas would be short, "and then dear, it will be all over. Won't that be great? . . . I will just bid you a very loving good-night, thinking and dreaming of you by day and by night. With much, much love my dear boy, and already looking forward to seeing you. . . . "[26] She became seriously ill while Joe was still in the West and he rushed home from Winnipeg to be with her. It seemed a false alarm — the doctors expected she would return to normal after several weeks' convalescence. Early in the New Year Joe left for Ottawa to attend more Royal Commission hearings.

The more the commissioners learned about the railway situation, the more serious it seemed. The CNR had never had a year when it could do without subsidies; now it was losing at least $40 million a year, perhaps much more, depending on the accounting methods used. The CPR was rapidly becoming less profitable, and more bitter at the way its shareholders' investment seemed imperilled by competition from the subsidized state-owned railway. Aside from the temporary effects of the Depression (by 1931 Flavelle was not sure how "temporary" it really was), both systems faced increasingly serious competition from motor trucks, motor buses, and private automobiles. Could the situation go on? Could the Dominion government, staggering under its debt load and cut off from foreign money markets by the breakdown in international finance, continue to meet the losses and carrying charges the CNR was incurring? The CN executives who testified to the commission saw nothing much else to do except to go on a little more economically. Beatty of the CPR revived Shaughnessy's notion that the salvation of the CPR, the CNR, and the country lay in leasing the government system to the private company.

Flavelle was in no mood to sympathize with either set of railwaymen. In his view, they had discredited themselves by spending hundreds of millions of dollars on wasteful competing facilities—branch lines, hotels, steamships—and had hidden the true cost of their operations even from themselves by failing to keep proper sets of accounts. Sir Henry Thornton's CNR was the more blatant sinner on both counts; it had spent more money competing aggressively with the older system and had substantially understated its losses by failing to make any significant allowances for depreciation. The CN reported aggregate operating earnings of $216.5 million for the years 1923 − 31; proper accounting shrunk the earnings to $74.6 million! These did not begin to cover the debt charges on the system, of course, and the friendly federal treasury met the deficits plus all capital expenditures. In fifteen years, from 1917 through 1931, the Canadian National Railways lines had swallowed over $1 billion of Canadian taxpayers' money on a correct reckoning, had accumulated no reserves, and were drawing about $100 million annually from the public teat.[27]

Flavelle had no more use than he had had ten years earlier for the idea of turning the CNR over to the CPR. When Beatty appeared before the commission Flavelle went round and round with him on the question of monopoly *versus* competition. Beatty became the interrogator. If the competition had been harmful and wasteful, why not get the savings from amalgamation? Because the "whip of competition" was necessary to keep the railways responsible. If 120 million Americans could be ruled by one man, why couldn't there be one railway for ten million Canadians? Because corporations were not democratic and absolute monarchies had been abolished years before. But you tell us competition hasn't worked? Because, Mr. Beatty, the competitors did not practise intelligent cooperation. It was possible — bankers, Flavelle suggested later in the proceedings, were "of all competitors the most savage I ever came in contact with . . . but they do come together; while the theory of operation is one of competition, the competitors do not necessarily need to bite one another." In any case, why should the commission accept the proposals of railway leaders whose record was of having just made "damn fools of themselves"?[28]

He could not go on the Royal Commission's Maritime trip because Clara was not recovering as quickly as she should. At the end of January her condition began to deteriorate. She was taken to Toronto General Hospital and died there on February 8, 1932. A simple funeral service was held at Holwood. Joe received thousands of letters and telegrams of condolence. "Her life was spent in unselfish, devoted service to her husband and children and all others whom she could reach in loving and gentle ministry," he wrote. "I would be unworthy of her devoted unselfish life if I were to allow myself to be dismayed in the presence of inevitable loneliness." They would have been married fifty years that September.[29]

He was back in Ottawa by February 15 for the final hearings on the railways, took a few weeks' vacation in Georgia, then returned to Ottawa for weeks of study and discussion about the shape of the final report. One night he was the only person in the compartment car travelling to Ottawa. It made him think about the problems of the railways, and about what was left of his life. "The time passes," he wrote Clara junior, "the profound difference being not in being alone and on duty, but that there is a sense that life is done, the share and share alike which gave each day a vital force and power, has gone, and one is an atom floating around, in some indefinite way."[30]

VIII

Flavelle's role in framing the Royal Commission's report is not clear; the evidence suggests that very little would have been changed if he had written it all himself. Some key passages in the September 1932 report, including those condemning the CNR's management for extravagance, were taken from a long memorandum he wrote. During the hearings he had opposed railway amalgamation — it was rejected in the report. The two major recommendations — that the CNR be placed under a three-man trusteeship and that an Arbitration Tribunal be set up with authority to compel cooperation between the railways — would, if implemented, achieve exactly his goals.

The chairman of the trustees would have the same kind of executive authority Flavelle had wielded at the IMB and had always claimed was needed by a "superman" for the CNR. As for the Arbitration Tribunal, the railways were "but children" in the matter of cooperation; "they require education accompanied at times by needed discipline," he wrote R. B. Bennett. He also thoroughly agreed with the report's several recommendations to protect the railways from unfair competition from the motor vehicle, particularly the suggestion that the true costs of highways be paid for by the motorists who used them. "The presentation of the railways' side of the case to the Commission left the impression that they underestimated the seriousness of this new form of competition," he noted. The one theme of Flavelle's memorandum that the other commissioners would not include in the final report was his extended argument that wages had to be reduced.[31]

As they wound up their work, Dr. Webster wrote Flavelle that some day the historian would record his "remarkable" share in the "great investigation . . . so that the country may justly give you the credit which is due." It was a great investigation, involving an immense commitment of time and effort by the commissioners, but it has been almost completely forgotten because so little came of it. Almost all MP's were opposed to loosening Parliament's control over the CNR. The CPR was fiercely opposed to giving the Arbitration Tribunal any power over its property. Legislation brought in to implement the major recommendations was considerably watered down before final passage. Bennett was not able to appoint the CN's trustees until December 1933, and they were not men of national stature (Flavelle had recommended J. S. McLean as the best executive administrator in Canada). The Arbitration Tribunal was never used. The railways achieved minor savings through voluntary cooperation, but Beatty continued to insist on a CPR-dominated railway monopoly as the only lasting solution. As the commissioners had understood, motor vehicles were provincially regulated; the provinces did not cooperate, and continued to subsidize motorists and truckers.

As conditions began to improve slightly in 1933, some politicians thought they saw glimmers of light at the end of the railway tunnel. Flavelle's last letter to Bennett's Minister of Railways, R. J. Manion, was a devastating critique of his and the CNR's optimism. "I know of no more deplorable mistake in business organizations, great or small, than that the men in charge should fool themselves as to the truth of their operations. . . ." By late 1934 he thought that the only consequence of the great investigation had been to make things worse by showing how little interested Parliament and the railways were in working out a sensible approach to the problem.[32]

IX

By 1932 Canadians were beginning to talk about the need to do something about debts. Deflation had increased every debtor's real burdens. In thousands and thousands of cases the burdens could not be borne. And why should they? Why should a farmer have to sell three thousand bushels of wheat to clear debts that a thousand bushels would have covered a few years ago? Why should a city homeowner have to work forty per cent longer to cover his monthly mortgage payment? Why should the creditors, the big banks and the big-shot rich men, get big windfall profits out of other people's hard luck?

Flavelle saw the debt-adjustment issue as a matter of confidence and the economic future of the country. It was not quite as simple as the problem of how the defaulter would get credit again, though in international finance that was a real enough worry. Flavelle understood the situation of debtors and understood that many debts would have to be scaled down. He believed that financial institutions made generous settlements with individuals in trouble. What would tampering with the *system* achieve? Almost certainly it would not recognize the dual role of financial institutions as both creditors and debtors. Suppose banks and insurance companies and trust companies were not permitted to collect all the money due them. Would they also be permitted not to pay their depositors, their policyholders, and the people who had given them money in trust, all the money due to them? Not very likely. In the extreme case, if financial institutions went under because they had become insolvent, Canadians would experience hardship and suffering beyond imagination.

The more talk there was of debt adjustment, the less confidence lenders had. The more uncertainty there seemed to be about the terms of business in the future, the less likely businessmen were to risk their money. Similarly, the more extravagant any debtor was, including governments, the less likely lenders were to have enough confidence to risk their money. Until that confidence was restored, the Canadian economy would continue to stagnate as investors sat on their money or lent it only at high rates of interest.

The answer for Canadians was surely less talk ("if youse two old gents would talk less . . . it would be good for youse") and more hard work. The sooner people paid off their debts, the more likely they would be to get lent more money. As he reflected on the war and the 1920s, Flavelle replaced his images of drunkenness with metaphors of lunacy. There could never again be anything like the "mad" extravagance of the late 1920s, the insane, crazy spending sprees of individuals and governments. By 1933 Flavelle was talking about the need for a five-year period of "skeleton governments" in Canada until budgets were balanced; he saw no reason why Canadians should still be spending a million dollars a day maintaining their cars, let alone buying new ones, with some car owners still unable to pay their mortgage interest. The retrenchment would eventually be good for Canadians—"In due course, I do not know how soon, or how long, out of the discipline of suffering, and sorrow, and distress, and trouble, and pain, will emerge qualities of endurance, faithfulness, patience, and faith which are the earmarks of dependable people."[33]

That would not be enough. Canada's economy was so dependent on the easy flow of money and goods and services among nations that only the restoration of international confidence, some normalization of world economic relations, could revive the great exporting industries. But in 1931 world currency and trade seemed to have collapsed, and international conferences in 1932 and 1933 failed to put the pieces together again. Even the imperial preferences negotiated at the 1932 Ottawa conference resulted in a good deal of imperial ill will (Flavelle thought they should have been given voluntarily rather than in a selfish "trading" session. The bacon preference was enormously valuable to Canada Packers in restoring the lost British market). During his Georgia holiday in 1933 Flavelle watched the Americans endure the supreme crisis of their financial system when Roosevelt temporarily closed all the banks to head off worse collapse. When he came home to Toronto he saw the *Punch* cartoon of the War Lord stalking Europe and began to realize that perhaps his generation might send the young men to war again.[34]

He had a personal contact with events in Germany through John Wheeler-Bennett, the son of his former agent. With substantial encouragement from Flavelle (among other things Flavelle had persuaded the old man to give his twenty-year-old son some money of his own), young Wheeler-Bennett had become a specialist in international relations, wrote widely on world affairs, and made a point of first-hand observation. He was in Germany for the last days of Weimar and the advent of Hitler, and sent Flavelle copies of his speeches, articles, and letters. He stayed at Holwood whenever he was in Toronto ("I have so many things I want to learn from you that I may weary you with my questions," Flavelle wrote him before one of his visits), and was deeply pessimistic about Europe's future after 1934. Flavelle's other English friends—Brand, Lionel Curtis, Lord Lothian (Philip Kerr)—shared the gloom. Almost all of them believed that Hitler was a creature of the botched peace settlement, particularly the harsh terms of the Treaty of Versailles. The desire for revenge unleashed by the Great War led directly to the poisoning of international relations fifteen years later.[35]

The old man's puritanism and repetition of slogans about hard work and the discipline of suffering began to seem irrelevant to day-to-day problems in Canada. Some of his friends began to tell him so. "However necessary good will may be it is not always enough," Perry wrote from Montreal. Systematic changes had to be made to make the debt burden tolerable—"It is better for capital to get a moderate return than to insist on a return which will drive the whole world into a condition of bankruptcy as a result of which capital will probably get nothing at all." After receiving one of Flavelle's most platitudinous and unbending sermon-letters on debts, Robert Cromie of the Vancouver *Sun* lost patience:

... there is a Puritan side of your nature that hates to forgive a debt, that hates to see a fellow or nation get into debt through his folly, and then through some set of circumstances escape payment of that debt.

Well, I hate that just as much as you do, but you have lived your life; I have lived a good portion of mine, but my children and their civilization have only commenced to live theirs. It seems to me that a complete breakdown of Capitalism would injure my children and their civilization much more than their economic morality would be if the present world debts were forgiven. . . . why not cut them down to a point where they can be paid, so that the world can have hope and get back to business?

. . . You said my editorial was mischievous. I say that your attitude is out of date; it is harsh, cruel, and unbending, and, in my judgment, will hurt the civilization which has to follow you.[36]

Flavelle did not answer. After Clara's death he became much less concerned with specific issues and wrote and talked more often in generalities. He ignored most Canadian questions as he worried about the international situation. The "human family" had been torn apart in the war, had lost a generation of leaders, and now suffered from the deep, unhealed wounds.

Governments, he thought, had caused the war. It was folly to think that collectivism in either government or business was going to achieve anything. None of his friends could disagree with his pessimism about world affairs — most of them shared it — or dare to predict when the Depression was going to end.

> We carried over a legacy of ill will from the Peace Treaty, and left unredeemed all the ill will which occasioned the War. In consequence, we have international bitterness, distrust, hatred, fear, on a scale which denied to the members of the human family, natural intercourse, natural interchange of goods, natural relations incident to thriving business. We lost the earning power, and the leadership upon which we should depend during these anxious times, in the death of a generation of young men of all the nations who were in the War.
>
> When history comes to record what has occurred, the fact that there was great suffering, economic distress, and unemployment on a great scale, will be recited as a mere incident, but for the members of the human family who are passing through it now, it is a very real experience. And yet we must live through it, and some of us must die in it.[37]

X

He became a villain one more time.

The Flavelle family still had large holdings of Robert Simpson Company Limited preferred stock (the Robert Simpson Company survived as a wholly-owned subsidiary of Simpson's Limited; the preferred stock could not be called in). Clara's estate, valued at $170,000, consisted almost wholly of these shares. In late 1932 or early 1933 Flavelle learned of transactions between the Robert Simpson Company and Simpson's Limited which considerably reduced the preferred shareholders' security. Through complex property transfers the first charge on Robert Simpson earnings had become interest payments to Simpson's rather than the obligation to the preferred shareholders. Flavelle joined with the other preferred shareholders to insist that Simpson's Limited revise the arrangement in order to provide better security. Although C. L. Burton was able to put up a fair defence of the property transfers as necessary for the construction of a new Montreal store, Flavelle was shocked by what he considered a "dreadful" manipulation of securities.[38]

The new Simpson's was also under scrutiny in Ottawa. In early 1934, H. H. Stevens, R. B. Bennett's Minister of Trade and Commerce, began to attack department and chain stores for ruthless buying practices. Bennett and other members of the cabinet doubted Stevens' competence and objectivity. Faced with threats of resignation from the popular minister, however, the Prime Minister agreed to make Stevens chairman of a House of Commons Select Committee to investigate price spreads and mass buying. Simpson's cooperated with the committee's auditors as they prepared a report on the firm's business. Reading newspaper accounts of some of the early testimony before the Stevens Committee, Flavelle was not alarmed to learn of very low wages. "I could not help but think how fortunate it was that these girls could get $8 or $9 a week, rather than be like so many other girls and women who cannot get anything," he wrote Sir Thomas White.[39]

The report on Simpson's was presented to the committee in June. It set out the company's entire financial history from 1898 to 1933. The committee members were not friendly to Simpson's, were obviously impressed at the millions Flavelle had "taken out" of the operation in 1925 and 1929, and found the use of holding companies, multiple issues of securities, and tricky inter-company transactions all rather suspicious.[40]

Just before Parliament prorogued in July, H. H. Stevens spoke to a Conservative MP's study group on the committee's findings. He singled out Simpson's as the "classic" example of an irresponsible refinancing. In the 1929 deal, he charged, Sir Joseph Flavelle and associates had pressured Simpson's employees to buy stock, offering to loan them the purchase price through the Bank of Commerce. The stock the employees bought "is not worth a snap of the fingers. There is no chance of its ever being worth a snap." And the bonds the public bought were not properly secured either. Sir Joseph had the right to sell out, Stevens admitted, but should have told people he was selling out:

If you will take the prospectus you will find that his name was prominent in them [sic] all. . . . the inevitable impression was that Sir Joseph Flavelle was still in the business. The employees were asked to participate in the prosperity of a business institution of which he was the head. Nothing was said about the fact that they were going to take 10 million out and leave a lot of liabilities in its place. I think it is safe to say that had the public known the facts, namely, that they were pulling out of the partnership [sic] and pulling out 10 million on their personal account, no one would have bought a single dollar of those bonds or that stock. I do not think there is any doubt about that.

Because of the burden of fixed interest Simpson's had to meet on its bonds, it had raised its average mark-up from thirty per cent to forty-seven per cent, thus exploiting Canadian consumers.[41]

Stevens gave the stenographic record of his speech to James Muir of the Dominion Bureau of Statistics to be printed as a pamphlet. As a reporter for the *Ottawa Journal*, Muir had broken the bacon scandal in 1917; he may well have marvelled at the opportunity to break another story about J. W. Flavelle's misdoings. Acting under vague authorization from Stevens, Muir had three thousand copies of the pamphlet run off in identical format to other DBS publications, and sent copies to the editors of a number of daily papers.[42]

Having heard about the speech and the pamphlet, C. L. Burton persuaded Bennett to attempt to stop its distribution. The attempt failed, and in early August 1934 Stevens' version of Flavelle's misdeeds at Simpson's was published across Canada. The old bugger was exposed again.

The most remarkable feature of the Stevens affair was not Muir's role, not the impropriety of using the DBS for political pamphleteering, not the impropriety of the chairman of a committee reaching conclusions halfway through the presentation of the evidence. It was the simple absurdity of Stevens' charges.

Everyone knew the Flavelle–Fudger–Cox interests were being bought out in 1929. The employees knew it first, and the public learned it in the ads selling the new securities. Flavelle's name was not on the prospectus; the new officers' names were. Stevens had confused that prospectus with two earlier ones issued to raise capital when Flavelle was still in the company! Rather than there having been pressure on employees to buy stock, they had been anxious to do so for years. Flavelle had not known of the Bank of Commerce loans to employees until after the fact because collateral loans were not brought before the board (and would not have expected the loans to be made because the main banker in the sale was the Royal Bank). Simpson's common stock was selling very cheaply (the employees who had bought it had taken a beating), but was worth more than "a snap of the fingers" and had every prospect of recovering. Simpson's mark-up on its goods had not increased since 1929; instead it had fractionally declined.[43]

Flavelle was deeply hurt by the publicity, by the obvious implication that he had looted Simpson's, its employees, and the public of millions. He considered writing a pamphlet answering the charges, and gave Floyd Chalmers of the *Financial Post* a long background interview on the truth about Simpson's. "He had never been quite happy since the war-time profits episode,"

Chalmers recorded in his memo of the interview, "and realized that he was never popular in the country." After more thought, Flavelle decided it was not worth the effort to defend himself. "A lie put on its way cannot be overtaken and corrected," he wrote to Cromie. That had been the lesson of 1917 and there was nothing to do but ignore the incident.[44] There is no evidence that he had any contact with Bennett or anyone in the cabinet about the affair.

It was not surprising that charges like this should be made in 1934. There had to be some identifiable villain in such hard times. And there probably would be little point in fighting back. Who would believe anything that the high priests of a discredited, failed capitalism would say in their own defence? They were surely responsible for the country's misery, and at last Harry Stevens had come along to uncover their machinations. Flavelle had been caught and found guilty before. Holy Joe Flavelle—now there was the only man in Canada who could pray a man's shirt off his back—that sanctimonious old Methodist who could hold you up with a Bible better than most crooks could with a revolver.[45]

J. S. McLean had also received widespread unfavourable publicity testifying before the Stevens Committee. Just before the Stevens pamphlet was published, police uncovered a highly developed plot to kidnap him. Two weeks later, John S. Labatt, the brewer, was kidnapped. "FOUR-X Spike" threatened to kidnap Flavelle and hold him for $4 million ransom. Flavelle stopped his 8:40 a.m. walks to the office through Queen's Park and down University Avenue. When he started again in late September, an article in the *Mail* described the actions of the "stocky businesslike individual with his hands casually in his coat pockets" who was never more than six feet away. "If any other pedestrian — man or woman — gets between him and Sir Joseph, he quickly closes the gap. He takes a good eye-ful of any car stalled at the curb *en route*. Any figures at windows of buildings attract his particular attention." The grandchildren remembered how the bodyguard used to sit out on the lawn at Holwood outside Flavelle's study while he was working.[46]

R. B. Bennett had left for England shortly after the publication of Stevens' pamphlet. When the cabinet finally met again on October 25, Bennett and C. H. Cahan, who were appalled by Stevens' demagoguery ("the rich are entitled to justice as well as the poor," Bennett told his minister), demanded that he apologize to Flavelle and Burton. Instead, Stevens resigned from the cabinet, to the applause of thousands of Canadians who thought he was being "crucified on the altar of big interests."[47]

A former small businessman, who desperately wanted to "show these fellows" that he could succeed,[48] Stevens was little more than a front man for the leaders of the Retail Merchants' Association, an organization formed to attack the department stores in 1898, the year Flavelle bought Simpson's. After his resignation Stevens continued to trade on the small man's envy of wealth and power, founding his own Reconstruction party. It won as many votes in the 1935 election as the CCF, elected only Stevens, and then disappeared. It was not clear whether Stevens attacked Flavelle in 1935 out of his general resentment of successful businessmen, personal animosity stemming back to their quarrels over patronage during the war, or his deep ignorance of corporation finance. The animosity surely could not have begun back in 1887 when nine-year-old Henry Herbert Stevens was a member of J. W. Flavelle's Sunday School at George Street Methodist Church.

The irony of the Stevens affair was that Flavelle, presented as the villain, in fact considered himself victimized by the new Simpson's owners because of the preferred-stock problem. More ironically, Flavelle shared the view that the 1929 reorganization of Simpson's had been reckless. In a perfectly legal manoeuvre, quite common when conservatively managed companies with large reserves were taken over, the Gundy—Burton group had apparently used the $5 million in surplus profits Simpson's had accumulated since 1925 to offset part of the costs of the purchase.*[49] Conservative businessmen like Flavelle accumulated large reserves to be ready for depressions. Lacking the reserves, Simpson's was less fit to face the 1930s. It was still a profitable company in most years of the decade, considerably outperforming the much larger Eaton's operation, but stopped paying dividends on class-"A" common in 1930 and Simpson's preferred (not Robert Simpson preferred) in 1932. With the reserves it would have been able to pay dividends much longer.

To Flavelle the Simpson's transaction was another chapter in the old story of brokers and promoters loading companies with debt and debt charges so they could sell more stock. It happened in every boom—the "filibusters" [sic] who went after the well-managed companies. He had seen it—in fact been part of it—thirty years earlier in CCM, Carter—Crume, and other reorganizations. National Trust had wrestled with its effects in Nova Scotia in the

---

* It is not clear how the transaction took place, or even that Flavelle's charges were correct. But it was not at all surprising that new owners, who, in effect, had bought large cash reserves, would (in a phrase of the day) "cut the melon" and pay the cash back to themselves. In a sense, that was what Flavelle himself had allowed to happen in the 1925 refinancing.

BESCO—DISCO affair—and Flavelle had worried at the time about Harry Gundy's plans for that reorganization. In the 1920s the leading Canadian bond houses had begun calling themselves "investment bankers." By 1935 all of them, except A. E. Ames & Company (which probably remembered 1903), were technically insolvent. "It was not that men intended to do wrong," Flavelle wrote. "They were simply carried away with the prevailing passion to make money, to make it fast, and to make it in big blocks."[50]

XI

He spent an increasing portion of his time, almost half of it Miss Gladman estimated, trying to help people whose attempts to make money had floundered. There are virtually no records of the help he gave to other businessmen. After his death an unnamed associate estimated that it totalled a million dollars in the 1930s. It was said that $50,000 went to help the owners of one men's clothing store. They failed anyway. In instructions to National Trust accompanying his will, Flavelle mentioned two pages of Loan Accounts Receivable on his Trial Balance records, "the great body of which have no value," which his trustees were not to attempt to collect. They could expect repayments from several people who had borrowed money from him against Simpson's stock, and from two brokers he had helped, Draper Dobie and Col. F. H. Deacon. In 1935 Aird Flavelle's sawmill in British Columbia was shut down and about to go into bankruptcy when Uncle Joe put up bonds as collateral for new credits which allowed it to reopen. The Flavelle businesses in Lindsay were also in serious trouble. For several years Joe gave substantial sums to help his brother Will. "You will not think of what is being done . . . as a favor, but as an act natural in outcome as it would be with any of us, because of our mutual love, confidence, and with you and me, an abiding memory of what mother would expect."[51]

As chairman of the Board of Governors, Flavelle seems to have felt personally responsible for the survival of St. Andrew's College, partly because his own generosity had helped create a larger college than student fees in the 1930s could maintain. Its situation was desperate in 1933 when he contributed $50,000.00 to help reduce the building-fund deficit, and was no better in 1935 when he paid the Imperial Bank $110,718.98 to wipe out St. Andrew's overdraft. He appears to have arranged each year to protect the college against losses from students who could not pay their fees.[52]

Miss Gladman was authorized to give small sums of money to needy people who came to the office in Room 2610 of the Bank of Commerce building. On her index cards she recorded the $1 "loan" F. Cole got for three weeks to buy a car licence so he could get a job delivering telephone books, the $5 Mrs. Lepard was given for rent, the $1 for M. J. Shannon to buy wire for an egg beater, the $10 to William Thom to get him to Copper Cliff to take up a job with INCO, the $10 to buy William Sullivan a new glass eye. From experience she had learned to ask the Reverends J. O. Johnston or W. E. Wilson to investigate those who needed larger sums and whose stories might be fictitious. Flavelle was more kind-hearted, or gullible, and would often send cheques to strangers who wrote in about being unemployed, needing clothes for their children, having to meet rent payments. From January 1932 he gave Guy Salls more than $250 in answer to requests for help with rent, clothing, glasses, etc., until Johnston investigated in September 1935 and found that Salls was an experienced chiseller. There were other chisellers—perhaps the man who got $33 from Flavelle in 1933 and was then arrested for stealing a coat from Simpson's; certainly one of them was Miss Edith Bickle—the details of her case do not survive, but according to Flavelle it was "a shocking story of a designing, dishonest woman."

He occasionally talked about the people to whom he gave regular help as his "list." They ranged from ninety-nine-year-old J. P. Morgan, who at one time had his tradesmen sending their bills to Flavelle, all the way to an unrelated namesake, Joseph Flavelle, who had been getting periodic help from Clara. One of Clara's personal servants was given $5 a week for fourteen months after she was let go at Holwood, with occasional help afterwards. In 1933 Flavelle stumbled across an old William Davies employee at the Toronto General Hospital Christmas Tree pageant and gave him several hundred dollars over the next few years, despite not being sure whether he needed it. When he heard that the former general manager of the Davies retail stores was unemployed and too old to get a new job, he sent him $14 weekly for two years, $10 weekly after that. A second cousin had made a bad marriage and been repudiated by her family; her husband was a wastrel. Flavelle gave the couple $3,679.89 in seven years. Mrs. Guinn, the wife of the deaf minister with the crippled son, plagued Flavelle with requests for money to send a daughter to Normal School, a misbehaving son to Albert College (when the son was killed in a car accident Flavelle helped pay the funeral expenses), money to buy a hearing aid for her husband, and more money to support the crippled son. He would turn down one request only to give in to the next. At Holwood extra food was left in the big milkbox by the tradesmen's entrance. Flavelle often went out and talked with the down-and-outers who came for meals.

He supported his usual range of organized charities, cutting down on some of his donations to spread his money farther. New organizations were added: the Toronto Symphony Orchestra, the Dominion Drama Festival, the Toronto Man-A-Block Committee, the Community Gardens Committee, and others. In 1934 the National Labour Day Committee got $15 to help unemployed workers get a free lunch at the Canadian National Exhibition; in 1933 Flavelle gave Jimmy Simpson $250 to help pay back taxes on the Toronto Labor Temple. There were mysterious donations—the $1,000 he gave to Tom Russell in January 1937 "concerning the matter you discussed with me today"—and trivial ones—the $10 he gave toward a fund Howard Ferguson was raising to help an old man dying of heart disease pay his taxes. He took over all the charities Clara had been supporting, including a commitment to pay the meat bill at the Earlscourt Children's Home. Although he frequently mentioned that his own investments were suffering and his income shrinking, Flavelle gave away more than $1,100,000 in the 1930s, probably twice that.[53]

The church desperately needed his help. Congregations could not pay their debts or their ministers, ministers could not pay their debts, the national organization was having trouble paying its debts. In the winter of 1933–4, eighty-seven per cent of J. O. Johnston's Berkeley Street United Church congregation were on relief. Flavelle gave Johnston and W. E. Wilson at King Street almost a blank cheque for their Poor Funds. He increased his donations to the church's Missionary and Maintenance Fund in the 1930s, including extra thousands he gave when Endicott or Arnup appealed for help making up the deficit. In the mid-1930s Flavelle began giving the Rev. D. D. Cochrane, the United Church Home Missionary Secretary, money to help ministers in distress. Every year Cochrane distributed $1,000 to $2,500, usually in $25-to-$50 gifts at Christmas time, to ministers with sick wives and children, unemployed ministers, ministers whose congregations had not paid their salaries, ministers on their deathbeds. Flavelle insisted on anonymity.[54]

West China Union University was the one institution Flavelle was connected with that flourished. Its financial position improved spectacularly as the devaluation of the American dollar doubled the purchasing power of its North American grants. Chiang Kai-shek's Nationalists briefly unified the country against the Japanese threat, and the leader himself made Chengtu his capital for several months, while driving the Communists out of Sze-chuan. President Beech persuaded the board to accept Sinoization, found several prominent Nationalist bankers to sit on his Chinese Board of Direc-tors, and controlled a substantial endowment gained from currency specula-tion. Flavelle ended his connection with West China in 1935. By then the North American Board had become little more than a finance committee. It was still unclear whether or not West China had a glowing future. Placing his university's savings as well as his faith in China, Beech had invested much of the endowment through the Raven Trust Company of Shanghai. He ignored Flavelle's warning that the British banks in China had a good reason for offering only one-third the interest given by these new Chinese banks. In 1935 the Raven Trust Company failed.[55]

XII

Various conferences and councils of the United Church denounced cap-italism and capitalists with good socialist rhetoric. When the Toronto Con-ference denounced the wealthy in 1933, a minister wrote Flavelle denounc-ing the conference. "There is so much suffering in all classes in the commu-nity, including preachers," Flavelle answered, "that perhaps in a Conference representing a church which has always been thinking of the under-dog, the action of the Toronto Conference will be understood by those of us who belonged to the old Methodist Church better than it can be understood by the outsider."[56]

His dissatisfaction with the United Church in the 1930s was that it did not have enough of the true old Methodism. It seemed to be spiritually bank-rupt, its preaching so little able to move its members that they would not support their ministry and the church's work. The United Church needed a "spiritual arousement," he told Richard Roberts (then serving as Mod-erator), and had to stop relying on centralization and organization as a sub-stitute.[57]

Many Toronto churchmen, especially middle- and upper-class laymen, were finding spiritual arousal in the genteel conservative revivalism of Frank Buchman's Oxford Group (later Moral Re-armament). Others were attracted to Denton Massey's nationally famous Bible classes at Metropol-itan United. In 1933, in response to the thirst for spiritual quickening,

Roberts called a meeting of Sherbourne Street laymen. Flavelle spoke to the group, describing the old "class-meeting" days in the Methodist Church. He spoke with "conspicuous power and feeling" according to a newspaper report. "Emotion, even to the point of tears, was perceptible over all the company and on many a face, Sir Joseph's not excepted." The group decided to form a Sunday-morning class with Flavelle as the leader. It met a few times and faded away.[58]

CHAPTER TWENTY

REST

I

He aged perceptibly after Clara's death, and again during the Stevens affair. His mind began to lose its quickness. His ideas hardened, and he had little to contribute at board meetings beyond pleas for cutbacks and economizing. His role at the trust company, the bank, and the university was little more than ceremonial. His English friends even let him give up Canadian Marconi in 1936, two years after it had been sold to I & IC. In his last letter on university affairs he urged president Cody to accept budget cuts so the U. of T. could live within its means. His last word on hospital affairs was a letter to the new chairman, E. C. Fox, urging him not to allow any further expansion until Toronto General's operating accounts were balanced.[1] (The two had a reconciliation of sorts when Flavelle invited Fox back to tea one Saturday after they found themselves sitting close to each other at an Argonaut football game.)

The slowing down was relative. At seventy-six he could still write a splendidly detailed nine-page letter attacking a "mischievous" editorial on the bacon trade.[2] His reading in 1935 and 1936 included Breasted's *Conquest of Civilization*, Gunther's *Inside Europe*, and Jack Wheeler-Bennett's *Hindenburg*. He constantly exchanged reading material with Will Rundle, in 1938 sending him the Hansard debate on Anthony Eden's resignation, Keynes writing in the *New Statesman*, an article on Boeing's development of seaplanes, and Nicholas Murray Butler on "The Abdication of Democracy." The university History Club still had an annual meeting at Holwood. In 1935, after the students had finished debating the New Deal, Flavelle made a long statement about his own career and the Depression. Young Claude Bissell, who had shared the general view of Flavelle as an arch-villain, was so impressed by the talk that a week later he wrote out a recreation of the remarks which exactly captured Flavelle's phraseology and speech cadences.[3]

His pessimism did not lift. The moderate economic recovery of 1934–6 more than disappeared in the 1937 collapse. Flavelle had voted for Mackenzie King in 1935, and even helped raise money for the Liberals, apparently because they were more likely to give Canada a majority government (from 1931 his preference was for a coalition National Government like Britain's).[4] He soon decided that King had once again failed to rise to his opportunities, and he was not impressed with Dr. R. J. Manion, Bennett's successor as Conservative leader. The Liberals lifted the CNR trusteeship, bringing the system back under political control. Perhaps there was some hope for the railways, though: Flavelle had heard that the new Minister of Transportation and Communications, C. D. Howe, was able, and thought he started off competently. In Ontario politics Flavelle seems to have been encouraged by Mitch Hepburn's economy programme and resistance to industrial unions.[5]

But there was no real reason to expect anything from governments—the organizations which had come so close to destroying civilization in the Great War. In the late 1930s Canada was rife with sectionalism, disunity, and political posturing. In one of his last comments on Canadian politics, Flavelle viewed with alarm "the increasing body of discontent in the provinces of this fair Dominion, to whom God has given so much and to whom we have paid so little in return. Our conduct has been unworthy of a free people, privileged in the opportunity to work out a national policy with a will for goodwill."[6]

The news from Europe was almost uniformly bad as the nations prepared for apparently inevitable war. Some of Flavelle's British friends—Lothian, Curtis, Geoffrey Dawson—were champions of appeasement, who hoped Hitler could be bought off. The realism and pessimism of Jack Wheeler-Bennett's letters and speeches convinced Flavelle that there could not be peace with Naziism.

The last IMB shells had still to be destroyed. In 1935 the Dominion Archivist learned that the shells in the War Trophy building were still live and could blow up the neighbourhood at any time. Flavelle referred him to Colonel Ogilvie, who was still with the Ministry of Militia and Defence. The next year a Toronto businessman asked Flavelle how Canadians might get some of the new contracts being let in Britain for shells and other war materials. The brokers and adventurers were already in England looking for business.

In early 1937 Ogilvie came to Flavelle to discuss the work he was doing appraising the capacity of Canadian plants. Fitzgerald supplied Ogilvie with samples of IMB contracts. In England Brand had a long talk with the Minister of Defence about the Canadian situation, and described it to Flavelle. "It seems quite like old times writing to you about these matters." The old men thought it was important that politicians remember how they had done things in the Great War. In May 1938, Flavelle went to Ottawa for several hours' conversation with British officials. He particularly warned them not to let their contracts be supervised by the Canadian government, "because the mischief of political patronage would not and could not be eliminated." [7]

The routine of his life went on. After Clara's death he stopped using Ashburnham, but continued to go south in February and March, usually with Mina. In 1935 they took a Cunard cruise of the Mediterranean, visiting Spain, Egypt, the Holy Land, Turkey, Greece, Yugoslavia, and Italy. His letters home were filled with wonder and delight at the new experiences. They went on to Paris, where he felt he appreciated the majesty of grand opera for the first time, and to London for luncheons and dinners with his old friends. There was a special luncheon with John Buchan, who wanted to talk with Flavelle about his new duties as Governor General. In 1937 Joe and Mina circumnavigated South America on the *Aquitania*; in 1938 they wintered in La Quinta, California, with the Whites, the Woods, and the Russells. During one of the trips, a tramp wintered comfortably in the attics of Holwood, slept in Sir Joseph's bed, and tried on his suits.

Holy Joe finally relaxed a little bit. In 1933 he received vice-regal permission in advance not to serve alcoholic beverages when the Governor General came to dinner at Holwood. Soon after that Clara told her father to stop imposing his principles on others, and liquor began to be served at Holwood. People who remembered Flavelle disagreed, but some thought he took the occasional glass of sherry. On a fishing trip in 1936 Horace Speakman could not see any difference in colour between the Scotch he was drinking and the glass of amber liquid Flavelle insisted was purely medicinal. He started playing cards on Sundays at Swannanoa—"What else is there to do?" And in California he had unusual feelings about the "half dressed women, perhaps quarter dressed" he saw on the streets: "My old fashioned training could easily if I would permit develop in sensuousness. I am fortunate in a steady enlargement of a spirit of tolerance toward all & sundry who carry on so different from my upbringing." [8]

He was still a member of half a dozen United Church boards and committees. In 1936 he attended his first General Council of the United Church. He was worried about going "because I know among our Church people there is a query mark concerning myself," but found himself treated with great kindness and an absence of suspicion. The council did not assuage his concern for the future of the church "and the absence as I see it, of intellectual understanding or moral purpose to look the matter fairly in the face. . . . " In his last letters to his minister at Sherbourne Street he tried to explain his view that the church should stop its noisy scolding about social and economic conditions and get on with its duty to preach a gospel of grace and salvation — the gospel he had heard at the revival services when he was a boy.[9]

There were always the claims. The rebuilt Metropolitan United had a $200,000 deficit. Could Flavelle help, and help persuade others to help? The Browns needed more help; would Sir Joseph please see Sarah so that she could explain? Thanks for the $5,000 you contributed to the Board of Home Missions' relief fund for ministers in the drought areas of the West. Could you help with the deficit in the Missionary and Maintenance Fund? It would not be wise to give anything to Charles Stacey, who is already on relief and drinks excessively. The Federation for Community Service might as well have the sixteen shares of Imperial Oil stock someone had left at Holwood after a party two years ago. The meat bill at the Earlscourt Children's Home rose from $298 in 1933 to $534 in 1937, apparently because soup bones and scrap meat were disdained; better to stop the open promise and give them $20 a month instead. November 1938: "There is a constant stream of callers, and letters covering requests for all sorts of things from Newfoundland to Victoria and I really do not know what to do with them."[10]

II

Some of his friends thought Flavelle should write his autobiography or allow his biography to be written. Several authors, including Newton MacTavish and W. J. Loudon, asked to be allowed to write the story of his life. Flavelle declined. "I have been a busy, active man, doing a lot of useful things for myself, or others, and for the State," he wrote Loudon, "but they are only the every-day sort of things that men ought to perform, and there is no distinction about them, which is an occasion for publicity, in the form of a written record."

It was just as well. Flavelle thought of biographies as inspirational memorials. He spent several thousand dollars paying A. H. U. Colquhoun to write a sycophantic, useless biography of their friend Willison. He agreed to suppress Willison's place-hunting ("I would like to forget that he had done so"), and even Willison's criticisms of other people, on the ground that nothing "disagreeable" should be put in a biography "if it does not serve a needed public purpose." [11] Flavelle would have disapproved of this book.

His modest denials of having done anything worth writing about did not hide his intense desire to be honoured. Because he was so unsure of himself —partly because of the public criticisms, partly because he had come so far in his lifetime, partly because he was a Methodist—Flavelle gloried in tributes and honours. His was the vanity of insecurity. Knowing that he was not "Sir" Joseph, "Baronet," and suspecting that other people knew it, Joe Flavelle tried to remain humble. He only became transparent. As a boy he had been taught to tip his hat to distinguished Peterboroughnians. Replying to a letter of congratulations on his seventy-first birthday, he wrote:

You will acquit me of playing the humble, if I say that I have repeated wonderment, each time as fresh as the previous one, when someone whose opinion must be respected, pays me tribute. In another form I have the surprise that as I go along the street, some workman or some important citizen, touches his hat to me. In many ways, I have not grown up. I am still the boy in simple life, struggling under indebtedness to home, to church and to kind friends. [12]

He loved praise and congratulations. The luncheon Mark Irish gave to honour him on his seventy-eighth birthday and the ceremonies when he retired as chairman at the Bank of Commerce's 1938 annual meeting were deeply gratifying.*[13] But never enough. On these occasions, and in one letter after

---

* On both occasions Sir Thomas White was the most prominent speaker testifying to Flavelle's achievements. Flavelle was especially delighted with E. R. Wood's telegram from California replying to the luncheon invitation: " . . . There must be some mistake about this Party. Sir Joseph never had a birthday, never did, and never will know nothing about them. . . . May he long continue his interest in finance bridge hockey golf football curling billiards fishing research music education and the bank's earning power." And he was moved by a particularly fine letter from R. B. Bennett after his retirement from the Bank of Commerce: "You have touched life at many points. You were endowed not only with great ability but even greater capacity, which has enabled you to render outstanding service to the business organizations with which you have been connected as well as to the religious, educational, social and political life, not only of the community in which you lived but to the Dominion and, in a very special sense, to the

another, he felt compelled to deny business wrongdoings, sordid motives, ambition, or place-hunting. I was not guilty. I had no ulterior motives. I did not ask for all this. I never sought an honour.

He had kept copies of his correspondence and sometimes mentioned that he was saving special letters (usually honouring him or from prominent people) for his grandchildren to read after his death. He wanted the family, above all others, to understand his work and understand that he had done no wrong. After Christmas dinner in 1938, with his children and grandchildren gathered around him, he talked for hours about his boyhood, his struggles to succeed, and the untrue charges made against him.

He knew that he was a product of his mother's training and George Street Methodist Church. Taking hard work, sobriety, and honesty for granted, he thought that his stress on accounting and his ability to get along with the people working for him explained most of his success in business. He would probably have agreed that accounting came naturally to an earnest Methodist, and that his style of executive leadership had been moulded in the Methodist class. There were two other characteristics of his Methodism, reinforced by his mother and his family experience, which were particularly evident in Joseph Wesley Flavelle:

First, both the Methodist way of life and the "spirit of capitalism" were rooted in an ideal of self-denial. All his business life Flavelle differentiated between his operations and those of the greedy businessmen—the "traders" looking for fast profits, the financial men looting companies to sell bonds and stock, the imprudent directors and shareholders who paid out all their profits in dividends, never looking to the future. Flavelle's was the pure capitalist's approach to accumulating wealth: deferring gratification so that wealth could be reinvested, building up even greater blessings in the future. Flavelle was too austere, too good at his work, too able to live up to his principles, to be thought of as anything like a typical Canadian businessman. He was archetypal, as near an incarnation of the capitalist ideal as Canada ever had.

Flavelle approximated the spirit of capitalism so closely that he became thoroughly entangled in its contradictions. He did well in business because he learned not to overvalue a high standard of living. By the early 1900s

---

Empire in its time of greatest peril. . . . Despite unwarranted attacks, the fact remains that your life will serve as an inspiration to Canadians of future years and as an example that great material success is not incompatible with an active, sympathetic and sincere interest in the real business of Christian living,—preparing for Life Eternal."

there seemed to be no point to making still more money, and Flavelle rejected the opportunity to create a business empire so that he could spend his time more congenially. Being only a capitalist, not finding self-fulfilment in empire-building or game-playing for its own sake, Flavelle did not become a great entrepreneur.

As an observer of society, Flavelle was haunted in the 1920s by the baffling dilemma of modern capitalism — that habits of self-denial create affluent societies which lose their habits of self-denial. During the war he had already learned that Canadian society was in no mood to honour his values. Canadians would not honour excellent businessmen who made money wearing one hat and then gave public service wearing another hat. Wartime highlighted what was already becoming obvious in the twentieth century: business, money, the wealthy were suspect; the slightest misjudgment or misunderstanding, and a reputation was destroyed. The capitalist system was self-destructive in this way also: that those who did best under it were bound to be hated.

The second characteristic of Methodism, and the one which distinguished it from most other Protestant denominations, was the impulse toward perfection in a faith which centred on man's will, rather than God's. Before it was diluted in Canada by secularism and Church Union, the Methodist impulse shaped the characters of great businessmen and great social reformers. Flavelle and the "social gospellers" —J. S. Woodsworth, Salem Bland, and others —shared a belief in the necessity of achieving perfect patterns of living. In Flavelle the perfectionist drive was intensely personal, directed to personal habits, to the perfecting of his business organizations, and then to personal social service. He succeeded splendidly within an economic and social system that was structured and hierarchical, but very open to talent. For the rest of his life he urged other young men to develop the drive and habits to make the system work for them as it had for him.

Flavelle drifted away from his early prohibitionist beliefs because he decided that it was not up to the state to make men sober. The Methodist social gospellers assumed that the state should not only abolish drunkenness, but that it should abolish poverty, inequality, and immorality as well. Flavelle wanted to perfect the individual, and believed the state could not do for a man what he had to do for himself. The Methodist socialists wanted to perfect society and believed that the state had to do for the individual what the system would not let him do for himself. All of these Methodists were Utopians in the sense that perfectionists tend to set impossibly high standards. They believed man could be saved. They disagreed on the means of salvation. Flavelle perfectly summarized their disagreement in the comment, "There is no such thing as mass salvation, either in religion or in politics."[14]

They were all moralists—all obsessed with doing the right thing, doing good, serving man and society. Flavelle's sense of stewardship or trusteeship was rooted in the same impulse as the social reformers' disdain for the idea of private property. In his business life Flavelle tried to be as saintly as any minister in private life. He faced considerably more temptations than most ministers — or social reformers — and did not do badly. A journalist once suggested that his life's story could be subtitled "the financial career of a conscience."

The masses were on the side of the social reformers. By the end of Flavelle's life it was clear that Canadians had rejected individualism and laissez-faire capitalism. Prewar social-reform agitation, the Great War and wartime profiteering, and the Great Depression, led them to form organizations and pass legislation which restricted the free actions of individuals, business, and markets, in a multitude of ways. In championing individualism against the centralizing, coercive, and stultifying effects of organization, Flavelle spoke for a lost set of values. His pure liberal-conservatism, blending a concern for a productive economic system with a belief in a community bound by spiritual ties, was a lost political cause. Most of the rest of the parameters of his way of life were crumbling. In two generations after Flavelle's death the Canadian world of missionaries, English butlers, coats of arms, tramps at the door, white flannels, ginger ale, and long walks on the Sabbath, disappeared. It was occasionally recreated on television — not very effectively.

III

After he came back from California in the spring of 1938 his days were filled with weddings, teas, convocations, funerals, and board meetings. "My pink cheeks and blue eyes are quite an object of envy on the part of young and middle-aged ladies, who say they have pleasure in meeting me and looking at me. . . ." At the end of June there was the annual migration to Swannanoa —"Here we are sweetheart, 2 trucks, 5 cars, a retinue of servants, a beautiful property, all for one man. Why should there not be storms and uproar from the under dog . . .?"[15]

The fishing was not good that summer. Joe alarmed June McEachren and Bill Barrett, who were staying with him, by going out almost every day, no matter how threatening the weather. Sometimes friends came up for a day-long fishing excursion. At noon they would beach the boats, set up a table, and eat off fine china. "Be sure not to step in the moose shit, Sir Joseph," Archie Ellery, his handyman and guide, always warned him.[16]

He slept well and felt reasonably fit, but cut back his golf to nine holes. He began to find his memory letting him down for names and places he had recently heard of. His health became more irregular that autumn, and in January his doctors realized that he was suffering from cancer of the bowel. When he was given the news he spent six hours talking with Reverend Cockram of Sherbourne Church, then went on with his life.

He went into the office for a few hours most days in January, and had social or business engagements almost every afternoon. When there was nothing else to do in the evenings he played billiards or cribbage with Payne, his butler. Friends commented on how well he looked at the tea Clara gave before he left for Florida in early February. The group took a sleeper to New York and the Orange Blossom Special to West Palm Beach, where they had reservations at The Breakers.

Joe walked a mile or two every day, sometimes played golf, and went on long drives. He sent cases of grapefruit back to Clara, Ellsworth, and Miss Gladman. On February 23 he wrote Clara, who was soon to join him, about the plans to motor to Virginia where they would meet Jack Wheeler-Bennett and then go on to Washington. He was fit, "but a bit short in pep. . . . I have been so long possessed of Vitality I feel I have lost something when it is not quite up to par." Clara had always been his favourite. "Again dear," he concluded, "my deep gratitude for the fidelity, simplicity and understanding of your love for me—it just stays with me as a comfort and assurance and with it a reminder always of mother's devotion."[17]

He played golf on Saturday, March 4. On Sunday, while travelling to Miami on a train, he took sick. Early Tuesday morning his heart failed. Clara and Mina were with him when he died.

The body was brought back to Toronto and placed in a bronze casket at Holwood. Floral tributes covered the south and west sides of the dining room from floor to ceiling as friends came to pay their last respects. After a private service at Holwood, then a public service at Sherbourne Street, Flavelle was buried in Mount Pleasant cemetery. The church was jammed with dignitaries and business leaders (many of whom went on to Sir Henry

Pellatt's funeral later that afternoon). In a letter to his son Aird, Will Flavelle described an incident at the church:

Three old ladies of humble place whom he had helped in their need managed to reach the over-crowded church only to be told there was no more room. Mr. Tory, one of the ushers, knowing one of them, said "Come along, I will find a place for you" and ushered them into Uncle's vacant pew, thus leaving vacant only the place he personally had occupied which simply had a bouquet of flowers attached to it. I thought it was just such an act as he would have done himself under the circumstances. . . .

Canada has not produced anyone to whom he was second. We lived too close to him to realize his bigness and his outstanding qualities. We knew him as Joe or Uncle Joe and in all his gracious kindness, for he never had the superior twist that so frequently is part of big men.[18]

The newspapers contained glowing tributes to Flavelle's work, character, and generosity from business associates, editors, and churchmen. Writing in *Saturday Night*, which editorially apologized for its 1917 articles, Hector Charlesworth best captured the scope of Flavelle's achievement: "In the end, Sir Joseph touched the life of Canada at more points than any man of his time."[19]

IV

Flavelle's estate totalled $6,053,038. He held stock valued at just under $4 million, bonds worth just over $1,500,000; at least two-thirds of his securities were Canadian. His children and grandchildren received bequests totalling about $2 million. There were gifts or annuities to all his nieces, nephews, and cousins, Miss Gladman, and the servants. The hospital, university, Sherbourne Street Church, and the United Church of Canada received gifts totalling about $175,000. Holwood was given to the University of Toronto to be used as "a club or meeting place" for women staff and students. The Province of Ontario took about one-third of Flavelle's wealth in succession duties.* The residue of the estate, about $1 million, was di-

---

* Flavelle directed that his estate pay any succession duties owing on all the bequests as well as gifts made during his lifetime. The province attempted to tax those payments as part of the bequests and gifts. Eight years after Flavelle's death the province's last appeal was denied. The cases are still considered to have established important principles.

vided equally between the children and a charitable foundation to be controlled by Flavelle's descendants. Ellsworth inherited the baronetcy.

Dispersed so widely, Flavelle's wealth effectively disappeared. The Flavelle Foundation continued as a very small charitable foundation, spending a few tens of thousands each year in useful attempts to supplement the tens of millions governments and lotteries lavished on education and the arts. The corporations whose history Flavelle helped shape — Canada Packers, Simpson's, National Trust, the Bank of Commerce — survived and prospered. Toronto General Hospital remained at the centre of health-service provision in Toronto, with the buildings erected during Flavelle's chairmanship eventually becoming considered part of historic Toronto. The governing structure of the University of Toronto that Flavelle helped to establish in 1906 was destroyed in 1971. Holwood was used as a residence during the war, a home for the history department afterwards,* and from 1961 housed the Faculty of Law. It was never used as a centre for women staff and students, was renamed Flavelle House, and had its interior gutted. Sir Joseph's bedroom, for example, became the men's washroom.

Sherbourne Street Church merged with Carlton Street Church in 1959 to become St. Luke's United, and carried on its downtown social work. In the 1960s the Ontario Government lavished money on the Ontario Research Foundation. Speakman Street and Flavelle Boulevard are the main thoroughfares in the Sheridan Park research complex in Mississauga, where it is located. Christian missionary and educational work in China were ended by the Communist revolution. The West China Union University disappeared. In Canadian politics the Conservative party survived.

Most Canadians forgot about J. W. Flavelle. If the name remained vaguely familiar, you might be able to place him as one of those old pirates who'd made their money exploiting somebody or had done well out of the war or had sold the spoiled meat.

---

* The present author was first tutored in history in one of the servants' bedrooms.

A NOTE ON SOURCES

Flavelle left behind him approximately 250,000 pages of correspondence. His business and philanthropic correspondence is at Queen's University (it would have been at the University of Toronto, which he served so well, if the university library had been interested enough to approach the family and ask for it). His IMB and Grand Trunk correspondence is in the Public Archives of Canada. The family retained a collection of scrapbooks, miscellaneous documents, and several hundred personal letters. These were made available to me and are to become part of the Flavelle papers at Queen's; they will be supplemented by some of the research notes compiled for this book. Canada Packers retains a small collection of very important letters and memoranda relating to the William Davies Company. The late Stuart Flavelle of Lindsay had a small but valuable collection of documents relating to the Flavelle family. As listed in the notes, a wide range of company records, Minutes, personal papers, newspapers, and other sources has also been used.

I have tried to make the footnoting unobtrusive and concise, but reasonably comprehensive. The citations should be intelligible to historians. Anyone who finds unintelligible or incorrect or inadequate references should write to me at the University of Toronto.

Abbreviations

BP   Robert L. Borden Papers
CAR   *Canadian Annual Review*
CEF   Clara Ellsworth Flavelle
CFM   Clara Flavelle McEachren (Clara junior)
FA   *Farmer's Advocate*
FCP   Flavelle Papers, Canada Packers

FFP   Flavelle Family Papers
FQ   Flavelle Papers, Queen's University
FO   Flavelle Papers, Public Archives of Canada
JSW   John S. Willison
JWB   John Wheeler-Bennett
JWF   Joseph Wesley Flavelle
LI   *Report and Proceedings of the Royal Commission on Life Insurance*, 1906
PAC   Public Archives of Canada
RLB   Robert Laird Borden
SFP   Stuart Flavelle Papers
UCA   United Church Archives
UTA   University of Toronto Archives
UTL   University of Toronto Library

NOTES

INTRODUCTION — THE ROBBER BARONET (pp.ix-xii)

1 FFP, JWF to CFM, Nov. 2, 1918.

2 Ibid., Sept. 14, 1917.

CHAPTER ONE — THE FLAVVLES OF PETERBOROUGH (pp.1-26)

1 Stuart Flavelle Family Papers, MSS. of Flavelle family history, inc. Bishop Darley to Rev. Dr. McCall, July 26, 1847.

2 Ibid.; Sir Joseph Flavelle, "Fragments": Being an Unfinished Story of His Life, privately published pamphlet, 1967.

3 SFP, John Flavelle to "Sister," Aug. 15, 1878.

4 SFP, family history, "Card," Dec. 13, 1849.

5 Camilla Sanderson, John Sanderson the First (Toronto, 1910), p. 123.

6 Ibid., p. 121; also FQ, Case 63, Address to Staff of National Trust, Jan. 25, 1934.

7 Fragments.

8 Ibid.

9 Ibid.

10 Peterborough: Land of Shining Waters (Toronto, 1967), p. 182.

11 Sanderson, John Sanderson the First, p. 168.

12 Flavelle Family Papers, Dorothea Flavelle to JWF, Dec. 19, 1892.

13 FQ, pp. 112-22, JWF to J. S. Willison, April 8, 1903.

14 FQ, 57, Address to Simpson's Staff, Feb. 2, 1924.

15 SFP, John D. Flavelle to William Flavelle, March 7, 1871.

16 Fragments.

17 Ibid.; FQ, 38, JWF to Dr. R. P. Bowles, Jan. 9, 1919.

18 FFP, JWF to CEF, June 6, 1904.

19 Fragments.

20 FQ, 66, Address to Canada Packers Junior Club, Oct. 12, 1937.

21 FFP, JWF to Clara Ellsworth, undated.

22 Peterborough Examiner, Nov. 2, 1885.

23 John Macdonald, "Leaves from the Portfolio of a Merchant," Canadian Methodist Magazine, May, June 1886.

24 Fragments.

25 FQ, supplementary: excerpts from JWF newspaper advertisements compiled by David Bell.

26 Peterborough Examiner, Sept. 21, 1882; income taken from Peterborough Municipal Assessment Rolls, donations from Collection books in the archives of George Street United Church; on his business see also Fragments, and FQ, 23, Memo for Mr. Ruddick, enc. in JWF to Ruddick, April 20, 1934.

27 FFP, JWF to Clara Ellsworth, June 10, 1881; JWF to "Uncle," July 24, 1881.

28 FFP, JWF to CEF, Sept. 10, 1885.

29 SFP, Margaret Flavelle to William Flavelle, April 12, 1883; *Christian Guardian*, Aug. 27, 1884; PAC, John A. Macdonald Papers, pp. 195165-6, JWF to Macdonald, June 3, 1884.

30 For his interest in the West see FQ, JWF to Willison, April 8, 1903; for the possibility that he lost money in land speculation see the unsigned, undated article about Flavelle in FQ, 52. There is no corroborating evidence whatsoever, though, for the statements in the article (which is otherwise quite accurate), and the sums mentioned are highly implausible.

31 FQ, JWF to Willison, April 25, 1903.

32 The description of the struggles to apply and enforce the Scott Act is taken from a research paper prepared by David Bell, now deposited in the FQ, supplementary collection. All quotations are from the Peterborough daily papers.

33 *Fragments*; FQ, 23, Memo for Mr. Ruddick, enc. in JWF to Ruddick, April 20, 1934.

34 *Peterborough Review*, Dec. 31, 1886.

35 FFP, undated clipping, spring or summer of 1887.

36 FFP, JWF to CEF, March 15, 1887.

CHAPTER TWO — HOGTOWN (pp. 27-52)

1 FFP, JWF to CEF, Jan. 27, March 16, 1887.

2 *Ibid.*, Feb. 10, March 15, 1887.

3 *Ibid.*, March 24, 1887.

4 *Ibid.*, March 23, 1887.

5 *Ibid.*, June 27, 1887.

6 FQ, 66, Address to Canada Packers Junior Club, Oct. 12, 1937; *Toronto Star*, March 8, 1939.

7 *Fragments*.

8 FQ, 20, Indenture, Feb. 24, 1888, enc. in John A. Gunn to JWF, Dec. 22, 1932.

9 FFP, CEF Scrapbook; JWF to CEF, June 6, 1904.

10 *Fragments*; Flavelle Papers, Canada Packers (FCP), Memo of agreement between Egg Dealers' Association of Ontario and Gunn, Flavelle & Company of Toronto, March 20, 1888; *Canadian Journal of Commerce*, March 30, 1888, p. 607.

11 *Fragments*.

12 FQ, 44, JWF to James Harris, Dec. 9, 1912.

13 *Fragments*.

14 Canada Packers Ltd., *The Story of Our Products* (1943); J. Frank Willis, *This Packing Business* (Canada Packers, n.d.).

15 W. Sherwood Fox, ed., *Letters of William Davies, Toronto 1854—1861* (Toronto, 1945); Willis, *This Packing Business*, p. 29; for Davies' volume see his letters in the *Farmer's Advocate* (FA), March 1889, p. 71, Dec. 1889, p. 374; for his profits see FCP, loose sheet of paper in JWF Quality Book.

16 *Fragments*.

17 FCP, William Davies Company Ltd., *Minutes*, copy of original agreement June 6, 1892; A. J. E. Child, "The Predecessor Companies of Canada Packers Limited: A Study of Entrepreneurial Achievement and Entrepreneurial Failure" (Unpublished MA thesis, University of Toronto, 1960), chap. 2. The agreement between Flavelle and the Davies family setting up the company contained several clauses designed to protect the family interest. As long as he was alive William Davies had veto power over "any radical departure from the lines of business which . . . William Davies & Co. have so successfully followed." As long as Davies continued to take an active interest in the business, Flavelle was not to dismiss any trusted employees without his consent, although it was also agreed that Davies as president was not to issue any instructions in conflict with Flavelle's. Most important, article twelve of the agreement required seventy-five per cent of its annual net profits to be paid to the shareholders in dividends, and this provision was eventually written into the charter. Another article set limits on the amounts of depreciation that could be written off annually without the Davies family's consent. The aim of these clauses was to safe-

guard the family, even if Flavelle obtained control of the company, against any tendency on his part to defer his own income and reinvest most of the profits in expansion. Flavelle's and the company's apparent scope for expansion was thus restricted so the family could ensure itself a substantial dividend income. On the other hand Flavelle was given the option to buy a controlling interest in the event of Davies' death.

18 FFP, JWF to CEF, July 31, 1892.
19 C. W. Towne and E. N. Wentworth, *Pigs: From Cave to Corn Belt* (Norman, Oklahoma, 1950); personal observation.
20 FA, Dec. 1889, p. 374.
21 FQ, 44, Edward Adie to JWF, April 3, 1917; JWF to Professor Day, April 5, 1917. In the late 1880s Davies considered moving his plant to the United States and stayed in Toronto only when the federal government agreed to relax the bonding regulations. See his letter in the *Sun*, Jan. 10, 1906.
22 FA, Dec. 1889, p. 375.
23 *Ibid.*, Nov. 20, 1897, p. 4; Aug. 1, 1898, p. 351.
24 FCP, Davies' *Minutes* and unbound financial statements; Child, "The Predecessor Companies of Canada Packers." These and all succeeding figures on profits, dividends, and killings are compiled from these three sources. When A. J. E. Child, who was then an executive of Canada Packers, prepared his MA thesis, he relied on some documents which have since been lost at Canada Packers. I have been able to confirm almost all of the figures given in his thesis, with only slight variations, but for an occasional year he quotes figures I was unable to locate.
25 FCP, JWF to Wm. Davies, April 18, 1894.
26 See note 24.

27 FFP, JWF Quality Book, "Memorandum Covering Our Trouble with Tainted Sides." An 1891 Davies letter to the *Farmer's Advocate* (December, p. 476) suggests he had come to believe the cause of the problem was Canadian farmers shipping in unspayed sows. He thought all his defective carcasses were unspayed Canadian sows. Flavelle found this untrue. The modern packer would find it remarkable that the company was trying to cure sows at all, something that was never done in Denmark.
28 *Ibid.*, anon. to JWB, July 29, 1893.
29 *Ibid.*, Memo on tainted sides.
30 *Letters of William Davies*, pp. 137-8; interview with Sir John Wheeler-Bennett.
31 FCP, JWF to Wm. Davies, April 18, 1894.
32 *Ibid.*, JWF to JWB, April 25, 1894; JWF to Wm. Davies, April 18, 1894.
33 *Ibid.*, JWB to JWF, Feb. 5, 1902, March 30, 1895; JWF to JWB, April 25, 1894.
34 *Ibid.*, JWF to Wm. Davies, April 18, 1894.
35 FFP, JWF Quality Book, JWB to JWF, Oct. 6, 1896.
36 FCP, JWF to Wm. Davies, April 18, 1894.
37 *Ibid.*, JWF to JWB, Feb. 18, 1897.
38 See note 24; FCP, Davies *Minutes*, May 26, 1896; JWF to Wm. Davies, June 10, 1897.
39 FCP, JWF to JWB, Feb. 18, 1897; FA, Feb. 20, 1897, p. 77, Aug. 5, 1897, p. 149.
40 Interview with Sir John Wheeler-Bennett; FCP, JWF to Wm. Davies, June 10, 1897; JWF to JWB, Feb. 18, 1897.
41 FQ, 66, Address to Canada Packers Junior Club, Oct. 12, 1937.
42 See note 24.
43 M. C. Urquhart and K. A. H. Buckley, eds., *Historical Statistics of Canada* (Toronto, 1965), p. 379; FCP, JWF memos, June 30, Aug. 27, 1900. Davies' proportion of the business in 1900 may have been higher.
44 *Letters of William Davies*, pp. 27-8.

CHAPTER THREE — ALL IN THE FAMILY (pp. 53-82)

1 H. J. Morgan, ed., *The Canadian Men and Women of the Time* (Toronto, 1912); *Toronto Daily Star*, Jan. 16, 1914; *Globe*, Jan. 16, 17, 1914; UCA, Sherbourne Street Church, Board of Trustees, *Minutes*, April 29, 1914; G. Wilson Craw, *The Peterborough Story: Our Mayors 1850-1951* (Peterborough, 1967), p. 38.

2 Annual reports, Central Canada Loan and Savings, published in the *Monetary Times*.

3 Victor Ross, *A History of the Canadian Bank of Commerce* (Toronto, 1922), II, p. 113.

4 *Report and Proceedings of the Royal Commission on Life Insurance*, 1906 (hereafter LI), pp. 949-50, 9-10, 137-61; UTL, Walker Papers, Walker to J. H. Dwight, March 22, 1899; to R. W. Smylie, March 27, 1899; to F. H. Peavey, April 5, 1899.

5 FFP, J. R. Dundas to JWF, April 6, 1892; *A. E. Ames & Co. Limited* (privately published pamphlet, Toronto, 1969).

6 FQ, 3274-6, Lash to JWF, April 22, 1916.

7 LI, pp. 963-4.

8 *Ibid.*, pp. 84, 1138-49.

9 *Ibid.*, pp. 86-7, 967-8, 1162. In 1906 Flavelle gave a correspondent this account of the subsidies: "The gift outright of large sums of money yearly by three gentlemen first, and two gentlemen afterward, cannot be easily understood at this distance. You would have to know of the peculiar relations during the early years of the Imperial—the passionate loyalty of Bradshaw's effort: the almost pedantic service given by myself and Ames and when Bradshaw said 'I must have a contribution in cash to help pay the organization and other heavy charges incident to a new company,' why, we just gave it to him. My relation though ceased when I gave up my directorship and subsequent gifts, I suppose, were made by Mr. Ames and Mr. Cox." FQ, 544-7, JWF to Mr. James, June 9, 1906.

10 National Trust Company Limited Library, A. D. Morrow, MSS. "Memories of the National Trust Company Ltd., 1898–1903"; National Trust Company, *Annual Reports*, 1898–1905.

11 *Memoirs and Writings, Harris Henry Fudger, 1852–1930* (privately printed, Toronto, 1931), pp. 1-6; C. L. Burton, *A Sense of Urgency: Memoirs of a Canadian Merchant* (Toronto, 1952), pp. 49-51.

12 FQ, 23, JWF to J. M. Macdonnell, June 7, 1934; *Fragments*; Burton, *A Sense of Urgency*, pp. 75-6.

13 William Stephenson, *The Store That Timothy Built* (Toronto, 1969); William Ferry, *A History of the Department Store* (New York, 1960).

14 Burton, *A Sense of Urgency*, p. 74.

15 *Shoppers Hand-Book and Fashion Catalogue of R. Simpson*, No. 51, Fall 1893; No. 56, Spring & Summer, 1896.

16 Robert Simpson Company Limited, *Minutes*, 1898–1902.

17 *Ibid.*, March 11, 1903.

18 Robert Simpson Company, *Spring and Summer Catalogue*, 1899.

19 National Trust, *Minutes*, Sept. 30, 1898.

20 Central Canada, *Annual Reports*, 1892–1900; E. P. Neufeld, *The Financial System of Canada* (Toronto, 1972), pp. 486-8; Walker Papers, Walker to G. J. Hinde, May 10, 1899.

21 Canadian Bank of Commerce, *Minutes*, April 21, 1891, Aug. 11, 1892.

22 Carter–Crume prospectus, *Monetary Times*, Sept. 15, 1899, p. 350; Moore Corporation, *The Moore Story, 1882–1957* (Toronto, 1957).

23 CCM prospectus, *Monetary Times*, Sept. 1, 1899, pp. 278-9.

24 G. R. Stevens, *Canadian National Railways* (Toronto, 1962), II, pp. 20, 36; H. V. Nelles, *The Politics of Development* (Toronto, 1974), pp. 228-34; PAC, C. L. Porteous Papers, Letterbooks, vol. 20, p. 551, Porteous to F. A. Carolan, Dec. 3, 1901.

25 FQ, 23-6, JWF to JSW, Oct. 10, 1902.

26 Bank of Commerce, *Minutes*, Jan. 21, 1902.

27 LI, p. 1164.

28 PAC, Laurier Papers, 63501-2, Laurier to L. O. David, 11 mars, 11 avril, 1902; 63633-5, P. B. Dumoulin to Laurier, 12 mars, 1902, and reply.

29 FCP, JWF to JWB, April 7, 1902; FQ, 23-6, JWF to JSW, Oct. 10, 1902.

30 LI, pp. 14, 17, 88-91.

31 Morrow, "Memories of National Trust."

32 From accounts of the special meeting in *Mail and Empire*, *Daily Star*, and *Globe*, March 31, 1902; also *Monetary Times*, Dec. 13, 1901, April 4, 1902, July 11, 1902.

33 *Mail and Empire*, April 1, 1902; *Monetary Times*, April 4, 1902; National Trust, *Minutes*, Aug. 28, 1899.

34 *Mail and Empire*, Dec. 16, 1904; *Globe*, Oct. 30, 1903; "A Canadian-Named Automobile," *Business Magazine* (*Maclean's*), Oct. 1905; for Russell see *Mail*, April 2, 1927, Feb. 21, 1928.

35 LI, pp. 1151-3; Walker Papers, Walker to B. W. Smylie, June 3, 1903; FQ, 8123-9, JWF to John E. Goldring, Sept. 12, 1925.

36 *Monetary Times*, June 10, 1903; LI, pp. 1153-4, 1168ff.; *Canadian Annual Review*, 1903, pp. 496-7; FQ, 8123-9, JWF to John E. Goldring, Sept. 12, 1925.

37 FQ, 270-3, JWF to JSW, June 17, 1903.

38 FFP, JWF to CEF, Jan. 20, 1904.

39 Simpson's, *Minutes*, Jan. 25, 1904; LI, p. 983; *A. E. Ames & Co. Limited*.

40 T. D. Regehr, "The Canadian Northern Railway: The West's Own Product," *Canadian Historical Review*, 1970.

41 LI, p. 1023.

42 FQ, 2699-3000, C. W. Irwin to JWF, May 7, 1918.

43 LI, p. 1064.

44 Senate, *Debates*, April 4, 1907, p. 552.

45 Walker Papers, Walker to J. H. Plummer, Sept. 9, 15, 1902; on personal relationships and capital markets see also Ian M. Drummond, "Canadian Life Insurance Companies and the Capital Market, 1890-1914," *Canadian Journal of Economics and Political Science*, May 1962.

46 JWF obituary, *Star*, March 8, 1939.

47 FQ, 544-7, JWF to Mr. James, June 9, 1906.

48 *Ibid.*, 121-38, JWF to JSW, April 8, 1903; 327-9, to RLB, Aug. 24, 1903.

49 *Ibid.*, 121-38, JWF to JSW, April 8, 1903.

50 *Ibid.*, 318-23, JWF to S. J. Moore, Aug. 12, 1903.

51 FFP, JWF to George A. Cox, Nov. 30, 1903.

52 FQ, 46-7, JWF to Cox, Nov. 28, 1902.

CHAPTER FOUR — METHODIST MILLIONAIRE (pp. 83-109)

1 FFP, JWF to CEF, "Monday," probably 1897.

2 *Ibid.*, CEF to CF, July 19, 1896.

3 *Ibid.*, JWF to CEF, May 7, 1897.

4 *Ibid.*, Aug. 24, 1895.

5 *Ibid.*, "Saturday," probably 1894.

6 *Ibid.*, May 1, 7, 1897, June 1, 1904.

7 *Ibid.*, Jan. 20, 1904.

8 *Ibid.*, Dec. 6, 1895; CEF to Muriel Gladman, Feb. 1930. Letter in the possession of the late Miss Gladman.

9 FFP, JWF to Mina Flavelle, July 12, 1896; JWF to Ellsworth Flavelle, July 19, 1896.

10 *Ibid.*, JWF to Mina and Clara Flavelle, Nov. 11, 1894.

11 *Ibid.*, JWF to CEF, July 10, 1896.

12 *Ibid.*, Dorothea Flavelle to Mina Flavelle, Sept. 20, 1904; Dorothea to CEF, Feb. 17, 1904.

13 FQ, 71, R. Harvey to JWF, Jan. 26, 1933; *Fragments*.

14 FQ, 33, JWF to Rev. Carey Bonner, Sept. 3, 1909.

15 Augustus Bridle, "A. E. Kemp—Manufacturer," *Saturday Night*, April 22, 1911. Details on Sherbourne Street Church are drawn from the church records, catalogued as St. Luke's United Church, in the United Church Archives.

16 Individual givings are recorded in two published Sherbourne Street *Year Books*, for 1896 and 1900. There is some evidence that the congregation nonetheless still leaned heavily on its pillars. The charitable interpretation of A. E. Ames's 1896 motion, seconded by Fudger, to have each member's contributions put in the *Year Book*, is that he felt ordinary members were relying too much on the wealthy few. It was passed only over strong objections. See Quarterly Official Board, *Minutes*, Sept. 18, 1896. A study of Sherbourne Street's income over the years suggests that most of the increase came through higher givings by its wealthy members. Without its five millionaires,

the congregation's stewardship was not overly impressive.

17 *Christian Guardian*, Jan. 23, 1901; CAR, 1902, p. 353; UCA, Nathanael Burwash Papers, JWF to Burwash, May 28, 1900; *Christian Guardian*, Oct. 4, 1899.

18 *Christian Guardian*, March 9, 1898; FO, 75, University of Toronto File, JWF Superintendent's Report, April 19, 1896.

19 Salem Bland, *James Henderson, DD* (Toronto, 1926), p. 324.

20 FQ, 67, Miscellaneous Speeches file, "Opportunities and Responsibilities," "Death of Walter Massey," "Business Success."

21 FQ, 67, Religious topics undated file, "The Significance of the Layman's Missionary Movement"; "Our Educational Work from the Layman's Standpoint," *Christian Guardian*, July 24, 1901; FQ, 67, Religious topics file, untitled address on spiritual force.

22 FFP, JWF to CF, Sept. 2, 1906, Sept. 27, 1908; JWF to Ellsworth Flavelle, July 26, 1896.

23 PAC, W. C. Good Papers, 577-80, JWF to Good, March 19, 1901.

24 FQ, 71, R. Harvey to JWF, Jan. 26, 1933.

25 FFP, JWF Superintendent's Report, April 8, 1904. "All arbitrary rules, regulations and interpretations of man," he said in the same report, "which intrude themselves between God and man, are wrong, misleading, mischievous, and are barriers between those who would seek the truth to practice it, and the Lord Himself."

26 FQ, 33, JWF to Rev. Carey Bonner, Sept. 3, 1909.

27 Good Papers, 577-80, JWF to Good, March 19, 1901.

28 FQ, 67, Miscellaneous Speeches file, "Opportunities and Responsibilities."

29 The description of Holwood and comments on its design are based on a tour of the house, photographs, and discussions with Douglas Richardson and William Dendy, neither of whom would agree with my conclusions. See also Michael Bliss and William Dendy, "Holwood," *Canadian Collector*, November/December 1975, pp. 18-21.

30 *Holwood, Keston, An Historical Sketch* (London, n.d.).

31 FFP, JWF Balance Sheets, June 30, Nov. 2, 1917, Dec. 10, 1918.

32 *Ibid.*, JWF to CEF, Oct. 8, 1929.

33 *Ibid.*, March 19, 1901.

34 Interview with Dr. John A. Ralph.

35 FFP, Minto to JWF, March 18, 1903.

36 FQ, 219-20, JWF to JSW, May 8, June 3, 1903; 17, undated clipping from *Goblin*, c. Feb. 1929.

37 Walker Papers, JWF to Walker, May 15, 20, 1903.

38 This account of life at Holwood in the winter of 1903 −4 is based on some three hundred letters in the Flavelle family papers written by the members of the family and Hannah Fudger to Clara Ellsworth Flavelle. Rather than list every reference, I assume that with careful attention to chronology the sources can be located quickly.

39 FFP, JWF to CEF, March 5, 1904; CAR, 1904, p. 550.

40 Interview with Sir John Wheeler-Bennett.

41 FFP, JWF to CEF, June 6, 1904.

CHAPTER FIVE — METHODIST MANAGEMENT (pp. 110-37)

1 FCP, JWF memo, Aug. 27, 1900.

2 *Ibid*. He estimated that by 1910 exports would double again to $25 million.

3 FFP, JWF to Wm. Davies, May 28, 1901; FCP, JWF memo, March 22, 1900.

4 FCP, JWF memo, March 22, 1900.

5 FFP, JWF to Wm. Davies, May 28, 1901.

6 FCP, JWF memo, Nov. 5, 1903.

7 *Ibid.*, JWF memo, Nov. 5, 1903; JWF to JWB, Feb. 12, 1903.

8 *Ibid.*, JWF memo, Dec. 1904 (misdated 1900).

9 *Ibid.*, JWF memo, Nov. 5, 1903; JWF report to shareholders, May 1, 1905.

10 *Ibid.*, JWF memo, March 22, 1900.

11 *The William Davies Company*, advertising booklet, 1915; former employees and others emphasized this point in interviews.

12 On Harris Abattoir see FQ, 44, JWF to James Harris, Dec. 9, 1912; 45, JWF memo, Oct. 24, 1919, enc. in JWF to Glyn Osler, Oct. 24; Child, "The Predecessor Companies of Canada Packers," chap. 6; FCP, JWF report to shareholders, May 1, 1905.

13 FQ, 20, JWF to R. B. Bennett, Oct. 14, 1932.

14 FCP, B. Brittain memo, April 1, 1896.

15 PAC, RG 17, I-1, vol. 988, Agricultural Department Correspondence, File 159525, W. W. Moore, "Report on the Conditions in Canadian Meat Packing Houses." The file also contains all correspondence relating to the investigation and 1907 legislation.

16 FCP, JWF undated memo "Re Workmens' Bonus"; Davies *Minutes*, May 2, 1893, and *passim*.

17 PAC, Willison Papers, 10187, JWF to JSW, Feb. 17, 1914.

18 FCP, JWF memo, June 30, 1900; Moore, "Report on Conditions in Canadian Meat Packing Houses"; FFP, JWF to CEF, March 20, 1901.

19 Interview with W. E. Bosnell.

20 FCP, Davies *Minutes*, Sept. 3, 1902.

21 After studying Flavelle's letters on accounting, Mr. R. M. Parkinson of Clarkson Gordon concluded that Flavelle was ahead of his contemporaries' practice in almost every respect. Flavelle's accounting methods and use of them as motivational tools conform very closely with enlightened management practice today. His best letter on accounting is in FQ, 50, to J. M. Sparrow, Nov. 29, 1935.

22 Simpson's *Minutes*; Ross Harkness, *J. E. Atkinson of the Star* (Toronto, 1963), p. 51; Ross, *History of the Canadian Bank of Commerce*, II, pp. 216, 222.

23 Alfred D. Chandler, *Strategy and Structure: Chapters in the History of the Industrial Enterprise* (Cambridge, Mass., 1962).

24 FCP, JWF to Wm. Davies, June 29, 1904.

25 On Smale see J. E. Middleton, *et al.*, *The Municipality of Toronto, A History* (Toronto, 1920), III, 91.

26 FCP, JWF to Wm. Davies, June 29, 1904; FQ, 44, JWF to E. C. Fox, March 6, 1917; 45, JWF Address to shareholders, enc. in JWF to A. F. Park, Sept. 10, 1919; FCP, Davies *Minutes*, Oct. 31, 1901, May 9, 1902.

27 FCP, JWF to Wm. Davies, June 29, 1904; also FQ, 44, R. N. Watt to JWF, May 22, 1912.

28 Interview with W. E. Bosnell; FCP, JWF to Wm. Davies, June 29, 1904.

29 FCP, JWF memo, May 1, 1905.

30 *Report of the Commissioners Appointed to Investigate the Business of William Davies and Co. Ltd. and Matthews—Blackwell Limited* (Ottawa, 1917), pp. 9-10; *Globe*, Oct. 12-13, 1917.

31 FCP, Wm. Davies & Co. to Messrs. duBois-Raymond, Wager & Lemke, July 30, 1913; interview with Dr. John A. Ralph.

32 FCP, JWF to JWB, Feb. 18, 1897; JWB to JWF, Feb. 5, 19, 1902, Feb. 4, 1909; JWF to JWB, Feb. 25, 1909.

33 *Ibid.*, JWF to Wm. Davies, June 10, 1897.

34 *Ibid.*, JWF memo, Nov. 5, 1903; Davies *Minutes*, March 24, 1900.

35 *Ibid.*, May 23, 1903.

36 *Ibid.*, JWF to JWB, Feb. 25, 1904.

37 *Ibid.*, JWB to JWF, Feb. 5, 19, 1902.

38 *Ibid.*, JWF to JWB, Jan. 22, 1902.

39 *Ibid.*, Feb. 11, 1902.

40 *Ibid.*, Feb. 19, April 5, 15, 18, May 1, 1902.

41 *Ibid.*, May 1, 3, 12, 1902; JWB to JWF, May 2, 1902.

42 *Ibid.*, JWF to Wm. Davies, June 20, 1902.

43 *Ibid.*, JWF to JWB, Feb. 12, 19, 1903.

44 *Ibid.*, March 9, 1903.

45 *Ibid.*, Feb. 19, 1903; Davies *Minutes*, May 23, 1903, Nov. 11, Dec. 4, 1904.

46 FA, March 15, April 15, 1902; *Weekly Sun*, Dec. 18, 1901.

47 FA, Dec. 14, 1904.

48 If the cooperatives fail, Flavelle had written, "it will only mean stronger people taking possession of them and buying them at a very low price, which enables them to compete on favored terms with the older curers." FCP, JWF to JWB, Feb. 12, 1903.

49 *Weekly Sun*, Aug. 30, Oct. 4, Nov. 29, Dec. 20, 1905; FA, Dec. 28, 1905, Jan. 11, 18, 25, 1906.

50 *Weekly Sun*, Jan. 10, 1906.

51 *World*, Jan. 23 to 31, 1906; *Weekly Sun*, Jan. 24, 31, 1906; FA, Feb. 1, 1906.

52 FA, Jan. 3, 1907. When farmers disputed an OAC study showing that hog-raising was still profitable, the Davies Company subsidized ten farmers who volunteered to keep costs. Including labour time and allowing for the fertilizer value of hog manure, their records showed costs of four to five cents per pound, confirming the OAC figures.

53 More properly, their return on pork was diminishing in relation to the return from simply marketing the grains directly rather than converting them into pork. In a process that was not yet consciously understood by packers or economists, farmers naturally adjusted production toward the more profitable product.

54 FCP, JWF to JWB, Feb. 25, 1904.

55 *Ibid.*, Nov. 25, 1902.

CHAPTER SIX — PROGRESSIVE CONSERVATIVE (pp. 138-58)

1 C. K. Clarke, *A History of the Toronto General Hospital* (Toronto, 1913); G. Harvey Agnew, *Canadian Hospitals, 1920 to 1970* (Toronto, 1974), p. 179; Toronto General Hospital, Board of Trustees, *Minutes*, Oct. 10, 1903, May 27, 1904.

2 FQ, 412-14, JWF to Dr. R. A. Reeve, Nov. 23, 1903.

3 Whitney, quoted in Loudon's unpublished, unpaginated MSS., "The Memoirs of James Loudon," University of Toronto Archives.

4 Walker Papers, JWF to Rev. Dr. Mulligan, April 24, 1902, enc. in JWF to Walker, April 24, 1902; for the situation at Toronto see W. S. Wallace, *A History of the University of Toronto, 1827–1897* (Toronto, 1927), Loudon's "Memoirs," and H. H. Langton, *James Loudon and the University of Toronto* (pamphlet, Toronto, 1927).

5 C. B. Sissons, *A History of Victoria University* (Toronto, 1952), pp. 180-1; for Cox's role in federation see Victoria University, Board of Regents, *Minutes*, May 8, 1914.

6 Victoria University Archives, Potts Letterbook #5, Potts to A. E. Ames, July 3, 1900.

7 Board of Regents, *Minutes*, Feb. 26, 1902; Board of Regents, Finance Committee, *Minutes*, Jan. 28, 1903, March 20, 1911; Board of Regents, Executive Committee, *Minutes*, Nov. 12, 1919.

8 UCA, Burwash Papers, Burwash to JWF, Feb. 22, 1902; Board of Regents, *Minutes*, Feb. 26, 1902.

9 Victoria University, *Reports to the Board of Regents, 1894–1912: President's Report*, 1902.

10 Victoria University Archives, Potts Letterbook #5, Potts to Dr. J. Mills, March 19, 1902; Potts to A. E. Ames, Jan. 13, 1905.

11 Loudon, "Memoirs," *passim*; Walker Papers, Walker to S. H. Blake, Jan. 11, 1900. Loudon was particularly bitter at Walker, who had been a dominant layman in university affairs for years, for going over to the Methodists on the residence issue. He insinuates in his memoirs that this might have been expected from the man who was their employee at the Commerce.

12 FFP, *Scrapbooks*, undated clippings re scholarship; Walker Papers, Walker to S. H. Blake, Jan. 11, 1900; Walker Papers, JWF to Loudon, Feb. 8, 1900.

13 UTA, Loudon Papers, F11, JWF to Kylie, April 29, 1904; Falconer Papers, JWF to Falconer, March 17, 1909.

14 TGH, *Minutes*, Dec. 1, 1902, March 4, April 8, 15, 1904, Nov. 20, 1903; FQ, 412-14, JWF to Dr. R. A. Reeve, Nov. 23, 1903.

15 TGH, *Minutes*, May 14, 1904.

16 *Ibid.*, May 27, July 5, Sept. 15, Nov. 4, Dec. 2, 1904, Jan. 6, 1905.

17 *Fragments*; TGH, *Minutes*, Oct. 3, 1904.

18 Walker Papers, John Hoskin to Walker, Dec. 1, 1904; JWF to Walker, Dec. 2, 1904; Walker to J. P. Whitney, April 10, 1905; Walker to Mr. Justice Moss, March 17, 1905.

19 FQ, JWF to Senator Beique, Jan. 18, 1927.

20 FCP, JWF to JWB, April 5, 1902; FQ, JWF to A. H. U. Colquhoun, Jan. 27, 1932; CAR, 1902, pp. 385, 124.

21 Richard Clippingdale, "J. S. Willison, Political Journalist: From Liberalism to Independence, 1881 – 1905" (PHD thesis, University of Toronto, 1970), chap. 7.

22 P. W. F. Rutherford, "The People's Press: The Emergence of the New Journalism in Canada, 1869 – 99," CHR, June 1975, pp. 169-91.

23 PAC, Goldwin Smith Papers, JWF to Smith, Dec. 13, 1904; also FQ, JWF to A. H. U. Colquhoun, Jan. 27, 1932.

24 FQ, 19-20, JWF to JSW, Oct. 3, 1902; 55-8, JWF to JSW, Dec. 1, 1902; JWF to A. H. U. Colquhoun, Jan. 27, 1932.

25 FQ, 38-9, JWF to JSW, Nov. 26, 1902.

26 FQ, 46-7, JWF to George Cox, Nov. 28, 1902; 102, JWF to JSW, Feb. 3, 1903.

27 FQ, 380, JWF to JSW, Oct. 31, 1903.

28 FQ, 110-15, JWF to JSW, March 4, 1903.

29 FQ, 404-7, JWF to JSW, Oct. 1903; 334-9, JSW to JWF, (misdated) Aug. 30, 1903; 396-403, JWF to JSW, "Sunday," Oct. 1903.

30 Walker Papers, JWF to Walker, Feb. 24, 1903. In this case he did suggest and Willison agreed that the other side of the case be published to "clearly indicate the dependence of the public upon these same selfish men whose methods at other times he so roundly abuses." This is the only instance of Willison having to balance his judgments.

31 Goldwin Smith Papers, JWF to Smith, Dec. 13, 1904.

32 FQ, 565-8, S. D. Chown to JWF, Oct. 3, 1906; JWF to Chown, Oct. 4.

33 CAR, 1902, p. 124; 1904, p. 280.

34 FQ, 121-33, JWF to JSW, April 8, 1903.

35 FQ, 430-9, JWF to JSW, Dec. 3, 1903; 84-99, JWF to JWB, Oct. 30, 1903.

36 *News*, Jan. 19, 1903.

37 FQ, 121-33, JWF to JSW, April 8, 1903.

38 FQ, 74-81, JWF to RLB, Aug. 16, 1903.

39 Walker Papers, J. H. Plummer to Walker, Oct. 4, 1902; pencilled note on FQ, 74-81, JWF to RLB, Aug. 16, 1903; on the Canadian Northern see also T. D. Regehr, *The Canadian Northern Railway, Pioneer Road of the Northern Prairies, 1895 – 1918* (Toronto, 1976).

40 FQ, 121-33, JWF to JSW, April 8, 1903; 327-9, JWF to RLB, Aug. 24, 1903.

41 FQ, 92, JWF to JWB, Oct. 30, 1903; on Borden see Robert Craig Brown, *Robert Laird Borden*, vol. 1 (Toronto, 1976).

42 Walker Papers, JWF to Rev. Dr. Mulligan, April 24, 1902, enc. in JWF to Walker, April 24, 1902.

43 FQ, 356-9, JWF to Rev. S. J. Shorey, Sept. 22, 1903; *News*, March 12, 1903.

44 FQ, 270-3, JWF to JSW, June 17, 1903; CAR, 1902, p. 54. S. H. Blake coined the phrase "carnival of corruption."

45 FQ, 419-24, JWF to Rev. S. J. Shorey, Nov. 26, 1903.

46 Charles Humphries, "The Sources of Ontario 'Progressive' Conservatism, 1900 – 1914," Canadian Historical Association, *Annual Report, 1967*.

47 CAR, 1904, p. 208.

CHAPTER SEVEN — "DOING ALL THE GOOD HE CAN" (pp. 159-78)

1 UTA, Royal Commission of 1906 Papers, JWF to Whitney, April 27, 1905.
2 *Speech Delivered by the Hon. J. P. Whitney . . . On Introducing the Act respecting the University of Toronto on Wednesday, May 17, 1905* (Toronto, 1905).
3 Walker Papers, JWF to Walker, Nov. 8, 1905.
4 *Ibid.*, JWF to C. D. Massey, July 12, 1905; JWF to George Cox, July 13, 1905, enc. in JWF to Walker, July 14; FFP, JWF to CEF, July 13, 1905.
5 *Fragments*; Walker Papers, JWF to Walker, Sept. 19, 1905.
6 *Ibid.*, clipping in P. C. Larkin to Walker, Oct. 24, 1905; JWF to Walker, Nov. 8, 1905; list of subscribers in FQ, 41, *Memoranda Relating to the Reorganization of the Toronto General Hospital*.
7 FFP, JWF to CEF, July 13, 1905.
8 CAR, 1902, p. 385; 1905, p. 281.
9 FQ, 500-11, JWF to W. K. McNaught, Jan. 4, 1906.
10 Walker Papers, Walker to Earl Grey, June 5, 1905; Grey to JWF, April 30, 1905, enc. in Grey to Walker, April 30.
11 Loudon Papers, A26, "Notes re what J. A. McDonald etc. said"; *Saturday Night*, May 21, 1904.
12 Loudon, "Memoirs"; CAR, 1905, pp. 295-6.
13 *Evening Telegram*, Oct. 3-5, 1905.
14 Daily press, Nov. 28 – Dec. 10, 1905; PAO, Whitney Papers, J. P. Whitney to E. C. Whitney, Nov. 29, 1905; C. W. Humphries, "The Political Career of Sir James P. Whitney" (unpublished PHD thesis, University of Toronto, 1966), p. 359ff.
15 Daily press, March 12-20, 1906; Royal Commission of 1906, *Papers*, case 3, Walter Bretz to A. H. U. Colquhoun, March 26, 1906; Arthur Hawkes to Colquhoun, March 13, 1906.
16 Royal Commission on the University of Toronto, *Report* (Toronto, 1906), *passim*.
17 Loudon Papers, Loudon to Whitney, Feb. 22, March 14, July 14, 1906. Also FQ, 38,

JWF to Whitney, March 3, 1906: "The capacity to incorporate a new spirit into the University body, the wisdom with which it is done, the encouragement which only good sense and grasp can give are wanting in president Loudon, not through lack of desire or want of loyalty, but because the good Lord denied him a plus quantity of these qualities when he was made. Kind heartedness and a certain sense of justice suggests giving him a chance under new conditions, particularly when one remembers how handicapped he was in the past, but I am persuaded that action directed upon such generous impulses would result unfortunately and to no one more so than the president himself." This was a gentle phrasing of the consensus of opinion about Loudon.
18 Goldwin Smith Papers, JWF to Smith, June 6, 1906, and reply; UCA, Burwash Papers, JWF to Burwash, May 29, 1906: "I am not a little troubled about my course in this matter. I have long held that honorary degrees should only be given to eminent public servants and to those who in the field of science or letters earned distinction, or if given for service rendered to University life, the recipient should be either a graduate of some university or a man of literary or scientific culture.

"The accident of my service upon the University Commission does not yet seem to me to constitute a sufficient reason for a plain business man to qualify for such an honour.

"I can see how my refusal might be misunderstood, and how if the chairman of the Commission declines, it might place the other members awkwardly."
19 *Fragments*; TGH *Minutes*, Feb. 6, 17, 1906.
20 Willison Papers, 10154, JWF to JSW, undated but April 1906.
21 Clippingdale, "J. S. Willison, Political Journalist," chap. 9; A. H. U. Colquhoun, *Press, Politics and People: The Life and Letters of Sir John Willison* (Toronto, 1935), chap. 10.

22 PAC, Borden Papers, JWF to RLB, March 23, 1905.

23 *News*, Dec. 15, 1906.

24 Walker Papers, JWF to Zebulon Lash, Dec. 19, 1906, enc. in JWF to Walker, Dec. 19; *News*, Dec. 20, 1906; FFP, *Scrapbooks*, clipping of an Augustus Bridle profile of JWF, c. 1909.

25 FQ, 51, Fifth Annual Report of the News Publishing Company, Jan. 29, 1908.

26 FQ, 552-3, JWF to Charles F. Clark, June 25, 1906.

27 FQ, 458-67, JWF to A. H. U. Colquhoun, Sept. 6, 1905.

28 FQ, 581-3, JWF to JSW, Dec. 19, 1907; Willison Papers, 10170-7, JWF to JSW,

Dec. 26, 1907; H. V. Nelles, *The Politics of Development: Forests, Mines & Hydro-Electric Power in Ontario, 1849–1941* (Toronto, 1974), chap. 7; CAR, 1907, pp. 515-24; Whitney Papers, J. P. Whitney to E. C. Whitney, Dec. 4, 1907.

29 FQ, 4201-5, JWF to A. Bridle, Dec. 15, 1921; 38, JWF to Goldwin Smith, May 8, 1906; Walker Papers, Walker to Prof. Walter C. Murray, Sept. 18, 1908.

30 FQ, 38, JWF to D. Bruce Macdonald, Dec. 30, 1906; JWF to Goldwin Smith, April 7, 1906.

31 *Evening Telegram*, May 29, 1906.

32 FFP, Dorothea Flavelle to CEF, Oct. 7, 1906; CF to CEF, March 21, 1909.

CHAPTER EIGHT — TRYING TO RETIRE (pp. 179-207)

1 FQ, 38, JWF to Falconer, Jan. 7, 1908; FFP, JWF to CEF, Dec. 29, 31, 1907, Jan. 1, 2, 1908; Middleton, *The Municipality of Toronto*, III, 91.

2 FFP, JWF to CEF, March 25, 1907; FQ, 38, J. P. Whitney to JWF, JWF to Whitney, Feb. 18, 1907.

3 Walker Papers, JWF to Walker, Dec. 21, 1907, enclosing JWF to Alexander Bruce, Feb. 18, 1907.

4 *Ibid.*, Canada Life Insurance File, report "To the Directors of the Canada Life Insurance Company," Jan. 22, 1908.

5 *Ibid.*, Z. A. Lash to J. H. Plummer, March 3, 1911, enc. in Lash to Walker, March 3.

6 *Ibid.*, JWF to E. W. Cox, March 4, 1908; JWF to George Cox, March 4, 1908.

7 FFP, JWF to CEF, March 8, 26, and April 1, 1908; James G. Harris, "The *News* and Canadian Politics, 1903–1914" (unpublished MA thesis, University of Toronto, 1952), p. 92; Colquhoun, *Press, Politics and People*, p. 150.

8 FQ, JWF to J. Macdonnell, Sept. 5, 1934; undated *World* clipping in UTA, Flavelle file.

9 FFP, JWF to CEF, March 26, 1908.

10 *Weekly Sun*, July 10, 1907; FA, July 11, 1907, April 2, 1908; FQ, 45, file 9, JWF to Wm. Davies, June 1909.

11 FCP, Wm. Davies Company, *Minutes*, June 7, 1909; Child's notes of Davies *Minutes*, Jan. 18, 1912; JWF, two handwritten memos, 1906.

12 *Ibid.*, JWF memo, May 1, 1905.

13 FFP, JWF to CEF, April 1, 1908.

14 For the succession problem see FCP, JWF to JWB, June 1, Nov. 20, 1908; also JWF to James Harris, Dec. 9, 1912.

15 *Ibid.*, JWB to JWF, "Easter Monday," 1908.

16 *Ibid.*, JWF to JWB, Nov. 20, 1908; FFP, JWF to CEF, Dec. 5, 1908 (2).

17 FFP, JWF to CEF, Dec. 10, 11, 1908.

18 FCP, JWF memo, Jan. 6, 1909; JWB to JWF, Feb. 4, 1909.

19 *Ibid.*, JWF and JWB agreement, May 17, 1909; JWF memo, June 7, 1909.

20 Interview with Sir John Wheeler-Bennett.

21 FQ, 45, file 9, JWF to Wm. Davies, June 1909; FCP, JWF to JWB, June 10, 1909.

22 FCP, JWF to James Harris, Dec. 9, 1912.

23 FQ, 655-65, JWF to Mrs. J. Wheeler-Bennett, June 17, 1911.

24 FQ, 44, E. C. Fox to JWF, March 1, 1910; FFP, JWF to Harry L. Stark, Dec. 10, 1909; Child, "The Predecessor Companies of Canada Packers." The problems involved in moving Davies to the Union stockyards are not clear. The fact that Swift's had the controlling interest in the new

yards may have made it impossible for Davies to move, and/or the Harris decision to rebuild may have come when it still seemed that fusion with Davies was likely.

25 FQ, 45, Fox to JWF, Nov. 24, 1911; JWF to Fox, undated (1912).

26 FCP, JWF memo, Oct. 9, 1912.

27 FQ, 45, JWF to Fox, undated (1912).

28 *Report of the Commissioners Appointed to Investigate the Businesses of William Davies Co. Ltd. and Matthews—Blackwell Ltd.* (Ottawa, 1917).

29 National Trust, Executive Files, Rundle, reply to toast at twenty-fifth annual meeting (1924); FQ, 577-80, JWF to JSW, April 10, 1907.

30 FQ, 2024-7, Rundle to JWF, Sept. 4, 1917.

31 Simpson's, *Minutes, passim*.

32 Burton, *A Sense of Urgency*, chap. 16.

33 Arthur Conrad, "The Line-Up of the Financiers," *Maclean's* magazine, Aug. 11, 1911. I am indebted to Mr. David Millar for bringing this article to my attention.

34 Walker Papers, Canada Life Assurance File, Lash to George Cox, Sept. 17, 1909; also Walker to Fisher A. Baker, Nov. 6, 1906.

35 FFP, JWF memo for Lash, Oct. 4, 1909.

36 Walker Papers, Canada Life Assurance File, Lash to George Cox, Oct. 8, 1909, Jan. 1, Sept. 26, 1910; Cox to Lash, Sept. 22, Oct. 4, 1910.

37 *Ibid.*, Walker to H. B. Walker, Oct. 24, 1910; Lash to J. H. Plummer, March 3, 1911, enc. in Lash to Walker, March 3; Canada Life Insurance File, excerpts from *Minutes*, April 24, 1911, and draft letter of resignation.

38 *Ibid.*, H. B. Walker to Walker, June 3, 1911; *Maclean's*, Aug. 11, 1911. There are two hints in the sources that Cox wanted to retaliate against those who challenged his family's control of Canada Life. The first is an entry in the *Minutes* of the Victoria College Board of Regents (May 23, 1910) in which Cox takes exception to the commission charged by National Trust for handling the college's finances; the

second is a letter to Walker (Walker Papers, Oct. 6, 1910) suggesting the time had come for the Commerce to organize its own trust company no matter what damage it did to National Trust. The difficulty in interpreting evidence like this—which seems to suggest a Cox attack on Flavelle as perhaps the most bothersome of his enemies—is that the Cox family still held a controlling interest in National Trust!

39 Aird Flavelle, "Timber Staking in British Columbia," MS. interview April 20, 1957, in the possession of Mrs. John Ballem, Calgary.

40 W. A. Craik, "Saving the Pennies of Young Canada," *Saturday Night*, Nov. 25, 1911.

41 *World*, Sept. 20, 1906; *Star*, Sept. 21, 1906; UCA, Albert Carman Papers, Carman memo, May 14, 1910.

42 For fuller accounts of the Jackson/Carman dispute see Sissons, *History of Victoria University*, pp. 233-9, and Margaret Prang, *Newton Rowell: Ontario Nationalist* (University of Toronto Press, 1975), chap. 5.

43 UCA, Sherbourne Street Quarterly Board, *Minutes*, Feb. 16, 1906, Sept. 22, 28, 1910; PAC, Rowell Papers, 8282-99, Jackson to Rowell, July 2, 1910.

44 *Globe*, Feb. 28, 1909.

45 Carman Papers, Carman Memo, May 14, 1910; Rowell Papers, 8214ff.; Prang, *Newton Rowell*, chap. 5.

46 Victoria University Archives, "Case of Prof. George Jackson" envelope, Geo. E. Dewey to the Board of Regents, April 29, 1910; Rowell Papers, 8321, C. D. Massey to Rowell, Aug. 9, 1910; 8260-3, Rowell to Rev. J. S. Ross, June 3, 1909.

47 Burwash Papers, Burwash to Rev. C. B. Spencer, Feb. 21, 1912; Edward Trelawney (Ernest Thomas), "Submerged Millionaires—A Plea for the Rich," undated *Christian Guardian* clipping in FFP, Flavelle *Scrapbooks*.

48 Falconer Papers, Falconer to JWF, Jan. 28, 1908.

49 FQ, 38, JWF to Falconer, Sept. 10, 1911.

In this handwritten draft Flavelle crossed out what would have been a prescient concluding sentence: "Certainly the appointment would be a most interesting one and might give the University a man whose brilliance would bring to it much honor in later years." See also Falconer Papers, Box 21, History file.

50 FQ, 38, A. G. MacKay to JWF, Nov. 14, 1907; JWF to MacKay, Nov. 7, 20, 1907; Falconer Papers, Box 4, salary increases file, JWF to Falconer, Nov. 12, 1908; Walker Papers, JWF to W. T. White, Aug. 17, 1906, enc. in JWF to Walker, Feb. 17, 1907; *World*, Jan. 14, 1908.

51 TGH, *Minutes*, Oct. 3, 1906.

52 *Ibid.*, *passim*.

53 FQ, 41, "Meeting of Toronto General Hospital Board on Staff Re-Organization with the Permanent Members of the Medical Faculty of the University of Toronto," Oct. 10, 1907. This document is a seventy-four-page transcript of the discussion and has considerable importance for the history of hospital organization in Canada. The businessmen argued for single-service departments on a German model; the doctors advanced a British model of decentralization and physician autonomy. The 1908 compromise was to create multiple co-equal services in the departments of medicine and surgery. In 1920, however, these were unified to create the single-service departments Flavelle had earlier advocated. See also FQ, 41, "Interim Report of the Committee of the Board of Trustees . . . on Staff Reorganization," and *Memoranda Relating to the Reorganization of the Toronto General Hospital*; W. G. Cosbie, *The Toronto General Hospital 1819–1965: A Chronicle* (Toronto, 1975), pp. 146, 174-5.

54 Loudon Papers, file T11; undated pamphlet, *The General Hospital and the University of Toronto*; TGH *Minutes*, May 5, 1908; Falconer Papers, JWF to Sir W. R. Meredith, May 13, 1908.

55 TGH *Minutes*, May 16, July 2, 1908, April 6, 20, 1910; Falconer Papers, JWF to Falconer, March 18, 1910; Walker Papers, JWF to Walker, March 18, 1910.

56 CAR, 1913, p. 342; Walker Papers, JWF to Walker, Feb. 17, 1910; *Fragments*.

57 Walker Papers, JWF to Walker, Feb. 17, 1910; TGH *Minutes*, Oct. 19, 1911.

58 TGH *Minutes*, Sept. 7, 1910, and *passim*.

59 *Ibid.*, Oct. 19, 1911; pamphlet, *Toronto General Hospital* (1913); Cosbie, *Toronto General Hospital*, pp. 147-8, which, however, misdates the June 19 opening as June 13.

60 FQ, 651, JWF to D. Malcolm, May 31, 1911; Flavelle family safety-deposit box, Lt.-Col. F. Farquhar to JWF, Dec. 17, 1913; FQ, 791-4, JWF to Farquhar, Dec. 23, 1913.

CHAPTER NINE — PUBLIC BUSINESSMAN (pp. 208-32)

1 FFP, *Scrapbooks*, Augustus Bridle, "A Man Who Does the Unexpected," undated clipping, c. 1913.

2 *Ibid.*, undated editorial, c. 1911.

3 *Ibid.*, JWF to CEF, Oct. 11, 1909, March 23, 1907.

4 *Ibid.*, March 22, 1908.

5 FQ, 756-9, JWF to JSW, March 17, 1912.

6 FFP, JWF to CEF, April 28, 1907.

7 *Ibid.*, Dec. 8, 1908.

8 *Ibid.*, Mina Flavelle to CEF, Feb. 13, 1907; also CF to CEF, Feb. 12, 13, 1907.

9 FQ, 748-64, JWF to JSW, March 6, 24, 1912; Walker Papers, JWF to Walker, Feb. 24, 1912; FFP, JWF to CEF, April 25, 30, 1907, May 2, 1909.

10 FFP, CF to Mina Flavelle, Dec. 14, 1908; JWF to CEF, May 2, 1909.

11 FQ, 23, Rev. Solomon Cleaver to JWF, May 14, 1935.

12 FQ, 784-5, King to JWF, Oct. 28, 1908; Prang, *Newton Rowell*, p. 136; FQ, 616-19, JWF to JSW, Jan. 12, 1910.

13 *Star*, Jan. 27, 1911.

14 FQ, 671-3, JWF to JSW, Jan. 31, 1911.
15 Walker Papers, Walker to H. R. S. Hemming, Jan. 31, 1911; JWF to Walker, Feb. 2, March 4, 1911.
16 *Star*, *Mail and Empire*, Feb. 14, 1911; *Globe*, Feb. 16, 17, 1911.
17 FQ, 677, JWF to Walker, Feb. 15, 1911; Walker Papers, Walker Diary, Feb. 21, 1911. Flavelle's involvement in the Toronto Liberal revolt has not been noticed; unfortunately the sources disclose only the bare facts.
18 Brown, *Borden*, I, 176-80; FQ, 683, JWF to JSW, March 7, 1911.
19 *Weekly Sun*, Sept. 6, 20, 1911; *Side Lights on Pork Packing Establishments*, unsigned Liberal election pamphlet, 1911.
20 *Star*, Sept. 18, 19, 1911; *Globe*, advertisements, Sept. 16, 18, 19, 1911; FQ, 44, JWF to Rev. J. A. Macdonald, Sept. 16. The arguments over relative prices could become very complex. Flavelle had claimed repeatedly that quotations for hogs on the Toronto cattle market were misleadingly low because of the unusual custom in Toronto of stuffing the hogs just before weighing. To discount the effect of the pigs' last supper, which would not be digested by killing time, packers offered about five per cent less for hogs on the Toronto market than on other markets, but the raw quotations never revealed the reason. On the other hand some of the packers' comparisons of their prices for premium hogs with Chicago prices for lard-type hogs may have been misleading in the other direction. On balance, there does not seem to have been a wide diversity one way or another between Canadian and American hog prices; what worried Flavelle was the prospect of Canadian prices moving independently of the requirements of the export trade under reciprocity, and the difficulty this would cause in procuring regular supplies. The comparison of retail prices with Buffalo seems to have favoured the Toronto consumer, for the Davies Company was at that time exporting bacon and cooked meats to Buffalo stores, where they were sold at substantially higher prices than in Toronto, having had the American tariff added.
21 FQ, 699-700, JWF to JSW, Nov. 9, 1911; 780-1, JWF to JSW, July 16, 1912.
22 FQ, 703-16, JWF to JWB, Dec. 8, 1911.
23 FQ, 718-24, JWF to JSW, Dec. 12, 1911; 788-90, JWF to RLB, Oct. 23, 1913; 774-9, JWF to JSW, June 6, 1912.
24 FQ, 774-9, JWF to JSW, June 6, 1912.
25 The best statement of Flavelle's views on imperialism is FQ, 84-99, JWF to JWB, Oct. 30, 1903; also 274-6, JWF to JSW, June 19, 1903. On the formation of the Round Table see John E. Kendle, *The Round Table Movement and Imperial Union* (Toronto, 1975), pp. 103-5.
26 FQ, 810-12, JWF to JSW, Jan. 9, 1913; CAR, 1912, pp. 44-5.
27 FQ, 936-41, JWF to RLB, May 19, 1915; 848-50, JWF to JSW, April 26, 1913; 834-40, JWF to JWB, April 21, 1913.
28 FQ, 848-50, JWF to JSW, April 26, 1913.
29 FQ, 906-9, JWF to Rundle, April 22, 1914; on railway policy generally see Regehr, *The Canadian Northern Railway*, chaps. 13, 14; Brown, *Borden*, I, pp. 222-8.
30 FQ, 906-9, JWF to Rundle, April 22, 1914.
31 FQ, 916-17, JWF to White, April 30, 1914.
32 FQ, 913-15, JWF to Walker, April 28, 1914, apparently not a final draft.
33 FQ, 879-85, JWF to JSW, Nov. 11, 1913.
34 JWF to King, Feb. 1, 1910, in papers as yet uncatalogued at the PAC; FQ, 67, Miscellaneous Speeches file, "An Insufficiently Considered Side of the Food Question"; for public concern about the cost of living see CAR, 1910, pp. 298-304.
35 *An Open Letter addressed to the Honourable the Minister of Agriculture for Ontario by Mr. J. W. Flavelle* (pamphlet, 1910); also FQ, 67, Address to the Canadian Club, Orillia, 1910; Miscellaneous Speeches file, "An Insufficiently Considered Side of the Food Question," and "Part of a Speech at Hamilton, fall, 1910."
36 Willison Papers, 10225, JWF to JSW, Nov. 23, 1914.

37 JWF to King, Feb. 14, 1910, in papers as yet uncatalogued at the PAC; most of this letter is quoted in RLB Papers, JWF to RLB, Feb. 21, 1910.

38 Willison Papers, 10187, JWF to JSW, Feb. 17, 1914.

39 FQ, 19, university correspondence, JWF (to George Wrong), Jan. 20, 1931.

40 FQ, 67, Miscellaneous Speeches file, prewar address on cooperation.

41 Ibid.

42 Ibid.

43 R. C. Brown and G. R. Cook, A Nation Transformed (Toronto, 1974), pp. 186-7.

44 FFP, CEF travel diary.

CHAPTER TEN — THE BUSINESS OF WAR (pp. 233-56)

1 FQ, 1345-55, A. L. Smith to JWF, June 17, 1916, and reply.

2 Willison Papers, 10204-6, JWF to JSW, Aug. 1, 1914.

3 Ibid., 10207, JWF to JSW, Aug. 4, 1914; Walker Papers, JWF to Walker, Aug. 13, 1914.

4 CAR, 1914, p. 247.

5 FQ, 54, Address to the Canadian Club, Ottawa, Nov. 14, 1914; Address to the Canadian Club, Hamilton, Sept. 28; Willison Papers, 10217-19, JWF to JSW, Sept. 23, 1914. Without government direction, Flavelle wrote Willison, the financial community was unlikely to do much on its own: "We must not look for leadership from Bankers. From the time they have any responsible position, they are trained to be critical, their whole effort to govern their conduct with prudence that will procure safety. They must not be imaginative . . . imagination up to the limits of romance belongs to the customers, not the Bankers. Hence for the conditions which we are passing through, Bankers cannot be leaders. . . ."

6 Globe, Oct. 22, 1917.

7 FQ, 44, Fox to JWF, Sept. 28, 1915; 45, Memo re Disposition of Lower Grade Cattle During Fall Run, Sept. 22, 1915.

8 CAR, 1914, pp. 247-58; Brown and Cook, A Nation Transformed, p. 240.

9 David Carnegie, The History of Munitions Supply in Canada, 1914–1918 (London, 1925), chaps. 1 and 2; History of the Ministry of Munitions (6 vols., London, 1920–4), vol. 2, pt. 4, "Munitions Organization in Canada," p. 6. Hereafter cited as Off. Hist.

10 Off. Hist., pp. 8-10; CAR, 1914, p. 255.

11 FO, JWF to Sir George Foster, June 16, 1915.

12 Christopher Addison, Politics from Within, 1911–18, vol. 1 (London, 1924), p. 79; Addison, Four and a Half Years, vol. 1 (London, 1934), p. 93; History of the Ministry of Munitions, vol. 3, pt. 3, pp. 16-19.

13 For the Allison group see BP, files OC 235 and 446, esp. p. 47666, Perley to RLB, Dec. 16, 1914.

14 Ibid., esp. 47090, Perley to RLB, Jan. 19, 1915; Royal Commission on Shell Contracts, Minutes of Evidence (Ottawa, 1916), pp. 789-92, 957, 1043ff. There is considerable confusion about the obtaining of the Russian order. F. H. Clergue may also have had a hand in it.

15 Off. Hist., pp. 1-10.

16 CAR, 1914, 264-9; UTA, German professors clipping file.

17 University of Toronto, Board of Governors, Minutes, Dec. 3, 4, 1914; Falconer Papers, 37, German File, JWF to an unnamed correspondent, Dec. 15, 1914; ibid., JWF to Falconer, Dec. 17, 1914.

18 CAR, 1915, pp. 240-8; John Swettenham, To Seize the Victory; The Canadian Corps in World War 1 (Toronto, 1965), pp. 56-9.

19 Addison, Politics from Within, p. 83.

20 RLB Diary, June 17, 1915; Off. Hist. p. 12.

21 Off. Hist. pp. 14-15; CAR, 1915, pp. 230-3.

22 BP, 23192, RLB to Senator J. A. Lougheed, June 28, 1915; 23092-3, RLB to J. R. Shaw, June 14, 1915.

23 Addison, *Four and a Half Years*, p. 91; *Off. Hist.*, pp. 12-14.

24 FQ, 1096-9, JWF to Rundle, April 2, 1915; 1104-10, Rundle to JWF, May 7, 14, 1915.

25 FQ, 1070-2, JWF to Rundle, June 15, 1915.

26 FO, JWF to Kemp, June 30, 1915; JWF to Foster, June 16, 1915; FQ, 959-62, JWF to RLB, June 25, 1915.

27 FQ, 949-55.

28 *Off. Hist.*, p. 15.

29 BP, 23335-6, Foster to RLB, Aug. 31, 1915; *Off. Hist.*, pp. 15-16; BP, 23692-7, D. A. Thomas to Alex. Bertram, Oct. 10, 1915.

30 BP, 23631-5, Bertram to D. A. Thomas, Oct. 5, 1915; also 24364-70, David Carnegie to RLB, April 2, 1916.

31 *Off. Hist.*, p. 16.

32 BP, 23596-9, T. A. Russell to RLB, Oct. 2, 1915; 23659-63, Memorandum of visit, Oct. 10, 1915.

33 BP, 23375-6, Memorandum, Sept. 9, 1915; 23905-13, Memorandum Regarding Manufacture of War Munitions in Canada; 23663, White to RLB, Oct. 11, 1915.

34 BP, 23861-8, Reports from A. F. Riddell and John F. Orde, Oct. 30, Nov. 15, 1915; 23494-503, Cantley to Bertram, Sept. 20, 1915; 23650-3, Riddell to Bertram, Oct. 8, 1915; 24271, Harold Daley to A. E. Blount, March 6, 1916.

35 BP, 47195-7, 23671-7, 23924-31, Carnegie to RLB, Nov. 22, Oct. 12, Nov. 22, 1915; RLB Diary, Oct. 27, Nov. 20, 1915.

36 *Off. Hist.*, pp. 15-19; Carnegie, *History of Munitions Supply*, chaps. 11-13; for British and American experience see *History of the Ministry of Munitions*, I, 1, pp. 120-9, III, 2, p. 2.

37 RLB Diary, Sept. 2, 5-23, Oct. 27, Nov. 20, 1915.

38 Bank of Commerce, *Minutes*, June 25, 1915, ff.; Regehr, *Canadian Northern*, pp. 406-8. The allegation, repeated in Regehr, that the directors did not know of these guarantees does not appear to be true.

39 FQ, JWF to RLB, June 28, 1915, enc. in Laurence Code to JWF, Jan. 6, 1917.

40 FQ, 924-8, JWF to RLB, Sept. 20, 1915.

41 FQ, 1158-60, White to JWF, June 30, 1915.

42 Bank of Commerce, *Minutes*, Sept. 17, Oct. 15, 1915.

43 Regehr, *Canadian Northern*, p. 407n.

44 RLB Diary, Nov. 26, 1915; Stevens, *Canadian National Railways*, II, p. 466.

45 BP, 24024, Hichens to RLB, Dec. 8, 1915.

46 FQ, 21, Brand to Lloyd George, Dec. 20, 1933.

47 *Fragments*; FQ, 38, JWF to Falconer, Dec. 4, 1915; PAC, Brand Papers, 6E, Brand to Christopher Addison, March 10, 1917.

CHAPTER ELEVEN — THE SHELL GAME (pp. 257-77)

1 FQ, 3629-31, Fitzgerald to JWF, Dec. 7, 1920. Fitzgerald did not become a formal member of the IMB until 1917.

2 FQ, 1650-2, JWF to JSW, Feb. 1, 1916.

3 FO, JWF to RLB, Dec. 3, 1915; White to JWF, Dec. 4, 1915; also RLB Diary, Jan. 19, 28, 1916.

4 FQ, 1182-3, JSW to JWF, Dec. 14, 1915; reply Dec. 15; FO, Secretaries to Governors General File, JWF to E. A. Stanton, Jan. 31, 1916; FQ, 1128-9, JWF to Rundle, Dec. 10, 1915.

5 FO, #7, JWF Memorandum Covering Time Fuzes, Dec. 31, 1915.

6 FO, Hughes to JWF, Dec. 8, 1915; Hichens File, Hughes to RLB, Dec. 8; JWF to Hichens, Dec. 9; #7, JWF Memorandum of Fuzes, Dec. 31; Hughes File, "Notes of remarks made by Major General Sir Sam Hughes at the first meeting of the Imperial Munitions Board . . . Dec. 10, 1915."

7 FO, #64, esp. Col. H. M. Elliott to Alex. Bertram, Dec. 1, 1915; *ibid.*, JWF to Elliott, Dec. 8; JWF to Hichens (2), Dec. 10; #6, JWF to RLB, Dec. 11, Crothers to JWF, Dec. 11.

8 FO, RLB to JWF, Dec. 11, 1915; JWF telegram and letter to RLB, Dec. 13; RLB

Diary, Dec. 6, 11; RLB to Perley, Nov. 27, 1915, quoted in Stevens, *Canadian National Railways*, II, p. 466.

9 FO, #7, JWF Memorandum on Fuzes, Dec. 31, 1915; JWF to Carnegie, Dec. 23; FFP, JWF to CEF, Dec. 15.

10 FO, JWF to Carnegie, Dec. 23, 1915; JWF to Hichens, Dec. 30; #7, JWF Memorandum on Fuzes, Dec. 31; FQ, 3026-8, JWF to Brand, March 4, 1919.

11 FO, #8, Hughes to JWF, Dec. 23, 1915; JWF to Hichens, Dec. 30; PAC, Mossom Boyd Papers, vol. 460, Sam Hughes to Boyd, March 8, 1892; John A. Macdonald Papers, 50137-40, Hughes to Macdonald, Nov. 22, 1890.

12 FO, #14, JWF to Nova Scotia Steel & Coal Co., Dec. 18, 1915; BP, 24181-7, Memorandum on Comparative Shell Prices, Feb. 7, 1916.

13 FO, Gordon File, JWF to G. H. Duggan, Dec. 28, 1915; #203, Chairman's letter, Dec. 31; #203, Memorandum of Conversations, Collingwood Shipbuilding, Dec. 28.

14 FQ, 9118, JWF to W. H. Heard, Dec. 24, 1926.

15 FO, JWF to Hichens, Jan. 18, 1916; #203, *passim*.

16 FO, JWF to Frank Cochrane, Dec. 28, 1915; JWF to Perley, Aug. 22, 1916; JWF to RLB, March 29, 1916.

17 FO, JWF to Arthur Meighen, June 9, 1916.

18 FO, JWF Memo. to Fitzgerald, Feb. 11, 1916.

19 FO, Morgan File, Edward Stettinius to JWF, Jan. 21, 1916; reply Jan. 25.

20 FO, #10, JWF to J. A. Milne, Jan. 6, 1916, ff., esp. JWF to Brig.-Gen. Ellershaw, Jan. 24.

21 FO, Borden File, Perley to Lloyd George, Jan. 18, 1916; JWF cable to Ministry of Munitions, Jan. 15; RLB cable to Perley, Jan. 14; War Office to JWF, Jan. 26; JWF to RLB, Jan. 29; Hughes File, JWF to Hughes, Jan. 29.

22 FO, #11, *passim*, esp. H. H. Macrae to H. H. Brown, Jan. 31, 1916, and JWF to Chapman Double Ball Bearing, Feb. 22.

23 FO, JWF to G. H. Dawson, Feb. 3, 1916; see also JWF to Arthur Meighen, Jan. 27, 1916; JWF to Dawson, March 17.

24 FO, Hughes to JWF, Dec. 13, 1915; RLB File, JWF to Hughes, Jan. 21, 1916.

25 *Saturday Night*, Jan. 8, 15, 1916; FQ, 1648, clipping; FQ, 1184-5, Peter Bain to JWF, Feb. 9, 1916.

26 FQ, 1650-2, JWF to JSW, Feb. 1, 1916; 1083-4, JWF to Rundle, Feb. 1; FO, JWF to Hichens, Feb. 25; JWF to Dawson, Feb. 3.

27 FQ, 1650-2, JWF to JSW, Feb. 1, 1916; 1083-4, JWF to Rundle, Feb. 1.

28 House of Commons, *Debates*, Jan. 25, 1916, pp. 235ff.; RLB Diary, Jan. 24, 28; FO, Hichens to JWF, Feb. 23.

29 FO, Hichens to Ministry of Munitions, Nov. 19, 1915.

30 *Off. Hist.*, pp. 56-8; FO, JWF to Hichens, Feb. 26, 1916; FQ, 1566-8, JWF to White, Feb. 26.

31 FO, JWF to Hichens, March 2, 1916; JWF to E. R. Wood, March 2.

32 FO, JWF to Perry, March 14, 1916; FQ, 1674-6, JWF to JSW, March 20.

33 FO, JWF to Sir George Foster, March 10, April 10, 12, 1916; #16, *passim*, esp. JWF to E. M. Macdonald, Feb. 24; #24, G. Ogilvie to JWF, Feb. 17, 1916.

34 FO, G. H. Dawson to JWF, Jan. 20, 1916; #31, *passim*; #32, *passim*.

35 FO, case 56, JWF Memorandum, May 19, 1916; *ibid.*, Fitzgerald Memorandum of Conversation, Feb. 23, 1916.

36 FO, #11, JWF Memo. of Conversation, March 3, 1916; RLB Diary, Jan. 19, 20, 24, 25.

37 FO, #11, *passim*, esp. Thomas Finlay to Crothers, March 31, 1916.

38 FO, JWF to E. R. Wood, April 5, 1916.

39 FO, JWF to Brand, March 14, 1916.

40 FQ, 1548-50, White to JWF, Feb. 16, 1916; 1085-92, Rundle to JWF, Feb. 16. Flavelle's letter to White has not survived.

41 FQ, 1654-60, JWF to JSW, March 5, 1916.

42 FO, JWF to Hichens, April 5, 1916; JWF to Brand, April 1.

43 FO, JWF to Hichens, April 5, 1916.

44 FO, JWF to E. R. Wood, April 6, 1916.

45 FQ, 1684-5, JWF to JSW, April 6, 1916; 1693-4, JWF to JSW, April 28.

46 Royal Commission on Shell Contracts, *Minutes of Evidence*, pp. 901-5, 949, 1010-1, 1130.

47 CAR, 1916, p. 286; FQ, 1702-3, JWF to JSW, May 29, 1916.

48 John A. Macdonald Papers, 50137-40, Hughes to Macdonald, Nov. 22, 1890; C. E. Porteous Papers, Correspondence, vol. 4, *passim*, esp. Hughes to Porteous, Dec. 5, 1896.

CHAPTER TWELVE — TO HELL WITH PROFITS (pp. 278-302)

1 FO, JWF to E. R. Wood, July 21, 1916.

2 FQ, 1471-5, JWF to Rundle, April 19, 1916; FO, JWF to Perry, April 19; JWF to Brand, June 29; JWF to Hichens, Aug. 4.

3 FO, IMB Minutes, March 23, 1916; JWF to Hichens, April 5; JWF to Brand, June 2; Hichens to JWF, May 1.

4 Brand Papers, 5B, Brand to JWF, July 12, 1916; FO, #203, Memorandum of meeting, June 26, 1916.

5 FO, Brand to JWF, June 9, 1916.

6 FO, JWF to Brand, July 26, 1916.

7 FO, JWF to RLB, Feb. 17, 1916; JWF to Hughes, Jan. 18; #1, *passim*.

8 FO, #168, A. H. Abbott to JWF, May 23, 1916; reply May 19.

9 *Ibid.*, undated memo, "Labour Conditions in Munitions Industry—Toronto."

10 FO, Case 56, *Report of the Commissioners Appointed to Inquire into Unrest Alleged to Exist in Industries in Toronto and Hamilton Producing Munitions of War, May 6, 1916*; #11, JWF to R. Hobson, May 30; reply May 31; #11, JWF to "All Manufacturers in Toronto and Hamilton," June 1.

11 FO, #11, Russell to JWF, June 5, 1916; Canadian Cartridge Co. to JWF, June 9; Paul J. Myler to JWF, June 5; also National Steel Car Co. to JWF, June 7.

12 FO, #11, JWF to Crothers, June 12, 1916.

13 FQ, 1500-3, JWF to Rundle, June 19, 1916.

14 FO, #11, JWF to Manitoba Engines Ltd., June 27, 1916.

15 *Ibid.*, JWF to Vulcan Iron Works, Sept. 12, 1916; reply Sept. 15.

16 FO, JWF to Hichens, Aug. 4, 1916; JWF to Brand, Aug. 18.

17 FO, JWF to E. R. Wood, July 21, 1916; JWF to Hichens, Aug. 4.

18 FO, JWF to Hichens, March 14, 1916; JWF to Perry, Sept. 16.

19 FO, #22, W. C. Franz to Fitzgerald, July 28, 1916.

20 FQ, 4472-7, JWF to C. H. Hale, Jan. 11, 1921; FO, IMB Minutes, July 12, 1916; #66, JWF to Brand, July 31; #19, H. V. F. Jones to JWF, July 28.

21 FO, JWF to Brand, June 23, 29, 1916.

22 FO, JWF to Brand, July 14, 1916; Brand to JWF, July 20.

23 *Off. Hist.*, pp. 59-61.

24 FO, JWF to Brand, Aug. 4, 1916.

25 FO, Brand to JWF, Aug. 8, 1916; Perry to JWF, Aug. 23; JWF to Perry, Aug. 17.

26 FO, JWF to Brand, Aug. 18, 1916; JWF to Perry, Sept. 15; also JWF to Brand, June 21.

27 FO, JWF to Perry, Sept. 16, 1916.

28 FO, Perry to JWF, Sept. 11, 1916.

29 FO, W. E. Edwards to JWF, Nov. 3, 25, 1916; Brand Papers, 6D, JWF to Brand, July 10; FO, Perry to JWF, Sept. 11.

30 In anticipation of those reductions the Canadian government and the IMB gave much thought to the possibility of getting Russian business. In the spring of 1916 Perry visited Russia on behalf of Canada, looking for business. Little, if anything, came of the effort because Canada had so few contacts with Russia and because the Russians were so angry about the messed-up Canadian Car & Foundry contract. As well, Canadian manufacturers were leery of Russian business because their inspection was impossibly erratic. See FO, JWF to Brand, June 23, 1916; #46, *passim*; Brand Papers, 5A, Brand to Mr. Booth, May 1, 1916, ff.; 6D, RLB to M. de Likatsieff, May 19, 1916.

31 FQ, 1500-3, JWF to Rundle, June 19, 1916; 1219, JWF to C. G. Creelman, Aug. 14.

32 FO, JWF to Perry, Sept. 26, 1916.

33 FFP, JWF to CFM, Oct. 17, 1916.

34 Addison, *Four and a Half Years*, p. 259; FO, JWF to Gordon, Oct. 18, 1916.

35 FO, JWF to Gordon, Nov. 16, 1916.

36 FQ, 1605-8, JWF to White, Nov. 9, 1916; FO, White to JWF, Nov. 10.

37 FFP, JWF to CFM, Oct. 28, 1916.

38 FFP, undated JWF memorandum; CEF to JWF, Oct. 29, 1916.

39 Flavelle, *Munitions in Canada, An Address . . . Ottawa Canadian Club, December 16, 1916* (pamphlet, n.d.).

40 *Ibid.*; *History of the Ministry of Munitions*, vol. 8, part 2, pp. 58-61; FQ, 1376-7, JWF to Walker, Nov. 4, 1916; also FFP, JWF to CEM, Nov. 9.

41 FO, Brand to JWF, March 2, 1917; JWF to Gordon, Oct. 28, 1916.

42 FO, Gordon to JWF, Oct. 28, 1916; FQ, 54, Address to Canadian Club, Toronto, Dec. 18, 1916.

43 FQ, 1535-6, JWF to Rundle, Nov. 14, 1916; FFP, JWF to CFM, Nov. 12; on Hughes's resignation see RLB Diary, Jan. 3, 1917.

44 See Donald Jack, *Three Cheers For Me* (rev. ed. Toronto, 1973), pp. 46-60.

45 Flavelle, *Munitions in Canada*.

46 FQ, 54, Address to Canadian Club, Toronto, Dec. 18, 1916.

47 FQ, 1541-2, JWF to Rundle, Dec. 15, 1916;

FO, JWF to Brand, Dec. 16, 29.

48 *Star*, Dec. 8, 1916; FQ, 1614-16, White to JWF, Dec. 10.

49 FFP, JWF to Newton McTavish, Sept. 4, 1921.

50 *Star*, Dec. 13, 1916; also Frederick Griffin, *Variety Show* (Toronto, 1936), pp. 6-12.

51 Laurier Papers, 193844-7, C. B. Sissons to Laurier, Nov. 18, 24, 1916; FO, Hawkes to JWF, Dec. 13.

52 FO, JWF telegram to RLB, Dec. 13, 1916; reply Dec. 14; BP, 32151, Blount Memo for the P.M., Dec. 13; RLB Diary, Dec. 16.

53 FO, JWF to Hawkes, Dec. 14, 1916; FQ, 54, Address to Canadian Club, Toronto, Dec. 18; FO, JWF to Brand, Feb. 13, 1917.

54 Flavelle, *Munitions in Canada*; *Star*, Dec. 18, 20, 1916.

55 Laurier Papers, 193961-6, H. F. Gadsby to Laurier, Nov. 27, 1916; Charles Murphy Papers, C. K. Kerr to J. E. Atkinson, Feb. 14, 1917; RLB Diary, Dec. 27, 1916.

56 FQ, 54, Address to Canadian Club, Toronto, Dec. 18, 1916.

57 FQ, 4649-56, JWF to Wm. Noxon, Dec. 23, 1921.

58 Ramsay Cook, *The Politics of John W. Dafoe and the Free Press* (Toronto, 1963), p. 74; CAR, 1916, p. 417.

59 FQ, 1745-8, Wrong to JWF, Dec. 22, 1916; reply Dec. 26; also 38, Falconer to JWF, Dec. 11, 1916.

CHAPTER THIRTEEN — PLOUGHSHARES INTO SHELLS (pp. 303-28)

1 FO, vol. 55, Memorandum of Information from Mr. W. A. Peterson, Feb. 10, 1919.

2 FO, Imperial Munitions Board File, memo, "The Imperial Munitions Board," July 7, 1918.

3 FO, memo enc. in JWF to Perry, Sept. 12, 1916; Gordon to JWF, Oct. 13, 1916; #203, Summary of Minutes of Meeting of 6″ Machining and Assembling Manufacturers, June 28, 1917; Perry File, W. A. Peterson to JWF, Aug. 16, 1917.

4 FQ, 1235-7, Fitzgerald to CEF, Oct. 18, 1916.

5 FO, #96, memo, Work of the Imperial Munitions Board, Dec. 4, 1918; McAvity File, memo re Organization of the Production Department, March 28, 1916.

6 FO, JWF to Brand, Dec. 16, 28, 1916.

7 FO, JWF to Brand, Feb. 13, 1917; also Edwards to JWF, Jan. 18, 1917, reply Jan. 19; Edwards to JWF, Jan. 23, Feb. 1, 1917; Edwards File, JWF memo for Fitzgerald, Aug. 24, 1917; Case 55, draft history of the IMB, p. 44; *Off. Hist.*, p. 54.

8 FO, Irish to JWF, Oct. 12, 1916; FQ, 2231-7, JWF to White, April 25, 1917.

9 FO, Irish File, Irish to Newton Rowell, May 31, 1918; *ibid.*, W. S. Fowler to Irish, Nov. 10, 1916; Irish to JWF, Oct. 18, 1916.

10 Interview with Mrs. Lillian Hamilton; FO, Irish to JWF, Feb. 3, Dec. 2, 1916; Mabel Irish to JWF, Jan. 8, 1917; reply Jan. 17.

11 *Off. Hist.*, pp. 31-2; Carnegie, *History of Munitions Supply*, pp. 268-9; *Fragments*.

12 FO, JWF to Lt.-Col. W. E. Edwards, Feb. 7, 1917.

13 FO, Gordon to JWF, Oct. 28, 1916; also Carnegie to JWF, Jan. 18, 1916; JWF to RLB, Sept. 12, 1916.

14 FO, Gordon to JWF, Feb. 15, 1916, and reply; JWF to Brand, Feb. 23, 1916; also file #58.

15 FO, JWF to Gordon, Nov. 14, 1916; Gordon to JWF, Oct. 28.

16 Quote from FQ, 2238-46, draft of JWF to White, sometime in spring 1917; on steel, see also FO, JWF to RLB, Jan. 11, 25, 1917; Morgan File, JWF to E. R. Stettinius, Jan. 30, 1917; JWF to Kemp, Feb. 23, 1917; #97, JWF to Mark Workman, Dec. 28, 1916, Jan. 5, 1917, reply Jan. 9; JWF to A. K. McLean, Aug. 17, 1918.

17 S. F. Wise, "The Borden Government and the Formation of a Canadian Flying Corps, 1911 – 1916," in Michael Cross and Robert Bothwell, eds., *Policy by Other Means: Essays in Honour of C. P. Stacey* (Toronto, 1972), pp. 121-44; FO, #39, *passim*.

18 FQ, 1629-30, JWF to White, Dec. 22, 1916; JWF to RLB, Dec. 28; JWF to Brand, Dec. 28.

19 FO, #109, JWF to RLB, Feb. 12, 1917; *ibid.*, McCurdy to JWF, Jan. 8, 1917; *ibid.*, McCurdy to RLB, Feb. 5; also Brand Papers, 6D, Perry to Brand, May 31, 1916: referring to McCurdy, "[Loring] Christie has a very bad opinion of him, and the general impression seems to be that he is out for what he can get and does not much care how he gets it."

20 FO, JWF to E. R. Wood, Jan. 9, 1917; Wood to JWF, Jan. 9; FQ, 2238-46, draft of JWF to White, undated, spring 1917; Carnegie, *History of Munitions Supply*, pp. 182-4.

21 FO, #80, JWF to Hon. D. Jamieson, March 19, 1917; JWF to Brand, March 1.

22 FO, JWF to White, Dec. 26, 1916.

23 FQ, 1635-7, Norcross report, Dec. 28, 1916; FO, JWF to RLB, Dec. 27; FQ, 1633-4, JWF to White, Dec. 28.

24 FO, JWF to RLB, Jan. 11, 1917; FQ, 2436-40, JWF to JSW, March 21, 1917.

25 FO, JWF to Brand, Feb. 7, 23, 1917; FQ, 2429-30, JWF to Hon. R. D. Reid, March 2; 2412-16, JWF to JSW, March 2; FO, #107, JWF to Sir Henry Drayton, Feb. 2.

26 FO, JWF to RLB, Dec. 29, 1916; FQ, 2407-9, JWF to JSW, Feb. 27, 1917; FO, #107, JWF to R. B. Bennett, Feb. 26.

27 FQ, 2367-70, JWF to JSW, Jan. 24, 1917; 2360-3, JWF to JSW, Jan. 9.

28 FQ, 966-7, undated, JWF to RLB; 2391-3, JWF to JSW, Feb. 8, 1917; 2412-16, JWF to JSW, March 2.

29 FO, JWF to Brand, Feb. 13, 1917; FQ, 2412-16, JWF to JSW, March 2.

30 FQ, 2391-3, JWF to JSW, Feb. 8, 1917; FO, JWF to Brand, Feb. 13; FQ, 2436-40, JWF to JSW, March 21.

31 FQ, 2412-16, JWF to JSW, March 2, 1917; FO, JWF to Brand, April 3.

32 FO, JWF to Brand, Dec. 29, 1916.

33 FQ, 1620-5, JWF to White, Dec. 15, 1916, reply Dec. 16.

34 *Off. Hist.*, pp. 65-6.

35 FO, JWF to Brand, March 9, 22, 28, 1917.

36 FO, JWF to Martin Burrell, Nov. 8, 1917.

37 FFP, JWF to CEF, Feb. 27, 1917.

38 FQ, 44, JWF to Fox, April 3, 1917; 2457-9, JWF to JSW, May 1; 2467-9, JWF to JSW, May 7; FO, JWF to Brand, April 3, 17; FQ, 2463-6, JWF to JSW, April 30.

39 Carnegie, *History of Munitions Supply*, Appendix III; Brand Papers, 9(1), Memo on IMB, Nov. 14, 1918.

40 Brand Papers, 5B, Brand to Mr. Montague, July 18, 1916.

41 *Ibid.*, 9(1), Brand to Sir L. Worthington Evans, Feb. 7, 1917; JWF, *Canada and Its Relations to the Empire* (1917), pamphlet of address at Convocation Hall, Toronto, April 27, 1917; also FQ, 2148-51, JWF to JWB, Jan. 16, 1917.

42 Brand Papers, 9(1), Brand to Christopher

Addison, April 16, 1917; 6E, Brand to
Addison, March 10.

43 FQ, 2484-7, JWF to JSW, June 5, 1917.

44 FO, #64, Trades and Labor Congress,
"Pronouncement of Organized Labor in
Canada on War Problems," June 11, 1917;
Ottawa *Citizen*, *Ottawa Journal—Press*,
June 4.

45 FO, JWF to Irish, Feb. 21, 1917; Irish file,
Irish to E. R. Wood, Jan. 4, 1917; FQ,
2231-7 draft of JWF to White, April 25.

46 FO, JWF to Col. H. G. Henderson, June 4;
FQ, 1848-9, JWF to Rev. E. W. Halpenny,
June 7.

47 FO, #64, "Memorandum re Munitions
Contracts, Fair Wages Clause, etc.," June
11, 1917; #64, JWF to Col. H. G.
Henderson, June 4.

48 FO, #64, JWF to RIMB, June 29, 1917; #64,
Irish to JWF, June 15; BP, 123319-23,
Crothers to RLB, June 9.

49 Ottawa *Citizen*, June 6, 18, 1917.

50 FO, Consolidated Mining and Smelting
File, *passim*; #99, JWF to Butchart, May
28, 1917.

51 *Labor Gazette*, March 1921, pp. 451, 462;
Sept. 1917, p. 717.

52 FO, JWF to Irish, Feb. 21, 1917.

53 FO, Irish to JWF, Jan. 18, 1917; reply Jan.
19; Irish to JWF, Jan. 23, 1917; reply Jan.
25.

54 BP, 123319-23, Crothers to RLB, June 9,
1917; FO, Irish to JWF, June 15; #64, JWF to
RLB, Aug. 24, 1917; Fitzgerald to JWF,
Aug. 29, 1917.

55 FO, Irish to JWF, June 14, 1917; reply
June 15.

56 FO, JWF to Sir Hardman Lever, May 21,
June 4, 1917.

57 *Off. Hist.*, pp. 66-9.

58 FO, Irish to JWF, July 10, 1917; FQ, 44, Fox
to JWF, July 11.

59 FQ, 1921-34, JWF to A. B. McCoig, MP,
June 7, 1917; 44, JWF to Fox, July 9; reply
July 10; 1190-1, Rundle to JWF, July 6;
reply July 9.

60 FQ, 1995-8, JWF to Rundle, July 10, 1917;
2015-23, JWF to Rundle, Aug. 22; RLB
Diary, July 10, 1917.

61 RLB Diary, June 23, 1917; FFP, JWF to CEF,
July 10.

CHAPTER FOURTEEN — HIS LARDSHIP (pp. 329-62)

1 *Globe*, Sept. 20, 1917; *Report of the
Commissioners Appointed to Investigate the
Businesses of William Davies Co., Ltd. and
Matthews—Blackwell Ltd.* (Ottawa, 1917),
p. 24.

2 FQ, 44, Fox to JWF, Dec. 27, 1915, Jan. 25,
1916.

3 FQ, 44, Fox to James Harris, Jan. 25, May
26, 1916; Fox to JWF, May 16, 1916; JWF to
Fox, May 19, Jan. 28, 1916.

4 FQ, 44, Fox to JWF, May 15, 1916; reply
May 17; Fox to JWF, May 29; reply June 2;
Fox to JWF, Aug. 11; JWF to Fox, Jan. 10,
1917; JWF to Aird, April 17, 1917.

5 FQ, 44, Fox to JWF, April 5, 1916; JWF to
Fox, Dec. 22, 30, 1915, Sept. 29, Feb. 17,
1916.

6 FQ, 44, Fox to W. S. Fowler, April 26, 1916,
et seq.; Fox to JWF, May 22 (there was also
a problem with one batch of twenty

thousand cases of corned beef Davies had
sold to Armour & Company in 1914.
Armour's claimed the meat was unsalable
because of a paraffin taste, perhaps caused
by chicken gizzards, and demanded
compensation. Fox denied any quality
problem, either a paraffin taste or the use
of chicken gizzards, and suspected the
American packer was having trouble
because its own reputation in the
corned-beef business was so bad); JWF to
F. E. White, Aug. 14, 1916; White to JWF,
Aug. 1; Fox to JWF, Aug. 11.

7 *Report of the Commissioners*, p. 5; Child,
"The Predecessor Companies to Canada
Packers," pp. 87-8.

8 FQ, 44, Fox to JWF, May 31, Aug. 30, 1916;
Report of the Commissioners, pp. 11-12; FQ,
44, JWF to Fox, July 25, 26, 1916; FFP, JWF
to CEF, "Wednesday, 9:30 a.m."

9 FQ, 44, Fox to JWF, March 8, May 31, 1916.

10 FQ, 45, JWF to Rev. Ernest Thomas, June 25, 1919; *Globe*, Oct. 20, 1917.

11 Sheed Thomson to Davies, July 15, 1916, reply July 17, quoted in *Globe*, Oct. 20, 1917.

12 FQ, 44, Fox to JWF, Aug. 28, 1916; JWF to Fox, Nov. 4, 1916.

13 FQ, 44, JWF to Fox, Aug. 14, Nov. 4, 1916, March 5, 1917.

14 FQ, 44, Fox to Department of Labour, Jan. 8, 1917; Fox to W. F. O'Connor, Feb. 5; Fox to Minister of Finance (2), April 13; JWF to Fox, June 5, 21, 1917.

15 *Report of the Commissioners*; FQ, 44, speech enc. in JWF to Fox, April 13, 1917.

16 FO, JWF to Gordon, July 19, 1917.

17 FQ, 1769-70, JWF to RLB, July 13, 1917.

18 Peter H. Rider, "The Imperial Munitions Board," (PH D thesis, University of Toronto, 1975), p.337.

19 Canada, *Sessional Papers*, 1917, No. 210a, *Report of W. F. O'Connor, K.C., Acting Commissioner re Cost of Living, Cold Storage Conditions in Canada*.

20 FO, RLB to JWF, July 14, 1917; FQ, 44, JWF to Fox, July 18; RLB Diary, July 18. After the *Journal*'s story appeared, Crothers had tabled the report in the House of Commons on the afternoon of the thirteenth, making it public without Borden's, or, apparently, the cabinet's, authorization.

21 FQ, 2000-1, Rundle to JWF, July 14, 1917; 1749-50, George Allan to JWF, July 16; 44, Adie to JWF, July 14; FFP, JWF to CEF, July 16.

22 FQ, 44, Fox to JWF, July 31, 1917; 45, Fox to JWF, Aug. 15.

23 *Globe*, July 17, 1917.

24 FQ, 44, JWF to Fox, July 18, 1917; *Christian Guardian*, Aug. 4.

25 Ottawa *Citizen*, July 16, 1917; *Toronto World*, July 20; BP, 44680, W. B. Northrup to RLB, July 21, 1917; also 44656, John Rowland to RLB, July 16; *Toronto Star*, July 14; *Globe*, July 17; *World*, July 14, 16; House of Commons, *Debates*, July 24, p. 3896.

26 Interview with W. E. Bosnell.

27 House of Commons, *Debates*, July 24, 1917, pp. 3894-904; July 30, pp. 4071-102; Aug. 1, pp. 4171-2.

28 *Globe*, July 20, 1917; *Star*, July 18; *Citizen*, July 14; *Leader*, Aug. 7, 10; *Bulletin*, Aug. 6; *Saturday Night*, July 21, Aug. 4.

29 FFP, Scrapbooks, JWF to F. O. Mitchell, July 21, 1917; JWF to CEF, July 31.

30 FFP, JWF to CFM, July 27, 1917; also JWF to CFM, July 18; FO, JWF to Gordon, July 19.

31 FQ, 45, Fox to JWF, Aug. 14, 1917, and enclosure.

32 FFP, JWF to CEF, Aug. 21, 1917.

33 FQ, 45, Fox to JWF, Aug. 4, 1917; JWF to Fox, Aug. 3.

34 FQ, 44, Fox to JWF, July 31, 1917; 45, JWF to Fox, Aug. 1.

35 FQ, 45, Fox to JWF, Aug. 2, 6, 1917; JWF to Fox, Aug. 7.

36 FQ, 45, Fox to JWF, Aug. 1, 1917; reply Aug. 2; Fox to JWF, Aug. 3.

37 FFP, CEF to CFM, Sept. 9, 1917.

38 FFP, JWF to CFM, Sept. 14, 1917; JWF to Clara and Frank McEachren, Sept. 11, 1917; on Waldron, see Brand Papers, 8, Brand to Perry, Oct. 20, 1917.

39 *Globe*, Sept. 18, 19, 20, 1917.

40 BP, 44652-5, John T. Wardle to Lloyd George, July 16, 1917; FO, JWF to Perry, Sept. 26.

41 *Ottawa Journal—Press*, Sept. 19, 1917; *Globe*, Sept. 22; Regina *Leader*, Oct. 2; Gadsby in *Charlottetown Patriot*, Oct. 3; *Saturday Night*, Oct. 27; *Citizen*, Sept. 27; FQ, 2491-7, JWF to JSW, Oct. 26.

42 FO, JWF to Brand, Sept. 26, 28, 1917; also JWF to Perry, Sept. 26; FFP, JWF to CFM, Sept. 28.

43 Brand Papers, 8, Brand to Perry, Oct. 20, 1917.

44 FFP, JWF to CFM, Sept. 28, 1917; Rider, "The Imperial Munitions Board," p. 348.

45 FFP, JWF to CFM, Oct. 16, 1917.

46 *Globe*, Oct. 12, 13, 1917; *Report of the Commissioners*, pp. 9-10.

47 *Globe*, Oct. 15, 19, 20, 1917.

48 FFP, JWF to CFM, Oct. 16, 17, 1917.

49 "On Being Investigated," *Saturday Night*, Nov. 3, 1917; BP, 44710, JWF to RLB,

"Wednesday Evening" (Oct. 17, 1917); RLB Diary, Oct. 18.

50 *Globe*, Oct. 22, 1917.

51 *Report of the Commissioners*, *passim*.

52 FFP, JWF to CFM, Nov. 19, 1917.

53 *Telegram*, Oct. 22, 1917; for similar comments see *Toronto Star*, Oct. 23; *Globe*, Oct. 22, 24; *Winnipeg Free Press*, Oct. 23, Nov. 29; *Ottawa Journal—Press*, Nov. 20, 26; *Christian Guardian*, Nov. 28.

54 FQ, 2238-46, JWF to White, undated (spring, 1917).

55 FQ, 44, July 10, 1917.

56 FFP, "Financial" File.

57 FQ, 44, Adie to JWF, July 14, 1917.

58 FO, Churchill file, Churchill to Northcliffe, Oct. 23, 1917.

59 FQ, 2502-6, JWF to JSW, Dec. 5, 1917.

60 Laurier Papers, 197719, R. J. Hartley to Laurier, Oct. 23, 1917; 197968, Gadsby to Laurier, Nov. 1, 1917; Rider, "The Imperial Munitions Board," p. 369.

61 FO, JWF to Newton Rowell, Nov. 8, 1917.

62 Rowell Papers, 2456, James E. Jones to Rowell, Dec. 27, 1917.

63 FFP, JWF to CFM, Dec. 19, 1917.

CHAPTER FIFTEEN — SEEING IT THROUGH (pp. 363-83)

1 FFP, JWF to CFM, Sept. 5, 1917.

2 FO, JWF to Gordon, July 26, 1917.

3 FO, JWF to Gordon, Aug. 23, 1917; *Globe*, Oct. 19, 20.

4 FO, JWF to Gordon, Sept. 10, 1917; JWF to Brand, Aug. 7, 11; JWF to Sir Hardman Lever, Aug. 10, 22; JWF to White, Aug. 25.

5 FO, JWF to Perry, Oct. 15, 1917; JWF to Gordon, Oct. 17; Borden file, JWF to Hon. F. B. Carvell, Jan. 1, 1918.

6 FO, JWF to Gordon, Oct. 23, 1917; JWF to Perry, Oct. 25; JWF to Brand, Nov. 6.

7 FQ, 2326-9, JWF to White, Nov. 8, 1917; Carnegie, *History of Munitions Supply*, pp. 215-29.

8 FO, JWF memo for Lloyd Harris, Aug. 9, 1918.

9 On the Ordnance agreement see R. C. Cuff and J. L. Granatstein, *Canadian—American Relations in Wartime* (Toronto, 1975), chaps. 2, 3.

10 FO, Borden file Dec. 1917; JWF to Brand, Nov. 19, Dec. 6; #203, Meeting of Machining and Assembling Manufacturers, Nov. 23, 1917; #182, JWF to A. E. Frapp, Jan. 27, 1919.

11 FO, #121, G. Morrow to JWF, Nov. 6, 1917; JWF to Morrow, Nov. 7, 13, ff.; #114, JWF to RLB, Jan. 28, 1918.

12 FO, JWF to Carnegie, Aug. 21, 1918; JWF to E. R. Wood, March 25; JWF to Brand, Nov. 22, 1917.

13 FO, #36, JWF to Brand, Dec. 21, 1917; #163, Noble Pirrie to JWF, July 2, 1918.

14 For Trenton see FO, files #88, #205.

15 FO, JWF to RLB, July 26, 1917.

16 FO, #91, Stevens to RLB, Nov. 27, 1917, ff.; also #91, Stevens to JWF, Aug. 10, 1917, ff.

17 FO, #103, esp. letter to members, B.C. Loggers Association, Nov. 24, 1917; #103, W. Astly to George Perley, Feb. 13, 1918.

18 FO, #99, esp. Butchart to JWF, Feb. 28, 1918. The contract situation on the Coast was supremely confused: some of the ships were being built at fixed prices, other ships on cost-plus contracts, and some assembling and equipping was going on in yards owned and operated by the Board itself.

19 FO, JWF to Perry, April 11, 1918.

20 FO, file #223.

21 RLB Diary, Feb. 3, 14, 19, 21, 26, 1918; FO, JWF to A. K. McLean, Feb. 13; JWF to Brand, Feb. 15.

22 FO, JWF to McLean, April 3, 17, 19, 1918; JWF to RLB, April 25.

23 RLB Diary, Feb. 26, 1918; Brand Papers, 7, Reading to Minister of Munitions, Feb. 23.

24 FQ, 2741-5, JWF to Rundle, March 28, 1918.

25 FFP, JWF to CFM, March 27, 1918; FQ, 2999-3003, JWF to E. R. Wood, April 8; also 2926-9, JWF to White, April 8.

26 FQ, 2754-8, JWF to Rundle, April 3, 1918.

27 FQ, 45, Fox to JWF, March 20, 1918; FO, JWF to RLB, April 2; FQ, Fox to JWF, Aug. 23, 30.

28 FQ, 23, Fitzgerald to JWF, Dec. 10, 1935; BP, 135264-301.

29 Prang, *N. W. Rowell*, p. 240; House of Commons, *Debates*, May 2, 1918, p. 1390ff.

30 FFP, JWF to CFM, April 16, 1918; FQ, JWF to JSW, April 12.

31 FFP, JWF to CFM, April 1, 1918; CEF to CFM, June 9; JWF to CFM, May 2.

32 FQ, 1774-5, Rev. R. P. Bowles to JWF, Oct. 10, 1917; 1825-7, Wm. Elliott to JWF, Oct. 19; FFP, Fudger to JWF, Oct. 3, 1917.

33 FFP, JWF to CFM, April 29, 1918; JWF to Rev. R. P. Bowles, July 11; JWF to CFM, May 14.

34 FQ, 2774-9, JWF to Rundle, May 23, 1918; also FFP, JWF to CFM, May 14.

35 FO, JWF to Carnegie, Nov. 29, 1918.

36 FQ, 67, pencilled memo in Speeches Miscellaneous file.

37 FO, #113; Fitzgerald file, April 19, 1918, ff.; #99, Butchart to JWF, May 3, 1918, ff.

38 FO, #94, JWF to Irish, March 26, 1918; Irish to JWF, March 28.

39 FO, JWF to Brand, June 11, 1918.

40 FQ, 2999-3003, JWF to E. R. Wood, April 8, 1918.

41 FO, #91, JWF to Hon. F. P. Carvell, April 18, 1918, ff.

42 FQ, 2776-9, JWF to Rundle, May 23, 1918; FFP, JWF to CFM, May 22.

43 FO, Irish to JWF, June 20, 1918; Irish file, Irish to Fitzgerald, June 28.

44 FO, JWF to Brand, June 12, 1918; #11, JWF to Russell, July 9, 1918.

45 FO, #99, JWF to Butchart, May 31, 1918; FQ, 2602-6, Butchart to JWF, June 7, 1918.

46 FQ, 2414-16, JWF to Butchart, June 25, 1918.

47 FO, #11, Irish to Fitzgerald, Sept. 11, 1918, ff.; FQ, 45, JWF to Fox, July 31.

48 FQ, 45, JWF to Fox, July 31, 1918; Fox to JWF, July 26.

49 FO, JWF to Brand, Oct. 3, 28, 1918; JWF to RLB, Sept. 14; JWF to Churchill, Oct. 9.

50 FO, #175, esp. JWF to Lloyd Harris, Oct. 15, 17, 1918; JWF to Carnegie, Oct. 31.

51 FO, JWF to F. A. Rolph, Oct. 30, 1918; JWF to N. W. Rowell, Oct. 22.

52 FO, JWF to Carnegie, Nov. 1, 1918; also FQ, 2834-7, JWF to Rundle, Nov. 4.

53 FFP, JWF to CFM, Nov. 2, 16, 1918.

CHAPTER SIXTEEN — NEW WINESKIN, OLD WINE (pp. 384-417)

1 FO, case 43, transcript, Banquet to the Staff, Nov. 25, 1918.

2 FO, #182, JWF to A. E. Frapp, Jan. 27, 1919; #177, *passim*; Willys—Overland file, *passim*.

3 FO, #143, JWF to George E. Wishart, Jan. 21, 1919; #185, George Edwards to Austin Taylor, Jan. 9; JWF to Sir Frederick Williams-Taylor, Jan. 17, ff.; JWF to Senator D. O. L'Esperence, March 29; #185, JWF to Austin Taylor, Jan. 11.

4 FQ, 3069-75, JWF to Brand, Sept. 25, 1919; FO, JWF to Lloyd Harris, Dec. 16, 1918; JWF to Brand, Jan. 7, 1919; FQ, 3305-7, JWF to Wm. Noxon, March 26, 1919.

5 FO, #177, JWF to Brand, March 28, 1919; Gear file, esp. Gear to JWF, Feb. 2, 1920.

6 FO, #174 and Lt.-Col. H. G. Henderson files, *passim*.

7 FO, #183, #176, *passim*.

8 FO, #180, Gordon to JWF, Nov. 7, 1919, and reply.

9 Carnegie, *History of Munitions Supply*, Appendices I, III.

10 FQ, 44, Fox to JWF, Jan. 31, 1916; reply Feb. 3; William Davies Company, *Minutes* (A. E. Child notes), March 11, May 18, 1917.

11 FQ, 45, Fox to JWF, Oct. 19, 1918; reply Oct. 21; "Memo" enc. in Fox to JWF, Aug. 2, 1918; JWF to Fox, Sept. 24, 1919; JWF to D. A. Cameron, Dec. 6, 1918.

12 FQ, 3354-9, JWF to J. R. Robinson, Dec. 15, 1919; 45, JWF to D. A. Cameron, Dec.

6, 14, 1918; Child, "The Predecessor Companies of Canada Packers," p. 96.

13 Child, "The Predecessor Companies of Canada Packers," pp. 91-5; FQ, 3354-9, JWF to J. R. Robinson, Dec. 15, 1919.

14 FQ, 45, file 8, "Memo concerning particulars of sale . . ."; Child, "The Predecessor Companies of Canada Packers," pp. 248-9.

15 Robert Simpson Company, *Minutes*, Jan. 23, 1919.

16 *Memoirs and Writings, Harris Henry Fudger*; FQ, 45, A. T. Park to JWF, Jan. 8, 1920.

17 Floyd S. Chalmers, memorandum of conversation with JWF, Aug. 12, 1934; copy in FFP, courtesy of Mr. Chalmers.

18 FFP, JWF to Sir Augustus Nanton, Dec. 11, 1920.

19 FQ, 45, Fox/Flavelle letters, Dec. 9-11, 30-1, 1918; 2858-65, JWF to Rundle, Dec. 21; 3281-7, JWF memo, Feb. 1919.

20 FO, JWF to Sanford Evans, April 1, 1919.

21 FQ, 3281-7, JWF memo, Feb. 1919; 3114-7, JWF to Carnegie, April 2, 1919.

22 FQ, 3069-75, JWF to Brand, Sept. 1, 1919; also 3525-30, JWF to Carnegie, July 2, 1920.

23 FQ, 3453-5, JWF to Willison, Oct. 18, 1919; also 3551-6, JWF to Carnegie, Dec. 10, 1920; FO, JWF to Fitzgerald, Nov. 1, 1919.

24 FQ, 3831-4, JWF to Noxon, May 25, 1920; 3850-3, JWF to Noxon, July 21; 3861-4, JWF to Noxon, Oct. 11.

25 FQ, 3780, JWF to Meighen, Oct. 14, 1920; Thomas D. Traves, "The Board of Commerce and the Canadian Sugar Refining Industry: A Speculation on the Role of the State in Canada," CHR, June, 1974, pp. 159-175.

26 FQ, 3551-6, JWF to Carnegie, Dec. 10, 1920.

27 FO, case 66, JWF to J. W. Dafoe, Sept. 7, 1921; FQ, 2540-1, JWF to Rev. Peter Addison, Nov. 19, 1918; FFP, JWF to CFM, Jan. 21, 1918.

28 FQ, 5378-81, Will Flavelle to JWF, April 17, 1922; reply April 19; 4613-14, JWF to Rev. J. W. Macmillan, Nov. 23, 1921.

29 FQ, 6401-7, JWF to Noxon, May 3, 1923.

30 FQ, 4785-6, JWF to Rev. Ernest Thomas, Feb. 21, 1921.

31 FQ, 3504-8, JWF to Carnegie, Feb. 16, 1920.

32 FQ, 3961-4, JWF to JSW, March 21, 1920; 6670-9, JWF to JSW, March 11, 1923; FFP, JWF to CFM, Feb. 26, 1920.

33 JWF, *Individualism as a Factor in Affairs* (pamphlet, Toronto, 1922).

34 FQ, 5229-36, JWF to Carnegie, Oct. 14, 1922.

35 FQ, 3010-18, E. R. Wood, to JWF, Dec. 1, 5, 1918; 3432-5, JWF to JSW, Jan. 5, 1919; 3229-31, JWF to Gordon, Dec. 17.

36 FQ, 3229-31, JWF to Gordon, Dec. 17, 1919; 3016-18, JWF to E. R. Wood, Dec. 5, 1918; FQ, JWF to Home Smith, Dec. 6; 3467-8, JWF to G. W. Allan, July 15, 1920.

37 FQ, 4072-4, JWF to JSW, Nov. 5, 1920; 3778, Meighen to JWF, July 14, 1920.

38 FQ, 4128-32, JWF to JSW, Dec. 24, 1920.

39 PAC, Meighen Papers, 9145-7, JWF to Meighen, March 30, 1921; Willison Papers, 10377, JWF to JSW, March 31.

40 FO, 75, Minutes of meeting of deputation re Chairmanship of Can. Nat. Rwys., Sept. 14, 1921.

41 SFP, JWF to Will Flavelle, April 22, 1921; Meighen Papers, 9145-7, JWF to Meighen, March 31, 1921.

42 FQ, 4668-9, 4761-2, JWF to Perry, May 17, 20, 1921; 4763-5, F. N. Southam to JWF, June 7; also 4359-60, JWF to Fitzgerald, June 2; FQ, 67, Speeches Miscellaneous file, undated pencilled memorandum.

43 FQ, 5012-17, JWF to JSW, April 30, 1921.

44 FO, 71, #326, JWF to F. N. Southam, Dec. 10, 1921.

45 JWF, *The Canadian National Railway System, Letter Addressed to The Rt. Hon. Arthur Meighen . . . August 12, 1921* (pamphlet, Toronto, 1921); FQ, 4564-5, JWF to Stewart Lyon, Oct. 7, 1921.

46 FO, 75, Minutes of meeting of deputation re Chairmanship of Can. Nat. Rwys., Sept. 14, 1921.

47 FO, 73, #392, JWF to C. G. Bowker, Aug. 10, 1921; JWF to W. D. Robb, Oct. 30, 1921.

48 FO, 70, #324; 59, #45, JWF to J. A. Stewart, Oct. 26, 1921.

49 FO, 70, #322, JWF to A. J. Mitchell, Oct. 31, 1921; #322a, Minutes of Special Meeting on Pension Questions, Nov. 9, 1921.

50 FO, 71, #326, JWF to F. N. Southam, Dec. 10, 1921.

51 FO, 71, #362, *passim*.

52 *Montreal Star*, Nov. 30, 1921 ff.; FQ, 4372-4, JWF to Fitzgerald, Dec. 15, 1921.

53 FQ, 5114-15, JWF to Allan S. Bond, Dec. 14, 1921; for Meighen and his problems with Atholstan and Montreal see Roger Graham, *Arthur Meighen* (Toronto, 1963), vol. 2.

54 FO, 71, #362, JWF to Fitzgerald, Jan. 6, 1922.

55 Graham, *Arthur Meighen*, 11, 163, quoting Meighen to Calder, Dec. 13, 1921; FO, 71, #362, JWF to Fitzgerald, Jan. 6, 1922.

56 FQ, 4272-8, JWF to Carnegie, March 31, 1921.

57 King Papers, Diary, Jan. 16, 1922; FQ, 5168-70, JWF to Brand, Jan. 17; 5734-9, JWF to JWB, Jan. 20.

58 FO, 60, #73; 59, #42; 70, #322, JWF to King, April 12, 1922.

59 FQ, 5871-2, JWF to JSW, Aug. 15, 1922; 5557-8, JWF to Col. J. B. Maclean, Aug. 31; Meighen Papers, 73464-5, JWF to Meighen, Oct. 4.

60 FQ, 55, Address to Montreal Board of Trade, Dec. 5, 1922.

61 FQ, 6413-14, Col. C. Ogilvie to JWF, May 12, 1923, and reply; FFP, Baronetage File.

62 FQ, 6517-31, JWF to Rundle, Nov. 8, 15, 1923; also 5922-34; FFP, JWF to Frank McEachren, Nov. 9; JWF to CFM, Nov. 16.

63 FQ, 6517-27, JWF to Rundle, Nov. 8, 1923.

64 FQ, 10493-501, JWF to JSW, Nov. 14, 12, 1923.

65 FQ, 45, JWF to E. C. Fox, Dec. 27, 1923.

CHAPTER SEVENTEEN — ELDER STATESMAN (pp. 418-47)

1 FQ, 49, Memo, May 22, 1924; Bank of Commerce, *Minutes*, April 25, May 2, 1924.

2 FQ, 6494-8, JWF to Rundle, June 20, 1923.

3 See correspondence in FQ with various editors, esp. 10347-65 and 10467-80, exchanges with M. E. Nichols and Fred Southam.

4 JWF letter, Aug. 29, 1920, Guy Flavelle letter, Aug. 30, both in Guy Flavelle's correspondence from his Western trip, in the possession of Mrs. John Ballem, Calgary; Willison Papers, 10293-9, JWF to JSW, Aug. 29, 1920; 10300-4, JWF to JSW, Sept. 6.

5 FQ, 61, Address to Peterborough Kiwanis Club, Oct. 15, 1928 (re 1921 Winnipeg speech); 55, Thornton Dinner file, JWF to Sanford Evans, Dec. 15, 1922; headlines from clippings in FFP scrapbook.

6 FQ, 6483-6, JWF to Rundle, May 25, 1923.

7 FQ, 57, clipping from *Halifax Herald*, April 29, 1925; 8199-8203, JWF to E. R. Peacock, June 29.

8 FQ, 7673-7, JWF to Carnegie, Feb. 9, 1925; also 8393-6, JWF to Dr. Charles Knister, Oct. 8, 1925.

9 FQ, 7118-20, JWF to Col. A. F. Gault, Dec. 15, 1924.

10 FQ, 8318-19, JWF to JSW, Feb. 14, 1925; 7464-5, JWF to JSW, Jan 21, 1924; 5780-2, JWF to White, Dec. 30, 1922.

11 FQ, 56, JWF to Editor, *Edmonton Journal*, Jan. 23, 1924.

12 FQ, 8331-3, JWF to JSW, Feb. 28, 1925.

13 FQ, 7118-20, JWF to Col. A. F. Gault, Dec. 15, 1924; 7327-31, JWF to C. A. Magrath, May 13, 1924; 8485-8, JWF to Macdonnell, Jan. 10, 1925.

14 FQ, 8327-8, JWF to Andrew Thompson, Feb. 26, 1925; 7687-90, JWF to Carnegie, Sept. 10, 1925; 7673-7, JWF to Carnegie, Feb. 9, 1925.

15 FQ, 7177-81, JWF to Hichens, April 14, 1924; Willison Papers, 10596-8, JWF to George Allan, March 2, 1925; FQ, 7964-6, JWF to Gordon, Jan. 10, 1925.

16 FQ, 7961-6, Gordon to JWF, Jan. 5, 1925;

reply Jan. 10; 9080-5, Gordon to JWF, April 26, 1926; reply April 27.

17 FQ, 8521-31, Macdonnell to JWF, April 14, 1925; reply April 14.

18 FQ, 57, Railway Problems file, JWF to Macdonnell, Sept. 29, 1925; 8541-3, JWF to Macdonnell, Oct. 1; 8367-9, JWF to JSW, Sept. 29; 8021-4, JWF to Lionel Curtis, Nov. 10.

19 FQ, 8541-3, JWF to Macdonnell, Oct. 1, 1925.

20 FQ, 7695-8, JWF to Carnegie, Oct. 12, 1925; 8173, JWF to Meighen, Sept. 19.

21 FQ, 7897-7902, JWF to Carnegie, Nov. 30, 1925; 7934-8, JWF to Carnegie, Dec. 29.

22 FQ, 8905-11, JWF to Lionel Curtis, July 2, 1926; 9560-2, JWF to Sir Campbell Stuart, Sept. 2, 1926; 8771-6, JWF to Carnegie, Oct. 5.

23 FQ, 8898-8901, JWF to M. A. Cunningham, Nov. 19, 1926; also 8336-40, JWF to S. D. Chown, Nov. 19; 9066-76 for JWF statements; 9096-108, exchange with D. B. Harkness.

24 FQ, 10397-435, esp. JWF to Senator Pope, 10402-17; 8771-6, JWF to Carnegie, Oct. 5, 1927.

25 FQ, 10256-60, JWF to Macdonnell, Oct. 19, 1927. Meighen's use of his speaking time at the convention to defend his Hamilton speech was the last straw for Flavelle: "that a man who had been honored by his party in being selected as leader, and supported in his position as Prime Minister, should so disregard his responsibility to a great party gathered in convention, as to make use of it for purely selfish purposes, is about as evil a thing as a mean, selfish-spirited man could perform."

26 FQ, 60, Address to Association of Canadian Advertisers, Oct. 5, 1927; 10256-60, JWF to Macdonnell, Oct. 19, 1927; 8781-94, JWF to Carnegie, Dec. 3, 1926.

27 FQ, 9001-3, JWF to D. H. Gibson, Nov. 4, 1926; 8608-11, JWF to Aird Flavelle, June 24, 1926.

28 FQ, 9814-27, JWF to Brand, Jan. 8, 1927;

8994-9, Fitzgerald to JWF, Dec. 20, 1926; 8612-18, JWF to Aird Flavelle, Dec. 1, 1926.

29 FQ, 60, Address to Advertisers, Oct. 5, 1927; 9983-90, JWF to Byng, Jan. 1927.

30 FQ, 6509-14, JWF to Rundle, Aug. 3, 1923.

31 Burton, *A Sense of Urgency*, p. 211; memorandum of a JWF conversation with Floyd Chalmers, Aug. 12, 1934, courtesy of Mr. Chalmers; FQ, 7078-84, William Flavelle to JWF, April 12, 1924, and reply; information on budgeting in Canadian business supplied by Mr. R. M. Parkinson of Clarkson Gordon.

32 National Trust, *Annual Report, 1923*, p. 22.

33 Bank of Commerce, *Minutes*, Jan. 27, 1922, Nov. 2, 1923.

34 FQ, 6799-6803, JWF to JSW, Oct. 19, 1923.

35 FQ, 49, JWF memo, May 22, 1924.

36 FQ, 8207-8, Rhodes to JWF, July 27, 1925; 8035-51, various telegrams; 8215, Rhodes to JWF, Aug. 7.

37 FQ, 17, Fitzgerald to JWF, Aug. 4, 1929; on National Trust and BESCO see FQ, 49, *passim*; also National Trust Company, J. W. Macdonnell correspondence, Macdonnell to Rundle, July 12, 1928.

38 FQ, 49, JWF to Macdonnell, Sept. 21, 1929.

39 *Ibid*.

40 FQ, 45, Fox to JWF, June 28, 1920, Jan. 26, 1921; Child, "The Predecessor Companies of Canada Packers," chaps. 10, 11.

41 FQ, 19, JWF to J. S. McLean, July 8, 1931.

42 Child, "The Predecessor Companies of Canada Packers," chaps. 10, 11.

43 FQ, 45, Fox to JWF, Jan. 1, 1920; 4823-9, JWB to JWF, Aug. 16, 1921; 6622-8, JWB to JWF, Dec. 14, 1923.

44 FQ, 10132-3, JWF to Aird Flavelle, Nov. 8, 1927.

45 On the formation of Canada Packers see Child, "The Predecessor Companies of Canada Packers"; FQ, 10276-80, J. S. McLean to J. A. C. Kemp, June 8, 1927; case 45, 1927 file.

46 Interview.

47 FQ, 9684-6, JWB to JWF, May 18, 1926.

48 FQ, 10878-9, JWF to Fitzgerald, May 11, 1928.

49 FQ, 9877-84, 9890-3, Brand to JWF, Aug.

27, Oct. 17, 1927; on Canadian Marconi generally see FQ, 46, 47, *passim*, esp. memo enc. in Perry to JWF, Jan. 11, 1928; W. J. Baker, *A History of the Marconi Company* (London, 1970).

50 FQ, 46.

51 FQ, 46, Perry to JWF, Aug. 11, Oct. 10, 1928.

52 Bowman, quoted in FQ, 46, JWF to Brand, Oct. 11, 1928.

53 FQ, 46, JWF to Perry, Oct. 23, 1928.

54 FQ, 46, JWF to Brand, Nov. 19, 1928; JWF to Breckenridge, Dec. 14, 1927. He was also uncomfortable in one other minor venture, his investment in the Amulet Realty Company, which was formed in 1926 by Home Smith to purchase land on the south side of Queen Street from the Sir William Mackenzie estate. According to Smith the aim was to make it easy for the city to extend University Avenue southwards because the syndicate would resell the property to the city at cost. Smith got into a row with City Council, however; there was considerable public criticism of the whole affair, and the property was finally sold to the city under arbitration in 1931. Flavelle advised Smith many times to make a settlement with the city and not to try to make a profit on the transaction. Smith realized the whole matter had embarrassed Flavelle and apologized for having asked him to become involved. Flavelle made $21,000

on a $26,000 investment on which he had hoped to make no profit. See FFP, Amulet Realty Company file.

55 FFP, Ellsworth Flavelle file, undated draft letter; Burton, *A Sense of Urgency*, chap. 23.

56 *Ibid.*; Chalmers memo, Aug. 12, 1934; FQ, 23, JWF to Macdonnell, June 7, 1934; FFP, Simpson's file, pencilled list of Simpson's shareholdings, 1929.

57 Chalmers memo, Aug. 12, 1934; FFP, Ellsworth Flavelle file, draft letter.

58 Burton, *A Sense of Urgency*, pp. 222-4.

59 *Ibid.*, chap. 23; FQ, 23, JWF to Rev. C. H. Huestis, Sept. 4, 1934; 17, JWF to Macdonnell, Aug. 7, 1929.

60 *Memoirs and Writings, Harris Henry Fudger*.

61 FQ, 10971-3, JWF to Larkin, Dec. 29, 1928; 10752-3, JWF to Carnegie, Dec. 29.

62 FQ, 17, JWF to Wm. C. Noxon, Jan. 3, 1929; 11006-11, JWF to Macdonnell, Jan. 6, 1928.

63 FQ, 60, JWF to H. S. Southam, Feb. 11, 1928; 17, JWF to Tyson, Feb. 14, 1929.

64 FQ, 49, White to JWF, April 7, 1928; 10958-60, JWF to Larkin, Oct. 17, 1928; 46, JWF to Perry, Nov. 29, 1928; Brand to JWF, Dec. 18, 1928.

65 FQ, 61, Notes for Address to Simpson's Annual Meeting; 17, JWF to Tyson, Feb. 14, 1929.

66 FQ, 17, JWF to Fred R. Robertson, June 21, 1929.

CHAPTER EIGHTEEN — "OPEN HOUSE FOR BEGGARS" (pp. 448-68)

1 FQ, 41, Rundle to A. F. Miller, May 13, 1916, enc. in Miller to JWF, May 16; Rundle to JWF, Jan. 12, 1917; Toronto General Hospital, *Minutes*, Aug. 2, June 7, July 5, 1916.

2 FQ, 41, JWF to T. A. Russell, Feb. 11, 1918; JWF to Jim Harris, Feb. 11; TGH, *Minutes*, July 9, Sept. 11, Nov. 13, 1919, Oct. 20, 1920; FQ, 41, JWF to C. S. Blackwell, Dec. 27, 1919; JWF to E. C. Drury, Jan. 8, 1920; 42, Blackwell to JWF, May 27, 1922.

3 FQ, 41, Rundle to JWF, Oct. 24, 1917; Brittain to Board of Trustees, July 9, 1919; TGH, *Minutes*, Oct. 15, 1917 ff.

4 FQ, 41, *passim*; 42, JWF to Dr. Duncan Graham, Feb. 11, 1921; TGH, *Minutes*, May 18, 1921.

5 UTA, clipping files re Select Committee on the University of Toronto; CAR, 1922, pp. 611-13; 1923, pp. 563-5; JWF, *The Present Administration of the University of Toronto* (pamphlet, Toronto, 1922).

6 FQ, 39, Falconer to JWF, April 4, 1929; interview with Horace Speakman.

7 FQ, 10858-62, Pelham Edgar to JWF, Dec. 17, 28, 1928, and replies; 38, JWF to Prof. MacIver, May 19, 1925; annual correspondence with E. R. Peacock.

8 FQ, 50, JWF to Ferguson, Dec. 4, 1930; D. H. Gibson to JWF, March 30, 1928; 18, Muriel Gladman to Ralph Skelton, April 1, 1930. On the ORF see Peter Oliver, "Government, Industry and Science in Ontario: The Case of the Ontario Research Foundation," in *Public and Private Persons: The Ontario Political Culture, 1914–1934* (Toronto, 1975), pp. 156–79.

9 FQ, 50, JWF to C. A. Magrath, Oct. 1, 1929; JWF to Ferguson, Jan. 13, 1930; J. S. McLean to JWF, May 16, 1928.

10 FQ, 26, JWF to G. A. Warburton, April 15, 1924; JWF to Sir James Aikins, June 22, 1925; JWF to E. R. Wood, July 23, 1926; 27, JWF to Newton Rowell, Feb. 13, 1926.

11 FQ, 27, JWF to Rev. John W. Woodside, July 3, 1928.

12 FQ, 28, JWF to Rev. Peter Bryce, Aug. 8, 1929; 62, Address of Welcome to the Delegates . . . Massey Hall, June 10, 1929.

13 FQ, 27, Roberts to JWF, Jan. 25, March 7, 1928; JWF to Roberts, Feb. 21; Kemp to JWF, Oct. 31; JWF to Roberts, Nov. 2; Roberts to JWF, Nov. 5; 28, Roberts to JWF, April 1, 1929; 27, JWF to J. H. Gundy, Oct. 13, 1928.

14 FQ, 37, Rev. J. H. Arnup to JWF, Jan. 31, 1930.

15 For West China Union University see the correspondence in FQ, 34–7; Joseph Taylor, *History of the West China Union University, 1910–1935* (Chengtu, 1936); John W. Foster, "The Imperialism of Righteousness: Canadian Protestant Missions and the Chinese Revolution, 1925–1926" (unpublished PH D thesis, University of Toronto, 1977).

16 FQ, 34, JWF to Beech, Feb. 1, 1927.

17 FQ, 35, JWF to Rev. James Endicott, Nov. 29, 1928; 37, JWF to Rev. Frank Anderson, Aug. 1, 1930.

18 FQ, 34, Beech to JWF, Nov. 25, 1926; 35, JWF to Arnup, Feb. 2, 1927;

JWF to Rundle, June 2, 1927.

19 FQ, 36, JWF to Rowell, May 2, 1929; 34, JWF to Geo. Vaux, Oct. 15, 1925; JWF to Arnup, Feb. 23, 1927; re houses, 34, JWF to H. T. Silcock, Oct. 17, 1927; 37, JWF to Beech, Oct. 16, 1929.

20 FQ, 37, Beech to JWF, June 9, 1930; letters enc. in E. A. Evans to Board, July 31, 1930.

21 Flavelle's general correspondence at Queen's contains hundreds of letters relating to individual donations. There are many more letters on church givings in the Methodist and United Church files. Cases 68–78 consist entirely of philanthropic files. Copies of my synoptic notes and tabulations are in the supplementary Flavelle papers at Queen's.

22 FQ, 27, Roberts to JWF, June 13, 1927.

23 FQ, 4388-9, Fitzpatrick to JWF, June 10, 1921.

24 FQ, 22, Victor Ross to JWF, Oct. 23, 1933.

25 FQ, 17, H. E. Kirkpatrick to JWF, March 2, 1929.

26 FQ, 50, Macdonald to JWF, Jan. 16, 1926; all other details from FQ, 50, *passim*; FFP, Appleby School file, J. S. H. Guest to JWF, March 15, 1917.

27 *Fragments*.

28 For individuals mentioned see named files in FQ, 68–78; for Jarvis, see 8453, Jarvis to JWF, July 15, 1925, and Peter Oliver, "Scandal in Ontario Politics: The Jarvis–Smith Affair, an Ontario Dreyfus Case," in *Public and Private Persons*, pp. 180–262.

29 FQ, 11081-8, H. C. Miller to JWF, Aug. 15, 1928, ff.

30 FQ, 70, R. A. Flack file, JWF to G. T. Little, Feb. 26, 1927.

31 FQ, 26, JWF to Rev. W. H. Douglas, 1925; JWF to Rev. W. A. Whattam, Jan. 5, 1920.

32 FQ, 26, JWF to Rev. S. W. Dean, Sept. 13, 1919.

33 FQ, 7100, JWF to Fitzpatrick, Dec. 24, 1923; 28, JWF to George W. McLaughlin, Feb. 9, 1929.

34 FQ, 26, JWF to Fudger, Dec. 5, 1921; 28, JWF to Geo. Wilson, Feb. 2, 1929; for the opposite view of charity see Burton, *A Sense of Urgency*.

CHAPTER NINETEEN — THE MORNING AFTER (pp. 469–98)

1 FQ, 17, JWF to Sir Campbell Stuart, Oct. 15, 1929.

2 FQ, 46, JWF to Perry, Oct. 29, 1929.

3 FQ, 49, JWF to Fitzgerald, Nov. 18, 1929; 17, JWF to Larkin, Nov. 20; 49, JWF to G. R. Cottrelle, Dec. 28.

4 FQ, 62, Address to Border Cities Chamber of Commerce, Nov. 14, 1929, clipping.

5 FQ, 18, JWF to Byng, May 28, 1930; JWF to Cromie, June 18; JWF to T. Lloyd Williams, June 10.

6 FQ, 18, JWF to Rundle, Oct. 11, 1930; 63, Address at St. Andrew's College, Oct. 30.

7 FQ, 18, White correspondence, Dec. 12, 1930.

8 FQ, 18, JWF to Rundle, Dec. 3, 1930; JWF to Aird Flavelle, Oct. 27; JWF to Carnegie, Nov. 22; JWF to Stuart Flavelle, Nov. 7; JWF to Byng, Dec. 31. I have analysed Flavelle's attitudes toward Western agriculture at more length in an article, "The Ideology of Domination: An Eastern Big-Shot Businessman Looks at Western Canada," in Henry Klassen, ed., *The Canadian West* (Calgary, 1977).

9 FQ, 18, JWF to Carnegie, April 22, 1931; FFP, JWF to CFM, May 3; FQ, 19, JWF to Howard Ferguson, March 4.

10 FFP, JWF to CFM, May 3, 1931.

11 JWF, *How Are Prices of World Commodities Established?* (pamphlet, Address to Canadian Credit Men's Trust Association, Toronto, 1931); see FQ, 63 for subsequent correspondence; *Star*, June 12, 20, 1931; *Mail and Empire*, June 19; FQ, 19, JWF to Sir Arthur Duckman, June 15.

12 FQ, 19, JWF to Hon. E. B. Ryckman, Nov. 5, 1931; also JWF to Howard Ferguson, Dec. 31; on the financial crisis see CAR, 1932, p. 429 ff.

13 FQ, 19, JWF to W. M. Southam, Nov. 16, 1931; JWF to Howard Ferguson, Dec. 31.

14 Flavelle got caught in one brief conflict of interest between chairmanships. In November 1931, Sir Charles Gordon asked him to serve on a committee to represent the banks in discussions with the newsprint industry. Gordon and Beatty of the CPR and M. W. Wilson of the Royal Bank would be the other members. The committee's aim was to help negotiate an end to all-out competition, perhaps even a merger, in an industry where surplus capacity and price-cutting were creating almost universal insolvency. Flavelle agreed to serve on the committee, provided there was no interference with his freedom to advise National Trust's officers in their capacity as Receivers of one of the insolvent companies, Great Lakes Paper. He attended one meeting before his officers told him that it was not in the interests of Great Lakes' bondholders to go along with the negotiations. He immediately resigned from the committee. National Trust became one of the mavericks which frustrated the committee's efforts during the next year. FQ, 19, JWF to Gordon, Nov. 6, 1931; Beatty to JWF, Nov. 16; MacKelcan to JWF, Nov. 18; JWF to Beatty, Nov. 25; 20, Beatty to JWF, Nov. 6, 1932.

15 FQ, 47, esp. Perry to JWF, Aug. 16, 1932; JWF to Perry, Nov. 5, 1931; JWF to Perry, May 28, 1931, Dec. 18, 1933.

16 FQ, 19, university correspondence, JWF to [George Wrong], Jan. 20, 1931; Wrong to JWF, Jan 18, 21.

17 University of Toronto, Board of Governors, *Minutes*, Jan. 22, Feb. 11, 26, 1931; FQ, 19, Macdonnell to JWF, Jan. 21, 1931.

18 *Star*, March 14, 1931.

19 FQ, 65, Barrie Address file, JWF to C. H. Hale, Feb. 26, 1934.

20 *Mail*, Nov. 28, 1927; *Star*, Dec. 3, 1928.

21 Wilder, *Theophilus North* (Avon edition), p. 143.

22 FQ, 61, Address at Ross Memorial Hospital, Lindsay, Oct. 12, 1928.

23 FQ, 19, JWF to Lionel Curtis, June 4, 1931.

24 FQ, 18, Bennett to JWF, July 8, 1931, and reply; JWF to Bennett, Oct. 19; FFP, JWF to CEF, Nov. 11.

25 FQ, 19, JWF to Duff, Nov. 16, 1931, ff.

26 FFP, JWF to CEF, Dec. 13, 1931; CEF to JWF, undated.

27 FQ, 52, Royal Commission on Railways and Transportation, Memorandum by JWF, June 15, 1932; on depreciation see *Proceedings of the Royal Commission on Railways and Transportation* (Ottawa, 1932), pp. 2506ff.

28 *Proceedings*, 950ff., 2240.

29 FFP, Bereavement File, JWF to Rev. W. A. Cameron, Feb. 12, 1932; JWF to Rev. Solomon Cleaver, Feb. 12.

30 FFP, JWF to CFM, April 7, 1932.

31 *Report of the Royal Commission on Railways and Transportation* (Ottawa, 1932); FQ, 52, JWF Memo, June 15, 1932; 21, JWF to R. B. Bennett, Feb. 2, 1933; 20, JWF to F. I. Ker, Nov. 14, 1932.

32 FQ, 21, Dr. J. C. Webster to JWF, Sept. 6, 1932; 22, JWF to Manion, Dec. 29, 1933; 23, JWF to Macdonnell, Oct. 29, 1934.

33 FQ, 22, JWF to Tyson, Aug. 25, 1933; 20, JWF to Cromie, March 15, 1932; 22, JWF to Peacock, March 29, 1933; JWF to Rowell, March 30, 1933; 65, Barrie Address file, JWF to C. H. Hale, Feb. 26, 1934.

34 FQ, 22, JWF to Rowell, March 30, 1933.

35 See FQ, general correspondence, Wheeler-Bennett correspondence, 1933 ff., esp. Wheeler-Bennett to JWF, Aug. 8, 1933; reply Aug. 24; also 21, JWF to Brand, Oct. 16, 1933; Lothian correspondence.

36 FQ, 21, Perry to JWF, March 18, 1932; 20, Cromie to JWF, June 21, 1932.

37 FQ, 21, JWF to J. H. Dennis, Jan. 28, 1933.

38 FQ, 22, JWF to Wm. Noxon, Feb. 13, 1933; FFP, Simpson's file, Glyn Osler to JWF, March 20, 1934, with enc.; Chalmers memo, Aug. 12, 1934; Burton's defence in *Financial Post*, June 30, 1934.

39 FQ, 49, JWF to White, Feb. 28, 1934; White to JWF, March 19.

40 House of Commons, Select Committee on Price Spreads and Mass Buying, *Proceedings*, pp. 2740ff.

41 PAC, H. H. Stevens Papers, vol. 43, *Price Spreads and Mass Buying: An Explanation of the Work Done and Results Achieved by the Special Select Committee on the House of Commons* (pamphlet, dated July 27, 1934).

42 Richard Wilbur, *H. H. Stevens* (Toronto, 1977), pp. 134-5.

43 *Globe*, *Star*, June 19, 1929; for the prospectuses see H. H. Stevens Papers, vol. 104, Robert Simpson File; FQ, 23, JWF to Dr. C. H. Huestis, Sept. 4, 1934; *Financial Post*, Aug. 11, 18.

44 Chalmers memo, Aug. 12, 1934; FQ, 23, Muriel Gladman to JWF, Aug. 31; 23, JWF to Cromie, Oct. 9.

45 Mr. George Spence remembered these quips about JWF in the 1930s.

46 *Mail*, Sept. 19, 24, 1934; interviews.

47 Wilbur, *H. H. Stevens*, pp. 139-42; *Star*, Oct. 30, 1934.

48 Wilbur, *H. H. Stevens*, pp. 75-80.

49 FQ, 23, JWF to Macdonnell, June 7, 1934; FFP, Simpson's file, financial statement.

50 FQ, 18, JWF to Carnegie, June 11, 1931. Flavelle described the operations of the "investment bankers," probably with Gundy and Simpson's in mind, as follows:
... No longer were they interested specially in well ordered corporations using their services for a moderate commission, whereby the needed capital was secured, but they became purchasers of businesses on their own account, and on account of a select company of friends. They sought to choose businesses which were doing well, which had been managed conservatively, and which had accumulated important cash reserves. Following the purchase, a new company, bearing the same, or a kindred name, was formed, and the assets of the old company were passed over, and in the process, frequently important sums of cash out of liquid resources, or secured through bonded indebtedness placed against the real property, provided an important sum of money which was used to help the purchase price of the business concerned.

This done, the debilitated business issued a fresh body of securities, including a great mass of no par shares. The unfortunate administrators, who had been frequently innocent of any association with the whole thing, found themselves saddled with a heavy capital structure, and with new chiefs in command. The securities in turn were placed widely, because there was madness in the air, which led to speculative buying on an immense scale.... FQ,

18, JWF to Carnegie, June 11, 1931; also JWF to
W. M. Southam, Jan. 16, 1933. On the
insolvency of investment houses see E. P.
Newfeld, *The Financial System of Canada*
(Toronto, 1972), p.509.

51 *Star*, March 9, 1939; *Telegram*, March 7,
1939; FFP, JWF to National Trust, Jan. 31,
1935; SFP, Aird Flavelle to JWF, Sept. 9,
1935 ff.; JWF to William Flavelle, April 21,
1934.

52 FQ, 50, *passim*.
53 See named files, FQ, 68–78.
54 FQ, 30, Cochrane correspondence.
55 FQ, 37, *passim*.
56 FQ, 72, JWF to Rev. Ashley Latter, July 13,
1933.
57 FQ, 30, JWF to Roberts, Oct. 4, 1935.
58 *Star*, Jan. 23, 1933.

CHAPTER TWENTY — REST (pp. 499–509)

1 FQ, 39, JWF to H. J. Cody, April 30, 1935;
43, JWF to E. C. Fox, Feb. 15, 1937.
2 FQ, 23, JWF to J. W. Tyson, April 30, 1934.
3 FQ, Claude Bissell to M. Bliss, April 19,
1971.
4 FQ, 23, JWF to J. W. McConnell, Dec. 12,
1934; 24, JWF to Kindersley, June 7, 1935;
J. L. Granatstein, "Financing the Liberal
Party, 1935–1945," in Michael Cross and
Robert Bothwell, eds., *Policy by Other
Means: Essays in Honour of C. P. Stacey*
(Toronto, 1972), pp. 179–200.
5 FQ, 24, JWF to Lord Ashfield, Nov. 13,
1936; 25, JWF to Peacock, Dec. 21, 1937;
24, JWF to Hepburn, May 2, 1935; 25, JWF
to Hepburn, Dec. 12, 1934.
6 FQ, 25, JWF to Will and Ada Rundle, Dec.
27, 1938.
7 FQ, 23, Sir Arthur Doughty to JWF, June
26, 1935; FQ, 24, Brand to JWF, Dec. 23,
1937; 25, JWF to Brand, May 25, 1938.
8 FFP, JWF to CFM, Feb. 27, March 9, 1938.
9 FQ, 30, JWF to George Pidgeon, July 30,
1936; FFP, JWF to CFM, Sept. 30; FQ, 25,

JWF to Rev. W. E. Cockram, Nov. 8,
1938 (2).
10 FQ, 31, JWF to Rev. J. O. Johnston, Nov.
17, 1938.
11 FQ, 22, JWF to W. J. Loudon, Jan. 31, 1933;
23, JWF to Colquhoun, March 5, 1934; 21,
JWF to Colquhoun, May 30, 1933.
12 FFP, 71st Birthday File, JWF to Dr.
J. H. Coyne, Feb. 16, 1929.
13 FFP, 78th Birthday File, Wood to Rundle,
Feb. 14, 1936; FQ, 25, R. B. Bennett to
JWF, July 28, 1938.
14 FQ, 7934-8, JWF to Carnegie, Dec. 29,
1925.
15 FFP, JWF to CFM, June 30, 1938.
16 Interview with Floyd Chalmers.
17 FFP, JWF to CFM, Feb. 23, 1939; also FQ,
39, Muriel Gladman to T. A. Russell, Feb.
8, 1939; FFP, JWF to CFM, Feb. 8; JWF
Pocket Diary, 1939.
18 SFP, William Flavelle to Aird Flavelle,
March 1939.
19 *Saturday Night*, March 18, 1939.

INDEX